The Tail End System

How to Find Long-Odds Winners in Jumps Racing

Ross Newton

highdown

A *RACING POST* COMPANY

ACKNOWLEDGEMENTS

I am indebted to my friends Brian King, Steve Butterworth, Andy Smith, the late Fred Anderton and Maurice Field in whose company I have attended countless jump meetings in all weathers. This book is the result of those memorable trackside experiences.

I am equally indebted to my farming friends in the Lake District, Gordon Harrison, Frances Marrs, the late Ronnie Harrison and Reg Peet who introduced me to Horses, Cattle, Sheep and Hound Trails; an education which undoubtedly kindled my interest in National Hunt Racing.

My thanks also to the following friends who have accompanied me to race meetings and provided me with a host of memories which have influenced the style and content of this book. They are Bob Alford, Rick Brown, and the late Paul Carbutt; Janet Carbutt and the late Ray Coleing; Jim Demetre, Terry Feasey, Barry Field, Gordon Finney, and the late Sandy Goodbrand, Brian Jackson and Alf James; Fred Jackson, Bob Jinks, Ron Jones, Glen Powell, Derek Smith, Glen Smith, Jeff Smith, Alan Ward and Mick Whittle.

Special thanks to Lynsey Davis of Birmingham who gave up many hours of her valuable spare time to produce the original manuscript received by Raceform, and Sue Williams of Devon who produced the final version.

A big thank you to Robert Cooper of At The Races whose on-screen request gave me the idea to write this book and also Gill Jones, owner of the fabulous Gambling Prince, for the career details which she kindly supplied.

Last but not least, my heartfelt thanks to Julian Brown, Adrian Morrish and all the team at Raceform for their enthusiasm, commitment and support.

Published in 2007 by Raceform
Compton, Newbury, Berkshire, RG20 6NL

A catalogue record for this book is available from the British Library.

ISBN 978-1-905153-67-1

Cover designed by Adrian Morrish
Interiors designed by Fiona Pike

Printed iby Creative Print and Design, Wales

Contents

Preface

I am delighted to report that I am not an ex-jockey nor a retired trainer, neither am I a retired bookmaker, professional tipster, racehorse owner, stable spy or TV presenter. Delighted because I have always viewed my non-racing background as a very big bonus when it comes to the task of finding winners. Since becoming involved with jump racing I have always believed that a non-orthodox approach can be extremely successful in a sport which is hidebound by misconception and misleading opinion, all of which, whether by design or not, can lead the punter into a very confused state of mind and, worst of all, a bad attack of indecision.

With 25 years experience of following jump racing at a wide variety of courses I have a sound knowledge of the sport; in addition, and most importantly, I have developed a thorough understanding regarding what information should be taken into consideration in making selection decisions and, equally important, what information should be totally disregarded.

I have always been a fanatic as far as 'outsiders' are concerned because not only do they provide tremendous value for money betting opportunities but also the ultimate experience in terms of sporting excitement. If anybody doubts this last statement I would ask them to consider whether they would rather be shouting home a 3/1 shot having staked £110 to win or a 66/1 shot having staked £5 to win.

For many years now I have been a disciple of the 'keep it simple' approach to problem solving and as a result I have developed a very successful approach to betting, namely The Tail End System, which can be understood by all.

My interest in jump racing first started in 1977 and I have always considered that from that date until the end of 2000 I was serving a comprehensive apprenticeship embracing all aspects of the sport. Throughout that period I was on a continuous learning curve with lots of highs, and just as many lows. However, an apprenticeship it certainly was because I never felt sufficiently at ease with my selection methods to consider I was working to a system which would provide me with the type of success levels which I would be happy with on an ongoing basis.

At the end of 2000 my wife Carol and I sold our business in Birmingham and we were then able to realise our long term ambition to move to Devon. Free from the encumbrances and commitments a business provides I was able to devote more time to the sport of jump racing and, without any conscious decision on my part, I found myself working to a different set of selection criteria which then provided me with long-priced winners at a rate that I had never experienced before. By the end of 2001 I was confident the selection system I had adopted would be successful on an ongoing basis; I named it The Tail End System.

Before I describe the system I think it is important that you know at least something about the apprenticeship to which I have already referred but, more importantly, that you understand the lessons which I learnt along the way which provide the cornerstones and foundations of The Tail End System itself.

Introduction

There are a lot of good things which can be said about the media circus which has attached itself to British Jumps racing but its treatment of outsiders has to be classified as very poor at best. Outsiders, which big races apart, can loosely be defined as horses with a starting price of 10/1 or longer, win approximately one in six of all jump races in Britain and yet their very presence is either ignored completely, briefly mentioned or even ridiculed on occasions. Television commentators and presenters and a whole army of racing experts react with a combination of shock and incredulity when a long-priced outsider prevails and invariably such results are dismissed as something of a fluke.

However, if you regard yourself as a punter and you believe in the saying 'never look a gift horse in the mouth', the situation I have described is simply wonderful news. If the racing industry and its media experts like to think all races should be won by horses with the best form, or trainers with the classiest strings, or jockeys with the best record, then let them think that because it means the starting prices of outsiders will remain relatively generous when compared with the prices on offer for fancied horses.

In the 2006/2007 racing season, out of 3,102 jump races held in Britain, 523 were won by outsiders at an average price of 18/1. Obviously, from a punters point of view, traditional methods of selection rarely result in long-priced horses being given serious consideration let alone actual selection so there is a need for a system which automatically rectifies this situation. The Tail End System is highly successful at picking long-priced winners because it has been designed specifically to carry out this task by giving priority of consideration to outsiders.

The System has a number of attractive features which are:

1) It can be used with equal success by punters new to the sport of jump racing as well as extremely well experienced followers of the sport.

2) The system is successful because it is based on simple, straightforward logic coupled with only factual information related to a horse's form and level of ability as published by the *Racing Post*.

3) The most complex part of the system is reading a horse's form, as published by the *Racing Post* on the day of the race, in a specified manner. As you would expect, the advice which is included in this book on the form reading process is extremely comprehensive and includes 33 examples of previous races so that it can be seen precisely how the process works.

4) It takes a very short time to understand and remember the rules on the system but it takes a good deal longer to fully appreciate the significance of the form reading exercise to a point where you feel confident of not making obvious mistakes.

5) One of the most attractive merits of the system is the fact that in order to follow it, all you need is the *Racing Post* on the day of the races in question and sufficient time to be able to devote 10-15 minutes to the form studying process for each race you have chosen for possible betting purposes.

It is important to note that in order to complete the form studying process and make your selections, you will require no prior knowledge of either the horses, the trainers or the jockeys involved.

6) The system makes no use of tipster advice, expert opinion or indeed advice or opinion from any source other than this book itself. Your selections will therefore be based entirely upon the factual information contained in that day's *Racing Post*.

7) When you are searching for long-priced winners there is no such thing as a failsafe method for determining which races to bet on. What the system does, however, is to define the class and types of races and the racetracks which, when combined, produce the best chances of a long-priced horse succeeding.

8) It is a system which gives you, the punter, an opportunity to achieve long-priced winners on a scale which is simply not achievable by either traditional or conventional selection methods.

9) Given the fact that it is a system for finding long-priced winners, it is one which is just as suitable for small stake punters as high rollers.

10) Because of the long starting prices which can be achieved it is very definitely a system which can be followed on a win only betting basis. The long starting prices also means that each way betting, place only betting and forecast betting can be extremely attractive propositions for system followers.

The Tail End System was invented by myself at the end of 2000 on the back of 20 years' experience of serious jump race following which embraced all of the Midlands racetracks. As soon as I started to follow the system it proved to be extremely successful and this situation has continued ever since.

Almost from day one when I first started attending jump meetings I have had a passion for outsiders and it took me 20 years to come up with The Tail End System, which I am confident is as good as is practically possible to achieve in identifying outsiders for selection purposes.

I have already mentioned that the system is simple and straightforward and therefore you, the reader, will probably be wondering why it contains 256 pages. There are two main reasons.

Firstly, the form reading section of the book, containing as it does examples of previous races and the form reading process attached to them, is voluminous, as you would expect, because this is the critical part of The Tail End System, which needs to be thoroughly understood.

Secondly, and just as important, The Tail End System is based on a philosophy which brings into question the traditional and conventional methods of selection which are so dreadfully poor in locating long-priced winners. The experience and philosophy I have just mentioned is included in the book because you, the reader, need to understand fully why The Tail End System is designed the way it is. Quite simply, if you do not appreciate why the system is the way it is you may be tempted to deviate from it and believe you me that could prove extremely costly.

At this stage I would like to digress a little and mention how this book came about because, although I am responsible for inventing The Tail End System and writing this book, the idea of the book does not belong to me.

On the 19 April 2005 I was watching At The Races, which was coming from Towcester, one of my two favourite tracks (the other is Stratford on Avon). In the first race, a Beginner's Chase, using The Tail End System, I backed Camdenation which won at 28/1 after the two fancied horses ridden by Tony McCoy and Richard Johnson both departed the race in dramatic fashion on the downhill run. In the second race, a Handicap Hurdle, again using The Tail End System, I backed Rose of York, which finished first at 20/1 and Macreater which finished second at 25/1. My only disappointment was the fact that the reverse exacta which I had placed paid only £217.80 compared with the Computer Straight Forecast, which was £405.96.

As the second race finished, Robert Cooper, the At The Races presenter, said something on the lines "Well blow me down, another long-priced winner. If anybody has picked the first two winners can they please email me immediately and tell me how they did it".

I thought long and hard about what Robert had said and my immediate thoughts were that, with what I have got to say about The Tail End System, I would never fit it into an email. The idea of a book soon followed and although it has taken me a time to get there I will remain indebted to Sir Bob as Matt Chapman in the At The Races Booth has christened him.

Returning now to the subject of The System itself I must emphasise that in order to obtain the best possible results from The Tail End System you must fully understand how it works and you need to be completely in tune with the form reading process. It therefore pays to read the important sections of the book including the form reading examples at least two or three times and to the point where you feel satisfied that you have understood everything correctly. Once you have reached this stage, you should then embark on a dry run where you operate the system exactly as you would if you were about to bet but without actually betting. I would suggest that your dry run should last at least two months so that you can check and recheck everything that you are doing without any mistakes costing you money.

Once you are ready to start betting you will need to be very selective about the races you use for actual betting purposes.

As already mentioned, approximately one race in six produces an outsider victory, so it can immediately be seen that the selection of races for betting purposes is a critical factor which will ultimately determine whether operating the System is a profitable exercise in the longer term.

Putting it bluntly, if you bet on too many races you are bound to lose money, so the emphasis is on taking great care only to choose races where you have made a very carefully considered decision that an 'outsider' victory is a distinct possibility.

Selection of races is a subject which is examined in depth in the following chapters but it is important that you understand right from the beginning that patience, discipline, experience of the System itself and your own intuition are all qualities which you will need to display in abundance if you are going to end up on the right side of the bookies.

From a personal point of view I have found three principal benefits from operating The Tail End System.

Firstly, when I started to operate The Tail End System at the end of 2000, I found myself in a situation for the first time in my betting life where I knew when I opened my *Racing Post* exactly how I would select my races and my horses.

Secondly, The Tail End System breathed new life into my form reading activities to a point where I now thoroughly relish the challenge it represents. My form reading skills have certainly improved and I now find it far easier to recognise race winning form belonging to outsiders simply because I can recognise it as being similar to the form shown by previous Tail End System winners.

Thirdly, having moved from a situation of having an occasional long-priced winner to one where I now have a lot of long-priced winners, the levels of excitement I have experienced seem to me to be well above the level that any punter has the right to expect.

To give you a good idea what can be achieved with The Tail End System and also its potential as a serious method of winning money you will need to study the actual race examples for the 2006/2007 season which appear in Section 3 of Chapter 23 – Reading the Form. These examples will show you exactly how and why the system works.

It is important to point out that the whole process of choosing which races to bet on, and reading the form and deciding which horses to bet on, is very definitely an art and not a science, which means that you, the punter, will have to make a series of critical decisions and your level of success will depend on how often you get those decisions right. The Tail End System cannot and does not make the decisions for you but what it does do is to provide you with a very definite order and method of doing things and comprehensive training in how to choose races and how to read form, so that you have the best possible chance of being successful.

I have followed British Jumps racing for such a long period that I know long-priced 'outsider' victories will always be an integral part of our sport. The Tail End System has been designed to give you the best possible chance to predict a sufficient number of those 'outsider' victories to make your participation in the challenge which is punting on British Jumps racing a successful one.

Chapter 1
AN APPRENTICESHIP IN JUMP RACING

I would have liked to be able to say that my dad, Jimmy Newton, taught me a lot about the sport but unfortunately during the last 12 years of his life, when he managed to pick five winners of the Grand National and backed them all heavily at long odds ante post, I had no interest whatsoever in the sport. As a result I knew nothing of the selection techniques which he employed and when I finally started betting of my own accord I was very much a raw beginner gleaning what information I could from the racing press.

Fortunately the company I worked for at the time, Metro Cammell (the Birmingham based train and bus manufacturers), was a large one and it didn't take long to identify working colleagues with similar interests to myself. Initially I started visiting Stratford on Avon racecourse with Fred Anderton, a Captain Tim Forster (trainer) fan. However, after a couple of years, Fred's interest in racecourse visits declined and I linked up with Brian King, Metro Cammell's Site Manager, and his friend Maurice Field, a retired policeman and committed Toby Balding follower. Immediately, my racecourse visits were extended to include Warwick, Worcester, Uttoxeter and Towcester as well as Stratford, all on a regular basis, with Ludlow, Hereford and Huntingdon being visited occasionally. In addition, we became annual visitors to the Cheltenham Festival on Champion Hurdle and Queen Mother Chase days and these became the highlights of our racing year.

As the years passed and Maurice's course visits became more infrequent we were joined by Steve Butterworth, an international croupier who had returned to Birmingham from the casinos of Baghdad and Moscow. Soon afterwards, Andy Smith, a heating engineer connected with Metro Cammell, joined us as well and from then on we were a four-man team visiting the Midlands' tracks.

All the members of our group, with the exception of myself, had started betting in their teens and all are committed students of form. From the very beginning of our friendship there has always been a full and open exchange of views and information related to the betting process. As a result we have all learnt a great deal along the way and there have been many occasions where, as a group, we have been successful. I should stress at this stage that none of our members could be described as high rollers; we are all relatively low stake punters searching for value for money bets.

As you can imagine, with frequent visits to such a wide variety of courses over a 20-year period, with a group of jump racing fans who work very hard at the task of finding winners the experience was second to none. As a result of all this experience, by the time 2000 rolled around I had formed some definite viewpoints about the sport of jump racing. These viewpoints, which provide the cornerstones and the foundations of The Tail End System, are not rocket science; they are a set of very basic lessons which have been put together on the basis of extensive experience, observation and analysis.

Chapter 2
THERE IS NO SUCH THING
AS A RACING CERTAINTY

I would urge anybody who is new to jump racing to visit a race meeting and take the trouble to walk at least part of the course, either before or after racing, to see what horse and jockey have to contend with. It is only when you see the size of the fences and the hurdles and you see for yourself the ground conditions which can prevail that you start to appreciate the difficulties the competitors experience in getting round a course in one piece, let alone getting in the prizes.

When I was very new to the sport I attended a Boxing Day meeting at Huntingdon with my brother-in-law, Ivor Robinson, and we both backed the outsider in a two horse chase where the favourite was something like 1/6 on in the betting and the other runner 7/2 against. Although the favourite's paper form justified the odds being offered, for the vast majority of punters its prohibitive price meant that the horse was not a betting proposition. When the race set off the favourite immediately went into a clear lead which extended to a distance of two fences by the time it entered the finishing straight. As the favourite tackled the last fence he ploughed through the top of it and deposited his jockey on the turf, an incident which prompted a huge roar from the crowd, a large proportion of which had backed the outsider on the assumption that the favourite could slip up, rather than the long-priced horse making a race of it. The 'outsider' meanwhile continued at his own pace and swept past the favourite as it was being remounted and proceeded to the finish to a rapturous applause from the many punters who appreciated their good fortune.

Although since that Huntingdon meeting in the late Seventies I have witnessed hundreds of incidents where both fancied and unfancied horses and their jockeys have thrown away clear winning opportunities for a multitude of reasons, it was that particular race which has left me with the view that there is no such thing as a certainty in jump racing.

An even earlier incident than the one I have just described has also profoundly affected my thinking with regard to the sport. When I was in my early teens and on my annual farm based holiday close to Keswick in the Lake District I was persuaded by Frances (one of the farmer's daughters), to take a ride with her on a fell pony. Allocated Frances' sister Anne's pony I coped OK with the first half mile of the ride across fields high above Keswick at the rear of the farm, trotting along at walking pace. However, problems developed when we stopped to take in the view and my pony decided to plant itself. Gentle urgings on my part failed to draw any response so I gave the pony a light tap with my heels and without warning it bolted. In the space of 25 yards the animal reached a speed approaching 30mph with me hanging onto the reigns for grim death. By the time we had crossed one pasture field into another on a downhill run and through an open gateway I had sufficient presence of mind to realise that my safest bet was to decamp from the pony before it reached the farmyard to which it was heading. I managed to do this by the simple but decidedly dodgy procedure of rolling off the side of the pony, tucking my head into my chest as I did so. Miracle of miracles, with no helmet to protect me I survived the fall with no worse than bruises and fortunately the pony escaped unscathed from the rest of its journey across the cobbled farmyard, a country lane and another field before a stone wall caused it to pull up.

As a result of that incident in the Lake District I have never been totally surprised at any of the very many dramatic episodes which I have witnessed during my racecourse visits since then. I certainly do appreciate the fact that the vast majority of falls and mishaps which arise during the course of a race are unavoidable, however skilled the jockey on board is.

The overriding lesson which I have learned from the Huntingdon race and my fall at Keswick and the multitude of races I have witnessed, is that in jump racing anything can happen. In this setting it is my view that in any race with more than three or four or more runners, a starting price which is less than 5/1 against is not worth taking if you are looking to make a profit from the sport on an annual basis. Secondly, I would advise that any approach to jump racing which is based on making large wagers on short priced horses is doomed to failure.

Chapter 3
JUMP RACING CAN PROVIDE
A MARVELLOUS BETTING OPPORTUNITY

In the 2006/2007 British jump racing season there were a total of 3,102 races over hurdles or fences of which 523 were won at a starting price of 10/1 or longer. The average starting price of those 523 'outsider' winners, which represent 16.86 percent of all winners, was 18/1. In practical terms this meant that on average there was one winning outsider with a starting price of 18/1 for every six jump races which were contested.

It can be seen from the chart entitled Outsider Statistics at all British Racecourses 2006/2007 Season which appears below, that winning outsiders are a significant feature at practically all British jump courses.

Obviously, with the number of outsiders that do prevail, some at huge prices, a significant betting opportunity exists. However, to actually make money from the exercise it is necessary to identify both the class and type of races where it is most feasible to pick winning long price horses, and also the racecourses where such outsiders are more likely to be successful.

'OUTSIDER' STATISTICS AT ALL BRITISH RACECOURSES 2006/2007 SEASON

Course	No of Races	No of Outsider Winners	Average Outsider Winner Starting Price	Outsider Winners as a Percentage of Races (%)	No of Blank Meetings (No 'Outsider' winners)
Aintree	42	13	18/1	30.95	2
Musselburgh	49	14	15/1	28.57	0
Ludlow	82	22	18/1	26.82	2
Haydock	64	17	18/1	26.56	0
Cheltenham	98	25	19/1	25.51	1
Towcester	98	25	16/1	25.51	3
Carlisle	49	12	14/1	24.48	1
Catterick	43	10	13/1	23.25	2
Lingfield	23	5	45/1	21.73	1
Kelso	92	20	21/1	21.73	2
Chepstow	80	16	15/1	20.00	4
Perth	73	14	16/1	19.17	4
Worcester	118	22	17/1	18.64	6
Stratford	99	18	17/1	18.18	6
Taunton	79	14	14/1	17.72	2
Hereford	104	18	18/1	17.30	5
Sedgefield	111	18	15/1	16.21	7
Wincanton	99	16	21/1	16.16	6
Huntingdon	93	15	18/1	16.12	6
Fakenham	56	9	22/1	16.07	3

Exeter	90	14	15/1	15.55	4
Ayr	65	10	19/1	15.38	3
Hexham	98	15	17/1	15.30	6
Ascot	53	8	21/1	15.09	3
Newbury	68	10	17/1	14.70	5
Bangor	75	11	14/1	14.66	4
Uttoxeter	137	20	23/1	14.59	7
Kempton	62	9	20/1	14.50	5
Folkestone	49	7	16/1	14.28	3
Newton Abbot	100	14	23/1	14.00	6
Wetherby	113	15	16/1	13.27	5
Market Rasen	126	16	22/1	12.69	8
Leicester	49	6	15/1	12.24	3
Cartmel	37	4	16/1	10.81	2
Southwell	56	6	13/1	10.71	5
Newcastle	56	6	41/1	10.71	5
Warwick	56	6	13/1	10.70	3
Plumpton	94	10	16/1	10.63	6
Fontwell	123	11	15/1	8.94	7
Sandown	43	2	20/1	4.65	6

OVERALL 'OUTSIDER' STATISTICS AT ALL BRITISH RACECOURSES 2006/2007 SEASON

Races	3,102
Outsider Winners	523
Average Outsider Starting Price	18/1
'Outsider' Winners as a Percentage of Races	16.86%
Total Number of Blank Meetings (No 'Outsiders')	159

The Tail End System is, therefore, about identifying the races to bet on and providing the method by which horses should be selected for those races.

Chapter 4
BETTING ON OUTSIDERS
CAN BE A PROFITABLE BUSINESS

Very early on in my jump racing career I became hooked on outsiders simply because I could not get excited about any horse winning a race at odds of less than 10/1, given the small amounts of money I was willing to invest. In my first couple of years of racecourse visits I witnessed a 100/1 shot win a seven runner chase at Stratford on Avon racecourse, and I saw Baron Blakeney at the same odds provide Martin Pipe with his first winner at the Cheltenham Festival. Although I backed neither of those two horses they inspired me to concentrate on outsiders and it wasn't that long before I started to get successful. My earliest recollection of a big price winner which I had backed with a worthwhile sum of money was a horse called Duart, trained by John Spearing, which won a chase at Stratford by a country mile at the price of 50/1.

Since that Duart victory I have had a lot of long-priced winners, but I have to confess that despite 50/1, 66/1, 70/1, and 80/1 winners it was not until November 2001 that I achieved my first 100/1 winner (Latimers Place, Exeter Racecourse) thanks to the Tote dividend, as opposed to the official starting price.

From the start of 2001 my adoption of what I now call The Tail End System, coupled with changed personal circumstances allowing me to follow racing every day of the week, led to a huge increase in the number of long-priced winners I was selecting at all prices, from 10/1 to 100/1 and over.

As you will see in the following chapters, simply by studying the statistics it is a straight forward exercise to identify the classes of races, the types of races and the racetracks which produce the most outside winners. Having identified the most likely races to bet on, The Tail End System has its own form reading procedure for selecting possible 'outsider winners' and it is this form reading procedure which helps to narrow down still further the best betting opportunities.

The other big advantage of The Tail End System is the fact that, given an average starting price for 'outsider' winners which is in the region of 18/1, it provides the scope to indulge in multiple choice betting, which obviously greatly increases your chances of winning without significantly denting your chances of making serious profits.

Chapter 5
THE CLASS OF RACE IS AN IMPORTANT CONSIDERATION

Whilst the television racing presenters and the racing press will always save their greatest enthusiasm for the top class races at the high profile tracks, it is definitely not these races which provide the best betting opportunities when searching for long-priced winners. The principal object of betting on horses is to make a profit, so it makes sense to concentrate on the classes and types of races and the tracks which produce the best results in the 'outsider' category.

All jump races are allocated a class category which determines the entry qualifications for each CHASE or HURDLE race, starting with Class 1, the highest category, followed by Class 2, 3, 4 and 5, the latter being the lowest category. Class 6 is the category which embraces Hunter Chase races and also National Hunt Flat races, although, to complicate the situation, the type of races just mentioned can be given a higher category than 6 if the prize money reaches certain levels.

The 'top class' races, which are the class 1 and 2 categories, carry the most prize money, attract the best horses and the attention of the top trainers and, as a result, are the subject of intense competition. Most of the horses competing in such races are very well known and, whilst the risk of an 'upset' is always a possibility, the chances of this happening are much less likely than it happening in the lower category races. In those Class 1 and Class 2 races where there are a large number of runners, ie 16 plus, there is often a higher chance of an 'upset', but by the same token, and due to the number of runners, it becomes far more difficult to identify the winner.

In the case of the Class 6 category (Hunter Chase) it is very difficult to get a handle on the form of the competitors because most of it is related to Point to Point races, which are an entirely different set up to that of National Hunt Chases. Unless, as a punter, you follow the Point-to-Point circuit very closely it is best to accept that Hunter Chases should be categorised as 'very difficult' for betting purposes. It is very important to point out that as far as the statistics in this book are concerned relating to Hunter Chases, that they have all, with the exception of the lists of race winners in the Appendices to this book, been categorised as Class 6 to avoid creating misleading statistics in Classes 1, 2, 3, 4 and 5, which are not in any way related entry qualification wise to Hunter Chases.

The Class 6 category also embraces the National Hunt Flat races, or 'Bumpers', as they are known. With these Flat/bumper races it is very difficult to get a handle on the form of the competitors primarily because, for a large proportion of runners, there is either no form at all or alternatively Flat racing form on both All Weather and grass tracks over shorter distances than the standard Bumper race distance (2m). Given these conditions it is best to consider Bumper races as a lottery type bet which is best left alone, and it is for this reason that The Tail End System and this book exclude National Hunt Flat races and Bumper races all together.

Looking at the 2006/2007 season, the 523 winning 'outsiders' (odds of 10/1 or greater) achieved their victories in the following numbers according to the class of race concerned:

	'OUTSIDER' WINNERS 2006/2007 SEASON						
Class of race	1	2	3	4	5	6	Total
Number of winning outsiders	37	31	96	246	97	16	523

* NB In the above, chart Class 6 shows all Hunter Chase winners regardless of the official classification of their race.

The figures in the above chart indicate that race classes 3, 4 and 5 are the logical ones to concentrate on if you are looking for 'outsider' winners. It would be wrong to say never look for outsiders in the class 1, 2 and 6 categories but it is wise to accept that, given the fact that they produce far fewer 'outsider' victories, and are frequently far more difficult to solve, such contests should be treated with extreme caution and generally left alone.

Chapter 6
THE TYPE OF RACE IS AN
IMPORTANT CONSIDERATION

In just the same way as the Class of race is important when betting on 'outsiders', so is the type of race. Types of jump races can be divided into two main categories – Handicaps and Non Handicaps. When we look again at the 523 winning outsiders in the 2006/2007 jumps season, the relevant figures in respect of type of races are as follows:

'OUTSIDER' WINNERS FOR 2006/2007 SEASON

Handicap Chase Winners	Handicap Hurdle Winners	Non-Handicap Winners	Non-Handicap Hurdle Winners	Total Winners
155	201	46	121	523

Looking at the above figures, the fact that there were 356 handicap winners compared with 167 non handicap winners would seem to indicate that, in the search for 'outsider', winners it is best to concentrate on handicap races; however, there are other factors to be taken into consideration.

In handicap hurdle races and handicap chases all competing horses are allocated a handicap rating based on previous performances over either hurdles or fences, as appropriate. If the handicapper has interpreted past performances correctly, and all the horses run to form, then in theory all the contestants should cross the finish line together. However, as we all know, horses run above and below their true form, the handicapper doesn't always get it right, a horse's true form is often disguised in previous performances and in jump racing there are a thousand different things which can happen to change the outcome of a race. As a result of all these factors, plus a few more, handicap races produce a higher proportion of 'outsider' winners than non-handicap races. The real bonus, however, as far as the punter is concerned, is that there is usually far more relevant 'form' related information for handicap races, compared with non-handicap races, with which to assess the winning potential of any runner, including outsiders.

Although handicap races can be complicated, non handicap races can be far more complicated for a variety of reasons. Non handicap races include the Top Class Level Weight races as well as a variety of Novice, Juvenile, Seller, Maiden, Claiming, Beginner and Classified races, many of which include weight allowances and weight penalties, the effect of which is often difficult to evaluate. In addition, in many of these races there is often a scarcity of relevant form for a considerable section of the runners, particularly in the Juvenile and Beginner categories. As a result of the factors mentioned, whilst the non-handicap races produce a significant number of outsider victories, often at very big starting prices, many of these victories are of the 'out of the blue' type, which cannot be picked up easily by the form reading process simply because relevant form either does not exist or is decidedly inconclusive. It should also be pointed out that there is a Racing Post Rating System for non-handicap races but because these ratings, for reasons associated with absence of relevant form, are generally incomplete (eg they do not cover the whole field), the rating system is very rarely a worthwhile guide when trying to weigh up the form of the runners.

To conclude: when determining which type of races to concentrate on when looking for 'outsider' winners the handicap races undoubtedly provide the best prospects. As far as the non-handicap races are concerned they have got to be rated as very difficult. However, this does not mean that they should necessarily be ruled out all together because there will be certain races where there is sufficient relevant form to make informed selection decisions.

Chapter 7
CERTAIN RACECOURSES ARE BETTER FOR 'OUTSIDER' WINNERS THAN OTHERS

There is no doubt whatsoever that certain racecourses consistently produce more 'outsider' winners than others. The reasons for this are abundantly clear to see in certain cases, principally the tough tracks (eg Towcester, Hexham, Cheltenham, Chepstow), but far less obvious on some of the flatter/easier tracks (eg Ludlow, Worcester, Stratford, Huntingdon). In any search for 'outsider' winners there is a necessity to know which racecourses are most likely to produce 'outsider' victories and at the same time be aware when a racecourse goes from a 'hot' rating to a 'cold' rating, so to speak, and the 'outsiders' dry up.

Looking first at the tough tracks, it becomes abundantly clear that a large number of horses, including ones that are quite outstanding on flat courses, have extreme difficulty in coping with the hills and the descents that are a real feature at the likes of Towcester, Hexham and Chepstow. Frequently the odds makers, the bookies and the punters fail to take proper account of this situation and some very long-priced winners result.

The good thing about tough tracks is that their undulations never change and the punter is more or less guaranteed at least an average number of 'outsider' victories. Having said that, the situation can still alter to a degree. Exeter is, to me, a prime example of such a happening because up to a couple of years ago really long-priced winners were cropping up on that track on an extremely frequent basis.

More recently, however, Exeter has hit a bit of a flat spot and although the contours of the course are unchanged, the size of fields seem smaller on average and the ground conditions may also have contributed to a reduction in the attractiveness of the course from an 'outsider' point of view. Exeter is, at the moment, still on my Preferred list of racecourses but it now has an "approach with caution" tag and if the situation does not improve during the current season, its name will be withdrawn from the Preferred list.

Still on the subject of tough tracks, I must mention that Cheltenham, particularly at the Festival, has one of the best records for providing 'outsiders', but stages the type of races that are probably the toughest in the country to crack from a betting point of view. The reason is the fact that in the 2006/2007 season, 21 of the 25 'outsider' victories at that venue were in Class 1, 2 or 6 races, which are the toughest to get right from a form reading point of view.

When you also take into account the very large fields at Cheltenham, which can easily double the degree of difficulty in picking winners, you end up with an almost impossible scenario if you are looking to make a profit from your betting activities.

Turning now to the subject of the easier tracks, I am afraid I possess no earth shattering theories as to why certain of them consistently produce a higher percentage of 'outsider' victories than others. Ludlow for example has been consistently close to the top of the charts for producing 'outsiders' in the past three seasons and yet the course, which is more or less flat and has no particularly sharp turns, appears to offer the easiest type of conditions for every type of horse, apart from those with a preference for left hand courses. (NB Ludlow is right handed.)

Unable to provide a satisfactory explanation for the situation that exists I have been forced to reply on the statistics for 'outsider' victories to guide me in preparing a list of Preferred and Non-Preferred racecourses and I don't want to go back further than the last season's results because the situation can change quite quickly.

Take, for example, Musselborough, a track which only produced 8 'outsider' victories from 48 races in the 2004/2005 season, has now produced 14 'outsider' victories from 49 races in the 2006/2007 season, which gives a win to race percentage of 28%, which is extremely high.

On a gloomier note, Warwick, which a few years back had an excellent record for producing a healthy tally of long-priced winners, has had a reversal of form over the past few seasons to an extent where I have been forced to avoid the course for betting purposes all together.

When following The Tail End System, the existence of Preferred and Non-Preferred lists of Racecourses is in my view a necessity because it can save a lot of time in wasted form reading activities if you know that a particular racecourse is far less likely to produce 'outsider' victories than others.

In preparing a list of Preferred racecourse and Non-Preferred racecourses I have relied on two principal pieces of information: firstly, the number of 'outsider' winners that were produced by each racecourse in the 2006/2007 season and secondly, the classification of those racetracks which you would regard as high profile courses whose favoured activity is to provide Class 1 and Class 2 racing.

Controversially though it may appear, I have automatically relegated all the high profile courses to the Non-Preferred group quite simply because betting on the type of racing they aim to provide, namely Class 1 and 2 events which frequently feature big fields, particularly in the handicap races, is doubly more difficult than betting on Class 3, 4 and 5 contests which are the bread and butter fare of the lower profile tracks.

The result of the exercise I have carried out can be seen on the next two pages entitled Preferred racecourses and Non-Preferred racecourses.

Commenting firstly on the Preferred Racecourses list, I do not regard the inclusion of any of the courses that appear on this list as particularly controversial because their inclusion is merited by the number of 'outsider' wins they have produced.

However, and this is most important, the Preferred Racecourse list must always be considered with a degree of caution for two main reasons.

Firstly, the 'outsider' wins, which are the reason for a racecourse being on the list, are historical information and therefore there is no guarantee that a similar percentage of 'outsider' wins will occur in the future. Secondly, in the last column on the chart you will see a record of the number of blank race meetings that have taken place at the course, where no 'outsider' victories were recorded. Now, again this information is historical, but nevertheless of importance because it warns you that a run of blank meetings can occur at any time for all sorts of reasons.

Given the situation I have just described it is important to stress that, in making use of the Preferred Racecourse list to shape your betting strategy, you must always keep abreast of the jump racing results as the season progresses so that you are fully aware when either the number of quality of 'outsider' victories has either fallen or risen significantly or a series of blank meetings has either started or finished.

Keeping in close touch with the results is not very difficult and it can make a huge difference to your levels of success if you can avoid betting at racecourses when they are "cold" and increase your betting activity when they are "hot".

Blank meetings and low levels of 'outsider' winners are frequently a feature of summer racing, when good jumping ground conditions are sometimes difficult to provide and when entry levels in races start to plummet. This is a strategy that is explained in greater depth in Chapter 9.

I must conclude this section on the Preferred Racecourse list by emphasising the point that knowing how a racecourse can produce 'outsider' winners can be of huge assistance to your betting activities but you must make sure that your knowledge of the course in question is up to date.

Turning now to the Non-Preferred racecourses I make no apologies for the fact that Aintree, Cheltenham, Haydock, Newbury and Wetherby, despite their records for producing high numbers of 'outsider' winners, appear on the list. The objective of The Tail End System is to select winners and the combination of high profile racecourses, Class 1 and 2 events and extra large fields, particularly in the handicap races, makes the task doubly difficult than that encountered when betting on Class 3, 4 and 5 handicap races at the low profile tracks. This whole subject of the high profile tracks is explored in further detail in Chapter 24.

As well as containing the high profile tracks, the Non-Preferred racecourse list includes the six racecourses with the lowest level of 'outsider' victories in the 2006/2007 season. It is interesting to note that of those six racecourses, two of them, Fontwell and Plumpton, appeared on the Preferred List in the 2004/2005 season, which again demonstrates the importance of keeping tabs with how individual courses are performing as the racing season progresses. The list of Preferred and Non-Preferred Racecourses are as follows:

PREFERRED RACECOURSES

Course	Number of Races (2006/2007 Season)	Number of 'Outsider' Winners (2006/2007 Season)	Average Starting Price of 'Outsider' winners	Number of 'Outsider' Winners as a Percentage of Number of Races	No of Blank Meetings (No 'Outsiders')
Musselborough	49	14	15/1	28%	0
Ludlow	82	22	18/1	26%	2
Towcester	98	25	16/1	25%	3
Carlisle	49	12	14/1	24%	1
Catterick	43	10	13/1	23%	2
Lingfield	23	5	45/1	21%	1
Kelso	92	20	21/1	21%	2
Chepstow	80	16	15/1	20%	4
Perth	73	14	16/1	19%	4
Worcester	118	22	17/1	18%	6
Stratford	99	18	17/1	18%	6
Taunton	79	14	14/1	17%	2
Hereford	104	18	18/1	17%	5
Sedgefield	111	18	15/1	16%	7
Wincanton	99	16	21/1	16%	6
Huntingdon	93	15	18/1	16%	6
Fakenham	56	9	22/1	16%	3

Exeter	90	14	15/1	15%	4
Ayr	65	10	19/1	15%	3
Hexham	98	15	17/1	15%	6
Bangor	75	11	14/1	14%	4
Uttoxeter	137	20	23/1	14%	7
Folkestone	49	7	16/1	14%	4
Newton Abbot	100	14	23/1	14%	6
Market Rasen	126	16	22/1	12%	8
	Total	**Total**	**Average**	**Average**	**Total**
	2088	**385**	**18/1**	**18.4%**	**101**

The courses which have failed to reach the 'Preferred List' are as follows:

NON-PREFERRED RACECOURSES

Course	Number of Races (2006/2007 Season)	Number of 'Outsider' Winners (2006/2007 Season)	Average Starting Price of 'Outsider' winners	No of 'Outsider' Winners as a Percentage of Number of Races	No of Blank Meetings (No 'Outsiders')
Aintree	42	13	18/1	30%	2
Haydock	64	17	18/1	26%	0
Cheltenham	98	25	19/1	25%	1
Ascot	53	8	21/1	15%	3
Newbury	68	10	17/1	14%	5
Kempton	62	9	20/1	14%	5
Wetherby	113	15	16/1	13%	5
Leicester	49	6	15/1	12%	3
Cartmel	37	4	16/1	10%	2
Southwell	56	6	13/1	10%	5
Newcastle	56	6	41/1	10%	5
Warwick	56	6	13/1	10%	3
Plumpton	94	10	16/1	10%	6
Fontwell	123	11	15/1	8%	7
Sandown	43	2	20/1	4%	6
	Total	**Total**	**Average**	**Average**	**Total**
	1014	**148**	**18/1**	**14.6%**	**58**

Looking at the list of 'Non-Preferred' courses the reasons for categorising them as such can be summarised as follows:

Courses		Principal Reason For Non-Preferred Tag		
Aintree	9	out of	13	outsider wins were Class 1 or 2 events
Cheltenham	19	out of	25	outsider wins were Class 1 or 2 events
Haydock	7	out of	17	outsider wins were Class 1 or 2 events
Newbury	3	out of	10	outsider wins were Class 1 or 2 events
Sandown	1	out of	2	outsider wins were Class 1 or 2 events
Kempton	3	out of	9	outsider wins were Class 1 or 2 events

Wetherby	3	out of	15	outsider wins were Class 1 or 2 events
Ascot	6	out of	8	outsider wins were Class 1 or 2 events

Courses	Principal Reason For Non-Preferred Tag
Cartmel	Insufficient outsider victories
Southwell	Insufficient outsider victories
Newcastle	Insufficient outsider victories
Warwick	Insufficient outsider victories
Plumpton	Insufficient outsider victories
Fontwell	Insufficient outsider victories

In the appendices at the back of this book is a comprehensive record of the 'outsider' victories in each of the British Jump racing courses during the 2006/2007 season. These records are worth studying in detail because they show at a glance all of the information relevant to the task of finding 'outsider' winners as well as providing the reasons why the 'Preferred racecourses' have been categorised as such.

The subject of 'Preferred' and 'Non-Preferred' racecourses is examined in the conclusion in Chapter 8 dealing with how to select races for betting purposes, talking into account the class of race, type of race and racecourses.

Chapter 8
IT IS NECESSARY TO CONSIDER CLASS OF RACE, TYPE OF RACE AND RACECOURSE IN DETERMINING WHICH RACES TO SELECT FOR BETTING PURPOSES

I will start by summarising the conclusions of Chapters 5, 6 and 7. These conclusions are as follows:

In any search for 'outsider' winners the following information should be taken into account:

a) Class 3, 4 and 5 races produce the overwhelming majority of 'outsider' winners and are therefore preferred to class 1, 2 and 6 races which are normally very difficult to solve from a betting point of view.

b) Handicap races produce the overwhelming majority of 'outsider' winners and are therefore preferred to non-handicap races which are normally more difficult to solve from a betting point of view.

c) The high profile tracks place an emphasis on top class races and the handicap races which they promote frequently attract large fields. For both these reasons their races are normally very difficult to solve.

d) As far as the remaining tracks are concerned certain racecourses have a better record for producing 'outsider' winners than others.

By taking all of the above information into account it is possible to produce a Preferred list of both races and racecourses which can enhance the chances of identifying long-priced winners.

Looking at the information so far, the logical conclusion is to examine the record of 'outsider' winners at preferred racecourses in Class 3, 4 and 5 handicap races compared with the record of 'outsider' winners at the same racecourses in all classes of non-handicap races.

In the chart entitled 'outsider' winners at Preferred Courses overleaf it can be seen that in the Class 3, 4 and 5 handicap races the outsider percentage was 22%, compared with a figure of 13% for all classes of non-handicap races. The outsider percentage of 22% is the best I have seen so far comparing favourably with the figure of 18% for all races at Preferred racecourses, 14% for all races at Non-Preferred racecourses and 16% for **all** racecourses.

It is worth noting that the average 'outsider' starting price in Class 3, 4 and 5 handicap races at Preferred Racecourses is 17/1, compared with 19/1 for all classes of non-handicap races for the same courses. Although the average starting price figure of 19/1 appears to make the non-handicap races an attractive betting proposition I would repeat my earlier statement that these races are normally more difficult to solve.

'OUTSIDER' WINNERS AT PREFERRED COURSES 2006/2007 SEASON

Preferred Racecourses	Number of Class 3, 4 & 5 Handicap Races	Number of 'Outsider' Winners	'Outsider' Winners as a Percentage of Races	Average 'Outsider' Starting Price	Number of Non-Handicap Races, All Classes	Number of 'Outsider' Winners	'Outsider' Winners as a Percentage of Races	Average 'Outsider' Starting Price
Musselborough	26	12	46%	16/1	19	3	15%	13/1
Ludlow	38	14	29%	14/1	38	6	15%	25/1
Towcester	50	13	26%	18/1	44	10	22%	15/1
Carlisle	30	9	30%	13/1	18	3	16%	19/1
Catterick	24	8	33%	13/1	18	2	11%	14/1
Lingfield	13	5	38%	41/1	10	1	10%	33/1
Kelso	45	13	28%	19/1	35	6	17%	31/1
Chepstow	36	8	22%	17/1	35	6	17%	12/1
Perth	40	8	20%	14/1	26	3	11%	24/1
Worcester	64	15	23%	16/1	54	7	12%	17/1
Stratford	52	11	21%	15/1	41	6	14%	21/1
Taunton	38	9	23%	14/1	41	5	12%	15/1
Hereford	56	11	19%	22/1	44	7	15%	14/1
Sedgefield	56	15	28%	16/1	51	2	3.9%	16/1
Wincanton	53	11	20%	19/1	31	2	6.4%	26/1
Huntingdon	51	12	23%	19/1	34	1	2.9%	16/1
Fakenham	29	8	27%	22/1	22	1	4.5%	14/1
Exeter	47	10	21%	14/1	34	5	14%	18/1
Ayr	33	6	18%	19/1	19	2	10%	23/1
Hexham	47	8	17%	16/1	41	6	14%	19/1
Bangor	36	7	19%	13/1	33	3	9.0%	14/1
Uttoxeter	73	10	13%	22/1	54	7	12%	25/1
Folkestone	22	4	18%	14/1	19	3	15%	19/1
Newton Abbot	45	8	17%	29/1	50	4	8.0%	18/1
Market Rasen	72	11	15%	17/1	44	3	6.8%	42/1
TOTAL	1,076	246	22%	Average 17/1	799	104	13%	Average 19/1

On the basis of all the 'outsider' winner statistics I have examined so far, it appears logical to adopt a strategy of restricting betting to the Class 3, 4 and 5 handicap races at the Preferred list of racecourses, in order to have the best possible chance of achieving a good level of profit on a long term basis. However, although such a strategy means you are looking at 246 'outsider' winners from 1,076 races and a winner to race percentage of 22% (2006/2007 season) you still have an extremely tough task in achieving a high enough success rate to produce an overall profit in those races which you select for actual betting purposes.

As a result of this situation it is essential that you examine each of the Class 3, 4 and 5 handicap races at the preferred list of racecourses and try to determine whether or not they appear to be a sound betting proposition in the quest for 'outsider' winners. If you are able to identify correctly the bad betting races and leave them out of your betting activities then you are left with a far better chance of making a good level of profit on an overall basis.

The task of working out which races to drop is not an easy one because when you compare the details of races which have produced 'outsider' winners with those which have not, there is no easily identifiable difference between the two groups. I have to report that I have studied the obvious factors such as distance of races, type of going and number of runners and it would appear, on the surface at least, that any Class 3, 4 and 5 handicap race with at least seven runners is just as likely to produce an 'outsider' winner as any other race, categorised in the same way.

However, I am pleased to report that help is at hand because simply by following The Tail End System you automatically end up becoming something of an 'outsider' expert. As you will discover in the later stages of the book, The Tail End System dictates that, to select a horse for betting purposes, you have to be satisfied that its form is good enough to achieve a place in the first three in the class, type and distance of race in which it is entered without reference to the form of any other runner. By studying the form of the outsiders in this way you, the punter, end up becoming very proficient in determining whether these outsiders have a genuine chance of a placing or not. It will probably take you a period of a few months to achieve the level of proficiency I am talking about but by that time you will have enough confidence to say whether the race in question is worth betting on or not. In other words, if you are not really sure that any of the outsiders could obtain a placing in the first three you will obviously be leaving the race alone.

Sometimes, however, you can eliminate races for betting purposes without having to go to the trouble of an in depth study of the outsiders form. I am sure you will be familiar with a low entry race card for a whole meeting where you know at a glance that the chances of picking up a good priced winner are either nonexistent or practically zero. It is race meetings like this that should be left well alone. If you study the racecourse statistics for the 2006/2007 season in appendices 1/A to 40/A you can see the details of all the 'outsider' winners which includes the number of runners in each race.

By looking through the racecourse statistics you will see that there are only a very few races which provided an 'outsider' winner where the number of runners were less than seven. Whilst this would seem to indicate a policy of bypassing all races of six runners or fewer, it is as you would probably guess not quite as simple as that. If my memory serves me correctly, it was in 2002 that I backed a horse called Parsons Pride in a six runner hurdle race at Worcester Racecourse.

In this race there were in effect four favourites at short prices and two outsiders at long prices, both of which I backed. Parsons Pride stretched the field from the start and it was only at the exit from the back straight at the end of the final circuit that its jockey gave it a breather, allowed its two closest pursuers to overtake, and then tucked in behind them. As the three leaders rounded the final bend and entered the finishing straight Parsons Pride accelerated into a lead which was some 20 lengths and growing by the time he cleared the final hurdle and headed to the line for a silent welcome. The starting price was 100/1 and the tote dividend was in excess of that figure.

The Parsons Pride race strengthened my view that before dismissing a small-field race you should always check very carefully to ensure that it isn't harbouring a long-priced runner, which has a solid chance of success.

At this stage of the proceedings it is necessary to point out that when I refer to Preferred and Non-Preferred racecourses and Preferred races (Class 3, 4, 5 Handicap Races) and Non-Preferred races (Class 1 and 2 handicap and non handicap races; Class 3, 4 5 non handicap races) I mean just that – Preferred and Non-Preferred.

It doesn't mean to say that you either cannot or should not bet on Non-Preferred races at any course or any type of race at a Non-Preferred course, or Non-Preferred races at Non-Preferred racecourses, but you should approach such contests with far greater caution because both experience and the statistics will teach you that you will have far less chance of winning than if you stick to the Preferred races and courses.

In Chapter 23, section 3, Race Examples, there are a number of examples where either the class of race, type of race or racecourse is of the Non-Preferred Category and yet The Tail End System worked successfully. What is necessary therefore is to get your priorities right and give priority to the Preferred races/courses and to consider betting on the Non-Preferred races/courses only when you think an exceptionally good betting opportunity exists. Getting this delicate balance right is not easy and is explored further not only in the remainder of this chapter, but also in Chapter 24, The High Profile Tracks and Meetings.

Returning to the overall subject of which races to bet on, you will not have to follow The Tail End System for very long on a dry run, no betting basis, before you start to appreciate that the choice of races to bet on is an absolutely critical factor in determining whether you make a profit overall.

The more you study the results the more you start to appreciate how certain racecourses consistently produce more 'outsider' victories than others. You will appreciate also that if you do restrict your betting activities to Class 3, 4 and 5 Handicap Races at the preferred racecourses, you will have a far better chance of being successful in the longer term.

Also, the more proficient you get at the actual form reading part of the System, you will find that the form pattern of certain 'outsiders' stands out in impressive fashion, relative to what you would term normal form patterns. It is when you start to get gut feelings during form reading, possibly based on form patterns that you have experienced with winning horses previously, that you realise you have acquired a skill which will help you enormously with your selections and also making the final decision as to whether to bet on a certain race or not.

In making The Tail End System work for you, you have to keep the thought firmly in the back of your mind that given the fact that, on average, only one race in six falls to an outsider, you need to be very selective in choosing your faces to bet on.

Fortunately, because of the starting prices you are likely to achieve, you will probably find that even if you are betting on two or three selections per race, you will only need to be successful in one race in five to be in profit. (NB The statement I have just made assumes that you are placing win bets only and staking the same amount of money on each selection.)

The words I have just used, namely 'you will only need', implies the task is a simple one and this of course is a far cry from the truth. What you need to be is very selective in choosing your races to bet on and that will require patience, caution and the application of a good deal of skill when reading the form.

Most horse race followers find the process of gambling very exciting and for many there is a strong tendency to jump into betting on the very first race of the day without a great deal of thought about betting strategy for the remainder of the races to follow.

When you are following The Tail End System, it is essential that you make a considered, but not necessarily lengthy, appraisal of all the races at all the jump meetings that day, with a view to determining which meetings and which races you are going to be particularly interested in. If, for example, you decide to follow the Class 3, 4 and 5 handicap races at the preferred courses only, you will undoubtedly make life a lot easier for yourself because you will not be wasting valuable time studying races which are either less likely to produce an outsider victory or alternatively far harder to crack from a selection point of view, because of factors such as the size of the field or the shortage of relevant form information.

I must again emphasise at this point that I am not trying to indicate that you should only bet on Class 3, 4 and 5 Handicap Races. However, if you are going to be successful, I think you will probably end up with a situation where:

a) Class 3, 4 and 5 Handicap Races at the preferred tracks are your priority.

b) Class 3, 4 and 5 Handicap Races at the Non-Preferred racetracks are occasionally a consideration when you feel that, despite the track, the race has the necessary ingredients to produce an outsider victory.

c) Class 1 and 2 races of all types and Class 3, 4 and 5 Non Handicap Races and Hunter Chases merit occasional consideration when there are very significant form clues to indicate that an outsider victory is on the cards.

Finally, and this is very important, you will get to the point where the experience of looking at countless races to determine whether they are likely to be a betting possibility will give you the ability to use your gut feelings to decide which races to concentrate on for form reading purposes.

However, and this point is critical, any decisions which you may make on race selection must not be based on any assessment on your part as to whether any of the shorter priced horses (shorter that is than the long-priced horses) are either likely or not likely to be successful in the race in question.

The reason for this is quite simple: if you try to assess whether the more favoured horses are going to give a good account of themselves, you could very well end up making the wrong decision and removing a race from the reckoning which ends up providing a massive payout for Tail End System followers.

The criteria which must be looked at when sorting out which races to concentrate on are:

a) The racecourse involved and its record, past and present, for producing outsider victories

b) The class of race

c) The type of race, Handicap or Non Handicap, Hurdle, Chase or Hunter Chase

d) Distance

e) Going

f) Number of runners

g) Betting Forecast

Having selected the races you are concentrating on, the final decision as to whether you bet on any of these races will be based entirely upon your findings and decisions in the clearly defined form reading process of The Tail End System (described in Chapters 22 and 23), which requires you to determine whether specific 'outsiders' in the race have a reasonable chance of a top three placing in the race in question, totally disregarding the form of the other runners.

Chapter 9
WHEN TO BET IN THE RACING CALENDAR

In Chapters 5, 6, 7 and 8 I have discussed *which* races to bet on but when it comes to 'outsiders', *when* to bet is equally important.

Before summer racing came into being a few years back, the jumping racing season always finished at the end of May or very early June, culminating with the Stratford meeting on Saturday afternoon and Market Rasen the same evening. There was then a complete break in racing in June and July, before a gradual resumption in August. When summer racing was introduced the summer break for horses, courses and connected staff was effectively scrapped and we now have a season of 12 months, which finishes the last Saturday in April when the Sandown meeting featuring the Betfred Gold Cup Chase is staged.

It is not the purpose of this book to discuss the merits or otherwise of summer racing but what needs to be considered is the spread of racing throughout the whole year and its effect on the number of 'outsider' winners which occur.

Looking once more at the 2006/2007 season the following chart shows the number of 'outsider' winners on a month by month basis.

NUMBER OF 'OUTSIDER' WINNERS 2006/2007 SEASON

Month	Number of 'Outsider' Winners
April (part month)	4
May	51
June	30
July	18
August	18
September	20
October	53
November	54
December	67
January	43
February	46
March	62
April (part month)	57
TOTAL	523

If we take a look now at the comparison between the number of 'outsider' winners in the summer months against the number in the remainder of the year, the figures are revealing.

**NUMBER OF 'OUTSIDER' WINNERS SUMMER MONTHS
AND REMAINDER OF THE 2006/2007 RACING SEASON**

	No of 'Outsider' Winners	No of Races	No of 'Outsider' Winners as a Percentage of Races
June July August September	86	558	15.4%
Remainder of The Racing Season	437	2544	17.1%

The above chart highlights the quiet period in the Jumps racing calendar from the 1st June to the 30th September because, in theory, if 2006/2007 had been a perfectly balanced racing year, 33.33 per cent of that year (ie four months) should have resulted in 174 'outsider' winners from 1,033 races from June to September, compared with the actual figures of 86 'outsider' winners from 558 races. By the same token, the remainder of the season (ie 1st of October to 31st May), which represents 66.66 per cent of the year, should have produced 348 'outsider' winners from 2,067 races when in fact there were 437 'outsider' winners from 2,544 races.

The above figures certainly endorse my long held view that if you are looking for long-priced winners you should concentrate your activities on the period when there is the most activity (ie October to May) because busy periods of racing generally mean more races, more runners, a wider spread of starting prices and also more opportunities for trainers to place their horses in races they can win. There is certainly a strong case from a betting point of view in taking heed of the old Stock Market adage "Sell in May and go away".

If however you feel that you must have a bet during the summer months, you will have to be doubly selective if you are to avoid losing money. That said, in 2006/2007 there were some cracking betting opportunities amongst the 558 races and 86 'outsider' winners in the summer but a great deal of care was needed to identify them.

In Chapter 7, when debating the whole question of which racecourses to select, I touched on the problem of blank meetings (ie meetings when there are no 'outsider' victories). Blank meetings can, of course, occur at any time in the race calendar and a run of blank meetings at a particular racecourse or even a number of racecourses, is sometimes a feature of summer racing when the ground firms up, or becomes waterlogged as it did in 2007, and the entries start to plummet as a result.

This highlights the need to always follow what is happening not only at the individual courses but also at all jumps courses. Even on days when I am leaving the racing alone I still make a quick study of the results and a careful study of any result of interest, eg where an 'outsider' has won or been placed at a decent price. By staying in touch with the racing in this way you identify situations where either a particular course or alternatively the whole of the sport has hit a flat spot with a complete absence of outside winners. When such a situation occurs it makes a lot of sense to back off altogether and wait for 'normal service' to be resumed. It is at such times that your patience will be tested but you have to accept that when a blank spot is occurring there is no point whatsoever in losing money unnecessarily. When 'normal service' is resumed and the 'outsider' winners reappear, that is the time to actively consider betting again, but not before.

Chapter 10
THE SEARCH FOR 'OUTSIDER' WINNERS DEMANDS A NON-ORTHODOX APPROACH TO BE SUCCESSFUL

Having dealt with the question of which races to bet on and when to bet, and before we deal with the subject of horse selection, we need to consider the task which is facing us when it comes to 'outsiders'.

The difficulties of selection are highlighted by the multitude of reasons which make a horse an 'outsider' in the betting.

Some of the reasons are as follows:
1) Bad position in the weights.
2) No recent relevant form.
3) Poor recent form.
4) No relevant form for the type of race or distance of race entered.
5) Going is considered unsuitable.
6) Odds compilers have got the price wrong.
7) Punters have deserted the horse in the betting and the price has drifted.
8) Horse's trainer is one of the 'lesser knowns'.
9) Horse's trainer is going through a quiet spell or a bad patch.
10) Jockey is considered to be in the lower order or inexperienced.
11) Jockey is going through a bad patch.
12) Horse's trainer has two or more entries in the same race and this is not the stable pick.
13) Horse is having its first race following a fall.
14) Horse is attempting to move up in class of race without the form to justify it.
15) There are half a dozen fancied runners in the race and this isn't one of them.
16) The age of the horse is considered to be against it.
17) The breeding of the horse does not appear particularly suitable for the race in question.
18) All the horse's best runs have been on a right hand track and today's is left handed.
19) The horse has never won a race before.
20) The horse has shown a marked tendency to under perform at the business end of a race.
21) There is no indication from the horse's form that he is likely to be suited by the racetrack hosting today's race.
22) Horse's recent high placing was considered to be a fluke which could not be repeated.
23) The trainer has chosen an unsuitable race.
24) Horse's previous form was in Ireland, the value of which is hard to determine.
25) Horse is moving to National Hunt from the Point to Point circuit, where the form is very hard to evaluate.

Obviously there are quite a lot more reasons than the 25 listed here but just by looking at them it can be seen that, if you follow the traditional methods of trying to determine which horse is going to win a race, you will be unlikely to pick an outsider. For this reason any system for picking 'outsider' winners has to be unorthodox to have any chance of success. So when you read the following parts of the current chapter you should always bear this in mind.

It is worth stating that I didn't have any difficulty thinking about the twenty five reasons listed above because all are very familiar descriptions of 'outsiders' which I have backed successfully. It is a fact that the majority of punters automatically dismiss long-priced winners as a fluke either because: a) the long price on offer meant that they had not even considered the horse as a possible betting proposition, or b) they did look at the horse's form but were unable to recognise any pointers which may have been present in that form to suggest the horse could possibly win the race.

There are not many jumps races where the result could be considered a complete fluke, with all the runners bar the winner falling or impeded, as in Foinavon's victory in the Grand National in the dim and distant past. If an 'outsider' has won a race it is because it has beaten the entire field and therefore any hard luck stories from any of its rivals on the day do not change the result. Particularly in handicap races there is nearly always some sort of clue in an 'outsider' winner's form to suggest a capability to achieve success and this is a point which will be examined in depth in the coming pages.

I would conclude this section by making the important point that 'outsider' winners in jump racing are not a rare breed because 523 wins from 3,102 races (2006/2007 season) is a sizable group which deserves serious consideration. However, in giving them that consideration you have to recognise that the form profile of these 'outsiders' is often markedly different from that of the shorter priced winners. In this setting the message, corny though it sounds, has to be: 'Think outsider – think different'.

Chapter 11
THE SELECTION OF 'OUTSIDERS' CAN ONLY BE BASED ON THE FORM OF THE HORSE

There are very sound reasons for saying that when it comes to selecting 'outsiders' only the form of the horse and factual information related to that form should be taken into account. This means that any information which constitutes an opinion as opposed to fact should be totally disregarded.

Firstly, although there is a whole army of racing pundits, professional tipsters, TV presenters and so called experts employed by the media to predict the winners of races, it is a fact that this group rarely concern themselves with 'outsiders'. There are valid reasons for this, and given the fact that in the 2006/2007 jump season 83 percent of all the winners had a starting price of 9/1 or less, it is obvious that the 'professionals' will concentrate on shorter-priced horses because their main objective is to pick as many winners as possible. Given this situation you have to conclude that the information emanating from these media professionals must be regarded as being of no assistance.

Secondly, although trainers, jockeys and stable insiders occupy the best position to assess the chances of any horse they are training or riding, the information they impart is so frequently wrong that it has to be dismissed as thoroughly unreliable.

This last comment does not imply any criticism of trainers, jockeys or stable staff but is merely an observation based on the facts that horses can be notoriously unpredictable in some cases and gloriously predictable in others but either way the racing public has no right to expect correct predictions from a horse's connections.

Thirdly, although many punters like to select a horse because of the record of its trainer, with 'outsider' selection it is not possible to do this without forsaking a lot of winners. Many 'outsider' winners are the 'out of the blue' variety trained by a trainer who, for example, is either:

a) Training his first winner
b) Trains very few winners
c) Is ending a long running cold spell
d) Comes from Ireland and is an unknown quantity
e) Is a low profile trainer

As a result of this situation you cannot exclude any horse from the selection process because of who is training it.

Fourthly, punters also like to select a horse because of the record of its jockey and again it is not possible to do this without giving up a lot of winners. Many 'outsiders' have a long price because their jockey is either inexperienced, relatively unsuccessful in terms of number of winners, unfashionable or female. As is discussed in Chapters 12 and 13, which follow, trainers have got to be trusted to pick the jockey and jockeys have got to be trusted because the standard of jockeyship has never been any higher. Whilst the decision to ignore who is riding a horse may not appeal to many punters, in my experience they are not taking any undue risks in doing so.

Finally, having already made the point that the media professionals cannot be entrusted with the task of picking 'outsider' winners neither can their opinions be taken into account with regard to the capability or suitability of a horse. If you study most of the professionals' pre-race notes relating to the 'outsiders' which go on to win the race, you will find that their chances are frequently either dismissed, ridiculed or seriously underestimated. As a result you must automatically disregard any comments from a professional which amounts to an opinion. The important thing here is to differentiate between opinion and fact, because there are occasions where a media professional will impart useful, factual information about a horse's record which cannot be gleaned from the form record which is published in the *Racing Post* on the day of the race. For example, if a professional in a race preview states "the horse looks equipped to cope with a move up in distance", the comment should be disregarded because it is merely an opinion. If however a professional states "the horse's Point to Point record in Ireland demonstrated a capability to deal with heavy going", the comment can be considered because it is based on fact rather than surmise.

In conclusion, I would stress that the importance of the advice contained in this section will become much clearer when you have studied chapter's 22 and 23.

Chapter 12
TRAINERS

I have every admiration for trainers because of the range of skills they possess in order both to survive and to be successful is simply amazing. By following the sport closely, it becomes clear that you have to assume that any accredited trainer is capable of winning any race providing the horse in his charge has sufficient natural ability. The evidence in support of this statement is the large number of apparent no-hoper type horses that achieve unexpected victories against all odds who are trained by trainers at the bottom end of the trainer's table, who have a relatively small string of horses in their care. I am not trying to say that trainers do not make mistakes because the very nature of their task involves a lot of trial and error, but what I am saying is that you have to place your trust in this group of stalwarts because to do otherwise will undoubtedly cost you money. The first trainer related golden rule in the search for 'outsider' winners is never, ever pass over the selection of a horse because you do not have sufficient knowledge of, or confidence in, its trainer.

The second golden rule is to think very hard indeed before dismissing any horse on the grounds that the trainer has chosen a race where the conditions ie going, distance, weight, type of race, class of race or time interval between races appear to be against the horse in question. There have been occasions in the past when I thought I knew better than the trainer about what conditions would suit the horse and have been proved wrong at considerable cost and as a result I very rarely argue now with the trainers' judgement about such matters.

The third golden rule concerns state of fitness, because it is notoriously difficult for a trainer to maintain a horse at peak racing fitness for any length of time. The classifications of fitness vary between:

a) Fit to start a race but not necessarily fit enough to complete the distance.
b) Fit to race but barring incidents affecting the other runners, not fit enough to win or be placed in the first three.
c) Fit enough to win or be placed in the first three.
d) Fit to race but possibly beyond peak fitness and therefore unlikely to win or be placed in the first three.

From the classifications outlined it can be seen that a trainer can be running a horse to get it fit for a subsequent outing rather, than running the horse to win, and, therefore, if this information can be gleaned from the horse's form record it can be extremely helpful in determining whether to select a horse for betting purposes.

The fourth golden rule is to recognise the fact that trainers are committed to the task of training winners and wherever possible landing a touch on behalf of their owners. In this setting they are entitled to use all the legitimate tricks in their trade to pull off a surprise victory. Fortunately, because all races are a matter of public record, it is possible in some cases to study the form book and second guess the trainer's plans for a particular horse. As you would expect, in order to unearth these plans you need to know what you are looking for and this is a subject which is explored in depth in Chapter 23.

The final golden rule is to always bear in mind the fact that situations do and will arise where you will be reading the form of an outsider and although there are no obvious form pointers to indicate that the horse concerned can achieve a top three placing, the trainer, by your own observations, is somebody capable of pulling off a shock victory and possibly landing a touch in the process. In this book I make no attempt to identify trainers who fit into this category, for the following reasons:

a) Any list of such trainers would quickly become out of date.
b) Any publicity given to such trainers will adversely affect their chances of landing long-priced winners in the future.
c) Anybody following on a daily basis all the 'outsider' winners over the jumps will, after a few months, become well aware of the trainers I am referring to.

As a result of the situation I have described you must automatically adopt a suspicious and very questioning approach to indifferent form records belonging to such trainers' horses and it may be that in such circumstances you decide to select a horse which otherwise would be passed over in the selection process.

Chapter 13
JOCKEYS

When I first started to attend race meetings in the late seventies, I soon realised that jockeys are a group of sportsmen possessing amazing courage and skill, entrusted with enormous responsibility in guiding valuable thoroughbreds around difficult courses, where tactical brilliance and an ability to get maximum effort from their charge is a prime requirement.

Although over the years I have on occasions criticised the riding tactics employed by a jockey, such criticism has been rare and not fully justified considering the difficulties involved in getting everything just right.

During recent years I have heard a number of the top ex-jockeys say that the current standard of jockeyship is as high as it has ever been and I definitely agree fully with this point of view. Furthermore, I would say that there are so many excellent jockeys around now that it must be impossible for a sub-standard jockey to get sufficient rides to justify his or her continuance in the profession.

As a result of my genuine confidence in the current crop of jockeys, I am very happy to accept the trainer's choice of jockey, male or female, for any horse I select. I therefore think it would be totally wrong and unnecessary to bypass the selection of my chosen horses because of their jockeys, particularly when such decisions would automatically lead to the loss of a large number of long-priced winners.

Chapter 14
PADDOCK JUDGING AND GOING TO POST

Two of the three years after I started to attend race meetings at Stratford Racecourse, I went through a phase where I visited the paddock before a race to see if I could spot any pointers for selection purposes. This phase was brought to an abrupt end when I was taught an expensive lesson. I had studied the form intently for this particular chase and had selected a horse ridden by Hwyel Davies, father of the current jockey, James Davies. Before placing a bet I visited the paddock, only to find my selection, a grey, was awash with sweat and looking quite agitated. Horrified at the discovery, I promptly reached for my *Sporting Life* and re-read the form before picking an alternative to the grey, which I was convinced would run a bad race. I am sure by now you can guess the rest of the story but, for the record, Hwyel Davies and his sweating grey won the race at a canter at a price of 16/1. Totally gutted I resolved never to visit the paddock again with serious intent, a resolution I have never broken.

It is also interesting to note that in all my racecourse visits over the years with Brian, Steve, Andy, Maurice and Fred, it has been extremely rare for any of us to have selected a horse for betting purposes which won the 'best turned out award' and then went on to win the race. As a result of this situation our racing group to a man has always issued some choice words if they have heard over the tannoy that the horse they had backed has been given the paddock prize.

I am sure by now that some of you readers will be saying, 'it isn't the paddock you should be looking at, you should be looking at how the horse goes to post.' I must admit that as a non horseman I have never attempted to judge a horse by the way it travels to post; in my defence, however, I would point to the appalling record of Channel Four Racing in this regard and I am sure you will agree that if the likes of John Francome are unable to get it right, what chance have us lesser mortals.

In conclusion I would say that, in all available evidence, the unanimous verdict on paddock judging and going to post has to be that a horse's appearance is not a reliable guide to how it will perform. The lesson therefore is stick to the form book and don't be deviated by what amounts to another example of misleading opinion.

Chapter 15
HORSES AND BREEDING

It is very important to understand that, for many long-priced winners of jump races, the combination of a long price with a win is either a 'one off' career event or a very rare occurrence for the horse concerned. The majority of lower grade horses competing in lower class races do not win very often and it is very common for them to only clock up a single victory. The number of lower grade horses that do manage to win at a big price, and then go on to win again, also at a big price, is extremely few because by the time of their next victory they will be known and remembered by many more punters as well as the handicapper and their price will be much lower.

Unexpected long-priced results normally originate from either the wrong interpretation of form, or lack of it, by the odds compilers and/or the punters, and as a result a long-priced winner is created.

long-priced winners are not, of course, confined to low grade horses because there are frequently low graded runners that are asked to compete in higher class races than previously and spring a total surprise having performed at a far higher level than their ratings indicated. In so many cases however, this is a one off occurrence because by the time the horse is ready to move up in class again, the market and the handicapper has got their measure and their starting price is nothing like the generous odds which were offered on the occasion of their first victory. There are exceptions to the rule and big priced wins can be repeated by the same horse. This is particularly possible where there is a long time gap since the horses last victory and as a result it has slipped to a more generous handicap mark and/or the odds compilers and punters have either written the horse off as a winning proposition or failed to recall the ability it once had. The exceptions which I have just mentioned are like to occur in the following situations:

a) The horse is a course specialist, who after a recent run of poor form, has returned to his favourite track and runs above the level of his most recent form.
b) The horse is getting on in years, eg 12, 13 or 14, and has been written off by the punters for that reason.
c) The horse has just returned from a long lay off and was not expected to go well fresh or alternatively its first one or two runs after its break were interpreted by the odds compilers and punters as meaning the horse has lost its way and is therefore very unlikely to win.

One particular important lesson to be learnt from all that has been stated in this section is that you, the punter, must avoid having favourite horses. This is because. given the fact that you are looking for long-priced winners which rarely win more than once or twice at such odds, you must look at each race as a one off and follow your adopted selection system without any deviation. In just the same way that owners find difficulty in resisting the temptation to lump money on their own horse, regardless of whether it has a genuine chance of winning, so betting system followers are often easily tempted to dump their system and plump for a horse which has won for them before. This is a massive mistake which can cost you, the punter, a lot of money. Past successes should always be regarded as what they are, namely a piece of history.

It is important you appreciate that The Tail End System has been deliberately constructed in such a way that System followers require no prior knowledge of either the horses, trainers or jockeys involved in any particular race, because all of the selection decisions are based entirely on the form of the horse as published in the *Racing Post* on the day of the contest. There are very sound and logical reasons for this, namely:

a) Trainer and jockey form is excluded from the equation simply because its inclusion would automatically result in the elimination of a large number of horses which win races at long prices.

b) A horse's previous form is only relevant when It is considered against all of the information appertaining to the race in which it is entered, eg Racecourse, Type of Race, Class of Race, Distance, Going, Handicap Ratings.

Given the above situation it has to be noted that, in certain circumstances, making use of prior knowledge of a horse can be dangerous because it can encourage you to either overlook or short circuit the form reading procedure which is an integral part of The Tail End System and this could have disastrous consequences.

When you read Chapters 22 and 23, you will see that The Tail End System incorporates a strict procedure and order by which horses are chosen for form reading purposes with a view to possible selection for betting purposes. The dangerous situation that I have referred to is therefore one where previous knowledge of a horse causes you to either select or reject a horse without following the procedure and order of form reading as it is written.

What you have to get used to with The Tail End System is the discipline of following a strict procedure which requires you to consider the form of horses in a particular order with a view to determining their ability to be placed in the first three places in the particular race you are looking at. It is for these reasons that you need to look at each race as a unique event, never to be repeated, and always complete the form reading process in the prescribed manner, regardless of whether you do or don't know anything about any of the horses involved.

Finally, I must make a brief mention of the subject of breeding. Quite deliberately, the breeding of horses, which is an extremely complicated subject, is not taken into consideration in any way by The Tail End System, simply because such consideration could result in a lot of long-priced winners being excluded from the reckoning for incorrect reasons.

Chapter 16
NEVER BE PUT OFF BY A LONG STARTING PRICE AND NEVER CHANGE YOUR MIND

It is probably fair to say that, because of what you read in the newspapers, see on TV or hear on the radio, you are brainwashed into thinking that a long starting price for any kind of sporting event means the competitor concerned has no realistic chance of winning. In horse racing there is not a doubt that the TV presenters, the newspaper columnists and the tipsters generally give the 'outsiders' a wide berth. This situation is completely understandable considering that in the case of the TV presenters they have limited time available and in the case of the columnists and tipsters they are normally restricted to picking one horse per race only, and for the sake of their own reputation and their success rates they are generally going to stick with the more obvious form choices.

In the case of the odds compilers, their task is to evaluate the form and allocate a price and therefore, by awarding the shortest prices to the best form horse and the longest prices to the worst form horses, they are doing their job correctly. As a result of this traditional approach by both the media and bookmakers, the punter is guided into thinking that the shorter priced horses are worth serious consideration whilst the longer price horses are worthy only of limited consideration.

In the search for 'outsider' winners the punter has to recognise the situation I have described and treat all starting prices as merely an opinion which could well be proved an unreliable guide to the horse's chances. By operating in this fashion the punter can ensure that when he is studying the form of a long-priced horse he gives the task just as much attention as he does with any other long-priced horse.

Over the years there have been a number of famous occasions on TV and radio where the presenter has asked the trainer to explain how his/her runner was able to win at a ridiculously long price and the response has usually been: 'The horse didn't know his starting price.' So if you can always remember the horse's angle on things when you are studying form to make your selections you will automatically keep yourself in the right frame of mind and avoid being sidetracked.

The other trap that you must avoid falling into is that of changing your mind after you have made your selection decision. It is Sod's law that if you have followed your adopted selection system but subsequently change your mind and select another horse in preference to your original choice, you will be proved wrong. I'm not saying that this will always be the case but over the years I have witnessed so many tearful incidents amongst my racing friends, including myself, where a selection has been made after careful consideration, only to be changed at the last minute with disastrous consequences. There is of course an easy remedy; if you have followed your adopted selection system and made a selection decision for carefully considered reasons then stick with that selection even if you have second thoughts afterwards. If you are convinced, however, from those second thoughts that you are about to back the wrong horse, then back your original choice anyway but place an additional bet on your 'second thought' selection. Fortunately in the case of outsiders the starting prices are likely to be sufficient to justify an additional investment on your part without serious effect on either potential winnings or your overall starting budget.

If you are not entirely convinced by what I have stated in this section so far I would like to recall an incident at the Cheltenham Festival in 1990 concerning one of my racing colleagues, Steve Butterworth. Steve is an ex casino croupier whose first love is roulette but he is also a very experienced jump race follower and an excellent reader of form. Cheltenham for Steve is the highlight of his betting year and an event which he regards as something of a holiday, away from the more intensive atmosphere associated with the green baize of the roulette table. Steve, Brian, Andy and myself were all at Cheltenham on the Wednesday of the Festival, which was the day before Norton's Coin's fabulous victory in the Cheltenham Gold Cup.

By the time we had reached the last race on the card, none of our group had achieved a memorable pick up but, true to form, we all buckled down to the task of trying to save our bacon on the lucky last, the Mildmay of Flete Handicap Chase.

Steve, following the normal practice within our group, made his selection quite separately from anybody else and, having convinced himself that New Halen (18lb out of the Handicap) was going to win the race, he made his way over to a tote kiosk and placed £10 on it to win. In the course of making his way back to where we were all based, Steve visited a line of bookmakers and was horrified to discover that his selection was freely available at a price of 66/1. Convinced from the price that New Halen was not going to win he restudied the form in the *Racing Post* and made an alternative selection. He then retraced his steps to the same tote lady who had taken his bet and asked her if he could change his selection. 'You should never change your bet young man,' came the response. Steve being Steve, recounted the full story of his visit to the Bookies but it cut no ice with Mrs Tote who insisted he would be taking the wrong step by changing but conceded that if he still wanted to go ahead with his request he could. The bet was changed and Steve made his way back to our group to watch the race. Like so many of the Festival events the race was another classic; as the runners made their descent for the final time and started to negotiate the famous finishing hill we could see a horse sprinting clear from the pack at an uncatchable pace. By the time it reached the finishing line it was eight lengths clear and still going away. 'New Halen wins,' the commentator boomed!

Chapter 17
SOD'S LAW (ANYTHING THAT CAN GO WRONG WILL GO WRONG)

Although I do not know either the origins or history of Sod's law I know enough about betting to appreciate that it is *the* determining factor which makes the majority of Bookies rich and the majority of punters poor. Sod's law dictates that if you have to make a choice between two or more horses you will choose the wrong one. There will, of course, be occasions when you make the right choice and there will be other occasions when you have a winning streak, but overall you will be wrong more times than you are right. It is for all these reasons that there is no future in pursuing a system which relies on backing short priced favourites because as we all know there are far too many favourites that get beaten and those that win will offer insufficient odds to overcome the losses which will be an unavoidable feature of such a system.

The best example I know to illustrate the difficulties posed by Sod's law are the even money bets which are available at any casino on the roulette table where you have 36 numbers to bet on from 1 to 36. (There is also one zero on all UK tables which takes 50% of all even money stakes when it drops.)

There are three different even money bets which are:
   a)   Black or Red
   b)   Odd or Even
   c)   High (19 – 36) and Low (1 – 18)

On the face of it, the chances of the punter landing any of these bets are 50/50 which reflects the even money on offer, but you have to ask yourself how the casinos can afford to offer such an opportunity to the punter without giving themselves a financial edge to ensure a profit. The answer I would suggest is the fact that it is the punter who has to make the selection decision (eg between black or red) and the casino industry therefore knows that Sod's law will dictate that in the long term the odds of winning will always fall in favour of the casino and not the punter.

However, although many casinos' punters do chance their arm on even money bets, the vast majority of roulette betting is staked on single numbers where the odds are 35 to 1 with the punter retaining his stake if he wins. Although these odds have a small bias in favour of the casino (because there are 37 single numbers including the zero), the odds are big enough to make single number betting very attractive to punters who can indulge in multiple choice staking and make handsome profits if they are good enough or lucky enough to predict the numbers being thrown up by the wheel.

I have used the example of roulette because it provides two very important lessons in relation to betting which can be extremely helpful in establishing a suitable strategy for horse racing. These lessons are:

a) Where the punter has to choose between two even money shots with identical chances of winning, Sod's law will dictate that he/she will make the wrong selection more times than he/she makes the right selection in the long term.

b) Where the punter has to make a selection from a large field of runners with comparable chances of winning, he/she can take advantage of the high starting prices which are frequently associated with such contests by adopting a multi selection approach in order to drastically reduce any adverse effects of Sods Law on his chances of winning.

When you read Chapter 22, which describes The Tail End System, you will discover how lessons a) and b) have been taken into account in the system's construction.

Chapter 18
HORSES FOR COURSES

The saying "Horses for Courses" is a very true statement as far as jump racing is concerned. When I first started attending race meetings at Stratford on Avon Racecourse, I was lucky enough to see Gambling Prince run on a number of occasions. Gambling Prince always seemed to run above himself at Stratford and to see his enthusiasm for that particular racetrack was a sight to behold. For a horse that cost 300 guineas his record was quite exceptional. He clocked up a grand total of 19 victories (eight of them at Stratford) over both fences and hurdles, including victories in both the Greenham Hurdle and the Game Spirit Chase at Newbury.

He also achieved third place in the Triumph Hurdle at Cheltenham and a 100/1 ante-post success in a big chase at Haydock. Gambling Prince's last victory at Stratford was achieved at the age of 13 and his overall record at that track is evidence in itself that horses can run above their ratings at tracks they take a liking to.

Although of course there are horses that demonstrate an ability to win at a wide variety of tracks, the majority of runners seem to prefer:

a)   Either left hand or right hand tracks and are rarely just as comfortable on both.
b)   Either flat or alternatively hilly/undulating tracks.
c)   Tracks that incorporate either sharp bends or alternatively easy turns

Practically all racetracks have a current course specialist and if you consult the racing history books you will find many of the best remembered horses of yesteryear showed a particular liking for certain tracks but not others.

When it comes to reading form, it is essential that a horse's record at the racecourse where it is running is taken into account, regardless of whether the form relates to wins, places in the first three or merely a satisfactory outing.

It is amazing how frequently a horse that has been given experience of a particular track without winning subsequently goes on to win at the same course. If a horse has had no relevant course experience but its form reads as if it is ready to win a race, it is always a worthwhile exercise to try and judge from its past performances and record if it is likely to put in a good performance at the particular racetrack in question. This exercise is carried out by comparing the type of racecourses it has performed well at in the past and comparing the conditions appertaining to those courses with the conditions it will experience in its current race.

There are so many 'outsider' wins that can be attributed to the horse's record at a particular track that course form is an important and integral part of The Tail End System. There is, therefore, further reference to this subject in Chapter 22 The Tail End System and Chapter 23 Reading the Form.

Chapter 19
RACING POST

When the *Racing Post* was first published in 1986 I became an immediate fan, primarily because the paper's style of presentation of racing form was not only superb but infinitely better than that of its rival, the *Sporting Life*. As the years have passed, the *Racing Post* has gone from strength to strength and it remains the essential daily guide to all UK horse racing as well as an invaluable guide to all forms of sports betting.

I never cease to be amazed at just how much information is crammed into the 100 plus pages of what I regard as horse racing's daily bible.

The big advantage which the *Racing Post* has over the racing pages of the national dailies is the fact that its horse racing form is a complete and comprehensive guide to each and every runner in every single race, enabling the punter to make informed selections with no prior knowledge of the horses that are participating.

As a result of the advantage I have just described, The Tail End System has been constructed in such a way that all you require to make your selections is the *Racing Post* for the day in question and approximately ten to fifteen minutes of your time to study the form for each of the races you intend betting on.

It is important to point out that the *Racing Post* does, in fact, publish more form related information than is actually desirable to use as far as The Tail End System is concerned and therefore it is essential that The Tail End System is adhered to strictly as it is written.

Chapter 20
KEEP IT SIMPLE

My first sporting passion, which started at the age of 14, was cycle racing, and though I rode my last road race at the age of 24 my interest in the sport continues to the present day. Over the years I have travelled to various parts of Europe to see the world Professional Road Race Championship, a single day event which is held annually and attracts the biggest stars in what is a massive sport in the main common market countries.

On one such occasion in the seventies, together with one of my friends and work colleague Ron Jones, we travelled on an organised coach trip to the Championships which were being held at the Nürburgring motor racing circuit in Germany. We had written instructions from Chequers Travel to board their number 2 coach at an address close to Victoria Station in London, where we arrived an hour before our scheduled departure time to find two Chequers Travel coaches parked in the street with signs 'Number 1' and 'Number 2 posted on their windscreens. Although there were already a few passengers on the coaches there was no sign of either the drivers or the couriers so we boarded the 'Number 2 coach and asked a couple of the passengers if it was indeed the 'Number 2' coach. We were given a thumbs up sign so we dumped all our bags on one of the seats and told the couple that we are going to grab a cup of tea at the nearby café before we departed.

Forty minutes later, we arrived back to find two empty spaces where our coaches had been but another couple of Chequers Travel coaches parked some fifty yards away. Again they were marked up 'Number 1' and 'Number 2' but this time one of the Chequers Travel's most experienced couriers, Jim, was on hand to explain where the original 'Number 2' coach had disappeared to, together with our bags. It didn't take a minute of listening to Jim to discover that Chequers Travel were also running a trip to a motor cycle Grand Prix in Belgium and that is where our bags were heading, together with our wallets and passports and everything else you need for a three day trip. By this time, we were in panic mode, which was only slightly alleviated by the laconic Jim, who ventured that the bikers were highly likely to be making their way to Dover for the Channel crossing, in which case there was a chance that we would catch them up there. We thought about it for a couple of minutes and decided that, although there was a good chance of being stranded in Dover with no money, it was a chance worth taking rather than give up the trip.

We then had a tense journey to Dover with our eyes never far from our coach driver, wiling him to keep the accelerator flat to the board in order to reduce the twenty minute gap between our coach and the one carrying the motorbikers.

There is a steep descent on the road into Dover and as the Docks and the ferries hove into view an earnest looking Jim made his way up to us from his seat by the driver.

'Look lads,' he said, 'with a bit of luck, when we reach the Docks in a couple of minutes we will be able to find the biker's coach. If we do, I want you to remember that you won't have a lot of time. So board the coach and speak to the driver but keep it simple; bags on the wrong coach, think it's this one, can we have them? Have you got that lads?'

'Yes we've got it Jim,' we replied, trying hard to suppress our laughter as he made his way back to the front of the coach.

As luck would have it when we reached a garage a couple of hundred yards from the

Docks there were the two bikers' coaches filling up with diesel. On Jim's instructions our coach immediately jerked to a halt and as Ron and I leapt out, Jim was shouting, 'remember lads, keep it simple!'

We reached the missing 'Number 2' coach and, following Jim's advice almost to the letter, we said to the driver: 'We're from the Chequers trip to Germany, we put our bags on your coach by mistake, can we have them?'

'Help yourself,' came the reply and as we made our way up the coach there were our bags sitting on the seat just as we left them.

The rest of our trip was without incident and Jim proved to be a brilliant courier who we travelled with again on a number of occasions.

As a result of the Dover incident we declared Jim a legend and thereafter whenever Ron and I were trying to solve a difficult problem at work, and believe you me, in a heavily unionised plant we had plenty of those, we'd always say: "Remember, keep it simple, bags on the wrong coach, think it's this one, can we have them?"

There is no doubt that, if you are trying to solve a tricky problem the more complicated you make the intended solution, the more likely it will be unsuccessful. Once you appreciate the fact that horse racing is always made to appear far more complicated than it actually, is as a result of the 1,001 pieces of form related information that are readily served up to you the punter, by both the media and the bookies, you will recognise the need to keep to a minimum the amount of information you actually use in the selection making process.

I issue this warning because The Tail End System is a simple solution to what can appear to be a very difficult problem. Unless you the reader understand the philosophy behind the system there will be a tendency for you to add bits on, for example trainer form, jockey form, speed ratings, previous knowledge of one of the runners etc, usually with disastrous consequences. I have to be honest and say that when I first started working on The Tail End System I was guilty on the odd occasion of not sticking rigidly to the system as it is written, thereby triggering Sod's law and causing me to lose very significant amounts of money. The Tail End System is very successful but abuse it at your peril because it has a very nasty habit of biting you on the backside.

Chapter 21
DISCIPLINE

Having already examined the need to keep it simple and stick to the system we need to consider the high level of discipline which is required when betting on horses. Whether you are at the racetrack, sitting at home with your wife, husband or partner, or merely sitting alone in a quiet room, you need to discipline yourself to switch off from all distractions around you and concentrate hard on what you are doing. Horse racing may be a hobby to you but at the same time you are trying to both win money and avoid losing it also. In this setting, you need to concentrate extremely hard when you are making your selections because it is all too easy to deviate from the system by mistake or to overlook or misread a vital bit of form and before you know it, you have chosen the wrong horse, a winning opportunity has been missed and you have lost money. The golden rule is always to give yourself ample time to make your selections because if you are forced to rush this process it will inevitably lead to mistakes. I cannot emphasise enough that attention to detail in both the race selection process and form reading process is absolutely critical if you are to be successful.

I have already mentioned in Chapter 19 that it takes approximately ten minutes to study the form for each race when working to The Tail End System. Ten minutes may not seem very long but when you are at a racetrack it is often extremely difficult to achieve that sort of period without constant interruptions. The answer is to plan your day as much as possible so that if you do have a necessity to study form before you arrive at the racetrack you have made the necessary arrangements to achieve this.

Disciplining yourself to make the time to study the form properly may seem like a bit of a chore but there is nothing like picking a big priced winner and you will always find the time to party afterwards.

Chapter 22
THE TAIL END SYSTEM

In order to operate The Tail End System it is necessary to follow the instructions listed below to the letter and in the order in which they appear:

a) *Racing Post*
Purchase the *Racing Post* on the day in question – no other paper will provide you with   the information required to operate the system.

b) **The Courses**
Identify which race meetings you are interested in. The preferred race courses are:

Ayr
Bangor
Carlisle
Catterick
Chepstow
Exeter
Fakenham
Folkestone
Hereford
Hexham
Huntingdon
Kelso
Lingfield
Ludlow
Market Rasen
Musselborough
Newton Abbot
Perth
Sedgefield
Stratford
Taunton
Towcester
Uttoxeter
Wincanton
Worcester

The above courses, based on their record, should provide a better chance of winning but as the System can work at any course the non-preferred courses can be considered if they are featuring races which appear to offer what you perceive to be an outstanding opportunity for an 'outsider' victory.

c) Identify the races which you are interested in

The preferred races are Class 3, 4 and 5 Handicap chases and Handicap Hurdle races. These races are based on their record should provide the best chance of winning but as the System can work in any event, consideration can be given to Class 3, 4, 5 and 6, non-handicap events and any type of Class 1 or 2 event, if such events appear to provide an outstanding opportunity for an 'outsider' victory.

d) Examine the races in greater depth

Having identified certain races as being a possibility for betting purposes you need to look at the Betting Forecast (displayed at the foot of each list of runners and riders appearing in the *Racing Post*) to determine whether prices of 10/1 or longer are likely to be on offer.

Bearing in mind the objective of The Tail End System is to select long-priced winners with an average starting price in the region of 17/1, it is probably best to dismiss those races where odds of 10/1 or greater are not achievable.

One word of caution, the Betting Forecasts published by the *Racing Post* should always be viewed as a forecast because the prices offered by the Bookmakers, Tote and the Betting Exchanges on the day of the race, and indeed the Official Starting Prices are frequently different from the Betting Forecast, and sometimes exceptionally different.

As a result of this situation, races which appear to be a betting proposition when you view your *Racing Post* in the morning, are sometimes no longer that nearer the race and vice versa. The golden rules therefore are never to commit yourself to a bet unless the price or prices you are being offered are acceptable and never dismiss a race for betting purposes on the grounds of the prices until you are certain that a betting opportunity does not exist.

e) Objectives

Having determined which races are a serious betting proposition, the next step is to choose long-priced horses to bet on. Before we examine the procedure for doing this you need to understand the principle objectives of The Tail End System which are:

i)   To select horses with the longest possible forecast prices which have a reasonable chance of finishing in the first three placings.

ii) To avoid as far as it is possible to do so, any deliberate choice between two or more horses so as to avoid the problems of 'Sods Law'.

iii) To take advantage of the long prices on offer by making multiple selections (ie two or more horses) where it appears sensible to do so in order to increase the chances of success.

f) Horse Selection Procedure

In order to meet the objectives of The Tail End System (outlined in e) above), the procedure for selecting horses is as follows:

i)   All horses are selected by reading the form of those horses as set out in the *Racing Post*, in accordance with the instructions and guidance which is contained in Chapter 23 which follows.

ii) Horses are only selected if. having read the form of the horse in the prescribed manner, you, the punter, are satisfied that 'the horse has a reasonable chance of finishing the race in the first three totally disregarding the form of the other runners'.

iii) The order in which you study the form of the horses is a critical part of the exercise and is based on the order in which they appear in the Betting Forecast displayed in the *Racing Post* for each race.

iv) The first horse to have its form studied is the last horse named in the *Racing Post*'s Betting Forecast, always providing that all of the horses in the race have been named in the Betting Forecast.

v) In the cases where the Betting Forecast ends with a BAR price (eg 25/1 BAR) it means that there are at least one or more runners that have not been named in the Betting Forecast which have a forecast price which is at least as long or longer than the BAR price (eg 25/1).

In such cases, you need to work out which horses have not been named in the Betting Forecast and that will provide you with a list of names in the BAR group. The first horse to have its form studied is the horse in the BAR group which appears nearest to the bottom of the list of runners and riders published by the *Racing Post*. (Note that this is because the System assumes that Forecast price wise all BAR group horses are equal, so priority is given to the horse with the lowest weight).

vi) Having determined which is the first horse to have its form studied (ie the last named horse in the Betting Forecast or the bottom listed horse in the BAR group) you read the form of the horse in accordance with the instructions/ guidance given in Chapter 23, Reading the Form.

vii) If, after you have studied the form of the first horse, you conclude that 'it has a reasonable chance of finishing in the first three regardless of the form of the other runners', this horse becomes your first selection.

viii) If you dismiss the chances of the first horse to be studied, or alternatively if you want to make a second selection, you move on to the next to last horse in the Betting Forecast (where all horses are named in the Betting Forecast) or the next bottom listed horse in the BAR group (where a BAR group exists in the Betting Forecast).

Again you study the form and again you make a decision either to select the horse or dismiss the horse and move on to the next horse to be studied.

ix) You continue to move to the next named horse in the Betting Forecast or the next bottom listed horse in the BAR group until you have made your first two selections. It should be noted that if you have started with a BAR group of horses, once you have exhausted this group you move to the last named horse in the Betting Forecast and so on.

x) It is very important to point out that if you dismiss a horse and then move to the next horse to study its form, you should automatically go back to the dismissed horse and double check your dismissal decision before making any decision on the next horse.

This double checking procedure is an essential feature of the System because it is very easy to dismiss horses by overlooking a significant pointer in their form. This is a matter which is discussed in detail in the following chapter.

xi) If you decide to make more than two selections, the procedure alters from automatically moving to the next horse in the Betting Forecast to either or both of the following two options:

Option 1 – Consider any course winners in the field (providing they have a forecast price of 10/1 or longer) starting with the course winner with the longest forecast price if there is more than one. If there is more than one course winner on the same forecast price, always start with the last named course winner in the Betting Forecast. *Special note:* Do not differentiate between course winners (marked C), course, distance winners (marked CD), course and distance winners (marked C&D).

and/or

Option 2 – Proceed as if Option 1 does not exist and continue with the procedure for making the first two selections, ie move to the next horse in the Betting Forecast. In those cases where there are both course winners and other horses remaining to be considered, the choice between taking option 1 or option 2 in making additional selections is always for you to make and sometimes not at all easy.

You can of course look at what both Option 1 and Option 2 have to offer and make your decision on which horse appears to have the strongest form. Alternatively you could do what I do, which is always to use the course winner Option 1 first of all and only consider the use of Option 2 if you are convinced that the course winner/s on offer has/have no chance of making the top three placings.

One further alternative, which is a failsafe approach, is to commit yourself to two additional selections instead of one and make a selection from both Option 1 and Option 2.

xii) By following the horse selection procedure described in i) to xi) immediately above, situations will occur where you dismiss all the horses priced 10/1 or longer because you are satisfied that none of them have a reasonable chance of achieving a placing in the first three. In these circumstances, you automatically dismiss the whole race from the reckoning. There will be other situations where you have made your selections but you are left with a 'gut feeling' that the form of your selections is really not strong enough to justify a bet. Again, in these circumstances it is probably best to dismiss the whole race from the reckoning.

As indicated in previous chapters, a dry run of at least two months where you are operating the System without actually placing bets should prove invaluable in giving you experience of when to bet and when to leave a race alone.

xiii) So that you can see clearly the order in which you study the form of the runners, on the following four pages are examples of two races. The first example has all the runners named in the Betting Forecast whilst the second example has a BAR group.

EXAMPLE 1 – All Runners Named in the Betting Forecast
New Hexham Website Handicap Hurdle (Class 4) 3m

3.50 RACE 4 New Hexham Website Handicap Hurdle (Class 4) Winner £3,083.40 ATR 3m

£4500 guaranteed **For** 4yo+ Rated 0-100 **Minimum Weight** 10-0 **Penalties** after May 5th, each hurdle won 7lb **True North's** Handicap Mark 100 **Entries** 42 pay £10 **Penalty value 1st** £3,083.40 **2nd** £898.65 **3rd** £449.55

1 4FPP/P- **TRUE NORTH** (IRE) [148] [D]
b g Black Monday-Slip A Loop
James Moffatt Maurice W Chapman
p 12 11-12 Brian Hughes(5)

2 1546PP/ **FLORRIES SON** [827] [CD]
b g Minster Son-Florrie Palmer
M Todhunter Miss T M Gray
12 11-12 Steven Gagan(10)

3 PP9/40- **RELIX** (FR) [26] [D]
gr g Linamix-Resleona
A M Crow Stuart Taylor, David Hardy, Lee Seaton
t 7 11-10 Mr M Ellwood(7) (99)

4 71450-6 **LITTLE TASK** [13] [D]
b g Environment Friend-Lucky Thing
J S Wainwright Keith Jackson
9 11-7 Paddy Aspell (102)

5 F30P3P- **SUPRENDRE ESPERE** [14]
b g Espere d'Or-Celtic Dream
C C Bealby Ricochet Management Limited
7 11-5 Tom Messenger(5) (104)

6 42583-4 **PANTHERS RUN** [13]
b g Jendali-Dorado Beach
J C Haynes J C Haynes
t 7 11-5 Michael McAlister(3) (103)

7 76349F- **TOBESURE** (IRE) [58] [D]
b g Asir-Princess Citrus
G A Charlton Richard Nixon
13 11-4 Andrew Thornton (103)

8 PP867-5 **POINT** [8]
b g Polish Precedent-Slxslip
W Jenks Mrs W P Jenks
10 11-2 Miss J C Williams(7) (105)

9 86367P- **FESTIVAL KING** (IRE) [40]
br g King's Theatre-Mary Linda
L Lungo Mr & Mrs Raymond Anderson Green
t5 11-2 Brian Harding (95)

10 57804-1 **MENELAUS** [12]
b g Machiavellian-Mezzogiorno
K A Morgan Rex Norton
p6 11-2 S E Durack (102)

11 634246- **CAESAR'S PALACE** (GER) [17] [D]
ch g Lomitas-Caraveine
Miss Lucinda V Russell Peter J S Russell
p 10 11-1 D J Oakden(10) (103)

12 7PP944- **SILVER BOW** [14]
b m Silver Patriarch-Isabeau
J M Jefferson Terry Pryka, John Cleeve & Peter Birch
6 11-1 Fergus King (107)

13 /9PP7-6 **NATIVE HEIGHTS** (IRE) [7]
b g Be My Native-Shirley's Dream
J K Hunter K Hunter
9 10-13 T J Dreaper(3)

14 4/30U0- **THE RIGHT PEOPLE** (IRE) [127]
ch g Deploy-Marlousion
L Lungo Contract Scotland Limited
7 10-13 Mr T Greenall (104)

15 573524- **POLITICAL SOX** [17] [D]
br g Mirror Boy-Political Mill
R Nixon Rayson & Susan Nixon
13 10-13 Tony Dobbin (100)

16 2P7477- **WESTMORLAND** (IRE) [58] [CD]
b g Phardente-Ticking Over
James Moffatt Maurice W Chapman
b1 11 10-7 P J McDonald(3) (105)

17 /8P4P3- **JUSTWHATEVERULIKE** (IRE) [58]
b g Courtship-Rose Of Summer
Miss S E Forster Peter Innes
ψ 6 10-4 Ryan Cummings(7) (98)

2006 (12 ran) Primitive Poppy Mrs A Hamilton 7 10-5 8/1   Phil Kinsella (7) OR86

BETTING FORECAST: 7-2 Silver Bow, 6 Little Task, 13-2 Menelaus, 9 Political Sox, 10 Caesar's Palace, The Right People, 12 Festival King, Justwhateverulike, Panthers Run, Relix, Tobesure, 16 Westmorland, 20 Suprendre Espere, 25 Florries Son, Point, 33 True North, 66 Native Heights.

In the above race the order in which you study the form to make your first two selections is as follows:

Order of Form Study Exercise	Name of Horse
First	Native Heights
Second	True North
Third	Point
Fourth	Florrie's Son
Fifth	Suprendre Espere
Sixth	Westmorland
Seventh	Tobesure
Eighth	Relix
Ninth	Panther's Run
Tenth	Just Whatever U Like

Let us assume that you select Native Heights and True North. If you then decide to make more than two selections you have either or both of the following two options:

Option 1 Consider any Course Winner. The order in which you study the form of the Course Winners based on the longest price first or the last in the Betting Forecast if two are on the same forecast price, is as follows:

Order of Form Study Exercise	Name of Horse
First	Florrie's Son
Second	Westmorland
Third	Tobesure

and/or

Option 2 Assume Option 1 does not exist and continue with the procedure for making the first two selections. As you had already selected Native Heights and True North you may consider the remaining horses in the following order:

Order of Form Study Exercise	Name of Horse
Third	Point
Fourth	Florrie's Son
Fifth	Suprendre Espere
Sixth	Westmorland
Seventh	Tobesure
Eighth	Relix
Ninth	Panther's Run
Tenth	Just Whatever U Like

EXAMPLE 2 – Betting Forecast with BAR Group of Unnamed Runners
Totesport Trophy Hurdle (Handicap) Class 1 2m

3.15 RACE 4 — *totesport Trophy Hurdle (Handicap) (Grade 3) (Class 1)* — Winner £85,530 — 2m¹⁄₂f — CH4

£150000 guaranteed For 4yo+ Weights raised 4lb Minimum Weight 10-0 Penalties after January 13th, a winner of a Class 1 or 2 hurdle 4lb; a winner of 2 Class 1 or 2 hurdles 6lb (no penalty to increase a horse's weight above 11st 12lb) Acambo's Handicap Mark 146 Entries 69 pay £150 1st Forfeit 60 pay £250 Confirmed 29 pay £200 Penalty value 1st £85,530 2nd £32,085 3rd £16,065 4th £8,010 5th £4,020 6th £2,010

1350-11 **1 ACAMBO** (GER) 56 [D] — gr g Acambaro-Artic Lady — D E Pipe D A Johnson — 6 11-12 — Timmy Murphy (154)

8F-9412 **2 MISTER HIGHT** (FR) 27 [D] — bl g Take Risks-Miss High — W P Mullins (IRE) Peter Garvey — 5 11-11 — Robert Thornton (148)

206-156 **3 SELF DEFENSE** 46 [CD] — b g Warning-Dansara — Miss E C Lavelle Fraser Miller Racing — 10 11-10 — Liam Treadwell (3) (144)

10-2163 **4 CROW WOOD** 63 (7F) [D] — b g Halling-Play With Me — J J Quinn Mrs Marie Taylor — 8 11-10 — Dougie Costello (3) (149) *N R*

101-869 **5 QUATRE HEURES** (FR) 27 [D] — b g Vertical Speed-Macyrienne — W P Mullins (IRE) John Mc's Winchester Syndicate — 5 11-8 — R Walsh (141)

74-2426 **6 KAWAGINO** (IRE) 76 [D] — b g Perugino-Sharakawa — J W Mullins K J Pike — 7 11-6 — Wayne Kavanagh (5) (155)

093-711 **7 PAPINI** (IRE) 35 [CD] — ch g Lomitas-Pariana — N J Henderson Newbury Racehorse Owners Group — 6 11-6 — Mick FitzGerald (147)

8-01103 **8 OVERSTRAND** (IRE) 21 [D] — b g In The Wings-Vaison La Romaine — Dr R D P Newland Dr R D P And Mrs L J Newland — 8 11-3 — S P Jones (5) (150) *2 ND*

1150-12 **9 TARLAC** (GER) 56 [D] — ch g Dashing Blade-Tintina — N J Henderson John P McManus — 6 11-2 — A P McCoy (153)

585-820 **10 CARACCIOLA** (GER) 70 [CD] — b g Lando-Capitolina — N J Henderson P J D Pottinger — 10 11-2 — Andrew Tinkler (152) *33 1 4 TH*

123-171 **11 PEDROBOB** (IRE) 43 [D] — ch g Pierre-Jazzelle — Anthony Mullins (IRE) Barry Connell — 9 10-13 — Noel Fehily (150) *3 Rd 11 1*

2212-12 **12 PRIVATE BE** 24 [D] — b g Gunner B-Foxgrove — P J Hobbs David And Daphne Walsh — 8 10-11 — Richard Johnson (153)

P19-130 **13 VICTRAM** (IRE) 27 [D] — b g Victory Note-Lady Tristram — Adrian McGuinness (IRE) Pinheads Pizza Syndicate — 7 10-10 — J W Farrelly (7) (153)

10-25 **14 ORCADIAN** 35 [BF] — b g Kirkwall-Rosy Outlook — J M P Eustace J C Smith — 6 10-9 — Mark Bradburne (152)

344-121 **15 MOORE'S LAW** (USA) 20 [D] — b g Technology-Brass Needles — M J Grassick (IRE) Mrs S Grassick — 9 10-8 — D F O'Regan (155)

01-1427 **16 PIRATE FLAGSHIP** (FR) 56 [CD] — b g River Mist-Sacadu — P F Nicholls Mr & Mrs Mark Woodhouse — b¹ 8 10-7 — Paddy Merrigan (3) (150)

62d263-1 **17 MY IMMORTAL** 129 [D] — b g Monsun-Dame Kiri — D E Pipe The Betfair Million Partnership — 5 10-7 — R J Greene (144)

-037829 **18 HEATHCOTE** 14 [D] — b g Unfuwain-Chere Amie — G L Moore B Siddle & B D Haynes — 5 10-6 — Jamie Moore (148) *50/1*

80-312P **19 BONGO FURY** (FR) 35 [D][BF] — b m Sillery-Nadivelee — D E Pipe Lord Donoughmore & Countess Donoughmore — v 8 10-5 — Andrew Glassonbury (5) (150)

11P-043 **20 NEW FIELD** (IRE) 27 [D] — b g Supreme Leader-Deep Steel — Thomas Mullins (IRE) John P McManus — 9 10-5 — R M Power (149)

8-31351 **21 RIO DE JANEIRO** (IRE) (4ex) 7 [D] — b g Sadler's Wells-Alleged Devotion — Miss E C Lavelle Fraser Miller Racing — 6 10-4 — P J Brennan (153)

BETTING FORECAST: 4 Acambo, 6 Tarlac, 9 Quatre Heures, 10 Moore's Law, Papini, Pedrobob, 12 New Field, 14 Mister Hight, 16 My Immortal, Orcadian, Victram, 20 Caracciola, Overstrand, 25 Private Be, 33 Pirate Flagship, Rio de Janeiro, 40 Bongo Fury, Heathcote, 50 bar.

In the above race not all the runners are named in the Betting Forecast so there is a BAR group which in this case is 50/1 BAR.

The first step is therefore to determine the runners in the BAR group and place them in order, starting with the horse which is nearest to the bottom of the list of runners and riders. When the BAR list has been exhausted you move on to the last named horse in the Betting Forecast, followed by the next to last and so on.

The order in which you study the form to identify your first two selections is as follows:

Order of Form Study Exercise	Name of Horse	
First	Kawagino	
— (Non Runner)	Crow Wood	Bar Group
Second	Self Defense	
Third	Heathcote	
Fourth	Bongo Fury	
Fifth	Rio de Janeiro	
Sixth	Pirate Flagship	Named Horses
Seventh	Private Be	
Eighth	Overstrand	

NB The above list can continue with named horses in Betting Forecast order up to and including Moore's Law, which is the first horse in the Betting Forecast with a price of 10/1 or more.

Let us assume that you dismiss Kawagino and Self Defense and select Heathcote and Bongo Fury. If after making your first two selections you want to make additional selections then you have either or both of the following options:

Option 1 Consider any Course Winner
Having dismissed Self Defense (course winner) the remaining course winners and the order in which you should study their form, based on the longest price first or the last in the Betting Forecast if two are on the same forecast price, is as follows:

Order of Form Study Exercise	Name of Horse
First	Pirate Flagship
Second	Caracciola
Third	Papini

and/or

Option 2 Assume Option 1 does not exist and continue with the procedure for making the first two selections. As you have dismissed Kawagino and Self Defense and selected Heathcote and Bongo Fury, you can now consider the remaining horses in the following order:

Order of Form Study Exercise	Name of Horse
Fifth	Rio de Janeiro
Sixth	Private Flagship
Seventh	Private Be
Eighth	Overstrand

NB The above list cancontinue with named horses in Betting Forecast order up to and including Moore's Law which is the first horse in the Betting Forecast with a price of 10/1 or more.

Chapter 23
READING THE FORM

Section 1 – Overall Principles

Reading the form is very much an art as opposed to a science and as such it encourages unwary punters to make the whole process much more complicated than is either absolutely necessary or desirable, given the object of the exercise is to find winners.

In many respects form reading is a bit like mixing a cake, and followers of racing are encouraged by all of the traditions which surround the sport to throw every single piece of information that is available into the mix. Unfortunately, this frequently leads to a situation where very capable horses can be automatically excluded from the reckoning because their form, as defined by the various pieces of information which have been included in the form reading exercise, bears no comparison with the form of other more fancied runners.

Because of the dangers I have described, the form reading process, which is an integral part of The Tail End System, is restricted to the following pieces of information published by the *Racing Post* on a daily basis:

- Runners and riders plus Betting Forecast
- Spotlight
- Handicap ratings
- Individual form of the horses

The form reading exercise always starts with either the last horse named in the Betting Forecast or alternatively if there is a BAR group, the horse from the BAR group which occupies the bottom most position in the list of runners and riders.

The reason for choosing this order of form reading is because any other method is likely to result in the horses with the longest forecast prices either being ignored completely or alternatively being given a very scant appraisal because their form is obviously inferior to that of the shorter priced horses.

Therefore by starting with the longest priced horse and by making sure that the form reading exercise is restricted to determining if a top three placing is a reasonable possibility (without considering the form and/or chances of any other runner) the system ensures the following:

a) The longest price horse will be given the same degree of consideration as any other horse whose form is studied.

b) No horse will be excluded from the reckoning because of form comparisons with another horse and therefore the problems which are posed by Sods Law are avoided as far as it is possible to do so.

Once the form reading exercise has started, the important elements to concentrate upon are:

c) Making sure that you apply just as much diligence to the study of any particular horses form as you do with any other.

d) If you have studied the form of a horse and decide to dismiss it from the reckoning, move to the next horse, study its form, but before making a decision go back to the previous horse and recheck your decision to dismiss it.

Once you have rechecked and, if necessary, changed your decision, you can then move on again to the next horse assuming of course that you have not already made your final selection.

e) Make sure you never ever make a decision to select or dismiss a horse because you have compared its form with that of another horse.

f) Never ever deviate from the order of form consideration laid down by the system ie always take the next horse on the Betting Forecast list regardless of whether it shares the same forecast price as another runner.

g) Never let personal knowledge of a horse persuade you to deviate from the order of form consideration or to unfairly dismiss a horse because you think there is a 'better' horse further down the line.

h) It is also necessary to comment upon the selection option which is available after making the first two selections, namely:

Option 1 – Consider a course winner
  and/or
Option 2 – Continue with the system as if Option 1 does not exist, ie move to the next horse in the Betting Forecast.

The availability of the above options introduces an element of choice which is contrary to one of the principal philosophies on which the system is founded, namely that of restricting choice to avoid the problems of Sod's law.

However, given the fact that a considerable number of 'outsider' winners are previous Course Winners, it is necessary to design the system so that it can pick up runners which fall into this category.

There will obviously be occasions when a course winner is picked up automatically in the first two selections but even if this is the case there may well be other Course Winners in the field which Option 1 gives you the possibility of considering. I say possibility because you have to stick to the rules regarding moving on to the next horse and consider Course Winners in an order determined by the length of their Betting Forecast price, ie longest price first, and if there are two Course Winners on the same forecast price you must always give first consideration to the horse which is nearest to the end of the list of named horses in the Betting Forecast.

It often pays to remember that when there is a BAR group in the Betting Forecast there are many occasions when the last named horse in the Betting Forecast goes on to win the contest.

Therefore in those situations where the BAR group has provided you with your first two selections you should always consider extending the form reading exercise up to and including the last named horse in the Betting Forecast. I appreciate that this could possibly mean making an additional bet or bets more than you planned but it is sometimes better to be safe than sorry.

Section 2 – A Code of Practice for Reading the Form

The best way to understand how to read the form is to look at actual examples of races and take yourself through the form reading process from start to finish. As a result in Section 3 which follows you will find examples of races and if you study these carefully you will understand the pieces of information which you need to evaluate in order to obtain the best possible idea of how a horse is likely to perform.

Shown immediately below is a Code of Practice which sets down guidelines and basic rules to be followed when studying the form.

Code of Practice

a) Study all of the details which describe the race ie class of race, type of race, entry conditions, weight allowances/penalties, distance, going, so that you are in a position to form a general opinion as to whether the contest is likely to suit any particular runner whose form you are studying.

b) Study what 'Spotlight' in the *Racing Post* has to say about any horse you are considering but make sure that you only take notice of the factual information and totally disregard any information which constitutes an opinion.

c) If the race is a handicap, study the handicap ratings to determine how the horse's previous ratings compared with the rating it has been allocated for today's contest.

d) If the race is a non-handicap, ignore the *Racing Post* ratings because they can be misleading.

e) Ignore Top Speed information in the *Racing Post* because it can be misleading.

f) Ignore all Post Data information in the *Racing Post* primarily because it is based on opinion rather than fact.

g) Study the horse's individual form record which appears in the *Racing Post*, paying particular attention to the following details:
   - Age of horse
   - List of previous placings
   - Jump win details: date, course, race description
   - Record (wins – places – runs) on fast (good to firm – hard) and softish (good to soft – heavy) going, and course and distance.
   - Comprehensive details of recent outings (NB *Racing Post* normally publishes last two or three outings)

h) Always pay particular attention to course wins and course runs as these are frequently significant pieces of information.

i) Where a horse has recent flat race form it is frequently because the trainer is attempting to 'tune the horse up' for a jumps contest. Finishing positions in such races are less important than the number of lengths they are beaten by. In any flat race where the horse in question has finished within 10 to 12 lengths of the winner, this should be interpreted as a good sign of race fitness.

Another good sign from recent flat race form is where a horse has either led the field or been up with the pace for a long way before being allowed to lose ground before the finish. In such cases the fact that a horse has finished a race a considerable distance behind the winner should not necessarily be regarded as a problem.

j) Always try to assess whether a horse's form indicates:
   - Fit to race but not necessarily fit enough to complete the distance.

- Fit to race but barring incidents affecting the other runners not fit enough to win or be placed in the first three.
- Fit enough to win or be placed in the first three.
- Fit to race but possibly beyond peak fitness and therefore unlikely to win or be placed in the first three.

The above considerations can help you make the correct decision to select or dismiss. Always double check your reasons for wanting to select or dismiss a horse before you confirm your decision.

Section 3 – Race Examples

By studying the form reading exercise which has been conducted on all of the following races you should have a comprehensive understanding of how to identify long-priced winners in British jump races.

Whilst every race is different from any other, long-priced winners are practically always identifiable because there is something in the form which indicates that they are likely to improve in their next race. By studying the form reading process in each of the actual examples of the races which follow, you will build up a picture in your mind of what to look for in future races.

Course form, whether it is winning form or simply course experience, is frequently a significant factor which should never be overlooked.

EXAMPLE 1

10.02.07 Newbury – Good to Soft – Class 1 – Handicap Hurdle – 2m1½f
Winner HEATHCOTE – 50/1 (last named horse in Betting Forecast)

3.15 RACE 4	totesport Trophy Hurdle (Handicap) (Grade 3) (Class 1) Winner £85,530	CH4 2m½f

£150000 guaranteed For 4yo+ Weights raised 4lb Minimum Weight 10-0 Penalties after January 13th, a winner of a Class 1 or 2 hurdle 4lb; a winner of 2 Class 1 or 2 hurdles 6lb (no penalty to increase a horse's weight above 11st 12lb) Acambo's Handicap Mark 146 Entries 69 pay £150 1st Forfeit 60 pay £250 Confirmed 29 pay £200 Penalty value 1st £85,530 2nd £32,065 3rd £16,065 4th £8,010 5th £4,020 6th £2,010

1 1350-11 **ACAMBO** (GER) 56 ⒷⒹ
gr g Acambaro-Artic Lady
D A Johnson — Timmy Murphy (154) — 6 11-12
D E Pipe

2 8F-9412 **MISTER HIGHT** (FR) 27 ⒷⒹ
b/ g Take Risks-Miss High
W P Mullins (IRE) Peter Garvey — Robert Thornton (148) — 5 11-11

3 206-156 **SELF DEFENSE** 46 ⒸⒹ
b g Warning-Dansara
Miss E C Lavelle Fraser Miller Racing — Liam Treadwell(3) (144) — 10 11-10

4 10-2163 **CROW WOOD** 63 (7F) Ⓓ
b g Hailing-Play With Me
J J Quinn · Mrs Marie Taylor — Dougie Costello(3) (149) — 8 11-10

5 101-869 **QUATRE HEURES** (FR) 27 Ⓑ
b g Vertical Speed-Macyrienne
W P Mullins (IRE) John Mc's Winchester Syndicate — R Walsh (141) — 5 11-8

6 74-2426 **KAWAGINO** (IRE) 76 ⒷⒹ
b g Perugino-Sharakawa
J W Mullins · K J Pike — Wayne Kavanagh(5) (155) — 7 11-6

7 093-711 **PAPINI** (IRE) 35 ⒸⒹ
ch g Luso-Pariana
N J Henderson Newbury Racehorse Owners Group — Mick FitzGerald (147) — 6 11-6

8 8-01103 **OVERSTRAND** (IRE) 21 Ⓓ
b g In The Wings-Valson La Romaine
Dr R D P Newland Dr R D P And Mrs L J Newland — S P Jones(5) (150) — 8 11-3

9 1150-12 **TARLAC** (GER) 56 ⒷⒹ
ch g Dashing Blade-Tintina
N J Henderson John P McManus — A P McCoy (153) — 6 11-2

10 585-820 **CARACCIOLA** (GER) 70 ⒷⒹ
b g Lando-Capitoline
N J Henderson · P J D Pottinger — Andrew Tinkler (152) — 10 11-2

11 123-171 **PEDROBOB** (IRE) 43 ⒷⒹ
ch g Pierre-Jarzelle
Anthony Mullins (IRE) Barry Connell — Noel Fehily (150) — 9 10-13

12 2212-12 **PRIVATE Be** 24 ⒷⒹ
b g Gunner B-Foxgrove
P J Hobbs · David And Daphne Walsh — Richard Johnson (153) — 8 10-11

13 P19-130 **VICTRAM** (IRE) 27 ⒷⒹ
b g Victory Note-Lady Tristram
Adrian McGuinness (IRE) Pinheads Pizza Syndicate — J W Farrelly(7) (153) — 7 10-10

14 10-25 **ORCADIAN** 35 ⒷⒻ
b g Kirkwall-Rosy Outlook
J M P Eustace · J C Smith — Mark Bradburne (152) — 6 10-9

15 344-121 **MOORE'S LAW** (USA) 20 ⒷⒹ
b g Technology-Brass Needles
M J Grassick (IRE) Mrs S Grassick — D F O'Regan (155) — 9 10-8

16 01-1427 **PIRATE FLAGSHIP** (FR) 56 ⒸⒹ
b g River Mist-Sacadu
P F Nicholls Mr & Mrs Mark Woodhouse — Paddy Merrigan(3) (150) — b/ 8 10-7

17 62d263-1 **MY IMMORTAL** 129 ⒷⒹ
b g Monsun-Dame Kiri
D E Pipe The Betfair Million Partnership — R J Greene (144) — 5 10-7

18 -037829 **HEATHCOTE** 14 ⒷⒻ
b g Unfuwain-Chere Amie
G L Moore · B Siddle & B D Haynes — Jamie Moore (146) — 5 10-6

19 80-312P **BONGO FURY** (FR) 35 ⒹⒺⒻ
b m Siliery-Nativelee
D E Pipe Lord Donoughmore & Countess Donoughmore — Andrew Glassonbury(5) (150) — v 8 10-5

20 11P-043 **NEW FIELD** (IRE) 27 ⒷⒹ
b g Supreme Leader-Deep Steel
Thomas Mullins (IRE) John P McManus — R M Power (149) — 9 10-5

21 8-31351 **RIO DE JANEIRO** (IRE) (4ex) 7 ⒷⒹ
b g Sadler's Wells-Alleged Devotion
Miss E C Lavelle Fraser Miller Racing — P J Brennan (150) — 6 10-4

BETTING FORECAST: 4 Acambo, 6 Tarlac, 9 Quatre Heures, 10 Moore's Law, Papini, Pedrobob, 12 New Field, 14 Mister Hight, 16 My Immortal, Orcadian, Victram, Overstrand, 25 Caracciola, Overstrand, 25 Private Be, 33 Pirate Flagship, Rio de Janeiro, 40 Bongo Fury, Heathcote, 50 bar.

SPOTLIGHT

Acambo Reported stronger horse by connections after his summer break and duly showed fair bit of improvement when beating a host of today's rivals in top Ascot handicap in December, when he would have won bit more easily but for mistake at the last and idling on the run-in; connections have Champion Hurdle aspirations and, with more possibly to come, good chance he will be involved despite 10lb rise since last time.

Mister Hight Smart juvenile at his best last season and back to that level of late, notably when second in valuable Leopardstown handicap last time; handicapper hasn't been especially kind though and Ruby Walsh again partners stablemate Quatre Heures.

Self Defense Slipped down to a feasible mark on recent efforts, albeit back from seven form of late, albeit in face of stiff tasks, and basically vulnerable to younger legs in race of this nature; wouldn't want much of the forecast rain to materialise either.

Crow Wood Useful dual-purpose horse but weighted up to best on balance off 4lb higher than when scrambling home in decent Wincanton handicap in November, latest third of four to two top notchers at Cheltenham coming in muddling affair and probably misleading form; flat run on AW last week and fair bit to prove.

Quatre Heures Needs to step up on recent efforts, albeit back from seven months off when running respectably in competitive Leopardstown handicap last time; Ruby Walsh keeps faith in preference to stablemate Mister Hight though and would have a shout on last April's win in a Punchestown Grade 1; chance would be enhanced if the preliminaries go smoothly (can get overwrought beforehand).

Kawagino Didn't take to chasing and ran badly returned to hurdles last time, so lots to prove on the face of it; however, ran very well when 20l seventh when 500-1 for last season's Champion Hurdle, fast-paced 2m (which he should have here) bringing out best in him, so not a total no-hoper.

Papini Fair bit more needed off 10lb higher mark than when taking decent Sandown handicap last time but clearly in the form of his life and stable has good recent record in this, so another bold show entirely possible; another win may just be asking for too much off this mark, though.

Overstrand Coaxed right back to his best by rookie trainer this winter, one blip coming when suffering from a respiratory infection on penultimate start at Ascot in December; ran as well as he was entitled to in Haydock Grade 2 last time but does look weighted up to the hilt now and others preferred at the weights.

Tarlac Progressive second-season hurdler who came on again when second to Acambo in valuable Ascot handicap last time, 4lb pull suggesting it should be close between the pair this time; stable has good record in this and everything looks in place for a very bold show.

Caracciola Talented sort who has reportedly been targeted at this race but high enough in the weights on balance of recent form and definitely wouldn't want much of the forecast rain to materialise.

Pedrobob Late-maturing 9yo who was useful in bumpers and showed comparable form for the first time over hurdles when making all and easily seeing off reasonable opposition in minor event on heavy at Leopardstown last time (2m5f round Cheltenham might well have been too far the time before); has coped fine in big fields before, raising hopes that he can reproduce that latest improved form in this different type of race; good chance if he can.

Private Be Two wins apart right-handed but has often had steering problems that way round and best suited by left-handed track such as this; good effort when second of three to smart sort over fences here last time but 9lb hike for previous win in Exeter handicap hurdle looks on the steep side and though likely to give it a good shot up front for a long way, better-weighted rivals may pick him off this time.

Victram Trainer inclined to put a line through latest flat effort at Leopardstown; previous third to Acambo and Tarlac entitles him to consideration, closely matched with that possibly more progressive pair now, but shade better than bare form as waiting tactics looked a little overdone; possibilities if new 7lb claiming rider times it right.

Orcadian Smart if quirky Flat-racer who hasn't as yet shown comparable form over hurdles, last time failing to build on promising Kempton second when well held behind progressive Papini at Sandown (handles heavy, so that ought not be an excuse); plus that he ran some of his very best races on the Flat at this track but bit to prove on what he has achieved overall over hurdles.

Moore's Law Proven in big-field handicaps, comes here in top form after easy win in minor event at Cork last time (even if most of those in behind not at best on one count or another) and forecast rain very much in his favour, so high on the list off fair enough mark.

Pirate Flagship Wouldn't want the ground to deteriorate, so worth keeping an eye on this morning's weather; more exposed than some, so though he again ran well enough in big-field handicap when seventh to Acambo returned to hurdles at Ascot last time, may be vulnerable tried blinkered now.

My Immortal High enough in the weights on what he has achieved over hurdles but hasn't had that many chances and wouldn't be the greatest surprise to see him show improvement, given that he was decent on the Flat and has been brought along with this race in mind; handled soft on the Flat so some rain shouldn't be a problem.

Heathcote Couple of good runs in useful handicaps this season confirm that last season's ability is still there but found it tough going more often that not and looks on too high a mark on balance of form; surprise if he can be involved.

Bongo Fury Second in this race from 2lb higher mark in 2005 but good bit to prove now, pulled up over fences at Sandown last time, albeit after going off too quickly and rather losing her nerve at some of the fences; may be happier returned to hurdles but this is a very tough race to bounce back in.

New Field Two wins at longer trips over fences last winter but done every bit as well returned to hurdles in useful handicaps of late, last time third in valuable contest at Leopardstown; place possibilities again on that but bit more needed to win.

Rio de Janeiro Quietly progressive novice who showed good battling qualities when grinding it out to take competitive Stratford handicap over a bit farther last week; likely less testing ground here may well help but effectively 6lb higher if absence of good claimer's allowance this time is factored into calculations, so more to do this time.

VERDICT PEDROBOB (nap) is preferred, his latest improved form to win at Leopardstown suggesting he is on a good mark. He has won in big-field bumpers and run well in a 20-runner race over hurdles, raising strong hopes this different type of race will not faze him at all. **Acambo** looks bound to give it a bold shot despite a 10lb rise for his latest Ascot win, and together with Ascot third **Victram**, may be the pick of the opposition. [MCu]

OFFICIAL RATINGS LAST SIX OUTINGS-LATEST ON RIGHT	3.15 HANDICAP	TODAY FUTURE	RP RATING LATEST / BEST / ADJUSTED
118¹ — 129⁰ 128⁹ 128¹ 136¹	Acambo	11-12 146	154 ◄ 154 154
— — — — 130²	Mister Hight	11-11 145 -9	148 148 148
— 149⁰ — — —	Self Defense	11-10 144	132 134 144
124¹ — 134² 140¹ —	Crow Wood	11-10 144	149 149 149
— — — — 130⁹	Quatre Heures	11-8 142 -13	140 141 141
— — — — 147⁶	Kawagino	11-6 140	127 162 ◄ 155 ◄
125⁰ 123⁹ 121³ 123⁷ 122¹ 130¹	Papini	11-6 140	147 147 147
138⁶ 121⁶ 120¹ 126¹ 137⁰	Overstrand	11-3 137 +1	149 150 150
— 115¹ 123⁵ 125⁰ 124¹ 130²	Tarlac	11-2 136	153 153 153
136⁵ — 135⁸ 134² 140⁰	Caracciola	11-2 136	141 152 152
— — — 129⁷	Pedrobob	10-13 133 -3	150 150 150
— — 120² 122¹	Private Be	10-11 131	— 147 153
111⁹ 114¹ 119⁹ 118¹ 128³ 128⁰	Victram	10-10 130 -3	141 153 153
— — — 123² 130⁵	Orcadian	10-9 129	139 152 152
114³ 116⁴ 117⁴ — 119²	Moore's Law	10-8 128	154 ◄ 154 155 ◄
128⁶ — — — —	Pirate Flagship	10-7 127	150 150 150
— — 126⁶ 126⁹	My Immortal	10-7 127	132 144 144
120⁰ 123⁷ 126⁷ 125⁸ 123² 126⁹	Heathcote	10-6 126 -1	126 148 148
130⁸ 128⁰	Bongo Fury	10-5 125	— 150 150
— — 116⁰ 114⁴ 113³	New Field	10-5 125 -8	149 149 149
— — — — 120¹	Rio de Janeiro (4x)	10-4 124 +1	147 153 153

Kawagino — 11-6

7-y-o b g Perugino - Sharakawa (Darshaan)
J W Mullins — Wayne Kavanagh (5)

Placings: 71/24U8U174-2426

OR140F75	Starts	1st	2nd	3rd	Win & Pl
Hurdles	10	2	2	–	£23,201
All Jumps races	14	2	3	–	£26,656
108 3/06 Winc	2m Cls3 99-120 Hdl Hcap soft £6,506
6/04 NAbb	2m1f Cls4 Nov Hdl gd-frm £3,385
	Total win prize-money £9,891

GF-HRD 1-0-2 **GS-HVY** 1-1-7 **Course** 0-0-2 **Dist** 2-2-10

26 Nov 06 Fontwell 2m2½f Cls2 122-147 Hdl Hcap £19,014
7 ran GD-SFT 9hdls Time 4m 33.00s (slw 19.00s)
1 Fenix 7 10-4 b ....Leighton Aspell 4/1
2 Gods Token 8 10-6 ......Liam Treadwell (3) 13/2
3 Fait Le Jojo 9 10-9 ....Howie Ephgrave (5) 7/1
6 KAWAGINO 6 11-7 ....Wayne Kavanagh (5) 14/1
never going well in rear, hard ridden 5th, lost touch next (jockey received two-day ban: failed to ride out to the line (Dec 7-8))
[RPR119 TS110 OR147] [op 20/1]
Dist: 7-4-4-21-1 **RACE RPR:** 134+/132+/131
Racecheck: Wins - Pl 1 Unpl 4

16 Nov 06 Wincanton 2m Cls4 105-115 Ch Hcap £5,999
5 ran GOOD 13fncs Time 4m 2.10s (slw 12.10s)
1 Jurado Express 10 11-12 ....Sam Thomas 5/1
2 KAWAGINO 6 11-9 ....Jamie Moore 10/11F
jumped left virtually throughout, held up, headway to track winner after 9th, mistake and lost place next, soon ridden, kept on same pace from 3 out
[RPR119 TS93 OR112] [op 4/5 tchd Evs]
3 Wizard Of Edge 6 11-2 b ......Timmy Murphy 3/1
Dist: 10-1½ **RACE RPR:** 128+/119+/106
Racecheck: Wins - Pl 1 Unpl 3

31 Oct 06 Exeter 2m1½f Cls3 Nov Ch £10,410
6 ran GOOD 12fncs Time 4m 11.60s (slw 2.60s)
1 Denman 6 10-12 ....R Walsh 1/3F
2 Penzance 5 11-4 ....Robert Thornton 6/1
3 Keepthedreamalive 8 10-9 .Daryl Jacob (3) 22/1
4 KAWAGINO 6 10-12 ....Jamie Moore 8/1
behind, slipped badly 3rd, stayed on from 2 out, never dangerous [RPR123 TS115]
Dist: 10-5-6-29-11 **RACE RPR:** 141+/140+/123
Racecheck: Wins 2 (2) Pl 3 Unpl 3

14 Oct 06 Kempton 2nd, see SELF DEFENSE

Self Defense — 11-10

10-y-o b g Warning - Dansara (Dancing Brave)
Miss E C Lavelle — Liam Treadwell (3)

Placings: 0012/42102/04206-156

OR144F106	Starts	1st	2nd	3rd	Win & Pl
All Jumps races	26	4	6	2	£154,704
10/06 Kemp	2m Cls2 Hdl good £12,526
2/05 Sand	2m1½f Cls1 List Hdl gd-sft £17,400
3/04 Newb	2m1½f Cls3 Nov Hdl good £5,252
11/03 Chel	2m1½f Cls1 Nov Gd2 Hdl gd-frm ..£17,400
	Total win prize-money £52,578

GF-HRD 1-0-1 **GS-HVY** 1-4-13 **Course** 1-0-4 **Dist** 4-5-22

26 Dec 06 Kempton 2m Cls1 Gd1 Hdl £57,020
7 ran GD-SFT 8hdls Time 3m 59.80s (slw 6.80s)
1 Jazz Messenger 6 11-7 ....N P Madden 10/1
2 Noble Request 5 11-7 ....Richard Johnson 7/1
3 Desert Quest 6 11-7 b ....R Walsh 8/1
6 SELF DEFENSE 9 11-7 .....Timmy Murphy 25/1
dropped to last after 3rd, struggling from 5th, no chance when mistake 3 out, tailed off
[RPR128 TS86 OR150] [tchd 20/1]
Dist: 4-6-¾-24-13 **RACE RPR:** 164/160/154
Racecheck: Wins 1 (1) Pl 1 Unpl 1

18 Nov 06 Ascot 2m3½f Cls1 Gd2 Hdl £56,340
7 ran SOFT 11hdls Time 4m 47.80s (slw 15.80s)
1 Hardy Eustace 9 11-0 v ....C O'Dwyer 11/8F
2 Mighty Man 6 11-8 ....Richard Johnson 15/8
3 Lough Derg 6 11-0 v ......Tom Scudamore 16/1
5 SELF DEFENSE 9 11-4 .....Mick FitzGerald 12/1
held up towards rear, no danger from 8th
[RPR130 TS93 OR152] [op 14/1 tchd 16/1]
Dist: 11-10-9-5-8 **RACE RPR:** 167+/159+/142+
Racecheck: Wins 2 (1) Pl 1 Unpl 6

14 Oct 06 Kempton 2m Cls2 Hdl £12,526
4 ran GOOD 8hdls Time 3m 48.80s (fst 4.20s)
1 SELF DEFENSE 9 11-8 ...Mick FitzGerald 6/5F
tracked leader, challenged 2 out, led just after last, ridden clear
[RPR125 TS125 OR152] [op 11/10 tchd 5/4]
2 KAWAGINO 6 11-5 ....Jamie Moore 11/4
held up in last, closed after 3 out, led after 2 out, headed and one pace soon after last
[RPR121 TS121 OR147] [op 100/30]
3 Castleshane 9 11-0 ....Mick FitzGerald 14/1
Dist: 1½-1¾-8 **RACE RPR:** 125+/121+/114
Racecheck: Wins - Pl - Unpl 6

4 Feb 06 Sandown 2m1½f Cls1 List Hdl £17,106
8 ran GOOD 8hdls Time 3m 58.60s (slw 11.60s)
1 Royal Shakespeare 7 11-4 Tom Scudamore 9/4F
2 Alph 9 11-0 ....Mattie Batchelor 25/1
3 Mister McGoldrick 9 11-0 ..Dominic Elsworth 4/1
6 SELF DEFENSE 9 11-8 ......Mick FitzGerald 5/2
in touch, jumped slowly and behind 4 out, kept on from 2 out but never going pace to reach leaders [RPR134 TS109 OR152] [op 7/2 tchd 4/1]
Dist: 1¼-2-½-hd-4 **RACE RPR:** 136/134+/132+
Racecheck: Wins 3 Pl 1 Unpl 12

Heathcote — 10-6

5-y-o b g Unfuwain - Chere Amie (Mr Prospector)
G L Moore — Jamie Moore

Placings: 1211-037829

OR126F66	Starts	1st	2nd	3rd	Win & Pl
All Jumps races	10	3	2	1	£27,890
4/06 Towc	2m Cls4 Nov Hdl 4yo gd-sft £4,437
2/06 Plum	2m1f Cls4 Nov Hdl 4yo gd-sft £5,205
12/05 Ling	2m1½f Cls3 Nov Hdl 3yo soft £5,195
	Total win prize-money £14,821

GF-HRD 0-0-1 **GS-HVY** 3-2-9 **Course** 0-0-0 **Dist** 3-2-9

27 Jan Cheltenham 2m1f Cls2 115-130 Hdl Hcap £16,265
13 ran HEAVY 7hdls Time 4m 20.00s (slw 23.00s)
1 Ashley Brook 9 11-6 ....P J Brennan 11/2
2 French Saulaie 6 11-1 ...Richard Johnson 12/1
3 Ma Yahab 6 10-9 ....Liam Treadwell (3) 14/1
4 HEATHCOTE 5 11-8 ....Jamie Moore 14/1
always towards rear
btn 43 lengths [RPR104 TS94 OR126] [op 16/1]
Dist: 20-2½-13-¾-1 **RACE RPR:** 148+/122+/115+
Racecheck: Wins - Pl - Unpl -

6 Jan Sandown 2m1½f Cls2 113-139 Hdl Hcap £31,225
12 ran HEAVY 8hdls Time 4m 12.00s (slw 25.00s)
1 PAPINI 5 11-3 ....Richard FitzGerald 6/1
led 2nd, ridden after 2 out, driven out
[RPR139 TS135 OR130] [op 8/1]
2 HEATHCOTE 5 10-5 ...Eamon Dehdashti (5) 8/1
in touch, headway after 3 out, stayed on from 2 out, chased winner soon after last, one pace
[RPR126 TS121 OR123] [op 14/1]
3 Ma Yahab 6 9-12 ....Liam Treadwell (3) 10/1
5 ORCADIAN 6 11-3 ....Mark Bradburne 9/2F
chased leader after 2nd, challenged 3rd, ridden and every chance 2 out, soon weakened
[RPR120 TS110 OR130] [op 4/1 tchd 5/1]
Dist: 5-1¾-6-7-18 **RACE RPR:** 139+/126/115
Racecheck: Wins - Pl 1 Unpl 5

30 Dec 06 Ascot 2m3½f Cls3 103-125 Hdl Hcap £9,295
10 ran GD-SFT 11hdls Time 4m 58.10s (slw 26.10s)
1 Lord Of Beauty 6 11-3 ....Tom Doyle 8/1
2 Kelrev 8 11-0 ....Richard Johnson 9/2
3 Cold Mountain 4 10-6 ....Richard Young (3) 14/1
8 HEATHCOTE 4 11-12 ....Jamie Moore 11/2
in rear, hit 6th and 3 out, never going pace to be competitive
btn 30 lengths [RPR104 TS63 OR125] [op 15/2 tchd 8/1]
Dist: ¾-15-10-nk-½ **RACE RPR:** 124+/120/100
Racecheck: Wins - Pl 2 Unpl 7

2 Dec 06 Sandown 2m1½f Cls1 List 114-140 Hdl Hcap £28,510
17 ran HEAVY 8hdls Time 4m 7.80s (slw 20.80s)
1 OVERSTRAND 7 10-5 ex6 .....S P Jones (7) 8/1
held up early, went prominent 3rd, going much

the best of leaders before 2 out, led before last, ridden clear [RPR139 TS140 OR126]
2 Whispered Promises 5 11-7 ..Alan O'Keeffe 25/1
3 Nation State 5 10-3 p ....R Walsh 7/1
7 HEATHCOTE 4 10-7 .Eamon Dehdashti (5) 10/1 prominent, ridden and outpaced before 2 out, gradually weakened
btn 18 lengths [RPR121 TS118 OR126] [op 11/1]
11 CARACCIOLA 9 11-7 ..Mr J Snowden (5) 25/1 held up in midfield, effort before 2 out, soon no progress under pressure, weakened last
btn 24 lengths [RPR129 TS125 OR140]

Dist: 7-2-³/₄-7-nk . RACE RPR: 139+/141/121+
Racecheck: Wins 1 Pl 5 Unpl 17

Bongo Fury 10-5

8-y-o b m Sillery - Nativelee (Giboulee)
D E Pipe Andrew Glassonbury (5)

Placings: 17/95U11205/080-312P

OR**125**F75	Starts	1st	2nd	3rd	Win & Pl
Hurdles	20	7	4	–	£91,155
All Jumps races	24	8	5	1	£101,044
12/06 Chep	2m¹/₂f Cls3 Ch soft £6,506				
123 1/05 Donc	2m¹/₂f Cls2 109-135 Hdl Hcap good				
	...........................£20,163				
115 1/05 Sand	2m¹/₂f Cls3 103-125 Hdl Hcap gd-sft				
	..............................£9,048				
2/03 Sand	2m¹/₂f Cls3 Nov Hdl heavy £5,210				
12/02 Sand	2m¹/₂f Cls3 Nov Hdl 3yo soft £5,376				
108 11/02 Chel	2m¹/₂f Cls3 Nov 84-109 Hdl Hcap gd-sft				
	.............................£10,440				
100 10/02 Strf	2m¹/₂f Cls4 Nov 70-100 Hdl Hcap good .				
	..............................£3,523				
10/02 Ludl	2m Cls4 Mdn Hdl 3yo firm £3,465				
	Total win prize-money £63,731				

GF-HRD 1-1-2 GS-HVY 5-3-15 Course 0-1-1 Dist 8-5-23

6 Jan Sandown 2m Cls2 118-139 Ch Hcap £12,572
6 ran SOFT 13fncs Time 4m 0.30s (slw 15.30s)
1 Bohemian Spirit 9 10-9 Miss R Davidson (5) 11/4
2 Charlton Kings 9 10-5 ....Timmy Murphy 4/1
3 Jacks Craic 8 11-12 ....P J Brennan 7/1
P BONGO FURY 8 11-3 v ....A P McCoy 9/4F with leader to 5th, jumped slowly 7th and weakened, mistake next, tailed off when pulled up before 3 out (trainer had no explanation for the poor form shown)
[OR130] [op 5/2 tchd 11/4]

Dist: 18-8-hd-7 RACE RPR: 141+/120+/129+
Racecheck: Wins - Pl - Unpl 2

12 Dec 06 Sedgefield 2m¹/₂f Cls3 111-130 Ch Hcap
£9,429
8 ran HEAVY 13fncs Time 4m 34.50s (slw 38.50s)
1 Transit 7 10-8 tp ....T J Dreaper (3) 16/1
2 BONGO FURY 7 11-7 v ....A P McCoy 5/4F led to 6th, close up, ridden to lead 2 out, hung left, headed after last, rallied under pressure
[RPR132 TS131 OR125] [op Evs tchd 11/8]
3 Ela Re 7 10-11 ....David O'Meara 11/1

Dist: 1-6-³/₄-3¹/₂ RACE RPR: 124+/132/121+
Racecheck: Wins 1 Pl 1 Unpl 7

2 Dec 06 Chepstow 2m¹/₂f Cls3 Ch £6,506
5 ran SOFT 12fncs Time 4m 21.00s (slw 19.00s)·
1 BONGO FURY 7 10-11 v ..Tom Scudamore 7/4J chased leader, blundered 1st, led 5 out, clear 3 out, unchallenged
[RPR122 TS116] [op 2/1 tchd 9/4 & 13/8]
2 Hashid 6 11-4 ....Andrew Thornton 40/1
3 Master Albert 8 11-4 ....Noel Fehily 3/1
Dist: 7-shd-15-10 RACE RPR: 122+/115/117+
Racecheck: Wins - Pl 2 Unpl 5

22 Nov 06 Lingfield 2m Cls4 Ch £3,904
7 ran SOFT 12fncs Time 4m 0.80s (slw 2.80s)
1 My Way de Solzen 6 11-5 Robert Thornton 4/11F
2 Gentleman Jimmy 6 11-5 ...Andrew Tinkler 50/1
3 BONGO FURY 7 10-12 v ....A P McCoy 16/1 led until 2nd, stayed prominent, chased winner from 7th until before 3 out, ridden and beaten 3 out [RPR111 TS109]

Dist: 14-7-6-18-¹/₂ RACE RPR: 145+/125/111
Racecheck: Wins 3 (3) Pl 2 Unpl 5

8 Apr 06 Aintree 2m¹/₂f Cls1 List 119-145 Hdl Hcap
£26,510
17 ran GD-SFT 9hdls Time 4m 18.30s (slw 24.30s)
1 Wellbeing 9 10-2 ....P J Brennan 7/1
2 Noble Request 5 11-6 ......Richard Johnson 9/1
3 Double Vodka 5 9-7 oh10 .Phil Kinsella (7) 66/1
11 BONGO FURY 7 10-9 v ..Tom Scudamore 40/1 chased leader, ridden approaching 3 out, weakened next
btn 30 lengths [RPR117 TS83 OR118]
15 TARLAC 5 10-6 ....A P McCoy 9/2F chased leaders, ridden and mistake 2 out, soon weakened, eased run-in
btn 44 lengths [RPR101 TS63 OR125] [tchd 4/1 & 5/1]

Dist: 9-6-5-hd-nk RACE RPR: 147+/149+/123
Racecheck: Wins 5 (1) Pl 6 Unpl 7

11 Mar 06 Sandown 2m¹/₂f Cls1 List 114-137 Hdl Hcap
£34,212
21 ran SOFT 8hdls Time 3m 59.57s (slw 12.57s)
1 VICTRAM 6 9-12 ....A E Lynch (5) 8/1 held up in rear, hit 4 out, headway on bit to track leaders and hit 2 out, slight lead and hit last, ridden run-in, held on all out
[RPR121 TS112 OR114]
2 Dusky Warbler 7 11-10 p ....Jamie Moore 20/1
3 Verasi 5 11-7 b ....Philip Hide 33/1
5 TARLAC 5 10-12 ....A P McCoy 9/2F tracked leaders, went 2nd and ridden 2 out, one pace under pressure run-in
[RPR127 TS117 OR123] [tchd 5/1 & 11/2]
12 BONGO FURY 7 11-0 v ....
...............................Andrew Glassonbury (7) 33/1 chased leaders, ridden 3 out, weakened next
btn 19¹/₂ lengths [RPR119 TS107 OR132]

Dist: nk-¹/₂-1¹/₄-1¹/₄-3¹/₂ RACE RPR: 121+/141/138
Racecheck: Wins 3 Pl 3 Unpl 26

Rio de Janeiro 10-4

6-y-o b g Sadler's Wells - Alleged Devotion (Alleged)
Miss E C Lavelle P J Brennan

Placings: 8-31351

OR**124**F69	Starts	1st	2nd	3rd	Win & Pl
All Jumps races	6	2	–	2	£23,309
120 2/07 Strf	2m3f Cls2 108-134 Hdl Hcap gd-sft				
	...........................£13,779				
5/06 Strf	2m¹/₂f Cls3 Nov Hdl gd-sft £6,889				
	Total win prize-money £20,668				

GF-HRD 0-1-1 GS-HVY 2-0-3 Course 0-0-0 Dist 1-2-5

3 Feb Stratford 2m3f Cls2 108-134 Hdl Hcap £13,779
12 ran GD-SFT 10hdls Time 4m 53.30s (slw 30.30s)
1 RIO DE JANEIRO 6 10-7 ....
...............................Wayne Kavanagh (5) 7/2F held up in mid-division, headway 7th, ridden to lead 2 out, driven out
[RPR123 TS81 OR120] [op 9/2 tchd 5/1]
2 Absolut Power 6 11-0 p ....Paul Moloney 25/1
3 Magic Sky 7 10-9 ....Charlie Poste (5) 12/1
Dist: 1¹/₄-nk-¹/₂-6-2 RACE RPR: 123+/123/124+
Racecheck: Wins - Pl - Unpl -

6 Jan Sandown 2m¹/₂f Cls1 Gd1 Hdl £25,659
7 ran HEAVY 8hdls Time 4m 12.10s (slw 25.10s)
1 Silverburn 6 11-7 ....R Walsh 5/1
2 Perce Rock 5 11-7 ....A P McCoy 2/1F
3 Astarador 5 11-7 ....P J Brennan 4/1
5 RIO DE JANEIRO 6 11-7 Wayne Kavanagh 100/1 in rear but in touch, headway 4 out, chased leaders and ridden 3 out, not fluent and weakened 2 out
[RPR129 TS114 OR120] [op 66/1]
Dist: 4-7-1¹/₂-7-11 RACE RPR: 146+/142/138+
Racecheck: Wins 1 Pl 1 Unpl 1

18 Jun 06 Stratford 2m¹/₂f Cls3 Nov Hdl £6,338
12 ran GD-FM 9hdls Time 3m 52.10s (slw 4.10s)
1 Lord Baskerville 5 11-5 ...Adam Pogson (5) 16/1
2 Traprain 4 11-4 ....T J O'Brien (3) 8/11F
3 RIO DE JANEIRO 5 11-10 ......Barry Fenton 7/2 led until 2nd, prominent until ridden and outpaced after 3 out, regained 3rd 2 out but no chance with leaders
[RPR100 TS92 OR120] [op 4/1 tchd 9/2]
Dist: 3¹/₂-2¹/₂-4-6-3 RACE RPR: 106+/101+/100
Racecheck: Wins 1 (1) Pl 1 Unpl 9

26 May 06 Stratford 2m¹/₂f Cls3 Nov Hdl £6,889
13 ran GD-SFT 9hdls Time 3m 56.10s (slw 8.10s)
1 RIO DE JANEIRO 5 10-12 ....Barry Fenton 3/1F settled tracking leaders, pushed ahead after 3 out, edged left between last two, kept on well, comfortably [RPR122 TS114] [op 9/2]
2 Sou'wester 6 11-4 ....Joe Tizzard 7/2
3 Don And Gerry 5 10-11 ....Tony Evans 6/1
Dist: 4-10-³/₄-15-13 RACE RPR: 122+/118/101
Racecheck: Wins 3 (1) Pl 3 Unpl 17

	KAWAGINO
Form Reading	
Spotlight	20 length seventh in last seasons Champion Hurdle
Handicap Ratings	Allocated a mark of 147 for last outing when 6th but down to a mark of 140 for today's outing.
Significant Items of Form	Seven year old with two hurdle victories in March 2006 and June 2004, Class 3 and 4 events. Last outing on 26.11.06 when 6th of 7 in Class 2 Handicap Hurdle over 2m2½f marked a move away from chasing for a horse whose previous two outings were in Class 4 (2nd) and Class 3 (4th) events. Has had two runs at Newbury with no success. Form indicates preference for right hand tracks.
Verdict	To give the horse a six week break after a disappointing return to hurdling does not really inspire confidence for a Grade I contest.
Hence:	DISMISS.

Form Reading	**SELF DEFENSE**
Spotlight	Slipped down to a feasible mark on very best form.
Handicap Ratings	Last run in a Handicap Race was five outings ago when allocated a mark of 149 and was unplaced. Today's mark 144.
Significant Items of Form	Ten year old with four Hurdle victories (two Class 1, one Class 2, one Class 3) over 2 miles on mainly Good going (one on Good to Soft), one being at Newbury (today's course). Last win at Kempton was in October 2006. Significantly no handicap victories and last four outings were all in Non Handicaps.
Verdict	It would require a leap of faith to think that a ten year old horse which has been campaigned extensively in the top grade races would be given sufficient latitude by the handicapper to be competitive in such a hot race as this one.
Hence:	DISMISS.

Form Reading	**HEATHCOTE**
Spotlight	Couple of good runs in useful Handicaps this season.
Handicap Ratings	Ran off a mark of 123 two outings ago in a Class 2 event at Sandown when 2nd and was raised to a mark of 126 for last two outings when unplaced. Handicapper has ignored last run when keeping mark at 126 for today's event.
Significant Items of Form	Five year old with three victories in Class 3 (two) and Class 4 (one) Novice Hurdles, last one being in April 2006. All wins on Soft and Good to Soft over 2 miles and demonstrated ability to handle both left and right handed tracks. Good 2nd in Class 2 Handicap Hurdle at Sandown two outings ago, beaten by Papini (5th paper favourite in today's contest) who is now 2lbs worse off. Last run at Cheltenham on Heavy in a Class 2 Handicap Hurdle when carrying 11st 8lbs was nothing to write home about.
Verdict	If you ignore last run at Cheltenham the form reads like a progressive hurdler capable of handling left and right hand tracks and all ground conditions. Second to Papini gives confidence that the trainer thinks his horse is at the right stage of fitness to tackle today's contest and bearing in mind how close Papini is to favouritism and the fact that Heathcote is only 2lbs away from bottom weight; a SELECT decision is a no brainer.

Form Reading	**BONGO FURY**
Spotlight	Second in this race from 2lb higher mark in 2005.
Handicap Ratings	On a mark of 125 for today's contest, which is below its last mark of 128 five outings ago when unplaced.
Significant Items of Form	Eight year old with seven hurdle victories, the last of which in January 2005 was a Class 2 Handicap Hurdle at Doncaster with £20,000 prize money. Most recent campaign from 22.10.06 to 06.01.07 has consisted of four 2 mile Chases that has resulted in 1 win, a 2nd and a 3rd. Has won on all ground conditions and at both left and right handed tracks.
Verdict	Too good a record to dismiss from the reckoning considering horse is only 2lb higher than bottom weight.
Hence:	SELECT.

Form Reading	**RIO de JANEIRO**
Note	Course winner option not taken up.
Spotlight	Quietly progressive novice.
Handicap Ratings	Allocated a mark of 120 for last race seven days ago when winning a Class 2 Hurdle at Stratford, which has given him a 4lb penalty and a mark of 124 for today's contest.
Significant Items of Form	Six year old with two Hurdle victories both at Stratford on Good to Soft over 2m3f (03.02.07) and 2m½f (26.05.06). Current campaign started on 06.01.07 with 5th of 7 in a Class 1 Grade 1 Hurdle on Heavy at Sandown, beaten 19½ lengths, which appears very respectable considering it was first run after a six month break.
Verdict	Form is definitely progressive and ability to perform on a left hand track and today's ground conditions makes the horse a sensible selection considering it is running off bottom weight.
Decision:	SELECT.

Overall Comment

This race, a Class 1 contest at a Non-Preferred track (Newbury) demonstrates that The Tail End System can be successful when the odds appear to be against it because of the strength of the opposition and the number of runners. It helped of course that this was a Handicap Contest, which always has to be preferred to a Non Handicap Race because all the form information you need is at your disposal to guide you in the right direction.

For me the most interesting feature of the result is that once again the last named horse in the Betting Forecast has prevailed and once again it has occurred when there is a BAR group. Such a situation is a fairly regular occurrence, so call it coincidence, call it uncanny, call it what you like, it emphasises the point that if there is a BAR group, you have to make sure that your form reading exercise reaches the last named horse in the Betting Forecast.

What I am not saying, however, is that you should automatically select the last named horse in the Betting Forecast or indeed give it preference, but you should make sure that if there is a BAR group that you are prepared to make sufficient selections to actually reach the last named horse in the Betting Forecast in the form reading process. Whether you actually select the horse must depend on the quality of its form.

I should also make a point about the Course Winner option because on this occasion having already dismissed Kawagino and Self Defense (course winner), the two members of the BAR Group, and having selected Heathcote and Bongo Fury I then had the option of either taking the Course Winner route or continuing to consider horses in the order of the Betting Forecast. I did look at the Course Winner option first but having looked at Pirate Flagship (the longest priced Course Winner) I wasn't at all impressed and it therefore made more sense to me to go down 'the next in the Betting Forecast route', which was offering me Rio de Janeiro on bottom weight and possessing what I saw as a more impressive form record for today's contest.

Interestingly enough, had I gone further down the Course Winner route than Pirate Flagship, the next course winner to have been considered would have been Caracciola which finished in the place money at 33/1.

For the record the Forecast Heathcote with Overstrand paid £1,380.90 for the Tote Exacta and £702.76 for the Computer Straight Forecast.

EXAMPLE 2

04.01.07 Lingfield – Heavy – Class 5 – Handicap Chase – 3 mile
Winner STAR GLOW – 100/1

3.00 RACE 5	**Lingfield Park For Weddings Handicap Chase (Class 5)** Winner £3,253	ATR 3m

£5000 guaranteed For 5yo+ Rated 0-95 Minimum Weight 10-0 Penalties after December 21st, a winner of a chase 7lb Before The Mast's Handicap Mark 95 Entries 33 pay £15 Penalty value 1st £3,253 2nd £955 3rd £477.50 4th £238.50

1 232F1U2 **BEFORE THE MAST** (IRE) [37]
br g Broken Hearted-Kings Reserve
M F Harris Walk The Plank Partnership
10 11-12 **Dave Crosse** (99)

2 05P-F67 **FLYING SPUR** (IRE) [21]
b g Norwich-Moorstown Rose
D E Pipe Stuart M Mercer
p 6 11-6 **Tom Scudamore**

3 3P-P422 **STORMY SKYE** (IRE) [12] [CD]
b g Bluebird-Canna
G L Moore Jayne Moore, T Pollock, J Driscoll
b 11 11-5 **Jamie Moore** (111) *3RD 7/1*

4 093P4/1 **AQUA PURA** (GER) [23]
b g Acatenango-Actrephane
B J Curley Curley Leisure
8 11-4 **Paul Moloney**

5 115P-P3 **TALLOW BAY** (IRE) [24]
b g Glacial Storm-Minimum Choice
Mrs S Wall Mrs S Wall
12 11-4 **Gerard Tumelty** (5) (106)

6 1PP2-P5 **STAR GLOW** [12] [B]
b g Dunbeath-Betrothed
R H York R H York
13 11-2 **Mr P York** (7) (99) *100/1*

7 /P-44PP **JOHNSTON'S SWALLOW** (IRE) [20]
b g Commanche Run-Mirror Of Flowers
Jonjo O'Neill John P McManus
b[1] 9 10-13 **Noel Fehily** (94)

8 453-325 **EBONY JACK** (IRE) [30] [BF]
b/br g Phardante-Ebony Jane
C L Tizzard K S B Bloodstock
b[1] 10 10-13 **Joe Tizzard** (111)

9 4-42322 **DR MANN** (IRE) [23]
b/br g Phardante-Shuil Le Laoi
Miss Tor Sturgis And Mrs J Allen And Brig C K Price
9 10-12 **Leighton Aspell** (103)

10 2U4P/5U **DADS LAD** (IRE) [24] [B]
b g Supreme Leader-Furryvale
Miss Suzy Smith Miss Suzy Smith
b 13 10-11 **David Boland** (10) (97)

11 82-32F1 **PEVERIL PRIDE** [30]
b g Past Glories-Peveril Princess
J A Geake Mrs E A Haycock
t 9 10-8 **Richard Young** (3) (102) *N.R*

12 50263-6 **GUNSHIP** (IRE) [34] [BF]
b g Needle Gun-Teajay's Future
P J Hobbs Mrs Karola Vann
6 10-6 **NON-RUNNER** (91)

13 95/4-PF **BOSUNS MATE** [9] [B]
ch g Yachtsman-Langton Lass
M Keighley M Keighley
p 14 10-5 **Tom Siddall**

14 8/P82PF **SUPREMELY RED** (IRE) [40]
b g Supreme Leader-Her Name Was Lola
D A Rees The Supreme Racing Club
10 10-0 **Lee Stephens** (3) (101) *NR*

15 45-P3P3 **RIVER INDUS** [12]
b g Rakaposhi King-Flow
R H Buckler Mrs C J Dunn
7 10-0 **Liam Treadwell** (3) (123) *2ND 9/2*

16 /2R3-5 **NATIVE CUNNING** [39]
b g Be My Native-Icy Miss
R H Buckler Nick Elliott
9 10-0 **Matthew Batchelor**

LONG HANDICAP: River Indus 9-8 Native Cunning 9-0

BETTING FORECAST: 4 Peveril Pride, 5 Stormy Skye, 6 Aqua Pura, 7 River Indus, Tallow Bay, 10 Dr Mann, Ebony Jack, 12 Before The Mast, Flying Spur, 20 Dads Lad, Johnston's Swallow, Star Glow, 33 bar.

SPOTLIGHT

Before The Mast Winner over 2m5.5f at Fakenham three runs ago (good ground) but a well-beaten last of two on this 7lb higher mark last time; no problems with the ground, but perhaps best watched on his first run at 3m.

Flying Spur Bumper winner on fast ground on debut; failed to win over hurdles, and didn't run up to his best on two previous runs over fences; first run at this trip, cheek pieces on again (beaten over hurdles with them latest) and others appeal more.

Stormy Skye Both chase wins have been over C&D, and comes into this in fair form having finished runner-up over 3m2f at Fontwell on his last two starts; goes on the ground, and one with a chance.

Aqua Pura Ex-German; returned from more than two years off to win a 2m1f selling handicap hurdle at Folkestone last time; first run over fences, first over this trip and now 18lb higher, so plenty to prove.

Tallow Bay All career wins have been in January or February (three last year); in snatches, but his last time out third suggests he's coming back to himself; chance.

Star Glow Has done well in point-to-points and is a hunter chase winner, but hasn't shown a great deal in two runs over regulation fences (held by River Indus on Fontwell form last time).

Johnston's Swallow Ex-Irish hurdles winner who has shown very little over fences for current yard; drop of 32lb reflects that lack of form, and even though blinkered for first time, is best watched for the time being.

Ebony Jack Stays well, goes in the mud, and though a bit disappointing this time, is back on a good mark and first-time blinkers may sharpen him up; quite interesting.

Dr Mann Only win was in a maiden point in 2004, but has run well enough over this trip on last two starts to suggest he is capable of giving another decent show, though hasn't always looked straightforward.

Dads Lad Thorough stayer who goes in the soft, but below par in two runs on return from a long break recently, and best watched for now.

Peveril Pride Fell at the final fence on last run here, but went on to win his first race over jumps with an easy success at Fontwell next time no problems with trip or ground, but facing tougher task on a 9lb higher mark.

Bosuns Mate Last success was in a hunter chase nearly four years ago; a few fair efforts since then, but now in the veteran stage, and with two poor efforts to his credit this season, is passed over this time.

Supremely Red Maiden hurdle winner in 2002, but yet to win over fences; fair effort when second at Uttoxeter in October, but below that since and others appeal more.

River Indus Maiden jumper who seemed to show vastly improved form when third to Classified in a novices chase at Fontwell latest; handicapper taken note and put him up 19lb, so though out of the handicap is 13lb well in here; however, chances are that was a one-off and not certain to be able to take advantage.

Native Cunning Low-grade chaser who is 14lb out of the handicap and looks the yard's second string here.

VERDICT A race that won't take a great deal of winning, and though **Stormy Skye** is in good form, and Ebony Jack should benefit from first-time blinkers, the tentative choice is **TALLOW BAY**, who shaped better last time and has done all his winning at this time of year.[CR]

	OFFICIAL RATINGS						**3.00**		TODAY	FUTURE		RP RATING	
	LAST SIX OUTINGS-LATEST ON RIGHT							HANDICAP			LATEST	BEST	ADJUSTED
88³	87²	90F	99¹	—	96²	Before The Mast	11-12	95		87	99	99
—	—	—	95F	95⁶	—	Flying Spur	11-6	89		—	55	—
99³	98P	98P	96⁴	92²	88²	Stormy Skye	11-5	88	+3	106	111	111
—	—	—	—	—	—	Aqua Pura	11-4	87		—	—	—
73¹	85¹	91⁵	90P	90F	87³	Tallow Bay	11-4	87	-2	95	106	106
—	—	—	—	90P	—	Star Glow	11-2	85	-3	75	75	99
—	—	—	—	—	—	Aqua Pura				—	94	94
—	—	115⁴	—	119P	100P	Johnston's Swallow	10-13	82		46	111	111
86⁴	87⁵	86³	86³	85²	85⁵	Ebony Jack	10-13	82		103	103	103
77⁴	76⁴	76²	76³	79²	80²	Dr Mann	10-12	81		—	92	97
102²	102U	102⁴	101P	94⁵	88U	Dads Lad	10-11	80		—	—	—
72⁶	62²	69³	62²	69F	68¹	Peveril Pride	10-8	77		100	100	102
—	—	—	—	80³	78⁶	Gunship	10-6	75		82	86	91
—	—	—	—	—	—	Bosuns Mate	10-5	74		—	—	—
—	—	79⁸	71²	71F	69F	Supremely Red	10-0	69		—	101	101
92⁴	87⁵	78P	—	74P	—	River Indus	9-8	69	+13	123 ◄	123 ◄	123 ◄
74⁶	72P	64F	64⁶	—	—	Native Cunning	9-0	69	-14	—	—	—

Native Cunning 10-0

9-y-o *b g Be My Native - Icy Miss (Random Shot)*
R H Buckler Matthew Batchelor

Placings: 165/55UP56PF6/2**R35**-5

OR69 H74	Starts	1st	2nd	3rd	Win & Pl
Chase	9	–	–	–	–
All Jumps races	22	1	1	–	£3,691

72 3/04 Plum 3m1½f Cls4 70-95 Hdl Hcap gd-sft £2,639
GF-HRD 0-0-2 **GS-HVY** 1-0-9 **Course** 0-0-0 **Dist** 0-0-4

26 Nov 06 Fontwell 3m3f Cls4 74-95 Hdl Hcap £3,448
9 ran GD-SFT 13hdls Time 7m 3.90s (slw 41.90s)
1 English Jim 5 11-1 ....Liam Heard (3) 9/4F
2 Star Time 7 10-12 v ....Tom Scudamore 5/1
3 Rebelle 7 11-12 p ....S E Durack 9/2
5 **NATIVE CUNNING** 8 10-2 ...Daryl Jacob (3) 5/1
led until 3rd, hard ridden and weakened 3 out
[RPR51 TS62 OR74] [op 6/1]
Dist: 1¾-3½-15-1¼-5 RACE RPR: 91+/79+/91+
After a stewards' inquiry, the placings remained unaltered.
Racecheck: Wins - Pl - Unpl 5

5 Mar 06 Kingston St Mary (PTP) 3m Conf
14 ran GOOD Time 6m 36.00s
1 Touch Of Flame 7 12-0 ....J Guerriero 5/1
2 Southwestern 7 12-0 ....N Harris EvensF
3 Bak On Board 9 12-0 ....Miss C Tizzard 12/1
5 **NATIVE CUNNING** 8 12-0 p Miss C Buckler 20/1
lost tch 11
Dist: 1½-dist-3-12-½
Racecheck: Wins - Pl 1 Unpl 2

19 Feb 06 Milborne St Andrew (PTP) 3m Ladies Open
5 ran GD-SFT Time 6m 35.00s
1 Reviewer 7 11-0 ....Miss R Green 2/1
2 Let's Fly 11 11-0 ....Miss P Gundry 5/4F
3 **NATIVE CUNNING** 8 11-0 p Miss C Buckler 20/1
w ldrs til outpcd 15
Dist: 6-8-2
Racecheck: Wins - Pl - Unpl 4

Supremely Red 10-0

10-y-o *b g Supreme Leader - Her Name Was Lola (Pitskelly)*
D A Rees Lee Stephens (3)

Placings: 4/3P100P/P/08/P82PF

OR69 H79	Starts	1st	2nd	3rd	Win & Pl
Chase	5	–	1	–	£859
All Jumps races	15	1	1	1	£4,007

6/02 NAbb 2m6f Cls4 Mdn Hdl good £2,961
GF-HRD 0-1-5 **GS-HVY** 0-1-5 **Course** 0-0-0 **Dist** 0-1-4

25 Nov 06 Towcester 3m½f Cls5 69-95 Cond Ch Hcap £3,253
11 ran HEAVY 12fncs Time 6m 56.90s (slw 46.90s)
1 Tradingup 7 10-3 ....W T Kennedy 15/2
2 Levallois 10 10-7 b .....Wayne Kavanagh 100/30
3 Apple Joe 10 9-12 ex7 Willie McCarthy (3) 13/8F
F **SUPREMELY RED** 9 10-0 ......Daryl Jacob 10/1
held up, fell 7th [OR69] [op 12/1]
Dist: 6-12-71 RACE RPR: 92+/89/72+
Racecheck: Wins - Pl 1 Unpl 6

30 Oct 06 Plumpton 3m2f Cls5 Nov 62-80 Ch Hcap £3,143
7 ran GOOD 17fncs Time 6m 37.70s (slw 15.70s)
1 Hill Forts Henry 8 9-7 tp Wayne Kavanagh (7) 5/2F
2 Strolling Vagabond 7 10-4 Jamie Goldstein 16/1
3 Emily Abby 6 10-12 b¹ ....Barry Fenton 11/2
P **SUPREMELY RED** 9 10-4 .Lee Stephens (5) 7/2
in touch until mistake 8th, blundered next, soon well behind, tailed off when clambered over 3 out and pulled up [OR71] [op 9/2 tchd 5/1]
Dist: 12-2-hd-45 RACE RPR: 77+/68/74
Racecheck: Wins 1 (1) Pl - Unpl 6

11 Oct 06 Uttoxeter 3m Cls5 64-90 Ch Hcap £2,928
12 ran SOFT 18fncs Time 6m 30.40s (slw 44.40s)
1 Frosty Jak 8 11-3 ....Joe Tizzard 5/1J
2 **SUPREMELY RED** 9 10-2 Lee Stephens (5) 33/1
always prominent, led after 13th to 14th, went 2nd last, no chance with winner
[RPR73 TS29 OR71] [op 40/1]
3 Solway Sunset 7 11-0 ....Dale Jewett (5) 11/2
Dist: 9-2½-8-11-13 RACE RPR: 94+/73+/86+
Racecheck: Wins 2 (2) Pl 1 Unpl 12

Bosuns Mate 10-5

14-y-o *ch g Yachtsman - Langton Lass (Nearly A Hand)*
M Keighley Tom Siddall

Placings: 123/P**33**U3U5/P**95**/4-PF

OR74 H74	Starts	1st	2nd	3rd	Win & Pl
Chase	31	4	3	5	£50,387
All Jumps races	41	8	5	5	£72,637

2/03 Sand 2m4½f Cls6 Am Hunt Ch soft £2,373
118 10/01 Extr 3m1½f Cls3 90-118 Ch Hcap gd-fm £5,440
4/00 Sand 3m½f Cls2 Nov Ch soft £16,884
3/00 Bang 3m½f Cls3 Nov Ch good £4,719
1/99 Newb 3m½f Cls3 Nov Hdl heavy £4,782
12/98 Chel 3m Cls1 Nov Gd2 Hdl good £9,375
5/98 Worc 2m Cls6 NHF 4-6yo gd-fm £1,560
3/98 Ludl 2m Cls6 NHF 4-6yo good £1,203
Total win prize-money £46,336
GF-HRD 2-0-5 **GS-HVY** 3-5-21 **Course** 0-0-0 **Dist** 4-4-16

26 Dec 06 Towcester 3m½f Cls5 Ch £3,578
13 ran SOFT 18fncs Time 6m 50.20s (slw 40.20s)
1 Solid As A Rock 6 10-7 ...Mr J Snowden (5) 15/2
2 Chopneyev 8 11-5 b .....Matthew Batchelor 9/4F
3 Optimistic Alfie 6 10-12 tb¹ Mark Bradburne 12/1
F **BOSUNS MATE** 13 10-5 b ...Mr M Wall (7) 33/1
chased leader, pushed along 7th, fell 10th
[OR74] [op 40/1 tchd 50/1]
Dist: 1¼-20-4-1½-7 RACE RPR: 105+/110+/84+
Racecheck: Wins - Pl 2 Unpl -

4 Nov 06 Sandown 2m4½f Cls4 78-104 Cond Hdl Hcap £3,253
14 ran GOOD 9hdls Time 5m 1.40s (slw 16.40s)
1 Fort Ord 7 10-10 ....J W Farrelly (8) 9/2
2 Adlestrop 6 10-7 ....Sean Quinlan (8) 9/1
3 Indigo Sky 5 9-6 oh14 ....R J Killoran (8) 66/1
P **BOSUNS MATE** 13 10-0 oh4 Gerard Tumelty 33/1
chased leaders, lost place 3rd, tailed off when pulled up before 2 out [OR78]
Dist: 1¾-7-4-¾-¾ RACE RPR: 104+/99+/78+
Racecheck: Wins 1 Pl 3 Unpl 8

30 May 05 Chaddesley Corbett (PTP) 3m Conf
6 ran GD-FM Time 5m 56.00s
1 Captain O'Neill 11 12-0 t ....R Armson 5/1
2 Totland Bay 9 12-3 ....T Weston EvensF
3 Suaverof 10 12-0 ....D Mansell 7/4
4 **BOSUNS MATE** 12 12-0 .....Mrs B Keighley 9/1
nvr gng wl; lost tch 14; fin lame
Dist: ¾-7-12-2½-20
Racecheck: Wins - Pl 1 Unpl 4

Star Glow 11-2

13-y-o *b g Dunbeath - Betrothed (Aglojo)*
R H York Mr P York (7)

Placings: 1111F2/1/16/21PP2-P5

OR85 H72	Starts	1st	2nd	3rd	Win & Pl
Chase	3	1	–	–	£1,378
All Jumps races	13	1	1	1	£2,245

2/05 Hntg 3m Cls6 Nov Am Hunt Ch gd-sft £1,378
GF-HRD 0-0-1 **GS-HVY** 1-2-10 **Course** 0-0-0 **Dist** 1-0-2

23 Dec 06 Fontwell 2m6f Cls3 Nov Ch £6,506
5 ran GD-SFT 13fncs Time 5m 56.60s (slw 33.60s)
1 Classified 10 11-10 ....Timmy Murphy 4/6F
2 Ommega 4 10-8 ....A Duchene (5) 9/4
3 **RIVER INDUS** 6 11-1 ......Daryl Jacob (3) 100/1
led, mistake 8th, headed 10th, soon ridden, 4th and beaten 2 out, kept on under pressure, went 3rd soon after last [RPR95 TS82 OR63]
5 **STAR GLOW** 12 10-11 ....Mr P York (7) 66/1
chased leader until 4th, ridden and outpaced after 8th, no chance from 10th
[RPR63 TS50 OR85]
Dist: 2½-9-7-25 RACE RPR: 115+/100+/95
Racecheck: Wins - Pl - Unpl -

4 Jun 06 Southwell 3m2f Cls5 68-90 Ch Hcap £3,578
14 ran GOOD 19fncs Time 6m 37.30s (slw 4.30s)
1 Lambrini Bianco 8 11-0 b ..Robert Thornton 9/2F
2 Blazing Hills 10 11-9 ....Andrew Thornton 12/1
3 Trovaio 9 11-3 ....Peter Buchanan 8/1
P **STAR GLOW** 12 11-5 ....Mr P York (7) 25/1
headway and prominent 9th, lost place 12th, tailed off 9th when pulled up before last
[OR90] [op 16/1]
Dist: ½-22-1¼-1¼-4 RACE RPR: 98/106/78
Racecheck: Wins 3 (3) Pl 3 Unpl 8

22 Apr 06 Kingston Blount (PTP) 4m2½f Club Memb
8 ran GOOD Time 9m 36.00s
1 Strong Tea 15 12-0 ....Miss A Goschen 3/1
2 **STAR GLOW** 12 12-0 ....P York 5/2J
prog to ld 18; hdd & nt qckn flat
3 Blasket Sound 14 12-0 ....D Renney 16/1
Dist: 4-nk-6-4-3
Racecheck: Wins - Pl - Unpl 2

Dads Lad 10-11

13-y-o *b g Supreme Leader - Furryvale (Furry Glen)*
Miss Suzy Smith David Boland (10)

Placings: F4B3/21P13/2U2U4P/5U

OR80	Starts	1st	2nd	3rd	Win & Pl
All Jumps races	29	3	3	6	£32,526

96 1/04 Asct 3m½f Cls3 84-106 Ch Hcap gd-sft £6,864
89 12/03 MRas 3m4½f Cls4 85-101 Ch Hcap gd-sft £3,268
90 3/02 Bang 3m½f Cls3 Nov 66-90 Ch Hcap soft £4,232
Total win prize-money £14,364
GF-HRD 0-0-0 **GS-HVY** 3-5-25 **Course** 0-0-0 **Dist** 2-1-10

11 Dec 06 Plumpton 3m2f Cls4 85-109 Ch Hcap £5,010
8 ran HEAVY 15fncs Time 7m 16.70s (slw 54.70s)
1 Zimbabwe 6 9-11 p ....Jay Harris (5) 2/1F
2 Blunham Hill 8 11-4 ....Charlie Poste (5) 15/2
3 **TALLOW BAY** 11 9-13 ...Gerard Tumelty (5) 7/1
ran in snatches, reminders off the pace after 6th, progress to press winner after 10th, outpaced after next, kept on from 2 out, nearly snatched 2nd [RPR85 TS37 OR87]
U **DADS LAD** 12 10-2 b ....Colin Bolger (3) 11/2
prominent, ridden after 10th, gradually lost touch, 17 lengths behind winner in 5th when blundered and unseated rider 4 out
[OR88] [op 9/2]
Dist: 7-shd-31-33-19 RACE RPR: 93+/104/85
Racecheck: Wins 1 (1) Pl - Unpl 3

30 Nov 06 Market Rasen 3m4½f Cls4 86-107 Ch Hcap £4,554
5 ran SOFT 16fncs Time 8m 8.40s (slw 1m 0.40s)
1 Kilbeggan Blade 7 11-12 ....Jason Maguire 5/4F
2 Kitski 8 11-12 ....G Lee 2/1
3 Moscow Leader 8 10-4 p ...Mr A Merriam (7) 9/1
5 **DADS LAD** 12 10-10 b ......Colin Bolger (3) 13/2
chased leader, upsides 11th, driven 3 out, lost place before next [RPR75 TS3 OR94] [op 5/1]
Dist: 3½-14-2½-14 RACE RPR: 125+/120+/89
Racecheck: Wins 2 (2) Pl - Unpl 4

20 Jan 05 Taunton 3m3f Cls3 101-127 Ch Hcap £8,132
10 ran GD-SFT 19fncs Time 7m 25.40s (slw 53.40s)
1 Brave Spirit 7 10-10 p ....Joe Tizzard 4/1
2 Levallois 9 10-7 ....Philip Hide 7/1
3 Yann's 9 11-0 ex7 ....Richard Johnson 6/4F
P **DADS LAD** 11 9-11 b ....Colin Bolger (3) 8/1
prominent until 12th, soon behind, tailed off and pulled up before 4 out (trainer said gelding was unsuited by drying ground) [OR101]
Dist: 1¼-5-11-½-½ RACE RPR: 124+/120+/121+
Racecheck: Wins 1 (1) Pl 6 Unpl 13

Form Reading	**NATIVE CUNNING**
Spotlight	14lb out of the handicap.
Handicap Ratings	Handicap mark of 64 three outings ago and mark of 69 for today's contest making it 14lb out of the handicap.
Significant Items of Form	Nine year old with one victory, March 2004 in Class 4 Handicap Hurdle over 3m1½f. Last run in a Class 4 Hurdle over 3m3f November 2006 was after a nine month break that followed a Point to Point campaign where running as an outsider.
Verdict	Nothing to excite in the form.
Hence:	DISMISS.

Form Reading	**SUPREMELY RED**
Spotlight	Yet to win over fences, fair effort when 2nd at Uttoxeter in October.
Handicap Ratings	Allocated a mark for 79 four outings ago which was reduced to 71 for next run when 2nd at Uttoxeter, but significantly was not raised afterwards. Mark today is 69.
Significant Items of Form	Ten year old with one Maiden Hurdle victory, June 2002. Last three runs in October and November 2006 have all been in Class 5 Handicap Chases over 3 miles/3miles plus; the results being: 2nd; pulled up; and fell latest.
Verdict	Handicapper did not react to 2nd at Uttoxeter in October and given the fact that the horse has got worse since then, there is little reason for optimism.
Hence:	DISMISS.

Form Reading	**BOSUNS MATE**
Spotlight	Veteran with two poor efforts this season.
Handicap Ratings	No handicap runs last six outings. Mark of 74 for today's contest.
Significant Items of Form	Fourteen year old with four chase victories, the last of which was in February 2003 in a Hunter Chase. Placings since then indicate deteriorating form and last two runs have done nothing to alter the position.
Verdict	No reason to do anything other than: DISMISS.

Form Reading	**STAR GLOW**
Spotlight	Has done well in Point to Points and is a Hunter Chase winner.
Handicap Ratings	One rating of 70 (two outings ago) in the last six runs and down to a mark of 65 for today, which indicates leniency.
Significant Items of Form	Thirteen year old with one National Hunt win in a Hunter Chase at Huntingdon in February 2005 but six Point to Point wins in last sixteen outings. Last run twelve days ago at Fontwell in a Class 3 Novice Chase over 2m6f resulted in a 5th of 5 runners at 43½ lengths on Good to Soft was perfectly satisfactory considering it was first race for 6½ months. Good to Soft – Heavy figures of 1-2-10 indicate it will like today's ground conditions.
Verdict	Always impossible to compare Point to Point form with National Hunt form but the fact that the horse had had a bucket load of wins and only one fall in the last sixteen outings, and has had a not disappointing return from a break, would indicate that it could be in with a shout in today's difficult ground conditions.
Decision:	SELECT.

Form Reading	**DAD'S LAD**
Spotlight	Thorough stayer who goes in the Soft.
Handicap Ratings	In the last six outings has had four handicap marks over 100 (highest 102) and only in the last two outings has mark reduced to 94 and 88. Today's mark of 80 gives horse a real chance if it can rekindle previous form.
Significant Items of Form	Thirteen year old with three chase wins in excess of 3 miles, the most recent being a Class 3 event at Ascot in January 2004. 5th of 5 in a Class 4 Chase at Market Rasen over 3m4½f on 30.11.06, beaten 34 lengths on Soft when returning from a twenty two month break. Bounce factor could have had its influence on last run on 11.12.06 when unseating 4 out in 3m2f Handicap Chase at Plumpton on Soft. All form has been on Good Soft – Heavy; figures 3-5-25.
Verdict	Today's conditions are going to suit and given the fact that the horse has a 10lb claimer on board and does not appear to have lost its enthusiasm, its record justifies support.
Hence:	SELECT.

Overall Comment

Yet another example where the last named horse in the Betting Forecast prevailed in a race in which there was a BAR group, emphasising the need to make sure the form reading extends to at least the last named horse.

100/1 for the winner was a brilliant return but if you read Spotlight's comments on River Indus you can see that the forecast which paid £517 (Tote Exacta) £428 (Computer Straight Forecast) was achievable.

EXAMPLE 3

13.02.07 Folkestone – Heavy – Class 4 – Novice Hurdle – 2m1½f
Winner SAFARI ADVENTURES – 25/1

3.10 RACE 4 — Hobbs Parker Novices' Hurdle (Class 4) ATR
Winner £3,253 — 2m1½f

£5000 guaranteed For 4yo+ which have not won more than three hurdles Weights 4yo 10st 7lb; 5yo+ 11st 3lb Penalties for each hurdle won 7lb Allowances fillies and mares 7lb Entries 57 pay £15 Penalty value 1st £3,253 2nd £955 3rd £477.50 4th £238.50

1	5241 KANAD 15 b g Bold Edge-Multi-Softt C J Mann Colin Gordon And Terry Moyise	5 11-10 Noel Fehily (127)	2 nk 7/2
2	43346-3 CRUISE DIRECTOR 86 b g Zilzal-Briggsmaid Ian Williams Mrs Maggie Bull	7 11-3 Wayne Hutchinson (115)	N R
3	DUELLING BANJOS (55F) ch g Most Welcome-Khadino J Akehurst Tattenham Corner Racing 2	8 11-3 Barry Fenton	
4	10-78 SAFARI ADVENTURES (IRE) 14 ▣ b g King's Theatre-Persian Walk P Winkworth Mrs Tessa Winkworth	5 11-3 Philip Hide (105)	25/1
5	90 STRIDER 14 ch g Pivotal-Sahara Belle D C O'Brien D C O'Brien	6 11-3 Mattie Batchelor (61)	
6	0108/8 THE THUNDERER 24 gr g Terimon-By Line H J L Dunlop Tom Wilson	8 11-3 Andrew Tinkler (71)	
7	31 BOYASTARA (FR) 113 b g Astarabad-Boya Girl P F Nicholls ROA Racing Partnership V	4 11-0 R Walsh	3RD 6/1
8	3132 WARNE'S WAY (IRE) 23 (BF) ch g Spinning World-Kafayef B G Powell Nigel Stafford	4 11-0 Timmy Murphy (130)	
9	P5 FAITH AND REASON (USA) 20 b g Sunday Silence-Sheer Reason B J Curley Curley Leisure	4 10-7 Paul Moloney (95)	
10	66 KHAZAR (FR) 28 b c Anabaa-Khalisa T Doumen (FR) John P McManus	4 10-7 A P McCoy (114)	
11	25 SAHF LONDON 40 (24F) b g Vettori-Lumiere d'Espoir G L Moore Longshot Racing	4 10-7 Jamie Moore (109)	

2006 (13 ran) Topkat M C Pipe 5 11-3 4/1 — A P McCoy RPR122

BETTING FORECAST: 2 Warne's Way, 100-30 Boyastara, 4 Kanad, 8 Khazar, 10 Cruise Director, 12 Sahf London, 16 The Thunderer, 20 Duelling Banjos, Faith And Reason, Safari Adventures, 200 Strider.

SPOTLIGHT

Kanad Improved for first try at handicapping when convincing winner over 2m on good ground at Ludlow last month and these conditions obviously very different but handled soft on Flat and should find this trip within his range.

Cruise Director Fair 1m4f Flat handicapper on his day, happy in testing conditions; respectable return to hurdling when third in Plumpton handicap in November but official figures give him something to find back in novice company.

Duelling Banjos Not rated as highly on Flat as some of these but was running well on AW in December; may be best watched this time.

Safari Adventures Brother to smart jumper Royal Shakespeare and looked good prospect himself in winning bumper debut; flopped in that sphere next time but hinted there's a race over hurdles in him even though well beaten when eighth of 14 behind useful sort in C&D novice late last month; may be better handicapping.

Strider Minor Flat winner season before last for David Evans but a couple of street lengths behind Safari Adventure over C&D last month and hard to fancy.

The Thunderer Very promising when landing good-ground bumper event for Nicky Henderson three years ago and looked after once clearly beaten on hurdling debut the following season; returning from monster lay-off and reported by jockey to have run too free when beaten best part of 50l in Wincanton novice hurdle last month but trainer going well with some near-misses of late and interesting to see if there's support this time.

Boyastara Wore blinkers when opening account over hurdles in France in October (soft ground) and of obvious interest representing top stable if market vibes are right but lack of headgear today a slight cause for concern.

Warne's Way Crumbled up the final hill at Towcester last month when odds on after creditable third on testing going in Class 1 juvenile event at Chepstow's Christmas fixture; had beaten dual subsequent winner Raslan to open account at Fontwell and looks the pick on pure form.

Faith And Reason Second off 84 in 1m2f AW handicap in June when with Godolphin and some promise in his 50-1 fifth of 13 finishers in Huntingdon novice hurdle last month; stable 2-30 in novice hurdles in recent seasons and handicapping may be better option, but never ignore market confidence with this yard.

Khazar Progressive middle-distance performer on Flat in France for Aga Khan but yet to translate that ability to hurdles and effort petered out very tamely on soft over this C&D last month; something to prove now for sure, but dangerous to write off.

Sahf London Successful in neo-banded event on AW last month but flopped in blinkers next time and two efforts over hurdles leave him with plenty to find; may need sights lowering a tad, but stable landed a big pot on Saturday.

VERDICT **WARNE'S WAY (nap)** was outslogged up the ferocious finish at Towcester last time but his previous form reads well enough for him to merit being given another chance. **Boyastara**, representing a top stable, must be monitored for market confidence, while the other previous winner, **Kanad**, can't be underestimated given his rate of progress.[PJ]

Strider — 11-3

6-y-o ch g Pivotal - Sahara Belle (Sanglamore)
D C O'Brien — Mattie Batchelor

Placings: 90

	Starts	1st	2nd	3rd	Win & Pl
All Jumps races	2	–	–	–	–
GF-HRD 0-0-0	GS-HVY 0-0-2		Course 0-0-1	Dist 0-0-1	

F58

30 Jan Folkestone 13th, see SAFARI ADVENTURES

4 Jan Lingfield 2m1½f — Cls4 Nov Hdl £3,253
11 ran HEAVY 8hdls Time 4m 22.00s (slw 26.00s)
1 Grecian Groom 5 11-5 ....Noel Fehily 33/1
2 Reidwil 4 10-7 ....Timmy Murphy 33/1
3 Polinarnix 4 10-5 ......Tom Scudamore 10/11F
9 STRIDER 6 11-5 ....Tom Siddall 100/1
always well in rear, lost touch after 5th, tailed off
btn 60 lengths [RPR50 TS13]

Dist: ½-½-16-13-12 RACE RPR: 110+/97/103
Racecheck: Wins - Pl - Unpl 7

Flat Form

28 Aug 05 Yarmouth 1m2f — Cls6 £3,073
15 ran GD-FM Time 2m 9.12s (slw 4.12s)
1 Sunshine On Me 4 9-0 .Slade O'Hara (7) 3 11/8F
2 Mink Mitten 3 8-4 1 ....Saleem Golam (5) 6 14/1
3 Love You Always 5 8-13 Josephine Chini (7) 1 7/1

---

12 STRIDER 4 9-6 t ....Francis Ferris 7 12/1
held up, ridden over 3f out, never dangerous
btn 19 lengths [RPR34 TS20 OR60] [op 14/1]

Dist: 2½-6-1¾-1-1 RACE RPR: 71/62/54
Racecheck: Wins 1 (1) Pl 3 Unpl 23

Safari Adventures — 11-3

5-y-o b g King's Theatre - Persian Walk (Persian Bold)
P Winkworth — Philip Hide

Placings: 10-78

	Starts	1st	2nd	3rd	Win & Pl
Hurdles	2	–	–	–	–
All Jumps races	4	1	–	–	£1,713
1/06	GF-HRD 0-0-0	GS-HVY 1-0-4	Course 0-0-2	Dist 1-0-3	

30 Jan Folkestone 2m1½f — Cls4 Nov Hdl £3,253
14 ran SOFT 9hdls Time 4m 26.70s (slw 18.70s)
1 Hobbs Hill 8 11-4 ....P J Brennan 1/2F
2 William Bonney 7 11-11 ....Noel Fehily 3/1
3 Cathedral Rock 5 11-4 ......Leighton Aspell 20/1
8 SAFARI ADVENTURES 5 11-4 J M McCarthy 33/1
held up well in rear and well off the pace,
mistake 3rd, nudged along and kept on steadily
from 2 out, never near leaders
btn 37 lengths [RPR94 TS90]

---

13 STRIDER 6 11-1 .Robert Lucey-Butler (3) 100/1
jumped slowly 1st, last and weakening after 3rd,
tailed off from next btn 118 lengths [RPR-]

Dist: 17-4-3-7-3½ RACE RPR: 137+/120/109
Racecheck: Wins - Pl - Unpl -

12 Jan Huntingdon 2m1½f Cls4 Nov Hdl 4-7yo £4,554
16 ran SOFT 8hdls Time 4m 12.80s (slw 32.80s)
1 French Saulaie 6 11-11 ...Richard Johnson 4/6F
2 Niver Bai 6 11-5 ....Sam Thomas 8/1
3 Cathedral Rock 5 11-5 ......Leighton Aspell 12/1
7 SAFARI ADVENTURES 5 11-5 Barry Fenton 16/1
held up, headway approaching 3 out, weakened
before next btn 19 lengths [RPR86 TS30]

Dist: 7-9-hd-1½-1 RACE RPR: 118+/100+/89
Racecheck: Wins - Pl 2 Unpl 10

14 Feb 06 Folkestone 2m1½f Cls6 NHF 4-6yo £1,713
13 ran SOFT Time 4m 27.50s (slw 26.50s)
1 Pangbourne 5 11-11 eb .....Robert Thornton 5/1
2 Fredensborg 5 11-4 ....Sam Thomas 4/1J
3 Boston Strong Boy 6 11-4 ....Andrew Tinkler 6/1
11 SAFARI ADVENTURES 4 11-1 Philip Hide 13/2
held up, in touch until well outpaced 5f out,
eased final 2f
btn 58 lengths [RPR58 TS23] [tchd 6/1]

Dist: 20-1¼-1¼-5-10 RACE RPR: 126+/99/97
Racecheck: Wins 4 (4) Pl 3 Unpl 15

Form Reading	**STRIDER**
Spotlight	Minor Flat winner season before last.
Handicap Ratings	Non Handicap.
Significant Items of Form	Six year old with two runs in Novice Hurdles 04.01.07 and 30.01.07 beaten out of sight both occasions.
Verdict	No reason to do anything other than: DISMISS.

Form Reading	**SAFARI ADVENTURES**
Spotlight	Brother to smart jumper Royal Shakespeare and looked good prospect himself when winning bumper debut.
Handicap Ratings	Non Handicap.
Significant Items of Form	Five year old Bumper winner on Soft at Plumpton over 2m2f January 2006. Ran unplaced in follow up Bumper in February 2006 at Folkestone. Rested until 12.01.07 when made hurdle debut in a Class 4 Novice Hurdle at Huntingdon (2m½f) when finished 7th of 16, beaten 19 lengths after being help up and making headway 3 out. Raced again (last outing) in Class 4 Novice Hurdle at Folkestone (Soft) over 2m1½f when 'held up in rear well off the pace, mistake 3rd nudged along and kept on steadily from 2 out, never rear leaders, beaten 37 lengths'.
Verdict	Classic form for a result (see overall comment below).
Hence:	SELECT.

Overall Comment

I have included this example because although it was a Non Handicap race and therefore a Non-Preferred event, the winner Safari Adventures had the classic form profile to achieve a good result at a long price. Classic for the following reasons:

a) Had already showed it could get its head in front by its Bumper victory over 2m2f on Soft.

b) Hurdle debut after twelve month break was very satisfactory with midfield finishing position after being held up and making headway three out.

c) Second hurdle race (last outing) when held up in rear well off the pace on today's course before keeping on steadily two out to achieve another midfield (8th of 14) finishing position gave every indication of a horse close to peak fitness, which is ready to show its true worth if given its head in the right race on the right course and under the right conditions (going/distance).

d) The trainer had made sure that the horse had become accustomed to the track and had obviously satisfied himself that Folkestone suited his running style.

I have lost count of the form profiles very similar to this one which belong to horses who have won races at long prices and therefore it is an example you should never tire of reading for future reference purposes.

I should also point out that I was so impressed with the form profile of Safari Adventures that I restricted myself to one selection only. It is also worth adding that the forecast was easily achievable given the fact that the runner was one of the most fancied runners at a price of 7/2.

The Tote Exacta paid £119.70 and the Computer Straight Forecast £107.23.

EXAMPLE 4

15.10.06 Hereford – Good to Firm – Class 4 – Handicap Hurdle – 3m2f
Winner JUG OF PUNCH – 50/1

4.20 | *Herefordshire Cider Handicap Hurdle (Class 4)* | ATR
RACE 5 | *Winner £3,578.30* | **3m2f**

£5500 guaranteed For 4yo+ Rated 0-105 Weights raised 5lb Minimum Weight 10-0 Penalties after October 7th, a winner of a hurdle 7lb Business Traveller's Handicap Mark 100 Entries 38 pay £10 Penalty value 1st £3,578.30 2nd £1,050.50 3rd £525.25 4th £262.35

1 625-519 **BUSINESS TRAVELLER** (IRE) [8]
ch g Titus Livius-Dancing Venus · tv 6 11-12 · Mark Nicholls(5) (103)
R J Price Karl And Patricia Reece

2 7904P-8 **ETENDARD INDIEN** (FR) [11]
b g Selkirk-Danseuse Indienne · 5 11-9 · Mick FitzGerald (101)
Simon Earle Mrs M Findlay

3 -131111 **TERRAMARIQUE** (IRE) [21] [D]
b g Namaqualand-Secret Ocean · v 7 11-7 · Marcus Foley (105)
N J Henderson Mr & Mrs Sandy Orr

4 3444F54 **DELAWARE** (FR) [11]
ch g Garde Royale-L'Indienne · 10 11-6 · Andrew Glassonbury(5) (98)
H S Howe Horses Away Racing Club

5 9-45316 **WAYWARD MELODY** [38]
b m Merdon Melody-Dubitable · v 6 11-3 · W T Kennedy(3) (101)
R Flint R Flint

6 00-97P5 **FORT ORD** (IRE) [42]
br g Norwich-Newtown Rose · 7 11-3 · J W Farrelly(10) (91)
Jonjo O'Neill John P McManus

7 P84140P **WEE DANNY** (IRE) [11] [CD]
b g Mandalus-Bonne Bouche · 9 11-1 · Justin Morgan(7) (97)
L A Dace Let's Have Fun Syndicate

8 5280324 **FOURPOINTONE** [21]
b g Overbury-Praise The Lord · p 5 11-0 · B C Byrnes(5) (94)
E McNamara (IRE) Erinvale Syndicate

9 2845422 **DEO GRATIAS** (POL) [12]
b g Enjoy Plan-Dea · v 6 11-0 · Carl Llewellyn (101)
Carl Llewellyn Dave Brown & Ted Henderson

10 1-4PPP0 **VIVANTE** (IRE) [21]
b m Toulon-Splendidly Gay · tp 8 10-12 · Mr D England(7) (100)
A J Wilson The Up And Running Partnership

11 0-03640 **JUG OF PUNCH** (IRE) [11]
ch g In The Wings-Mysistra · 7 10-12 · Colin Bolger(3) (102)
S T Lewis Simon T Lewis

12 23527-5 **MISTER ZAFFARAN** (IRE) [105]
ch g Zaffaran-Best Served Cherry · 7 10-11 · Jodie Mogford (92)
Mrs N S Evans P T Evans

13 840447P **CAPER** [11] [C]
b g Salse-Spinning Mouse · p 6 10-11 · David Dennis (100)
R Hollinshead Cecil W Wardle

14 6-U6631 **SUNDAWN LADY** [21] [B]
b m Faustus-Game Domino · b 8 10-8 · Gerard Tumelty(5) (101)
C P Morlock Michael Padfield & Philip Dean

15 P-UP0P8 **BARNEYS REFLECTION** [24]
b g Petoski-Annaberg · b 6 10-5 · Liam Heard(5) (79)
J L Flint J L Flint

16 06-PP08 **SANDYWELL GEORGE** [23]
ch g Zambrano-Farmcote Air · t 11 10-3 · Dave Crosse (74)
L P Grassick David Lloyd & Mrs Carole Lloyd

2005 (13 ran) Harbour View E McNamara 6 10-1 5/2 · B C Byrnes (7) OR87

BETTING FORECAST: 7-4 Terramarique, 6 Deo Gratias, 7 Fourpointone, Sundawn Lady, 12 Delaware, Wayward Melody, 14 Business Traveller, Fort Ord, 20 Etendard Indien, Wee Danny, 25 Jug Of Punch, 33 Caper, Mister Zaffaran, 50 bar.

SPOTLIGHT

Business Traveller Lacks consistency and doesn't win that often, but is capable of a big run on his day, highlighted by ready Ludlow success in May; disappointed on recent comeback and yet to defy a mark this high; opposable.

Etendard Indien Useful on Flat in France and looked a bright hurdling prospect when running away with British bow for Nicky Henderson; however, has been bitterly disappointing since, including off 3lb higher on recent debut for current yard; this longer trip will need to help.

Terramarique Has been in blinding form over hurdles and fences since joining Nicky Henderson; defied lower marks in impressive fashion with visor over summer and has kept winning as a chaser since, including off just 2lb lower latest; clearly in form of his life and will handle conditions; obvious contender.

Delaware Losing run stretches back to 2002 and, although has steadily crept down to present lenient mark, recent efforts in similar company suggest he'll find a few too strong again here; opposable over trip that might just stretch.

Wayward Melody Not the most reliable on view; finished 13l behind Terramarique in August and unlikely to turn tables on these terms; has won a less competitive handicap hurdle since, but could only plug on mid-division with visor back on latest; place claims at best.

Fort Ord Won a minor bumper in Ireland, but failed to threaten as a hurdler there and no improvement over fences and hurdles since joining current yard; significant hike in trip will need to help.

Wee Danny Paid price for winning four on the trot back in 2003; has dropped back to a winnable mark, is proven over C&D and stopped the rot with a game success in August, but finished 17l behind Terramarique soon after and form continued to deteriorate since; work to do.

Fourpointone Irish challenger; still a maiden, but has run some solid races in defeat in competitive races this year, not least when denied by a neck at Galway last month; acts on any ground; interesting if market speaks in favour.

Deo Gratias Dual Flat winner who, although yet to taste success as a hurdler, comes here after a couple of big runs under similar conditions with visor; unlucky to meet an in-form rival latest and should go well.

Vivante Has lost the plot since defying 3lb lower mark in April; not much better latest, though did at least manage to complete, and clearly something amiss; best watched.

Jug Of Punch Very much has two ways of running and was fortunate when left clear to win a selling handicap in February; didn't convince that he stayed when last seen over this trip and couldn't be confident after latest disappointment.

Mister Zaffaran Didn't show much as a pointer and only hints of ability in bumpers last season; flattered by placing on hurdle debut and when tailed-off fifth on return to fray in July; not badly treated for handicap debut, but others boast more convincing form.

Caper Sole career win came in a selling hurdle last year and has lacked consistency since; lost his way over fences more recently and showed no interest in game latest; looks harshly treated for this return to hurdles and will probably struggle.

Sundawn Lady Lived up to previous placed potential when bravely shading Deo Gratias in a similar race latest; may well improve for that much-needed confidence booster, stays well and no surprise to see her go well again.

Barneys Reflection Twice defied higher hurdle ratings last year, but has done nothing of note since and no real signs of a revival last month; look elsewhere.

Sandywell George Rarely wins and, although potentially well treated on pick of form, recent lacklustre efforts suggest he won't take advantage.

VERDICT TERRAMARIQUE (nap) can do little wrong at present and, with conditions to suit, can complete the five-timer back over hurdles. **Deo Gratias** and **Sundawn Lady** appeal as likely dangers.[BDO]

OFFICIAL RATINGS LAST SIX OUTINGS-LATEST ON RIGHT	**4.20** HANDICAP	TODAY FUTURE	RP RATING LATEST / BEST / ADJUSTED
87⁶ 86² 95⁵ 97⁵ 94¹ 102⁹	Business Traveller 11-12	100	58 103 103
117⁷ 113⁹ 110⁰ 108¹ 105ᴾ 100⁸	Etendard Indien 11-9	97	84 106 ◄ 101
— — 78¹ 85¹ — —	Terramarique 11-7	95	— 105 ◄ 105
— — — 95ᶠ 95⁵ 95ᶜ	Delaware 11-6	94	98 98 98
— — 88⁶ 88³ 87¹ 91⁶	Wayward Melody 11-3	91	95 101 101
— — — 88⁷ — 95⁵	Fort Ord 11-3	91	91 91 91
85⁸ 84⁴ 81¹ 88⁴ 90⁰ —	Wee Danny 11-1	89	— 97 97
77² 79⁸ 78⁰ 77³ 77² 81⁴	Fourpointone 11-0	88	84 94 94
82⁸ — 82⁴ 82² 84² —	Deo Gratias 11-0	88	101 ◄ 101 101
83¹ 91⁴ 91ᴾ — — 90⁰	Vivante 10-12	86	81 100 100
128⁰ 89⁰ 89³ 89⁶ 89⁴ 88⁰	Jug Of Punch 10-12	86	72 102 102
— — — — — —	Mister Zaffaran 10-11	85	71 71 92
— — — — — —	Caper 10-11	85	— 100 100
80⁶ 78ᵁ 78⁶ 76⁶ 74³ 75¹	Sundawn Lady 10-8	82	101 ◄ 101 101
— — 95ᴾ — 85ᴾ 82⁸	Barneys Reflection 10-5	79	79 79 79
— — — 84⁰ 80⁸	Sandywell George 10-3	77	61 74 74

Sandywell George 10-3

11-y-o *ch g Zambrano - Farmcote Air (True Song)*
L P Grassick Dave Crosse

Placings: U5868/573060406-PP08

OR77	Starts	1st	2nd	3rd	Win & Pl
Hurdles	35	1	4	5	£8,272
All Jumps races	48	1	4	5	£8,720

88 12/03 Wwck 2m3f Cls4 Nov 71-92 Am Hdl Hcap gd-sft £2,457

GF-HRD 0-6-20 GS-HVY 1-0-13 Course 0-0-1 Dist 0-0-0

22 Sep Worcester 3m Cls4 74-100 Hdl Hcap £2,928
14 ran GOOD 12hdls Time 6m 3.50s (slw 27.50s)
1 Veverka 5 11-1 ....Sean Fox 11/2
2 Good Potential 10 10-8 t .....Warren Marston 9/1
3 Needle Prick 5 10-7 ....Mr D England (7) 10/1
8 **SANDYWELL GEORGE** 11 10-6 t ....Dave Crosse 80/1
chased leaders until 8th, plodded on and soon well beaten
btn 47 lengths [RPR36 TS2 OR80] [op 66/1]
10 **WEE DANNY** 9 10-13 ....Colin Bolger (3) 9/1
prominent, ridden after 9th, dropped out rapidly before next, tailed off
btn 83 lengths [RPR10 OR90] [op 15/2]
Dist: nk-12-2½-11-3½ RACE RPR: 92/87+/80+
Racecheck: Wins 1 Pl - Unpl 4

3 Sep Worcester 2m4f Cls4 84-110 Hdl Hcap £3,904
17 ran GOOD 10hdls Time 4m 43.00s (slw 5.00s)
1 Rabbit 5 10-6 ....P J Brennan 15/2
2 Veverka 5 10-3 ....Sean Curran 20/1
3 Orion Express 5 10-7 ....Liam Heard (5) 7/2F
14 **SANDYWELL GEORGE** 11 10-0 tv oh1 ....Dave Crosse 66/1
behind from 7th
btn 40 lengths [RPR49 TS14 OR84]
Dist: 5-1½-nk-3-1½ RACE RPR: 97+/89+/97+
Racecheck: Wins 3 (3) Pl 2 Unpl 12

14 May Worcester 2m7½f Cls4 Ch £3,904
12 ran GOOD 18fncs Time 6m 3.00s (slw 18.00s)
1 Oakfield Legend 5 10-5 ow1 ....James Diment (5) 33/1
2 Rosemauve 6 11-2 b ......Tom Scudamore 11/4J
3 Club Royal 9 10-9 ......Mrs Lucy Rowsell (7) 14/1
P **SANDYWELL GEORGE** 11 10-13 tv ....Tom Malone (3) 80/1
always behind, tailed off when pulled up before 4 out [OR69] [op 66/1]
Dist: nk-5-18-6 RACE RPR: 80+/91+/80
Racecheck: Wins - Pl - Unpl 9

Barneys Reflection 10-5

6-y-o *b g Petoski - Annaberg (Tirol)*
J L Flint Liam Heard (5)

Placings: 4811/40457P6PP-UP0P8

OR79	Starts	1st	2nd	3rd	Win & Pl
Hurdles	14	2	-	-	£5,447
All Jumps races	23	2	-	-	£6,073

90 4/05 MRas 2m1½f Cls5 70-95 Sell Hdl Hcap good £2,296
83 3/05 Fknm 2m Cls5 60-83 Sell Hdl Hcap good £2,597
Total win prize-money £4,893

GF-HRD 0-0-7 GS-HVY 0-1-7 Course 0-0-0 Dist 0-0-0

21 Sep Fontwell 2m2½f Cls5 67-83 Sell Hdl Hcap £2,082
12 ran GD-FM 9hdls Time 4m 22.40s (slw 8.40s)
1 Lojo 4 10-6 ....Paddy Merrigan (5) 13/2
2 Before The Mast 9 11-6 ....Charlie Poste (5) 13/2
3 Westfield Dancer 7 11-7 b ....Paul Moloney 13/2
8 **BARNEYS REFLECTION** 6 11-6 b ....Liam Heard (5) 25/1
chased leaders, mistake 4th, ridden after next, weakened approaching 2 out
btn 34 lengths [RPR56 TS29 OR82]
Dist: hd-10-5-7-8 RACE RPR: 76/90+/77+
Racecheck: Wins - Pl 1 Unpl 1

26 Aug Newton Abbot 2m1f Cls4 69-95 Cond Hdl Hcap £4,554
7 ran GD-FM 6hdls Time 3m 59.30s (slw 8.30s)
1 Blandings Castle 5 10-0 oh5 ..Daryl Jacob 13/2
2 Spitfire Bob 7 11-4 ....Owyn Nelmes 7/1
3 Brochrua 6 10-13 ....Byron Moorcroft (8) 5/2
P **BARNEYS REFLECTION** 6 11-2 p ....W T Kennedy 7/2
prominent, ridden after 3rd, weakening when blundered 3 out, soon pulled up
[OR85] [op 4/1 tchd 9/2]
Dist: 22-1¾-35 RACE RPR: 74/70/71
Racecheck: Wins - Pl - Unpl 2

4 Jul Southwell 3m½f Cls5 Claim Hdl £2,741
14 ran GD-FM 13hdls Time 6m 7.50s (slw 25.50s)
1 Chockdee 6 11-7 t.................A P McCoy 7/4F
2 Rushneeyriver 8 10-11 p ....Noel Fehily 6/1
3 Shared Account 12 10-8 p ...P C O'Neill (3) 11/2
11 **BARNEYS REFLECTION** 6 10-6 b ....Declan McGann (5) 66/1
unseated rider leaving paddock and ran loose, chased leaders until hard ridden 7th, soon behind, mistake 9th, tailed off after 3 out
btn 106 lengths [RPR- OR90]
Dist: ½-¾-19-4-1¼ RACE RPR: 108+/98+/97+
Racecheck: Wins 3 (3) Pl 2 Unpl 7

Vivante 10-12

8-y-o *b m Toulon - Splendidly Gay (Lord Gayle)*
A J Wilson Mr D England (7)

Placings: 0/87964/532251-4PPP0

OR86	Starts	1st	2nd	3rd	Win & Pl
Hurdles	16	1	2	1	£6,189
All Jumps races	18	1	2	1	£6,180

83 4/06 Hntg 2m5½f Cls4 83-109 Hdl Hcap gd-fm £3,426

GF-HRD 1-2-5 GS-HVY 0-0-2 Course 0-0-0 Dist 0-1-3

24 Sep Huntingdon 3m2f Cls5 69-90 Hdl Hcap £2,741
20 ran GD-FM 12hdls Time 6m 7.50s (slw 9.50s)
1 **SUNDAWN LADY** 8 10-6 b Gerard Tumelty (5) 7/1
chased leaders, led last, edged left flat, all out
[RPR81 TS77 OR75] [tchd 15/2]
2 **DEO GRATIAS** 6 11-4 v ......Carl Llewellyn 15/2
chased leader until led 9th, ridden and headed last, stayed on [RPR87 TS84 OR82] [op 8/1]
3 Dizzy Future 4 11-0 ....W T Kennedy (3) 15/2
12 **VIVANTE** 8 11-5 tp ....Mr D England (7) 33/1
prominent to 7th
btn 30 lengths [RPR65 TS70 OR90]
Dist: hd-¾-10-1½-1½ RACE RPR: 81+/87/85
Racecheck: Wins - Pl 2 Unpl 4

3 Sep Worcester 3m Cls4 Nov Hdl £2,928
12 ran GOOD 12hdls Time 5m 43.70s (slw 7.70s)
1 Waynesworld 8 10-12 ....Tom Scudamore 3/1
2 Ladino 6 11-10 ....Richard Johnson 2/1F
3 Possextown 8 11-10 ....Tony Dobbin 7/2
P **VIVANTE** 8 10-11 tp .....Wayne Hutchinson 33/1
towards rear, jumped right 5th, lost touch 7th, tailed off when pulled up before 9th [OR90]
Dist: 1½-½-1¾-45 RACE RPR: 110+/119+/119+
Racecheck: Wins - Pl 1 Unpl 4

5 Jul Stratford 2m3f Cls4 Nov Hdl £4,554
9 ran GOOD 10hdls Time 4m 30.10s (slw 7.10s)
1 Wee Dinns 5 12-0 ....A P McCoy 2/5F
2 Sonoma 6 10-11 ....Johnny Levins (5) 5/1
3 Persian Carpet 4 10-2 ....Mark Nicolls (5) 50/1
P **VIVANTE** 8 10-9 tp ....Mr D England (7) 16/1
prominent to 5th, tailed off when pulled up before 3 out (jockey said mare had a breathing problem) [OR90] [op 14/1]
Dist: 6-4-6-16-12 RACE RPR: 117+/95+/81
Racecheck: Wins 2 (2) Pl 1 Unpl 10

17 Apr Huntingdon 2m5½f Cls4 83-109 Hdl Hcap £3,426
12 ran GD-FM 10hdls Time 5m 11.00s (slw 19.00s)
1 **VIVANTE** 8 9-7 tp oh2 ....Mr D England (7) 14/1
soon led, headed after 5th, led approaching 3 out, driven out [RPR84 TS34 OR83] [op 16/1]
2 Orange Street 6 11-12 ..Benjamin Hitchcott 4/1F
3 Coralbrook 6 10-12 b ....J A McCarthy 11/2
P **ETENDARD INDIEN** 5 11-8 Andrew Tinkler 11/2
prominent, led after 5th to 6th, weakened 3 out, pulled up before 2 out [OR105] [op 7/1]
Dist: 1¼-12-1½-2½-5 RACE RPR: 84/110+/84+
Racecheck: Wins - Pl 1 Unpl 8

Mister Zaffaran 10-11

7-y-o *ch g Zaffaran - Best Served Cherry (Sheer Grit)*
Mrs N S Evans Jodie Mogford

Placings: P/P/P23527-5

OR85	Starts	1st	2nd	3rd	Win & Pl
Hurdles	3	-	1	-	£1,066
All Jumps races	5	-	1	1	£1,609

GF-HRD 0-0-3 GS-HVY 0-1-1 Course 0-0-0 Dist 0-0-0

2 Jul Uttoxeter 2m4½f Cls5 Mdn Hdl £2,602
15 ran GD-FM 11hdls Time 4m 54.40s (slw 8.40s)
1 Ladino 6 11-0 ....Richard Johnson 6/5F
2 Able King 6 11-0 ....Jamie Goldstein 9/4
3 Capt Jack 7 11-0 ....G Lee 9/1
5 **MISTER ZAFFARAN** 7 11-0 Jodie Mogford 50/1
close up, ridden 7th, weakened after 9th, tailed off [RPR54 TS26] [op 40/1]
Dist: 1½-20-35-2-hd RACE RPR: 114+/111/91
Racecheck: Wins 4 (4) Pl - Unpl 7

23 Oct 05 Wincanton 2m6f Cls4 Nov Hdl £3,435
9 ran GOOD 11hdls Time 5m 12.80s (slw 3.80s)
1 Denman 5 10-11 ....Christian Williams 5/6F
2 Lyes Green 4 10-11 ....Leighton Aspell 16/1
3 Alphabetical 6 10-11 ....Noel Fehily 4/1
7 **MISTER ZAFFARAN** 6 10-11 t Jodie Mogford 12/1
chased leaders until weakened after 8th (jockey said gelding hung left-handed)
btn 81 lengths [RPR33 TS37] [op 16/1]
Dist: 1¼-14-13-23-½ RACE RPR: 117+/112+/98
Racecheck: Wins 3 (3) Pl 1 Unpl 8

6 Oct 05 Worcester 3m Cls4 Nov Hdl £3,465
4 ran GD-FM 12hdls Time 5m 59.30s (slw 23.30s)
1 Harry's Dream 8 10-12 ....Richard Johnson 1/6F
2 **MISTER ZAFFARAN** 6 10-12 Jodie Mogford 8/1
chased leader, led 6th until approaching 3 out, soon beaten, hung badly right to paddock exit soon after last [RPR75 TS14] [op 10/1]
3 Great Escape 9 10-12 ....Sean Curran 20/1
Dist: 15-3-dist RACE RPR: 105+/75+/63
Racecheck: Wins - Pl 1 Unpl 4

Caper 10-11

6-y-o b g Salse - Spinning Mouse (Bustino)
R Hollinshead David Dennis

Placings: 2658U4445P36-84O447P

OR85	F30		Starts	1st	2nd	3rd	Win & Pl
Hurdles			16	1	1	2	£5,747
All Jumps races			27	1	1	3	£7,233
	3/05	Hrfd	2m3³/₄f Cls5 Nov Sell Hdl 4-8yo gd-fm				£2,233

GF-HRD 1-0-12   GS-HVY 0-3-9   Course 0-0-1   Dist 0-0-2

4 Oct Towcester 3m¹/₂f Cls5 64-86 Ch Hcap £3,253
12 ran GOOD   -18fncs Time 6m 17.50s (slw 7.50s)
1 Lucky Luk 7 10-12 ....J A McCarthy 4/1F
2 Carriage Ride 8 11-2 b ....Philip Hide 25/1
3 Missy Moscow 8 9-7 b oh7 J W Stevenson (7) 14/1
P CAPER 6 10-5 p ....Tom Doyle 13/2
  jumped slowly in detached last and never took
  any interest, tailed off and pulled up 10th
  (jockey said gelding was never travelling)
  [OR69] [op 8/1]

Dist: 22-9-³/₄-6-1¹/₂   RACE RPR: 100+/82+/56
Racecheck: Wins - Pl - Unpl -

24 Sep Huntingdon 3m   Cls4 Nov 78-104 Ch Hcap
£3,904
12 ran GD-FM   19fncs   Time 6m 1.50s (slw 11.50s)
1 TERRAMARIQUE 7 11-1 v ex7 ....
..................................Marcus Foley 15/8F
  chased leader, led 4 out, blundered last, soon
  headed, rallied to lead post
  [RPR106 TS70 OR93] [op 13/8]
2 Spanchil Hill 6 10-0 oh2 ....G Lee 16/1
3 Rakalackey 8 11-11 ....Richard Johnson 7/2

---

7 CAPER 6 10-0 b¹ oh9 ....Tom Doyle 25/1
  held up, never dangerous
  btn 31 lengths [RPR61 TS29 OR78]

Dist: hd-7-1¹/₂-³/₄-14   RACE RPR: 106+/88/108+
Racecheck: Wins - Pl - Unpl 5

3 Sep Worcester 2m7¹/₂f Cls5 62-88 Ch Hcap £3,253
17 ran GOOD   18fncs   Time 5m 48.00s (slw 3.00s)
1 Sam Adamson 11 9-11 t oh3 ....
..................................Richard Young (3) 33/1
2 Mollycarrsbrekfast 11 10-12 ...P J Brennan 9/2F
3 Vandante 10 11-9 ....Robert Thornton 10/1
4 CAPER 6 10-9 p ....David Dennis 11/1
  held up in mid-division, ridden and headway
  13th, no further progress from 4 out
  [RPR66 TS57 OR71] [op 14/1]

Dist: 6-4-9-2-25   RACE RPR: 76+/84+/91+
Racecheck: Wins - Pl 1.Unpl 10

Jug Of Punch 10-12

7-y-o ch g In The Wings - Mysistra (Machiavellian)
S T Lewis Colin Bolger (3)

Placings: 2PP/7581068170-03640

OR86	F50		Starts	1st	2nd	3rd	Win & Pl
All Jumps races			22	2	1	3	£9,441
	2/06	Ludl	2m5f Cls5 Nov Sell Hdl 4-7yo good £2,602				
79	11/05	Ludl	2m5f Cls4 59-85 Hdl Hcap good .£3,533				
			Total win prize-money £6,135				

GF-HRD 0-1-6   GS-HVY 0-0-8   Course 0-0-1   Dist 0-0-1

4 Oct Towcester 2m   Cls4 74-100 Hdl Hcap £3,904
15 ran GOOD   8hdls   Time 3m 46.40s (fst 2.10s)
1 Optimum 4 9-9 ....Liam Treadwell (5) 14/1
2 Robbie Can Can 7 11-2 Wayne Hutchinson 3/1F
3 Pilca 6 10-13 ....W T Kennedy (3) 7/1

---

8 ETENDARD INDIEN 5 11-12 Mick FitzGerald 10/1
  prominent, jumped slowly 5th, soon driven,
  faded befoe next
  btn 33 lengths [RPR79 TS71 OR100][tchd 11/1]
12 JUG OF PUNCH 7 10-11 Colin Bolger (3) 22/1
  prominent, driven 4th, faded after next
  btn 44 lengths [RPR56 TS45 OR88] [op 20/1]

Dist: 4-3¹/₂-3¹/₂-4-11   RACE RPR: 85+/98+/94
Racecheck: Wins - Pl 1 Unpl 1

26 Aug Market Rasen 2m3¹/₂f Cls5 85-91 Hdl Hcap
£3,083
9 ran GOOD   10hdls Time 5m 9.80s (slw 36.80s)
1 Black Rainbow 8 11-2 ...Miss T Jackson (7) 11/2
2 Gondolin 6 11-6 ....S E Durack 9/1
3 Erins Lass 9 10-13 v¹ .....J W Stevenson (10) 5/1
4 JUG OF PUNCH 7 11-7. ....Chris Honour (3) 9/1
  went prominent 5th, outpaced after 3 out, stayed
  on run-in [RPR80 OR89] [op 10/1]

Dist: nk-11-³/₄-6-4   RACE RPR: 91/91 +/81+
Racecheck: Wins - Pl - Unpl 6

22 Aug Worcester 2m   Cls5 63-89 Cond Hdl Hcap
£2,398
10 ran GD-FM   8hdls   Time 3m 40.70s (slw 0.80s)
1 Silver Island 5 10-6 t :................T J O'Brien 7/2
2 Lawaaheb 5 11-12 ....Adam Pogson 12/1
3 So Cloudy 5 11-1 ....S J Craine (3) 5/2
6 JUG OF PUNCH 7 11-12 ..Tom Messenger 25/1
  behind, bumped 1st, hampered approaching 3
  out, never dangerous
  [RPR69 TS50 OR89] [op 22/1]

Dist: 11-2-1-3-16   RACE RPR: 82+/92+/81
Racecheck: Wins 1 (1) Pl 3 Unpl 8

Form Reading	**SANDYWELL GEORGE**
Spotlight	Potentially well treated on pick of form.
Handicap Ratings	Today's mark 77, down from 80 and 84 previous two outings, so handicapper not impressed.
Significant Items of Form	Eleven year old with one Novice Handicap Hurdle victory over 2m3f December 2003 Warwick. Placings record very unimpressive, particularly last ten runs.
Verdict	No sign of improvement coming.
Hence:	DISMISS.

Form Reading	**BARNEYS REFLECTION**
Spotlight	Twice defied higher hurdle ratings last year but nothing of note since.
Handicap Ratings	Allocated a mark of 95 for race four outings ago when pulled up but down to a mark of 79 for today's event.
Significant Items of Form	Six year old with two wins in Class 5 Selling Hurdles March and April 2005 but very poor record for last ten outings.
Verdict	No apparent danger in deciding to: DISMISS.

Form Reading	**VIVANTE**
Spotlight	Lost the plot since defying 3lb lower mark in April.
Handicap Ratings	Ran off mark of 83 when winning last April. Raised to a mark of 90 next outing and now down to a mark of 86 for today's contest.

Significant Items of Form	Eight year old with one Class 4 Handicap Hurdle victory on Good to Firm at Huntingdon April 2006 over 2m5½f. Current campaign has consisted of a Class 4 Novice Hurdle over 3 miles on 03.09.06 when pulled up and a Class 5 Handicap Hurdle over 3m2f at Huntingdon on 24.09.06 when 12th of 20 on Good to Firm.
Verdict	Last two runs show no signs of a return to race winning form particularly as last run was in a Class 5 Handicap and today's contest is a Class 4 event.
Decision:	DISMISS.

Form Reading	**MISTER ZAFFARAN**
Spotlight	Didn't show much as a Pointer and only hints of ability in Bumpers last season.
Handicap Ratings	Allocated a mark of 85 for today's contest but last six runs have been in Non Handicaps so no real clue if handicapper is being harsh or lenient.
Significant Items of Form	Seven year old with no victories but a 2nd of 4 in a Novice Hurdle Class 4 over 3 miles on Good to Firm at Worcester, October 2005, beaten 15 lengths. Only two runs since then in a 2m6f Class 4 Novice Hurdle at Wincanton on Good when beaten 81 lengths (hung badly left) at the end of October 2005, followed on 02.07.06 by a 5th of 15 in a Class 5 Maiden Hurdle over 2m4½f at Uttoxeter on Good to Firm when beaten 58½ lengths.
Verdict	No indication that trainer has got the measure of the horse and as evidence that horse has preference for left hand tracks. (NB Today's track is right handed), coupled with no evidence that horse goes well fresh, seems to point to the horse facing an uphill task on its handicap debut after a 3½ month break.
Decision:	DISMISS.

Form Reading	**CAPER**
Spotlight	Sole career win came in a Selling Hurdle last year and has lacked consistency since. Lost his way over fences more recently and showed no interest lately.
Handicap Ratings	Allocated a mark of 85 for today's contest but as no Handicap Hurdle runs in last six outings, it is very difficult to form an opinion as to whether under or over weighted.
Significant Items of Form	Six year old with one victory in a Class 5 Novice Selling Hurdle at Hereford over 2m3½f on Good to Firm March 2005. Has had at least eighteen runs since that win with no success and last three runs have been in Handicap Chases Class 4 and 5 around 3 miles within the period of the last six weeks. Although last run was particularly poor its run on 03.09.06 when 4th of 17 at Worcester over 2m7½f in a Class 5 event, beaten 19 lengths showed it is not without hope given the right race and conditions.
Verdict	Despite great concerns about current form the facts are that this horse was a course winner on today's ground conditions in a Hurdle Race (Class 5) 18 months ago. There is therefore a chance that a return to hurdling on a course it has performed well at previously, will rekindle its enthusiasm. Cannot discount the fact that this is a Class 4 event over 3m2f but is one of those occasions where you have to trust the trainer and take the view that the horse is too dangerous to leave out of the reckoning.
Hence:	SELECT.

Form Reading	**JUG OF PUNCH**
Spotlight	Fortunate when left clear to win a Selling Hurdle in February.
Handicap Ratings	Ran off an incredibly high mark of 128 six outings ago when unplaced and marks of 89 and 88 for last five outings, which has included a 3rd and a 4th place. Today's mark is 86, which leads you to believe that if it can reproduce its spring 2006 form, or even something approaching it, it will be in with a shout.
Significant Items of Form	Seven year old with two Hurdle wins both at Ludlow over 2m5f on Good, the first a Class 4 Handicap Hurdle in November 2005 and the second a Class 5 Selling Hurdle in February 2006. Last two runs have both been on right hand tracks. Run at Market Rasen on 26.08.06 over 2m3½f when 4th of 9, beaten 12 lengths was significant insofar as 'stayed on, run in'. Next and last run on 04.10.06 at Towcester over 2 miles when 12th of 15, beaten 44 lengths was far less impressive. However this was a Class 4 event over the shorter distance on the toughest track in the country, which probably didn't suit its style of running, which based on its Ludlow successes means a flat, right hand track over a distance of at least 2m4f.
Verdict	Previous Handicap mark of 128 is an indication that horse could be a lot better than its recent runs have suggested. Hereford is almost as flat as Ludlow and like that course is also right handed, so chances are that the trainer knows exactly what she is doing in choosing this 3m2f contest. Place in the first three a reasonable possibility.
Hence:	SELECT.

Overall Comment

This was one of those races where there were a number of horses to be studied and dismissed – four – before Caper and Jug of Punch were selected.

In this particular case there were no horses in the BAR group that appeared worth selecting but there are of course plenty of examples where the reverse is the case, so every care has to be taken to ensure that you have not missed something which could have affected your decision.

Jug of Punch was a worthy winner of this contest having picked off both Terramarique and Fort Ord on the run in and ran on strongly.

Jug of Punch, like most winners, had something in its form that was eye catching and this was its previous rating of 128 which added to its previous wins at Ludlow and respectable recent runs amounted to race wining form. In this race I stopped at two selections because having looked at the form of both Wee Danny (a Hereford course winner) and Etendard Indien (which were the next two in the Betting Forecast), I was not impressed and felt that it could be one of those contests where you could make half a dozen selections and still not find the winner.

For the record the Forecast Jug of Punch with Fort Ord paid £726.20 for the Tote Exacta and £845.09 for the Computer Straight Forecast.

EXAMPLE 5

16.02.07   Fakenham – Good to Soft – Class 5 – Selling Handicap Hurdle – 2m

Winner   QUEEN TARA – 66/1

2.00 RACE 2   *West Norfolk Sporting Trust*
Selling Handicap Hurdle (Class 5)   ATR
Winner £2,740.80   2m

£4000 guaranteed **For** 4yo+ **Rated** 0-90 **Minimum Weight** 10-0 **Penalties** after February 3rd, a winner of a hurdle 7lb Major Jon's Handicap Mark 89 Winner to be sold by auction for a minimum of 4000.00 **Minimum claiming price** 6000.00 **Entries** 22 pay £8 **Penalty value** 1st £2,740.80 2nd £798.80 3rd £399.60

1 P083420 **MAJOR JON** (IRE) 16 ⓑ   b 7 11-12
br g Sherdari-Slyguff Lord   S P Walsh(5)   98
Mrs T J Hill The Sunday Night Partnership

2 13P/P2 **A DOUBLE EWE BEE** 82 ⓑ   6 11-7
b m Kingsinger-Some Dream   T O'Connor(7)   84
W G M Turner R A Bracken

3 002 **SEAN OG** (IRE) 16   t5 11-5
gr g Definite Article-Miss Goodbody   M D Grant   90
E J Creighton Sean Dalton

4 6743 **BATHWICK ROX** (IRE) 57   p4 11-4
b g Carrowkeel-Byproxy   Tony Evans   87
P D Evans Mrs S Clifford

5 4056169 **NEEDWOOD SPIRIT** 14 ⒸⒹ   12 11-3
b g Rolfe-Needwood Nymph   Declan McGann(5)   89
Mrs A M Naughton Famous Five Racing

6 8-48640 **PRINCESS STEPHANIE** 215   9 11-2
b m Shaab-Waterloo Princess   Carey Williamson(10)   82
M J Gingell The Real Tadzio Partnership

7 00-80 **KOVA HALL** (IRE) 52 (25F)   tv1 5 11-1
ch g Halling-My Micheline   Charlie Poste(5)   73
M F Harris Christopher Shankland

8 6U/0 **ARABIE** 23   9 11-0
b g Polish Precedent-Always Friendly   Richard Hobson   61
B R Summers G Ferrigno

9 50/7P7- **ALASIL** (USA) 368 (19F)   7 11-0
b/br g Swain-Asl   Mr M Price(7)   98
R J Price Miss V J Price

10 46077U **QUEEN TARA** 45   p5 10-11
b m Kayf Tara-Lucy Tufty   Matty Roe(7)   88
Mrs C A Dunnett F Butler

11 06-903 **PERKY PEAKS** (IRE) 80   6 10-11
b/br g Executive Perk-Knockee Hill   Marc Goldstein(7)   81
N A Twiston-Davies N A Twiston-Davies

12 /5800-0 **MIALYSSA** 152   t7 10-3
b m Rakaposhi King-Theme Arena   James Diment(5)   82
M R Bosley The Judge 'N' Thomas Partnership

13 P4523-0 **MARIA BONITA** (IRE) 26   6 10-3
b m Octagonal-Nightitude   Chris Honour(3)   91
C N Kellett J E Tilley

14 POPF30P **EXPLODE** 13   b 10 10-0
b g Zafonic-Didicoy   Tom Siddall   91
Miss L C Siddall Lynn Siddall Racing II

● To claim for any horse except the winner, ring Weatherbys on 01933-303080 within 15 minutes of the off-time, stating your BHB Security Code, payment method & contact number.

2006 (10 ran) Needwood Spirit Mrs A M Naughton 11 10-2 11/2   T J Burrows (7) OR72

BETTING FORECAST: 7-2 Sean Og, 11-2 Alasil, 6 A Double Ewe Bee, 7 Needwood Spirit, 9 Bathwick Rox, 10 Major Jon, 11 Perky Peaks, 12 Kova Hall, 14 Princess Stephanie, 16 Maria Bonita, Mialyssa, 20 Explode, 25 Arabie, Queen Tara.

SPOTLIGHT

Major Jon Form this season has a most uneven look to it and turned in shoddy efforts last time; that's not to say he won't bounce back here but could not be confident about him.

A Double Ewe Bee Pulled up on fast ground on her last visit here but her only previous success came on a sharp track and she did look on way back when second in Leicester seller last month.

Sean Og Banded class on Flat but showed much improved form over hurdles when clear second in Leicester claimer last month wearing first-time tongue tie; prospects if building on that, though line through Viscount Rossini gives him something to find on Major Jon-and A Double Ewe Bee.

Bathwick Rox Operated in this grade much of her Flat career but couldn't cash in on drop to this grade for first time over hurdles when third to easy winner at Ludlow in December; may do better now handicapping.

Needwood Spirit Still effective in this grade, as he showed when decisive winner over 2m3f on soft at Catterick at New Year, but not in same form since; goes well here and did snatch victory in this last year but repeating trick off 8lb higher may be beyond him.

Princess Stephanie Runner-up in C&D seller two seasons ago but appeared to improve in Stratford novice hurdle in June; jacked up the handicap for that and ran respectably off new mark in non seller next time but ran no sort of race when last seen in mid-July.

Kova Hall Won modest 1m1f handicap in Ireland, and second off 82 at Nottingham last June hints at the sort of raw ability to land race like this; clearly needs to improve on hurdles form (last term for Philip Hobbs) but perhaps first-time visor will help, as he once ran creditably in blinkers on Flat.

Arabie Looks right handful these days, having regularly refused to race on Flat last year and pulled riders' arms out of their sockets over hurdles; can't trust even down in this grade.

Alasil Has had back problems but retained sufficient ability to land 1m2f seller at Chepstow last year; poor effort on AW last month but has claims on some of his old hurdling form for Dina Smith off this very feasible-looking mark.

Queen Tara Hasn't fulfilled promise of hurdling debut fourth over this C&D in May and locked on the retreat when unseating rider in cheekpieces off this mark in mares' handicap (33-1) last time; rejected despite this lower grade.

Perky Peaks Not easy to assess accurately his third in Hereford November seller in mud but respected off low weight on handicap bow given he represents top stable.

Mialyssa 100-1 all three starts over hurdles after showing only limited bumper ability but she could be open to improvement now handicapping off feather weight in bottom grade with tongue tied.

Maria Bonita Placed form off higher marks in sellers last term offers some hope and doubtless needed last month's well-beaten reappearance but others hold greater appeal.

Explode Third in Catterick seller late last year looked like a revival was on the way but hasn't backed that up in two starts since.

VERDICT **ALASIL** ran well enough in a Nottingham Flat handicap in October to suggest he can handle soft going and must have possibilities off this mark in the lowest grade over hurdles. The likely decent pace should enable last year's winner **Needwood Spirit** to run a decent race but perhaps downgraded **Kova Hall** could be the biggest threat if a first-time visor enables him to translate his Flat form to hurdles.[PJ]

OFFICIAL RATINGS						2.00	HANDICAP	TODAY FUTURE	RP RATING		
LAST SIX OUTINGS-LATEST ON RIGHT									LATEST / BEST / ADJUSTED		
100⁰	—	—	92⁴	—	89⁰	Major Jon	11-12	89	64	98 ◄	99 ◄
—	—	89³	—	90ᴾ	—	A Double Ewe Bee	11-7	84	84	84	84
—	—	—	—	—	—	Sean Og	11-5	82	90 ◄	90	90
—	—	—	—	—	—	Bathwick Rox	11-4	90	87	87	87
77⁰	80⁵	75⁶	75¹	84⁶	82⁹	Needwood Spirit	11-3	80	76	89	89
66⁸	62⁴	64⁸	—	81⁴	81⁰	Princess Stephanie	11-2	79	—	82	82
—	—	—	—	—	78⁰	Kova Hall	11-1	78	70	73	73
—	—	—	—	—	—	Arabie	11-0	77	61	61	61
85ᶠ	87⁵	85⁰	—	82ᴾ	79⁷	Alasil	11-0	77	—	—	98 ◄
—	—	—	—	—	74⁰	Queen Tara	10-11	74	—	88	88
—	—	—	—	—	—	Perky Peaks	10-11	74	74	74	81
—	—	—	—	—	—	Mialyssa	10-3	66	82 ◄	82	82
—	—	—	69²	73³	69⁰	Maria Bonita	10-3	66	28	28	91
66⁰	66ᴾ	69ᶠ	64³	63⁰	69ᴾ	Explode	10-0	63	—	91	91

Queen Tara — 10-11

5-y-o b m Kayf Tara - Lucy Tufty (Vin St Benet)
Mrs C A Dunnett — Matty Roe (7)

Placings: 46077U

OR**74**	F35	Starts	1st	2nd	3rd	Win & Pl
All Jumps races		6	–	–	–	£214
GF-HRD 0-0-1	GS-HVY 0-0-2	Course 0-0-1			Dist 0-0-4	

2 Jan Folkestone 2m1½f   Cls4 Nov 71-87 Hdl Hcap
£3,253
8 ran   SOFT   .9hdls   Time 4m 40.20s (slw 32.20s)
1 Tanzanite Dawn 6 10-0 ...Gerard Tumelty (5) 4/1
2 South Sands 6 11-2 ....Tom Scudamore 9/2
3 Sister Grace 7 11-7 ....Barry Fenton 9/2
U **QUEEN TARA** 5 10-8 p ....J A McCarthy 33/1
held up in last, weakening when jumped very slowly 4th, jinked and unseated rider soon after [or74]
Dist: 18-5-6-3½-1¾   RACE RPR: 88/81/81
Racecheck: Wins 1 Pl 1 Unpl 3

22 Nov 06 Lingfield 2m1½f   Cls4 Nov Hdl £2,928
.7 ran   HEAVY   8hdls   Time 4m 14.10s (slw 18.10s)
1 Gaelic Gift 4 10-10 ....Timmy Murphy 3/1
2 Pat Cohan 6 10-10 ....Mick FitzGerald 15/2
3 Lamanver Homerun 4 10-10 ....R Walsh 6/4F
7 **QUEEN TARA** 4 10-3 ......John Kington (7) 50/1
chased leaders until 4th, soon behind, tailed off from before 2 out btn 57 lengths [RPR37 TS23]
Dist: 5-2½-8-22-10   RACE RPR: 101+/90+/87+
Racecheck: Wins 1 (1) Pl 1 Unpl 8

5 Nov 06 Market Rasen 2m3½f Cls4 Nov Hdl £2,602
10 ran   GOOD   10hdls   Time 4m 47.60s (slw 14.60s)
1 Secret Pact 4 10-9 ....W T Kennedy (3) 5/4F
2 Golden Boot 7 10-12 ....G Lee 13/2
3 Water Pistol 4 10-10 ......Declan McGann (5) 16/1
7 **QUEEN TARA** 4 9-12 ......John Kington (7) 40/1
chased leaders, 2nd and ridden when hit 3 out, soon weakened, modest 6th when mistake last btn 51 lengths [RPR33 TS21]   [op 33/1]
Dist: 2-8-14-8-18   RACE RPR: 93+/90+/81
Racecheck: Wins - Pl - Unpl 9

22 Jun 06 Southwell 2m   Cls5 Mdn Hdl £3,083
13 ran   GD-FM   4hdls   Time 3m 50.60s (slw 9.60s)
1 Hugs Destiny 5 11-1 ....Andrew Thornton 7/1
2 Cayman Calypso 5 11-1 ....Warren Marston 9/2
3 War Pennant 4 10-12 ....Jamie Moore 9/1
13 **QUEEN TARA** 4 10-5 ......Jodie Mogford 33/1
ridden and struggling 5f out, tailed off before 2 out btn 66 lengths [RPR12]
Dist: 1¾-hd-shd-2½-3   RACE RPR: 88/86/83
Racecheck: Wins 1 (1) Pl 3 Unpl 15

Arabie — 11-0

9-y-o b g Polish Precedent - Always Friendly (High Line)
B R Summers — Richard Hobson

Placings: 6U/0

OR**77**	F68	Starts	1st	2nd	3rd	Win & Pl
All Jumps races		3	–	–	–	–
GF-HRD 0-0-1	GS-HVY 0-0-1	Course 0-0-0			Dist 0-0-3	

24 Jan Huntingdon 2m1½f   Cls4 Nov £1,952
17 ran   SOFT   8hdls   Time 4m 14.00s (slw 34.00s)
1 Monfils Monfils 5 11-4 ...Mick FitzGerald EvensF
2 Le Burf 6 11-6 ....Gerard Tumelty (5) 11/2
.3 King's Thought 8 11-4 ......Mark Bradburne 33/1
11 **ARABIE** 9 11-4 ....Richard Hobson 100/1
pulled very hard, held up in rear early, headway to lead after 3rd, hit next, soon headed, weakened next, tailed off btn 54 lengths [RPR47]
Dist: 1¼-11-¾-3-10 RACE RPR: 103+/108+/93+
Racecheck: Wins - Pl - Unpl 5

3 Mar 05 Ludlow 2m   Cls3 Nov Hdl £5,077
18 ran   GOOD   9hdls   Time 3m 54.50s (slw 15.50s)
1 Medison 5 11-8 ....Timmy Murphy 2/1F
2 Flying Enterprise 5 11-12 .....Sam Thomas 11/1
3 Queen Soraya 5 11-5 ....J Culloty 9/2
U **ARABIE** 7 11-2 ....David Dennis 22/1
pulled hard in rear, headway approaching 5th, weakening when blundered and unseated rider 3 out   [op 20/1]
Dist: shd-6-shd-12-11½ RACE RPR: 123+/127+/114
Racecheck: Wins 4 (3) Pl 1 Unpl 26

6 Jul 04 Uttoxeter 2m   Cls4 Nov Hdl £3,877
9 ran   GD-FM   10hdls   Time 3m 48.70s (slw 6.70s)
1 Debbie 5 10-6 ....James Davies (3) 11/2
2 Scapolo 6 11-0 ....Mick FitzGerald 9/4
3 Darab 4 10-12 p ....Paul Moloney 6/1
6 **ARABIE** 6 11-0 ....David Dennis 14/1
pulled very hard and prominent, hit 3rd, led after 4th, clear 6th, headed before 3 out, dropped out very tamely [RPR75 TS14]   [tchd 16/1]
Dist: 3½-2½-nk-13-14 RACE RPR: 100+/102+/95
Racecheck: Wins - Pl 1 Unpl 14

Flat Form

20 Nov 06 Southwell (AW) 1m Cls6 50-60 Am Hcap
£1,978
14 ran   STAND   Time 1m 44.77s (slw 4.27s)
1 Take It There 4 10-6 .....Miss Zoe Lilly (5) 11 16/1
2 Louisiade 5 10-6 ....Miss A Ryan (5) 2 8/1
3 Scottish River 7 11-3 ....Mr Lee Newnes 4 10/1
R **ARABIE** 8 11-0 b ......Mr C Ellingham (7) 10 80/1
refused to race [or60]   [op 66/1]
Dist: 1½-5-1¾-2-nk   RACE RPR: 61/58/53
Racecheck: Wins 2 (1) Pl 3 Unpl 13

Explode — 10-0

10-y-o b g Zafonic - Didicoy (Danzig)
Miss L C Siddall — Tom Siddall

Placings: P/5070/000-PP0PF30P

OR**63**	F48	Starts	1st	2nd	3rd	Win & Pl
All Jumps races		16	–	–	1	£399
GF-HRD 0-0-1	GS-HVY 0-1-9	Course 0-0-1			Dist 0-1-13	

3 Feb Wetherby 2m   Cls5 69-95 Sell Hdl Hcap £2,928
8 ran   GD-SFT   9hdls   Time 4m 3.50s (slw 23.50s)
1 Diamond Vein 8 10-8 b ....Anthony Ross 13/2
2 Seafire Lad 6 11-5 tp ....Kenny Johnson 5/2F
3 Migration 11 11-5 ....P J Benson (7) 4/1
P **EXPLODE** 10 9-9 b oh6 Tom Messenger (5) 16/1
in touch, went prominent 4th, weakened approaching 3 out, behind when hit 2 out, pulled up before last [or69]   [tchd 18/1]
Dist: 12-8-8-24   RACE RPR: 87+/87+/88+
Racecheck: Wins - Pl - Unpl -

24 Jan Catterick 2m   Cls5 63-88 Sell Hdl Hcap £2,056
12 ran   SOFT   8hdls   Time 4m 8.40s (slw 24:40s)
1 Karyon 7 9-12 ....Phil Kinsella (3) 10/1
2 Bayside 6 11-12 ....Alan Dempsey 4/1
3 Makandy 8 11-0 ....Mr R Armson (7) 20/1
10 **EXPLODE** 10 10-1 b ....Neil Mulholland 8/1
soon prominent, hit 5th, weakened next btn 55 lengths [RPR10 or63]   [op 6/1]
Dist: 2½-¾-5-4-4   RACE RPR: 64+/87/81
Racecheck: Wins - Pl - Unpl 4

28 Dec 06 Catterick 2m   Cls5 64-90 Sell Hdl Hcap £2,741
13 ran   GD-SFT   8hdls   Time 3m 58.30s (slw 14.30s)
1 Nebraska City 5 9-13 .Michael McAlister (3) 17/2
2 Mr Ex 5 11-12 p ....G Lee 9/4F
3 **EXPLODE** 9 10-0 b oh1 ......Tom Siddall 28/1
chased leaders, effort before 2 out, soon one pace [RPR63 TS61 OR64]   [op 25/1]
Dist: 3-6-8-5-1¾   RACE RPR: 76+/95+/63+
Racecheck: Wins 2 (2) Pl - Unpl 5

29 Nov 06 Catterick 2m   Cls5 69-95 Sell Hdl Hcap £2,741
17 ran   GD-SFT   8hdls   Time 3m 49.60s (slw 5.60s)
1 Caulkleys Bank 6 11-12 .....Mr T Greenall 11/4F
2 Grey Samurai 6 11-7 ....Padge Whelan 4/1
3 Armentieres 5 10-5 v .....Steven Gagan (10) 11/2
F **EXPLODE** 9 10-0 b oh6 ....R J Greene 33/1
chased leaders, handy 5th when fell 4th [or69]
Dist: 8-2½-4-3-8   RACE RPR: 114+/99/91
Racecheck: Wins 4 (4) Pl 1 Unpl 7

Form Reading	**QUEEN TARA**
Spotlight	Hasn't fulfilled promise of hurdling debut, 4th over this course and distance in May 2006.
Handicap Ratings	Allocated a mark of 74 for last outing (unseated) which was its first handicap race. Today's mark also 74.
Significant Items of Form	Five year old that according to Spotlight had its first run over hurdles at today's course last May when finished 4th. Has had only six outings altogether and current campaign has consisted of three Class 4 Novice Hurdles on 05.11.06 (7th of 10, beaten 51 lengths), 22.11.06 (7th of 7, beaten 57 lengths) and 02.01.07 (unseated after 4th hurdle). These runs have been on two right hand tracks and one left hand track on Good, Heavy and Soft, over 2m3½f, 2m½f and 2m1½f.
Verdict	Normally this horse's form wouldn't warrant selection but a quick glance at the

placings record of all the contestants shows that all have a very indifferent form record and therefore we are looking at any positive point in the form profile that could give the horse an edge. In Queen Tara's case its hurdling debut, 4th at Fakenham, must be taken as a positive sign that it likes today's course, which is always a good recommendation. The other positive is the fact that the horse has been campaigned in Class 4 contests and though two 7th placings appear none too clever, it did finish these races and as you will soon find out, 6th, 7th, 8th and 9th place finishes repeatedly feature in the recent form of outsider winners. Today's contest is a Class 5 Selling Handicap in which anything can happen. The last outing when unseated can be discounted and a placing in the first three places is a reasonable possibility bearing in mind its previous 4th place.

Decision: SELECT.

Form Reading	**ARABIE**
Spotlight	Regularly refused to race on flat last year and pulled riders arms out of their sockets over hurdles.
Handicap Ratings	No handicap hurdle form, mark of 77 for today's contest.
Significant Items of Form	Nine year old that seems to have been transferred to jumping late in its career but last three runs make grim reading and indicates an uncontrollable horse.
Verdict	Decision: DISMISS.

Form Reading	**EXPLODE**
Spotlight	3rd in Catterick seller late last year, indicated a revival was on the way.
Handicap Ratings	Last six outings (all Handicap Hurdles) show ratings from 63 to 69. Ran off a mark of 64 when 3rd three outings ago and on a mark of 63 for today's contest.
Significant Items of Form	Ten year old with no victories and two placings better than 7th in the past sixteen outings; however best placing of 3rd of 13 is a Class 5 Selling Handicap Hurdle at Catterick (left hand course) was on 28.12.06 when beaten only 9 lengths (Good to Soft). Two runs since then on 24.01.07 Catterick (Soft) and 03.02.07 Wetherby (Good to Soft), both left hand tracks, both over 2 miles and both Class 5 Selling Handicap Hurdles resulted in a 10th of 12, beaten 55 lengths and pulled up before last after hitting 2 out (latest run).
Verdict	On the basis that we are looking for a positive point, the 3rd place on 28.12.06 is proof that the horse has ability. Although the horse's two runs since then have both been disappointing, the proximity of that 3rd place means that it would not be unreasonable to think that it could achieve a top three placing in today's race.
Decision:	SELECT.

Overall Comment

Once you have followed The Tail End System for some time, you automatically acquire some very useful experience and one of them is spotting likely races for an upset.

Obviously the fact that the contest is a Class 5 Selling Handicap Hurdle on a Preferred Course tells you something and the poor placings record of all the contestants is a first class indicator that picking the winner will not be easy, and therefore the contest is just as likely to fall to an 'outsider' as it is to one of the more fancied horses.

In races as poor as these you have to be prepared to be more flexible than normal in considering indifferent form records, but you are still looking for something which stands out. In Queen Tara's case, its 4th place at the track was the clue and in Explode's case, its 3rd place three outings ago was an indicator of its ability.

Okay, you probably wouldn't have wanted to make any more than two selections, and neither would you have wanted to risk a lot of money, but at the odds on offer any kind of bet was worth having.

For the record the Forecast Queen Tara with Explode paid £637.00 for the Tote Exacta and £1,026.60 for the Computer Straight Forecast.

EXAMPLE 6

15.02.07 Chepstow – Heavy – Class 5 – Handicap Hurdle – 2m½f

4.25 RACE 6 — *Weatherbys Bloodstock Insurance Handicap Chase (Class 5)* — *Winner £3,568* — ATR — **2m½f**

£5485 guaranteed For 5yo+ Rated 0-90 **Minimum Weight** 10-0 **Penalties** after February 3rd, a winner of a chase 7lb **Caislean Na Deirge's Handicap Mark** 90 **Entries** 20 pay £10 **Penalty value 1st** £3,568 **2nd** £1,047 **3rd** £523 **4th** £261

No.	Form	Horse / Breeding / Trainer, Owner	Age, Weight / Jockey	Rating
1	0574046	**CAISLEAN NA DEIRGE** (IRE) 51 D — b g Boyne Valley-Bramble Lane — **Evan Williams** Michael J Harper 3rd 5/1	9 11-12 **Paul Moloney**	94
2	P23U12F	**ISLAND OF MEMORIES** (IRE) 70 D — ch m Beneficial-Coronea Sea Queen — **D P Keane** P Tory	b 7 11-10 **Neil Mulholland**	100
3	P-0P660	**BATTLEFIELD** 17 — b g Overbury-Tapua Taranata — **R Lee** Bevan Brereton Compton Greig Jackson	7 11-7 **Tom Doyle**	96
4	7798	**NATIVE CITY** (IRE) 20 — b g City Honours-Fourroads-Native — **Jonjo O'Neill** John P McManus	5 11-6 **A P McCoy**	
5	07-BP59	**LORRELINI** (IRE) 51 — ch h Among Men-Well Able — **R H Alner** Miss H J Flower	6 11-5 **Robert Walford**	
6	-97P2PP	**ALL SONSILVER** (FR) 14 D — b g Son Of Silver-All Licette — **P Kelsall** Peter Kelsall 16/1	10 10-12 **Derek Laverty**(5)	100
7	9757-41	**FEMME D'AVRIL** (FR) 51 D — b m Homme de Loi-Free Demo — **D E Pipe** Cdre Richard Bridges 2nd 7/4 F	5 10-8 **Andrew Glassonbury**(5)	
8	4PP0225	**KINKEEL** (IRE) 15 — b g Hubbly Bubbly-Bubbly Beau — **A W Carroll** Group 1 Racing (1994) Ltd	b 8 10-4 **Mattie Batchelor**	98
9	-025P46	**STAR GALAXY** (IRE) 21 — b g Fourstars Allstar-Raven Night — **M A Doyle** Donald Gould, David Prince, Mark Wadley	7 10-0 **S P Walsh**(5)	98

LONG HANDICAP: Star Galaxy **9-9**

BETTING FORECAST: 9-4 Femme d'Avril, 3 Island Of Memories, 5 Kinkeel, Native City, 9 Caislean Na Deirge, 16 Star Galaxy, 20 Lorrelini, 25 Battlefield, 33 All Sonsilver. FX 61.50 CSF 47.67

SPOTLIGHT

Caislean Na Deirge One win, in a 2m good-ground handicap hurdle off a mark of 80, from 31 tries over jumps (including points) at up to 3m and yet to be placed in eight attempts chasing; nevertheless entitled to respect on fourth in competitive Naas handicap in October and interesting if there is money for him on first outing since leaving Peter McCreery.

Island Of Memories Let down by jumping three times in seven starts over fences (stiff task last time) but sound claim if he runs to the form he showed to account for a subsequent dual winner at Uttoxeter and when clear second over C&D in November; has won on heavy.

Battlefield Ex-Irish maiden; best effort when third off 10lb higher at Clonmel (2m4f, yielding) last March but mainly well below that from since arriving in Britain, albeit faced with stiff task last time; slipping down the handicap.

Native City Has looked modest in a bumper and maiden hurdles but stable has been on target in similar circumstances recently - for example with High Calibre - and more realistic chance now handicapping (with help of weight-for-age allowance).

Lorrelini Poor form over hurdles, found wanting off slightly higher marks in handicaps when dropped back to this distance last twice; more needed with switch to fences.

All Sonsilver On a losing run and unable to take advantage of diminishing handicap mark though showed he retains some ability when second off 12lb higher at Warwick three outings ago; that was over 3m, however, and his best form is at 2m4f+.

Femme d'Avril Best efforts on the Flat on heavy (in France); improved form over hurdles for this stable this season, seemingly appreciating waiting tactics when winning modest if quite well contested novice handicap at Wincanton on Boxing Day; effectively 2lb lower with the 5yo weight-for-age allowance here and obvious chance if taking to chasing.

Kinkeel Still a maiden but been running well enough from the front in similar company, including from out of the handicap last twice, to give him place prospects at least again.

Star Galaxy Pick of form, at 2m3f/2m4f, before Christmas brings him into calculations but bit below that level more recently and likely to have to settle for minor placing again.

VERDICT Not an easy race to assess with two of the likely market principals, **Native City** and **FEMME D'AVRIL**, having their first taste of jumping fences in public. Both benefit from a 7lb weight-for-age allowance and this means the latter is potentially very well in and she is open to further improvement on just her third outing for David Pipe. **Island Of Memories** may prove best of those with chasing form.[FC]

OFFICIAL RATINGS LAST SIX OUTINGS-LATEST ON RIGHT						4.25 HANDICAP		TODAY	FUTURE	RP RATING LATEST	BEST	ADJUSTED
—	—	—	92^0	89^4	89^6	Caislean Na Deirge	11-12	90		57	94	**94**
82^2	85^3	83^U	83^1	88^2	—	Island Of Memories	11-10	88		—	98	**100** ◄
96^P	—	—	99^6	90^6	—	Battlefield	11-7	85		61	101	**96**
—	—	—	—	—	—	Native City	11-6	90		—	—	—
—	—	—	—	—	—	Lorrelini	11-5	83		—	—	—
85^9	89^7	82^P	88^2	82^P	88^P	All Sonsilver	10-12	76		—	105 ◄	**100** ◄
—	—	—	—	—	—	Femme d'Avril	10-8	78		—	—	—
65^P	75^P	—	60^2	69^2	73^5	Kinkeel	10-4	68		90 ◄	98	**98**
—	64^2	68^5	—	66^4	63^6	Star Galaxy	9-9	64	-5	80	98	**98**

All Sonsilver 10-12

10-y-o *b g Son Of Silver - All Licette (Native Guile)*
P Kelsall Derek Laverty (5)

Placings: 136/P/PPP64B5-97P2PP

OR76 H88	Starts	1st	2nd	3rd	Win & Pl
Chase	22	3	3	3	£20,823
All Jumps races	28	5	3	3	£27,245

106	2/04	Newc	3m Cls4 81-107 Ch Hcap heavy	£5,099
101	1/04	Newc	2m4f Cls4 75-101 Ch Hcap heavy	£4,371
93	2/03	Ayr	2m5½f Cls4 Nov 79-105 Ch Hcap gd-sft	£4,115
96	4/02	Hexm	2m½f Cls4 78-101 Hdl Hcap good	£3,360
	3/02	Kels	2m½f Cls4 Nov Hdl soft	£3,063

Total win prize-money £20,008

GF-HRD 0-0-0 **GS-HVY** 4-2-23 **Course** 0-0-2 **Dist** 2-0-8

1 Feb Wincanton 3m1½f Cls4 83-114 Ch Hcap £4,229
12 ran GD-SFT 21fncs Time 6m 37.00s (slw 19.00s)
1 Wizard Of Edge 7 10-11 ....R J Greene 25/1
2 Even More 12 11-9 ....Andrew Thornton 12/1
3 Treasulier 10 9-11 p ....Keiran Burke (7) 11/2
P **ALL SONSILVER** 10 9-9 oh7 ....Mr D England (5) 66/1
chased leaders until weakened after 12th, tailed off and pulled up before 17th [OR88]
Dist: ½-10-21-14-12 RACE RPR: 117+/127/98
Racecheck: Wins 1 (1) Pl 1 Unpl -

25 Jan Warwick 3m2f Cls4 82-106 Ch Hcap £3,253
12 ran HEAVY 20fncs Time 7m 2.10s (slw 39.10s)
1 Cinnamon Line 11 11-2 ....Tom Doyle 20/1
2 Durante 9 11-10 t ....Jason Maguire 14/1
3 Finzi 9 10-12 ....Tom Scudamore 8/1
P **ALL SONSILVER** 10 9-9 oh1 ....Gerard Tumelty (5) 10/1
dropped to rear 10th, tailed off and pulled up 14th [OR82] [op 11/1]
Dist: ½-16-¾-8-4 RACE RPR: 112+/118/90
Racecheck: Wins 1 (1) Pl - Unpl 3

31 Dec 06 Warwick 3m½f Cls4 88-114 Ch Hcap £3,904
11 ran HEAVY 14fncs Time 6m 39.60s (slw 34.60s)
1 Florida Dream 7 11-7 b .....Mr D England (5) 4/1
2 **ALL SONSILVER** 9 9-9 oh7 ....Gerard Tumelty (5) 50/1
always prominent, chased winner from 8th, ridden and every chance approaching 2 out, one pace [RPR89 TS69 OR88]
3 Flash Cummins 6 11-9 t....Timmy Murphy 11/4F
Dist: 12-6-7-22-6 RACE RPR: 130+/89+/112+
Racecheck: Wins - Pl 2 Unpl 9

Form Reading	**ALL SONSILVER**
Spotlight	Second off 12lb higher at Warwick three outings ago.
Handicap Ratings	Running off a mark of 88 three outings go when finished 2nd at Warwick but down to a mark of 76 today which indicates it is well in, based on most previous best form.
Significant Items of Form	Ten year old with three Class 4 Handicap Chase victories (two on Heavy and one on Good to Soft) on left hand tracks (distance 2m4f to 3 miles), most recent February 2004. Also two Hurdle victories in Class 4 events over 2m½f, again on left hand tracks on Good and Soft. Good 2nd of 11 in Class 4 Handicap Chase at Warwick 31.12.06 on Heavy. Two runs since then, both in Class 4 Handicap Chases over 3m2f and 3m1½f and both times pulled up after weakening around half distance.
Verdict	Dropped in class and dropped in distance for today's event and as age still only ten, there is no apparent reason why horse cannot succeed at what is close to the minimum distance, on ground it clearly likes and on a left hand track which is clearly its favourite.
Decision:	SELECT.

Overall Comment

I have included this race as a good example to note because when the trainer drops the horse in class and/or distance, you have to ask yourself the question why and then ask yourself whether the horse has the form credentials to take advantage of the situation.

The fact that All Sonsilver ran creditably enough to half distance in its last two outings provided a logical enough case for saying that it could be competitive in a 2m½f Class 5 contest which was providing its favourite conditions, ie left hand track and Heavy going.

It is in situations like this that you have to place your trust in the trainer that he/she has made the right choice of event to bring out the best in his/her horse.

For the record the Forecast All Sonsilver with the favourite Femme D'Avril paid £61.50 for the Tote Exacta and £47.67 for the Computer Straight Forecast.

EXAMPLE 7

18.02.07   Towcester – Heavy – Class 4 – Handicap Hurdle – 3m
Winner   WHITFORD DON – 33/1

3.50 RACE 4   ATR   *Mount Pleasant Golf Club Handicap Hurdle (Class 4)* Winner £3,253   **3m**

£5000 guaranteed **For** 4yo+ Rated 0-105 Weights raised 1lb Minimum Weight 10-0 **Penalties** after February 10th, a winner of a hurdle 7lb Eurocelt's Handicap Mark 104 Entries 43 pay £15 Penalty value 1st £3,253 2nd £955 3rd £477.50 4th £238.50

1 324-40P **EUROCELT** (IRE) 91   9 11-12
b g Eurobus-Seklo Lady   Wayne Hutchinson (106)
P G Murphy Midland Racing Partnership

2 5PUP909 **WHITFORD DON** (IRE) 19 ▣   9 11-8
b g Accordion-Whitford Breeze   Miss C Dyson(7) (98)
Miss C Dyson Miss C Dyson

3 60P-34P **GREEN PROSPECT** (FR) 33   v7 11-6
b g Green Tune-City Prospect   Noel Fehily (105)
M J McGrath P Whatley

4 841 **CLASSIC FAIR** 62 ▣   t6 11-6
b m Classic Cliche-Bay Fair   Joe Tizzard (109)
A J Honeyball Apple Pie Partnership

5 /68-423 **MOORLANDS RETURN** 32 ▣   p8 11-5
b g Bob's Return-Sandford Springs   S E Durack (109)
Mrs A M Thorpe Mrs Lynda M Williams

6 7PP-F4P **MONTECORVINO** (GER) 23 ▣   b16 11-3
ch g Acatenango-Manhattan Girl   Marc Goldstein(7) (103)
N A Twiston-Davies Three Off The Tee Partnership

7 P22/P0- **FABREZAN** (FR) 612   8 11-3
b g Nikos-Fabulous Secret   J A McCarthy
C N Kellett K O Warner

8 PP-6764 **YOUNG CUTHBERT** 23   t9 11-3
b g Homo Sapien-Deirdres Dream   Richard Hobson (85)
Mrs S E Handley P C & S E Handley

9 -8F8134 **RADNOR LAD** 23   7 11-2
ch g Double Trigger-Gabibti   Richard Johnson (100)
Mrs S M Johnson The Ever Hopeful Partnership

10 5/0625 **LISSARA** (IRE) 15   9 11-2
b g Glacial Storm-Bonnies Glory   W T Kennedy(3) (103)
Noel T Chance Mrs Rose Boyd

11 48809 **OMIKRA** (GER) 66   5 11-1
b m General Monash-Ost Tycoon   D F Flannery(5) (92)
Gerard Cully (IRE) John J Kelly

12 PP-535P **PARK QUEST** (IRE) 14   9 10-12
br g Jolly Jake-Ann's Fort   Gerry Supple
Mrs C J Ikin Mrs P J Ikin

13 4250406 **HAPPY HUSSAR** (IRE) 28   14 10-10
b g Balinger-Merry Mirth   Dr P Pritchard(5) (106)
Dr P Pritchard Mrs T Pritchard

14 87P-355 **THE RIVER JOKER** (IRE) 28 ▣   11 10-9
ch g Over The River-Augustaeliza   Charlie Poste(5)
John R Upson Graeme P McPherson

15 /7-26P7 **BDELLIUM** 49   v9 10-5
b m Royal Vulcan-Kelly's Logic   Chris Honour(3) (107)
B I Case Neil Hutley

16 23-8883 **ROYAL NIECE** (IRE) 25   8 10-4
b m Rakaposhi King-Sister Stephanie   Tom Siddall (109)
D J Wintle W Butler, J Gent And Mrs M Turner

17 0-6077P **DEVILS AND DUST** (IRE) 34   6 10-0
b g Needle Gun-Tartan Trouble   S J Craine(3) (88)
D McCain Jnr Jon Glews

LONG HANDICAP: Devils And Dust 9-11

2006 (18 ran) **Desert Tommy** Evan Williams 5 11-9 8/1   Nick Williams (5) OR107

BETTING FORECAST: 4 Moorlands Return, **9-2** Radnor Lad, **5** Lissara, **11-2** Classic Fair, **10** Royal Niece, **12** Happy Hussar, **14** Montecorvino, **16** The River Joker, **20** Green Prospect, **25** Bdellium, Devils And Dust, Eurocelt, Omikra, **33** Park Quest, **50** Fabrezan, Whitford Don, **66** Young Cuthbert.

SPOTLIGHT

Eurocelt Below best over jumps in Ireland since back from break; no stamina concerns but handicapper hasn't taken any chances and he runs without his usual headgear; best watched on UK debut.

Whitford Don Was rated 134 in his prime but that has looked a distant memory recently and beaten miles on debut for this yard at Taunton last month (3m1f, soft); down 5lb but makes no appeal.

Green Prospect Not beaten far in two runs last summer but pulled up back in selling company his first start for six months at Folkestone last month (2m6f, soft) and best watched with stamina unproven.

Classic Fair Stepped up on hurdle debut when showing a willing attitude to win at Taunton last time (3m, good to soft) in first-time tongue tie; not badly treated for handicap debut and should appreciate this thorough test of stamina so one for the shortlist.

Moorlands Return Three creditable efforts for this yard, last two showing that these conditions are fine, but been creeping up the handicap without winning and may have to settle for minor honours with cheekpieces back on for the first time in 18 months.

Montecorvino Sole success came here last January (2m, soft) but completed only twice since, some way behind Moorlands Return at Warwick in December (3m1f, heavy); visor no great help once in the past and remains to be seen if first-time blinkers will help.

Fabrezan Handles this ground and on fair mark on old form but can only watch after such a long absence on debut for new yard.

Young Cuthbert Off the track for 18 months and shown little at big prices in four runs for this trainer since, including in a similar contest at Haydock two starts ago (2m7f, heavy); makes no appeal.

Radnor Lad Defied a subsequent winner to score first success at Hereford in December (3m2f, good to soft) and has continued in good heart; up 13lb since that win but unlikely to be far away and Richard Johnson back in the saddle.

Lissara Off for two years after a promising debut in a Grade 2 bumper at Newbury in 2004 but has improved with each start since his return; was plugging on late at Sandown on his handicap debut last time out (2m4f, soft) and likely to be thereabouts in this weaker contest.

Omikra Not disgraced on hurdles debut at Cork in June (2m, good to firm) but struggled since, including over this trip; Ireland-based trainer hasn't had a winner since October but worth a precautionary check in the betting.

Park Quest Won maiden point in Ireland in 2005 but no sign of ability over fences in four starts this winter, pulled up on handicap chase debut at Fontwell last time; first start over hurdles in Britain but doesn't look well treated and no appeal.

Happy Hussar Beaten only 8l here last time (2m4f, heavy) when staying on in the closing stages; this longer trip should suit but hasn't won a race for more than two years and likely to find a couple of his younger rivals too good.

The River Joker Has done much of his recent racing here but poor form since back from break despite coming down the weights; 21lb higher over hurdles, having not run over the smaller obstacles for 18 months and couldn't fancy.

Bdellium Creditable return from absence in October but less good since and first-time visor didn't help last time when a long way behind Moorlands Return and Montecorvino; hard to see her reversing those placings on this ground.

Royal Niece Longstanding maiden over hurdles but not disgraced on chase debut at Huntingdon last time (3m, soft) and possible there may be more to come at this game; acts on the ground and possibilities.

Devils And Dust Hinted at some ability in bumpers, including here on his racecourse debut, but well beaten on all five starts over obstacles, pulled up on handicap debut at Plumpton most recently (3m1f, soft); cannot be fancied from 3lb out of the handicap.

VERDICT   **Classic Fair** and **Radnor Lad** look sure to be thereabouts, but **LISSARA** is open to improvement at this trip and is preferred on his second start in handicap company.[SR]

OFFICIAL RATINGS								TODAY FUTURE	RP RATING		
LAST SIX OUTINGS-LATEST ON RIGHT						**3.50**	**HANDICAP**		LATEST	BEST	ADJUSTED
—	—	—	—	—	—	Eurocelt	11-12	104	—	106	106
—	—	115⁹	110⁶	110⁹	105⁹	Whitford Don	11-8	100	70	98	98
108⁶	—	105ᴾ	101³	100⁴		Green Prospect	11-6	98	—	105	105
—	—	—	—	—	—	Classic Fair	11-6	98	—	109 ◄	109 ◄
—	92⁶	—	90⁴	85²	94³	Moorlands Return	11-5	97	105	109	109 ◄
104⁷	103ᴾ	101ᴾ	—	97⁴	95ᴾ	Montecorvino	11-3	95	—	95	103
115⁷	—	—	99²	104ᴾ	102⁰	Fabrezan	11-3	95	—	—	—
—	108ᴾ	—	100⁷	97⁶	—	Young Cuthbert	11-3	95	—	85	85
81⁸	89⁶	81⁸	81¹	88³	91⁴	Radnor Lad	11-2	94	100	100	100
—	—	—	—	—	94⁵	Lissara	11-2	94	103	103	103
—	—	—	85⁰	83⁹		Omikra	11-1	93	88	92	92
—	—	—	—	—	—	Park Quest	10-12	90	—	—	—
—	—	—	90⁴	99⁰	88⁶	Happy Hussar	10-10	88	102	102	106
—	—	—	—	—	—	The River Joker	10-9	87	—	—	—
87²	86⁷	82⁶	85⁶	85ᴾ	85⁷	Bdellium	10-5	83	66	107	107
83²	85³	86⁸	—	85⁸		Royal Niece	10-4	82	—	114 ◄	109 ◄
—	—	—	—	—	82ᴾ	Devils And Dust	9-11	78 -3	—	88	88

Whitford Don   11-8

9-y-o b g Accordion - Whitford Breeze (Le Bavard)
Miss C Dyson   Miss C Dyson (7)

Placings: 21PF1U1P/PP4-5PUP909

OR**100**		Starts	1st	2nd	3rd	Win & Pl
Hurdles		8	1	1	1	£8,573
All Jumps races		22	4	2	1	£33,443

3/05	Extr	2m7½f Cls3 Nov Ch soft £7,235
2/05	Wwck	3m2f Cls2 Nov Ch soft £10,108
12/04	Wwck	3m2f Cls3 Ch soft £5,499
3/04	Newb	3m½f Cls3 Nov Hdl good £6,786

Total win prize-money £29,628

GF-HRD 0-0-0   GS-HVY 3-3-17   Course 0-0-0   Dist 2-1-7

30 Jan Taunton 3m½f Cls4 84-110 Am Hdl Hcap £3,123
12 ran   SOFT   12hdls   Time 6m 1.90s (slw 28.90s)
1 Rockys Girl 5 9-7 oh5 .Mr Felix de Giles (7) 11/1
2 Pyleigh Lady 6 11-0 ....Mr I Popham (7) 3/1
3 Norton Sapphire 8 10-10 ....Mr J J Doyle (3) 7/4F
9 **WHITFORD DON** 9 11-2 .Miss C Dyson (5) 40/1
chased leaders, ridden from 4 out, weakened quickly next
btn 51 lengths [RPR64 TS66 OR105] [op 33/1]
Dist: 3-4-13-10-5   RACE RPR: 95+/112/101+
Racecheck: Wins - Pl 2 Unpl -

27 Dec 06 Chepstow 3m Cls3 96-120 Hdl Hcap £5,530
17 ran   SOFT   12hdls   Time 6m 2.70s (slw 27.70s)
1 The Real Deal 5 10-9 ....Wayne Hutchinson 18/1
2 The Sawyer 6 11-2 ....W T Kennedy (3) 15/2
3 Ile de Paris 7 10-11 v1 ....S E Durack 10/1
12 **WHITFORD DON** 8 11-2 tp ....R Walsh 20/1
behind from 2nd
btn 81 lengths [RPR38 TS49 OR110] [tchd 25/1]
Dist: 3½-1¼-3-5-5   RACE RPR: 113+/119+/109
Racecheck: Wins 5 (1) Pl 4 Unpl 9

16 Dec 06 Haydock 2m4f Cls3 92-118 Hdl Hcap £9,100
12 ran   HEAVY   10hdls   Time 5m 11.20s (slw 33.20s)
1 Vicario 5 11-10 ....Jason Maguire 4/1
2 Ile de Paris 7 10-13 p ....Tom Doyle 11/1
3 Green 'N' Gold 6 10-12 ....Eddie Ahern 10/1
9 **WHITFORD DON** 8 11-9 tp Andrew Thornton 33/1
midfield, headway 5th, weakened after 4 out
btn 32 lengths [RPR92 TS91 OR115]
Dist: 7-2-2½-3-7   RACE RPR: 125+/106/103
Racecheck: Wins 1 Pl 3 Unpl 11

Fabrezan   11-3

8-y-o b g Nikos - Fabulous Secret (Fabulous Dancer)
C N Kellett   J A McCarthy

Placings: 41P2321118/P7P22/P0-

OR**95**	F35	Starts	1st	2nd	3rd	Win & Pl
All Jumps races		23	4	4	4	£25,302

107	2/05	Plum	2m5f Cls3 98-115 Hdl Hcap soft ..£6,858
100	1/04	Plum	2m5f Cls3 91-112 Hdl Hcap soft ..£5,556
	1/04	Hrfd	3m2f Cls4 Nov Claim Hdl gd-sft ..£2,674
	7/03	Worc	2m4f Cls4 Nov Hdl good £3,514

Total win prize-money £18,604

GF-HRD 0-1-5   GS-HVY 3-2-9   Course 0-0-0   Dist 0-1-4

16 Jun 05 Aintree 3m½f Cls4 83-108 Hdl Hcap £3,757
15 ran   GOOD   13hdls   Time 6m 14.50s (slw 18.50s)
1 My Lady Link 6 10-13 ....Sam Thomas 5/1
2 Zygomatic 7 10-7 ....Keith Mercer (3) 25/1
3 Swansea Bay 9 11-6 ....Mick FitzGerald 13/2
11 **FABREZAN** 6 11-8 p ......Robert Thornton 20/1
with leader, led 7th to 3 out, soon weakened
btn 33 lengths [RPR73 TS70 OR102]
Dist: 4-shd-1¼-1¾-8   RACE RPR: 101+/90/100
Racecheck: Wins 1 (1) Pl 3 Unpl 20

---

14 May 05 Uttoxeter 3m Cls3 93-119 Hdl Hcap £5,207
11 ran   GOOD   12hdls   Time 6m 8.40s (slw 28.40s)
1 Hawthorn Prince 10 10-11 .Warren Marston 33/1
2 Just Beth 9 11-2 ....Derek Laverty (5) 8/1
3 Bohemian Boy 7 11-9 ....Andrew Tinkler 6/1
P **FABREZAN** 6 10-1 p ow2 Mr D R Cook (10) 20/1
prominent, lost place and mistake 5th, behind from 8th, tailed off when pulled up before 3 out
[OR104] [tchd 25/1]
Dist: 6-3-17-dist-dist RACE RPR: 114+/118+/117+
Racecheck: Wins 3 (2) Pl 1 Unpl 13

10 Apr 05 Newton Abbot 2m6f Cls3 99-125 Hdl Hcap £5,759
10 ran   GOOD   10hdls   Time 5m 22.10s (slw 21.10s)
1 Nick's Choice 9 10-8 ....Lee Stephens (5) 9/2
2 **FABREZAN** 6 10-0 p oh4 ......P J Brennan 12/1
tracked leader, led 3 out, headed approaching next, rallied well and every chance last, not quicken run-in
[RPR97 TS32 OR99] [op 10/1 tchd 16/1]
3 Kings Castle 10 10-11 ......Andrew Thornton 8/1
Dist: ¾-12-10-3½-10   RACE RPR: 112+/97/98+
Racecheck: Wins 3 (1) Pl 2 Unpl 12

Park Quest   10-12

9-y-o br g Jolly Jake - Ann's Fort (Crash Course)
Mrs C J Ikin   Gerry Supple

Placings: F2/1P38/FPP-535P

OR**90**		Starts	1st	2nd	3rd	Win & Pl
Hurdles		1	–	–	1	
All Jumps races		6	–	–	1	£716

GF-HRD 0-0-0   GS-HVY 0-1-5   Course 0-0-1   Dist 0-0-1

4 Feb Fontwell 2m6f Cls5 64-90 Ch Hcap £3,253
16 ran   GD-SFT   16fncs   Time 5m 49.20s (slw 26.20s)
1 Iris's Prince 8 11-2 p ....T J O'Brien 13/2
2 Ballyaahbutt 8 9-9 b oh5 .....S P Jones (5) 4/1F
3 Carroll's O'Tully 7 9-11 oh5 Colin Bolger (3) 16/1
P **PARK QUEST** 9 11-12 ....Gerry Supple 33/1
always behind, tailed off when pulled up after 10th [OR90] [op 25/1]
Dist: 1¾-10-9-1-5   RACE RPR: 98+/79/71+
Racecheck: Wins - Pl - Unpl -

21 Jan Towcester 2m3½f Cls4 Ch £3,578
8 ran   HEAVY   9fncs   Time 5m 44.10s (slw 53.10s)
1 Quirino 6 11-0 ....Jamie Moore 2/1
2 Esprit Saint 6 11-0 ....Robert Thornton 8/13F
3 Danse Macabre 8 10-9 ..Willie McCarthy (5) 28/1
5 **PARK QUEST** 9 11-0 ......Gerry Supple 100/1
blundered 4th, soon behind
[RPR55 OR90] [op 66/1]
Dist: hd-28-24-8-3   RACE RPR: 115/115/87
Racecheck: Wins - Pl - Unpl 3

27 Dec 06 Chepstow 2m3½f Cls4 Ch £4,880
10 ran   SOFT   16fncs   Time 5m 7.20s (slw 20.20s)
1 Afrad 5 11-4 ....Mick FitzGerald 13/8
2 Ballybough Jack 6 10-13 ......S P Jones (5) 20/1
3 **PARK QUEST** 8 11-4 ....Gerry Supple 100/1
always behind, left poor 3rd 3 out, tailed off
[RPR90]
Dist: 24-65-33   RACE RPR: 129+/107+/39
Racecheck: Wins - Pl 1 Unpl 9

Omikra   11-1

5-y-o b m General Monash - Ost Tycoon (Last Tycoon)
Gerard Cully (IRE)   D F Flannery (5)

Placings: 48809

OR**93**	F46	Starts	1st	2nd	3rd	Win & Pl
All Jumps races		5	–	–	–	£339

GF-HRD 0-0-1   GS-HVY 0-0-3   Course 0-0-0   Dist 0-0-1

---

14 Dec 06 Gowran Park 2m4f 81-106 Hdl Hcap £5,957
20 ran   HEAVY   Time 5m 26.50s (slw 39.50s)
1 Shining Lights 7 11-5 ...Mr C Motherway (5) 14/1
2 Idealrise 5 9-12 ....S G McDermott (3) 12/1
3 Killeen 6 10-2 ....D J Condon 11/2F
9 **OMIKRA** 4 10-1 ....T G M Ryan 20/1
towards rear, kept on same pace from 3 out
btn 17 lengths [RPR75 OR83]
Dist: 2½-1¼-4½-2-4   RACE RPR: 115/89/89
Racecheck: Wins 1 Pl - Unpl 16

29 Sep 06 Cork 3m 79-109 Hdl Hcap £5,957
24 ran   YLD-SFT   Time 5m 45.70s (slw 8.70s)
1 Ilringuback 6 9-10 ....G T Hutchinson 6/1
2 Bawn Og 8 11-3 ex4 ....Mr M Fahey (7) 4/1F
3 World Away 5 9-5 ....D G Hogan (3) 20/1
16 **OMIKRA** 4 10-2 ....D J Condon 25/1
always behind, never a factor
btn 83 lengths [RPR16 OR85]
Dist: 1-4-5-¾-1   RACE RPR: 93+/120/88+
Racecheck: Wins 1 Pl 4 Unpl 21

20 Sep 06 Listowel 2m Mdn Hdl 4yo £6,672
18 ran   SFT-HVY   Time 4m 16.40s (slw 23.40s)
1 Bobs Pride 4 11-5 ....R Walsh 11/4F
2 Salt Lake 4 11-5 ....B J Geraghty 7/2
3 Orbit O'Gold 4 11-5 ....P Carberry 3/1
8 **OMIKRA** 4 10-9 ....M J Ferris (5) 33/1
towards rear, kept on one pace from 3 out
btn 32 lengths [RPR79 TS21]
Dist: 4-10-1¾-8-1¼   RACE RPR: 119+/112/102
Racecheck: Wins 2 Pl 6 Unpl 20

Eurocelt   11-12

9-y-o b g Eurobus - Seklo Lady (Selko)
P G Murphy   Wayne Hutchinson

Placings: 3F134B/320/50324-40P

OR**104**		Starts	1st	2nd	3rd	Win & Pl
Hurdles		4	–	–	1	£731
All Jumps races		16	–	2	4	£6,150

GF-HRD 0-0-0   GS-HVY 0-6-15   Course 0-0-0   Dist 0-3-8

19 Nov 06 Punchestown 2m6f 72-96 Ch Hcap £6,433
14 ran   SOFT   Time 6m 12.40s (slw 41.40s)
1 Walk Over 8 11-6 ....P Carberry 6/1
2 Slow To Part 9 10-12 p ......R M Power 11/2J
3 Johnee Joblot 7 10-8 ....R Walsh 13/2
P **EUROCELT** 8 10-5 b ....A D Leigh (5) 14/1
mid-division, reminders before halfway, 7th 6 out, soon weakened, pulled up before 4 out
[OR83] [op 16/1]
Dist: 2½-3½-20-1½-2½   RACE RPR: 106+/95/88
Racecheck: Wins - Pl 4 Unpl 13

11 Nov 06 Naas 3m 74-104 Ch Hcap £5,957
17 ran   YLD-SFT   Time 6m 39.60s (slw 39.60s)
1 Cavallo Classico 5 10-10 ....P Carberry 7/1
2 Dosco 7 11-12 ....P W Flood 3/1F
3 Over Siberia 7 11-12 ....P A Carberry 14/1
12 **EUROCELT** 7 11-9 p ....M Darcy 14/1
in rear of mid-division, no extra after 5 out, tailed off btn 59 lengths [RPR39 OR85]
Dist: 1½-10-4-5½-2½   RACE RPR: 101/115/105
Racecheck: Wins 1 Pl 8 Unpl 14

19 Oct 06 Punchestown 3m1f 74-101 Ch Hcap £5,480
21 ran   SOFT   Time 6m 54.30s (slw 34.30s)
1 Walk Over 8 10-13 ......Mr J P O'Farrell (3) 8/1
2 Penny Hall 6 11-11 t ......Miss N Carberry 11/2J
3 Bitsandbobs 9 10-9 ....Mr R O Harding (5) 11/2J
4 **EUROCELT** 8 10-8 b ....Mr R P Quinlan (7) 14/1
in rear of mid-division, reminders 5th, progress after 4 out, moderate 5th 3 out, kept on same pace [RPR65 TS67 OR85] [op 12/1]
Dist: 4-8-20-14-11   RACE RPR: 98+/103+/84+
Racecheck: Wins 5 Pl 5 Unpl 21

Form Reading	**WHITFORD DON**
Spotlight	Was rated 134 in his prime, beaten by miles on debut for this yard at Taunton last month.
Handicap Ratings	Ran off a mark of 115 three outings ago (placed 9th) and down to a mark of 100 for today's contest which is a mile below its best mark of 134 (see Spotlight).
Significant Items of Form	Nine year old with three Chase wins (one Class 2, two Class 3) over distances from 2m7½f to 3m2f on both left hand and right hand tracks, all on Soft and also has one Hurdle victory in a Class 3 Novice Hurdle at Newbury. Last victory was in March 2005 at Exeter (right hand track). Placings since March 2005 have been distinctly uninspiring but last run on 30.01.07, which was the first for new trainer/jockey, in a Class 4 Handicap Hurdle over 3m½f at Taunton (right hand track) on Soft, was reasonable 'chased leaders, weakened three out, beaten 51 lengths'.
Verdict	High mark of 134 indicates that horse has previously been well above its recent level of form and at nine years old it should still have time on its side and therefore there is always a chance that new lady trainer/jockey can get the horse running again on a track which, like Exeter (last win), is right handed but even tougher. Ground conditions (Heavy) should suit so much too dangerous to dismiss from the reckoning.
Hence:	SELECT.

Form Reading	**FABREZAN**
Spotlight	Debut for new yard after long absence.
Handicap Ratings	Handicap Hurdle marks in last six outings ranged from 115 to 99 and down to a mark of 95 today, which reflects its absence from the racetrack for twenty months.
Significant Items of Form	Eight year old with four Hurdle victories over 2m4f to 3m2f in Class 3 and 4 events on Soft, Good to Soft and Good on relatively easy tracks including Hereford (right handed). Last victory February 2004.
Verdict	Long absence coupled with apparent lack of tough course experience makes a DISMISS decision the only logical one to make.

Form Reading	**PARK QUEST**
Spotlight	Won maiden Point in Ireland in 2005 but no sign of ability in four starts over fences this winter.
Handicap Ratings	No relevant ratings so almost impossible to value today's mark of 90.
Significant Items of Form	Nine year old whose last three runs in Class 4 and 5 Chases make dismal reading because even 3rd place was a beating of 89 lengths.
Verdict	No reason to make a decision any different from: DISMISS, particularly as a complete absence of any Hurdle form.

Form Reading	**OMRIKA**
Spotlight	Not disgraced on Hurdles debut at Cork in June 2006 (2m, Good to Firm) but struggled since.
Handicap Ratings	Marks of 85 and 83 in Ireland for last two outings but with mark of 93 today handicapper has taken no chances for British debut.
Significant Items of Form	Five year old with no victories and recent Hurdle form in Ireland shows no positive sign that it could make a place in the top three in today's contest.
Verdict	Irish Raiders should always be treated with respect but there are no signs to indicate that this particular Raider could make an impression.
Decision:	DISMISS.

Form Reading	**EUROCELT**
Spotlight	No stamina concerns but handicapper hasn't taken any chances, UK debut.
Handicap Ratings	No Handicap Hurdle entries in last six outings, so today's UK debut mark of 104 is difficult to interpret.
Significant Items of Form	Nine year old with apparently no victories under rules, but at least one Point to Point victory. All form is Irish and last three runs October and November 2006 in Handicap Chases from 2m6f to 3m1f include a 4th of 21 at Punchestown on Soft, beaten 32 lengths when 'kept on same pace'.
Verdict	Another case of beware Irish Raiders but in this instance we've got a horse with what looks like a reasonable placings record that is making its UK debut in a 3 mile Handicap Hurdle on Heavy at the toughest track in the country, having run its last three races over fences. Now given the fact that the horse has a British based trainer, you would have thought that if it was just a case of giving the horse a run, he would have picked a far easier racetrack than this one. You therefore have to assume that the trainer knows what he is doing and bearing in mind horse's last run was three months ago, you have to work on the basis that this is a serious attempt in a suitable race.
Hence:	SELECT.

Overall Comment

There are two important lessons to be learned from this race.

Lesson number one, never ever ignore the claims of a lady jockey, lady trainer or somebody who combines both roles; I make this statement because I have come across a number of punters who will never, ever consider a horse ridden by a lady.

Lesson number two, always be prepared to put your Sherlock Holmes hat on when you are reading the form, because if you can second guess what the trainer is likely to be thinking and planning, you can make a lot of progress in solving the mystery surrounding so many of our lower class races.

For the record the Forecast Whitford Don with Eurocelt paid £757.90 for the Tote Exacta and £820.26 for the Computer Straight Forecast.

EXAMPLE 8

26.01.07 Hereford – Soft – Class 3 – Handicap Chase – 2m3f
Winner LUCIFER BLEU – 28/1

3.50 *totesport.com Handicap Chase (Class 3)* ATR
RACE 6 *Winner £8,425.26* **2m3f**

£12950 guaranteed For 5yo+ Rated 0-120 **Weights raised 1lb Minimum Weight** 10-0 **Penalties** after January 13th, a winner of a chase 7lb **Maletton's Handicap Mark** 126 **Entries** 25 pay £20 **Penalty value 1st** £8,425.26 **2nd** £2,473.45 **3rd** £1,236.73 **4th** £617.72

6-34111 **MALETTON** (FR) (7ex) 6 — 7 12-5
1 *b g Bulington-Reine Dougla* — **Sam Thomas** (132)
Miss Venetia Williams Malcolm Edwards

13P-031 **ALPHABETICAL** (IRE) 31 — p 8 11-11
2 *br g Alphabatim-Sheeghee* — **Noel Fehily** (126)
C J Mann Hugh Villiers

6624-01 **HAUNTED HOUSE** 18 — 7 11-1
3 *ch g Opera Ghost-My Home* — **Mark Bradburne** (128)
H D Daly Gibson, Goddard, Hamer & Hawkes

413-P7U **GIVE ME LOVE** (FR) 55 D — tb 7 11-1
4 *ch g Bering-Cout Contact* — **Liam Heard**(3)
A G Juckes Barry Hine

552713/ **LUCIFER BLEU** (FR) 965 BF — 8 10-12
5 *b g Kadalko-Figa Dancer* — **Andrew Glassonbury**(5)
D E Pipe A J White 28/1

4/4-064 **JACK'S LAD** (IRE) 34 C — 8 10-11
6 *ch g High Roller-Captain's Covey* — **Tom Siddall** (115)
Mrs S M Johnson Batts Vaughany & Mason

P2-433 **ARTIPREUIL** (FR) 70 — 5 10-8
7 *gr g Saint Preuil-Artilute* — **Richard Johnson**
P J Hobbs Terry Warner

4F-3F34 **DONOVAN** (NZ) 27 — 8 10-1
8 *b g Stark South-Agent Jane* — **Wayne Hutchinson** (128)
Ian Williams Concertina Racing

BETTING FORECAST: 4-6 Maletton, 5 Alphabetical, 7 Haunted House, 15-2 Artipreuil, 11 Lucifer Bleu, 14 Donovan, 33 Jack's Lad, 40 Give Me Love.

SPOTLIGHT

Maletton Took time to acclimatise after coming over from France but found his form with a vengeance now, completing hat-trick over fences when sticking it out well to win valuable Wincanton handicap over extended 3m1f on Saturday; can compete off same mark here (officially 8lb well-in) and plenty pacey enough to cope with this shorter trip; main question is whether this third run in 12 days will be one too many but tough to beat if still in top form.

Alphabetical Back to winning ways in fair Wincanton handicap in first-time cheekpieces last time and, with forecast softer ground no problem, ought to run well off fair enough 7lb higher mark, softer ground here no problem.

Haunted House Sometimes too keen for his own good over hurdles and failed to win despite some fair efforts (including in testing ground); winning start despite some less than fluent jumping on chase bow in distinctly ordinary 2m novice handicap recently and capable of going well here, provided he holds it together on jumping front; shaped last time as if bit further at least would be within range.

Give Me Love Fair novice chaser last season but little encouragement in three runs for new, present yard this time; significantly down in the handicap but has lot to prove.

Lucifer Bleu Took weakish Exeter novice for this stable in April 2004 but off since a third of seven in run of the mill 3m Perth novice in June of that year; fitness unlikely to be an issue hailing from this stable but absence of Tony McCoy (on board for that Exeter win and riding in other races here today) could be construed as a negative and also needs to prove very soft ground is okay for him.

Jack's Lad Bumper winner at this track and also scored over hurdles (at Ludlow); hasn't shown much aptitude for chasing in two tries this season, albeit when facing stiff task here last time, and lots to prove in this context at present.

Artipreuil Lightly-raced maiden who stayed this trip in France and ran best race since joining current top stable when third in soft-ground Exeter novice hurdle last time; more needed on chase debut now but going the right way when last seen out and interesting that he is pitched straight into an open handicap.

Donovan All wins have been with cheekpieces though visor didn't do much for him last time and headgear dispensed with altogether this time; soft ground fine but needs to step up a notch on balance of recent form and this trip as far as he wants to go.

VERDICT A race that revolves around **MALETTON**, who will be extremely hard to beat if in the same form as when completing a hat-trick off this mark in a much more competitive Wincanton handicap on Saturday. The only real doubt concerns the fact that this will be his third demanding run in 12 days. Chase debutant **Artipreuil** may be next best. [MCu]

OFFICIAL RATINGS LAST SIX OUTINGS-LATEST ON RIGHT						3.50 HANDICAP		TODAY	FUTURE	RP RATING LATEST	BEST	ADJUSTED
—	115^{3}	115^{4}	—	119^{1}	126^{1}	Maletton (7x)	12-5	126	+8	132◄	132	132◄
98^{1}	115^{3}	113^{P}	—	111^{3}	111^{1}	Alphabetical	11-11	118		126	126	126
—	—	—	—	—	100^{1}	Haunted House	11-1	108		128	128	128
119^{4}	—	—	—	119^{7}	111^{U}	Give Me Love	11-1	108		—	137◄	—
—	—	—	—	—	—	Lucifer Bleu	10-12	105		—	—	—
—	—	—	—	—	—	Jack's Lad	10-11	104		115	115	115
—	—	—	—	—	—	Artipreuil	10-8	109	-1	—	—	—
94^{4}	93^{F}	93^{3}	92^{F}	96^{3}	96^{4}	Donovan	10-1	94		106	128	128

Give Me Love 11-1

7-y-o *ch g Bering - Cout Contact (Septieme Ciel)*
A G Juckes Liam Heard (3)

Placings: 42406/543UU22413-P7U

OR108H119	Starts	1st	2nd	3rd	Win & Pl
Chase	11	1	2	2	£10,593
All Jumps races	31	4	4	5	**£78,566**

4/06 Chep 2m3½f Cls4 Ch gd-sft £4,384
11/04 Autl 2m2f List Hdl 4yo Hcap heavy ...£25,352
11/04 Autl 2m3½f Hdl 4yo holding £7,099
10/04 Engh 2m1½f Hdl 4yo v soft £7,099
Total win prize-money £43,934

GF-HRD 0-0-1 GS-HVY 4-6-28 **Course** 0-0-0 **Dist** 2-0-7

2 Dec 06 Chepstow 2m3½f Cls3 107-129 Ch Hcap £9,108
8 ran SOFT 16fncs Time 5m 13.30s (slw 26.30s)
1 Wain Mountain 10 11-8 tb .....Jason Maguire 4/1
2 Il'athou 10 11-12 ....Joe Tizzard 5/1
3 Nice Try 7 11-0 ....Sam Thomas 7/2J
U **GIVE ME LOVE** 6 10-3 tb Richard Spate (5) 10/1
held up, headway after 5th, mistake and lost place 8th, soon ridden and struggling, tailed off 11th, blundered and unseated rider 4 out
[OR111] [op 20/1]
Dist: 2½-¾-¾-4 RACE RPR: 136+/134/122+
Racecheck: Wins - Pl 1 Unpl 10

18 Oct 06 Worcester 2m4½f Cls3 112-129 Ch Hcap £13,012
11 ran GD-SFT 15fncs Time 5m 13.40s (slw 11.40s)
1 Briery Fox 8 11-11 ....Mark Bradburne 12/1
2 Nayodabayo 6 11-12 ....Wayne Hutchinson 16/1
3 Caribou 4 10-5 ....Leighton Aspell 5/2F
7 **GIVE ME LOVE** 6 10-11 tb .Liam Heard (5) 50/1
held up in mid-division, headway after 6th, led 8th, ridden and headed 4 out, weakened quickly
btn 42 lengths [RPR86 TS42 OR119]
Dist: 1½-2½-12-5-11 RACE RPR: 137+/138+/114+
Racecheck: Wins 2 (2) Pl 4 Unpl 10

8 Sep 06 Bangor-On-Dee 2m4½f Cls4 Nov Ch £4,749
6 ran GD-FM 15fncs Time 4m 55.90s (fst 4.10s)
1 Amicelli 7 11-5 ....Richard Johnson 8/13F
2 Steppes Of Gold 9 10-12 ....J W Farrelly (7) 11/2
3 Cunning Pursuit 5 10-12 t ..Richard McGrath 6/1
P **GIVE ME LOVE** 6 11-5 t ....Ollie McPhail 10/1
always behind, pulled up before 11th (jockey said gelding was unsuited by the good to firm (good in places) ground) [OR119] [op 8/1]
Dist: ½-12-17-8 RACE RPR: 121+/119/100
Racecheck: Wins 1 (1) Pl 4 Unpl 6

Jack's Lad 10-11

8-y-o *ch g High Roller - Captain's Covey (Captain James)*
Mrs S M Johnson Tom Siddall

Placings: 15P714/4-064

OR104H109	Starts	1st	2nd	3rd	Win & Pl
Chase	2	–	–	–	£677
All Jumps races	10	2	–	–	**£7,494**

2/05 Ludl 2m Cls4 Mdn Hdl gd-sft £3,770
11/04 Hrfd 2m1f Cls6 Mdn NHF 4-6yo soft ...£1,981
Total win prize-money £5,751

GF-HRD 0-0-0 GS-HVY 2-0-5 **Course** 1-0-3 **Dist** 0-0-1

23 Dec 06 Hereford 2m Cls3 Nov Ch £7,606
7 ran GD-SFT 12fncs Time 4m 2.00s (slw 11.00s)
1 Trouble At Bay 6 11-3 ....J A McCarthy 3/1
2 Opera de Coeur 4 10-7 ..Richard Johnson 13/8F
3 Ursis 5 11-3 ....A P McCoy 5/1
4 **JACK'S LAD** 7 11-3 ....Tom Siddall 100/1
held up, mistake 3rd, no chance from 7th, tailed off when blundered last
[RPR98 TS73 OR109] [tchd 125/1]
Dist: 7-3½-37-shd-39 RACE RPR: 146+/129/136+
Racecheck: Wins - Pl 2 Unpl 2

7 Dec 06 Ludlow 2m Cls3 Nov Ch £6,263
7 ran GD-SFT 13fncs Time 4m 8.00s (slw 14.00s)
1 Ease The Way 5 11-4 p ....Paul Moloney 8/1
2 Muhtenbar 6 11-4 ....G Lee 11/10F
3 Carthys Cross 7 11-4 ....Jason Maguire 4/1
6 **JACK'S LAD** 7 11-4 ....Tom Siddall 33/1
behind, mistake 1st, tailed off after 5th (water)
[RPR55 TS29 OR109]
Dist: hd-8-10-shd-56 RACE RPR: 130+/130+/122+
Racecheck: Wins - Pl - Unpl 6

2 Nov 06 Haydock 2m Cls3 105-128 Hdl Hcap £8,133
12 ran GOOD 8hdls Time 3m 44.40s (slw 8.40s)
1 Papini 5 11-6 ....Mick FitzGerald 5/2F
2 Crathorne 6 11-6 ....Dominic Elsworth 6/1
3 Culcabock 6 10-3 ....Peter Buchanan 8/1
10 **JACK'S LAD** 7 10-10 ....Richard Johnson 25/1
blundered 4th, always behind
btn 49 lengths [RPR77 TS59 OR112] [op 33/1]
Dist: 2½-5-3½-5-6 RACE RPR: 132+/130+/107
Racecheck: Wins 2 (2) Pl 3 Unpl 10

Donovan				10-1

8-y-o b g Stark South - Agent Jane (Sound Reason)
Ian Williams   Wayne Hutchinson

Placings: 154/1466031464F-3F34

OR94 H108		Starts	1st	2nd	3rd	Win & Pl
Chase		11	1	–	3	£7,270
All Jumps races		35	5	1	4	£33,116
88	10/05	Towc	2m¹/₂f Cls4 Nov 71-96 Ch Hcap good			£4,154
102	4/05	Kels	2m2f Cls3 95-113 Hdl Hcap soft			£7,020
95	1/05	Weth	2m Cls3 95-115 Hdl Hcap gd-sft			£7,069
86	8/04	Bang	2m1f Cls4 Nov 74-103 Cond Hdl Hcap good			£3,424
81	5/04	Kels	2m¹/₂f Cls4 Nov 74-100 Hdl Hcap gd-fm			£4,836

Total win prize-money £26,503
GF-HRD 1-1-6 GS-HVY 2-1-14 Course 0-0-1 Dist 0-0-4

30 Dec 06 Ascot 2m3f Cls4 96-115 Ch Hcap £5,205
8 ran GD-SFT 16fncs Time 5m 4.50s (slw 30.50s)
1 Fast Forward 6 11-7 ....Liam Treadwell (3) 5/2F
2 Witness Run 6 11-12 ....Barry Fenton 5/1
3 Baodai 4 11-4 ....Richard Johnson 9/1
4 DONOVAN 7 10-10 v ....Dave Crosse 7/1
  chased leaders, ridden 10th, in rear next and
  never dangerous after
  [RPR79 TS25 OR96]   [tchd 15/2]
Dist: 2¹/₂-14-8-4-18 RACE RPR: 121+/117/100+
Racecheck: Wins - Pl - Unpl 3

30 Nov 06 Leicester 2m4¹/₂f Cls4 82-108 Ch Hcap £5,205
6 ran GOOD 15fncs Time 5m 17.80s (slw 20.80s)
1 Flash Cummins 6 11-11 t ..Timmy Murphy 8/13F
2 Tom Fruit 9 11-12 ....Russ Garrity 9/2
3 DONOVAN 7 11-0 ....David Dennis 7/1

held up, headway 9th, every chance
approaching last, soon ridden, found nil
[RPR99 TS78 OR96]   [op 13/2]
Dist: ¹/₂-1³/₄-6-18   RACE RPR: 116+/115+/99
Racecheck: Wins 2 (2) Pl 2 Unpl 4

26 Oct 06 Stratford 2m1¹/₂f Cls4 90-115 Ch Hcap £6,397
9 ran SOFT 13fncs Time 4m 28.20s (slw 25.20s)
1 Jarro 10 10-11 ....Mr W Biddick (7) 7/2
2 Twist Bookie 6 10-13 ....Keith Mercer 9/1
3 Schinken Otto 5 11-4 ....Fergus King (3) 14/1
F DONOVAN 7 10-3 ....David Dennis 6/1
  chased leaders, led fater 3 out, ridden and just
  headed when fell last [RPR101 OR92]
Dist: 7-16-46   RACE RPR: 117+/106+/100+
Racecheck: Wins 1 (1) Pl 3 Unpl 8

Lucifer Bleu				10-12

8-y-o b g Kadalko - Figa Dancer (Bandinelli)
D E Pipe   Andrew Glassonbury (5)

Placings: U175527/13/

OR105 H110		Starts	1st	2nd	3rd	Win & Pl
Chase		2	1	–	1	£5,370
All Jumps races		9	2	1	1	£18,639
	4/04	Extr	2m1¹/₂f Cls4 Nov Ch gd-fm			£4,533
	5/03	Autl	2m1¹/₂f Hdl 4yo heavy			£11,221

Total win prize-money £15,754
GF-HRD 1-0-3 GS-HVY 1-0-4 Course 0-0-0 Dist 0-1-2

5 Jun 04 Perth 3m Cls3 Nov Ch £5,447
7 ran GD-FM 17fncs Time 6m 2.30s (slw 5.30s)
1 Galileo 8 10-13 b ....Paul Moloney 9/4
2 Winter Garden 10 10-6 p Peter Buchanan (7) 10/1
3 LUCIFER BLEU 5 10-13 ....A P McCoy 7/4F

close up, led 12th, not fluent 5 out, soon ridden,
headed last, one pace [RPR108 TS60] [op 2/1]
Dist: 1³/₄-¹/₂-dist-1¹/₄-1¹/₂ RACE RPR: 111+/107/108+
Racecheck: Wins - Pl Unpl 7

28 Apr 04 Exeter 2m1¹/₂f Cls4 Nov Ch £4,533
5 ran GD-FM 11fncs Time 4m 9.50s (slw 0.50s)
1 LUCIFER BLEU 5 10-11 ....A P McCoy 5/2
  made all, stumbled just before 3rd, ridden 7th,
  edged left after 2 out, in command when left
  clear last
  [RPR109 TS99]   [op 3/1 tchd 100/30 & 7/2]
2 Distant Romance 7 10-4 ....Colin Bolger (5) 33/1
3 Investor Relations 6 10-11 .P J Brennan (3) 25/1
Dist: 19-17   RACE RPR: 109/88/76
Racecheck: Wins 2 (2) Pl - Unpl 4

14 Apr 04 Cheltenham 3m Cls3 Nov 110-115 Hdl Hcap £10,440
10 ran GD-FM 12hdls Time 5m 44.30s (slw 6.30s)
1 My Line 7 11-9 ....Andrew Thornton 9/1
2 Parsons Legacy 6 11-9 .....Richard Johnson 7/1
3 Vodka Bleu 5 11-9 v¹ ....A P McCoy 7/1
7 LUCIFER BLEU 5 11-3 ....Jamie Moore (3) 14/1
  held up in rear, some headway 3 out, never in
  contention and soon weakened
  btn 44 lengths [RPR76 TS77 OR110] [tchd 16/1 &
  20/1]
Dist: ³/₄-1-19-6-6 RACE RPR: 125+/122/121+
Racecheck: Wins 2 (1) Pl 2 Unpl 5

Form Reading	**GIVE ME LOVE**
Spotlight	Fair novice chaser last season but little encouragement in three runs for new, present yard this time.
Handicap Ratings	On a mark of 119 (placed 4th) six outings ago and now down to a mark of 108 which constitutes a very big drop.
Significant Items of Form	Seven year old with three French Hurdle victories and one Class 4 Chase victory in the UK at Chepstow April 2006 on Good to Soft. Current campaign has consisted of one Novice Chase (Class 4) September 2006 when pulled up, followed by two Class 3 Handicap Chases when 7th of eleven runners October 2006 and unseated December 2006.
Verdict	No recent evidence to suggest big improvement is on the cards.
Hence:	DISMISS.

Form Reading	**JACK'S LAD**
Spotlight	Bumper winner at this track and also scored over hurdles at Ludlow. Hasn't shown much aptitude for chasing in two runs this season.
Handicap Ratings	No previous runs in Handicap Chases, mark of 104 for today's contest.
Significant Items of Form	Eight year old with one Bumper victory at Hereford (Soft) and one maiden Hurdle victory at Ludlow (Good to Soft) February 2005. Only five runs since then and current campaign which started on 02.11.06 has consisted of a Class 3 Handicap Hurdle (10th, beaten 49 lengths) and two Class 3 Novice Chases, both over 2 miles where beaten 74 lengths and 47½ lengths without making any significant forward move in either contest.
Verdict	The form does not indicate any improvement is forthcoming.
Hence:	DISMISS.

Form Reading	**DONOVAN**
Spotlight	All wins have been with cheek pieces, headgear dispensed with altogether this time.
Handicap Ratings	Marks for last six outings have varied from 92 to 96 and today's mark is 94.
Significant Items of Form	Eight year old with one Class 4 Chase victory at Towcester October 2005 over 2m½f on Good. Also four Hurdle victories in Class 3 and 4 events over distances from 2m to 2m2f. Last three runs between 26.10.06 and 30.12.06 have all been in Class 4 Handicap Chases over distances from 2m1½f to 2m4½f, where places were: fell, 3rd of 6; 4th of 6.
Verdict	Form seems to have hit a flat spot and moving up a Class to a Class 3 event would not appear to be the answer.
Decision:	DISMISS.

Form Reading	**LUCIFER BLEU**
Spotlight	Took weakish Exeter Novice for this stable in April 2004 but off since a 3rd of 7 in a run of the mill 3 mile Novice in June of that year.
Handicap Ratings	No Handicap Chase ratings, mark of 105 for today's contest.
Significant Items of Form	Eight year old with one Class 4 Novice Chase victory at Exeter (Good to Firm), over 2m1½f in April 2004 and one French Hurdle victory on Heavy in May 2003. Last run in June 2004 was in a Class 3 Novice Chase at Perth (3 miles, Good to Firm) where 3rd, beaten 2¼ lengths after being headed at the last.
Verdict	Two years eight months off the track but no David/Martin Pipe runners race if they are not fit. French win showed horse can handle Heavy, Exeter win showed horse can handle a right hand track and last run at Perth showed that today's distance will not be a problem. If horse can win at Exeter (tough track) it should be able to win at Hereford (relatively easy track).
Decision:	SELECT.

Overall Comment

In 1989 at the Cheltenham Festival when Peter Scudamore was the Pipe Stables Number One Jockey, Peter was aboard a Pipe runner which was favourite for the Supreme Novices Hurdle won by a horse called Sondrio (also from the Pipe yard) which was ridden by Jonathon Lower, landing odds of 120/1 on the Tote.

I learned a big lesson that day, primarily because before the start I had announced to 'the gang' that Martin Pipe had a runner that was paying 120/1 and when it scorched home and I started to receive congratulations, I had to admit in a very distraught manner that I had changed my mind at the last moment and hadn't backed it.

The lesson of that race was of course that whether by design or not the riding arrangements of the stable jockeys had wrong footed the betting market.

With that lesson still firmly imprinted in my mind, I sensed something was going to happen as soon as I saw that Lucifer Bleu had opened at a price of 28/1, reflecting the fact that Andrew Glassonbury was on board despite the fact that Tony McCoy was at the meeting and presumably available to ride.

The Betting Forecast price of 11/1 in the *Racing Post* seemed pretty generous to me, but 28/1 looked like a belated monetary Christmas present plus a generous helping of interest.

If you read Spotlight's comment that the 'absence of McCoy could be construed as a negative', you will see how the market started to be wrong footed. Add to that the facts that the horse had been off the track for 965 days and Chester Barnes had refrained from tipping the horse on the stables Pipeline and you can see all too clearly why the betting market managed to make a complete fool of itself.

This race was another classic example of the rank outsider proving it could win the contest purely on merit without benefiting from any bad luck stories from its opponents. Going straight into the lead from the off Lucifer Bleu was asked by his jockey Andrew Glassonbury to constantly stretch the field some 4/5 lengths clear of his pursuers and at no stage, apart from a slight peck on landing at the last, did he look like getting pulled back.

The lessons to be learned from this race are as follows.

a)   Always let the form of a horse dictate whether you back it or not.

b)   Never ever try to determine a horse's chances by considering the jockey on board.

c)   Never, let a horse's price in the betting market influence your own opinion on whether it has a reasonable chance of winning or being placed in the first three.

For the record the Forecast Lucifer Bleu with the favourite Maletton paid £83.60 for the Tote Exacta and £58.40 for the Computer Straight Forecast.

EXAMPLE 9

10.01.07   Wincanton – Soft – Class 5 – Handicap Hurdle – 2m6f

Winner   CELTIC MAJOR – 50/1

2.10
RACE 3

betfredpoker.com Handicap Hurdle (Class 5)
Winner £2,740.80

RUK

2m6f

£4000 guaranteed For 4yo+ Rated 0-95 Minimum Weight 10-0 Penalties after December 30th, a winner of a hurdle 7lb Celtic Major's Handicap Mark 95 Entries 62 pay £10 Penalty value 1st £2,740.80 2nd £798.80 3rd £399.60

1	P/5PF9- **CELTIC MAJOR** (IRE) [335]	gr g Roselier-Dun Oengus	Andrew Glassonbury(5)	9 11-12
	Miss H Lewis Walters Plant Hire Ltd		**50/1**	
2	2-1958 **FLYING FORME** (IRE) [20]	b g Muroto-Coolavanny Queen	Darren O'Dwyer(7) [83]	7 11-11
	P J Hobbs C J O'Shea And Co Ltd			
3	P58P/0- **DR CHARLIE** [583] [CD]	ch g Dr Devious-Miss Toot	Miss C Dyson(7)	9 11-11
	Miss C Dyson Miss C Dyson			
4	0P4-905 **ANOTHER BURDEN** [34]	b m Alflora-Dalbeattie	Richard Johnson [91]	6 11-10
	H D Daly The Shropshire Lads Syndicate			
5	373P/60 **STORM PRINCE** (IRE) [34] [CD]	ch g Prince Of Birds-Petersford Girl	W T Kennedy(3) [94]	b 10 11-9
	Miss T Spearing D J Oseman			
6	05-56PP **MAXIMINUS** [30]	b g The West-Candarela	S P Jones(5) [96]	v¹ 7 11-8
	M Madgwick M Madgwick			
7	159-973 **NOT FOR DIAMONDS** (IRE) [41]	b g Arctic Lord-Black-Crash	Andrew Thornton [101]	7 11-6
	J W Mullins J M & J M Scott **3/1 F**			
8	741P-43 **DARKSHAPE** [20] [BF]	b g Zamindar-Shapely	Sam Thomas [97]	7 11-5
	Miss Venetia Williams Concertina Racing			
9	6-3P585 **MASSINI SUNSET** (IRE) [36]	b g Dr Massini-Burgundy Sunset	Tom Scudamore [93]	7 11-4
	N R Mitchell Mr And Mrs Andrew May			
10	75PU/95 **DEAR SIR** (IRE) [124]	ch g Among Men-Deerussa	Angharad Frieze(10) [88]	7 11-4
	Mrs P N Dutfield Unity Farm Holiday Centre Ltd			
11	0/3FP-0 **SEEMMA** [15]	b m Romany Rye-Shepani	Wayne Kavanagh(5) [88]	7 11-4
	K Bishop J A G Meaden			
12	8487 **HAZELBURY** [20]	b m Overbury-Mira Lady	Keiran Burke(7) [87]	6 11-2
	N J Hawke Mrs J McDermid			
13	006- **MONTENDA** [257]	b g Classic Cliche-Polly Leach	Miss L Gardner(7) [87]	6 11-0
	Mrs S Gardner Mr & Mrs Searle			
14	PP44563 **WONDERSOBRIGHT** (IRE) [8]	br g Magical Wonder-Brightness	C M Studd(5) [99]	tp 8 10-12
	P Butler Christopher W Wilson			
15	-836277 **GOTTA GET ON** [23]	br m Emperor Fountain-Lonicera	Daryl Jacob(3) [97]	6 10-12
	R H Alner Mrs Susie Old			
16	215982 **CANOPUS** [19]	b g Giant's Causeway-Brighteet Star **2ND 7/2**	A P McCoy [100]	p 4 10-12
	Jonjo O'Neill Charlie Blakemore And Steve Hammond			
17	9702-6 **COOL SOCIETY** [50]	b g Atraf-Cool Run	Robert Walford [90]	5 10-11
	R H Alner Donhead Stud			

BETTING FORECAST: 11-4 Not For Diamonds, 5 Canopus, 11-2 Darkshape, 8 Another Burden, 9 Flying Forme, 12 Gotta Get On, 14 Wondersobright, 16 Cool Society, Massini Sunset, 20 Maximinus, Seemma, Storm Prince, 25 Dear Sir, 33 Hazelbury, 40 Dr Charlie, Montenda, 50 Celtic Major.

SPOTLIGHT

Celtic Major With Jonjo O'Neill in 2004 and Peter Bowen last season, failing to accomplish much and looks on very stiff mark on this debut for current yard.

Flying Forme Won Irish maiden point in May; well held at increasingly long odds in three novice hurdles; tries new trip for this handicap debut but still plenty to prove off this mark.

Dr Charlie Three hurdle wins, latest in C&D handicap in May 2004, but below form in limited runs in 2005 and has been on the sidelines for 583 days; a little down the weights but probably best watched.

Another Burden Two handicaps have brought no significant improvement and hopes here seemingly pinned on the extra 6f; no striking evidence that it will turn things around but worth market check.

Storm Prince Won twice in March 2004, including over C&D, but absent 27 months before well beaten both starts this term; down the weights but questions to answer.

Maximinus Has done little in four starts, including last three, so perhaps that is an excuse but showed very little last two and now gets first-time headgear; bits of modest hurdles form (including twice over C&D) since sole win in November 2004, so there are straws to clutch at.

Not For Diamonds Won bumper in 2005; 25-1 but perked up dramatically on handicap hurdling debut over C&D (good to soft) latest, staying on for third in large field and although 13l behind the winner, that performance makes hugely more appeal than most of what's on offer from this line-up; shortlisted.

Darkshape Only three runs since win in December 2005 but twice made frame when favourite in big-field handicaps last month; handles soft ground but this trip is step in the dark.

Massini Sunset Ran in points in Ireland until this summer; low-level form in British novice hurdles over 2m3f-2m5f and no certainty to appreciate the extra distance.

Dear Sir Very lightly raced in this sphere last two years and latest fifth at Bangor (2m4f, good to firm) in September was best effort in that time; however, unraced on soft at 2m6f and plenty to prove.

Seemma No show on handicap debut over 2m here on Boxing Day but that was her first run for 19 months (new yard); failure to go on in 2005 (lame final start) to be considered but she is well related and showed a bit of ability on heavy ground on hurdling debut, so not entirely ruled out.

Hazelbury Promise in novice hurdles does not match up to this mark, as seemed to be confirmed when well beaten on handicap debut last month; this is over 5f further, but she's a bit speculative.

Montenda Well beaten in three novice hurdles last spring for Simon Burrough.

Wondersobright Won over fences in Ireland more than a year ago and has refound a bit of form over hurdles of late, on latest start passed by two after he had big lead in 2m6l selling handicap at Folkestone (soft); same mark and more needed with tongue tie added to cheekpieces.

Gotta Get On Poor maiden; second in novice at Newton Abbot in July over this trip and not discredited on good to soft next time after four-month break; today's return to handicap gives her better chance than on latest outing and, although not proven on soft, she's got a squeak.

Canopus Blinkers/cheekpieces last five starts, winning ordinary juvenile hurdle at Newton Abbot in August first occasion; latest second in soft-ground handicap at Hereford (2m1f) was best effort since and gives him a chance, but 2m6f is bit of a guess.

Cool Society Hard to know what ability there is as he was a hard puller initially and has since been held up out the back in an attempt to settle him; made useful late gains when reappearing in 2m Kempton handicap (good to soft) in November but another for whom this trip is unknown territory.

VERDICT There's a major shortage of solid claims, which may well make this a suitable opening for November's C&D third **NOT FOR DIAMONDS**. [RA]

OFFICIAL RATINGS							2.10 HANDICAP		TODAY FUTURE		RP RATING		
LAST SIX OUTINGS-LATEST ON RIGHT											LATEST	BEST	ADJUSTED
—	104P	99⁵	99P	—	—	Celtic Major	11-12	95	—		—	—	—
—	—	—	—	—	—	Flying Forme	11-11	94	—	70	83	83
107⁶	106P	106⁵	106⁸	105P	103⁰	Dr Charlie	11-11	94	—	—	—	—
—	—	98⁰	96⁵	—	—	Another Burden	11-10	93	91	91	91	
108³	108⁷	107³	106P	98⁶	95⁰	Storm Prince	11-9	92	71	82	94
97⁰	94⁵	92⁵	—	—	—	Maximinus	11-8	91	—	92	96
—	—	—	—	—	89³	Not For Diamonds	11-6	89	101 ◄	101 ◄	101 ◄
—	76⁴	76¹	87P	85⁴	84³	Darkshape	11-5	88	97	97	97
—	—	—	—	—	—	Massini Sunset	11-4	87	93	93	93
97⁷	96⁵	—	90⁸	88⁵		Dear Sir	11-4	87	88	88	88
—	—	—	—	92⁰		Seemma	11-4	87	-70	70	88
—	—	—	—	88⁷		Hazelbury	11-2	85	66	87 ·	87
—	—	—	—	—	—	Montenda	11-0	83	66	87	87
—	85⁴	85⁴	—	83⁶	81³	Wondersobright	10-12	81	87	99	99
—	77³	78⁶	—	83⁷		Gotta Get On	10-12	81	65 ·	97	97
—	—	94⁹	92⁸	90²		Canopus	10-12	94	100	100	100
—	—	—	—	82⁶		Cool Society	10-11	80	90	90	90

Celtic Major — 11-12

9-y-o gr g Roselier - Dun Oengus (Strong Gale)
Miss H Lewis   Andrew Glassonbury (5)

Placings: 2505/8P/5PF9-

OR95	Starts	1st	2nd	3rd	Win & Pl
Hurdles	6	–	–	–	
All Jumps races	10	–	1	–	£672
GF-HRD 0-0-0	GS-HVY 0-0-8		Course 0-0-0		Dist 0-0-0

9 Feb 06 Huntingdon 2m4¹/₂f Cls4 88-109 Ch Hcap £3,904

15 ran GOOD   16fncs   Time 5m 9.10s (slw 18.10s)
1 Runner Bean 12 11-6 ....Robert Thornton 33/1
2 Priscilla 8 11-2 ....John McNamara 11/1
3 Randolph O'Brien 6 10-10 .....Carl Llewellyn 8/1
9 CELTIC MAJOR 8 10-7 ..Lee Stephens (5) 66/1
mid-division, lost place after 5th, behind from
8th btn 42 lengths [RPR64 TS25 OR95]

Dist: 7-2-nk-³/₄-1   RACE RPR: 119+/103/95
Racecheck: Wins 4 (4) Pl 5 Unpl 16

21 Jan 06 Lingfield 3m Cls4 Nov 69-95 Ch Hcap £3,904

10 ran SOFT   16fncs   Time 6m 32.80s (slw 33.80s)
1 Trenance 8 11-7 ....Jason Maguire 9/2
2 Rosses Point 7 11-8 p ....Paul Moloney 11/4F
3 Mandingo Chief 7 11-9 ...Wayne Hutchinson 7/1
F CELTIC MAJOR 8 11-12 ......Dave Crosse 16/1
fell 3rd [OR95]   [op 14/1]

Dist: 3-shd-14-14   RACE RPR: 104+/104+/103+
Racecheck: Wins 3 (2) Pl 5 Unpl 6

11 Jan 06 Newbury 3m¹/₂f Cls4 91-109 Cond Hdl Hcap £3,083

15 ran GD-SFT   13hdls   Time 6m 10.20s (slw 20.70s)
1 Kilty Storm 7 10-13 .Andrew Glassonbury (8) 4/1
2 The Gangerman 6 11-1 .....Bernie Wharfe (8) 8/1
3 Captain Corelli 9 11-7 .Robert Stephens (3) 5/6F
P CELTIC MAJOR 8 11-2 ....W T Kennedy 12/1
with leader until weakened after 9th, behind and
pulled up before 3 out [OR99]

Dist: 5-2¹/₂-23-1³/₄-¹/₂   RACE RPR: 111+/106/105
Racecheck: Wins 4 (3) Pl 4 Unpl 12

Montenda — 11-0

6-y-o b g Classic Cliche - Polly Leach (Pollerton)
Mrs S Gardner   Miss L Gardner (7)

Placings: 006-

OR83	Starts	1st	2nd	3rd	Win & Pl
All Jumps races	3	–	–	–	–
GF-HRD 0-0-0	GS-HVY 0-0-2		Course 0-0-1		Dist 0-0-0

28 Apr 06 Chepstow 2m4f   Cls4 Nov Hdl £2,928

10 ran GOOD   11hdls   Time 4m 47.40s (slw 11.40s)
1 College Ace 5 11-7 ....Richard Johnson 5/4
2 Flemens River 5 11-0 p ......Leighton Aspell 50/1
3 The Glen Road 9 11-0 ....Paul Moloney 25/1
6 MONTENDA 5 11-0 ....R J Greene 50/1
hit 1st, always behind [RPR52 TS11]

Dist: 2¹/₂-11-2-22-4   RACE RPR: 108+/91/80
Racecheck: Wins - Pl 1 Unpl 4

22 Mar 06 Chepstow 2m¹/₂f Cls4 Nov Hdl £2,928

16 ran GOOD   11hdls   Time 5m 57.30s (slw 9.30s)
1 Chiaro 4 11-7 b ....Richard Johnson 5/4F
2 Anemix 5 11-2 ....Howie Ephgrave (5) 5/2
3 White On Black 5 11-7 ....Jamie Moore 8/1
10 MONTENDA 5 10-9 .....Chris Honour (5) 200/1
prominent until weakened 4th
btn 55 lengths [RPR73 TS38]

Dist: 18-13-2¹/₂-10-2 RACE RPR: 139+/124+/107+
Racecheck: Wins 1 (1) Pl 4 Unpl 16

9 Mar 06 Wincanton 2m   Cls4 Mdn Hdl £3,426

18 ran SOFT   8hdls   Time 4m 1.30s (slw 24.30s)
1 Gentleman Jimmy 6 11-2 ....Jim Crowley 25/1
2 Rapscallion 7 11-2 ....Andrew Tinkler 16/1
3 Inishturk 7 11-2 ....Robert Thornton 20/1
10 MONTENDA 5 11-2 ....Jason Maguire 150/1
always behind btn 65+ lengths [TS7][op 125/1]

Dist: 4-5-1-13-8   RACE RPR: 107 I/100+/95
Racecheck: Wins - Pl 4 Unpl 24

Dr Charlie — 11-11

9-y-o ch g Dr Devious - Miss Toot (Ardross)
Miss C Dyson   Miss C Dyson (7)

Placings: 8P714565P2/16P58P/0-

OR94	Starts	1st	2nd	3rd	Win & Pl
All Jumps races	24	3	1	–	£10,574
100 5/04	Winc	2m6f Cls4 84-100 Hdl Hcap good £3,507			
94 10/03	Hrfd	2m3¹/₄f Cls4 86-98 Hdl Hcap gd-fm £2,317			
4/02	Wwck	2m3f Cls4 Nov Hdl gd-fm £2,923			
			Total win prize-money £8,747		
GF-HRD 2-0-3	GS-HVY 0-0-10		Course 1-1-4		Dist 1-1-12

6 Jun 05 Newton Abbot 2m6f Cls4 77-103 Hdl Hcap £3,571

17 ran GOOD   10hdls   Time 5m 18.30s (slw 17.30s)
1 Spirit Of Tenby 8 10-3 ....James Davies 13/2F
2 Here Comes Harry 9 9-11 oh1 ....
....Owyn Nelmes (3) 16/1
3 Celtic Ruffian 7 10-0 oh9 Matthew Batchelor 25/1
12 DR CHARLIE 7 11-5 .....Miss C Dyson (7) 25/1
held up towards rear, ridden after 6th, soon
struggling
btn 32 lengths [RPR76 TS80 OR103] [op 20/1]

Dist: 1¹/₂-5-1³/₄-3¹/₂-8   RACE RPR: 87+/81+/75
Racecheck: Wins 4 (3) Pl 1 Unpl 19

17 Apr 05 Wincanton 2m6f Cls4 80-106 Hdl Hcap £3,591

18 ran GOOD   11hdls   Time 5m 22.00s (slw 13.00s)
1 Rift Valley 10 10-13 v ....Richard Johnson 5/2F
2 Roman Court 7 10-9 .....Robert Walford (3) 25/1
3 Hylia 6 10-12 ....J A McCarthy 14/1
P DR CHARLIE 7 11-4 ......Miss C Dyson (7) 16/1
in touch, weakened 7th, tailed off when pulled
up before 2 out [OR105]   [op 20/1]

Dist: 10-2¹/₂-6-6-1³/₄   RACE RPR: 112+/93+/89
Racecheck: Wins 2 (2) Pl 4 Unpl 12

20 Feb 05 Fontwell 2m6¹/₂f Cls3 87-115 Hdl Hcap £6,090

14 ran GD-SFT   11hdls   Time 5m 50.80s (slw 40.80s)
1 Tell The Trees 4 9-9 oh2 ..Tom Malone (5) 11/1
2 Ice Crystal 8 11-12 ....A P McCoy 7/2F
3 Kiwi Babe 6 11-9 ....Leighton Aspell 25/1
8 DR CHARLIE 7 10-10 .....Miss C Dyson (7) 25/1
chased leaders, shaken up and outpaced from
3 out, kept on from 2 out but never a danger
btn 11¹/₂ lengths [RPR97 TS24 OR106]

Dist: 4-2-2-2-shd   RACE RPR: 92+/114/110+
Racecheck: Wins - Pl 1 Unpl 22

CELTIC MAJOR

Form Reading	
Spotlight	With Jonjo O'Neill in 2004 and Peter Bowen last season. Debut for current yard.
Handicap Ratings	Raced off a mark of 104 (pulled up) five outings ago, down to a mark of 95 today so handicapper has relented a bit.
Significant Items of Form	Nine year old with no victories and according to placings (ten outings) lightly raced. Last Hurdle race on 11.01.06 was a Class 4 Handicap hurdle over 3m¹/₂f at Newbury (Good to Soft) where started at 12/1 in a 15 runner field and 'with leader until weakened after 9th, behind and pulled up before 3 out'. Only two races since then were in Class 4 Handicap Chases over 3 miles at Lingfield 21.01.06 when fell and over 2m4¹/₂f at Huntingdon (right hand track), 09.02.06 when 9th of 15.
Verdict	According to the handicapper, Celtic Major at top weight is the best horse in the race. Previously with two top trainers and although they didn't achieve a result with this horse, there is always a chance that new trainer can achieve a turnaround in today's race by taking the horse back to hurdling in a lower class event (Class 5) over a distance (2m6f) and on going (Soft) and type of track (right handed) which form suggests could suit. Last Hurdle run starting price of 12/1 in a Class 4 Handicap suggests today's forecast Starting Price of 50/1 for a Class 5 event is far too big. Too many 'ifs' to say horse has a reasonable chance of a top three placing but its top weight rating suggests that it is possibly far too good to be left out of the reckoning.
Hence:	SELECT.

Form Reading	**MONTENDA**
Spotlight	Well beaten in three Novice Hurdles last spring for Simon Burrough.
Handicap Ratings	No runs yet in a Handicap. Today's mark 83.
Significant Items of Form	Six year old with only three runs to date in March and April 2006, all in Class 4 Maiden and Novice Hurdles from 2 miles to 2m4f where beaten 65+, 55 and 39½ lengths with no sign of being competitive.
Verdict	Although horse is making its debut with new trainer today and although dropping down in Class, its inexperience would suggest that some kind of result would be most unlikely.
Decision:	DISMISS.

Form Reading	**DR CHARLIE**
Spotlight	Three Hurdle wins, latest in C & D Handicap in May 2004. On the sidelines for 583 days.
Handicap Ratings	Marks from 103 to 107 last six outings down to a mark of 94 today, which probably reflects the period off course.
Significant Items of Form	Nine year old with three Hurdle victories in Class 4 events (two Handicaps, one Novice Hurdle) over distances from 2m3f to 2m6f on Good and Good to Firm with the most recent (May 2004) over today's course and distance. Course record equals 1 win, 1 place and 4 unplaced. Has run ten times on Good to Soft – Heavy without being placed. Last three runs between 20.02.05 and 06.06.05 include an 8th of 14 at Fontwell on Good to Soft in a Class 3 Handicap Hurdle over 2m6½f, beaten 11½ lengths.
Verdict	Course win was two years eight months ago and impossible to determine from *Racing Post* information whether horse can go fresh after a break of nineteen months. However this is a Class 5 event and course form and the distance all seem to indicate that a top three placing is a reasonable possibility.
Hence:	SELECT.

Overall Comment

One significant advantage with The Tail End System is that you are frequently backing very long priced horses and as a result you find it easy to justify relatively small bets where losing is not a disaster and winning can produce an excellent profit.

In such a situation you can afford to adopt an optimistic approach to selection in the knowledge that though the form of your selections is not outstanding, you do not need to achieve that many wins to find yourself comfortably ahead of the bookies.

In this particular case, Celtic Major had a Starting Price of 50/1 but the Tote return was £93.40 (win), £11.90 (place); the Exacta, which involved linking Celtic Major with the second favourite in the Betting Forecast, Canopus, paid £666.90, and the Computer Straight Forecast £229.10.

It is interesting to note that Celtic Major went on to win its next event, a far stronger contest, also at Wincanton, at odds of 12/1.

I would hasten to add that it is very unusual for a Tail End System winner to have a follow up victory but its second success underlined the importance of course form, and this is a factor which frequently dominates the selection procedure.

EXAMPLE 10

15.12.06   Uttoxeter – Heavy – Class 4 – Handicap Chase – 3m

Winner   **CINNAMON LINE – 20/1**

3.00
RACE 6

Air And Ground Aviation Handicap Chase (For The Fred Dixon Memorial Trophy) (Class 4)
Winner £5,387

ATR

3m

£8500 guaranteed For 4yo+ Rated 0-105 Weights raised 4lb Minimum Weight 10-0 Penalties after December 2nd, a winner of a chase 7lb Ferimon's Handicap Mark 107 Entries 42 pay £15 Penalty value 1st £5,387 2nd £1,591 3rd £795 4th £397 5th £198

1 /53-921 **FERIMON** (7ex) [8] [D]
gr g Terimon-Rhyming Moppet   Richard Johnson
H D Daly Strachan Myddelton Gabb Stoddart Lawson
7 12-5
(116)

2 1/P-44P **JOHNSTON'S SWALLOW** (IRE) [14]
b g Commanche Run-Mirror Of Flowers   Dominic Elsworth
Jonjo O'Neill John P McManus
8 11-12

3 F1UP5-3 **HAPPY SHOPPER** (IRE) [23] [D]
b g Presenting-Reach Down   Tom Scudamore
D E Pipe Heli-Beds Racing
v1 6 11-11
(113)

4 P5P2-12 **WHAT'SONYOURMIND** (IRE) [20]
b g Glacial Storm-Granny Clark   A P McCoy
Jonjo O'Neill John P McManus
6 11-10
(101)

5 F-3532F **FARINGTON LODGE** (IRE) [7] [D][BF]
b g Simply Great-Lodge Party   Barry Keniry
J M Saville The Shaw Hall Partnership
8 11-3
(115)

6 5FP7-F6 **CINNAMON LINE** [13] [D]
ch g Derrylin-Cinnamon Run   Tom Doyle
R Lee Club Ten
10 11-1
(114)
20/1

7 PPP-734 **LAZY BUT LIVELY** (IRE) [30] [CD]
br g Supreme Leader-Oriel Dream   Keith Mercer
R F Fisher S P Marsh
10 10-13
(118)

8 P-PP933 **MOSCOW LEADER** (IRE) [7] [D]
ch g Moscow Society-Catrionas Castle   Mr A Merriam(7)
B N Pollock Medbourne Racing Club
p 8 10-13
(108)

9 -7PPP27 **PARDINI** (USA) [4] [CD]
b g Quest For Fame-Nobilissima   Charlie Poste(5)
M F Harris Prevention & Detection (Holdings) Ltd
7 10-12
(112)

10 523P-5U **AVADI** (IRE) [26]
b g Un Desperado-Flamewood   W T Kennedy(3)
P T Dalton Mrs Julie Martin
8 10-10
(113)

11 1-34P35 **CLOCKERS CORNER** (IRE) [8]
b g Eurobus-Pampered Finch VII   Warren Marston
J R Cornwall J R Cornwall
9 10-5
(103)

12 847-F77 **FULL ON** [22]
b g Le Moss-Flighty Dove   Paddy Merrigan(3)
A M Hales The Mossy Partnership
9 10-3
(118)

13 P5P-P85 **LOST IN NORMANDY** (IRE) [15] [D]
b g Treasure Hunter-Auntie Honnie   R J Greene
Mrs L Williamson Please Hold UK
b 9 10-2
(112)

14 -962577 **LITTLE VILLAIN** (IRE) [14]
b g Old Vic-Party Woman   Lee Edwards(10)
T Wall T Wall
8 10-0
(106)

LONG HANDICAP: Little Villain 9-2

2005 (17 ran) **Major Benefit** Mrs K Waldron 8 11-5 20/1   Richard Spate (7) OR105

BETTING FORECAST: 4 Ferimon, 5 Farington Lodge, 11-2 What'sonyourmind, 8 Happy Shopper, Lazy But Lively, 10 Avadi, 12 Full On, Pardini, 16 Clockers Corner, Lost in Normandy, Moscow Leader, 20 Cinnamon Line, 25 Johnston's Swallow, 50 Little Villain.

SPOTLIGHT

Ferimon Let down by jumping in early chase starts but made just the one notable error when opening chase account in Huntingdon novice handicap latest (3m, good to soft); handles mud but faces tough task under welter burden.

Johnston's Swallow Tailed off/pulled up all three tries over fences including on handicap debut latest; hard to fancy on first attempt at this trip.

Happy Shopper Landed small-field Lingfield handicap chase in February (heavy) but failed to complete in three of other five chase outings and tailed off third on reappearance latest; one to swerve now visored for the first time.

What'sonyourmind Mostly poor form over hurdles last term but made successful chase bow at Towcester early last month (2m4f, good to soft) before jumping poorly when distant second at same venue (2m6f, heavy); trip/ground no problem but needs to improve fencing.

Farington Lodge Opened account in 3m soft-ground handicap chase at Newcastle early last year and unlucky not to double up over same C&D next time (3l up when fell close home); jumping problems resurfaced at Southwell last time and looks opposable in this big field.

Cinnamon Line Seems happiest at Chepstow, scene of sole chase success (3m, good), but only sixth there latest and record over fences at other venues reads PFPFP; easily opposed.

Lazy But Lively Goes well in the mud but never convinced in the jumping department and no coincidence that last three wins have come in small fields; plodded on into distant fourth behind subsequent winner at Hexham last time (4m) and will be staying on when others have had enough.

Moscow Leader Best effort for current yard when 17l third of five at Market Rasen on penultimate start (3m5f, soft) but didn't build on that at Southwell next time and not hard to look elsewhere.

Pardini Both wins, including heavy-ground course success, came after very recent outings and back to form when runner-up at Folkestone last month on return from five-day break; poor effort over inadequate 2m4f at Plumpton four days ago but no surprise to see him bounce back.

Avadi 2m4f heavy-ground Market Rasen winner (sole success) early last term and since placed at 2m; in the process of running sound race before unseating at Towcester latest (2m3.5f) but best watched with stamina unproven.

Clockers Corner Faced some stiff tasks in non-handicap company prior to last-time out 22l fifth of 17 behind Ferimon at Huntingdon where he jumped out to his left on occasions; may do better now returned to left-handed track and not impossible to see him involved off light weight.

Full On 14l second of 17 in this race last year despite some hairy leaps but well held over C&D latest and still searching for first win; placed at best.

Lost In Normandy Blinkered when landing soft-ground Bangor handicap chase over shorter trip at this time last year and has done no winning mark after three moderate efforts without the headgear this term; one to watch closely in the market now blinkers back on.

Little Villain Beaten by 24l when 100-1 runner-up here in October (2m5f, heavy) but well beaten since and surprising if he were to break duck from 12lb wrong.

VERDICT **Ferimon** would have been the pick on faster going but he might struggle to carry 12st 5lb in this ground so a chance is taken on **PARDINI**, whose best efforts have come when making a quick return to action. **Lazy But Lively**, not disgraced from well out of the weights at Hexham last time, has each-way claims. [AM]

OFFICIAL RATINGS LAST SIX OUTINGS–LATEST ON RIGHT						**3.00** HANDICAP	TODAY FUTURE	RP RATING LATEST / BEST / ADJUSTED		
—	—	—	—	—	99[1]	Ferimon (7x) 12-5	107 +8	116 ◀ 116	116
—	—	115[4]	—	110[P]	Johnston's Swallow 11-12	100	—	81	—
93[F]	93[1]	102[U]	102[P]	102[5]	101[3]	Happy Shopper 11-11	99	85	113	113
—	—	—	88[1]	98[2]	What'sonyourmind 11-10	98	94	101	101
94[F]	—	94[5]	91[3]	91[2]	91[F]	Farington Lodge 11-3	91	—	115	115
104[5]	98[F]	98[P]	98[7]	96[F]	96[6]	Cinnamon Line 11-1	89	96	116	114
94[P]	94[P]	—	—	94[3]	109[4]	Lazy But Lively 10-13	87	110	118	118 ◀
97[P]	95[P]	95[5]	92[9]	92[3]	89[3]	Moscow Leader 10-13	87 -5	69	114	108
—	90[P]	87[P]	86[P]	86[2]	86[7]	Pardini 10-12	86	41	116	112
85[5]	85[2]	85[3]	85[P]	85[5]	—	Avadi 10-10	84	—	113	113
—	—	—	—	—	83[5]	Clockers Corner 10-5	79	103	103	103
—	—	—	92[F]	92[7]	84[7]	Full On 10-3	77	101	121 ◀ 118 ◀
92[P]	92[5]	90[P]	90[P]	86[8]	82[5]	Lost in Normandy 10-2	76	95	116	112
—	—	82[2]	—	—	78[P]	Little Villain 9-2	74 -12	76	106	106

Little Villain — 10-0

8-y-o *b g* Old Vic - Party Woman (Sexton Blake)
T Wall   Lee Edwards (10)

Placings: 923P0/0964B68-962577

		Starts	1st	2nd	3rd	Win & Pl
OR74 H62						
Chase		5	–	1	–	£1,309
All Jumps races		33	–	3	1	£3,589
GF-HRD 0-0-5	GS-HVY 0-3-17		Course 0-2-6		Dist 0-1-4	

1 Dec Exeter 2m7¹/₂f Cls4 Nov 74-100 Ch Hcap £5,855
13 ran SOFT   17fncs Time 6m 3.20s (slw 23.20s)
1 Zimbabwe 6 9-11 p ....Jay Harris (5) 10/1
2 Onyourheadbeit 8 11-5 ....Leighton Aspell 14/1
3 Just For Men 6 11-6 b¹ ....Sam Thomas 16/1
7 **LITTLE VILLAIN** 8 9-9 ow5 oh5 ....
....Lee Edwards (10) 66/1
in touch until weakened after 13th, tailed off
btn 48 lengths [RPR48 TS54 OR79] [op 50/1]
Dist: shd-6-11-2-62   RACE RPR: 128+/128+/121
Racecheck: Wins 1 (1) Pl - Unpl 5

23 Nov Uttoxeter 2m6¹/₂f Cls4 Ch £5,704
12 ran HEAVY   Time 6m 15.00s (slw 50.00s)
1 Heez A Dreamer 6 11-0 ....A P McCoy 3/1
2 L'Antartique 6 11-0 ....G Lee 7/2
3 Kilty Storm 7 10-9 t Andrew Glassonbury (5) 14/1
7 **LITTLE VILLAIN** 8 10-4 Lee Edwards (10) 100/1
hampered 1st, blundered 2nd, in touch,
reminders 7th, soon lost place and behind,
tailed off btn 88 lengths [RPR39 OR69]
Dist: 9-10-1¹/₄-9-18   RACE RPR: 93+/107+/94+
Racecheck: Wins 1 (1) Pl - Unpl 1

11 Nov Uttoxeter 3m Cls4 Nov Ch £3,904
7 ran GD-SFT   18fncs Time 6m 37.80s (slw 51.80s)
1 Kilbeggan Blade 7 10-12 ......Paul Moloney 9/4F
2 FERIMON 7 10-12 ....Tom Doyle 3/1
took keen hold in touch, headway 14th,
challenged 3 out, kept on same pace
[RPR92 TS19 OR104] [op 9/4]
3 Denada 10 10-5 ....Bernie Wharfe 7/2
5 **LITTLE VILLAIN** 8 10-2 ....Lee Edwards (10) 9/1
chased leaders, ridden 14th, upsides next, one
pace [RPR78 OR82] [op 12/1]
Dist: 7-5-5-2¹/₂-54   RACE RPR: 102+/92+/86
Racecheck: Wins 2 (2) Pl 1 Unpl 3

Johnston's Swallow — 11-12

8-y-o *b g* Commanche Run - Mirror Of Flowers
(Artaius)
Jonjo O'Neill   Dominic Elsworth

Placings: 32/0/P2461/P-44P

		Starts	1st	2nd	3rd	Win & Pl
OR100 H115						
Chase		3	–	–	–	£860
All Jumps races		12	1	2	1	£9,001
3/05	DRoy	2m Mdn Hdl yld-sft				£3,921
GF-HRD 0-0-0	GS-HVY 1-3-11		Course 0-0-0		Dist 0-0-0	

1 Dec Sandown 2m4¹/₂f Cls3 Nov 106-115 Ch Hcap
£6,506
6 ran GD-SFT   17fncs Time 5m 28.50s (slw 26.50s)
1 Idris 5 11-12 ....Jamie Moore 5/1
2 Topinambour 6 11-3 t ....Richard McGrath 8/1
3 Charlton Kings 8 11-0 ......Mr J Snowden (5) 9/2
P **JOHNSTON'S SWALLOW** 8 11-7 Noel Fehily 25/1
in rear, ridden approaching 7th, lost touch from
9th, no chance when hampered 12th, tailed off
when pulled up before 3 out [OR110]

Dist: 1³/₄-9-52   RACE RPR: 121+/108/103+
Racecheck: Wins - Pl - Unpl 1

12 Nov Fontwell 2m2f Cls4 Ch £4,554
5 ran GOOD   13fncs Time 4m 31.70s (slw 11.70s)
1 Priors Dale 6 11-5 ....Barry Fenton 6/4J
2 Idris 5 11-5 ....Jamie Moore 4/1
3 Only Vintage 6 11-5 ....Sam Thomas 6/4J
4 **JOHNSTON'S SWALLOW** 8 11-5 Noel Fehily 14/1
held up, losing touch when hit 9th, tailed off
[RPR79 TS72 OR113] [op 10/1]
Dist: 6-7-33-48   RACE RPR: 125+/121+/113+
Racecheck: Wins 3 (3) Pl - Unpl 3

26 Oct Stratford 2m1¹/₂f Cls4 90-115 Ch Hcap £6,397
9 ran SOFT   13fncs Time 4m 28.20s (slw 25.20s)
1 Jarro 10 10-11 ....Mr W Biddick (7) 7/2
2 Twist Bookie 6 10-13 ....Keith Mercer 9/1
3 Schinken Otto 5 11-4 ....Fergus King (3) 14/1
4 **JOHNSTON'S SWALLOW** 8 11-12 ....
....A P McCoy 11/2
held up, headway 8th, weakened next, left
remote 4th last
[RPR52 TS16 OR115] [op 9/2 tchd 4/1]
Dist: 7-16-46   RACE RPR: 114+/103+/97+
Racecheck: Wins - Pl 3 Unpl 5

Cinnamon Line — 11-1

10-y-o *ch g* Derrylin - Cinnamon Run (Deep Run)
R Lee   Tom Doyle

Placings: F35/F4/P212/P5FP7-F6

		Starts	1st	2nd	3rd	Win & Pl
OR89 H103						
Chase		10	1	2	–	£6,606
All Jumps races		23	1	3	3	£9,146
3/05	Chep	3m Cls4 Ch good				£3,900
GF-HRD 0-0-0	GS-HVY 0-5-15		Course 0-1-1		Dist 1-2-12	

2 Dec Chepstow 3m Cls4 85-109 Ch Hcap £3,904
11 ran SOFT   18fncs Time 6m 32.10s (slw 37.10s)
1 Ironside 7 10-9 b¹ ....Joe Tizzard 7/1
2 Surefast 11 9-10 ....Keiran Burke (3) 33/1
3 Back In Business 6 10-7 ......Paul Moloney 3/1J
6 **CINNAMON LINE** 10 10-13 ......Tony Evans 20/1
held up and behind, good headway
approaching 5 out, ridden and weakened 4 out
[RPR83 TS58 OR96] [op 16/1]
Dist: 5-6-8-1-4   RACE RPR: 106+/93+/93+
Racecheck: Wins - Pl - Unpl 1

2 Nov Towcester 2m6f Cls4 75-99 Ch Hcap £3,904
9 ran GD-SFT   16fncs Time 5m 38.10s (slw 11.10s)
1 Bay Island 10 11-10 tp ....Paul Moloney 6/4F
2 Blazing Hills 10 11-12 p ...Andrew Thornton 16/1
3 Never Awol 9 10-12 p ....Tom Messenger (5) 7/1
7 **FULL ON** 9 11-2 ....W T Kennedy (3) 12/1
chased leader to 7th, weakened approaching 3
out btn 35 lengths [RPR73 TS72 OR92][op 14/1]
F **CINNAMON LINE** 10 11-9 ....Tom Doyle 9/1
held up, behind when fell 5th
[OR96] [op 10/1 tchd 11/1 & 8/1]
Dist: 9-12-2¹/₂-2-nk   RACE RPR: 115+/107+/85
Racecheck: Wins - Pl 1 Unpl 10

18 Apr Chepstow 3m Cls4 83-106 Ch Hcap £4,229
10 ran GOOD   18fncs   Time 6m 2.10s (slw 7.10s)
1 Sissinghurst Storm 8 10-3 .....Henry Oliver 4/1F
2 Lucky Leader 11 10-1 b ...Owyn Nelmes (3) 17/2
3 Ebony Jack 9 10-6 p ....Joe Tizzard 8/1

Happy Shopper

5 **HAPPY SHOPPER** 6 11-8 .Tom Scudamore 6/1
prominent, ridden 13th, weakened approaching
5 out [RPR97 TS97 OR102]
7 **CINNAMON LINE** 10 11-4 ....Tom Doyle 8/1
held up in mid-division, blundered and lost
place 9th, short-lived effort approaching 5 out
btn 25 lengths [RPR87 TS85 OR98] [tchd 17/2]
Dist: nk-hd-4-11-6   RACE RPR: 95+/95+/96
Racecheck: Wins 1 (1) Pl 2 Unpl 10

Moscow Leader — 10-13

8-y-o *ch g* Moscow Society - Catrionas Castle
(Orchestra)
B N Pollock   Mr A Merriam (7)

Placings: 1F/P43/625572P-PP933

		Starts	1st	2nd	3rd	Win & Pl
OR87 H107						
Chase		21	1	3	4	£14,419
All Jumps races		31	4	5	7	£27,507
95	3/04	Carl	3m Cls3 Nov 89-101 Ch Hcap heavy			
						£7,182
102	12/03	Weth	2m4¹/₂f Cls4 Nov 81-102 Hdl Hcap good			
						£3,168
95	12/03	Kels	2m6¹/₂f Cls4 Nov 71-95 Hdl Hcap soft			
						£2,755
	8/03	Cttml	2m6f Cls4 Nov Hdl good			£4,102
			Total win prize-money £17,208			
GF-HRD 0-2-3	GS-HVY 2-3-13		Course 0-0-1		Dist 1-3-10	

8 Dec Southwell 3m¹/₂f Cls3 89-106 Ch Hcap £7,332
6 ran GD-SFT   19fncs Time 6m 41.70s (slw 35.70s)
1 Sharp Belline 9 11-7 ....David O'Meara 7/2
2 Sound Of Cheers 9 11-7 t Adrian Scholes (5) 18/1
3 **MOSCOW LEADER** 8 10-2 p Mr A Merriam (7) 8/1
left 2nd and 4th, led 6th until headed after 9th,
stayed close up, every chance when blundered
14th, weakening and mistake next, left poor 3rd
16th [RPR54 TS26 OR88] [op 9/1 tchd 10/1]
F **FARINGTON LODGE** 8 10-11 Barry Keniry 11/4
chased leader until fell 4th [OR91] [op 7/2]
Dist: 19-32   RACE RPR: 117+/103/54
Racecheck: Wins - Pl - Unpl -

30 Nov Market Rasen 3m4¹/₂f Cls4 86-107 Ch Hcap
£4,554
5 ran SOFT   16fncs Time 8m 8.40s (slw 1m 0.40s)
1 Kilbeggan Blade 7 11-12 ....Jason Maguire 5/4F
2 Kitski 8 11-12 ....G Lee 2/1
3 **MOSCOW LEADER** 8 10-4 p Mr A Merriam (7) 8/1
led, mistake 9th, headed after 3 out, lost place
approaching 2 out, kept on to take modest 3rd
run-in [RPR89 TS15 OR92] [op 14/1]
Dist: 3¹/₂-14-2¹/₂-14   RACE RPR: 125+/120+/89
Racecheck: Wins 1 (1) Pl - Unpl 2

23 Nov Uttoxeter 3m Cls5 67-93 Ch Hcap £3,253
14 ran HEAVY   14fncs Time 7m 2.30s (slw 1m 16.30s)
1 Southerndown 13 10-6 ....W T Kennedy (3) 14/1
2 Dr Mann 8 10-12 ....Leighton Aspell 4/1
3 Pip Moss 11 9-9 t oh5 ...Gerard Tumelty (5) 50/1
7 **FULL ON** 9 11-3 ....Mark Bradburne 10/1
chased leaders, 6th and outpaced when
blundered 3 out, soon weakened
btn 34 lengths [RPR76 OR84]
9 **MOSCOW LEADER** 8 11-4 p Mr A Merriam (7) 25/1
with leaders, led 4th to 8th, weakened 11th,
tailed off btn 95 lengths [RPR8 OR92]
Dist: 3-nk-9-13-8   RACE RPR: 87/87/75
Racecheck: Wins 1 (1) Pl 3 Unpl 2

Form Reading	**LITTLE VILLAIN**
Spotlight	Beaten 24 lengths when 100/1 runner up here in October 2006 (2m5f Heavy).
Handicap Ratings	Mark of 82 when finishing second in October 2006 (see Spotlight) but down to mark of 74 today making horse 12lb out of the weights.
Significant Items of Form	Eight year old with no victories and working on Spotlight's information, current campaign goes back to at least 2nd place in October at Uttoxeter, which has been followed by three disappointing runs in Class 4 Chases (two of them at Uttoxeter).
Verdict	All the indicators are of a horse which has passed the point of peak fitness and is in need of a break or alternatively a lower class event.
Decision:	DISMISS.

Form Reading	**JOHNSONS SWALLOW**
Spotlight	Tailed off/pulled up on all three tries over fences.
Handicap Ratings	Raced off a mark of 115 for Handicap debut three outings ago (NB Spotlight information incorrect) when distant 4th and down to a mark of 110 for last outing when pulled up. Down to a mark of 100 today so handicapper not impressed.
Significant Items of Form	Eight year old with one Maiden Hurdle victory in Ireland. Pulled up in last outing, a Class 3 Chase at Sandown 01.12.06, and in its two previous runs in Class 4 Chases in October and November, was beaten 69 lengths and 46 lengths.
Verdict	No reason for optimism.
Hence:	DISMISS.

Form Reading	**CINNAMON LINE**
Spotlight	Seems happiest at Chepstow, scene of sole Chase success (3m Good).
Handicap Ratings	Ran off a mark of 104 six outings ago when 5th but marks for next five outings were 98 and 96. Today's mark of 89 indicates a good degree of leniency by handicapper.
Significant Items of Form	Ten year old with one Class 4 victory over 3 miles at Chepstow (Good) March 2005. All form on Good to Soft and Heavy and two runs at today's course have produced one top three placing. Current campaign started on 02.11.06 following a six month break and resulted in a fall at the fifth fence at Towcester. Next and last run on 02.12.06 in a Class 4 Handicap Chase over 3 miles at Chepstow (Soft) resulted in a 6th of 11, beaten 24 lengths, after making good headway 5 out before weakening.
Verdict	Bearing in mind Towcester run was only around one third of the scheduled distance due to its fall, the horse's last run was therefore its first completed race after its six months break and one that can be viewed as very satisfactory and part of the process of getting fully race fit. Decision, logical to expect an improvement in performance this outing, so a top three placing a definite possibility.
Decision:	SELECT.

Form Reading	**MOSCOW LEADER**
Spotlight	Best effort for current yard when 17 lengths, 3rd of 5 at Market Rasen on penultimate start (3m5f Soft).
Handicap Ratings	Ran off a mark of 97 six outings ago (pulled up) which has steadily reduced to a mark of 89 last outing and down to 87 today. Handicapper obviously feels performance on a downward trend at present.
Significant Items of Form	Eight year old with one Class 3 Novice Handicap Chase victory at Carlisle (Heavy) over 3 miles, March 2004, plus three previous Class 4 Hurdle victories from 2m4½f to 2m6½f. Impossible to determine from *Racing Post* information when current campaign started but has had three Handicap Chases from 3 miles to 3m4½f between 23.11.06 and 08.12.06, the last one being a Class 3 event where 3rd of 6, beaten 51 lengths, after blundering the fourteen fence when having every chance.
Verdict	Although form reads as if it has hit a flat spot, this horse is finishing its races and as an eight year old it looks entitled to win again, given the right conditions. Has won on Heavy and on left hand tracks, so probably too dangerous to assume it will finish out of the top three places.
Decision:	SELECT.

Overall Comment

One of those contests when you look at the race card, the placings and the betting and you immediately get a feeling that an 'outsider' could prevail.

The dismissal of Little Villain and Johnston's Swallow was straightforward and the selection of Cinnamon Line was a confident one because you always like to see some demonstration of fitness in at least one of the horse's most recent runs.

However in the case of Moscow Leader, the selection was far from confident because whilst you could detect no significant recent demonstration of race winning fitness the horse's age and win record led you to believe it was too dangerous to leave out. Such situations are always a big dilemma because you know you are looking at a wide open contest and at the same time you appreciate you could make half a dozen selections and still not pick the winner.

On this occasion the sensible decision seemed to be to restrict the number of selections to two because the form of the two options for a third selection, namely Pardini (longest priced course winner), or Lost in Normandy (next in line in the Betting Forecast) appeared none too impressive, although as events transpired Pardini did finish third.

For the record the Forecast Cinnamon Line with Full on (equal third favourite in the betting) paid £192.10 for the Tote Exacta and £159.52 for the Computer Straight Forecast.

EXAMPLE 11

04.11.06   Kelso – Good – Class 3 – Handicap Hurdle – 2m6½f

Winner   BILLY BUSH – 40/1

2.55 | Graham Todd Haulage And Friends Handicap Hurdle (Class 3) | ATR
RACE 5 | Winner £5,204.80 | 2m6½f

£8000 guaranteed For 4yo+ Rated 0-125 Weights raised 1lb Minimum Weight 10-0 Penalties after October 28th, a winner of a hurdle 7lb Totally Scottish's Handicap Mark 120 Entries 22 pay £20 Penalty value 1st £5,204.80 2nd £1,528 3rd £764 4th £381.60

1 55-1162 **TOTALLY SCOTTISH** [7]   10 11-12
b g Moto-Glenfinlass   James Reveley (7) [123]
K G Reveley   The Phoenix Racing Co

2 /P90P-P **YOUR A GASSMAN** (IRE) [187]   8 11-12
b g King's Ride-Nish Bar   T J Dreaper (3) [117]
Ferdy Murphy   W J Gott

3 108/FP- **BILLY BUSH** (IRE) [271]   7 11-2
b g Lord Americo-Castle Graigue   P J McDonald (5) [116]
Ferdy Murphy   Oakview Racing

4 73931-1 **SILENT BAY** [182]   7 10-12
b g Karinga Bay-Lady Rosanna   Paddy Aspell [122]
J Wade   John Wade

5 -460938 **COLOURFUL LIFE** (IRE) [16]   10 10-9
ch g Rainbows For Life-Rasmara   Dominic Elsworth [121]
K G Reveley   Andy Peake

6 7BF2-47 **MUCKLE FLUGGA** (IRE) [39]   7 10-8
ch m Karinga Bay-Dancing Dove   P J Benson (7) [122]
N G Richards   Dr Kenneth S Fraser

7 6215-52 **POWERLOVE** (FR) [170]   5 10-6
b m Solon-Bywaldor   Keith Mercer [122]
Mrs S C Bradburne   Mark Fleming & Jane Cameron

8 4P/57-0 **HAYSTACKS** (IRE) [16]   10 10-6
b g Contract Law-Florissa   Alan Dempsey
James Moffatt   Mr & Mrs A G Milligan

9 4/151-8 **PIRAEUS** (NZ) [14]   7 10-6
b g Beau Zam-Gull Mundur   Kenny Johnson [122]
R Johnson   Jimmy Rogers

10 71-4386 **TALARIVE** (USA) [45]   tp 10 10-6
ch g Riverman-Explode   Brian Hughes (5) [123]
P D Niven   Ian G M Dalgleish

11 4F0212- **PRINCE ADJAL** (IRE) [197]   6 10-2
b g Desert Prince-Adjalisa   Tom Messenger (5) [123]
Miss S E Forster   C Storey

12 5F-4331 **FLEETFOOT MAC** [132]   5 10-1
b g Fleetwood-Desert Flower   Richard McGrath [116]
B Storey   K Ferguson

2005 (13 ran) Tynedale Mrs A Hamilton 6 10-8 15/2   T J Dreaper (7) OR114

BETTING FORECAST: 5-2 Silent Bay, 11-2 Piraeus, 6 Totally Scottish, 8 Powerlove, 9 Prince Adjal, 10 Colourful Life, Talarive, 12 Muckle Flugga, 16 Fleetfoot Mac, 20 Billy Bush, 25 Your A Gassman, 50 Haystacks.

SPOTLIGHT

Totally Scottish Has run three solid races since a mid summer break (two on the Flat) and a reproduction of his latest second at Wetherby would give him a chance here, although he is vulnerable to a better treated rival.

Your A Gassman Looked a decent prospect in 2004, when he won four, including a novice chase here, but he has completely lost his way and showed nothing last season; probably wants more of a stamina test and is hard to fancy.

Billy Bush Joined this yard after a promising novice hurdle campaign in Ireland but he failed to complete in two chases early this year; handicapper hasn't done him any favours and he would probably prefer softer ground.

Silent Bay Improved with experience and he galloped his rivals into submission in a novice race at Hexham in May (3m, good to firm); feasibly treated for handicap debut, but he is a big horse and he may not be at his best after six months off.

Colourful Life Decent chaser at his peak and third over hurdles at Stratford in September (2m6.5f, good to firm) would give him a chance here, but usual partner is on Totally Scottish and he hasn't won a race for nearly two years.

Muckle Flugga Came good with two wins in the spring of 2005 and hit form at the same time this year, but well held on first run for four months recently and booking of an inexperienced 7lb claimer suggests there will be other days for him.

Powerlove Won a handicap hurdle at Ayr in March (3m0.5f, good) but handicapper has looked in control in three runs since; off since May and no surprise if he needs this run.

Haystacks Lightly raced since winning in cheekpieces at Catterick in November 2003 but 66-1 and always struggling off this mark on first run for a year at Haydock last time (3m, good); can only be watched at present.

Piraeus Won over C&D in December but was comfortably held when a well backed favourite here last month on his first start since; would probably prefer softer ground and probably best to look elsewhere.

Talarive Needs decent ground to show his best and goes well fresh so short break shouldn't present a problem, but has no secrets from the handicapper and yet to win off a mark this high.

Prince Adjal Stole a race at Ayr in March (3m1f, soft) by getting a flyer at the start but the handicapper put him up 14lb and he was unable to cope with his new mark over the same C&D last time; best watched on seasonal debut.

Fleetfoot Mac Won a novices' handicap chase on his most recent start at Hexham in June (3m1f, good to soft) but he had previously been beaten in selling handicaps over hurdles off lower marks than this; opposable here, though conditions should be fine.

VERDICT **Silent Bay** is probably the only one of these open to significant improvement but he has a six-month absence to overcome and **TOTALLY SCOTTISH**, who won't be lacking for fitness, may be the one to come out on top. [SR]

	OFFICIAL RATINGS	2.55		TODAY FUTURE		RP RATING	
	LAST SIX OUTINGS-LATEST ON RIGHT		**HANDICAP**			LATEST / BEST / ADJUSTED	
117⁵ 117⁵	— 113¹ 119⁶ 119²	Totally Scottish	....11-12 120		119	119	123 ◄
—	— 129⁰ — —	Your A Gassman	....11-12 120		—	91	117
—	— — — —	Billy Bush	....11-2 110		—	—	—
—	115⁸ 110⁹ 105⁹ 103³ 105⁸	Silent Bay	....10-12 106		122 ◄ 122	122	
100⁷ 100⁸ 100⁶	9R² 102⁴ 102⁷	Colourful Life	....10-9 103		95	124	121
99⁶	— 97¹ 103⁵ 103⁵ —	Muckle Flugga	....10-6 102		103	122	122
110⁵ 110⁴ 112⁸	110⁶ 108⁷ 100⁶	Powerlove	....10-6 100		122 ◄ 124	122	
—	— — — —	Haystacks	....10-6 100		—	65	—
95⁸	85⁴ 85¹ 92⁶ 92¹ 100⁸	Piraeus	....10-6 100		53	123	122
95⁸	93¹ 101⁴ 100³ 101⁸ 101⁶	Talarive	....10-6 100		38	123	123 ◄
—	— 8¹⁰ 81² 82¹ 96²	Prince Adjal	....10-2 96		115	126 ◄ 123 ◄	
—	— — 92³ 92³ —	Fleetfoot Mac	....10-1 95		—	116	116

Haystacks   10-6

10-y-o b g Contract Law - Florissa (Persepolis)
James Moffatt   Alan Dempsey

Placings: 7/75634/1516/4P/57-0

OR **100** F40   Starts 1st 2nd 3rd   Win & Pl
All Jumps races 27   4   2   £19,811
104   11/03   Catt   3m1½f Cls3 91-108 Hdl Hcap gd-fm .....
     £4,147
99   5/03   Ctml   2m6f Cls3 94-118 Hdl Hcap gd-fm £5,866
103   5/00   Ctml   2m6f Cls3 97-121 Hdl Hcap gd-fm £3,721
      3/00   Kels   2m2f Cls4 Nov Hdl 4yo gd-sft £2,386
      Total win prize-money £16,100
GF-HRD 2-0-5   GS-HVY 2-1-10   Course 1-2-5   Dist 2-1-6

19 Oct Haydock 2m7¹⁄₂f Cls4 93-114 Hdl Hcap £4,554
11 ran   GOOD   12hdls   Time 5m 55.20s (slw 20.20s)
1 Gidam Gidam 4 11-7 p ....Phil Kinsella (5) 7/1
2 Sha Bihan 5 11-4 ....Robert Thornton 7/1
3 Michaels Dream 7 11-10 b .Wilson Renwick 14/1
6 HAYSTACKS 10 10-11 ...
.................................James Reveley (7) 15/2
held up, ridden and weakened after 4 out
btn 34 lengths [RPR76 TS46 OR105] [op 9/1]

10 HAYSTACKS 10 10-13 .....Alan Dempsey 66/1
reminders after 6th, always behind
btn 62 lengths [RPR43 TS17 OR100]

Dist: 1³⁄₄-1-14-5-5   RACE RPR: 119+/109+/113
Racecheck: Wins - Pl - Unpl 2

11 May 05 Perth 3m1½f Cls3 87-113 Hdl Hcap £5,577
10 ran   GOOD   12hdls   Time 5m 58.50s (slw 13.50s)
1 Thoutmosis 6 11-9 ....Gary Berridge (3) 3/1F
2 Political Sox 11 10-11 .....Gareth Thomas (7) 16/1
3 Speed Kris 6 11-6 p ....Mark Bradburne 4/1
7 HAYSTACKS 9 11-7 ....Jim Crowley 12/1
held up, headway and prominent before 2 out, soon ridden and beaten
btn 22 lengths [RPR89 TS69 OR108] [op 14/1]

Dist: 1¹⁄₂-3¹⁄₂-13-shd-¹⁄₂ RACE RPR: 117+/107/105
Racecheck: Wins - Pl 2 Unpl 13

30 Apr 05 Hexham 2m4¹⁄₂f   Cls3 96-122 Hdl Hcap
      £4,901
12 ran   GOOD   10hdls   Time 5m 5.40s (slw 12.40s)
1 River Mist 6 10-0 oh1 ....Wilson Renwick 20/1
2 Wet Lips 7 11-7 t ....Henry Oliver 7/1
3 Hugo de Perro 10 10-11 p Peter Buchanan (3) 40/1
5 HAYSTACKS 9 11-0 ....Jim Crowley 33/1

behind, struggling 5th, rallied before 2 out, no impression [RPR43 TS46 OR100]

Dist: 2¹⁄₂-3-11-15-12   RACE RPR: 100+/118/108
Racecheck: Wins 1 Pl 5 Unpl 14

Your A Gassman   11-12

8-y-o b g King's Ride - Nish Bar (Callernish)
Ferdy Murphy   T J Dreaper (3)

Placings: 7222/11211U69/P90P-P

OR **120**   Starts 1st 2nd-3rd   Win & Pl
Hurdles 7   2   3   –   £11,708
All Jumps races 19   5   4   1   £33,588
12/04   Kels   3m1f Cls3 Nov Ch gd-sft £8,015
11/04   Newc   3m Cls3 Nov Ch good £8,320
5/04   Ctml   3m2f Cls4 Nov Hdl good £3,566
5/04   Prth   2m4f Cls4 Mdn Hdl good £4,280
5/03   Sthl   2m1f Cls6 NHF 4-6yo gd-fm £2,079
      Total win prize-money £26,260
GF-HRD 1-0-1   GS-HVY 1-1-5   Course 1-1-3   Dist 0-1-1

1 May Sedgefield 3m4f Cls3 99-125 Ch Hcap £12,485
12 ran   GOOD   22fncs   Time 7m 9.40s (slw 24.40s)
1 Devil's Run 10 10-12 ....Paddy Aspell 4/1 J
2 Dark Ben 6 10-4 ....Dougie Costello (3) 9/1

3 Theatre Knight 8 10-7 ....Peter Buchanan 6/1
P **YOUR A GASSMAN** 8 11-7 b Keith Mercer 11/1
always in rear, behind when pulled up before 2 out [OR120]
Dist: 2½-4-4-3-dist RACE RPR: 125+/117/113
Racecheck: Wins 2 (1) Pl 4 Unpl 3

25 Feb Newcastle 4m1f Cls2 111-137 Ch Hcap £46,478
17 ran HEAVY 22fncs Time 9m 3.80s (slw 40.80s)
1 Philson Run 10 11-6 ....G Lee 10/1
2 High Cotton 11 9-4 oh9 James Reveley (10) 12/1
3 Korelo 8 11-4 ....Timmy Murphy 7/2F
P **YOUR A GASSMAN** 8 11-0 b Keith Mercer 33/1
midfield, driven and outpaced 17th, never dangerous after, tailed off when pulled up before last [OR125]
Dist: 1¼-½-1¼-dist-13 RACE RPR: 143+/120/140+
Racecheck: Wins 1 Pl 5 Unpl 19

9 Dec 05 Cheltenham 3m Cls2 129-155 Hdl Hcap £14,392
19 ran GD-SFT 12hdls Time 5m 56.80s (slw 18.80s)
1 Attorney General 6 10-3 ow2 Jason Maguire 9/1
2 Fire Dragon 4 10-3 ....Richard Johnson 8/1
3 Oodachee 6 10-0 oh2 ....D J Casey 4/1F
14 **YOUR A GASSMAN** 7 10-0 oh9 ....Brian Harding 66/1
behind most of way
btn 46 lengths [RPR89 TS36 OR129]
Dist: ½-1¼-4-5-2½ RACE RPR: 138+/137/134+
Racecheck: Wins 2 (2) Pl 7 Unpl 11

Billy Bush 11-2
7-y-o *b g Lord Americo - Castle Graigue (Aylesfield)*
Ferdy Murphy P J McDonald (5)
Placings: 0435108/FP-

OR110	Starts	1st	2nd	3rd	Win & Pl
Hurdles	6	1	-	1	£8,522
All Jumps races	9	1	-	1	£8,522

1/05 Thur 2m6f Nov Hdl soft £7,351
GF-HRD 0-0-0 GS-HVY 1-1-8 Course 0-0-0 Dist 1-0-2

6 Feb Sedgefield 2m5f Cls4 Ch £4,229
9 ran SOFT 14fncs Time 5m 34.30s (slw 34.30s)
1 Vicario 5 10-3 ....S J Craine (5) 100/30
2 Henry's Pride 6 10-11 ...Paddy Merrigan (5) 12/1
3 Dark Ben 6 10-11 ....Dougie Costello (5) 9/4F
P **BILLY BUSH** 7 10-11 ....T J Dreaper (5) 3/1
prominent, hit 3rd and next, ridden along and mistake 9th, soon behind and pulled up before 4 out (jockey said gelding never travelled) [tchd 100/30]
Dist: 2-½-dist-3½-25 RACE RPR: 113/122+/118
Racecheck: Wins 1 (1) Pl 1 Unpl 10

30 Jan Southwell 3m½f Cls4 Ch £5,332
8 ran GOOD 19fncs Time 6m 32.70s (slw 26.70s)
1 Shining Strand 7 11-5 ....Andrew Tinkler 3/1
2 Classic Rock 7 11-5 ....Andrew Thornton 66/1
3 Great As Gold 7 11-5 b ....Wilson Renwick 9/2
F **BILLY BUSH** 7 11-0 ....T J Dreaper (5) 8/1
chased leaders, disputing 2nd when fell 12th [op 11/2]
Dist: dist-hd RACE RPR: 132+/87/87
Racecheck: Wins 1 (1) Pl 3 Unpl 7

28 Mar 05 Fairyhouse 2m4f Hdl £9,234
18 ran SOFT 11hdls Time 5m 11.50s (slw 31.50s)
1 Major Vernon 6 11-12 ....R Walsh 11/2
2 In Compliance 5 11-10 ....B J Geraghty 6/4F
3 Simon 6 11-12 ....Mark Grant 8/1
8 **BILLY BUSH** 6 11-12 ....P Carberry 16/1
never a factor, kept on one pace from 3 out
btn 43 lengths [RPR85 OR113]
Dist: shd-20-nk-2½-3 RACE RPR: 128/126/108
Racecheck: Wins 2 Pl 2 Unpl 18

Fleetfoot Mac 10-1
5-y-o *b g Fleetwood - Desert Flower (Green Desert)*
B Storey Richard McGrath
Placings: U451008P/5F-4331

OR95 F55	Starts	1st	2nd	3rd	Win & Pl
Hurdles	11	1	-	2	£4,171
All Jumps races	14	2	-	2	£7,749

90 6/06 Hexm 3m1f Cls4 Nov 79-105 Ch Hcap gd-sft £3,578
12/04 Uttx 2m Cls5 Nov Sell Hdl 3yo heavy £2,366
Total win prize-money £5,944
GF-HRD 0-1-2 GS-HVY 2-0-9 Course 0-0-0 Dist 0-0-0

25 Jun Hexham 3m1f Cls4 Nov 79-105 Ch Hcap £3,578
11 ran GD-SFT 19fncs Time 6m 35.10s (slw 27.10s)
1 **FLEETFOOT MAC** 5 10-5 Dominic Elsworth 14/1
chased leaders, hit 2nd and 7th, led before 3 out, drew clear before last, stayed on well
[RPR97 TS83 OR90] [op 16/1]
2 The Masareti Kid 9 10-0 b oh3 Paddy Aspell 7/1
3 Trovaio 9 10-1 ....Peter Buchanan 9/2
Dist: 6-7-5-½ RACE RPR: 97+/83/78+
Racecheck: Wins 1 (1) Pl 3 Unpl 9

7 Jun Sedgefield 2m5½f Cls5 75-101 Sell Hdl Hcap £6,506
14 ran GD-FM 10hdls Time 5m 7.20s (slw 12.20s)
1 Moyne Pleasure 8 10-12 ....Kenny Johnson 9/2F
2 Crosby Dancer 7 10-0 .....P J McDonald (5) 11/2
3 **FLEETFOOT MAC** 5 11-3 Dominic Elsworth 10/1
prominent, lost place halfway, rallied before 2 out, kept on from last, not reach first two
[RPR89 TS68 OR92] [op 9/1]
Dist: shd-1½-4-4-½ RACE RPR: 86/79/89
Racecheck: Wins 1 (1) Pl 4 Unpl 10

24 May Sedgefield 2m1f Cls5 69-95 Cond Sell Hdl Hcap £2,082
15 ran GOOD 6hdls Time 4m 2.40s (slw 10.90s)
1 Crosby Dancer 7 10-1 .....P J McDonald (3) 14/1
2 From Little Acorns 10 11-6 Keith Mercer (3) 33/1
3 **FLEETFOOT MAC** 5 11-9 ....Brian Hughes 10/1
headway 4th, stayed on from 2 out, took moderate 3rd soon after last
[RPR89 TS78 OR92] [tchd 9/1]
Dist: 2½-8-shd-¾-3½ RACE RPR: 79/96/89+
Racecheck: Wins - Pl 3 Unpl 17

Form Reading	**HAYSTACKS**
Spotlight	Lightly raced since winning in cheek pieces at Catterick, November 2003.
Handicap Ratings	Handicap marks for last six outings ranging from 112 down to 100 on latest run; mark of 100 today.
Significant Items of Form	Ten year old with three Class 3 and one Class 4 Hurdle victories on Good to Firm and Good to Soft between March 2000 and November 2003 at Kelso, Cartmel (two) and Catterick, from 2m2f to 3m1½f. Only six runs since last win with two moderate outings in Class 3 Handicap Hurdles in the spring of 2005, followed by an eighteen month break before running again two weeks ago in a Class 4 event at Haydock when beaten 62 lengths, finishing 10th of 11 over 2m7½f.
Verdict	It would appear that horse must have experienced problems in getting back to racing and no evidence to feel optimistic today.
Decision:	DISMISS

Form Reading	**YOUR A GASSMAN**
Spotlight	Decent prospect 2004 but has completely lost his way and showed nothing last season.
Handicap Ratings	Only one handicap mark of 129 for outing three races ago (unplaced). Mark of 120 today.
Significant Items of Form	Eight year old with two Chase victories (Class 3) and two Hurdle victories (Class 4) all in 2004, plus one Bumper win 2003. Last win 3m1f Chase was at Kelso but placings in eight runs since then have been very poor with 3 pulled ups and 1

unseated and a best placing of 6th. Last two runs in a Class 2 and a Class 3 Handicap Chase in February and May 2006 resulted in pulled ups.

Verdict   Nothing in recent form to suggest a return to winning ways is on the cards.

Hence: DISMISS.

Form Reading   **BILLY BUSH**

Spotlight   Joined this yard after a promising Novice Hurdle campaign in Ireland, but failed to complete two Chases early this year.

Handicap Ratings   No handicap ratings from previous six runs, allocated a mark of 110 for today.

Significant Items of Form   Seven year old with one Irish Hurdle victory over 2m6f on Soft January 2005, which judging by the prize money (£7,351) was a decent event. Last Hurdle race in Ireland was in March 2005 when 8th of 18 over 2m4f on Soft in a £9234 event. Off the track for ten months before running in two Class 4 Chases at Southwell, 3m½f, Soft and Sedgefield 2m5f, Soft, falling at the 12th when 2nd in the former (30.01.06) and pulled up in the latter (06.02.06).

Verdict   Always beware horses moving over from Ireland and always be prepared to give them time to adapt to the British climate and scene. Nine months break since last run and though no evidence that goes well fresh, there is a decent chance that the break, plus a return to hurdling, will rekindle enthusiasm and spark a return to form. Top three placing a reasonable possibility.

Hence: SELECT.

Form Reading   **FLEETWOOD MAC**

Spotlight   Won a Novice Handicap Chase on most recent start at Hexham in June 2006.

Handicap Ratings   Mark of 92 for last two Handicap Hurdles which were two and three outings ago when placed 3rd on both occasions. Mark of 95 today.

Significant Items of Form   Five year old with one Class 4 Handicap Chase victory at Hexham in June 2006 (last outing) on Good to Soft, plus one Class 5 Selling Hurdle victory at Uttoxeter on Heavy, December 2004. The last two runs before Hexham victory were two 3rd places in Class 5 Selling Hurdles over 2m5½f Sedgefield, Good to Firm (07.06.06) and 2m1f Sedgefield, Good (24.05.06).

Verdict   Bearing in mind the horse is five years old you have to ask the question as to why the trainer has opted for a Class 3 event when last two Hurdle runs were in Class 5 events. Having won at Hexham and Uttoxeter, today's course (also left handed), distance and ground should suit and though no evidence that goes well fresh, it is probably safe to assume that trainer's decision is based on belief that horse could run well, particularly as running off bottom weight.

Decision: SELECT.

Overall Comment

Because of two non runners the field of 10 was an ideal size to provide value for money bets with a very reasonable chance of a result.

The form of both Billy Bush and Fleetwood Mac was not outstanding but sufficiently good to make a top three placing a reasonable possibility. In the case of Billy Bush, a reasonable Irish record, followed by a period of adaptation in Britain before gaining success, is a familiar story and one which should be committed to the memory cells for future reference purposes.

The forecast Billy Bush and Totally Scottish (paid £179.20 for the Tote Exacta and £177.77 for the Computer Straight Forecast) was definitely achievable considering that, by removing Piraeus (non runner) from the equation, the first two paper favourites were Silent Bay and Totally Scottish (course winner).

A reverse forecast involving the two System selections, plus the two paper favourites, would have secured the Forecast.

The same result could also have been achieved by selecting the first two Course Winners at the front end of the Betting Forecast (Totally Scottish and Prince Adjal) and pairing them with the two System selections. Given the fact that Prince Adjal finished 3rd, it is worth mentioning the fact that the Tricast was achievable as well.

EXAMPLE 12

21.10.06   Chepstow – Good to Soft – Class 3 – Handicap Chase – 3m
Winner   MR DOW JONES – 33/1

4.05 RACE 6

John And Iris Watts
Remembrance Day Handicap Chase
(Class 3)
Winner £6,506   ATR   3m

£10000 guaranteed For 4yo+ Rated 0-125 Weights raised 4lb Minimum Weight 10-0 Penalties after October 14th, a winner of a chase 7lb Squires Lane's Handicap Mark 119 Entries 21 pay £15 Penalty value 1st £6,506 2nd £1,910 3rd £955 4th £477

1 565216- SQUIRES LANE (IRE) [169] [D]
b g Mister Lord-Perks Glory
Andrew Turnell M Tedham
Mark Grant   7 11-12   (116)

2 6P434P- VICTORY GUNNER (IRE) [185] [C][D]
ch g Old Vic-Gunner B Sharp
C Roberts Ron Bartlett & F J Ayres
Lee Stephens(5)   8 11-10   (126)

3 37F5U-4 TRUST FUND (IRE) [14] [D]
ch g Rashar-Tuney Blade
R H Alner Tim Collins
Robert Walford   8 11-9   (130)
3RD 7/2

4 33371-2 NO GUARANTEES [15]
b g Master Willie-Princess Hotpot
N A Twiston-Davies Mrs M Slade And G MacEchern
Tony Evans   6 11-7   (126)
9/2 2ND

5 U65412- SHARP JACK (IRE) [182]
b g Be My Native-Polly Sharp
R T Phillips Bellflower Racing Ltd
Wayne Hutchinson   8 11-6   (129)

6 761F55- EVEN MORE (IRE) [166] [D]
b g Husyan-Milan Moss
R H Alner G Keirle
Andrew Thornton   11 11-6   (127)

7 128-FP7 BEAUCHAMP PRINCE (IRE) [14] [C][D]
gr g Beauchamp King-Katie Baggage
M Scudamore The Yes - No - Wait Sorries
Tom Scudamore   5 11-3   (119)

8 -113231 SUNGATES (IRE) [6] [C][D]
ch g Glacial Storm-Live It Up
Evan Williams The Blue Yonder Partnership
Paul Moloney   10 11-3   (130)

9 9/74-1 OVER THE BLUES (IRE) [16] [D]
b g Bob Back-Fiona's Blue
Jonjo O'Neill John P McManus
A P McCoy   6 11-0   (127)

10 26/P14- MALJIMAR (IRE) [191]
b g Un Desperado-Marble Miller
Nick Williams Mrs Jane Williams
David Dennis   6 10-9

11 2/8-2P6 MR DOW JONES (IRE) [58] [D]
b g The Bart-Roseowen
W K Goldsworthy Mrs L A Goldsworthy
Richard Johnson   14 10-4   (120)
33/1

BETTING FORECAST: 4 No Guarantees, 9-2 Sungates, Trust Fund, 11-2 Over The Blues, 6 Sharp Jack, 10 Victory Gunner, 12 Beauchamp Prince, 16 Maljimar, Squires Lane, 20 Even More, 25 Mr Dow Jones.

SPOTLIGHT

Squires Lane Couldn't win a maiden point in Ireland but done better under Rules, though they went pretty slow in the modest 3m beginners chase he won at Southwell in February; found wanting only start since in April and questionable how well treated he is for handicap debut.

Victory Gunner Well equipped for a slog through the mud round here, two good hurdle wins over this trip and decent effort when fourth in the Midlands National considering his inexperience; well beaten on reappearance last three seasons though.

Trust Fund Hasn't stood much racing and had his good and bad days but encouraging return to action here earlier in the month and not badly treated on his best form; decent chance.

No Guarantees Winning pointer at this trip though mostly raced at shorter over hurdles; decent first try over fences at Carlisle recently considering he ran into potentially useful sort and way he finished suggests he's worth another try at this trip; chance.

Sharp Jack Hurdle winner who didn't linger long over the smaller obstacles; already made his mark over fences and not going to have any problems with the trip on this surface so main question is how straight he is (needed run after year off in 2005, won on reappearance in 2004).

Even More Won after a summer break this time three years ago but has needed the run twice since and generally kept to much easier tracks so not hard to have reservations.

Beauchamp Prince Run some good races here in the past, including on testing ground, and better for recent run here after a break (well behind Trust Fund), but had problems with jumping and may be best watched.

Sungates String of decent efforts and wins for new connections on different ground surfaces; this the stiffest track he's raced on for them but won here over hurdles off this mark last February and couldn't rule out despite penalty.

Over The Blues No great shakes in three novice hurdle runs but made light of a year's absence and step up in trip when winning on handicap debut at Worcester recently; jumping faces tougher test on this stiffer track and do well to overcome these more experienced rivals.

Maljimar Promising in handful of runs for Henrietta Knight, novice hurdle winner in March; sold relatively cheaply since (9,000gns) but has potential off this mark now chasing for interesting new yard even if good deal to prove under these conditions.

Mr Dow Jones Run well here in the past but only one respectable effort in four runs since coming back from long absence and best watched.

VERDICT Several of interest here with **Sungates** high on the list though he's usually given more time between his races. **TRUST FUND** handles plenty of cut and should give a good account after an encouraging return here two weeks ago.[EMW]

OFFICIAL RATINGS LAST SIX OUTINGS-LATEST ON RIGHT	4.05 HANDICAP		TODAY	FUTURE	RP RATING LATEST / BEST / ADJUSTED		
— — — — — —	Squires Lane	11-12	119		107	109	116
123⁶ 126ᴾ 123⁴ 123³ 122⁴ 120ᴾ	Victory Gunner	11-10	117		—	129	126
122³ 119⁷ 116ᶠ 120⁵ 117ᵁ 117⁴	Trust Fund	11-9	116		124	134 ◄	130 ◄
— — — — — 111²	No Guarantees	11-7	114		126	126	126
110⁷ 109⁶ 107¹ 114² 114⁵ 114⁵	Sharp Jack	11-6	113		129 ◄	129	129
— — — — — —	Even More	11-6	113		126	127	127
— 113² — 119⁶ 119ᴾ 116⁷	Beauchamp Prince	11-3	112		107	119	119
85¹ 95¹ 106³ 106² 104³ 103¹	Sungates (7x)	11-3	110	-7	126	128	130 ◄
— — — — — 99¹	Over The Blues	11-0	107		127	127	127
— — — — — —	Maljimar	10-9	102		—	—	—
— — 104⁶ 99² 99ᴾ 99⁶	Mr Dow Jones	10-4	97		—	120	120

Mr Dow Jones **10-4**

14-y-o *b g The Bart - Roseowen (Derring Rose)*
W K Goldsworthy Richard Johnson

Placings: 1134216292/132/8-2P6

OR97 H105	Starts	1st	2nd	3rd	Win & Pl
Chase	41	9	5	9	£46,526
All Jumps races	46	10	7	10	£54,437

	4/04	NAbb	3m3f Cls4 Nov Hdl good	£3,465
108	2/04	Font	3m2½f Cls4 82-108 Ch Hcap good	£6,773
	5/03	Uttx	2m7f Cls6 Am Hunt Ch heavy	£3,017
	5/03	Hrfd	3m1½f Cls6 Am Hunt Ch good	£1,568
	4/02	Chel	3m2½f Cls6 Am Hunt Ch good	£5,798
	3/02	Hrfd	3m1½f Cls6 Am Hunt Ch good	£1,929
	2/02	Hrfd	3m1½f Cls6 Am Hunt Ch heavy	£1,866
	4/01	Hrfd	2m3f Cls6 Am Hunt Ch good	£2,720
	2/01	Ludl	3m Cls6 Am Hunt Ch gd-sft	£2,629
	4/99	Chep	3m Cls6 Am Hunt Ch heavy	£3,599
			Total win prize-money	£33,364

GF-HRD 0-2-9 GS-HVY 4-8-20 **Course** 1-2-3 **Dist** 2-7-11

24 Aug Fontwell 3m2½f Cls4 73-103 Ch Hcap £4,554
6 ran GD-FM 19fncs Time 6m 35.20s (slw 6.20s)
1 Waynesworld 8 11-9 ex7 .John Kington (7) 2/1F
2 Montys Tan 8 11-9 ....Christian Williams 9/4
3 Just Reuben 11 10-0 oh6 ..Tom Scudamore 4/1
6 **MR DOW JONES** 14 11-12 Timmy Murphy 10/1
held up, lost touch 14th, tailed off
[OR99] [tchd 11/1]
Dist: 8-18-11-9-69 RACE RPR: 117+/102+/61
Racecheck: Wins 1 (1) Pl 1 Unpl 3

4 Jun Hereford 3m1½f Cls4 78-104 Ch Hcap £5,205
15 ran GD-FM 17fncs Time 6m 22.70s (slw 10.70s)
1 **SUNGATES** 10 10-7 ....Paul Moloney 10/1
held up in mid-division, headway approaching 13th, led soon after last, driven out
[RPR105 TS89 OR85] [op 8/1 tchd 11/1]
2 Terrible Tenant 7 10-2 .....Richard Young (3) 7/1
3 Paddy The Optimist 10 9-9 ....Tom Messenger (7) 4/1F
P **MR DOW JONES** 14 11-7 ....Jamie Moore 16/1
held up in mid-division, headway 9th, ridden 11th. weakened 13th. tailed off when pulled up before 2 out (jockey said gelding lost both front shoes) [OR99] [op 14/1]
Dist: ¾-9-21-6-8 RACE RPR: 105/102/90
Racecheck: Wins 5 (4) Pl 6 Unpl 12

26 May Stratford 3m4f Cls3 99-125 Ch Hcap £8,801
10 ran SOFT 21fncs Time 7m 28.40s (slw 40.40s)
1 Elvis Returns 8 10-13 ex7 ..T J Dreaper (3) 7/2F
2 **MR DOW JONES** 14 10-0 ....Jamie Moore 50/1
held up towards rear, progress 9th, went 2nd 15th, led before 17th, driven and headed 3 out, one pace and soon no chance with winner
[RPR96 TS76 OR99] [op 40/1]
3 Around Before 9 11-7 t ....A P McCoy 7/1
P **BEAUCHAMP PRINCE** 5 10-13 ....Tom Scudamore 15/2
jumped very poorly in rear, no chance after blunder 14th, tailed off and pulled up 18th
[OR119] [tchd 8/1]
Dist: 9-3-29-27 RACE RPR: 130+/96/114
Racecheck: Wins - Pl - Unpl 11

Form Reading	**MR DOW JONES**
Spotlight	Run well here in the past.
Handicap Ratings	Four outings ago ran off a mark of 104 (finished 8th) that was reduced to 99 for next three races, which included one 2nd place. Slight reduction to 97 today, which has given it bottom weight.
Significant Items of Form	Fourteen year old with seven Hunters Chase victories and more recently in 2004 one Class 4 Handicap Chase victory 3m2½f Fontwell and one Class 4 Novice Hurdle victory 3m3f Newton Abbot. Course record consists of one win and two top three places in six outings. Majority of form has been on Good to Soft – Heavy which includes four wins and eight top three places. In current season finished good second on 26.05.06 in Class 3 Handicap Chase at Stratford 3m4f (Soft) followed nine days later by a Class 4 Handicap Chase at Hereford 3m1½f (Good to Firm) when pulled up before 2 out after losing both front shoes. Next and last outing was on 24.08.06 when 6th of 6 in a 3m2½f Class 4 Handicap Chase at Fontwell on Good to Firm.
Verdict	Fourteen year old whose 2nd at Stratford on 26.05.06 in a Class 3 event demonstrates that the horse has not lost its enthusiasm. Last run on Good to Firm at Fontwell can be discounted because it was not its ground, but a return to Chepstow where it has won before on Heavy going and running off bottom weight should suit well. Having been given a two month break to get over its last run has every chance of securing a place in the top three.
Decision:	SELECT.

Overall Comment

This race has been included because fourteen and fifteen year olds are frequently discounted by the odds compilers, pundits and punters simply on account of their age and as a result they go off at long prices despite the fact that they are still very capable of winning given the right set of conditions.

In Mr Dow Jones' case, he has an excellent record, albeit the majority of these have been Hunter Chases, and so it was simply a question of gauging whether the horse's form and the race conditions were both likely to be right. Mr Dow Jones' Chase record was the best of all the runners in the race, so it made sense to back it for the win and also to pair it with something else for the Forecast.

On this occasion, pairing Mr Dow Jones with the first three favourites in the Betting Forecast would have produced a Tote Exacta return of £153.70 or a Computer Straight Forecast return of £183.60, either of which would have made the exercise very worthwhile.

The messages to be gleaned from this race are: always give careful consideration to fourteen and fifteen year olds; try to determine whether they still have ability and enthusiasm; try and gauge whether the race conditions are right, and finally, try and assess whether the timing of the contest, having regard to the horse's form displayed in the horse's most recent outings, is going to be right for what you perceive to be the horse's current level of form.

EXAMPLE 13

10.12.06   Musselburgh – Good – Class 5 – Handicap Chase – 2m4f
Winner   BLACK CHALK – 11/1

12.20 Musselburgh News Amateur Riders' Handicap Chase (Class 5)   RUK
RACE 1   Winner £3,123   2m4f

£5000 guaranteed For 4yo+ Rated 0-95 Weights raised 3lb Minimum Weight 10-9 Penalties after December 2nd, a winner of a chase 7lb Barracat's Handicap Mark 91 Entries 29 pay £15 Penalty value 1st £3,123 2nd £968.50 3rd £484 4th £242

1	08P/841 **BARRACAT** (IRE) ¹⁶ ⓒⒹ		9 11-12	
	b g Good Thyne-Helens Fashion	Mr C Dawson(7)	96	
	W T Reed Roman Wall Racing			
2	36F-145 **TAGAR** (FR) ¹⁹		9 11-11	
	b g Fijar Tango-Fight For Arfact	Mr T Greenall(7)	102	
	C Grant Lord Daresbury			
3	644-533 **SCOTMAIL LAD** (IRE) ¹⁹³ Ⓓ		p 12 11-7	
	b g Ilium-Nicholas Ferry	Mr C Mulhall(3)	109	
	C A Mulhall Mrs C M Mulhall			
4	88-5313 **YANKEE HOLIDAY** (IRE) ¹⁶ 🏳		6 11-6	
	b g Oscar-Parloop	Mr D England	98	
	Mrs S C Bradburne Robb Cooper McIntosh & Hardie			
5	4P-0855 **SPORTS EXPRESS** ¹⁶		v 8 11-6	
	ch m Then Again-Lady St Lawrence	Mr D Oakden(7)	102	
	Miss Lucinda V Russell Powrie Valentine & McManus Brothers			
6	FU00-6P **HARRY THE DEALER** (IRE) ^{245 (8P)}		p 7 11-5	
	b g King Luthier-Ballygunaghan Babe	Mr C P Huxley(7)	82	
	Gerard Keane (IRE) F Sheedy			
7	P0-FUP8 **BARCHAM AGAIN** (IRE) ⁷		p 9 11-3	
	b g Aristocracy-Dante's Thatch	Mr J E Clare(7)		
	Mrs C J Kerr Mrs C J Kerr			
8	P44U-06 **SUPER DOLPHIN** ³¹		7 10-12	
	ch g Dolphin Street-Supergreen	Mr H Challoner(7)	99	
	R Ford Barrow Brook Racing			
9	60F/0P- **BLACK CHALK** (IRE) ^{631 (225U)}		8 10-12	
	br g Roselier-Ann's Cap	Mr N McParlan(5)		
	Daniel J P Barry (IRE) Mrs Tracey O'Hara			
10	F-7P071 **POLITICAL CRUISE** ⁴ Ⓓ		8 10-7	
	b g Royal Fountain-Political Mill	Mr M Ellwood(7)	109	
	R Nixon Rayson & Susan Nixon			
11	5-36F6P **GOODBADINDIFFERENT** (IRE) ¹⁵ Ⓓ		10 10-7	
	b/br g Mandalus-Stay As You Are	Mr H Haynes(7)	102	
	Mrs J C McGregor The Good To Soft Firm			
12	-28783P **CLASSIC CALVADOS** (FR) ¹⁶		tp 7 10-7	
	b/br g Thatching-Mountain Stage	Mr S W Byrne(7)	103	
	Mrs S A Watt David H Cox			
13	P434PP2 **GUNSON HIGHT** ¹⁶		t 9 10-7	
	b g Be My Chief-Glas Y Dorlan	Miss J Riding(7)	96	
	W Amos J L Gledson			
14	13U-1U9 **GOLLINGER** ³⁵		10 10-3	
	b g St Ninian-Edith Rose	Mr R Tierney(5)	107	
	P D Niven R H R Tierney			

2005 (10 ran) Bohemian Spirit N G Richards 7 11-9 13/8F   Miss R Davidson (3) OR95

BETTING FORECAST: 9-2 Barracat, 6 Gunson Hight, Political Cruise, 7 Scotmail Lad, Tagar, Yankee Holiday, 10 Classic Calvados, 14 Gollinger, Harry The Dealer, Super Dolphin, 20 Goodbadindifferent, Sports Express, 25 Black Chalk, 66 Barcham Again.

SPOTLIGHT

Barracat Good ground bumper winner who bettered modest hurdle form when beating a reliable yardstick on chase debut over C&D last time; 11lb higher in the weights but open to improvement and has claims.

Tagar Not the most consistent but won in heavy ground (also won on good) over 2m at Uttoxeter in May and seems to stay this longer trip; below best on latest start and, although yard back among winners this week, may find one or two too good.

Scotmail Lad Hasn't won over regulation fences for over three years but won point last year and far from disgraced when third to two subequent winners when last seen in May; place claims again if fully wound up after break.

Yankee Holiday Showed a good attitude to beat a couple of subsequent winners at Hexham on penultimate start (2m on fast ground) but didn't get home having failed to settle (set strong pace) over 2m at this course last time; will have to settle better if he is to see out this longer trip.

Sports Express Modest and inconsistent performer who has yet to win under any code in 32 starts; has a pull in the weights with Barracat on latest run over C&D but surprise if it's enough to enable her to better placings.

Harry The Dealer Point winner in 2004 but hasn't scored since and form over regulation fences is modest at best; cheekpieces on for the first time but one to watch unless there's significant market support.

Barcham Again Dual 3m chase winner in 2004 but missed whole of last year and well beaten all outings in 2006; returns to fences but isn't easy to recommend.

Super Dolphin Point and hurdle winner who hasn't been at best on two starts this year; far from certain to appreciate the step up to this trip and best watched at present.

Black Chalk Has achieved little over hurdles and failed to complete on last two starts in Irish points (ran out penultimate start); plenty to prove on debut over regulation fences.

Political Cruise Isn't very consistent but notched third win over hurdles (all in heavy ground) in amateur riders event at Hexham earlier this week and can race from 8lb lower mark over fences; obvious chance from handicapping perspective but 2m4f on good ground round here represents a very different test, unless there has been a real deluge by post time.

Goodbadindifferent Inconsistent chaser who is back on a fair mark and, as a 2m4f fast-ground Perth chase winner last year, should have conditions to suit; hasn't shown much of late but can't rule out from this mark in this company.

Classic Calvados Another inconsistent sort and yet to win in 26 career starts; creditable effort in eventful Leicester handicap over this trip on fast ground penultimate run but long way below that level behind Barracat over C&D last time with cheekpieces back on (on again); remains one to tread carefully with.

Gunson Hight Hurdle winner on second start in 2003 but hasn't scored since and isn't the most reliable; however, creditable effort over 2m at this course last time and shouldn't be inconvenienced by return to this trip; not one for maximum faith but can't rule out in ordinary event.

Gollinger Error-prone chaser over regulation fences but is a dual point winner on good ground this year; however, well beaten under similar conditions after break on first run for yard at Market Rasen last time and has nothing to prove.

VERDICT Not too many of these are reliable betting propositions and a hike in the weights may not be enough to prevent **BARRACAT** from following up his recent C&D win. As that was his first run over fences, there is almost certainly better to come and he looks highly likely to go close. At bigger odds, **Goodbadindifferent** wouldn't be without a chance. [RY]

OFFICIAL RATINGS									TODAY FUTURE	LATEST / BEST / ADJUSTED
LAST SIX OUTINGS-LATEST ON RIGHT						**12.20** HANDICAP			RP RATING	
—	—	—	—	—	80¹	Barracat	11-12	91	96	96
93³	93⁶	92^F	88¹	94⁴	92⁵	Tagar	11-11	90	80	102	102
—	94⁴	90⁴	89⁵	87³	87³	Scotmail Lad	11-7	86	104 ◀ 104	105 ◀
—	—	—	—	74¹	85³	Yankee Holiday	11-6	85	96	96	98
—	91^P	—	—	90⁵	90⁵	Sports Express	11-6	85	87	102	102
—	—	—	—	—	—	Harry The Dealer	11-5	84	82	82	82
96^P	93⁰	89^F	89^U	—	—	Barcham Again	11-3	82	—	—	—
85^P	85⁴	84⁴	92^U	82^U	81⁶	Super Dolphin	10-12	77	93	93	99
—	—	—	—	—	—	Black Chalk	10-12	77	—	—	—
—	80⁷	75^P	—	—	—	Political Cruise	10-7	72	—	119 ◀ 109 ◀
—	87³	87⁶	84^F	78⁶	77^P	Goodbadindifferent	10-7	72	—	102	102
—	—	—	—	75³	79^P	Classic Calvados	10-7	72	—	103	103
—	64³	69⁴	—	—	70²	Gunson Hight	10-7	72	96	96	96
—	—	—	—	—	76³	Gollinger	10-3	68	68	68	107

Barcham Again 11-3

9-y-o b g Aristocracy - Dante's Thatch (Phardante)
Mrs C J Kerr Mr J E Clare (7)

Placings: U85633FP1P1/P0-FUP8

		Starts	1st	2nd	3rd	Win & Pl
OR82 H80						
Chase		13	2	–	2	£11,967
All Jumps races		22	2	1	2	£13,063
90 5/04 Ludl	3m Cls4 Nov 81-100 Ch Hcap good					£6,773
						Total win prize-money £10,738
83 3/04 Hrld	3m1½f Cls4 64-90 Ch Hcap good					£3,965
GF-HRD 0-0-1	GS-HVY 0-2-13	Course 0-0-0		Dist 0-1-4		

3 Dec Kelso 2m6½f Cls4 Nov 79-105 Hdl Hcap £3,220
16 ran HEAVY 11hdls Time 6m 6.50s (slw 51.50s)
1 Witch Wind 6 11-0 ....Mr M Ellwood (7) 6/1
2 Stagecoach Opal 5 11-5 Michael O'Connell (7) 15/2
3 Super Revo 5 10-5 p ......Dominic Elsworth 11/1
8 **BARCHAM AGAIN** 9 9-12 p ow2 ....
..........................Declan McGann (5) 150/1
behind, driven halfway, never on terms
btn 88 lengths [RPR3 TS4 OR82] [op 100/1]
Dist: 5-29-9-5-16 RACE RPR: 108 +/109 +/58
Racecheck: Wins - Pl - Unpl -

17 Nov Kelso 2m6½f Cls4 84-108 Hdl Hcap £2,928
15 ran GD-SFT 11hdls Time 5m 48.70s (slw 33.70s)
1 Windy Hills 6 11-10 ....Tony Dobbin 5/1
2 Kempski 6 10-1 b ....Alan Dempsey 13/2
3 Crackleando 5 10-4 ......P J McDonald (5) 16/1
P **BARCHAM AGAIN** 9 9-11 p ow2 oh4 ....
..........................Declan McGann (5) 200/1
always behind, tailed off when pulled up before
3 out [OR86] [op 150/1]
Dist: 1-9-¾-6-7 RACE RPR: 113/89/88
Racecheck: Wins - Pl - Unpl 11

18 May Perth 3m Cls4 87-113 Ch Hcap £6,506
12 ran SOFT 18fncs Time 6m 53.90s (slw 56.90s)
1 Burwood Breeze 10 11-8 ....P J Brennan 6/1
2 Very Very Noble 12 10-13 t .Neil Mulholland 16/1
3 **GOODBADINDIFERENT** 10 10-0 oh10 ....
..............................Keith Mercer 33/1
behind, mistake and reminders 6th, headway
and remote third before 4 out, no impression
before next (jockey received caution: used whip
with excessive force) [RPR34 OR87]
U **BARCHAM AGAIN** 9 9-11 b ....
..........................Declan McGann (5) 40/1
behind, no chance when mistake and unseated
rider 12th [OR89]

Dist: 9-54-17 RACE RPR: 125 +/101/34
Racecheck: Wins - Pl 1 Unpl 13

Black Chalk 10-12

8-y-o br g Roselier - Ann's Cap (Cardinal Flower)
Daniel J P Barry (IRE) Mr N McParlan (5)

Placings: 060/F/OP-

		Starts	1st	2nd	3rd	Win & Pl
OR77 H82						
All Jumps races		4	–	–	–	–
GF-HRD 0-0-0	GS-HVY 0-0-4	Course 0-0-0		Dist 0-0-1		

29 Apr Taylorstown (PTP) 3m Open Mdn
11 ran FIRM Time 6m 25.00s
1 Poolbouy Lad 8 12-0 ....J T Keeling 7/1
2 Jack Monday 7 12-0 ....J Smyth 6/4F
3 Mr Ejecta 7 12-0 ....J W Farrelly 12/1
P **BLACK CHALK** 8 12-0 ....N McParlan 6/1
lft @ start, cto til pu 7 out
Dist: ½-15-4-5-8 RACE RPR: 82/81/56
Racecheck: Wins - Pl 2 Unpl 3

25 Feb Farmaclaffley (PTP) 3m Open Mdn
18 ran SOFT Time 7m 18.00s
1 Its All About Luck 7 12-0 ....J W Farrelly 5/1
2 Willie's Opinion 8 12-0 ......P McAleese 4/1
3 Glenwilliam 9 12-0 ....C Cully 14/1
O **BLACK CHALK** 8 12-0 ....N McParlan 8/1
prom til ro 4th
Dist: 15-20-¾-dist-20 RACE RPR: 81/61/41
Racecheck: Wins - Pl 1 Unpl 7

19 Mar 05 Newcastle 2m4f Cls4 Nov 69-95 Hdl Hcap £2,751
10 ran HEAVY 9hdls Time 5m 26.80s (slw 43.80s)
1 Lady Past Times 5 10-10 ....Jim Crowley 10/1
2 Nifty Roy 5 10-10 ....P Robson 28/1
3 Casas 8 10-5 t ....Mr S F Magee (7) 20/1
F **BLACK CHALK** 7 10-13 ....Paul Moloney 5/2
close up going well, led 4 out, headed before 2
out, 8 lengths down and weakening when fell
last [RPR66 OR82] [op 5/1 tchd 9/4]
Dist: 2-13-6 RACE RPR: 77 +/75/65 +
Racecheck: Wins - Pl 3 Unpl 12

Sports Express 11-6

8-y-o ch m Then Again - Lady St Lawrence (Bering)
Miss Lucinda V Russell Mr D Oakden (7)

Placings: /4P4554/22/P34P-0855

		Starts	1st	2nd	3rd	Win & Pl
OR85 H90						
Chase		5	–	–	1	£1,050
All Jumps races		20	–	6	1	£7,788
GF-HRD 0-0-2	GS-HVY 0-6-14	Course 0-0-1		Dist 0-4-12		

24 Nov Musselburgh 2m4f Cls4 Nov 79-105 Ch Hcap £3,904
12 ran GOOD 16fncs Time 5m 4.50s (slw 11.50s)
1 **BARRACAT** 9 9-10 ....Tom Greenway (5) 40/1
always close up, led 5 out, ridden along 3 out,
stayed on well approaching last
[RPR94 TS29 OR80] [op 50/1]
2 Three Mirrors 6 11-12 ....G Lee 11/10F
3 Ebac 5 11-2 t ....P J Brennan 20/1
5 **SPORTS EXPRESS** 8 10-11 v ....
..........................Peter Buchanan 28/1
held up in midfield, headway and in touch 5 out,
soon ridden and no impression from next
[RPR79 TS14 OR90] [op 20/1]
P **CLASSIC CALVADOS** 7 9-9 tp oh4 ....
..........................Phil Kinsella 12/1
chased leaders, ridden along and weakened 5
out, pulled up before next [OR79] [tchd 14/1]
Dist: 12-7-4-1½-11 RACE RPR: 94 +/111 +/92 +
Racecheck: Wins - Pl - Unpl 1

15 Nov Hexham 2m4½f Cls4 81-99 Ch Hcap £4,229
8 ran SOFT 15fncs Time 5m 34.60s (slw 34.60s)
1 Uneven Line 10 10-8 p ....Neil Mulholland 8/1
2 Posh Stick 9 11-6 ....S J Craine (3) 11/4
3 Ruggtah 5 10-9 b ....Tony Dobbin 13/2
5 **SPORTS EXPRESS** 8 11-3 v¹ Peter Buchanan 16/1
held up, struggling before 10th, never on terms
[RPR40 OR90]
Dist: 6-29-15-11 RACE RPR: 94 +/105 +/70 +
Racecheck: Wins - Pl - Unpl 2

27 Oct Uttoxeter 3m Cls4 82 105 Hdl Hcap £4,229
9 ran SOFT 12hdls Time 6m 17.50s (slw 37.50s)
1 Chickapeakray 5 11-7 ....S J Craine (3) 7/2J
2 Bdellium 8 10-0 ....Chris Honour (3) 10/1
3 Wayward Melody 6 10-5 p ....
.............................Wayne Kavanagh (7) 11/2
8 **SPORTS EXPRESS** 8 11-2 Richard Johnson 12/1
led 2nd, hit 6th, headed next, lost place 8th,
tailed off next
btn 100 lengths [RPR- TS9 OR95] [tchd 14/1]
Dist: 2-1-1½-5-36 RACE RPR: 111 +/84/93 +
Racecheck: Wins - Pl - Unpl 2

Form Reading	**BARCHAM AGAIN**
Spotlight	Dual 3 mile Chase winner in 2004 but missed whole of last year and well beaten in all outings in 2006.
Handicap Ratings	On a mark of 96 six outings ago which reduced to a figure of 89 three outings ago, its last Handicap Chase. Down to a mark of 82 today which means the handicapper is none too impressed and has displayed leniency.
Significant Items of Form	Eight year old with two Class 4 Handicap Chase victories over 3 miles and 3m1½f on Good in 2004 but only six runs since then, with a best placing of 8th and four failures to complete. Current campaign, which has consisted of two runs on 17.11.06 and 03.12.06 in Class 4 Hurdle races at Kelso, has resulted in a pulled up and 8th of 16, beaten 88 lengths.
Verdict	Poor form has lasted two and a half years now and no sign that a return to chasing will do the trick even though it is a Class 5 event.
Decision:	DISMISS.

Form Reading	**BLACK CHALK**
Spotlight	Has achieved little over hurdles and failed to complete on last two starts in Irish Points.

Handicap Ratings	No handicap chase ratings. Allocated a mark of 77 for today's contest, the value of which is impossible to interpret.
Significant Items of Form	Eight year old with only six runs to its name and no victories. Irish trained and last two runs on 25.02.06 and 29.04.06 have been in Irish Points where ran out at 4th on Soft and then pulled up on Firm. However its most recent run prior to that was in a Class 4 Novice Handicap Hurdle at Newcastle on 19.03.05 over 2m4f on Heavy when still leading 3 out before weakening and falling at the last when 8 lengths down.
Verdict	Always beware the Irish Raider and in this case you have got to be very suspicious about a horse that has been brought all the way over from Ireland for a Class 5 Chase after a seven and a half month break, which was preceded by two indifferent Point to Points, but an encouraging run in a Class 4 Novice Handicap Hurdle at Newcastle. Decision, this is one of those cases where it is not what the form says, it is what it doesn't say that is important. There is a clue to the horse's potential ability in its Newcastle run, albeit a Handicap Hurdle, and that is enough to suppose that the horse's last two runs in Point to Points can be regarded as misleading. All the signs are that this horse if far too dangerous to leave out of the reckoning and this has possibly been confirmed by its board price of 11/1, compared with the Forecast price of 25/1.
Hence:	SELECT.

Form Reading	**SPORTS EXPRESS**
Spotlight	Modest and inconsistent performer who has yet to win under any code in 32 starts.
Handicap Ratings	Mark of 90 for last two outings when 5th on both occasions. Today's mark is 85, which appears to be a generous reduction.
Significant Items of Form	Eight year old with no wins but 8 placings of 5th or better. Last run was on 24.11.06 when 5th of 12 runners in a Class 4 Novice Handicap Chase, beaten 24½ lengths at Musselburgh (Good). It is important to note that in that race it was 'held up in midfield, headway and in touch 5 out'. The horse's two previous runs were on 15.11.06 at Hexham in a Class 4 Handicap Chase over 2m4½f on Soft, beaten 61 lengths and on 27.10.06 at Uttoxeter in a Class 4 Handicap Hurdle over 3 miles on Soft when finished 8th of 9 runners, beaten 100 lengths.
Verdict	Horse's last run at Musselburgh on 24.11.06 was solid enough and considering that was a Class 4 event, the drop in class today, coupled with a more lenient handicap mark and ground conditions that should suit, make a place in the top three a reasonable possibility.
Decision:	SELECT.

Overall Comment

I know nothing whatsoever about the Irish trainer of Black Chalk but I have seen so many races where a horse's Irish form belies the ability it shows in Britain, that I have become highly suspicious of Irish Raiders. In this particular case, the board prices on offer for Black Chalk (11/1), compared with a Betting Forecast price of 25/1, proved to be a giveaway clue, but you cannot always rely on the betting market to warn you. The clue to selection was of course the horse's Newcastle run, which was the one bright feature in an otherwise pretty dismal form record. The selection of Sports Express was a fairly straightforward affair, which coupled with Black Chalk in a Tote Exacta, paid £527.40 and for the Computer Straight Forecast paid £314.71.

EXAMPLE 14

03.03.07   Newbury – Soft – Class 3 – Handicap Chase – 3m

Winner   GREEN BELT FLYER – 20/1

2.40 RACE 3	VC Casino.com Handicap Chase (Class 3) Winner £10,020.80	CH4 3m

£16000 guaranteed **For** 5yo+ Rated 0-130 **Minimum Weight** 10-0 **Penalties** after February 24th, a winner of a chase 7lb **The Duckpond's Handicap Mark** 130 **Entries** 21 pay £70 **Penalty value** 1st £10,020.80 2nd £2,960 3rd £1,480 4th £740.80 5th £369.60 6th £185.60

1 FPF1/1- **THE DUCKPOND** (IRE) 445 ☐
ch g Bob's Return-Miss Gosling
J A B Old   W E Sturt
10 11-12   Jason Maguire (132)

2 230-885 **GREEN BELT FLYER** (IRE) 49 20/1
b g Leading Counsel-Current Liability
Miss Venetia Williams   Green Belt Foresters
9 11-12   Sam Thomas (130)

3 8B54535 **FOOL ON THE HILL** ☐
b g Reprimand-Stock Hill Lass
P J Hobbs   Louisville Syndicate
10 11-3   Richard Johnson (137)

4 315P-1P **NYKEL** (FR) 42 ☐
ch g Brier Creek-Une Du Chatelier
A King   The Unlucky For Some Partnership
6 11-2   Wayne Hutchinson (138)

5 P0-0U46 **HARRYCONE LEWIS** 70 2 v/o
b g Sir Harry Lewis-Rosie Cone
Mrs P Sly   The Craftsmen   7/1
9 11-0   Warren Marstor (136)

6 P11P-2F **YES MY LORD** (IRE) 113 ☐☐☐
b g Mister Lord-Lady Shalom
D E Pipe   D A Johnson
p8 10-10   Timmy Murphy (139)

7 56-3427 **MISS SHAKIRA** (IRE) 67
b m Executive Perk-River Water
N A Twiston-Davies   Cotswold Racing Club (Crc)
9 10-6   Tony Evans (139)

2006 (11 ran) Presenting Express Miss E C Lavelle 7 10-7 9/2   Marcus Foley OR111

BETTING FORECAST: 5-2 Yes My Lord, 4 Nykel, 9-2 The Duckpond, 11-2 Fool On The Hill, 6 Miss Shakira, 7 Harrycone Lewis, 10 Green Belt Flyer.

The Duckpond Won both completions over jumps, maiden hurdle at Newton Abbot nearly two years ago, then back from longish break to make good impression on chase debut at Warwick 15 months ago; delicate but promising and yard in good order so wouldn't necessarily assume he can't go well after the absence.

Green Belt Flyer Smart Irish form at shorter but well below that level in handful of runs in Britain over the last year or so, no improvement for the refitting of blinkers latest; much to prove taking big step up in trip.

Fool On The Hill Gone well here in the past but rather lacklustre at around this trip these days, including in blinkers latest; handicapper giving him a great chance but not doing quite enough to fancy at present.

Nykel Handles this ground and basically progressive chaser, though didn't jump well enough to do himself justice at Wincanton latest and eventually pulled up; something to prove after that but wouldn't surprise us to see him resume progress.

Harrycone Lewis Slight concern about ground as he's seemed best with sharper conditions in the past but on fair mark and went close in this race two years ago; one to bear in mind as he can go well fresh.

Yes My Lord Progressive last spring until below par at Fontwell in April; disappointing when wasn't up to giving 5lb to Mr Dow Jones at Stratford in October (odds-on) and none the wiser about current handicapping after falling at halfway when last seen in first-time cheekpieces at Cheltenham in November; Timmy Murphy back up and might resume upward curve.

Miss Shakira Not had much racing at this trip but stayed it perfectly well over hurdles on slow ground at Uttoxeter in the autumn; since run well back at shorter over fences and though below par when last seen on Boxing Day she's got possibilities off her light weight.

VERDICT These fences jump particularly well and that may help **Nykel** after a disappointing round of jumping at Wincanton last time. He can do a lot better here and is respected, along with **Yes My Lord**, but it will be interesting to see how **THE DUCKPOND** gets on after his break. He looked pretty useful when winning at Warwick last winter and his stable is in good form now.[EMW]

	OFFICIAL RATINGS LAST SIX OUTINGS-LATEST ON RIGHT					**2.40**	**HANDICAP**	TODAY FUTURE		RP RATING LATEST / BEST / ADJUSTED		
						The Duckpond	11-12	130	—	—	132	
135²	—	140⁰	140⁶	138⁵	135⁵	Green Belt Flyer	11-12	130	+100	123	130	
136⁶	135⁵	130⁴	129⁶	125³	123⁶	Fool On The Hill	11-3	121	115 ◄	154 ◄	137	
104³	104¹	112⁶	112⁶	112¹	121⁰	Nykel	11-2		—	138	138	
120⁰	—	—	120¹	120⁴	—	Harrycone Lewis	11-0	118	—	125	136	
—	—	—	100¹	109⁰	109²	Yes My Lord	10-10	114	—	139	139 ◄	
—	110⁶	—	—	107²	127	Miss Shakira	10-6	110	88	139	139 ◄	

Green Belt Flyer   11-12

9-y-o b g Leading Counsel - Current Liability (Caribo)

Miss Venetia Williams   Sam Thomas

Placings: 417/8746412FP230-885

OR**130**H130	Starts	1st	2nd	3rd	Win & Pl
Chase	21	3	2	1	£39,519
All Jumps races	32	6	3	3	£68,794

119 10/05 Naas 2m3f 98-129 Ch Hcap soft £9,234
     3/05 Naas 2m Nov Ch yld-sft £8,331
     1/05 Tram 2m Ch sft-hvy £5,146
122 2/04 Naas 2m 91-122 Hdl Hcap yield £9,169
    12/03 Gowr 2m Nov Hdl 4-8yo yiekl £6,273
     6/03 Baln 2m Mdn Hdl 4-5yo sft-hvy £4,705
          Total win prize-money £42,858

GF-HRD 0-2-2 GS-HVY 6-3-27 Course 0-0-1 Dist 0-0-0

13 Jan Warwick 2m   Cls3 110-135 Ch Hcap £6,506
5 ran   HEAVY   12fncs   Time 4m 8.10s (slw 18.10s)
1 Madison Du Berlais 6 11-5 Tom Scudamore 11/10F
2 Offemont 6 10-1 b ....Tom Doyle 9/2
3 No Visibility 12 10-7 t ....Robert Walford 8/1
5 **GREEN BELT FLYER** 9 11-12 b Sam Thomas 7/1
led to 5th, weakened 7th
    [RPR98 TS62 OR135]   [op 11/2]
Dist: 14-13-16-10   RACE RPR: 144+/116+/105
Racecheck: Wins 2 (2) Pl - Unpl 3

9 Dec 06 Cheltenham 2m½af Cls2 124-146 Ch Hcap
                                                        £12,526
10 ran   SOFT   14fncs   Time 4m 20.80s (slw 21.80s)
1 Kalca Mome 8 11-1 ....Richard Johnson 9/2
2 Bohemian Spirit 8 9-13 Miss R Davidson (5) 12/1
3 Baby Run 6 11-6 ....Tony Evans 5/1
8 **GREEN BELT FLYER** 8 11-4 ....T P Treacy 20/1
in touch from 5th, hit 10th, never dangerous after

btn 30 lengths [RPR121 TS110 OR138][op 16/1]
Dist: 2-6-9-6-4   RACE RPR: 147/134/148+
Racecheck: Wins 1 (1) Pl 1 Unpl 8

25 Nov 06 Newbury 2m1f   Cls2 118-142 Ch Hcap
                                                        £21,921
9 ran   SOFT   13fncs   Time 4m 17.70s (slw 13.70s)
1 Saintsaire 7 10-11 ....R Walsh 15/8F
2 Bambi de L'Orme 7 11-5 ....David Dennis 5/1
3 Whispered Secret 7 10-11 ......R J Greene 9/1
8 **GREEN BELT FLYER** 8 11-10 Alan O'Keeffe 16/1
chased leader, challenged from 5th until led 7th, headed 4 out, soon weakened
    btn 70 lengths [RPR80 TS61 OR140][tchd 14/1]
Dist: 1¾-1¼-1½-11-shd RACE RPR: 140+/143/134
Racecheck: Wins 2 (2) Pl 1 Unpl 8

Harrycone Lewis   11-0

9-y-o b g Sir Harry Lewis - Rosie Cone (Celtic Cone)

Mrs P Sly   Warren Marston

Placings: 1P212/2F96121P0-0U46

OR**118**H119	Starts	1st	2nd	3rd	Win & Pl
Chase	14	4	2	1	£31,439
All Jumps races	30	6	5	2	£43,847

     2/06 Hntg 3m2f Cls4 Nov Hdl good £3,904
    12/05 Hntg 3m2f Cls4 Nov Hdl good £3,310
115 1/05 Hntg 3m Cls3 97-117 Ch Hcap good £5,512
110 11/04 MRas 2m6½f Cls3 105-117 Ch Hcap soft £6,090
     2/04 Fknm 3m¹/sf Cls4 Nov Ch good £4,576
     1/04 Fknm 3m¹/sf Cls3 Nov Ch gd-sft £5,421
          Total win prize-money £28,813

GF-HRD 0-1-2 GS-HVY 2-2-15 Course 0-1-3 Dist 3-2-13

23 Dec 06 Bangor-On-Dee 3m Cls2 111-131 Hdl Hcap
                                                        £10,084
8 ran   SOFT   12hdls   Time 6m 3.00s (slw 29.00s)
1 Just Beth 10 10-10 ....Derek Laverty (5) 7/1

2 Magnifico 5 11-6 ...Andrew Glassonbury (5) 12/1
3 Carlys Quest 12 11-8 ....G Lee 9/2
6 **HARRYCONE LEWIS** 8 11-8 Warren Marston 9/1
led, headed and not fluent 4 out, soon weakened [RPR113 TS76 OR120] [tchd 10/1]
Dist: 1½-4-1¼-2-11   RACE RPR: 121/130/124+
Racecheck: Wins 2 (2) Pl 3 Unpl 7

2 Dec 06 Wetherby 3m1f Cls3 104 130 Ch Hcap £7,807
10 ran   SOFT   18fncs   Time 7m 2.00s (slw 56.00s)
1 Silver Knight 8 11-3 p ....Russ Garritty 5/2F
2 Kerry Lads 11 11-12 p ....Peter Buchanan 8/1
3 Jungle Jinks 11 10-13 ....Barry Keniry 9/1
4 **HARRYCONE LEWIS** 8 11-2 b ....
    ....Warren Marston 18/1
with leaders, outpaced 4 out, moderate 4th when blundered next, kept on from 2 out
    [RPR111 TS52 OR120]   [op 14/1]
Dist: 22-3½-1-21-17 RACE RPR: 137+/126+/108+
Racecheck: Wins 1 (1) Pl 3 Unpl 9

8 Nov 06 Bangor-On-Dee 3m¹/af Cls3 114-135 Ch
                                                        Hcap £10,141
13 ran   GD-SFT   18fncs   Time 6m 6.80s (slw 6.80s)
1 Bob Bob Bobbin 7 11-11 ....Joe Tizzard 9/1
2 Distant Thunder 8 11-8 ....Tom Doyle 9/2
3 Dunbrody Millar 8 11-2 ....T J O'Brien 12/1
U **HARRYCONE LEWIS** 8 10-11 b ....
    ....Warren Marston 50/1
chased leaders to 12th, in rear when hampered and unseated rider 2 out
    [RPR111 OR120]   [tchd 40/1]
Dist: 2-20-2-4-dist   RACE RPR: 150/145/119
Racecheck: Wins 2 (2) Pl 5 Unpl 12

Form Reading	**GREEN BELT FLYER**
Spotlight	Smart Irish form at shorter but well below that level in handful of runs in Britain over the last year or so.
Handicap Ratings	Lowest mark 135 and highest mark 140 for last five outings and with mark down to 130 today the handicapper appears to be lenient.
Significant Items of Form	Nine year old with three Irish Chase wins from 2 miles to 2m3f and three Irish Hurdle wins at 2 miles on going from Yielding to Soft – Heavy. Last Chase win was October 2005. Current campaign started on 25.11.06 at Newbury in Class 2 Handicap Chase 2m1f on Soft when 8th of 9 runners, beaten 70 lengths after leading from the 7th to 4 out. On 09.12.06 at Cheltenham (Soft) was 8th of 10 runners, beaten 30 lengths in a Class 2 Handicap Chase. Last run on 13.01.07 was at Warwick (Heavy) when last of 5 in a Class 3 Handicap Chase, beaten 53 lengths after leading to the 5th fence. Had blinkers on for that run, which have been left off for today's contest. Has had no runs at today's distance of 3 miles.
Verdict	Given the fact the horse is a transferee from Ireland, allowances can be made for its British form because it is a known fact that they can take a period of time to adapt. What is important is the fact that the horse has been finishing Class 2 Chases in Britain without being totally outclassed. Last run could be down to fitting of blinkers and is best ignored. Decision to run in a 3 mile event is obviously down to the trainer and given the fact that 2 miles to 2½ miles horses have won the Grand National, it cannot be viewed as a mistake unless events prove otherwise. Decision, Irish form is far too good to ignore and given the fact the horse is finishing his chases and the trainer is trying a different approach, there is room for optimism.
Hence:	SELECT.

Form Reading	**HARRYCONE LEWIS**
Spotlight	On fair mark and went close in this race two years ago, can go well fresh.
Handicap Ratings	Mark of 120 for last three Handicap Chase outings and down to a mark of 118 today.
Significant Items of Form	Nine year old with four Chase wins at distances around 3 miles on going varying from Good to Soft, three of which were Class 3 events and two were Handicaps. Last Chase win was January 2005 and since then has had two Class 4 Novice Hurdle wins over 3m2f at Huntingdon, the latest in February 2006. Most recent campaign goes back to at least 08.11.06 when unseated in a Class 3 Handicap Chase at Bangor, which was followed on 02.12.06 by a similar event over 3m1f at Bangor when 4th of 10, beaten 26½ lengths but 'kept on from 2 out' after blunder 3 out. Last run on 23.12.06 was in a Class 2 Handicap Hurdle, again at Bangor over 3 miles, when 6th of 8 runners, beaten 9¾ lengths. Has had three runs at Newbury with one top three placing.
Verdict	Has the ability to finish in the first three in this event and given the fact that horse has been given a seventy day break, goes well fresh and went close in this event two years ago, a SELECT decision appears to be sensible.

Overall Comment

Newbury is not on the Preferred list of racecourses but given the fact that it has already yielded a 50/1 winner in Heathcote less than a month ago, further consideration is merited when a Class 3 Handicap Chase with only 7 runners is offering a price of 20/1 on the last horse in the Betting Forecast, which had predicted a starting price of 10/1.

The first lesson to be learnt from this race is never, ever be put off by a longer price than that shown in the Betting Forecast; always let your form reading make the decisions for you.

In this particular case the two selections, which were the last two horses in the Betting Forecast, produced a Tote Exacta return of £143.60 and a Computer Straight Forecast of £140.07.

The second lesson to be learnt is that if you do notice that a Non-Preferred racecourse has started to produce long priced winners, then it is worth giving serious consideration to Preferred races that appear to have the necessary ingredients to produce an 'outsider' result.

This last statement does not mean placing bets regardless as to whether or not you are getting the right vibes; what it does mean, however, is considering the race very carefully and let the form reading exercise make the final decision as to whether to place a bet or leave the race alone.

EXAMPLE 15

03.03.07   Newbury – Soft – Class 3 – Novices Handicap Hurdle – 2m½f
Winner   STRAWBERRY – 20/1

4.20 RACE 6
VC Casino.com Novices' Handicap Hurdle (Class 3)
Winner £4,684.32
RUK
2m½f

£7200 guaranteed **For** 4yo+ Rated 0-115 Weights raised 5lb Minimum Weight 10-0 Penalties after February 24th, a winner of a hurdle 7lb **La Grande Villez's** Handicap Mark 110 Entries 45 pay £30 **Penalty value 1st** £4,684.32 **2nd** £1,375.20 **3rd** £667.60 **4th** £343.44

1 0F6331P **LA GRANDE VILLEZ** (FR) 65
   b m Villez-Grande Sultane
   A King   The Copper Bay Partnership
   5 11-12
   Wayne Hutchinson (99)

2 71B1432 **SWIFT SAILOR** 37 (D)(BF)
   gr g Slip Anchor-New Wind
   G L Moore   Mike Charlton And Rodger Sargent
   p 6 11-11
   Leighton Aspell (115)

3 FP/525- **STOOP TO CONQUER** 378 (161F)
   b g Polar Falcon-Princess Genista
   A W Carroll   Seasons Holidays
   7 11-9
   Timmy Murphy (115)

4 -5P4625 **CAPTAIN MARLON** (IRE) 37 (BF)
   b g Supreme Leader-Marionette
   C L Tizzard   Grass Roots Racing
   6 11-9
   Joe Tizzard (107)

5 20/564 **PERFECT STORM** 33
   b g Vettori-Gorgeous Dancer
   P J Hobbs   The Newchange Syndicate
   8 11-9
   Richard Johnson (111)

6 42-72P3 **STRAWBERRY** (IRE) 30
   b m Beneficial-Ravaleen
   J W Mullins   Dr R Jowett
   6 11-8
   Wayne Kavanagh(5) (107)

7 0-994 **ILLICIT SPIRIT** (IRE) 42
   ch g Pistolet Bleu-Hackler Poitin
   C R Egerton   P Byrne
   5 11-6
   J A McCarthy (109)

8 1684 **AMIR EL JABAL** (FR) 29
   b c Enrique-Premonitary Dream
   D E Pipe   Stef Stefanou
   4 11-4
   Tom Malone(3) (112)

9 59-656P **IT HAPPENED OUT** (IRE) 37
   gr g Accordion-Miss Hawkins
   J W Mullins   Mrs Sally Mullins
   6 11-2
   Andrew Thornton (107)

10 446 **RAYDAN** (IRE) 29
   b g Danehill-Rayseka
   D R Gandolfo   B R K Pain
   5 11-2
   Barry Fenton (109)

11 2541 **KICK AND PRANCE** 37
   ch g Groom Dancer-Unerring
   J A Geake   Sideways Racing III
   tp 4 11-1
   Daryl Jacob(3) (107)

12 0P592 **OISEAU DE NUIT** (FR) 12
   b g Evening World-Idylle Du Marais
   M G Rimell   Terry Warner
   5 10-11
   Jason Maguire (117)

13 906 **STRIDER** 18
   ch g Pivotal-Sahara Belle
   D C O'Brien   D C O'Brien
   6 10-11
   Mattie Batchelor (114)

14 /P-3P8B **RIDERS REVENGE** (IRE) 49
   b g Norwich-Paico Ana
   Miss Venetia Williams   Dr Moira Hamlin
   9 10-8
   Sam Thomas (114)

15 94/377- ● **PHOTOGRAPHER** (USA) 450 (33F)
   b/br g Mountain Cat-Clickety Click
   S Lycett   N E Powell
   9 10-6
   Tony Evans (114)

● PHOTOGRAPHER will only run if the ground is suitable, states trainer

2006 (14 ran) Wellbeing P J Hobbs 9 11-2 100/30   Richard Johnson OR103

BETTING FORECAST: 6 Swift Sailor, **13-2** Amir El Jabal, Stoop To Conquer, **7** Illicit Spirit, Oiseau de Nuit, Perfect Storm, **9** Kick And Prance, **12** Raydan, **14** Captain Marlon, **16** It Happened Out, La Grande Villez, Strawberry, Strider, **33** Photographer, Riders Revenge.

SPOTLIGHT

La Grande Villez Plenty of form over hurdles in France before winning debut for this yard in maiden hurdle at Fontwell during November; said to be unsuited by soft ground when pulled up on handicap debut in December which does rather raise questions about ability to handle this surface off the same mark.

Swift Sailor Never been as good over hurdles as on the Flat and would probably prefer better ground but holding his form in ordinary staying handicaps off ever-increasing marks; up another 3lb but return to this trip shouldn't bother him and should be involved in relatively uncompetitive event.

Stoop To Conquer Had an off day when last seen on the Flat in September and not translated his decent form on the level to hurdles so far, last seen over jumps a year ago; however looks more interesting on handicap debut with Timmy Murphy up as he had a decent record here on the Flat, 2-3 including on slow ground; well worth considering after break.

Captain Marlon Shown plenty of promise on slow ground in bumpers and over hurdles and though disappointing favourite on handicap debut in January, the race may have come too quickly after decent effort five days earlier; worth another chance.

Perfect Storm Not totally convinced about stamina on galloping tracks, effort petered out at Exeter on handicap debut in December and seemed to do better from off the pace at Ludlow latest; not overly well handicapped on what we've seen so far and ground may sap him.

Strawberry Held her own in competitive mares bumpers last spring and couple of fair efforts over farther since switched to hurdles; open to some improvement but has a bit to prove at the shorter trip/slower ground now handicapping.

Illicit Spirit Not show much in first two hurdle runs but more to like about recent Wincanton effort (33-1), winner won again since and probably fair effort; gives impression this more galloping track will suit now handicapping and more interesting than most.

Amir El Jabal Flat winner over extended 1m2f in French Provinces last spring, also wide-margin winner on hurdle debut at Auteuil in November; favourite for British debut in December but didn't deliver then, nor on two subsequent runs, but comes back into the picture on handicap debut off fair mark; market can guide.

It Happened Out Taken time to get his eye in over hurdles, better effort his third run when keeping on well in closing stages over C&D in December; didn't fare so well upped in trip and switched to handicap chase latest but worth another chance in handicap hurdle for first time.

Raydan Minor promise at up to 1m5f in handful of runs on the Flat in Ireland; shown a little ability over hurdles since trained in Britain and of more interest now handicapping, though may yet prove suited by easier test of stamina.

Kick And Prance Handles these conditions and winning handicap hurdle debut at Fontwell in January when having hard race in ordinary affair; tackling more galloping track and some rivals who have been nestling in the woodwork so likely work to do off 7lb higher with cheekpieces tried.

Oiseau de Nuit Very unfortunate animal, bumped into big improver who was also making handicap debut at Market Rasen last month and gone up 10lb for unavailing pursuit; winner apart, that didn't look particularly strong and remains to be seen if he's worth the mighty rise.

Strider 100-1 all three hurdle starts for this yard, but more encouragement latest (not saying much as he was beaten miles the first twice) when not beaten too far in competitive novice for the track at Folkestone latest; possibilities from strict handicapping point of view but it might flatter him.

Riders Revenge Had a disappointing winter following lengthy absence and return to hurdles didn't pay off latest, losing ground when brought down three out at Warwick in January; plenty to prove for now.

Photographer Beaten miles both starts on AW since returning from over a year off and early days for him on the comeback trail.

VERDICT **STOOP TO CONQUER** goes well fresh and has a fine strike-rate here on the Flat so he could be interesting on his handicap debut over hurdles with Timmy Murphy booked. **Amir El Jabal** is also worth a look in the market at this level for the first time.[EMW]

OFFICIAL RATINGS LAST SIX OUTINGS-LATEST ON RIGHT						4.20 HANDICAP		TODAY	FUTURE	RP RATING LATEST	BEST	ADJUSTED
—	—	—	—	—	110^{P}	La Grande Villez	11-12	110		—	99	**99**
90^{1}	96^{B}	95^{1}	103^{4}	103^{3}	106^{2}	Swift Sailor	11-11	109		112	115	**115**
—	—	—	—	—	—	Stoop To Conquer	11-9	107		—	—	**115**
—	—	—	—	—	95^{5}	Captain Marlon	11-9	107		86	107	**107**
—	—	—	—	110^{6}	108^{4}	Perfect Storm	11-9	107		111	111	**111**
—	—	—	—	—	—	Strawberry	11-8	106		104	104	**107**
—	—	—	—	—	—	Illicit Spirit	11-6	104		109	109	**109**
—	—	—	—	—	—	Amir El Jabal	11-4	110		78	112	**112**
—	—	—	—	—	—	It Happened Out	11-2	100		—	107	**107**
—	—	—	—	—	—	Raydan	11-2	100		70	109	**109**
—	—	—	—	—	100^{1}	Kick And Prance	11-1	107		107	107	**107**
—	—	—	—	—	85^{2}	Oiseau de Nuit	10-11	95		117◄	117◄	**117◄**
—	—	—	—	—	—	Strider	10-11	95		114	114	**114**
102^{P}	—	—	—	—	95^{8}	Riders Revenge	10-8	92		—	—	**114**
—	98^{9}	95^{4}	—	—	—	Photographer	10-6	90		—	—	**114**

Riders Revenge 10-8

9-y-o *b g Norwich - Paico Ana (Paico)*
Miss Venetia Williams Sam Thomas

Placings: 300/23/52BP4P/P-3P8B

OR92	Starts	1st	2nd	3rd	Win & Pl
Hurdles	8	-	1	1	£2,301
All Jumps races	16	-	2	3	£3,985

GF-HRD 0-0-0 GS-HVY 0-5-14 Course 0-0-0 Dist 0-4-9

13 Jan Warwick 2m Cls4 Nov 79-105 Hdl Hcap £3,904
12 ran HEAVY 7hdls Time 3m 58.40s (slw 21.40s)
1 Star Double 7 11-5 b ....Tony Evans 7/1
2 Florazine 6 10-2 ....W T Kennedy (3) 11/1
3 Oscar Jack 6 11-9 ....Liam Treadwell (3) 11/2
B **RIDERS REVENGE** 9 11-2 ......T J O'Brien 33/1
held up in touch, lost place 3rd, behind when brought down 5th [OR95] [op 28/1]
Dist: 3-6-9-½-1½ RACE RPR: 107+/89/104
Racecheck: Wins 1 (1) Pl 2 Unpl 7

26 Dec 06 Towcester 2m3½f Cls4 72-98 Ch Hcap £3,578
8 ran SOFT 14fncs Time 5m 32.40s (slw 41.40s)
1 Jacarado 8 10-5 v ....Henry Oliver 11/2
2 Monsieur Georges 6 10-6 ....Dave Crosse 7/1
3 Shaka's Pearl 6 11-0 ...Jay Pemberton (10) 13/2
8 **RIDERS REVENGE** 8 11-0 t Liam Treadwell (3) 6/1
in touch, soon pushed along, mistake 3rd, soon ridden, behind from 7th
btn 47 lengths [RPR50 OR89] [op 15/2]
Dist: 4-3½-6-5-8 RACE RPR: 88+/84+/96
Racecheck: Wins - Pl 1 Unpl 4

25 Nov 06 Towcester 3m1½f Cls5 69-95 Cond Ch Hcap £3,253
11 ran HEAVY 12fncs Time 6m 56.90s (slw 46.90s)
1 Tradingup 7 10-3 ....W T Kennedy 15/2
2 Levallois 10 10-7 b .....Wayne Kavanagh 100/30
3 Apple Joe 10 9-12 ex7 Willie McCarthy (3) 13/8F
P **RIDERS REVENGE** 8 11-9 Liam Treadwell (3) 14/1
held up, mistake 2nd, ridden after 4th, behind when hampered 7th, tailed off when pulled up before 3 out [OR95] [op 10/1]
Dist: 6-12-71 RACE RPR: 92+/89/72+
Racecheck: Wins - Pl 1 Unpl 14

Strider 10-11

6-y-o *ch g Pivotal - Sahara Belle (Sanglamore)*
D C O'Brien Mattie Batchelor

Placings: 906

OR95 F58	Starts	1st	2nd	3rd	Win & Pl
All Jumps races	3	-	-	-	-

GF-HRD 0-0-0 GS-HVY 0-0-3 Course 0-0-0 Dist 0-0-1

13 Feb Folkestone 2m1½f Cls4 Nov Hdl £3,253
10 ran HEAVY 8hdls Time 4m 45.80s (slw 37.80s)
1 Safari Adventures 5 11-3 ....Philip Hide 25/1
2 Kanad 5 11-10 ....Noel Fehily 7/2
3 Boyastara 4 11-0 ....R Walsh 6/1
6 **STRIDER** 6 11-3 ....Mattie Batchelor 100/1
in touch in midfield, slightly outpaced when mistake 2 out, no danger after [RPR97 TS93]
Dist: 2-5-1¼-9-5 RACE RPR: 118/123/108
Racecheck: Wins - Pl - Unpl 2

30 Jan Folkestone 2m1½f Cls4 Nov Hdl £3,253
14 ran SOFT 8hdls Time 4m 26.70s (slw 18.70s)
1 Hobbs Hill 8 11-4 ....P J Brennan 1/2F
2 William Bonney 7 11-11 ....Noel Fehily 3/1
3 Cathedral Rock 5 11-4 ......Leighton Aspell 20/1
13 **STRIDER** 6 11-1 .Robert Lucey-Butler (3) 100/1
jumped slowly 1st, last and weakening after 3rd, tailed off from next btn 118 lengths [RPR-]
Dist: 17-4-3-7-3½ RACE RPR: 137+/120/109
Racecheck: Wins 2 (2) Pl 2 Unpl 6

4 Jan Lingfield 2m½f Cls4 Nov Hdl £3,253
11 ran HEAVY 8hdls Time 4m 22.00s (slw 26.00s)
1 Grecian Groom 5 11-5 ....Noel Fehily 33/1
2 Reidwil 4 10-7 ....Timmy Murphy 33/1
3 Polinamix 4 11-0 ....Tom Scudamore 10/11F
9 **STRIDER** 6 11-5 ....Tom Siddall 100/1
always well in rear, lost touch after 5th, tailed off btn 60 lengths [RPR50 TS13]
Dist: ½-½-16-13-12 RACE RPR: 110+/97/103
Racecheck: Wins - Pl 1 Unpl 9

Strawberry 11-8

6-y-o *b m Beneficial - Ravaleen (Executive Perk)*
J W Mullins Wayne Kavanagh (5)

Placings: 242-72P3

OR106	Starts	1st	2nd	3rd	Win & Pl
Hurdles	3	-	1	1	£2,530
All Jumps races	7	-	3	1	£5,682

GF-HRD 0-0-0 GS-HVY 0-1-3 Course 0-0-0 Dist 0-2-4

1 Feb Wincanton 2m6f Cls4 Nov Hdl £3,578
17 ran GD-SFT 11hdls Time 5m 36.80s (slw 27.80s)
1 Karello Bay 6 11-1 ....Mick FitzGerald 2/5F
2 Star Award 6 11-1 ....T J O'Brien 33/1
3 **STRAWBERRY** 6 10-10 Wayne Kavanagh (5) 14/1
mid-division, headway from 7th, ridden to challenge winner approaching 2 out, lost 2nd run-in, kept on same pace
[RPR98 TS57] [tchd 12/1]
Dist: 3-3-1¼-19-2½ RACE RPR: 111+/101/98
Racecheck: Wins - Pl - Unpl 5

7 Dec 06 Huntingdon 2m4½f Cls3 Nov Hdl £5,205
16 ran GD-SFT 10hdls Time 5m 6.60s (slw 27.60s)
1 La Dame Brune 4 10-10 ....Mick FitzGerald 16/1
2 Knockara Luck 5 10-10 ....Tony Dobbin 5/1
3 Eden Linty 5 10-10 ....T J O'Brien 12/1
P **STRAWBERRY** 5 10-10 ....Jamie Moore 7/1
chased leaders until ridden and weakened 7th, blundered next, tailed off and pulled up last
[op 11/1]
Dist: 19-10-4-½-4 RACE RPR: 125+/103+/90+
Racecheck: Wins 2 Pl 3 Unpl 9

23 Nov 06 Taunton 2m3½f Cls3 Nov Hdl £6,831
12 ran GOOD 10hdls Time 4m 57.50s (slw 35.50s)
1 Tambourine Davis 4 10-10 ....Ollie McPhail 5/4F
2 **STRAWBERRY** 5 10-5 .Wayne Kavanagh (5) 3/1
tracked leaders, joined winner 7th, every chance approaching 2 out, kept on
[RPR98] [op 4/1]
3 Star Award 5 10-10 ....Timmy Murphy 9/1
Dist: 3½-4-11-15-7 RACE RPR: 105+/98+/93
Racecheck: Wins 3 (1) Pl 4 Unpl 13

La Grande Villez   11-12

5-y-o b m Villez - Grande Sultane (Garde Royale)
A King   Wayne Hutchinson

Placings: 39-030F6331P

OR110   Starts 1st 2nd 3rd   Win & Pl
Hurdles   10   1   –   4   £19,513
All Jumps races   11   1   –   4   £19,513
    11/06 Font 2m2½f Cls4 Mdn Hdl gd-sft £2,798
GF-HRD 0-0-0   GS-HVY 1-3-11   Course 0-0-0   Dist 0-0-2

28 Dec 06 Leicester 2m Cls3 99-121 Hdl Hcap £9,395
11 ran SOFT   9hdls   Time 4m 10.00s (slw 23.00s)
1 Nikola 5 11-7 ....Tony Evans 10/1
2 Dhehdaah 5 11-7 ....Warren Marston 5/2F
3 Magic Sky 6 11-7 ....Charlie Poste (5) 28/1
P LA GRANDE VILLEZ 4 11-1 Robert Thornton 11/2
   mid-division, weakened approaching 3 out,
   behind when pulled up before next (jockey said
   filly was unsuited by the soft ground)
   [OR110]   [op 7/2]
Dist: 1¾-4-1-¾-5   RACE RPR: 124+/124/121
Racecheck: Wins - Pl 3 Unpl 6

26 Nov 06 Fontwell 2m2½f Cls4 Mdn Hdl £2,798
10 ran GD-SFT   9hdls   Time 4m 47.10s (slw 33.10s)
1 LA GRANDE VILLEZ 4 10-10
   ....Robert Thornton 10/11F
   prominent, blundered 2nd, pecked 6th, led 2
   out, ridden 3 lengths ahead when mistake last,
   stayed on [RPR97 TS60]   [op 11/8 tchd 6/4]
2 Valley Hall 5 10-10 ....Dave Crosse 11/2
3 Launceston 4 10-10 ....G Lee 10/1
Dist: 6-25-3½-14-2   RACE RPR: 97+/89+/63
Racecheck: Wins - Pl - Unpl 13

Photographer   10-6

9-y-o bb g Mountain Cat - Clickety Click (Sovereign
Dancer)
S Lycett   Tony Evans

Placings: 474/5/94/377-

OR90 F53   Starts 1st 2nd 3rd   Win & Pl
All Jumps races   9   –   –   1   £370
GF-HRD 0-0-1   GS-HVY 0-1-4   Course 0-0-1   Dist 0-1-6

8 Dec 05 Taunton 2m1f   Cls3 Nov Hdl £7,319
14 ran GOOD   9hdls   Time 4m 4.70s (slw 17.70s)
1 Natal 4 11-8 t ....Mick FitzGerald 4/11F
2 Blaeberry 4 10-5 ....,.......Barry Fenton 50/1
3 Albarino 6 10-12 ....Brian Crowley 40/1
7 PHOTOGRAPHER 7 10-12 Jason Maguire 100/1
   led until 2nd, prominent, ridden and one pace
   after 3 out btn 18 lengths [RPR94 TS33 OR88]
Dist: 5-½-1¾-9-½ RACE RPR: 130+/102+/107+
Racecheck: Wins 1 (1) Pl 4 Unpl 20

26 Nov 05 Newbury 2m½f   Cls3 Nov Hdl £7,202
14 ran GOOD   8hdls   Time 3m 55.90s (slw 2.90s)
1 Natal 4 11-8 t ....R Walsh 5/2F
2 Fandani 5 11-5 ....Richard Johnson 5/1
3 Odiham 4 11-0 ....Tom Doyle 8/1

---

7 PHOTOGRAPHER 7 11-0 ....R J Greene 66/1
   chased leader until approaching 3 out, soon
   weakened
   btn 41 lengths [RPR92 TS67 OR88] [tchd 80/1]
Dist: 16-¾-9-4-6   RACE RPR: 143+/123+/116
Racecheck: Wins 2 (1) Pl 3 Unpl 17

4 Nov 05 Fontwell 2m2½f   Cls4 Hdl £2,542
9 ran SOFT   9hdls   Time 4m 40.80s (slw 26.80s)
1 Brave Spirit 7 11-0 p ....Joe Tizzard 3/1J
2 Presenting Express 6 11-0 ......Barry Fenton 4/1
3 PHOTOGRAPHER 7 11-0 ....R J Greene 10/1
   waited with, headway after 5th, led briefly 2 out,
   weakened and lost 2nd run-in
   [RPR94 TS84 OR88]   [op 12/1]
Dist: shd-12-7-3½-23 RACE RPR: 105/107+/94+
Racecheck: Wins 3 (2) Pl 3 Unpl 7

Flat Form

29 Jan Lingfield (AW) 2m Cls6 50-60 Hcap £2,389
12 ran STAND   Time 3m 22.99s (fst 1.01s)
1 Dolzago 7 9-6 b ....George Baker 3 33/1
2 Josh You Are 4 8-6 ...William Buick (7) 4 EvensF
3 Pocket Too 4 9-2 p ....Seb Sanders 1 9/1
12 PHOTOGRAPHER 9 9-9 ......L P Keniry 6 40/1
   tracked leaders, ridden on outer 3f out,
   weakened rapidly, eased, tailed off
   btn 38 lengths [RPR25 TS24 OR60] [op 50/1]
Dist: 4-1½-½-¾-nk   RACE RPR: 67/62+/63
Racecheck: Wins - Pl - Unpl 6

Form Reading	**RIDERS REVENGE**
Spotlight	Had a disappointing winter following long absence.
Handicap Ratings	Mark of 95 for last outing (brought down). Previous Handicap Hurdle mark, which was six outings ago, was 102 (pulled up). Today's mark of 92 reflects a downward trend in performance but probably insufficient to make any real difference to the horse's chances.
Significant Items of Form	Nine year old with no wins. Last six outings show three pulled ups and one brought down. Looking at most recent campaign, ran on 25.11.06 in a Class 5 Handicap at Towcester (Heavy) over 3m1½f when pulled up and again on 26.12.06 at Towcester (Soft) in a 2m3½f Class 4 Handicap Chase when last of 8, beaten 47 lengths. Next and last run was on 13.01.06 in a Class 4 Novices Handicap Hurdle over 2 miles at Warwick (Heavy) when brought down at the fifth.
Verdict	Although the horse's trainer had a winner (Green Belt Flyer) in an earlier race at this meeting, there is nothing in the published form in the *Racing Post* to show that this horse has the capability or the current form to finish in the first three places in this event.
Decision:	DISMISS.

Form Reading	**PHOTOGRAPHER**
Spotlight	Beaten by miles both starts on AW since returning from a year off.
Handicap Ratings	Handicap Hurdle marks of 98 (finished 9th) and 95 (finished 4th) for runs that were five and four outings ago. Today's mark of 92 doesn't appear generous for a horse that appears to be going nowhere at present.
Significant Items of Form	Nine year old with no wins but a 3rd of 9 runners in a Class 4 Hurdle on Soft over 2m2½f at Fontwell November 2005. Has had two National Hunt outings since then in Class 3 Novice Hurdles over 2m½f at Newbury (November 2005) Good,

and 2m1f at Taunton (December 2005) Good, beaten 41 lengths and 18 lengths respectively. Last run was on 29.01.07 when last in an All Weather Flat Race over 2 miles at Lingfield, beaten 38 lengths.

Verdict	Given the fifteen month break from National Hunt racing, and with no positives to be gleaned from last All Weather outing at the end of January 2007, it would require a leap of faith to think horse could figure at the finish on this occasion.
Decision:	DISMISS.

Form Reading	**STRIDER**
Spotlight	Not beaten too far in competitive Novice Hurdle at Folkstone latest.
Handicap Ratings	No previous Handicap Hurdle ratings. Mark of 95 for today's contest, the value of which is hard to evaluate.
Significant Items of Form	Six year old with only three outings, all of them recent, in Class 4 Novice Hurdles on either Soft or Heavy, over 2m½f or 2m1½f. Beaten 60 lengths and 118 lengths in first two races, but last outing on 13.02.06 when 6th of 10 runners on Heavy at Folkestone, beaten 22¼ lengths was a better performance.
Verdict	Although last run was an improvement, it is difficult to see further improvement being achieved in horse's first Handicap, which is in a higher Class event (Class 3 as opposed to the Class 4 events it has contested so far).
Decision:	DISMISS.

Form Reading	**STRAWBERRY**
Spotlight	Held her own in competitive mares Bumper last spring and couple of fair efforts over longer distance since switched to hurdles.
Handicap Ratings	Allocated mark of 106 for today's contest, its first Handicap, and impossible to say whether well treated or not.
Significant Items of Form	Six year old with no wins but placings record shows three second places and one third place in only seven outings. Placed 2nd at Taunton 23.11.06 in a Class 3 Novice Hurdle over 2m3½f (Good) 12 runners, beaten 3½ lengths. Ran next on 07.12.06 in a Class 3 Novice Hurdle over 2m4½f on Good to Soft at Huntingdon when pulled up at the last. Gven a break of almost two months before running again in a Class 4 Novice Hurdle at Wincanton on 01.02.06 over 2m6f on Good to Soft when finished 3rd of 17 runners, beaten 6 lengths after losing place on the run in. Form record shows that at today's distance has had a total of six runs with two top three placings.
Verdict	The horse's form record is very respectable and though the horse has run on right hand tracks at distances of 2m3½f, 2m4½f and 2m6f in last three outings, the trainer's decision to run on a left hand track at the shorter distance of 2m½f must be for a reason. Although handicap mark is impossible to evaluate, the horse's recent form is good enough to suggest a top three placing is a very reasonable possibility.
Decision:	SELECT.

Form Reading	**LE GRANDE VILLEZ**
Spotlight	Plenty of form over hurdles in France before winning debut for this yard in Maiden Hurdle at Fontwell during November 2006.
Handicap Ratings	Ran off a mark of 110 for last outing in December 2006, which was horse's handicap debut (pulled up). Allocated same mark of 110 for today's event which makes the horse top weight.
Significant Items of Form	Five year old with eleven outings to date, the first of which were in France and included four third places. Last event in France was on 23.09.06 when 3rd of 13 on Very Soft at Auteuill in a 2m1½f Hurdle. Horse's next race on 26.11.06 was its first in Britain when winning a Class 4 Maiden Hurdle on Good to Soft over 2m2½f at Fontwell (10 runners). Next and last race was at Leicester on 28.12.06 in a Class 4 Handicap Hurdle over 2 miles on Soft when pulled up before 2 out after racing in mid division with jockey reporting 'filly was unsuited by Soft ground'.
Verdict	Undoubtedly horse has ability and jockey's remark that horse was unsuited by Soft ground does not stack up with the facts as we know them. Last run in France when 3rd was on Very Soft going and win at Fontwell was on Good to Soft. In addition all the horse's form has been on Good to Soft – Heavy with statistics reading 1-3-11. I have seen many such statements before where either jockeys or trainers have ignored previous evidence to the contrary and stated the going wasn't suitable, only to see their horse simply hack up in a following race on exactly the same going conditions. As a result I automatically dismiss such statements from the reckoning on the grounds that they are 'opinion not fact', which, as you already know, is one of the cornerstones of The Tail End System. What is more of a worry is whether the horse's handicap mark for its last contest, its Handicap debut, was a major contributory factor to its poor performance. It could well be the case, but on the basis that horses frequently have bad runs after a success, it is worth taking a calculated chance that until proved otherwise, the handicap mark should be regarded as neither a help nor a hindrance. The horse has been given a two month break since its last run; the trainer has made a decision today to run on Soft going so he must think it suits, so it is logical to assume the horse has a reasonable chance of obtaining a top three placing.
Decision:	SELECT.

Overall Comment

Another winner at Newbury, a Non-Preferred track, and at the same meeting but a later race, than that of Green Belt Flyer. However, both these victories have been in Class 3 Handicap events, which, as you know, are Preferred races.

It is always a dilemma in making a decision to either discontinue betting in a meeting when you already have a winner under your belt, or continue betting on the basis that as one double deck bus has arrived, there could well be another one arriving shortly. The answer to this problem is to let the form reading process make the decision for you. If you feel happy with your selections, place your bets. Alternatively, if your gut feeling is you haven't got a reasonable chance, leave the race alone.

One final point about this race, the forecast for Strawberry with the favourite in the betting, Illicit Spirit, paid £153.50 on the Tote Exacta and £95.28 for the Computer Straight Forecast.

EXAMPLE 16

03.12.06 Kelso – Heavy – Class 4 – Novices Handicap Chase – 2m1f
Winner FEARLESS FOURSOME – 11/2

1.30 RACE 3	*Eric Scarth Memorial Novices' Handicap Chase (Class 4)* *Winner £3,708.42*	ATR 2m1f

£5700 guaranteed For 4yo+ Rated 0-100 Minimum Weight 10-0 Penalties after November 25th, a winner of a chase 7lb Kristiansand's Handicap Mark 100 Entries 18 pay £20 Penalty value 1st £3,708.42 2nd £1,088.70 3rd £544.35 4th £271.89

1 132 **KRISTIANSAND** 22 □BF
b g Helling-Zonda   6 11-12 **Keith Mercer**
P Monteith P Monteith

2 464-P22 **LE ROYAL** (FR) 18 BF
b g Garde Royale-Caucasie   7 11-7 **James Reveley**(7)
K G Reveley Mrs Stephanie Smith (111)

3 323435P **AMALFI STORM** 25
b m Slip Anchor-Mayroni   b¹5 10-8 **Mr T Greenall**
M W Easterby The Lucky 5 Partnership (102)

4 66-1441 **MYSTIC GLEN** 9 □
b m Veittori-Mystic Memrory   7 10-8 **G Lee**
P D Niven Mrs J A Niven (102)

5 2377F64 **DELAWARE TRAIL** 9
b g Catrail-Dilwara   t7 10-5 **Kenny Johnson**
R Johnson Toon Racing (111)

6 90P-331 **TIN HEALY'S PASS** 30 □
b g Puissance-Shas Spin   v6 10-4 **Michael McAlister**(3)
I McMath W.E.B. Racing & Mrs A J McMath (107)

7 1246-77 **BAAWRAH** 57 □
ch g Cadeaux Genereux-Kronengold   5 10-3 **Dominic Elsworth**
M Todhunter J D Gordon

8 P2-28P6 **FEARLESS FOURSOME** 16 *1ST*
b g Perpendicular-Harrietfield *£11/2*   t7 10-0 **Peter Buchanan**
N W Alexander Alexander Family (101)

9 65237-0 **AZTEC PRINCE** (IRE) 29 *2ND*
ch g King Persian-China Doll *40/1*   t6 10-0 **Neil Mulholland**
Miss S E Forster C Storey (74)

10 R5424-P **JIMMYS DUKY** (IRE) 196 *3RD*
b g Duky-Harvey's Cream *8/1*   8 10-0 **Richard McGrath**
D M Forster D M Forster (104)

LONG HANDICAP: Aztec Prince 9-13 Jimmys Duky 9-7

2005 (10 ran) One Five Eight M W Easterby 6 11-7 20/1   Mr T Greenall (3) OR97

BETTING FORECAST: 7-2 Tin Healy's Pass, 4 Le Royal, Mystic Glen, 6 Baawrah, Kristiansand, 10 Amalfi Storm, 14 Delaware Trail, Fearless Foursome, 20 Jimmys Duky, 25 Aztec Prince.

SPOTLIGHT

Kristiansand Frustrating on the Flat but won on hurdle debut at Cartmel in August and has run creditably in defeat on both subsequent outings (including over 2m at this course); may be capable of better over obstacles but at an experience disadvantage with the majority for this chasing debut.

Le Royal Dual hurdle winner in 2004 but hasn't scored since and, although creditable efforts in defeat over 3m1f at this course on last two starts, hasn't really shaped as though this marked drop in distance is what is required to get him back in the winners enclosure.

Amalfi Storm Series of creditable efforts in bumpers and over hurdles and not disgraced behind Tin Healy's Pass on chase debut; probably found Bangor run coming too quickly when pulled up last time but, although yard among winners and blinkers fitted, is best watched until getting head in front where it matters.

Mystic Glen Finally off the mark over hurdles at Perth in July (good to firm) and bettered pick of hurdle form when scoring at Musselburgh (good) last time; 7lb higher but more of a worry is the weather forecast, as further easing of the ground wouldn't play to her strengths.

Delaware Trail Modest maiden on Flat and over obstacles; flattered by proximity to According To John (runs 1.00) penultimate run and soundly beaten back in handicap last time; down in trip and plenty to prove.

Tin Healy's Pass Point winner who has shaped well over regulation fences this term with solid effort in first-time blinkers at Carlisle and winning at Hexham in visor (on again) last time; 6lb higher but won't mind more rain and should give another good account.

Baawrah Flat (AW) and hurdle winner who hasn't been at best on either start this year but stable among the winners and interesting back in trip in ordinary event if there's any market support on this chasing debut.

Fearless Foursome Yet to win and hasn't shown much to date over fences but this represents easiest task to date and would be interesting if pick of hurdle form over this trip could be translated to fences from this much lower chasing mark; tongue tie back on and isn't one to write off just yet.

Aztec Prince Placed in points but only modest form to date over hurdles; tried tongue tied but something to prove from just out of the handicap on debut over regulation fences.

Jimmys Duky Modest and inconsistent maiden who was soundly beaten in handicap when last seen in spring; cheekpieces left off and down in trip so plenty to prove from 7lb out of the handicap.

VERDICT An ordinary event in which it could be worth chancing FEARLESS FOURSOME at decent odds. This represents his easiest test to date over fences, he has the tongue tie back on, he won't mind rain and the drop in trip and he would be very well treated if the pick of his hurdle form could be translated to this sphere.[RY]

OFFICIAL RATINGS LAST SIX OUTINGS-LATEST ON RIGHT						**1.30** HANDICAP		TODAY FUTURE	RP RATING LATEST / BEST / ADJUSTED		
—	—	—	—	—	—	Kristiansand	11-12	100	—	—	—
—	—	—	95²	95²	87⁵	Le Royal	11-7	95	106	111◄	111◄
—	—	—	87⁵	—	75¹	Amalfi Storm	10-8	82	—	102	102
—	—	—	—	—	75¹	Mystic Glen	10-8	82	102	102	102
82³	—	—	—	—	79⁴	Delaware Trail	10-5	79	92	106	111◄
—	—	—	77ᵖ	—	74³	Tin Healy's Pass	10-4	72¹	107◄	107	107
—	—	—	—	—	—	Baawrah	10-3	77	—	—	—
89ᵖ	—	—	—	86ᵖ	94⁶	Fearless Foursome	10-0	74	96	96	101
—	—	—	—	—	—	Aztec Prince	9-13	74 -1	—	—	—
—	72⁵	73⁴	—	—	67ᵖ	Jimmys Duky	9-7	74 -7	—	104	104

Aztec Prince   10-0

6-y-o ch g King Persian - China Doll (West China)
Miss S E Forster   Neil Mulholland

Placings: UU3/65237-0

OR74 H73	Starts	1st	2nd	3rd	Win & Pl
All Jumps races	3	–	–	–	–
GF-HRD 0-0-0	GS-HVY 0-0-1		Course 0-0-1		Dist 0-0-2

4 Nov Kelso 2m¹/₂f   Cls5 Nov Sell Hdl 4-6yo £2,193
15 ran GOOD 8hdls Time 4m 0.90s (slw 12.90s)
1 Taras Knight 4 10-12 t ....Russ Garritty 2/1F
2 Caulkleys Bank 6 10-12 ....Mr T Greenall 7/2
3 KRISTIANSAND 6 10-12 ..David Da Silva (7) 9/2
led, ridden before last, headed run-in, no extra near finish
[RPR103 TS82 OR108]   [op 7/2 tchd 3/1]
11 AZTEC PRINCE 6 10-7 Tom Messenger (5) 25/1
always behind, no chance from halfway
btn 45 lengths [RPR53 TS23]   [tchd 16/1]
Dist: nk-1³/₄-4-12-1³/₄   RACE RPR: 98/98/103
Racecheck: Wins 1 (1) Pl 3 Unpl 3

26 Apr Perth 2m4¹/₂f   Cls4 Mdn Hdl £5,205
15 ran GOOD 9hdls Time 5m 2.80s (slw 17.80s)
1 All Things Equal 7 11-0 ....T J Phelan (3) 7/2
2 Troll 5 11-3 ....Tony Dobbin 4/1
3 Fastaffaran 5 11-3 ....Richard McGrath 7/2
7 AZTEC PRINCE 6 11-0 .....Mr C Storey (3) 20/1
behind, ridden before 3 out, never on terms
btn 41 lengths [RPR58 TS25]
Dist: 10-4-3-6-18   RACE RPR: 106+/91+/86+
Racecheck: Wins - Pl 3 Unpl 14

8 Apr Dalston (PTP) 2m4f   Open Mdn
9 ran SOFT   Time 5m 44.00s
1 Senza Scrupoli 6 12-0 ....Miss W Gibson 3/1
2 Early Spring 7 11-7 ....L Morgan 4/1
3 AZTEC PRINCE 6 12-0 ....C Storey EvensF
led to 7; rdn & wknd app 2 out
Dist: 4-15
The stewards cautioned the rider of Smooth Attraction for continuing on an exhausted horse. Official Distances: 4, 15
Racecheck: Wins - Pl - Unpl 3

Jimmys Duky   10-0

8-y-o b g Duky - Harvey's Cream (Mandalus)
D M Forster   Richard McGrath

Placings: 0P80/4333P/R5424-P

OR74 H70	Starts	1st	2nd	3rd	Win & Pl
Chase	11	–	1	3	£3,878
All Jumps races	15	–	1	3	£3,878
GF-HRD 0-0-1	GS-HVY 0-2-11		Course 0-0-0		Dist 0-1-1

21 May Market Rasen 2m4f   Cls5 66-87 Ch Hcap £3,769
12 ran SOFT 14fncs Time 5m 13.30s (slw 19.30s)
1 Silver Dagger 8 9-13 et¹ Michael McAlister (5) 50/1
2 Be Telling 7 11-6 ....Paul Moloney 2/1F
3 Scotmail Lad 12 11-4 p ....Mr C Mulhall (7) 20/1
P JIMMYS DUKY 8 10-5 p ..Richard McGrath 11/2
prominent to 7th, soon lost place, lost place after 9th, soon behind, pulled up before 2 out
[OR67]   [tchd 6/1]
Dist: 11-2¹/₂-nk-15   RACE RPR: 90+/91/93
Racecheck: Wins 1 (1) Pl 4 Unpl 6

17 Apr Sedgefield 2m5f   Cls4 Ch £4,086
12 ran GD-FM   16fncs Time 5m 30.50s (slw 30.50s)
1 Show Me The River 7 11-2 ....G Lee 11/10F
2 Herecomestanley 7 10-11 h Charlie Poste (5) 9/1
3 Oneforbertandhenry 7 11-2 ....Barry Keniry 12/1
4 JIMMYS DUKY 8 11-2 p ..Richard McGrath 12/1
*prominent, outpaced 10th, never dangerous
after* [RPR76 TS11 OR67]   [op 16/1]

Dist: 3½-2½-14-17   RACE RPR: 96/92/91+
Racecheck: Wins - Pl 2 Unpl 5

28 Mar Sedgefield 2m1½f   Cls4 Ch £4,384
9 ran HEAVY   13fncs Time 4m 32.10s (slw 36.10s)
1 Red Man 9 10-6 p ....Steven Gagan (10) 13/8F
2 JIMMYS DUKY 8 10-13 p Dougie Costello (3) 8/1
*chased leaders, pushed along and outpaced
after 5 out, ridden along 3 out, stayed on
approaching last*
[RPR76 TS76 OR67] [op 17/2 tchd 9/1 & 15/2]
3 Missoudun 6 10-9 p ....Mr S F Magee (7) 66/1

Dist: 24-2-22-8-9   RACE RPR: 106+/76+/72
Racecheck: Wins - Pl 1 Unpl 11

Fearless Foursome   **10-0**

7-y-o b g Perpendicular - Harrietfield (Nicholas Bill)
N W Alexander   Peter Buchanan

Placings: 88842/396044P2-28P6

OR74 H95	Starts	1st	2nd	3rd	Win & Pl
Chase	4	-	-	-	-
All Jumps races	17	-	3	1	£5,644

GF-HRD 0-0-0 GS-HVY 0-4-16 Course 0-2-6 Dist 0-3-6

17 Nov Kelso 2m6½f Cls3 Nov 94-121 Ch Hcap £6,506
7 ran GD-SFT 17fncs Time 5m 54.50s (slw 22.50s)
1 Cloudless Dawn 6 11-2 ....Russ Garritty 6/1
2 Three Mirrors 6 10-11 ....G Lee 5/2J
3 Laertes 5 11-12 ....Mr T Greenall 14/1
6 FEARLESS FOURSOME 7 10-0 oh20 ....
..:...................................Peter Buchanan 100/1
*behind, mistake 8th, outpaced before 12th,
never on terms* [RPR68 TS51 OR94]

Dist: 9-10-hd-2½-17 RACE RPR: 123+/112+/113
Racecheck: Wins - Pl 1 Unpl -

4 Nov Kelso 3m1f   Cls5 Nov 69-95 Ch Hcap £2,277
10 ran GOOD   19fncs Time 6m 25.20s (slw 23.20s)
1 Orki Des Aigles 4 10-2 ......P J McDonald (5) 6/1
2 LE ROYAL 7 11-9 ....Fergus King (3) 7/2J
chased leaders, outpaced before 3 out, rallied

---

to chase winner run-in, no impression
[RPR104 TS66 OR95]   [tchd 4/1]
3 Jethro Tull 7 11-1 ....C J Callow (10) 8/1
P FEARLESS FOURSOME 7 11-0 t ....
....Tony Dobbin 14/1
*towards rear, hampered by faller 14th, soon lost
touch, tailed off when pulled up before 4 out*
[OR86]   [op 12/1 tchd 11/1]

Dist: 13-8-¾-2-5   RACE RPR: 97+/104+/95+
Racecheck: Wins 1 (1) Pl 2 Unpl 5

15 Oct Carlisle 2m   Cls3 Nov Ch £6,506
10 ran GD-SFT   12fncs Time 4m 8.00s (slw 7.00s)
1 Garde Champetre 7 11-0 ....A P McCoy 4/5F
2 Ela Re 7 11-0 ....David O'Meara 9/1
3 Altay 9 11-0 ....Padge Whelan 5/2
7 DELAWARE TRAIL 7 11-0 t Kenny Johnson 100/1
*held up in rear, behind from 6th, tailed off 9th
btn 40 lengths* [RPR81 TS60 OR78] [op 66/1]
8 FEARLESS FOURSOME 7 11-0 t ....
....Mark Bradburne 50/1
*jumped right, chased leaders to 5th, soon
behind, tailed off 9th
btn 71 lengths* [RPR50 TS17 OR86][tchd 66/1]

Dist: 3½-6-8-1¼-1¾ RACE RPR: 126+/118+/112+
Racecheck: Wins - Pl 6 Unpl 11

Form Reading	**AZTEC PRINCE**
Spotlight	Placed in Points but only modest form to date over hurdles. Just out of the handicap on debut over regulation fences.
Handicap Ratings	No previous Handicap Chase ratings. Allocated a mark of 74 for today's contest, which puts it 1 lb out of the weights.
Significant Items of Form	Seven year old with only nine outings to date and no wins, but three top three placings, the most recent of which was 3rd of 9 runners on 08.04.06 in a 2m4f Point to Point on Soft. That run was followed on 26.04.07 by a 7th of 15 in a 2m4½f Class 4 Maiden Hurdle at Perth (Good), beaten 41 lengths. Next and most recent run was on 04.11.06, after a six month break, at Kelso (Good) in a 2m½f Class 4 Novice Selling Hurdle, when 11th of 15 runners, beaten 45 lengths.
Verdict	Very little form to go on but most recent relevant form was 3rd of 7 in a 2m4½f Point to Point on Soft on 08.04.06. Point to point form is very difficult to evaluate but at least it shows that distance and going and fences should be no problem, and given the fact that horse is running off bottom weight in a Class 4 Novice Handicap, it is reasonable to think that a top three placing is a possibility. This is the second run after a break, therefore improvement can be expected.
Decision:	SELECT.

Form Reading	**JIMMYS DUKY**
Spotlight	Modest and inconsistent Maiden.
Handicap Ratings	Handicap Chase marks of 72, 73 and 67 in three of last six outings and mark of 74 for today's contest, which gives it bottom weight 7lb out of the handicap.
Significant Items of Form	Eight year old with no wins but a placings record which shows that in fifteen outings, has achieved four top three placings. Most recent campaign, which started on or before 28.03.06 and finished on 21.05.06 included a 2nd of 9 runners in a Class 4 2m½f Chase at Sedgefield on Heavy, a 4th of 12 runners in a Class 4 2m5f Chase at Sedgefield on Good to Firm and finally a pulled up in a Class 5 Handicap Chase over 2m4f on Soft at Market Rasen.

Verdict	Never discount a horse that is out of the handicap, even if it is as much a stone out. What is far more important is how the horse has been running and a 2nd and a 4th in Class 4 Chases in most recent campaign is respectable enough for this contest. Ignore horse's last run (pulled up) which was at the end of its campaign and look at the positives, namely fences, going, distance and course (Kelso is a left hand track similar in profile to Sedgefield) should all suit, coupled to which horse is running off bottom weight.
Decision:	SELECT.

Form Reading	**FEARLESS FOURSOME**
Spotlight	Yet to win and hasn't shown much to date over fences.
Handicap Ratings	Three Handicap Chase ratings of 89, 86 and 94 in last six outings, all of which resulted in pulled up. However down to a mark of 74 today which indicates that the horse has a lot better chance at today's weights where running off bottom weight.
Significant Items of Form	Seven year old with no wins but a placings record that shows seven top four placings in seventeen outings. All the horse's form has been on Good to Soft – Heavy, course record figures are 0-2-6 and distance figures are 0-3-6. Last three runs are all recent, best of which is probably its last outing on 17.11.06 when 6th of 7 in a Class 3 Handicap Chase at today's track on Good to Soft when beaten 38½ lengths.
Verdict	Today's contest should be easier (lower Class), distance more suitable (shorter), going will suit (Good to Soft) and having proved last time out that it can get over the fences at Kelso, a decent run should be expected, running as it is off bottom weight.
Decision	No reason to do anything other than: SELECT.

Overall Comment

This was one of the races where The Tail End System provided the top three placings.

At the same time the race posed something of a dilemma from a betting point of view because Fearless Foursome had been backed down from 9/1 to 11/2 and Jimmys Duky from 16/1 to 8/1, both below the 10/1 threshold you normally look for if you weren't able to catch the opening prices.

Usually in such circumstances, which actually are quite rare occurrences, I back all my selections to win providing the odds are not less than 5/1. If they are less than 5/1. I refrain from betting on those particular selections to win, but I do include them in any reverse forecast bet on the race.

What you must avoid in these situations is dumping a selection altogether because its price is less than 10/1 and trying to replace it with another longer priced selection, because such a move could prove fatal.

The safest option is, therefore, to pair the short priced (under 10/1) selections with the remainder of your selections in a reverse forecast, so that if a short priced selection prevails, you still have the chance of a decent pick up via the forecast.

For the record, the Exacta paid £237.50, the Computer Straight Forecast £147.49 and the Tricast £1,740.63.

EXAMPLE 17

03.12.06   Kelso – Heavy – Class 5 – Amateur Riders Handicap Hurdle – 2m2f
Winner   WINDYGATE – 12/1

2.30 **RACE 5** | *Glenrath Farms Catherine Campbell Amateur Riders' Handicap Hurdle (Class 5)* | ATR
Winner £2,637.20 | **2m2f**

£4000 guaranteed For 3yo+ Rated 0-90 Minimum Weight 10-0 Penalties after November 25th, a winner of a hurdle 7lb Lerida's Handicap Mark 90 Entries 43 pay £15 Penalty value 1st £2,637.20 2nd £811.20 3rd £405.60

1 P4-8049 **LERIDA** [29] *NON RUNNER* 4 11-12 Mr D Oakden (7) **92**
ch g Groom Dancer-Catalonia
Miss Lucinda V Russell D G Pryde

2 509 **KINGSBURY** (IRE) [21] 7 11-12 Mr S W Byrne (7) **88**
b g Norwich-Glen Na Mban
Ferdy Murphy Reg Joseph & Ferdy Murphy

3 74-P518 **NUZZLE** [29] (s) 6 11-11 Miss J R Richards (7) **89**
b m Salse-Lena
N G Richards Brian Morton & Paul Montgomery

4 1-P5648 **OSCAR THE BOXER** (IRE) [114] 7 11-10 Mr O Williams (7) **93**
b g Oscar-Here She Comes
J M Jefferson Boundary Garage (Bury) Limited

5 8180P20 **BARNEY** (IRE) [27] 5 11-9 Miss J Sayer (7) **88**
b g Basanta-Double Or Nothing
Mrs E Slack A Slack

6 0/69-36 **DANIEL'S DREAM** [186] 6 11-8 Mr T Davidson (5) **86**
b g Prince Daniel-Amber Holly
J E Dixon Mrs E M Dixon

7 P9070- **INCH HIGH** [252] (56F) 8 11-8 Mr H Haynes (7) **88**
ch g Inchinor-Harrken Heights
J S Goldie Thoroughbred Leisure Racing Club 2

8 41/30-G **INN FROM THE COLD** (IRE) [187] *3 RD* 10 11-7 Mr G Willoughby (7) **88** *8/1*
ch g Glaciel Storm-Silver Apollo
L Lungo Guy Willoughby

9 5F8/P-P **KEEP SMILING** (IRE) [199] p 10 11-5 Miss J Riding (5)
b g Broken Hearted-Laugh Away
Mrs C J Kerr Mrs C J Kerr

10 00008-7 **STATUTE** [112] t 4 11-4 Miss Caroline Hurley (5) **81**
b c Fasliyev-Unopposed
F J Bowles (IRE) Reginald Stephen Blandford

11 P-74434 **BELLA LIANA** (IRE) [18] b 6 11-4 Mr S Clements (7) **86**
b m Sesaro-Bella Galiana
J Clements (IRE) James Clements

12 31U31-7 **NIFTY ROY** [8] 6 11-2 Mr T Greenall (7) **92**
b g Royal Applause-Nifty Fifty
I McMath Mrs A McMath K Hogg

13 8077/04 **JIDIYA** (IRE) [30] b 7 11-2 Mr C Hughes (7) **90**
b g Lahib-Yaqatha
Mrs H O Graham F W W Chapman

14 P80-09 **LEPRECHAUN'S MAITE** [119] (102F) 4 11-2 Mr J A Richardson (7) **79** *2 Nd* *100/1*
b g Komaite-Leprechaun Lady
W G Young W G Young

15 999366- **NORMINSTER** [220] 5 11-2 Mr M Ellwood (7) **89**
ch g Minster Son-Delightfool
R Nixon Rayson & Susan Nixon

16 147775- **STAR TROOPER** (IRE) [250] p 10 11-0 Miss Carly Frater (7) **90**
b/br g Brief Truce-Star Cream
Miss S E Forster C Storey

17 6/760- **BEAU PEAK** [327] 7 10-12 Mr C Whillans (7)
ch m Meadowbrook-Peak A Boo
D W Whillans Mrs H M Whillans

18 860-07 **WINDYGATE** (IRE) [30] *1 ST* 6 10-12 Mr D England (79) *12/1*
b/br g Supreme Leader-Moscow Maid
A Parker A Parker

BETTING FORECAST: 5 Oscar The Boxer, 6 Nifty Roy, 8 Kingsbury, Nuzzle, 10 Inn From The Cold, 12 Barney, Norminster, Statute, 14 Lerida, 16 Bella Liana, Daniel's Dream, Inch High, Star Trooper, 20 Jidiya, 25 Beau Peak, 33 bar.

SPOTLIGHT

Lerida Failed to build on promising Haydock fourth for this jockey when well beaten over C&D latest; seems happiest on sound surface and best to look elsewhere.

Kingsbury Market springer in novice company at Carlisle latest but only ninth of the 13 runners (heavy); possible this track may suit better and worth market check on handicap debut.

Nuzzle C&D winner (good to soft) who has won both his starts in selling hurdles but again failed to cope with stronger company when only eighth over C&D latest; others more likely.

Oscar The Boxer 2m4f soft-ground winner in February before string of disappointments in the summer; 114-day absence to overcome but return to slow surface offers hope.

Barney Dual Sedgefield scorer on good/faster so soft surface probably to blame for last-time-out Carlisle flop; below par over C&D in October and wouldn't want further rain.

Daniel's Dream Close third at this venue in May on return from a break (2m, good to firm) before disappointing at Cartmel later the same month; opposable on ground softer than ideal.

Inch High 1m soft-ground winner on the Flat in May (first win) but never better than mid-division in five previous tries over hurdles; well held in Banded company on the level latest and hard to see him involved.

Inn From The Cold Won similar contest at Carlisle in 2004 (2m4f, heavy) but missed whole of last year before fair comeback third at Newcastle in January (2m); below par the next twice and best watched on first outing since May.

Keep Smiling Pulled up at big prices with both outings this year (hurdle/chase) after long absence and not hard to look elsewhere.

Statute Not beaten far at Downpatrick last time but remains a maiden after 18 starts Flat/hurdles and percentage call to oppose.

Bella Liana In the frame several times at up to 3m but still searching for first win after 23 attempts in varied company; only modest effort in first-time blinkers latest and best watched over trip short of optimum with headgear retained.

Nifty Roy Improved form on soft ground in 2m chases in first part of year but tailed off on last month's return; wouldn't be the easiest ride for an amateur (can race keenly) but much lower in this sphere and respected.

Jidiya Not disgraced (66-1 fourth of 15) in Hexham plating handicap latest but yet to score over hurdles and opposable with ground softer than preferred.

Leprechaun's Maite Lightly raced and little solid form Flat/hurdles, including in selling hurdles; easily opposed.

Norminster Close 20-1 third at Ayr only previous handicap outing with plenty of cut; yard's runners always worth second look here and couldn't rule out if ready for first outing since April.

Star Trooper Done most of winning in the mud and ended long losing run in Sedgefield selling hurdle in January but went off the boil afterwards; opposable on return from 250-day break.

Beau Peak Little promise in three novice hurdles and best watched on handicap debut/first run since January.

Windygate Beaten miles at big prices in three novice hurdles; massive improvement needed on handicap debut.

VERDICT **NORMINSTER**, whose small stable is going well, gets the vote in a tricky looking handicap hurdle. **Oscar The Boxer** and **Nifty Roy** are others to consider. [AM]

OFFICIAL RATINGS						**2.30** HANDICAP	TODAY FUTURE	RP RATING		
LAST SIX OUTINGS-LATEST ON RIGHT								LATEST	BEST	ADJUSTED
—	—	105⁸	100⁵	95⁴	94⁹	Lerida 11-12	90	63	93	92
—	—	—	—	—	—	Kingsbury 11-12	90	47	88	88
83⁷	83⁴	—	82⁵	82¹	90⁸	Nuzzle 11-11	89	85	89	89 ◄
86¹	92ᴾ	92⁵	91⁶	90⁴	90⁸	Oscar The Boxer 11-10	88	56	93	93 ◄
81¹	87⁸	87⁰	86ᴾ	85²	85⁰	Barney 11-9	87	—	88	88
—	—	—	—	—	—	Daniel's Dream 11-8	86	69	86	86
—	—	—	—	—	89⁰	Inch High 11-8	86	—	88	88
73¹	84⁴	84¹	86³	86⁰	85⁸	Inn From The Cold 11-7	85	69	88	88
94⁵	92⁵	90ᶠ	—	83ᴾ	—	Keep Smiling 11-5	83	—	—	—
—	—	74⁰	79⁰	—	74⁷	Statute 11-4	82	79	81	81
—	—	85⁷	—	—	—	Bella Liana 11-4	82	75	86	86
—	—	—	—	—	—	Nifty Roy 11-2	82	—	67	92
—	—	94⁰	93⁷	91⁷	83⁰	Jidiya 11-2	80	90 ◄	90	90
—	—	—	83⁰	83⁹	—	Leprechaun's Maite 11-2	80	47	51	79
—	—	85⁰	84⁰³	82⁶	—	Norminster 11-2	80	—	89	89
74¹	81⁴	80⁷	80⁷	79⁷	—	Star Trooper 11-0	78	—	95 ◄	90
—	—	—	—	—	—	Beau Peak 10-12	76	—	—	—
—	—	—	—	—	—	Windygate 10-12	76	79	79	79

Windygate 10-12

6-y-o bb g Supreme Leader - Moscow Maid
(Moscow Society)
A Parker   Mr D England

Placings: 860-07

OR76	Starts	1st	2nd	3rd	Win & Pl
Hurdles	3	–	–	–	–
All Jumps races	5	–	–	–	–
GF-HRD 0-0-0	GS-HVY 0-0-5	Course 0-0-1	Dist 0-0-0		

3 Nov Hexham 2m4½f   Cls4 Nov Hdl £3,448
18 ran GD-SFT   10hdls   Time 5m 11.65s (slw 18.85s)
1 Reel Charmer 6 10-2 ....W T Kennedy (3) 6/1
2 Bedlam Boy 5 10-12 ....Tony Dobbin 11/4F
3 Cash Man 5 10-9 ....Gary Berridge (3) 50/1
7 WINDYGATE 6 10-7 ......Phil Kinsella (5) 150/1
midfield, ridden 4 out, soon beaten
btn 46 lengths [RPR63 TS34]
Dist: 3-21-5-3½-1   RACE RPR: 102+/105+/85+
Racecheck: Wins 2 (2) Pl 2 Unpl 4

29 Oct Carlisle 2m4f   Cls4 Nov Hdl £3,063
16 ran HEAVY   -9hdls   Time 5m 17.70s (slw 28.70s)
1 Gunner Jack 5 10-12 ....Tony Dobbin 7/4F
2 Mr Preacher Man 4 10-12 Peter Buchanan 10/1
3 Bywell Beau 7 10-12 t ......Dominic Elsworth 8/1
12 WINDYGATE 6 10-12 ...Richard McGrath 250/1
not fluent, always behind
btn 81 lengths [RPR24]
                                            [op 200/1]
Dist: 10-7-6-7-nk   RACE RPR: 110+/95/88
Racecheck: Wins 1 (1) Pl 1 Unpl 6

3 Apr Kelso 2m½f   Cls4 Nov Hdl £3,253
16 ran SOFT   8hdls   Time 4m 11.10s (slw 23.10s)
1 Boulders Beach 6 11-0 .Dominic Elsworth 8/13F
2 Harry Flashman 5 11-0 .....Wilson Renwick 16/1
3 Stagecoach Opal 5 11-0 .....Padge Whelan 8/1
14 WINDYGATE 6 10-9 ......T J Dreaper (5) 200/1
always behind, no chance from halfway
btn 66 lengths [RPR33 TS1]
                                             [op 100/1]
Dist: shd-4-4-15-shd   RACE RPR: 99/99/95

Leprechaun's Maite 11-2

4-y-o b g Komaite - Leprechaun Lady (Royal Blend)
W G Young   Mr J A Richardson (7)

Placings: P80-09

OR80	Starts	1st	2nd	3rd	Win & Pl
All Jumps races	5	–	–	–	–
GF-HRD 0-0-1	GS-HVY 0-0-2	Course 0-0-0	Dist 0-0-1		

6 Aug Market Rasen 2m1½f Cls5 68-94 Sell Hdl 4-7yo
                        Hcap £2,398
14 ran GD-FM   8hdls   Time 4m 10.20s (slw 7.20s)
1 New Wish 6 10-0 oh2 ....Paddy Aspell 5/1
2 Champagne Rossini 4 9-11 Derek Laverty (5) 10/1
3 Kossies Mate 7 9-7 oh4 ......C M Studd (7) 33/1
9 LEPRECHAUN'S MAITE 4 10-9 v1 ....
..................................Tom Messenger (5) 20/1
prominent, disputed 2nd at 4th, weakened
under pressure 3 out, tailed off
btn 52 lengths [RPR35 TS21 OR83] [op 16/1]
Dist: 7-3¾-10-12-8   RACE RPR: 77+/70+/65
Racecheck: Wins - Pl 1 Unpl 15

---

27 Jul Uttoxeter 2m   Cls5 Nov 74-95 Hdl Hcap £2,277
15 ran GOOD   10hdls   Time 3m 50.40s (slw 8.40s)
1 Stokesies Boy 6 10-11 ....Ollie McPhail 50/1
2 Kingscourt Lad 8 10-10 t ...Adam Pogson (5) 7/2
3 Lord Rosskit 6 11-5 ex7 .Mr S F Magee (7) 2/1F
12 LEPRECHAUN'S MAITE 4 10-5 ....
..................................Mr A Merriam (7) 66/1
chased leaders, mistake 4 out, ridden and
weakened before next
btn 45 lengths [RPR39 TS29 OR83] [op 50/1]
Dist: hd-2-2-4-14   RACE RPR: 83/87/97+
Racecheck: Wins 3 (3) Pl 4 Unpl 12

1 Dec 05 Leicester 2m   Cls3 Nov Hdl 3yo £5,673
14 ran SOFT   9hdls   Time 4m 0.90s (slw 13.90s)
1 Caribou 3 10-12 ....Leighton Aspell 7/1
2 Cava Bien 3 10-12 ....Timmy Murphy 5/1
3 Copper Bay 3 10-12 ....Warren Marston 3/1F
10 LEPRECHAUN'S MAITE 3 10-12 ....
..................................Vince Slattery 66/1
prominent until weakened approaching 3 out
btn 46 lengths [RPR49 TS37]   [op 50/1]
Dist: 1-1-9-3-5   RACE RPR: 98+/94/93
Racecheck: Wins 1 Pl 3 Unpl 17

Flat Form

23 Aug Leicester 1m½f Cls5 Auct Mdn 3-4yo £4,534
12 ran GD-SFT   Time 1m 47.05s (slw 4.55s)
1 Our Faye 3 8-12 ....Frankie McDonald 9 5/1
2 Dan Buoy 3 9-3 ....Robert Havlin 2 10/1
3 Arabian Breeze 3 8-12 .Adrian McCarthy 8 100/1
8 LEPRECHAUN'S MAITE 4 9-4 ....
..................................Tom Messenger (5) 7 100/1
held up, ridden halfway, never troubled leaders
(jockey received one-day ban: used whip with
excessive frequency and on a horse showing no
response (Sep 3)) btn 7 lengths [RPR42 TS12]
Dist: 2-1-1-½-nk   RACE RPR: 53/54+/46
Racecheck: Wins - Pl 2 Unpl 13

Keep Smiling 11-5

10-y-o b g Broken Hearted - Laugh Away (Furry
Glen)
Mrs C J Kerr   Miss J Riding (5)

Placings: /F1UUP/333F/55F8/P-P

OR83	Starts	1st	2nd	3rd	Win & Pl
Hurdles	10	–	–	3	£1,603
All Jumps races	18	1	–	3	£7,399
10/02 Bang	2m4½f Cls3 Nov Ch gd-sft		....£5,796		
GF-HRD 0-0-3	GS-HVY 1-2-8	Course 0-0-0	Dist 0-0-2		

18 May Perth 3m   Cls4 87-113 Ch Hcap £6,506
12 ran SOFT   18fncs   Time 6m 53.90s (slw 56.90s)
1 Burwood Breeze 10 11-8 ....P J Brennan 6/1
2 Very Very Noble 12 10-13 t .Neil Mulholland 16/1
3 Goodbandiferent 10 10-0 oh10 ....
..................................Keith Mercer 33/1
P KEEP SMILING 10 9-9 oh4 ....
..................................Tom Greenway (5) 40/1
in touch, blundered and lost place 7th, tailed off
when pulled up after 11th [OR87] [tchd 33/1]
Dist: 9-54-17   RACE RPR: 125+/101/34
Racecheck: Wins - Pl 1 Unpl 13

---

26 Apr Perth 3m1½f Cls4 83-100 Am Hdl Hcap £4,997
18 ran GOOD   12hdls   Time 5m 59.80s (slw 14.60s)
1 Burren Moonshine 7 10-11 Mr P Sheldrake (7) 9/2F
2 Sir Rowland Hill 7 11-5 ......Mr S W Byrne (7) 7/1
3 Speed Kris 7 11-1 v .....Miss R Davidson (3) 16/1
P KEEP SMILING 10 10-9 ......Mr C Storey 100/1
behind, outpaced when hampered 8th, tailed off
when pulled up after 8th [OR83]
Dist: hd-12-2-6-5   RACE RPR: 101+/108/89+
Racecheck: Wins 1 (1) Pl 4 Unpl 18

26 Jul 04 Sedgefield 2m5f   Cls4 79-105 Ch Hcap
                        £4,381
12 ran GD-FM   16fncs   Time 5m 6.40s (slw 6.40s)
1 Karo de Vindecy 6 10-0 t oh5 Jim Crowley 9/2
2 Dragon King 12 11-5 b ....S E Durack 9/2
3 Brave Effect 8 10-12 ....G Lee 7/1
8 KEEP SMILING 8 11-5 ...Owyn Nelmes (7) 22/1
in touch to halfway, weakening when blundered
3 out
btn 42 lengths [RPR71 TS45 OR105] [op 16/1]
Dist: 3-6-3½-10-4   RACE RPR: 91+/105+/95+
Racecheck: Wins 2 (2) Pl 6 Unpl 11

Beau Peak 10-12

7-y-o ch m Meadowbrook - Peak A Boo (Le Coq
d'Or)
D W Whillans   Mr C Whillans (7)

Placings: 6/760-

OR76	Starts	1st	2nd	3rd	Win & Pl
Hurdles	3	–	–	–	–
All Jumps races	4	–	–	–	–
GF-HRD 0-0-0	GS-HVY 0-0-3	Course 0-0-0	Dist 0-0-0		

10 Jan Sedgefield 2m5½f   Cls4 Nov Hdl £3,253
13 ran SOFT   10hdls   Time 5m 49.60s (slw 14.60s)
1 Ile Maurice 6 11-8 ....Keith Mercer 5/6F
2 Verstone 4 10-3 ....J A McCarthy 33/1
3 Our Joycey 5 11-2 ....Richard McGrath 40/1
10 BEAU PEAK 7 11-2 ...Dominic Elsworth 50/1
in rear, behind from 5th, tailed off
btn 90 lengths   [op 40/1]
Dist: 11-¾-shd-12-½   RACE RPR: 110+/74+/85
Racecheck: Wins 1 (1) Pl 2 Unpl 12

5 Jun 05 Perth 2m4½f   Cls4 Nov Hdl £4,381
14 ran HEAVY   10hdls   Time 5m 28.60s (slw 43.60s)
1 Tandava 7 11-7 ....Wilson Renwick 5/2J
2 Kilty Storm 6 11-0 ....R J Greene 5/2J
3 Sarin 7 11-0 ....Sam Thomas 11/2
6 BEAU PEAK 6 10-4 .....Peter Buchanan (3) 50/1
in touch to 3 out, soon weakened [RPR61 TS45]
Dist: 1¼-14-12-4-3   RACE RPR: 110+/101/89+
Racecheck: Wins 2 (2) Pl 3 Unpl 17

30 Apr 05 Hexham 3m   Cls4 Nov Hdl £3,402
11 ran GOOD   12hdls   Time 6m 17.10s (slw 27.10s)
1 Bellaney Jewel 6 10-13 ....Tony Dobbin 6/4
2 Rogues Gallery 5 11-6 ....G Lee 6/5F
3 Uneven Line 9 10-4 ....Mr C Storey (3) 20/1
7 BEAU PEAK 6 10-0 ....Ewan Whillans (7) 20/1
prominent, headway to press leader 4th, every
chance until weakened between last two
btn 15 lengths [RPR76 TS12]   [op 14/1]
Dist: 1½-3-1¼-7-2   RACE RPR: 97+/102/86
Racecheck: Wins 1 (1) Pl 4 Unpl 12

	WINDYGATE
Form Reading	
Spotlight	Beaten by miles at big prices in three Novice Hurdles; Handicap debut.
Handicap Ratings	No previous ratings, mark of 76 and bottom weight for today's contest.
Significant Items of Form	Six year old with no wins and only five runs to date, but finished race on each occasion. Ran at today's track in a Class 4 Novice Hurdle over 2m½f on Soft on 03.04.06 when beaten 66 lengths, always behind. Near seven month break until 29.10.06 before running at Carlisle (Heavy) in a Class 4 Novice Hurdle over 2m4f, beaten 81 lengths, always behind. Next and last outing on 03.11.06 was at Hexham (Good to Soft) again in a Class 4 Novice Hurdle where 7th of 18 runners,

	beaten 46 lengths over 2m4½f, midfield, ridden 4 out, soon beaten.
Verdict	Has run without distinction in last three races, which were all higher Class (Class 4) events than today's contest. However has finished all its races and last run when occupying a midfield position indicates that the horse is improving. Betting Forecast puts the horse in the 33/1 BAR group, so on course price of 12/1 indicates confidence in a decent run off bottom weight. The facts – down in class, bottom weight, midfield position last run, getting fitter following long break, plus market support – all add up to a top three placing being a reasonable possibility.
Decision:	SELECT.

Form Reading	**LEPRECHAUN'S MATE**
Spotlight	Lightly raced and little solid form flat/hurdles.
Handicap Ratings	Mark of 83 for last two outings and down to a mark of 80 today.
Significant Items of Form	Four year old with only five National Hunt outings and no wins. In December 2005, as a three year old, ran in a Class 3 Novice Hurdle over 2 miles at Leicester (Soft) when 10th of 14, prominent until weakened 3 out, beaten 46 lengths. Next run was on 27.07.06 at Uttoxeter (Good) in a Class 5 Novice Handicap Hurdle over 2 miles when 12th of 15 runners, beaten 45 lengths, chased leaders, mistake 4 out. Last National Hunt run was on 06.08.06 when 9th of 14 in a Class 5 Selling Handicap Hurdle at Market Rasen over 2m1½f, beaten 52 lengths where prominent disputed second place at 4th, weakened under pressure 3 out. Last run was on the flat (turf) on 23.08.06 at Leicester, 1m½f (Good to Soft) when 8th of 12, beaten 7 lengths.
Verdict	The two items of significace in the form are its run in a Class 3 Novice Hurdle in December 2005, when prominent until 3 out, and its flat run in August 2006, when only beaten 7 lengths. Both these runs could indicate that the horse is somewhat better than its last two National Hunt runs on 27.07.06 and 06.08.06 suggest. This is a Class 5 Amateur Riders Handicap Hurdle, which probably won't take a lot of winning, so any glimmers of hope in the form should be viewed with interest. Although we do not know if this horse will go well fresh after what will have been a four month break, a risky prediction that horse could be placed in the first three does not seem entirely unreasonable.
Decision:	SELECT.

Form Reading	**KEEP SMILING**
Spotlight	Pulled up at big prices both outings this year.
Handicap Ratings	Ran off a mark of 94 six outings ago (finished 5th) but this has steadily reduced to 92, 90 and finally 83 two outings ago when pulled up. Same mark of 83 for today's event, which means horse has to improve considerably on latest form to figure in this contest.
Significant Items of Form	Ten year old with one Class 3 Novice Chase win on Good to Soft at Bangor October 2002. Last two runs were in April and May 2006, both at Perth in firstly a Class 4 Amateur Riders Handicap Hurdle over 3m½f on Good and secondly a Class 4 handicap Chase over 3 miles on Soft and resulted in horse being pulled up on both occasions. These two runs followed a one year and nine months break, which indicates horse has had its problems.

Verdict	Given lack of promise in last two runs, coupled with big time gap back to any performance of note, there is no sensible alternative other than to: DISMISS.

Form Reading	**BEAU PEAK**
Spotlight	Little promise in three Novice Hurdles, Handicap debut, first run since January 2006.
Handicap Ratings	Handicap debut allocated a mark of 76 for today's contest which puts horse on bottom weight.
Significant Items of Form	Seven year old with only five outings and no wins to date. Ran on 30.04.05 at Hexham (Good) in Class 4 Novice Hurdle over 3 miles when 7th of 11, prominent pressed leader 4th, every chance until weakened between last two, beaten 15 lengths. Ran next at Perth (Heavy) in a 2m4½f Class 4 Novice Hurdle when 6th of 14, beaten 34¼ lengths, in touch to 3 out. Last run was on 10.01.06 at Sedgefield (Soft) in a Class 4 Novice Hurdle over 2m5½f when 10th of 13, beaten 90 lengths.
Verdict	Considering today's contest is a Class 5 event, horse's runs at Hexham and Perth make good reading and although there is no information to show horse can go well fresh, for insurance purposes alone it is worth making the decision that a top three placing is attainable.
Decision:	SELECT.

Overall Comment

When I first looked at the list of runners, riders and forecast prices for this event, Windygate on the bottom weight and not amongst the named runners in the Betting Forecast, caught my eye.

When I found out its board price was down to 12/1 I was pretty sure that a big run was expected, despite the fact that its form was none too impressive, though it had been finishing its races.

In the case of Leprechaun's Mate, also not amongst the named runners in the Betting Forecast, its run on the flat when finishing within 7 lengths was a good pointer because you frequently see cases where a flat run within 10/12 lengths of the winner turns out to be significant.

Finally, in the case of Beau Peak, this horse was the last named horse in the Betting Forecast and I am always reluctant to dismiss such horses from the reckoning if there are some significant pointers in their form to indicate ability. The reason is quite simply the fact that I have lost count of the number of last named horses in the Betting Forecast which have ended up winning.

As it happens, Beau Peak was brought down during the race but it doesn't alter the fact that, as the last named horse possessing form to justify its inclusion, it would have been wrong not select it.

For the record, the Tote Exacta paid £1,031.40, the Computer Straight forecast £903.68 and the Tricast £9,788.21.

EXAMPLE 18

09.05.06   Kelso – Good to Firm – Class 4 – Novices Handicap Hurdle – 2m6½f

Winner   HEVERSHAM – 50/1

2.20 RACE 1   *John Smith's No Nonsense Novices' Handicap Hurdle (Class 4) Winner £5,010.40*   **ATR**   2m6½f

£8000 guaranteed For 4yo+ Rated 0-110 Minimum Weight 10-0 Penalties after April 29th, a winner of a hurdle 7lb My Final Bid's Handicap Mark 110 Entries 37 pay £20 Penalty value 1st £5,010.40 2nd £1,480 3rd £740 4th £370.40 5th £184.80 6th £92.80

1 /22223- **MY FINAL BID** (IRE) 51
b g Supreme Leader-Mini Minor
Mrs A C Hamilton J P G Hamilton
7 11-12
Alan Dempsey (106)

2 92P422- **CHIEF DAN GEORGE** (IRE) 13
b g Lord Americo-Colleen Donn
D R Macleod Maurice W Chapman
6 11-7
Declan McGann (5) (116)

3 436215- **POWERLOVE** (FR) 13
b m Solon-Bywaldor
Mrs S C Bradburne Mark Fleming & Jane Cameron
5 11-5
Mark Bradburne (111)

4 4211-U1 **JODANTE** (IRE) (7ex) 4
ch g Phardante-Crashtown Lucy
R C Guest R C Guest
p 9 11-4
Patrick McDonald (7) (120)

5 72847P- **LE MILLENAIRE** (FR) 13
b/br g Ragmar-Ezaia
S H Shirley-Beavan S H Shirley-Beavan
b 7 11-0
Wilson Renwick (109)

6 0F4324- **ROSCHAL** (IRE) 51
gr g Roselier-Sunday World
Miss Lucinda V Russell J R Adam
p 8 10-11
Peter Buchanan (111)

7 /P4643- **THE WEAVER** (FR) 109
ch g Villez-Miss Planette
L Lungo P Gaffney & J N Stevenson
7 10-10
Gary Berridge (3) (118)

8 93P32P- **BROMLEY ABBEY** 11
ch m Mandor Son-Little Bromley
Miss S E Forster Mrs A Eubank
p 8 10-6
Tom Messenger (7) (109)

9 535585- **BUFFY** 15
b m Classic Cliche-Annie Kelly
B Mactaggart Harlequin Racing
6 10-5
Paddy Aspell (113)

10 93655-8 **HEVERSHAM** (IRE) 8
b g Octagonal-Saint Ann
J Hetherton K C West
b 5 10-0
Paddy Brennan (117)

11 053P43- **COUNTRYWIDE SUN** 59
b g Denny The Dip-Sundae Girl
A C Whillans Jethart Justice
4 10-0
Dougie Costello (3) (104)

12 322/UP- **ALICE'S OLD ROSE** 13
b m Broadsword-Rosie Marchioness
Mrs H O Graham C J Pickering
9 10-0
Tom Greenway (5)

LONG HANDICAP: Countrywide Sun **9-13** Alice's Old Rose **9-9**

BETTING FORECAST: 11-10 Jodante, 13-2 Chief Dan George, 10 My Final Bid, Powerlove, The Weaver, 14 Buffy, Countrywide Sun, 16 Bromley Abbey, 25 Heversham, Le Millenaire, 33 Alice's Old Rose.

SPOTLIGHT

My Final Bid Runner-up in three bumpers and first two starts over hurdles before finishing third in maiden event over shorter trip here in March; close second to subsequently smart Money Trix needs to be viewed in most positive light if he's to be considered capable of defying top weight.

Chief Dan George Has progressed for step up in distance last twice, finishing clear of remainder when pipped by subsequent handicap winner Noir Et Vert over 3m at Perth last month; 6lb higher mark justifiable and should give good account.

Powerlove Looked on the up when scoring over 3m at Ayr but found wanting off this mark at Perth next time when behind Chief Dan George.

Jodante Translated good recent chasing form to hurdles when winning with head in chest on fast ground over slightly shorter trip than this at Southwell last week; still 9lb lower than chase rating with penalty and must take all the beating unless the ground softens up dramatically, in which case he'd presumably miss the gig.

Le Millenaire Winning pointer on good goung but hasn't built on promise of second to decent sort over 2m on soft on hurdles bow and needs positive reaction to first-time blinkers.

Roschal Well weighted on pick of chasing exploits when second at Ayr in March but completely failed to build on that off today's 4lb higher mark next time and something to prove now.

The Weaver Not one of the stable stars but has a race in him judged on third off 1lb higher over 3m at Musselburgh in January; break might have done him good.

Bromley Abbey Poor show on fast ground late last month raises doubts whether she's capable of reversing previous Ayr form with Powerlove despite 3lb pull for less than 2l beating.

Buffy Bit more like it when fifth over 2m at Hexham last month but best form to date has been at that trip and so reservations about this longest journey for her to date.

Heversham No improvement for step up to 2m4f last time after shaping as though needing farther than modest fifth in 2m1f Sedgefield handicap on previous start and needs first-time blinkers to work some magic.

Countrywide Sun Has shown some promise in minor company but will need to settle better than last time if he's to have any chance of benefitting from this much longer trip.

Alice's Old Rose Runner-up off lower marks than this two seasons ago but something to prove now after being tailed off when pulled up (25/1) over 3m at Perth last month.

VERDICT Unless the ground softens up dramatically, **JODANTE (nap)** ought to be capable of defying his cakewalk against modest rivals at Southwell last week. **Chief Dan George** is the most feasible alternative.[PJ]

	OFFICIAL RATINGS LAST SIX OUTINGS-LATEST ON RIGHT					2.20 HANDICAP			TODAY/FUTURE		RP RATING LATEST / BEST / ADJUSTED		
—	—	—	—	—	—	My Final Bid	11-12	110		106	106	106	
—	89²	94P	—	98²	99²	Chief Dan George	11-7	105		116	116	116	
—	—	99⁶	—	97¹	103⁵	Powerlove	11-5	103		99	111	111	
—	—	—	—	—	95¹	Jodante (7x)	11-4	102	-7	118 ◄	118 ◄	120 ◄
—	—	—	—	102⁷	100P	Le Millenaire	11-0	98		—	109	109	
—	—	—	—	91²	95⁴	Roschal	10-11	95		84	111	111	
98U	99⁹	99⁴	99⁶	97⁴	95³	The Weaver	10-10	94		115	118 ◄	118	
77⁹	—	—	85³	87²	90P	Bromley Abbey	10-6	90		—	109	109	
—	—	90⁵	99⁸	90⁵	96⁵	Buffy	10-5	89		112	113	113	
—	—	92⁶	87⁵	86⁵	84⁸	Heversham	10-0	84		82	117	117	
—	—	96⁵	—	95P	91⁴	Countrywide Sun	9-13	89		104	104	104	
72⁴	79³	72²	79²	81U	83P	Alice's Old Rose	9-9	84	-5	—	—	—	

Dist: hd-12-2-6-5   RACE RPR: 101 +/108/89 +
Racecheck: Wins - Pl - Unpl 3

2 Jan Ayr 3m½f   Cls5 65-91 Hdl Hcap £2,398
15 ran SOFT   11hdls Time 6m 40.50s (slw 55.50s)
1 Caesar's Palace 9 11-9 p Peter Buchanan (3) 5/1F
2 Moon Mist 8 10-9 ....Richard McGrath 6/1
3 Seeking Shelter 7 10-2 ....Brian Harding 10/1
U **ALICE'S OLD ROSE** 9 10-11 ....
....Dougie Costello (5) 9/1
held up towards rear, blundered and unseated rider 4th [OR81]   [op 7/1]
Dist: 1-3½-18-17-½   RACE RPR: 94/76/67 +
Racecheck: Wins 2 (2) Pl 3 Unpl 9

5 Dec 04 Kelso 2m6½f   Cls4 Nov 79-105 Hdl Hcap
    £3,563
13 ran GD-SFT   11hdls Time 5m 49.30s (slw 34.30s)
1 Basilea Star 7 10-11 t ....Keith Mercer (5) 5/1
2 **ALICE'S OLD ROSE** 7 10-0 oh3 Luke Fletcher 7/1
chased leaders, led approaching 2 out, hard ridden and headed last 200yds
    [RPR79 TS40 OR79]   [op 8/1 tchd 9/1]
3 Classical Ben 6 11-9 ......Padraig Whelan (3) 6/1

Alice's Old Rose   10-0

9-y-o b m Broadsword - Rosie Marchioness
(Neltino)

Mrs H O Graham   Tom Greenway (5)

Placings: U/PUP6P/U4864322/UP-

OR**84**	Starts	1st	2nd	3rd	Win & Pl
All Jumps races	9	–	2	1	£2,912

GF-HRD 0-0-1 GS-HVY 0-1-3 Course 0-1-1 Dist 0-1-1

26 Apr Perth 3m½f Cls4 83-100 Am Hdl Hcap £4,997
18 ran GOOD   12hdls Time 5m 59.60s (slw 14.60s)
1 Burren Moonshine 7 10-11 Mr P Sheldrake (7) 9/2F
2 Sir Rowland Hill 7 11-5 .....Mr S W Byrne (7) 7/1
3 Speed Kris 7 11-1 v .....Miss R Davidson (3) 16/1
P **ALICE'S OLD ROSE** 9 10-2 ow2 ....
....................................Mr D A Fitzsimmons (7) 25/1
led 3rd to 5th, weakened 4 out, tailed off when pulled up before last [OR83]
P **LE MILLENAIRE** 7 11-5 .Miss K Bryson (7) 33/1
led to 3rd, close up until weakened 7th, tailed off when pulled up before last [OR100]

Le Millenaire   11-0

7-y-o bb g Ragmar - Ezaia (Iron Duke)

S H Shirley-Beavan   Wilson Renwick

Placings: 0/1/712U/472847P-

OR**98**	Starts	1st	2nd	3rd	Win & Pl
Hurdles	5	–	1	–	£1,268
All Jumps races	7	–	1	–	£1,268

GF-HRD 0-0-0 GS-HVY 0-1-5 Course 0-0-1 Dist 0-0-1

26 Apr Perth Pulled Up, see ALICE'S OLD ROSE

3 Apr Kelso 2m6½f   Cls4 96-110 Hdl Hcap £3,904
17 ran SOFT   11hdls Time 5m 50.10s (slw 35.10s)
1 Imtihan 7 10-7 ....Michael O'Connell (10) 7/2F
2 **CHIEF DAN GEORGE** 6 10-9 ....
....................................Declan McGann (5) 10/1
took keen hold early, chased leaders, effort and chased winner 3 out, kept on same pace run-in
    [RPR98 TS64 OR98]   [op 9/1]
3 Roobihoo 7 11-12 t ....Richard McGrath 7/1

7 LE MILLENAIRE 7 10-11 Miss K Bryson (7) 33/1
close up, led 6th to next, ridden and weakened
before 2 out btn 25 lengths [RPR82 TS50 OR102]
Dist: 6-1-13-1½-½ · RACE RPR: 109+/98+/109+
Racecheck: Wins 1 (1) Pl 3 Unpl 6

23 Mar Ayr 2m4f   Cls4 Nov Hdl £3,253
8 ran   GOOD   11hdls   Time 4m 59.20s (slw 19.20s)
1 Aces Four 7 11-8 ....Keith Mercer EvensF
2 Canada Street 5 11-1 ....Graham Lee 3/1
3 Duke Orsino 6 10-12 ......Peter Buchanan 5/1
4 LE MILLENAIRE 7 10-8 .Miss K Bryson (7) 20/1
chased leaders, outpaced 8th, soon beaten
[RPR81 TS31 OR106]
Dist: 14-11-7-dist   RACE RPR: 125+/100+/91+
Racecheck: Wins 2 (1) Pl - Unpl 6

Heversham   10-0

5-y-o *b g Octagonal - Saint Ann (Geiger Counter)*
J Hetherton   Paddy Brennan

Placings: 793655-8

OR84 F40   Starts 1st 2nd 3rd   Win & Pl
All Jumps races......... 7   –   – 1   £349
GF-HRD 0-0-1   GS-HVY 0-1-5   Course 0-0-1 Dist 0-0-0

---

1 May Sedgefield 2m4f Cls5 75-90 Hdl Hcap £2,733
1 Leadaway 7 11-0 ....Richard McGrath 9/2F
2 Moyne Pleasure 8 11-7 .....Kenny Johnson 15/2
3 Amalfi Storm 5 11-0 ....Mr T Greenall (3) 13/2
8 HEVERSHAM 5 11-6 p ....Russ Garritty 16/1
raced wide, in touch, headway to chase leaders
3 out, soon ridden and beaten
btn 39 lengths [RPR54 OR84]
Dist: 5-3-3½-8-3   RACE RPR: 89+/88/81
Racecheck: Wins - Pl - Unpl -

17 Apr Sedgefield 2m1f   Cls5 Nov 80-90 Hdl Hcap
                                              £2,741
15 ran GD-FM   8hdls   Time 4m 13.50s (slw 22.00s)
1 Suprendre Espere 6 11-8 .....Joseph Byrne 18/1
2 Filey Flyer 6 11-1 ....Colm Sharkey (7) 16/1
3 Emerald Destiny 4 11-8 ....Brian Harding 11/1
5 HEVERSHAM 5 11-9 p ....Russ Garritty 20/1
raced wide, held up, outpaced 4 out, rallied 2
out, never dangerous
[RPR76 TS21 OR86]   [op 25/1]
Dist: 1¼-4-6-8-¾-shd   RACE RPR: 91/90/84
Racecheck: Wins - Pl - Unpl 8

26 Mar Market Rasen 2m1½f Cls5 80-90 Hdl Hcap
                                              £2,602
15 ran SOFT   8hdls   Time 4m 36.70s (slw 33.70s)

---

1 Theatre Tinka 7 10-13 ....Adam Hawkins (10) 4/1
2 Fixateur 4 11-5 ....Wayne Hutchinson 6/1
3 Before The Mast 9 11-2 Charlie Poste (5) 100/30F
5 HEVERSHAM 5 11-10 p ....Graham Lee 16/1
mid-division, headway to chase leaders 5th,
outpaced after next
[RPR76 TS60 OR87]
Dist: 3-6-8-¾-15   RACE RPR: 93/86/82
Racecheck: Wins - Pl 1 Unpl 8

10 Mar Ayr 2m   Cls4 Nov 75-100 Hdl Hcap £4,554
8 ran   SOFT   8hdls   Time 4m 10.70s (slw 29.70s)
1 Boris The Spider 5 11-7 ......Wilson Renwick 4/1
2 Bollin Thomas 8 11-12 ....Tony Dobbin 5/2
3 Norminster 5 9-13 ....Gareth Thomas (7) 20/1
5 BUFFY 6 11-2 ....Neil Mulholland 9/2
held up in touch, headway before 3 out,
weakened before next
[RPR59 TS53 OR90]   [op 5/1]
6 HEVERSHAM 5 11-1 p ....Paddy Aspell (3) 12/1
prominent, effort and every chance after 3 out,
weakened before next
[RPR32 TS15 OR92]   [op 9/1]
Dist: ¾-3-21-7-29   RACE RPR: 98+/101+/77
Racecheck: Wins 1 (1) Pl 1 Unpl 10

Form Reading	**ALICE'S OLD ROSE**
Spotlight	Runner up off lower marks than this two seasons ago.
Handicap Ratings	On a mark of 72 six outings ago and now on a mark of 84 for today's contest which puts it on bottom weight 5lb out of the handicap.
Significant Items of Form	Nine year old with no wins but a second at today's course and distance in December 2004 in a Class 4 Novice Handicap Hurdle. Handicap mark that day was 79 when carrying 10st (bottom weight). Has had only two runs since then, the first on 02.01.06 at Ayr (Soft) over 3m½f when unseated at the fourth, the second on 26.04.06 at Perth (Good) over 3m½f when pulled up before last after leading from 3rd to 5th and weakening 4 out.
Verdict	Considering horse had a thirteen month break before resuming racing in January 2006 its runs since then have been typical of a horse getting fit again. Although horse was pulled up in its last run, it practically raced the distance and therefore should not be far away from the form which gave its 2nd place at today's course and distance in 2004, which was also a Class 4 Novice Handicap Hurdle.
Decision:	One of those occasions where you have to trust the trainer that she has now got the horse fit enough to be placed in the first three places, therefore: SELECT.

Form Reading	**LE MILLENAIRE**
Spotlight	Winning pointer on Good going but hasn't built on promise of second to decent sort over 2 miles on hurdles bow.
Handicap Ratings	Allocated a mark of 102 for Handicap Hurdle run two outings ago when placed 7th. Mark of 98 for today's contest after pulling up on last run.
Significant Items of Form	Seven year old with no National Hunt wins but two Point to Point victories. Last three runs have all been in Class 4 hurdles. Current campaign goes back to at least 23.03.06 when 4th of 7 in a Class 4 Novice Hurdle at Ayr (Good) over 2m4f, beaten 32 lengths. Ran next on 03.04.06, 7th of 17 at Kelso (Soft) in a Handicap Hurdle (Class 4) over today's distance when beaten 25 lengths after leading between 6th and 7th before weakening 2 out. Last race was on 26.04.06 at Perth (Good) in a Class 4 Handicap Hurdle over 3m½f when pulled up before the last after leading to the 3rd and close up to the 7th.

Verdict	It is impossible to determine from form information available in the *Racing Post* exactly how long current campaign has lasted, so it is equally impossible to work out whether horse has already passed peak fitness or whether it is still getting fitter. However, as its last run was in the same race as Alice Old Rose and almost identical in description (ie led early on, pulled up before last), it would be nonsensical to make a different SELECT or DISMISS decision for the two horses, particularly as both of them have had a satisfactory run at Kelso in a Class 4 Handicap Hurdle event at today's distance (2m6½f), albeit on different dates.
Decision:	SELECT.

Form Reading	**HEVERSHAM**
Spotlight	No improvement for step up to 2m4f last time after shaping as though needing further when modest 5th in 2m1f Sedgefield Handicap on previous start.
Handicap Ratings	Ran off a mark of 92 four outings ago and down to a mark of 84 today, which puts it on bottom weight.
Significant Items of Form	Five year old with no wins in only seven outings but one third place and two fifths. Current campaign goes back to at least 10.03.06 when 6th of 8 in a Class 4 Novice Handicap Hurdle at Ayr (Soft) over 2 miles, beaten 60 lengths after having every chance after 3 out. Ran next at Market Rasen (Soft) on 26.03.06 in a Class 5 Handicap hurdle over 2m1½f when 5th of 15, beaten 17¾ lengths after making headway to chase leaders at the fifth. Next ran on 17.04.06 at Sedgefield (Good to Firm) when again 5th of 15 in a Class 5 Novice Handicap Hurdle, beaten 16 lengths over 2m1f after rallying 2 out. Last run on 01.05.06 at Sedgefield over 2m4f in a Class 5 Handicap Hurdle where finished 8th, beaten 39 lengths after making headway to chase leaders 3 out.
Verdict	Although today's race, a Class 4 event, represents a step up in Class and distance, the horse has carried weights of 11st 10lb, 11st 9lb and 11st 6lb in its last three runs, so today's feather weight of 10st should make life a lot easier for the horse. Place in the first three must be a reasonable possibility because horse has been making an effort in each of its last four runs and according to the course statistics, it has run once at Kelso previously.
Decision:	SELECT

Overall Comments

There were not many clues in this race to indicate a big upset was on the cards but a brief glance at the runners and riders showed that if the paper favourite failed to perform, the race appeared wide open.

In this particular case it would be wrong to say that the favourite failed to perform, but simply by not wining it created the opportunity for an outsider victory at a big price.

I always think that a betting profile, particularly in a Handicap race, where there is a short priced favourite and a very open betting market for the remainder of the field, is always worth serious consideration. With such races it is important that you do not rely on your skills in trying to determine whether the favourite will or will not win. Instead, rely on the fact that there are a million and one reasons why a favourite will lose a race and the odds are at least 50/50 of it doing so.

This leaves you in a situation where you are reading the form of the 'outsiders' to establish whether there are in fact long priced 'outsiders' in the field with sufficient form to be placed in the top three placings.

If you think there are and you have a reasonable degree of confidence in their form, then go ahead and bet and let fate determine the fortunes of the favourite without you worrying about it.

In this particular race, the form of the 'outsider' selections was nothing to write home about, but as the betting has indicated, if you ignore the favourite the race wouldn't take a lot of winning.

If you had taken out insurance by placing your selections in a reverse forecast with the favourite, you would have been well rewarded because the Tote Exacta paid £135.80 and the Computer Straight Forecast £121.22.

EXAMPLE 19

19.02.06   Carlisle – Soft – Class 4 – Novice Hurdle – 2m4f
Winner   DOUBLE EAGLE – 16/1

1.40 RACE 1   VC Bet "Front Runners In US Racing" Novices' Hurdle (Class 4)   RUK
Winner £2,740.80   2m4f

£4000 guaranteed **For** 4yo+ which have not won more than three hurdles **Weights** 4yo 10st 7lb; 5yo+ 11st 3lb **Penalties** each hurdle won 7lb **Allowances** fillies and mares 7lb **Entries** 52 pay £10 **Penalty value 1st** £2,740.80 **2nd** £798.80 **3rd** £399.60

1 67-6881 **ALLEGEDLY SO** (IRE) 33   t6 11-11
b g Flemensfirth-Celtic Lace   G Lee (112)
D W Whillans   The Optimistic Pessimists

2 31 **ROLE ON** (IRE) 36   5 11-10
gr g Bob's Return-Banderole   Tony Dobbin (113)
N G Richards   Mr & Mrs Duncan Davidson

3 87P **BOSTON MATE** 49   5 11-3
b g Bal Harbour-Grindalythe   Ewan Whillans (7) (71)
R D E Woodhouse   M K Oldham

4 5-9 **BOW SCHOOL** (IRE) 108   6 11-3
b g New Frontier-Salleghan   Alan Dempsey (63)
J Howard Johnson   J Howard Johnson

5 3-122 **CAMDEN GEORGE** (IRE) 55   6 11-3
b g Pastemak-Triple Town Lass   Padge Whelan (111)
Mrs S J Smith   Mrs S Smith

6 330-P68 **CLASSIC HARRY** 19   6 11-3
b g Classic Cliche-Always Shining   Russ Garritty (98)
P Beaumont   N W A Bannister

7 19433 **DOUBLE EAGLE** 37 C   5 11-3
b g Silver Patriarch-Grayrose Double   S J Craine (3) (108)
D McCain Jnr   Dr G M Thelwall Jones

8 P **INGLEWOOD LAD** (IRE) 45   5 11-3
gr g Environment Friend-Pretty Obvious   Michael McAlister (3)
I McMath   D Graves A McMath G Mitchell D Gillespie

9 249 **MR PREACHER MAN** 38 BF   5 11-3
b g Sir Harry Lewis-Praise The Lord   Peter Buchanan (106)
Miss Lucinda V Russell   Mr & Mrs A D Stewart

10 **QDOS** (IRE)   5 11-3
br g Presenting-Emma's Way   P J Brennan
J Howard Johnson   Andrea & Graham Wylie

11 3F212-2 **RAMSDEN BOY** (IRE) (93P)   6 11-3
b g Saddlers' Hall-Double Glazed   Mr P McNeilly (7)
R T J Wilson (IRE)   G Ramsey

12 325 **ROC TREDUDON** (FR) 38   7 11-3
b g Double Bed-La Belle Polonaise   Keith Mercer (94)
L Lungo   R J Gilbert

13 5255 **SCRAPPIE** (IRE) 19   7 11-3
b g Fourstars Allstar-Clonyn   NON-RUNNER (102)
Miss Lucinda V Russell   John R Adam & Sons

14 P **TARTAN SNOW** 19   7 11-3
b g Valseur-Whitemoss Leader   Paddy Aspell
W S Coltherd   Whitemoss Golf Syndicate

15 09 **WEST HIGHLAND WAY** (IRE) 71   6 11-3
b g Foxhound-Gilding The Lily   Owyn Nelmes (3) (62)
Mrs H O Graham   Laumar Racing

16 PF-77P0 **OBLIGEE DE SIVOLA** (FR) 55   5 10-10
b m Video Rock-Quine de Chalamont   P J McDonald (5)
Ferdy Murphy   R Whittaker & J Whittaker

17 9-049 **SUPREME PROSPECT** 33   6 10-10
b m Supreme Leader-Dubai Dolly   Kenny Johnson (53)
R Johnson   T L A Robson

18 4 **TOPAZ LADY** (IRE) 33   6 10-10
ch m Zaffaran-Miss Top   Brian Harding (92)
N G Richards   Lowthian, Blakeney & Porter

BETTING FORECAST: 6-4 Role On, 7-2 Camden George, 6 Allegedly So, Mr Preacher Man, 10 Ramsden Boy, 12 Qdos, 14 Double Eagle, Topaz Lady, 20 Roc Tredudon, 33 Bow School, Classic Harry, 100 Boston Mate, Obligee de Sivola, West Highland Way, 200 bar.

SPOTLIGHT

Allegedly So Stunned just about everyone when edging home in a 3m novice hurdle at odds of 100/1 at Newcastle but did show ability in winning a bumper and first-time tongue-tie clearly made a big difference; no reason to doubt the form with the second having gone close in a Grade 2 next time and the third also well regarded.

Role On Encouraging bumper debut here in November and fulfilled that promise with a winning start over hurdles in January, where he didn't beat much but did so in pleasing fashion given he looked green; up in trip here and a leading player despite penalty.

Boston Mate Shown zero in three starts and chasing will be more his game.

Bow School It was a modest bumper in which he showed some promise on debut but then well held on hurdling bow and clearly needs to have improved plenty since then to stand a chance.

Camden George The fact he's been keen in the past is a bit of a concern around here but battled hard in winning his bumper and just a matter of time before he collects over hurdles, his latest second at Market Rasen solid enough in the context of this race.

Classic Harry Soft-ground bumper form to his name and best run yet over hurdles at Newcastle last time, though even that gives him something to find.

Double Eagle Looked a useful prospect when winning his bumper here on soft ground last year but yet to really click over hurdles and distress signals were out some way from home at Wetherby latest.

Inglewood Lad Took a walk in the market (100/1) prior to hurdling debut and duly showed very little.

Mr Preacher Man Sent off favourite in the Kelso race won by Role On but fluffed his lines completely; earlier efforts confirm he's better than that and no surprise at all should he finish a lot closer this time.

Qdos Initially made 16,000euros but that jumped to 64,000 when resold last summer; pedigree makes encouraging reading, dam being a half-sister to good chaser Bitofamixup, from the same family as old favourites Golden Freeze and Sparky Gayle; looks the stable's main hope and market should be informative.

Ramsden Boy Merits respect on Rules debut having won a point in Ireland last year and not at all disgraced behind a good sort (easy winner) on final run in November.

Roc Tredudon Beaten a fair way on all starts but was sent off at odds-on for his bumper and has shaped with a degree of promise since sent hurdling, behind Role On on final start at Kelso; may need better ground and one for another day.

Tartan Snow 200/1 chance and tailed off on debut.

West Highland Way Maiden winner on the Flat in 2004 but not a lot since and beaten out of sight both times over hurdles.

Obligee de Sivola Runner-up in the French Provinces last year but hard to derive much encouragement from her two runs for this yard and remains best watched.

Supreme Prospect Soundly beaten all starts and low-grade handicaps probably beckon.

Topaz Lady Moved well for a long way when an encouraging fourth of 17 on Newcastle debut and, sent off only 4/1, had presumably been showing something at home; clearly has a future, though Tony Dobbin has jumped ship to stablemate Role On.

Supreme Prospect   10-10

6-y-o b m Supreme Leader - Dubai Dolly (Law Society)

R Johnson   Kenny Johnson

Placings: 9-049

	Starts	1st	2nd	3rd	Win & Pl
Hurdles	2	–	–	–	–
All Jumps races	4	–	–	–	–
GF-HRD 0-0-0	GS-HVY 0-0-4		Course 0-0-0		Dist 0-0-0

17 Jan Newcastle   9th, see TOPAZ LADY

3 Jan Wetherby 2m   Cls4 Nov Hdl £3,083
7 ran HEAVY   7hdls   Time 4m 37.90s (slw 57.90s)
1 Tabora 5 11-7 ....Richard Johnson 4/11F
2 Misleain 7 11-0 ....Paddy Aspell 22/1
3 Gouranga 4 10-2 ....Mattie Batchelor 4/1
4 **SUPREME PROSPECT** 6 11-0 ....
....Kenny Johnson 100/1
behind until plugged on one pace approaching last [RPR25]
Dist: 9-58-¾-shd-½   RACE RPR: 102+/85+/14
Racecheck: Wins - Pl - Unpl 1

3 Nov 06 Hexham 2m1½f   Cls5 NHF 4-6yo £2,398
10 ran SOFT   Time 4m 17.10s (slw 25.10s)
1 Issaquah 4 10-9 ....Fergus King (3) 4/1
2 Riverbank Rainbow 5 10-12 Richard McGrath 22/1
3 Flora May 5 10-7 ....Derek Nolan (5) 9/1
10 **SUPREME PROSPECT** 5 10-12 ....
....Kenny Johnson 66/1
raced wide in rear, outpaced halfway, never on terms btn 66 lengths [RPR21]
Dist: 4-2-1¼-¾-1½   RACE RPR: 88+/83/81
Racecheck: Wins 1 Pl 4 Unpl 21

Tartan Snow   11-3

7-y-o b g Valseur - Whitemoss Leader (Supreme Leader)

W S Coltherd   Paddy Aspell

Placings: P

	Starts	1st	2nd	3rd	Win & Pl
All Jumps races	1	–	–	–	–
GF-HRD 0-0-0	GS-HVY 0-0-1		Course 0-0-0		Dist 0-0-1

31 Jan Newcastle 2m4f   Cls4 Nov Hdl £2,928
18 ran SOFT   9hdls   Time 5m 20.80s (slw 37.80s)
1 Imperial Commander 6 10-12 Tony Evans 11/10F
2 Jass 5 10-9 ....Phil Kinsella (3) 14/1
3 Nevertika 6 11-5 ....Richard McGrath 7/2
5 SCRAPPIE 7 10-12 ....Peter Buchanan 100/1
prominent, driven after 4th, outpaced from 4 out [RPR91 TS32]
8 CLASSIC HARRY 6 10-12 .Anthony Ross 100/1
in touch until weakened after 5th btn 42 lengths [RPR87 TS27]
P **TARTAN SNOW** 7 10-12 ..Alan Dempsey 200/1
unseated rider twice before start, midfield, struggling after 4th, tailed off when pulled up before 2 out
Dist: 19-1½-11-6-1¼   RACE RPR: 132+/112+/115
Racecheck: Wins - Pl - Unpl 2

Inglewood Lad   11-3

5-y-o gr g Environment Friend - Pretty Obvious (Pursuit Of Love)

I McMath   Michael McAlister (3)

Placings: P

	Starts	1st	2nd	3rd	Win & Pl
All Jumps races	1	–	–	–	–
GF-HRD 0-0-0	GS-HVY 0-0-1		Course 0-0-0		Dist 0-0-1

5 Jan Newcastle 2m4f   Cls3 Nov Hdl £4,880
12 ran SOFT   11hdls   Time 5m 21.50s (slw 38.50s)
1 Dancer's Serenade 5 11-4 ..Jason Maguire 9/4F

---

2 Ballabriggs 6 11-4 ....Dominic Elsworth 33/1
3 Bouncing King 5 11-1 ....S J Craine (3) 4/1
5 SCRAPPIE 7 11-4 ....Peter Buchanan 18/1
mistake 1st, behind, outpaced halfway, some late headway, never on terms [RPR70 TS14]   [op 14/1 tchd 20/1]
P INGLEWOOD LAD 5 11-1 ....
..............................Michael McAlister (3) 100/1
held up, struggling halfway, never on terms, pulled up before 4 out
Dist: nk-8-shd-22-1½   RACE RPR: 101+/100/92
Racecheck: Wins - Pl - Unpl 6

West Highland Way   11-3

6-y-o b g Foxhound - Gilding The Lily (High Estate)

Mrs H O Graham   Owyn Nelmes (3)

Placings: 09

	Starts	1st	2nd	3rd	Win & Pl
F60					
All Jumps races	2	–	–	–	–
GF-HRD 0-0-0	GS-HVY 0-0-0		Course 0-0-0		Dist 0-0-0

10 Dec 06 Musselburgh 2m4f Cls5 Mdn Hdl £2,602
14 ran GOOD   12hdls   Time 4m 47.30s (slw 2.80s)
1 Sharp Reply 4 11-0 ....Mark Bradburne 9/2
2 Celtic Carisma 4 11-0 ....Richard McGrath 7/2
3 Wee Forbees 4 11-0 ....P J Brennan 5/4F
9 **WEST HIGHLAND WAY** 5 11-0 ....
....Dominic Elsworth 100/1
in touch to 4 out, soon ridden and beaten btn 45 lengths [RPR30 TS29]
Dist: 2-nk-9-1¼-43   RACE RPR: 100+/88/95
Racecheck: Wins 3 (3) Pl 2 Unpl 4

17 Nov 06 Kelso 2m½f   Cls3 Nov Hdl £5,205
13 ran GD-SFT   8hdle   Time 4m 7.50s (slw 19.50s)
1 Smart Street 4 10-13 ....Phil Kinsella (5) 8/1
2 To Tiger 5 10-5 ....David Da Silva (7) 14/1
3 Raining Horse 4 10-9 p ...Gary Berridge (3) 66/1
11 **WEST HIGHLAND WAY** 5 10-12 ....
....Keith Mercer 250/1
midfield, struggling 4th, soon beaten btn 58 lengths [RPR51 TS10]
Dist: 1¾-3-2½-4-5   RACE RPR: 115/107/104
Racecheck: Wins 3 Pl 1 Unpl 18

Flat Form

10 Oct 06 Newcastle 1m2f Cls5 58-70 Hcap £3,562
17 ran SOFT   Time 2m 16.15s (slw 9.45s)
1 Dium Mac 5 9-1 ......Suzzanne France (7) 18/1
2 Sudden Impulse 5 8-11 Silvestre de Sousa 5 5/2F
3 Mystical Ayr 4 8-7 ......Andrew Mullen (3) 10 14/1
15 **WEST HIGHLAND WAY** 5 9-1 ....
....Stephen Donohoe (3) 11 100/1
always towards rear btn 45 lengths [OR66]
Dist: 1¼-3-1½-nk-¾   RACE RPR: 82/69/63
Racecheck: Wins 3 (1) Pl 1 Unpl 16

Roc Tredudon   11-3

7-y-o b g Double Bed - La Belle Polonaise (Bold Lad)

L Lungo   Keith Mercer

Placings: 325

	Starts	1st	2nd	3rd	Win & Pl
Hurdles	2	–	1	–	£1,146
All Jumps races	3	–	1	1	£1,405
GF-HRD 0-0-0	GS-HVY 0-1-3		Course 0-0-0		Dist 0-0-0

12 Jan Kelso 2m2f   Cls4 Nov Hdl 4-7yo £3,253
16 ran HEAVY   8hdls   Time 5m 2.30s (slw 49.30s)
1 **ROLE ON** 5 11-5 ....Tony Dobbin 5/2
took keen hold, in touch, led 3 out, ridden and kept on strongly run-in [RPR109 TS55]   [op 15/8 tchd 7/4]
2 Cavers Glen 5 11-5 ....Barry Keniry 5/1
3 Nelson Du Ronceray 6 10-12 ....

....David Da Silva (7) 11/1
5 ROC TREDUDON 7 11-5 ......Keith Mercer 12/1
prominent, effort after 2 out, outpaced after last [RPR73 TS16]   [op 7/1]
9 MR PREACHER MAN 5 11-5 Peter Buchanan 2/1F
close up, driven 3 out, beaten after next (trainer had no explanation for the poor form shown) btn 68 lengths [RPR36]   [op 9/4 tchd 3/1]
Dist: 7-4-1½-19-1¾   RACE RPR: 109+/99+/93
Racecheck: Wins - Pl 2 Unpl 8

11 Dec 06 Ayr 2m   Cls4 Nov Hdl £3,904
10 ran HEAVY   9hdls   Time 4m 20.00s (slw 39.00s)
1 The Abbots Habit 5 10-12 ....Brian Harding 4/7F
2 ROC TREDUDON 6 10-12 ....Keith Mercer 20/1
held up in rear, steady headway approaching 4 out, in touch after next, kept on approaching last, no chance with winner [RPR70]   [op 16/1]
3 Classy Chav 4 10-12 ....G Lee 33/1
Dist: 25-6-hd-7-6   RACE RPR: 111+/83/77
Racecheck: Wins 1 (1) Pl - Unpl 8

15 Nov 06 Hexham 2m1½f   Cls6 NHF 4-6yo £1,782
7 ran SOFT   Time 4m 25.00s (slw 33.00s)
1 Tot O'Whiskey 5 10-13 ....Fergus King (3) 5/1
2 Heez A Steel 5 10-13 ....Jan Faltejsek (3) 20/1
3 ROC TREDUDON 6 11-2 ...Brian Harding 4/6F
took keen, close up until ridden and weakened from 2f out [RPR77]   [op 5/6]
Dist: 9-27-17-15-dist RACE RPR: 113+/100+/77+
Racecheck: Wins 2 (2) Pl 1 Unpl 7

Topaz Lady   10-10

6-y-o ch m Zaffaran - Miss Top (Tremblant)

N G Richards   Brian Harding

Placings: 4

	Starts	1st	2nd	3rd	Win & Pl
All Jumps races	1	–	–	–	£190
GF-HRD 0-0-0	GS-HVY 0-0-1		Course 0-0-0		Dist 0-0-0

17 Jan Newcastle 2m   Cls4 Mdn Hdl £2,602
17 ran SOFT   9hdls   Time 4m 15.50s (slw 32.50s)
1 Dance The Mambo 5 11-2 b1 ..Mr T Greenall 4/1
2 Freedom Flying 4 10-5 ....Barry Keniry 10/1
3 Bollin Ruth 5 11-2 ....Dominic Elsworth 5/1
4 **TOPAZ LADY** 6 11-2 ....Tony Dobbin 4/1
held up, headway and prominent 4 out, ridden and one pace from 2 out [RPR74 TS43]   [op 100/30]
9 SUPREME PROSPECT 6 11-2 ....
....Kenny Johnson 80/1
raced wide, never reached leaders btn 54 lengths [RPR35]
Dist: 14-½-nk-9-5   RACE RPR: 90+/64/75
Racecheck: Wins - Pl - Unpl 5

Double Eagle   11-3

5-y-o b g Silver Patriarch - Grayrose Double (Celtic Cone)

D McCain Jnr   S J Craine (3)

Placings: 19433

VERDICT A few with chances but **ROLE ON** looks the pick of them, having created a strong impression in his manner of victory at Kelso. Better was clearly expected of **Mr Preacher Man** in that same race and it will be interesting to see the level of confidence behind him this time.[AWJ]

OR111   Starts 1st 2nd 3rd   Win & Pl
Hurdles 3   –   –   2   £1,591
All Jumps races 5   1   –   2   £3,304
    10/06   Carl   2m1f Cls6 NHF 4-6yo soft £1,713
GF-HRE J-0-0   GS-HVY 1-1-5   Course 1-0-1   Dist 0-0-1
13 Jan Wetherby 2m4½f Cls3 Nov Hdl 4-7yo £5,665
6 ran   HEAVY   8hdls   Time 5m 59.30s (slw 1m 10.30s)
1 Shrewd Investor 7 11-11 .David O'Meara 11/10F
2 Major Oak 6 11-11 b ....Barry Keniry 3/1
3 **DOUBLE EAGLE** 5 11-3 ....S J Craine (3) 9/2
tracked leaders, weakened approaching 2 out, 25 lengths behind when blundered last
[RPR70 TS46]   [op 5/1 tchd 7/1]
Dist: ½-37   RACE RPR: 113+/110/70+
Racecheck: Wins - Pl - Unpl 1

23 Dec 06 Bangor-On-Dee 3m Cls4 Mdn Hdl £2,928
12 ran   SOFT   12hdls   Time 6m 3.50s (slw 29.50s)
1 Shrewd Investor 6 10-12 .....David O'Meara 13/2
2 Secret Ploy 6 10-9 ....P C O'Neill (3) 10/11F
3 **DOUBLE EAGLE** 4 10-9 ....S J Craine (3) 9/1
in touch, not fluent 6th, went 2nd after 7th to 3 out, weakened approaching 2 out
[RPR97 TS65]   [op 10/1]
Dist: hd-16-13-6-6   RACE RPR: 113/113/97
Racecheck: Wins 2 (2) Pl - Unpl 8

5 Dec 06 Sedgefield 2m5½f Cls4 Nov Hdl £2,928
9 ran   SOFT   10hdls   Time 5m 48.10s (slw 53.10s)
1 Silver Snitch 6 10-12 ....Tony Dobbin 15/8F
2 Senora Snoopy 5 10-5 ....G Lee 7/2
3 Greenock 5 10-9 ....T J Dreaper (3) 9/1
4 **DOUBLE EAGLE** 4 10-12 .Dominic Elsworth 5/2
prominent, driven before 3 out, no extra before next [RPR71 TS19]   [op 9/4 tchd 3/1]
6 **CLASSIC HARRY** 5 10-12 p ..Russ Garritty 16/1
led to before 2 out, soon weakened (trainer's rep said gelding had a breathing problem)
[RPR68 TS15]   [op 14/1]
Dist: 2-26-2-1¾-1½   RACE RPR: 105+/92/73
Racecheck: Wins - Pl 3 Unpl 6

Form Reading	**SUPREME PROSEPCT**
Spotlight	Soundly beaten all starts.
Handicap Ratings	Not applicable – Non Handicap.
Significant Items of Form	Six year old with only four runs to date, the last two of which were in Class 4 Hurdles on 03.01.07 when 4th of 7 runners, beaten 67¾ lengths over 2 miles at Wetherby (Heavy) and 17.01.07 when 9th of 17, beaten 54 lengths over 2 miles at Newcastle (Soft).
Verdict	No indication from last three races that horse is about to become competitive.
Hence:	DISMISS.

Form Reading	**TARTAN SNOW**
Spotlight	Tailed off on debut.
Handicap Ratings	Not applicable.
Significant Items of Form	Seven year old with only one run to date on 31.01.07 at Newcastle (Soft) in a Class 4 Novice Hurdle when unseated twice before start and struggling after 4th before pulling up 2 out.
Verdict	No evidence to promote optimism.
Hence:	DISMISS.

Form Reading	**INGLEWOOD LAD**
Spotlight	Showed very little, hurdle debut.
Handicap Ratings	Not applicable.
Significant Items of Form	Seven year old with only one run to date on 05.01.07 at Newcastle (Soft) in a Class 3 Novice Hurdle when pulled up before 4 out after struggling from halfway.
Verdict	No evidence to suggest a top three placing is likely.
Hence:	DISMISS.

Form Reading	**WEST HIGHLAND WAY**
Spotlight	Maiden winner on the flat in 2004, beaten out of sight on two hurdle runs.
Handicap Ratings	Not applicable.
Significant Items of Form	Six year old with only two hurdle runs on 17.11.06 and 10.12.06 in a Class 3 Hurdle at Kelso, beaten 58 lengths and a Class 5 Maiden Hurdle at Musselburgh, beaten 68 lengths.
Verdict	No indication of ability yet.
Hence:	DISMISS.

Form Reading	**OBLIGEE DE SIVOLVA, BOSTON MATE, CLASSIC HARRY** and **BOW SCHOOL** in the order as shown were all dismissed in the form reading process. See Overall Comment

---

Form Reading	**ROC TREDUDON**
Spotlight	Shaped with a degree of promise since sent hurdling.
Handicap Ratings	Not applicable.
Significant Items of Form	Seven year old with only three runs and no wins, but a 3rd of 7 runners at Hexham (Soft) in opening Bumper on 15.11.06, followed by a 2nd of 10, beaten 25 lengths in a Class 4 Novice Hurdle (2 miles) at Ayr (Heavy) on 11.12.06. Finished 5th of 16 in a Class 4 Novice Hurdle, beaten 31½ lengths by today's paper favourite on 12.01.07 over 2m2f at Ayr (Heavy) after making an effort 2 out.
Verdict	Form is impressive enough and recent enough to think a top three placing is achievable.
Hence:	SELECT.

Form Reading	**TOPAZ LADY**
Spotlight	Moved well for a long way when an encouraging 4th of 17 on Newcastle debut and sent off only 4/1.
Handicap Ratings	Not applicable.
Significant Items of Form	Six year old with only one run in a Class 4 Maiden Hurdle over 2 miles at Newcastle on Soft when 4th of 17, beaten only 14½ lengths.
Verdict	Only one run but finishing position and starting price indicates horse has good potential.
Decision:	Too good to overlook, hence: SELECT.

Form Reading	**DOUBLE EAGLE**
Spotlight	Bumper winner here (Carlisle) on Soft last year and yet to click over hurdles.
Handicap Ratings	Not applicable.
Significant Items of Form	Five year old Bumper winner at Carlisle (Soft) October 2006. Last three runs started with a 4th of 9 runners in a Class 4 Novice Hurdle at Sedgefield (Soft) over 2m5½f, beaten 30 lengths on 05.12.06. Ran next on 23.12.06 at Bangor (Soft) over 3 miles when 3rd of 12 runners in a Class 4 Maiden Hurdle, beaten 16 lengths after occupying 2nd until 3 out. Last ran on 13.01.06 at Wetherby (Heavy) in a Class 3 2m4½f Novice Hurdle when 3rd of 6 runners, beaten 37½ lengths after a blunder at the last.
Verdict	Course winner with decent recent form, best of which was run at Bangor when 3rd over 3 miles. Distance and ground should be suitable so top three placing a definite possibility.
Decision:	SELECT.

Overall Comments

This has been included in the form reading examples to demonstrate why a Non Handicap race, and particularly one which is a low grade contest, is always going to prove more difficult to unravel, form-wise than a Handicap contest.

Non Handicaps such as this one are frequently made up of lots of runners with very little form and therefore there is always a distinct possibility that one or more of them can produce a massive improvement in form relative to what they have shown so far or, alternatively, they can have no form at all (ie it is their first race) and they can pull off a win which is a complete surprise to the betting market.

Although there are *Racing Post* ratings for such contests they cannot be classed as a valuable guide because the form on which they are based is frequently incomplete, unreliable or hard to assess.

It is for all these reasons that as far as The Tail End System is concerned, Non Handicaps are classified as Non-Preferred contests.

There will, however, be Non Handicaps where there is something about one or more of the runners that catches the eye, and closer inspection reveals a possible betting opportunity.

As far as this particular race was concerned, the form reading was long and time consuming, which is why I have abbreviated my report on the exercise in the case of four horses, namely Obligee de Sivola, Boston Mate, Classic Harry and Bow School.

Looking at the list of runners and riders, one horse, Double Eagle, stood out because it was the only course winner in the field and the fact that it went on to win the race is evidence yet again that course form is always an extremely important factor.

From a *Racing Post* point of view, this race was important because the winner of the Search for a Tipster competition sealed his victory with the selection of Double Eagle. This prompted one of the *Racing Post* regular columnists to write that Double Eagle's selection was a complete fluke, a statement which I found very puzzling, to say the least.

You do not need to study the form of jump race horses for very long before you discover that course form, whether it be a win, place or a run, is frequently a significant factor in identifying winners, and it is for this very reason that the course winner option is built into The Tail End System.

It should be noted that, in the form reading exercise, two selections, Roc Tredudon and Topaz Lady, had already been made when the form of Double Eagle, which happened to be a course winner, was read because it was the next horse in the betting forecast.

So in this particular case, it was not necessary to make a decision to choose between reading the form of the next horse in the Betting Forecast or the longest priced course winner (which was Double Eagle) in order to make a third selection.

For the record the Forecast Double Eagle, with Camden George the second favourite, paid £58.70 for the Tote Exacta and £101.03 for the Computer Straight Forecast.

EXAMPLE 20

14.05.06 Uttoxeter – Good – Class 5 – Handicap Hurdle – 2m
Winner DONIE DOOLEY – 33/1

3.30
RACE 4
stratstone.com Jaguar Handicap **ATR**
Hurdle (Class 5)
Winner £2,602.40 **2m**

£4000 guaranteed For 4yo+ Rated 0-95 Weights raised 2lb Minimum Weight 10-0 Penalties after May 6th,
a winner of a hurdle 7lb Toulouse Express's Handicap Mark 93 Entries 70 pay £10 Penalty value 1st
£2,602.40 2nd £764 3rd £382 4th £190.80

06027-0	**1**	**TOULOUSE EXPRESS** (IRE) [14]	7 11-12	Kenny Johnson (95)
		b g Toulon-Miss Ivy		
		R Johnson Robert Johnson		
/7085P-	**2**	**DONIE DOOLEY** (IRE) [157] C	8 11-12	Marcus Foley (87)
		ch g Be My Native-Bridgeofallen	33/1	
		P T Dalton Mrs Julie Martin		
298717-	**3**	**IMPERIAL ROYALE** (IRE) [85] D	5 11-12	Thomas Burrows(7) (94)
		ch g All-Royal-God Speed Her		
		P L Clinton In The Clear Racing		
0P05P-	**4**	**DREAM ON MAGGIE** [85]	6 11-11	Paddy Brennan (93)
		ch m Dreams End-Allo Bella		
		P Bowen P Bowen		
/70098-	**5**	**RIVERTREE** (IRE) [21]	5 11-11	Daryl Jacob(5) (96)
		ch g Entrepreneur-French River		
		D P Keane Mrs P Corcoran		
/1P47-4	**6**	**LAWAAHEB** (IRE) [14] D	5 11-10	Chris Honour(3) (93)
		b g Alhaarth-Ajayib		
		M J Gingell Direct-Racing		
6P159-	**7**	**DISHDASHA** (IRE) [-87] (6F) D	4 11-9	Jodie Mogford (78)
		b g Desert Prince-Counterplot		
		C R Dore W Lunn Haulage		
77560-7	**8**	● **INSURGENT** (IRE) [1]	4 11-9	Barry Keniry (91)
		b g Fasliyev-Mountain Ash	N.R	
		R C Guest Billy Maguire		
P0/63-	**9**	**NIGHT WARRIOR** (IRE) [21]	b 6 11-9	Paul Moloney (93)
		b g Alhaarth-Miniver		
		N P Litimoden Nigel Shields		
8/4071-	**10**	**LOSING GRIP** (IRE) [35]	7 11-7	Dominic Elsworth (99)
		b/br m Presenting-Executivo Wonder		
		Mrs S J Smith The Victory Salute Group		
1P/P6P-	**11**	**MIKE SIMMONS** [22] C	p 10 11-7	Derek Laverty(5) (91)
		b g Dellacashial-Lady Crusty	25/1 (2nd)	
		L P Grassick L P Grassick		
0531-	**12**	**CITY OF MANCHESTER** (IRE) [15]	4 11-7	Robert Thornton (86)
		b g Desert Style-Nomadic Dancer		
		B D Leavy S H Riley		
056C0-6	**13**	**TINIAN** [14]	8 11-7	Miss C Metcalfe(7) (87)
		b g Mtoto-Housefull		
		Miss Tracy Waggott Miss T Waggott		
0/560-0	**14**	**FORBEARING** (IRE) [14] D	9 11-6	Mr D Greenway(7) (91)
		b g Bering-For Example		
		K G Wingrove L T Woodhouse		
214/P-P	**15**	**PRECIOUS LUCY** (FR) [12]	7 11-6	Richard Hobson
		gr m Kadrou-Teardrops Fall		
		G F Bridgwater Mrs Jennifer Hobson & Mrs Sharon Steward		
57B70-	**16**	**PATRONAGE** [31]	b[1] 4 11-5	Noel Fehily (95)
		b g Royal Applause-Passionate Pursuit	N.R	
		Jonjo O'Neill Gordon Hopkins		
67P/P8-	**17**	**PEERLESS MOTION** (IRE) [28] D	11 11-5	Keith Mercer (90)
		b g Caerleon-Final Figure	20/3 RD	
		S Lycett Mrs S J Branston		
573/0P-	**18**	**MAJOR BLADE** (GER) [71] (6F)	8 11-5	T J Phelan (91)
		b g Dashing Blade-Misnininki		
		Mrs H Dalton G Lloyd, G Allmond, R Barrs		

● INSURGENT 7th 5.40 Hexham yesterday

2005 (16 ran) Tinstre P W Hiatt 7 10-8 50/1   Sean Fox OR80

BETTING FORECAST: 11-4 Losing Grip, 5 City Of Manchester, 8 Insurgent, Major Blade, Night Warrior, 12 Lawaaheb, 14 Dishdasha, Dream On Maggie, Imperial Royale, Patronage, Rivertree, Toulouse Express, 25 Peerless Motion, Tinian, 33 Donie Dooley, Mike Simmons, Precious Lucy, 50 Forbearing.

SPOTLIGHT

Toulouse Express Narrowly beaten in Catterick seller on debut for this yard in March but well beaten in handicap company since; others more likely.

Donie Dooley Won fast-ground maiden hurdle over longer trip here in 2003 but well held since and pulled up at Huntingdon when last seen; opposable on first outing for 157 days.

Imperial Royale Won soft-ground lady riders' handicap hurdle at Leicester before disappointing on heavy going over this C&D; won't mind if the ground eases but consistency not his strong point.

Dream On Maggie Well held at big prices three of four starts in maiden/novice hurdles (pulled up and dismounted at Wincanton latest) but not disgraced at Fontwell previously (beaten around 12l); market will guide on handicap debut.

Rivertree Blanked all 21 starts for Joseph Crowley in Ireland and first win not imminent judging by two runs at Wincanton for Paul Keane last month; however, yard's runners always worth a second look here and couldn't rule out entirely with this trip likely to suit better than the 2m6f he tackled last time.

Lawaaheb Sole hurdles win for another yard in Fakenham seller but good fourth in big-field handicap at Wetherby last time offers hope; clearly appreciated removal of headgear that day and one to consider.

Dishdasha Surprise winner of Huntingdon juvenile novice event last November (good/firm) but winless since over hurdles and in Banded company on the Flat; fit after fair effort at Kempton six days ago (last win came after similar break) but improvement needed.

Insurgent Musselburgh bumper winner in January (good/firm) and far from disgraced when 33-1 fifth on hurdles debut at Kelso last month before two quick runs for handicap mark; however, didn't run very well at Hexham yesterday, weakening into seventh in modest novice hurdle.

Night Warrior Five-time winner on AW and only fair effort on first hurdles spin for this yard when third of four finishers at Wincanton latest; blinkers he wore for last three Flat wins but missing at Wincanton, are back on today and another to watch in the market.

Losing Grip First win when making all the running to account for Moyne Pleasure (runs in 3.00) in Market Rasen selling handicap latest (soft); this represents step up in class but respected from top yard, especially if rain arrives.

Mike Simmons Well beaten (pulled up twice) three outings this year on return from long break and seems best at longer trips; first-time cheekpieces will need to have huge effect.

City Of Manchester Third and first last two starts, both at plating level (well backed latest) but clearly in good heart and couldn't rule out in open contest.

Tinian Fair effort at Wetherby latest with usual cheekpieces dispensed with but overall profile unconvincing and still looking for first win in Britain.

Forbearing Changed yards frequently and shown some winners in the past after snatching defeat from the jaws of victory on more than one occasion; no show on debut for Ken Wingrove latest and easy chuck-out.

Precious Lucy Hereford winner on firm ground for another yard a couple of years ago but pulled up last twice and easily opposed.

Patronage Sole win for Michael Bell when long odds-on in Redcar maiden last summer; regressive since, including over hurdles for current connections and opposable in first-time blinkers.

Peerless Motion Punchestown bumper winner for Dermot Weld back in 1999 and off the mark over hurdles for Charlie Mann in 2001; well beaten two starts for current yard since returning from a break and best watched.

Major Blade Far from convincing over hurdles so far but won handicap on the Flat just six days ago and a possible if transferring that improvement to timber.

VERDICT A tricky puzzle to solve and, while support for handicap debutant **Night Warrior** would be significant, a chance is taken on **RIVERTREE**, whose shrewd trainer does well here.[AM]

OFFICIAL RATINGS								RP RATING		
LAST SIX OUTINGS-LATEST ON RIGHT						**3.30** HANDICAP	TODAY FUTURE	LATEST / BEST / ADJUSTED		
77[0]	77[6]	77[0]	—	93[7]	93[0]	Toulouse Express 11-12	93	60	95	95
—	100[7]	100[0]	97[6]	95[6]	93[P]	Donie Dooley 11-12	93	—	75	87
—	84[9]	—	—	87[1]	93[7]	Imperial Royale 11-12	93	52	94	94
—	—	—	—	—	—	Dream On Maggie 11-11	92	—	93	93
—	—	—	96[0]	97[9]	95[8]	Rivertree 11-11	92	54	96	96
—	—	95[P]	95[4]	92[7]	91[4]	Lawaaheb 11-10	91	85	93	93
—	—	—	—	95[5]	—	Dishdasha 11-9	94	59	78	78
—	—	—	—	—	—	Insurgent 11-9	91	70	91	91
—	—	—	—	—	—	Night Warrior 11-9	90	84	93	93
—	—	—	—	—	76[1]	Losing Grip 11-7	88	99 ◄	99	99 ◄
86[8]	83[1]	100[P]	95[P]	95[6]	92[P]	Mike Simmons 11-7	88	—	*61	—
—	—	—	—	89[0]	89[6]	City Of Manchester 11-7	92	86	86	86
—	—	—	—	—	—	Tinian 11-7	88	80	87	87
110[5]	—	—	—	—	—	Forbearing 11-6	87	74	91	91
—	—	90[1]	—	90[P]	90[P]	Precious Lucy 11-6	87	—	—	—
—	—	—	—	—	93[9]	Patronage 11-5	90	38	100 ◄	95
—	107[3]	110[6]	108[7]	95[P]	90[8]	Peerless Motion 11-5	86	82	82	90
—	—	95[3]	89[0]	89[P]	Major Blade 11-5		86	—	70	91

Forbearing 11-6

9-y-o *b g Bering - For Example (Northern Baby)*
K G Wingrove Mr D Greenway (7)

Placings: 1401170/582650/560-0

OR87 F56	Starts	1st	2nd	3rd	Win & Pl
All Jumps races	20	3	1	1	£17,293

106 3/04 Chep 2m½f Cls3 91-118 Hdl Hcap gd-fm £5,200
101 2/04 Leic 2m Cls4 78-104 Hdl Hcap soft £4,271
93 12/03 Tntn 2m1f Cls3 88-110 Hdl Hcap good £4,501
Total win prize-money £13,972

GF-HRD 1-1-9 GS-HVY 1-2-9 Course 0-2-3 Dist 2-3-11

30 Apr Ludlow 2m Cls5 Claim Hdl £2,928
17 ran GD-FM 9hdls Time 3m 44.50s (slw 5.50s)
1 Canadian Storm 5 10-13 p Richard Spate (7) 13/2
2 Waziri 5 11-2 ....Paul Moloney 7/1
3 Desert Spa 11 10-9 ....Mr T J O'Brien (5) 9/2J
10 **FORBEARING** 9 10-7 .Mr D Greenway (7) 40/1
in rear, some headway 5th, hit 4 out, jumped left when beaten 3 out
btn 18½ lengths [RPR66 TS43 OR90] [tchd 50/1]

Dist: 1¾-1¾-¾-shd-½ RACE RPR: 94+/85/81
Racecheck: Wins 1 (1) Pl 3 Unpl 4

10 Nov 05 Ludlow 2m Cls5 Cond Sell Hdl £2,440
14 ran GOOD 9hdls Time 3m 47.60s (slw 8.60s)
1 Auetaler 11 10-4 p................B C Byrnes (6) 7/1
2 My Sharp Grey 6 10-3 ....Robert Stephens 9/1
3 Ambersong 7 10-10 ....Gino Carenza 5/1
11 **FORBEARING** 8 10-7 p James Diment (3) 33/1
held up in mid-division, ridden 4th, hit 6th, soon behind btn 30 lengths [RPR70 TS56 OR95]

Dist: 2-5-3½-¾-1¾ RACE RPR: 100+/91/94+
Racecheck: Wins 3 (2) Pl - Unpl 19

4 Sep 05 Fontwell 2m4f Cls4 Claim Hdl £2,569
7 ran GD-FM 10hdls Time 4m 52.40s (slw 17.40s)
1 Outside Investor 5 10-12 p ..Robert Thornton 6/1
2 Red Nose Lady 8 10-9 p ....Jodie Mogford 3/1
3 Lightning Star 10 10-12 b ....Philip Hide 2/1F
6 **FORBEARING** 8 10-3 ....James Diment (5) 14/1
pulled hard and hung left throughout, not fluent, in touch until outpaced approaching 3 out (jockey said gelding hung left in straight)
[RPR83 TS31 OR100] [op 12/1 tchd 16/1]

Dist: ½-½-1¼-12-1 RACE RPR: 102/100+/101
Racecheck: Wins 1 (1) Pl 2 Unpl 6

Precious Lucy 11-6

7-y-o *gr m Kadrou - Teardrops Fall (Law Society)*
G F Bridgwater Richard Hobson

Placings: 08/214/P-P

OR87	Starts	1st	2nd	3rd	Win & Pl
All Jumps races	7	1	1	–	£5,454

90 6/04 Hrfd 2m1f Cls4 Nov 69-95 Hdl Hcap gd-fm £3,936

GF-HRD 1-1-3 GS-HVY 0-0-1 Course 0-0-0 Dist 0-0-1

2 May Wincanton 2m Cls4 74-97 Hdl Hcap £3,426
17 ran GOOD 8hdls Time 3m 48.90s (slw 11.90s)
1 Long Road 5 11-8 ....A P McCoy 11/4F
2 Brown Fox 5 10-1 t ....Owyn Nelmes (3) 16/1
3 Without Pretense 8 9-12 ow2 Mark Nicolls (5) 14/1
P **PRECIOUS LUCY** 7 11-5 .Richard Hobson 40/1
chased leader, blundered 3rd, weakened approaching 2 out, behind when pulled up before last [OR90] [op 33/1]

Dist: hd-8-3½-½-shd RACE RPR: 103+/84/75
Racecheck: Wins - Pl 1 Unpl 1

23 Apr Stratford 2m3f Cls3 90-105 Hdl Hcap £6,889
11 ran GOOD 10hdls Time 4m 30.80s (slw 7.80s)
1 Wee Dinns 5 11-8 ....Tom Scudamore 5/1
2 Treaty Flyer 5 11-7 ....A P McCoy 3/1F
3 Little Venus 6 11-7 ....Mark Bradburne 14/1
P **PRECIOUS LUCY** 7 10-11 Richard Hobson 20/1
held up and behind, headway approaching 7th, weakened after 3 out, behind when pulled up before 2 out [OR90] [op 33/1]

Dist: 4-nk-¾-5-4 RACE RPR: 110+/101+/100
Racecheck: Wins 1 (1) Pl - Unpl 3

2 Aug 04 Newton Abbot 2m3f Cls3 Nov Hdl £5,857
8 ran GD-FM 9hdls Time 4m 32.20s (slw 12.20s)
1 Harbour Bound 5 10-11 Christian Williams (3) 16/1
2 Tonic Du Charmil 4 11-4 ......Timmy Murphy 2/1
3 Gin 'N' Fonic 4 10-7 ....Chris Honour (5) 8/1
4 **PRECIOUS LUCY** 5 10-12 Richard Hobson (3) 9/2
held up, headway 5th, weakened after 3 out, finished lame (jockey said gelding was lame)
[RPR71 TS29 OR96] [op 5/1 tchd 7/2]

Dist: 1-25-20-6-¾ RACE RPR: 104/108+/78+
Racecheck: Wins 2 (1) Pl 3 Unpl 7

Mike Simmons 11-7

10-y-o *b g Ballacashtal - Lady Crusty (Golden Dipper)*
L P Grassick Derek Laverty (5)

Placings: 34P0/4596778/1P/P6P-

OR88 F30	Starts	1st	2nd	3rd	Win & Pl
All Jumps races	30	3	–	4	£11,727

83 5/04 Uttx 2m4½f Cls4 82-103 Hdl Hcap gd-sft £3,556
97 4/01 Font 2m4f Cls4 84-103 Hdl Hcap good £2,762
2/00 Tntn 2m1f Cls4 Mdn Hdl soft £2,472
Total win prize-money £8,790

GF-HRD 0-0-7 GS-HVY 2-2-16 Course 1-0-3 Dist 0-0-6

22 Apr Bangor-On-Dee 2m4f Cls4 87-100 Hdl Hcap £3,426
13 ran GD-SFT 11hdls Time 5m 5.30s (slw 27.30s)
1 Chickapeakray 5 10-13 ....Paddy Aspell 4/1F
2 Longueville Manor 5 11-5 ....Noel Fehily 9/2
3 Porak 9 11-7 ....Derek Laverty (5) 20/1
P **MIKE SIMMONS** 10 11-4 .....Barry Fenton 28/1
always behind, ridden approaching 6th, tailed off when pulled up before 3 out
[OR92] [op 25/1]

Dist: nk-12-3-shd-5 RACE RPR: 93/99/96+
Racecheck: Wins - Pl 2 Unpl -

9 Apr Worcester 3m Cls4 95-100 Hdl Hcap £3,083
10 ran GOOD 12hdls Time 5m 50.90s (slw 14.90s)
1 Rosses Point 7 11-7 p ......Christian Williams 3/1
2 Harry's Dream 9 11-12 ....Richard Johnson 4/5F
3 Sir Rowland Hill 7 11-0 ....Mr S W Byrne (7) 50/1
6 **MIKE SIMMONS** 10 11-2 Derek Laverty (5) 66/1
prominent, ridden after 9th, weakening when hit 3 out [RPR54 TS43 OR95] [op 40/1]

Dist: hd-1¼-7-27-14 RACE RPR: 103/108/102
Racecheck: Wins - Pl 2 Unpl 4

26 Jan Warwick 3m1f Cls3 95-120 Hdl Hcap £5,205
16 ran SOFT 12hdls Time 6m 22.00s (slw 34.00s)
1 Passenger Omar 8 10-4 t William Kennedy (3) 4/1J
2 Jiver 7 11-2 v1 ....Tom Scudamore 25/1
3 Clan Royal 11 11-1 ....A P McCoy 13/2
P **MIKE SIMMONS** 10 10-1 .....Ollie McPhail 66/1
prominent, ridden after 6th, weakened after 7th, tailed off when pulled up before 9th
[OR95] [op 50/1]

Dist: ½-12-hd-3½-hd RACE RPR: 111+/117/105+
Racecheck: Wins 1 Pl 6 Unpl 15

Donie Dooley 11-12

8-y-o *ch g Be My Native - Bridgeofallen (Torus)*
P T Dalton Marcus Foley

Placings: 43/9/9F510/7085P-

OR93	Starts	1st	2nd	3rd	Win & Pl
Hurdles	9	1	–	–	£5,284
All Jumps races	13	1	–	1	£7,137

6/03 Uttx 2m4½f Cls3 Mdn Hdl gd-fm £5,285

GF-HRD 1-0-2 GS-HVY 0-1-7 Course 1-0-6 Dist 0-1-5

8 Dec 05 Huntingdon 2m5½f Cls4 89-110 Hdl Hcap £3,920
13 ran GOOD 10hdls Time 5m 27.10s (slw 35.10s)
1 Welcome To Unos 8 11-2 ....Phil Kinsella (7) 9/2
2 Archduke Ferdinand 7 11-7 Robert Thornton 4/1
3 Common Girl 7 11-9 ....John McNamara 33/1
P **DONIE DOOLEY** 7 10-9 ......James Davies 40/1
held up, ridden and weakened approaching 6th, tailed off when pulled up before next, broke blood vessel (vet said gelding bled from nose)
[OR93] [op 33/1]

Dist: 8-2-1-4-2 RACE RPR: 116+/106/106
Racecheck: Wins 1 (1) Pl - Unpl 11

24 Nov 05 Uttoxeter 2m6½f Cls4 82-108 Hdl Hcap £3,832
10 ran SOFT 12hdls Time 6m 11.60s (slw 59.60s)
1 Arm And A Leg 10 11-12 ...Richard Johnson 6/1
2 Hi Laurie 10 9-10 ....John Kington (7) 6/4F
3 Ingres 5 11-0 ....Charlie Studd (7) 5/1
5 **DONIE DOOLEY** 7 10-13 Andrew Thornton 22/1
held up, headway to join leader 8th, led next, headed before 3 out, weakened last
[RPR68 OR95] [op 16/1]

Dist: 2½-1½-1¼-24-21 RACE RPR: 110/87+/101
Racecheck: Wins 1 (1) Pl 2 Unpl 12

1 Nov 05 Worcester 2m4f Cls4 75-101 Hdl Hcap £3,468
17 ran GOOD 10hdls Time 5m 8.80s (slw 30.80s)
1 Pardon What 9 11-0 b ....Keith Mercer (3) 28/1
2 Eljutan 7 10-13 ....Shane Walsh (7) 66/1
3 Hard N Sharp 5 11-0 .....William Kennedy (5) 6/1
8 **DONIE DOOLEY** 7 11-8 ..Andrew Thornton 50/1
chased leaders until weakened approaching 4 out btn 28 lengths [RPR73 TS27 OR97]

Dist: 5-5-1¾-1¾-9 RACE RPR: 99+/94+/89+
Racecheck: Wins 2 (1) Pl - Unpl 18

Form Reading	**FORBEARING**
Spotlight	Changed yards frequently, debut for K Wingrove.
Handicap Ratings	Ran off a mark of 110 six outings ago (placed 5th) which was last Handicap Hurdle outing. Down to a mark of 87 today, which indicates handicapper has not been impressed.
Significant Items of Form	Nine year old with three Handicap Hurdle wins (two Class 3, one Class 4) all around 2 miles on Good, Soft and Good to Firm, at Taunton, Leicester and Chepstow, the latest in March 2004. Last two runs have been in Class 5 Hurdles, both Non Handicaps on 10.11.05 and 30.04.06, both at Ludlow. Since last win has had twelve runs with only one placing (2nd) better than 5th place.
Verdict	Form definitely on a downhill slide and though last run on 30.04.06 after six months break resulted in a 10th of 17 runners, there is no solid evidence to suggest a return to winning ways.
Hence:	DISMISS.

Form Reading	**PRECIOUS LUCY**
Spotlight	Hereford winner two years ago for another yard.
Handicap Ratings	Mark of 90 four outings ago when placed 1st, mark of 87 today.
Significant Items of Form	Seven year old with only seven National Hunt outings and one win in a Class 4 Handicap Hurdle at Hereford in June 2004. Last two runs on 23.04.06 and 02.05.06 in a Class 3 and a Class 4 Handicap Hurdle over 2m3f and 2 miles on Good at Stratford and Wincanton followed a twenty one month break and result was a 'Pulled up' on both occasions.
Verdict	Today's contest represents a drop in Class but last two runs do not indicate the horse is ready to be competitive.
Hence:	DISMISS.

Form Reading	**MIKE SIMMONS**
Spotlight	Well beaten three outings this year; first time cheek pieces.
Handicap Ratings	Won off a mark of 83 five outings ago and was raised to a figure of 100 for next outing. Next three runs were off marks of 95 (pulled up), 95 (6th) and 92 (pulled up). Today's mark of 88 is a move in the right direction but still above 83 when last won.
Significant Items of Form	Ten year old with three Class 4 Hurdle wins from 2m1f to 2m4½f on Good, Good to Soft, and Soft, the last of which was in May 2004 at Uttoxeter (today's course). Only four runs since last win, three of which were this year and best of which was 6th of 10 runners at Worcester on 09.04.06 over 3 miles (Good) in a Class 4 Handicap Hurdle, prominent when ridden after 9th, beaten 49 lengths.
Verdict	Today's contest is a Class 5 race for 0-95 rated horses which resulted in a spread in the weights of only 7lb, which indicates a pretty even contest. In this setting you are looking for horses with an edge, and though Mike Simmons' placings for the last four runs since its May 2004 win of P-P-6-P make grim reading, the facts are that it is a Uttoxeter course winner and its run at Worcester on 09.04.06 over 3 miles was good enough to suggest that a top three placing over today's

distance of 2 miles is a reasonable possibility, particularly if the first time cheek pieces help.

Hence: SELECT.

Form Reading	**DONIE DOOLEY**
Spotlight	Won fast ground Maiden Hurdle over longer trip here in 2003.
Handicap Ratings	Ran off a mark of 100 five outings ago and down to a mark of 93 today, which is the same as far as its last outing when pulled up.
Significant Items of Form	Eight year old with one win in a Class 3 Maiden Hurdle over 2m4½f on Good to Firm over today's course in June 2003. Only six outings since then, with last campaign finishing with three Class 4 Handicap Hurdles over 2m4f, 2m6½f and 2m5½f on Good (twice) and Soft in November and December 2005. In the last of those three runs it was pulled up with a broken blood vessel, but on previous runs at today's course (Uttoxeter) over 2m6½f it made headway to join leader 8th, led next, headed before 3 out, weakened last and finished 5th of 10 runners, beaten 29 lengths.
Verdict	This course winner is only eight years old and given the fact that its Uttoxeter run in November 2005 showed that he retains both a liking for the course as well as the ability to be competitive for at least 2 miles (today's distance), it is worth taking a chance that it can perform when fresh after a five month break in a Class 5 event, which it should find easier than the ones it has been competing in.
Decision:	SELECT.

Overall Comment

This race provided two important lessons.

The first is to try to identify how difficult a race will be to win so that you can adjust your form reading standards for selection purposes to suit the contest.

The second lesson is the importance of course form which time and time again in jump races proves to be a factor in the form reading exercise that cannot be overlooked.

The fact that this was a Class 5 Handicap Hurdle with a weight spread amongst all the runners of only 7lbs showed that it was likely to be a pretty evenly matched field for a race which wouldn't take a lot of wining. The surprising element was the excellent starting price of the only two Course Winners in the field which, placed together in a reverse forecast, produced a Tote Exacta dividend of £2,161 and a Computer Straight Forecast of £655.

Returning to the subject of form reading, it is worth pointing out that although the recent form of both Course Winners was poor, the fact that this was a Class 5 contest meant that if either of them decided to show their liking for the course, there was a good chance that they would be in the final shake up. The fact that both Course Winners were selected meant that there was a reasonable chance that at least one of them would be competitive. In my view, trying to determine which of the two would come out on top, based on the form available, would have been an impossible task.

It all goes to show that in contests like these, you have got to be pretty damn sure your analysis of a horse is going to be proved correct to be content with only one selection. Making an additional selection or selections always gives you a degree of insurance, which is invaluable in a sport where lapses in form and mishaps are frequent occurrences.

EXAMPLE 21

06.09.06   Uttoxeter – Good – Class 3 – Handicap Hurdle – 2m4½f

Winner   RAGDALE HALL – 33/1

3.30 RACE 4

Allied Irish Bank (GB) Handicap Hurdle (Class 3)   ATR

Winner £5,704.20   2m4½f

£9000 guaranteed For 4yo+ Rated 0-125 Minimum Weight 10-0 Penalties after August 26th, a winner of a hurdle 7lb The Last Cast's Handicap Mark 125 Entries 18 pay £15 Penalty value 1st £5,704.20 2nd £1,684.80 3rd £842.40 4th £421.20 5th £210.60

1 9F-F7FP THE LAST CAST 51 C D
ch g Prince Of Birds-Atan's Gem
Evan Williams D P Barrie 
7 11-12
Paul Moloney

2 070P-P9 CAMPAIGN TRAIL (IRE) 63 D
b g Sadler's Wells-Campestral
Jonjo O'Neill Michael Tabor 
8 11-9
Dominic Elsworth (130)

3 32213-6 ABSOLUT POWER (GER) 17 C D
ch g Acatenango-All Our Dreams
J A Geake Dr G Madan Mohan 
p5 11-4
Richard Johnson (128)

4 112581- RARE COINCIDENCE 130 (20F) C
ch g Atraf-Green Seed
R F Fisher A Kerr 
p5 10-13
Keith Mercer (121)

5 3P3F/54 RAGDALE HALL (USA) 13 C D
b g Bien Bien-Gift Of Dance
J Joseph Jack Joseph
9 10-13
Shane Walsh (5) (127)

6 07-61U4 ALDIRUOS (IRE) 57 D
ch g Bigstone-Ball Cat
A W Carroll Aramis Racing Syndicate 
6 10-11
Wayne Hutchinson (127)

7 /104-29 TICKET TO RIDE (FR) 63 D
ch g Pistolet Bleu-Have A Drink
A J Wilson Tim Leadbeater 
t8 10-11
Timmy Murphy

8 347598- DEVITO (FR) 144
ch g Trempolino-Snowy
G F Edwards G F Edwards 
5 10-10
T J O'Brien (3) (129)

9 310475- CUMBRIAN KNIGHT (IRE) 248 (19F)
b g Presenting-Crashrun
J M Jefferson J M Jefferson 
8 10-9
G Lee (127)

10 8812311 PRESENT ORIENTED (USA) 18
ch g Southern Halo-Shy Beauty
M C Chapman Miss M Renaghan 
5 10-9
Tom Messenger (5) (131)

11 9971-43 TALARIVE (USA) 18 D
ch g Riverman-Estala
P D Niven Ian G M Dalgleish
p10 10-2
Brian Hughes (127)

2005 (8 ran) Xellance P J Hobbs 8 11-5 9/2   T J O'Brien (7) OR122

BETTING FORECAST: 4 Present Oriented, 9-2 Aldiruos, 5 Rare Coincidence, 11-2 Absolut Power, 7 Talarive, 10 Ticket To Ride, 12 Cumbrian Knight, Devito, 14 Campaign Trail, 20 The Last Cast, 33 Ragdale Hall.

SPOTLIGHT

The Last Cast Hinted at a return to form over fences at Stratford in June but four non-completions from last five starts spell danger and suggest that a confidence-boosting mission could be the reason for this return to hurdles (which he hasn't encountered for nearly two years).

Campaign Trail Decent effort at Cheltenham in March on his return to hurdling but shown precious little since and now over two and half years since last success over smaller obstacles; drying ground won't be ideal, either.

Absolut Power Developed into a useful handicapper last summer and reappearance effort in a warm handicap at Newton Abbot quite acceptable, given it was his first run for the best part of a year on ground soft enough; won the novice event on this card 12 months ago and big run anticipated.

Rare Coincidence Tough and dependable sort who dug deep to land a novice event at Market Rasen on final jumps start in April; running well on the Flat in recent weeks so fitness not an issue but has failed in handicaps off lower marks than today's.

Ragdale Hall Major player on old form but only had the three runs in last couple of years and couldn't muster much of a challenge in claiming company last time.

Aldiruos Back to winning ways at Wetherby in June and would have gone mighty close to following up over hurdles next time out but for saddle slipping at the last; disappointing last time as 3m trip didn't seem to present a problem but given a break since then and comfortably makes the shortlist.

Ticket To Ride Gradually finding his feet since arriving from France and placed off a 9lb higher mark over fences under this jockey two runs back; was just as capable over hurdles for former connections so potentially interesting if not finding the ground too fast.

Devito Signed off last season on a bit of a downer but consequently back on a reasonable mark now and interestingly obliged on his first start back last autumn; handles any ground and one to consider with a positive jockey booking.

Cumbrian Knight Multi-purpose performer who is having only his second spin over hurdles since November 2004, though did run respectably off 3lb higher at Musselburgh in January; AW winner later that month but no real fireworks on the Flat since then.

Present Oriented Seemingly going places over hurdles and only 4lb higher than when grinding out win number three this summer in a 2m6f handicap at Market Rasen last month; likes to front-run but those tactics not essential and, although all three wins have been at the same track, he has run well left-handed.

Talarive Similar chance to Present Oriented based on their recent Market Rasen encounter but not as progressive as his conqueror and this slightly shorter trip likely to find him out in this better grade.

VERDICT **DEVITO (nap)** wasn't pulling up any trees when last seen in action but he's run many of his better races after some time off and is sufficiently well handicapped to go close if continuing that trend. **Absolut Power** appeals most of the remainder.[AWJ]

	OFFICIAL RATINGS LAST SIX OUTINGS-LATEST ON RIGHT						3.30	HANDICAP	TODAY FUTURE		RP RATING LATEST / BEST / ADJUSTED		
—	—	—	—	—	—	The Last Cast	11-12	125		—	—	—
—	—	132⁰	130⁸	127⁶	125⁹	Campaign Trail	11-9	122	94	135 ◄	130
109³	110²	—	—	118³	118⁸	Absolut Power	11-4	117	115	123	128
89¹	—	105²	—	108⁶	—	Rare Coincidence	10-13	112	121	121	121
104⁰	100⁷	100⁶	98¹	105¹	105⁴	Ragdale Hall	10-13	112	97	127	127
125³	—	—	123⁶	115⁵	—	Aldiruos	10-11	110	112	127	127
—	117⁰	—	—	—	—	Ticket To Ride	10-11	110	—	66	—
118³	115⁴	114⁷	113⁵	112⁹	110⁸	Devito	10-10	109	122	134	129
—	—	—	—	—	111⁵	Cumbrian Knight	10-9	108	120	120	127
91¹⁸	—	95²	—	—	104¹	Present Oriented	10-9	108	127 ◄	131	131 ◄
100⁹	97⁸	95⁸	93¹	101⁴	100³	Talarive	10-2	101	127 ◄	127	127

Ragdale Hall   10-13

9-y-o b g Bien Bien - Gift Of Dance (Trempolino)
J Joseph   Shane Walsh (5)
Placings: /616151344/253P3F/54

OR**112**F72		Starts	1st	2nd	3rd	Win & Pl
Hurdles		23	4	6	2	£29,832
All Jumps races		28	6	6	4	£42,155
9/03	Prth	2m4½f Cls3 Nov Ch good				£5,623
8/03	NAbb	2m1½f Cls3 Ch gd-fm				£5,356
115 6/03	Strf	2m1½f Cls3 91-115 Hdl Hcap good				£5,564
109 4/03	Strf	2m1½f Cls3 102-123 Hdl Hcap gd-fm				....£4,849
9/02	Hrfd	2m3½f Cls4 Nov Hdl gd-fm				£3,196
6/02	Uttx	2m Cls4 Nov Hdl good				....£2,639
		Total win prize-money £27,227
24 Aug Fontwell 2m4f			Cls5 Claim Hdl £2,277
7 ran GD-FM	10hdls	Time 4m 38.80s (slw 3.80s)
1 Allaboveboard 7 10-10 ..Richard Johnson 8/11F
2 Smart Tiger 4 10-9 b ....Paul Moloney 12/1
3 Lupin 7 11-9 ....Wayne Hutchinson 4/1

4 RAGDALE HALL 9 11-7 ...Shane Walsh (5) 10/1 tracked leaders until ridden and weakened 7 out
[RPR82 TS81 OR115]   [op 7/1]
Dist: 11-17-5-22-7   RACE RPR: 96+/88+/81
Racecheck: Wins 1 (1) Pl - Unpl 2

3 Aug Stratford 2m1½f Cls3 94-115 Hdl Hcap £6,889
8 ran GD-FM   9hdls   Time 4m 1.20s (slw 13.20s)
1 Iffy 5 11-1 ....Robert Thornton 3/1
2 Smart Minister 6 9-12 ....Mr R Tierney (7) 9/1
3 Dyneburg 6 11-7 ....Jason Maguire 9/4F
5 RAGDALE HALL 9 11-7 ...Shane Walsh (5) 33/1 chased leaders, not fluent 4th, ridden and lost place after 3 out, weakened next, mistake last
[RPR112 TS46 OR115]   [op 20/1]
Dist: 5-hd-3-hd-3½   RACE RPR: 111+/93/109
Racecheck: Wins 1 (1) Pl 3 Unpl 3

23 Apr 05 Sandown 2m4½f Cls2 120-141 Hdl Hcap £15,857
17 ran GOOD   9hdls   Time 4m 43.80s (fst 1.20s)
1 Yes Sir 6 11-9 ....A P McCoy 13/2C
2 Penny Pictures 6 11-5 ......Robert Thornton 11/1
3 Fontanesi 5 11-9 ....Timmy Murphy 20/1

F RAGDALE HALL 8 10-4 ..Shane Walsh (7) 66/1 chased leaders, mistake 4th, hard ridden 3 out, soon beaten, 11th and weakening when fell 2 out [RPR112 OR123]

Dist: 1¼-3½-¾-1-3½ RACE RPR: 146+/139/140+
Racecheck: Wins 4 (2) Pl 3 Unpl 12

The Last Cast   11-12

7-y-o ch g Prince Of Birds - Atan's Gem (Sharpen Up)
Evan Williams   Paul Moloney
Placings: 1/8617/41290/9F-F7FP

OR**125**F75		Starts	1st	2nd	3rd	Win & Pl
Hurdles		10	4	1	1	£24,263
All Jumps races		20	5	1	1	£37,854
11/04	Uttx	2m Cls4 Ch heavy				....£4,792
119 3/04	Newb	2m5f Cls3 97-123 Hdl Hcap good				£5,272
1/03	Chel	2m Cls2 Nov Hdl 4yo heavy				....£9,526
12/02	MRas	2m1½f Cls4 Nov Hdl 3yo soft				....£3,094
11/02	Bang	2m1f Cls4 Nov Hdl 3yo soft				....£3,136
		Total win prize-money £25,820
GF-HRD 0-0-3 GS-HVY 4-2-12   Course 1-0-1   Dist 1-0-4

17 Jul Newton Abbot 3m2½f Cls3 106-132 Ch Hcap
£7,606
8 ran GD-FM 20fncs Time 6m 31.70s (slw 7.70s)
1 Bosham Mill 8 10-5 ....T J O'Brien (3) 7/4F
2 Comanche War Paint 9 11-2 Liam Heard (5) 10/1
3 Bengal Bullet 9 9-8 ....Miss T Cave (7) 4/1
P THE LAST CAST 7 11-12 Christian Williams 16/1
always in rear, tailed off from 15th, pulled up
before 2 out [OR132]

Dist: 11-20-8-34 RACE RPR: 125+/128+/87
Racecheck: Wins - Pl - Unpl -

18 Jun Stratford 2m7f Cls3 112-135 Ch Hcap £9,395
11 ran GD-FM 18fncs Time 5m 37.70s (slw 11.70s)
1 Celtic Boy 8 11-7 ....Richard Johnson 9/4F
2 Totheroadyouvgone 12 10-3 p Marcus Foley 16/1
3 On The Outside 7 10-7 t ....Mick FitzGerald 11/1
F THE LAST CAST 7 11-7 ......Paul Moloney 40/1

held several positions, headway to challenge
14th, driven and outpaced in 4th 3 out, staying
on again to dispute 4-length 2nd when fell last
[RPR134 OR130] [op 33/1]
Dist: 9-1¾-3-23-2 RACE RPR: 140+/111+/112
Racecheck: Wins 1 (1) Pl 2 Unpl 10

11 Jun Stratford 2m1½f Cls3 104-130 Ch Hcap £7,829
10 ran GD-FM 13fncs Time 4m 2.90s (fst 0.10s)
1 Rookery Lad 8 11-0 ....T J O'Brien (3) 9/2F
2 Master Rex 11 11-5 ....Noel Fehily 11/2
3 Lindsay 7 10-12 ....Mark Bradburne 8/1
7 THE LAST CAST 7 11-12 p Christian-Williams 12/1
chased leaders, lost place 3rd, behind from 5th
btn 50 lengths [RPR91 TS44 OR130]
Dist: 5-8-5-1¼-½ RACE RPR: 132/129/116+
Racecheck: Wins - Pl 1 Unpl 5

27 May Stratford 2m5½f Cls2 116-138 Ch Hcap
£12,526
8 ran SOFT 16fncs Time 5m 51.50s (slw 46.50s)
1 Fool On The Hill 9 11-3 .....Richard Johnson 8/1
2 TICKET TO RIDE 8 10-7 tp ..Timmy Murphy 9/1
prominent, lost place 7th, struggling 11th, rallied
approaching 2 out, went 2nd last, no chance
with winner [RPR114 TS87 OR119] [op 12/1]
3 East Tycoon 7 10-13 ....A P McCoy 3/1F
F THE LAST CAST 7 11-4 p Christian Williams 6/1
led to 3rd, led after 8th until after 3 out, 6
lengths 2nd and tired when fell 2 out
[RPR132 OR130] [op 7/1 tchd 15/2]
Dist: 14-4-10-4-10 RACE RPR: 143+/114/120+
Racecheck: Wins - Pl - Unpl 10

Form Reading	**RAGDALE HALL**
Spotlight	Major player on old form but only three runs in last couple of years.
Handicap Ratings	Mark of 125 six outings ago (placed 3rd) but down to a mark of 115 two outings ago (placed 5th). Today's mark 112 which looks attractive if horse can recapture some of its old form.
Significant Items of Form	Nine year old with two Class 3 Chase wins and four Hurdle wins (two Class 3, two Class 4) on going ranging from Good to Good to Firm and at distances from 2 miles to 2m4½f. Last win (Chase) was September 2003; first win (Hurdle) was at today's course (Uttoxeter) on Good in June 2002. Current campaign, which followed a fifteen month break, started on 03.08.06 with a 5th of 8 runners in a Class 3 Handicap Hurdle over 2m½f at Stratford, beaten 8 lengths. Next and last run on 24.08.06 in a Class 5 Claiming Hurdle over 2m4f at Fontwell (Good to Firm) when 4th of 7 runners, beaten 33 lengths, was less impressive but could have been the result of the 'bounce factor', which often happens on the second run back after a long break and usually if there is insufficient gap between the two races.
Verdict	Although the last two wins were in Chases, it looks as if trainer is making a determined attempt to succeed over hurdles again. Recent form is consistent with a return from a long break and providing horse can recapture old form, a top three placing is a definite possibility considering it has Class 3 Hurdle wins to its name and with course, distance and going all tailored to suit.
Decision:	SELECT.

Form Reading	**THE LAST CAST**
Spotlight	Hinted at a return to form over fences at Stratford in June.
Handicap Ratings	No Handicap Hurdle runs in last six outings.
Significant Items of Form	Seven year old with one Class 4 Chase Victory in November 2004 at Uttoxeter and four Hurdle wins (two Class 4, one Class 3, one Class 2) between November 2002 and March 2004 over distances from 2 miles to 2m5f on going from Good to Heavy. Most recent campaign, which has run from 27.05.06 to 17.07.06 has consisted of one Class 2 Handicap Chase over 2m5½f on 27.05.06 at Stratford when fell 2 out when lying 2nd, followed by three Class 3 Handicap Chases where 7th, beaten 50 lengths; fell at last when disputing 2nd place and finally pulled up before 2 out.

Verdict   Although last campaign has been over fences and relatively disappointing, the
                         fact that, on two occasions, it was lying 2nd when falling close to the finish,
                         coupled with the fact that it has been given a six week break before being sent
                         hurdling on a course where it has won before, all add up to a top three placing
                         being a possibility at least. Distance and going will also suit so too dangerous to
                         leave out.
Hence: SELECT.

Overall Comment

I have made it clear in earlier passages in this book that although trainer form is not part of
The Tail End System, you will encounter certain situations where, although the form of a
horse does not really justify selection, the ability of the horse's trainer to land a long priced
winner can, and on occasions should, influence your selection decisions.

I have also made very clear my reasons for stating that it will never be my intention to
publish a list of such trainers. However, in the case of Ragdale Hall, his trainer, Jack Joseph,
sadly passed away at the age of 87, only a matter of months after this victory, so I am at
liberty to make comment about his abilities without breaking my undertaking.

Together with my racing colleagues, Brian and Andy, I became aware of the special talent
of Jack Joseph when, a good few years ago, we witnessed a race at Stratford where a low
grade hurdler trained by Jack Joseph and called Milzig, who we had all backed
independently at long odds, made eye catching progress from the back of a large field of
runners on the final circuit. Its progress was far too late to reach the leaders but the *Racing
Post* race report the following day merely stated 'passed beaten horses closing stages' and
this statement effectively disguised the true value of its run to anybody who had not been
an eye witness to the backmarkers efforts.

Two weeks later Brian, Andy and myself were at Worcester where Milzig was again a
runner in a low class hurdle, but this time there were only 5 runners. Convinced we were
following a horse which had shown race winning form, we were absolutely delighted when
the betting opened up with Milzig the clear outsider and available in places at 20/1. We
waded in at 20/1 and continued to back the horse at all prices down to 12/1 until the off.

Half way down the back straight on the final circuit, Milzig was again at the back of the
field but this time it was close up and its jockey, Carl Llewellyn, had got it stoked up and
raring to go. As it tackled the bend at the top of the course it went into overdrive, overtook
the other runners by the time it reached the home straight and swept into a 10 length lead
that it continued to increase all the way to the line.

Since that red letter day I have always looked very closely at Jack Joseph trained horses
whose prices were long.

Our Milzig adventure gave me the confidence to put some money down on a good
number of occasions when, although the form of one of his runners did not look too
promising, you could sense with some certain degree of confidence that something was
possibly afoot.

Jack Joseph's record both as a trainer and an owner was a testament to his abilities, and
reading the tributes which were paid to him in the *Racing Post* on his passing by a number
of jockeys, you knew you had, over the years, witnessed the work of a horseman with a very
special talent.

Returning to the subject of Ragdale Hall, I think its form for this particular race was good enough to have made a selection without taking into account its trainer's special abilities and style. However, there will be many races in the future where you will look at the form of a horse which appeared quite ordinary and yet produced a victory, and it is then that you realise that, if you had known a bit more about the trainer's abilities to produce an 'outsider' victory, then your decision to DISMISS the horse might have been different.

Fortunately, by the process of studying the 'outsider' results over the period of a few months, you will find that there are a number of trainers who fit the description of an 'outsider' specialist and they all tend to be low profile miracle makers who make a deliberate point of not shouting about their achievements from the rooftops. The list of such trainers is an ever changing one, with new kids on the block making their presence felt and long standing members retreating back into the shadows.

To take advantage of this situation you have to be on your toes and it is impossible to always make the right predictions. You certainly have to be alert to newcomers because you often do not get a lot of warning before they are making their presence felt and if they are too successful too quickly, the market ensures that their runners do not start at long prices for very long.

Likewise, you have to be wary about the long standing members who appear to have hit a cold spell because this is often the time when they are at their most dangerous and liable to strike without warning.

Trainers like the late Jack Joseph are a very special breed, capable of producing the most exciting moments in racing you are ever likely to experience. Look out for them and recognise their importance because their good fortune can have a major effect on yours.

If Jack Joseph was planning a fitting epitaph to his life as a trainer, this was it. Held up at the back of the field under a patient ride by Shane Walsh, Ragdale Hall started to make progress on the descent at the far end of the course and moved into contention as they entered the finishing straight 3 out.

However, there was still a lot of work to be done and it was only as the leader Aldirous cleared the last that you thought there was a possibility that Ragdale Hall could get up. Galvanised by Walsh to make a final effort, he pulled alongside Aldirous in the last 20 yards and went a neck in front just as they passed the winning post. Horse racing does not get any better than this race – thank you Jack for all the memories.

For the record, the Tote Exacta paid £209.00 and the Computer Straight Forecast of £157.12.

EXAMPLE 22

21.06.06   Worcester – Good to Firm – Class 4 – Handicap Hurdle – 2m4f

Winner   HARRYCAT – 20/1

5.20
RACE 6

wbx.com World Bet Exchange
Handicap Hurdle (Class 4)
Winner £3,253   **2m4f**   ATR

£5000 guaranteed **For** 4yo+ **Rated** 0-110 **Minimum Weight** 10-0 **Penalties** after June 10th, a winner of a hurdle 7lb **Sky Warrior's** Handicap Mark 109 **Entries** 28 pay £10 **Penalty value** 1st £3,253 2nd £955 3rd £477.50 4th £238.50

1 3/2135- **SKY WARRIOR** (FR) [374] C D
b g Warrshan-Sky Bibi   **Mr N Williams**(5)   8 11-12
Evan Williams   Mr And Mrs Glynne Clay   (113)

2 /2170-8 **HARRYCAT** (IRE) [17]   **Liam Heard**(5)   p 5 11-10
b g Bahhare-Quiver Tree   (111)
C P Morlock   The S.I.R. Partnership

3 971753- **FARD DU MOULIN MAS** (FR) [54] C D   **Barry Fenton**   13 11-7
blbr g Morespeed-Soiree d'Ex   (113)
M E D Francis   Mrs Merrick Francis III

4 14/P7-P **PROGRESSIVE** (IRE) [31]   **Noel Fehily**   8 11-3
ch g Be My Native-Move Forward   (111)
Jonjo O'Neill   John P McManus

5 079-312 **COLTSCROFT** [9] C D   **Sean Fox**   6 10-13
b g Teenoso-Marquesa Juana   (113)
J C Fox   Mrs A Doyle

6 111P/3P **IN DISCUSSION** (IRE) [18] BF   **A P McCoy**   8 10-10
b g King's Theatre-Silius   (114)
Jonjo O'Neill   John P McManus

7 P4241-P **OSCAR THE BOXER** (IRE) [18] B   **G Lee**   7 10-9
b g Oscar-Here She Comes   (108)
J M Jefferson   Boundary Garage (Bury) Limited

8 0P4P9-0 **RESERVOIR** (IRE) [24]   **Richard Johnson**   5 10-8
b g Green Desert-Spout   (109)
J Joseph   Jack Joseph

9 50/2-P0 **GLENFIELD HEIGHTS** [24]   **Robert Lucey-Butler**(5)   11 10-7
b g Golden Heights-Cleeveland Lady   (112)
W G M Turner   Mrs Philomena Reich

10 1F550P- **QUEEN EXCALIBUR** [242]   **Ollie McPhail**   7 10-1
ch m Sabrehill-Blue Room   (112)
C Roberts   Dr Simon Clarke

11 6P8677- **MR DIP** [220] (190F)   **Colin Bolger**(3)   6 10-0
b g Reprimand-Scottish Lady   (104)
L A Dace   Let's Have Fun Syndicate

12 3F6-332 **TRUE TEMPER** (IRE) [4]   **Tom Messenger**(5)   9 10-0
b m Roselier-Diamond Rock   (108)
A M Crow   G M Crow

LONG HANDICAP: Mr Dip 9-9 True Temper 9-5

2005 (15 ran) Blue Hawk R Dickin 8 10-3 25/1   John Pritchard (7) OR94

BETTING FORECAST: 7-2 In Discussion, 4 Coltscroft, 9-2 Fard Du Moulin Mas, 11-2 Sky Warrior, 13-2 Oscar The Boxer, 12 Progressive, 20 Harrycat, Queen Excalibur, True Temper, 25 Glenfield Heights, Mr Dip.

SPOTLIGHT

Sky Warrior Couple of runs over hurdles for this yard two winters ago after switched from France but raced over fences since, best suited by this trip on sound surface; been off for a year but well handicapped back over hurdles judged on chase form and of interest.

Harrycat Acts on the ground and promising rider's 5lb claim a help but well beaten first start for new yard earlier in the month and stamina for this trip must be proved.

Fard Du Moulin Mas Generally hard to place off this sort of mark even if not beaten far off similar one at Doncaster in December but that's offset by this being weak so possibilities as he goes well fresh.

Progressive Lightly raced and not lived up to early promise on easy ground, well beaten over hurdles/fences since coming back from lengthy layoff last autumn; this better ground could help but stable second string and likely best watched.

Coltscroft Promise in bumper company not confirmed over hurdles to start with but doing better now handicapping and convincing in minor C/D handicap last month; taken big rise in weights but the 2m4f trip probably more of a problem latest and worth another chance back at this distance.

In Discussion Prolific jumps winner two years ago but lengthy absence after September 2004; encouraging chase return here last month but lost action and moderate effort only subsequent run so something to prove back over hurdles, albeit off much more favourable mark.

Oscar The Boxer Running well at this trip following layoff, won no whips conditionals race on slow ground at Ayr in February; might have needed run but still disappointing at Hexham earlier in the month considering he goes on this ground and question mark after that.

Reservoir Taken handy drop in weights following minor efforts for this yard following a break but though return to quick surface should suit he's yet to convince at this trip.

Glenfield Heights Creditable return from long absence last summer but not done so well in handful of runs since and hard to be confident he'll do much better here.

Queen Excalibur Pulled up over fences when last seen in October and though she acts on the ground she's got plenty to prove over this trip.

Mr Dip Modest form on sand when last seen before Christmas and form in handicap hurdles at around this trip previously suggests he has a tough task from out of the weights here.

True Temper Creditable effort in Hexham novice latest but invariably finds it tough off lowly marks in handicaps and today no exception on these unfavourable terms.

VERDICT In Discussion may yet be worth another chance now back over hurdles off a favourable mark, but COLTSCROFT (nap) has been in good form lately and has plenty going for him back at this trip.[EMW]

	OFFICIAL RATINGS						**5.20**		HANDICAP	TODAY FUTURE		RP RATING		
LAST SIX	OUTINGS	-LATEST	ON	RIGHT								LATEST	/ BEST	/ ADJUSTED
–	–	–	–	–	–		Sky Warrior		11-12	109				113
–	–	–	–	109⁷	107⁰ 107⁸		Harrycat		11-10	107		100	111	111
102⁹	100⁷	99¹	105⁷ 104⁵ 104³				Fard Du Moulin Mas		11-7	104		103	113	113
–	–	–	104⁷ 103ᴾ				Progressive		11-3	100			90	111
–	–	85³	85¹ 96²				Coltscroft		10-13	96 +5		110◄	110	113
–	–	–	–	–	–		In Discussion		10-10	93				114◄
00ᴾ	84⁴	84²	80⁴ 86¹ 92⁰				Oscar The Boxer		10-9	92			108	108
114⁹	110ᴾ	105⁴	105ᴾ 100⁹ 95⁰				Reservoir		10-8	91		88	118◄	108
107⁵	106⁶	103⁰	–	92ᴾ 92⁰			Glenfield Heights		10-7	90		96	117	112
78¹	85ᶠ	85⁵	85⁵ 85⁰	–			Queen Excalibur		10-1	84			112	112
–	–	86⁸	84⁶ 81⁷ 81⁷				Mr Dip		9-9	83 -5		67	104	104
–	–	–	–	76³			True Temper		9-5	83 +2		108	108	108

Mr Dip   10-0

6-y-o b g Reprimand - Scottish Lady (Dunbeath)
L A Dace   Colin Bolger (3)

Placings: 36P8677-

OR83 F38   Starts   1st   2nd   3rd   Win & Pl
All Jumps races 9   –   –   1   £548
GF-HRD 0-0-4   GS-HVY 0-0-2   Course 0-0-2   Dist 0-0-3

13 Nov 05 Fontwell 2m6¹⁄₂f Cls4 Nov 79-92 Hdl Hcap
£3,429
12 ran GD-SFT   11hdls Time 5m 48.10s (slw 38.10s)
1 English Jim 4 10-8 ....Matthew Batchelor 50/1
2 Justino 7 11-2 ....Benjamin Hitchcott 4/1
3 Waynesworld 7 10-11 ....John Kington (10) 3/1F
7 MR DIP 5 10-12 ....Colin Bolger (3) 25/1
always behind
btn 45 lengths [RPR39 OR81]   [op 33/1]
Dist: 2-4-8-29-2   RACE RPR: 77/83/84

---

31 Oct 05 Plumpton 2m5f Cls4 64-90 Cond Hdl Hcap
£2,681
12 ran GD-SFT   12hdls Time 5m 28.00s (slw 35.00s)
1 Saucy Night 9 10-1 ....Liam Heard (5) 11/10F
2 Coustou 5 11-6 p ....Shane Walsh (6) 11/1
3 Manque Neuf 6 10-9 p Eamon Dehdashti (3) 14/1
7 MR DIP 5 11-3 ....Colin Bolger 20/1
took keen hold, held up in last, lost touch with
leading group 8th, steady progress next, never
on terms, weakened after 2 out
btn 38 lengths [RPR55 TS1 OR81]   [tchd 22/1]
Dist: 11-5-5-8-1¹⁄₄   RACE RPR: 83/91/72
Racecheck: Wins 2 (1) Pl 3 Unpl 8

---

13 Dec 05 Southwell (AW) 1m4f   Cls7 £1,440
12 ran STAND   Time 2m 41.52s (slw 5.02s)
1 Bulberry Hill 4 9-0 ....Sam Hitchcott ⁵ 7/4F
2 Liquid Lover 3 8-9 ....Eddie Ahern ¹¹ 9/2

---

3 MR DIP 5 9-0 ....
held up, headway halfway
ridden, hung right and hea...
weakened [RPR38 TS37 OR35]   [op ...]
Dist: shd-7-3-1¹⁄₄-1³⁄₄   RACE RPR: 49/49/38
Racecheck: Wins - 0-0 Unpl 8

Glenfield Heights   10-7

11-y-o b g Golden Heights - Cleeveland Lady (Turn Back The Time)
W G M Turner   Robert Lucey-Butler (5)

Placings: 64P113/550/2-P0

OR90   Starts   1st   2nd   3rd   Win & Pl
All Jumps races 12   2   1   1   £6,959
11/99 Tntn   3m¹⁄₂f Cls3 Nov Hdl good £3,141
10/99 Font   2m6¹⁄₂f Cls4 Mdn Hdl good £2,583
Total win prize-money £5,724
GF-HRD 0-1-4   GS-HVY 0-0-2   Course 0-0-0   Dist 0-0-1

28 May Fontwell 2m2½f Cls4 81-105 Hdl Hcap £3,383
16 ran GOOD 9hdls Time 4m 21.40s (slw 7.40s)
1 Hail The King 6 11-7 .Robert Lucey-Butler (5) 7/1
2 Khaysar 8 10-13 ....Owyn Nelmes (3) 25/1
3 Shaman 9 10-13 ....Philip Hide 6/1
10 **GLENFIELD HEIGHTS** 11 10-3 t ....
....Richard Gordon (10) 20/1
held up towards rear, ridden and headway 6th,
weakened 3 out
btn 17½ lengths [RPR75 TS22 OR92]
13 **RESERVOIR** 5 10-11 ....T J O'Brien (5) 25/1
prominent to 6th
btn 27 lengths [RPR68 TS15 OR95]
Dist: nk-nk-¾-3-½   RACE RPR: 105/95/91
Racecheck: Wins 1 Pl 2 Unpl 6

12 May Wincanton 2m6f Cls4 77-100 Hdl Hcap £3,083
12 ran GD-FM 11hdls Time 5m 20.00s (slw 11.00s)
1 Annie Fleetwood 8 11-10 ..Andrew Thornton 4/1
2 Dawn Wager 5 10-10 ....James Davies 33/1
3 Minster Park 7 10-12 t ....R J Greene 12/1
P **GLENFIELD HEIGHTS** 11 10-8 ....
....Richard Gordon (10) 14/1
in touch until 6th, ridden after 3 out, weakened
quickly and pulled up before next
[OR92]   [op 13/2]

True Temper   10-0

9-y-o b m Roselier - Diamond Rock (Swan's Rock)
A M Crow   Mark Bradburne

Placings: 0FP4/33d4553443F6-332

OR**83**		Starts	1st	2nd	3rd	Win & Pl
Hurdles		18	–	1	3	£2,465
All Jumps races		28	–	1	5	£3,611
GF-HRD 0-3-8		GS-HVY 0-3-17		Course 0-0-0		Dist 0-2-9

17 Jun Hexham 2m½f   Cls4 Nov Hdl £2,741
10 ran GD-FM 8hdls Time 4m 7.40s (slw 8.40s)
1 Glen Harley 6 10-12 t ....Alan Dempsey 7/2
2 **TRUE TEMPER** 9 10-12 .....Mark Bradburne 9/2
in touch, ridden after 3 out, rallied to chase
winner before last, one pace run-in
[RPR80 TS46 OR74]   [op 4/1]

---

3 Ro Eridani 6 10-9 ....Mr C Storey (3) 25/1
Dist: 3-16-8-¾   RACE RPR: 83+/80/68+
Racecheck: Wins - Pl - Unpl -

27 May Cartmel 2m6f Cls5 Nov 69-95 Hdl Hcap £2,602
12 ran GD-SFT 11hdls Time 5m 33.80s (slw 19.80s)
1 Optimistic Harry 7 10-0 ....Peter Buchanan 5/1
2 Thorn Of The Rose 5 10-6 ..Neil Mulholland 12/1
3 **TRUE TEMPER** 9 10-2 p Declan McGann (5) 7/1
led until approaching 2 out, one pace
[RPR69 TS40 OR76]   [op 8/1]
Dist: 9-7-6-8-3   RACE RPR: 77+/74/69+
Racecheck: Wins - Pl 2 Unpl 2

Queen Excalibur   10-1

7-y-o ch m Sabrehill - Blue Room (Gorytus)
C Roberts   Ollie McPhail

Placings: 0P/F5651F550P-

OR**84**	F40	Starts	1st	2nd	3rd	Win & Pl
Hurdles		11	1	–	–	£2,723
All Jumps races		12	1	–	–	£2,723
78 7/05	Uttx	2m Cls4 Nov 72-88 Hdl Hcap gd-fm				£2,723
GF-HRD 1-0-9		GS-HVY 0-0-3		Course 0-0-3		Dist 0-0-1

22 Oct 05 Chepstow 3m   Cls3 Ch £5,785
8 ran SOFT 18fncs Time 6m 29.30s (slw 34.30s)
1 Red Georgie 7 11-0 ....Carl Llewellyn 3/1
2 Reflected Glory 6 11-0 ...Christian Williams 9/4F
3 Jolejoker 7 11-0 ....Richard Johnson 16/1
P **QUEEN EXCALIBUR** 6 10-7 .Ollie McPhail 66/1
always in rear, jumped slowly 8th, pulled up
before 9th   [op 50/1]
Dist: 10-25-29   RACE RPR: 130+/123+/93
Racecheck: Wins 1 (1) Pl 3 Unpl 10

23 Sep 05 Worcester 2m Cls4 Nov 79-105 Hdl Hcap
£4,232
16 ran GD-FM 7hdls   Time 3m 41.40s (fst 1.60s)
1 Sunnyland 6 10-11 ....Richard Johnson 7/2F
2 Smart Boy Prince 4 11-12 ....David Dennis 6/1
3 Dont Ask Me 4 10-2 t ....Timmy Murphy 7/1
13 **QUEEN EXCALIBUR** 6 10-1 ....
....Lee Stephens (5) 16/1

---

held up in mid-division, jumped slowly 3rd,
behind from 5th
btn 32 lengths [RPR63 TS52 OR85]   [op 14/1]
Dist: ¾-1-8-1½-1¾   RACE RPR: 100/114/90
Racecheck: Wins 5 (5) Pl 9 Unpl 6

Harrycat   11-10

5-y-o b g Bahhare - Quiver Tree (Lion Cavern)
C P Morlock   Liam Heard (5)

Placings: 426P/2170-8

OR**107**	F65	Starts	1st	2nd	3rd	Win & Pl
All Jumps races		9	1	2	–	£9,806
8/05	Strf	2m1½f Cls3 Nov Hdl gd-fm £6,322
GF-HRD 1-1-3		GS-HVY 0-0-4		Course 0-1-1		Dist 0-0-0

4 Jun Hereford 2m1f   Cls3 95-121 Hdl Hcap £9,395
15 ran GD-FM 8hdls Time 3m 53.00s (slw 3.00s)
1 Mac Federal 4 10-6 ....Jamie Goldstein 25/1
2 Traprain 4 10-12 ....T J O'Brien (5) 9/4F
3 Tom Bell 6 9-12 v ....Steven Crawford (5) 14/1
8 **HARRYCAT** 5 10-12 p .....Jimmy McCarthy 66/1
prominent until weakened 3 out
btn 25 lengths [RPR96 TS90 OR107]
Dist: ½-5-½-9-7   RACE RPR: 115/130+/107
Racecheck: Wins 1 Pl 2 Unpl 3

8 Dec 05 Huntingdon 2m1½f Cls3 98-124 Hdl Hcap
£5,530
12 ran GOOD 8hdls Time 4m 2.50s (slw 22.50s)
1 Hernando's Boy 4 11-1 .....Phil Kinsella (7) 7/2F
2 Irish Wolf 5 10-11 ....Tom Greenway (5) 9/2
2 Silver Prophet 6 10-12 ......Sean Curran 15/2
10 **HARRYCAT** 4 10-9 p ....Philip Hide 20/1
mid-division, mistake and lost place 4th,
weakened after next
btn 49 lengths [RPR61 OR107]
Dist: dht-shd-8-4-9 RACE RPR: 124+/117/114+
Racecheck: Wins 2 (1) Pl 1 Unpl 16

Form Reading	**MR DIP**	
Spotlight	Out of the weights here.	
Handicap Ratings	Mark of 86 four outings ago (finished 8th) and down to a mark of 83 today which leaves it 5lbs out of the weights.	
Significant Items of Form	Seven year old with no wins whose last jumps campaign ended October/November 2005 with two runs in Class 4 Handicap Hurdles over 2m5f and 2m6½f on Good to Soft where 7th of 12 on both occasions beaten 38 lengths and 45 lengths. One run since then in December 2005 on the All Weather where 3rd of 12 over 1m4f, beaten 7 lengths.	
Verdict	No indication from form that it can return from an eighteen month break and immediately be competitive in an event where it is out of the weights.	
Decision:	DISMISS.	

Form Reading	**GLENFIELD HEIGHTS**	
Spotlight	Creditable return from long absence last summer.	
Handicap Ratings	Ran off a mark of 107 six outings ago (placed 5th) and down to 92 for last two outings (pulled up and out of the top 10). Mark of 90 for today's event, which would indicate it needs to recapture previous form to figure.	

Significant Items of Form	Eleven year old with two hurdle wins in 1999, a Class 3 over 3m½f and a Class 4 over 2m6½f, both on Good. 2nd place last season (details not shown) was followed by two runs in May 2006 which followed a long break. In its first run over 2m6f at Wincanton, it was pulled up 2 out. Next and last run however a Class 4 handicap Hurdle over 2m2½f at Fontwell (Good) on 28.05.06 it made headway at the 6th before weakening 3 out, beaten 17½ lengths.
Verdict	Last run, which was just over three weeks ago, indicated that the horse was getting fitter after its break and it was close enough at the finish to show it could be competitive again in a Class 4 event. No problems with today's distance and going, so a top three placing is a reasonable possibility.
Hence:	SELECT.

Form Reading	**TRUE TEMPER**
Spotlight	Creditable effort in Hexham Novice latest.
Handicap Ratings	Ran off a mark of 76 two outings ago when 3rd but up to a mark of 83 today which puts it 9lbs below the weights.
Significant Items of Form	Nine year old with no wins but a total of seven places in the first three in the last nineteen outings. Third of 12 runners in a Class 5 Handicap Hurdle over 2m6f at Cartmel on 27.05.06, beaten 16 lengths after leading until 2 out. Second of 10 runners in a Class 4 Novice Hurdle over 2m1½f at Hexham on 17.06.06, beaten 3 lengths.
Verdict	Handicap ratings indicate horse is unlikely to win from 9lbs out of the handicap, but the horse's good form in its last two races, which were probably a lot easier than today's contest, is sufficient to suggest a top three placing is a reasonable possibility.
Decision:	SELECT.

Form Reading	**QUEEN EXCALIBUR**
Spotlight	Pulled up over fences when last seen in October.
Handicap Ratings	After winning off a mark of 78 six outings ago horse ran off a mark of 85 for next four outings, two of which resulted in a 5th place. Mark of 84 for today's race.
Significant Items of Form	Seven year old with one win in a Class 4 Novice Handicap Hurdle over 2 miles at Uttoxeter on Good to Firm July 2005. Last run eight months ago was a Class 3 Chase at Chepstow over 3 miles when pulled up before 9th. Previous run in September 2005 was in a 2 mile Class 4 Handicap Hurdle at Worcester when 13th of 16 runners on Good to Firm, beaten 32 lengths.
Verdict	Statistics show three runs at today's course (Worcester) but only one run at today's distance and two last runs indicate that the horse may have a problem with distances over two miles. Combination of an eight month break and the distance question mark suggests that a competitive run in today's contest is unlikely.
Hence:	DISMISS.

Form Reading	**HARRYCAT**
Spotlight	Acts on the ground and promising riders 5lbs claim a help.
Handicap Ratings	Mark of 109 (placed 7th) and 107 (placed 0 and 8th) for last three outings which places it 2lbs below top weight.
Significant Items of Form	Five year old with a Class 3 Novice Hurdle victory at Stratford (Good to Firm) over 2m½f in August 2005. Last run on 04.06.06 followed a six month break when 8th of 15 in a Class 3 Handicap Hurdle at Hereford, beaten 25 lengths, after being prominent until 3 out. Has had two runs at today's course, one of which resulted in a top three placing, but no runs at today's distance.
Verdict	This horse is only five years old but has demonstrated that it is competitive in Class 3 events. Last run was encouraging considering it was returning from a six month break and though today's distance is an unknown factor, it is worth taking a chance that the trainer knows what he is doing in placing the horse in a Class 4 Handicap Hurdle at a course and on going, both of which should suit, providing this horse's second run after a break is not affected by the bounce factor. Decision, top three placing a definite possibility.
Hence:	SELECT.

Overall Comment

Yet another contest where a horse that achieved a midfield finishing position (8th) in its first run following a long break has gone on to win its next contest.

Harrycat had showed it was competitive in Class 3 events so it was not surprising that it prevailed in a lower class (Class 4) event.

The bonus was the fact that a Reverse Forecast on the three System selections yielded £331.80 for the Tote Exacta and £855.53 for the Computer Straight Forecast.

EXAMPLE 23

29.03.07   Towcester – Good – Class 5 – Handicap Chase – 2m3½ f

Winner   ROMNEY MARSH – 33/1

5.00
RACE 6

gg.com Tipzone Handicap Chase (Class 5)   ATR

Winner £2,927.70   2m3½f

£4500 guaranteed for 5yo+ Rated 0-90 Weights raised 2lb Minimum Weight 10-0 Penalties after March 17th, a winner of a chase 7lb Iaskofyou's Handicap Mark 86 Entries 30 pay £15 Penalty value 1st £2,927.70 2nd £859.50 3rd £429.75 4th £214.65

1 680-75P IASKOFYOU (IRE) 140 D
br g Jolly Jake-Deep Bart   10 11-12
Mr P Mason(7)   95
A J Chamberlain   A J Chamberlain

2 U-73652 HIGHLAND CHIEF (IRE) 18
b/br g Taipan-Catatonia   p7 11-11
Sam Thomas   93
Miss H C Knight   P J Dunkley And D F Reilly

3 P08-6P0 CASHEL DANCER 7
b m Bishop Of Cashel-Dancing Debut   8 11-11
Phil Kinsella(3)   85
S A Brookshaw   Ken Edwards

4 2498726 LUSAKA DE PEMBO (FR) 18 D BF
b g Funny Baby-Creakeline   8 11-9
P J Brennan   104
N A Twiston-Davies   Trevor Hemmings

5 68337 ARCHWAY COPSE 18
ch m Anshan-Finkin   7 11-7
Wayne Hutchinson
Ian Williams   The Duck Racing Partnership

6 -2PPU5F ARCTIC SPIRIT 123 C
b g Arctic Lord-Dickies Girl   12 11-4
R J Greene   99
R Dickin   The Lordy Racing Partnership

7 6342221 BALLYAAHBUTT (IRE) (7ex) 8
b g Good Thyne-Lady Henbit   b 8 11-4
S P Jones(5)   94
B G Powell   Mrs A Ellis

8 2P654P0 ACERTACK (IRE) 45
b g Supreme Leader-Ask The Madam   10 11-3
Barry Fenton   96
R Rowe   Keith Hunter

9 9-8P8PP ROMNEY MARSH 31
br m Glacial Storm-Mirador   6 11-1
C M Studd(5)
R Curtis   The Romney Marsh Partnership

10 P04-P45 MR MICKY (IRE) 30
b g Rudimentary-Top Berry   9 10-6
Gerry Supple   98
M B Shears   J B Shears

11 825U666 AUDITOR 130 C
b g Polish Precedent-Annaba   v 8 10-0
Colin Bolger(3)   101
S T Lewis   Simon T Lewis

12 53P4P0F KILTIMONEY (IRE) 31
gr g Kasmayo-Rosie's Midge   7 10-0
Mr C P Huxley(7)   107
N R Mitchell   Dunplush

LONG HANDICAP: Auditor 9-13 Kiltimoney 9-12

2006 (8 ran) Tipp Top 0 Brennan 9 11-3 100/30   John McNamara OR79

BETTING FORECAST: 5-4 Ballyaahbutt, 3 Lusaka de Pembo, 6 Highland Chief, 16 Acertack, Archway Copse, Iaskofyou, Mr Micky, 25 Arctic Spirit, Kiltimoney, 33 Auditor, 50 Cashel Dancer, Romney Marsh.

SPOTLIGHT

Iaskofyou Ex-Irish gelding suited by about this trip and good to firm/good to soft; lightly raced in recent times and possibly not the force he was though is edging down the handicap; left D. E. Fitzgerald since last seen nearly five months ago.

Highland Chief Modest maiden; seemed to find 3m stretching him on a couple of occasions and apparently more at home over extended 2m6f when runner-up in ordinary race at Market Rasen latest; this trip on stiff track should suit but may well find one or two too good again.

Cashel Dancer Trip/ground should suit but failed to take advantage of slipping handicap mark over hurdles last season and no hint of revival over fences/hurdles this term.

Lusaka de Pembo Difficult to win but 30lb lower than a year ago and done enough this season, including when second off this mark over 2m here last month (third and fifth won next time), to suggest he will win a race before long; disappointing favourite since but capable of getting involved with trip/ground likely to suit.

Archway Copse Moderate novice hurdler, well-beaten third on two occasions and last of seven to finish upped to this trip on handicap debut latest; plenty to prove on chasing debut.

Arctic Spirit Goes well here and suited by a sound surface but best at around 2m and shown his form, when second at Exeter last May, just once over the last couple of seasons; plummeting in the handicap but even if he can revive at the age of 12 the trip is likely to find him out.

Ballyaahbutt Knocking on the door this season and, despite creeping up the handicap, came up with the right answer at Lingfield last week; rider's allowance will help to offset the penalty and another bold bid from the front anticipated provided he handles the ground (has form on good but pulled up three starts on good to firm).

Acertack Lean time of it this season and last and basically on the downgrade; trip/ground should suit and down in the weights again but not hard to look elsewhere.

Romney Marsh Showed a little ability in bumpers but looked moody and no closer than eighth on the two occasions she has completed the course over hurdles; no obvious reason to expect better with switch to fences.

Mr Micky Lightly raced in recent seasons but showed he retains a little ability here last month (closely matched with Lusaka de Pembo); possibly found extra half-mile beyond him last time (well behind Ballyaahbutt) but trip/ground could be negatives again.

Auditor Gained only jumping win here more than three years ago, distance farther than ideal and only the merest glimmer of ability this season.

Kiltimoney Maiden pointer in Ireland; showed a little ability in face of stiff task, albeit a remote last of three, on British debut at Plumpton (2m4f, good) in November but failed to build on that on softer ground since; something to learn about jumping but is a possible longshot.

VERDICT   BALLYAAHBUTT (nap) stands out as a progressive type but firming ground should be a concern. Lusaka de Pembo is capable of making his presence felt but is not one to rely on and, in the circumstances, a small interest in Kiltimoney may be the best each-way alternative. [FC]

OFFICIAL RATINGS LAST SIX OUTINGS-LATEST ON RIGHT							5.00 HANDICAP	TODAY FUTURE		RP RATING LATEST / BEST / ADJUSTED		
06⁶	06⁵	04⁰	92⁷	90⁵	00⁹	Iaskofyou 11-12	86		—	84	95
93ᵁ	93⁷	91³	88⁶	83⁵	83²	Highland Chief 11-11	85	88	88	93
				92ᴾ		Cashel Dancer 11-11	85		—	85	85
101⁴	104⁹	92⁵	90⁷	83²	83⁶	Lusaka de Pembo 11-9	83	64	104	104
						Archway Copse 11-7	81		—	—	—
96²	96ᵁ	—	96ᵁ	92⁵	89⁷	Arctic Spirit 11-4	78		109	99
59³	66⁴	59²	64²	67²	72¹	Ballyaahbutt (7x) 11-4	78 +1	94◄	94	94
89ᴾ	93⁶	89⁵	87⁴	84ᴾ		Acertack 11-3	77		105	96
						Romney Marsh 11-1	75		—	—	—
—	—	—	—	72⁴	70⁵	Mr Micky 10-6	66	38	98	98
60²	88⁵	65ᵁ	85⁶	78⁶	62⁶	Auditor 9-13	60 -1	76	107	101
—	—	—	81ᴾ	76⁰	84ᶠ	Kiltimoney 9-12	60 -2	—	112◄	107◄

Romney Marsh   11-1

6-y-o br m Glacial Storm - Mirador (Town And Country)

R Curtis   C M Studd (5)

Placings: 0469-8P8PP

OR75 H75   Starts 1st 2nd 3rd Win & Pl
All Jumps races 9   -   -   -
GF-HRD 0-0-2 GS-HVY 0-0-6 Course 0-0-0 Dist 0-0-1

26 Feb Plumpton 2m5f Cls4 79-99 Hdl Hcap £3,253
11 ran HEAVY   12hdls Time 5m 44.60s (slw 51.60s)
1 Cusp 7 10-9 ....S E Durack 10/1
2 Ruling Reef 5 10-9 ....Mr Lee Newnes (7) 7/2F
3 Up At Midnight 7 11-12 ......Mick FitzGerald 9/2
P ROMNEY MARSH 6 10-1 ....C M Studd (5) 33/1
made most at decent pace, hit 9th, headed soon after 3 out, still 3rd 2 out, weakened and pulled up before last (jockey said mare was tired after last flight) [OR79]

Dist: 10-6-7-8-6   RACE RPR: 94+ /88/94+
Racecheck: Wins 1 (1) Pl - Unpl 3

12 Feb Plumpton 2m Cls5 73-90 Am Hdl Hcap £2,056
14 ran HEAVY   9hdls Time 4m 21.20s (slw 40.20s)
1 It's Rumoured 7 11-9 p ......Kevin Tobin (3) 20/1
-2 Silistra 8 11-0 p ....Miss K Jewell (5) 16/1
3 Tirailleur 7 11-2 ....Carey Williamson 16/1
13 ACERTACK 10 10-13 ....Mr R Hodson (5) 14/1
prominent until weakened rapidly from 6th, tailed off and going very slowly after last
btn 73 lengths [OR77]   [op 12/1]

P ROMNEY MARSH 6 11-1 Mr T Copeland (5) 16/1
never went a yard, tailed off when clambered over 2nd, pulled up before 5th
[OR79]   [tchd 20/1]

Dist: 1½-27-6-3½-¾   RACE RPR: 95/86/63+
Racecheck: Wins 1 (1) Pl 2 Unpl 8

29 Dec 06 Taunton 2m3½f Cls4 Nov Hdl £3,253
12 ran SOFT   10hdls Time 5m 8.30s (slw 46.30s)
1 Armariver 6 11-5 ....Sam Thomas 8/11F
2 Lincoln's Inn 4 10-12 ....T J O'Brien 6/1
3 Warpath 5 11-5 ....Mr J E Tudor (7) 10/1
8 ROMNEY MARSH 5 9-12 John Kington (7) 150/1
chased leaders until weakened 3 out
btn 38 lengths [RPR59 TS23]   [op 66/1]

Dist: 6-6-17-5-½   RACE RPR: 115+ /98/106
Racecheck: Wins 1 (1) Pl 1 Unpl 13

Cashel Dancer   11-11

8-y-o b m Bishop Of Cashel - Dancing Debut (Polar Falcon)

S A Brookshaw   Phil Kinsella (3)

Placings: 0/60P25126/83P08-6P0

OR85 H90   Starts 1st 2nd 3rd Win & Pl
Chase 2   -   -   -   £92
All Jumps races 30 3   3   5 £22,565
89 2/05 Ludl 2m Cls3 84-110 Hdl Hcap gd-sft .£4,726
   6/03 Uttx 2m4½f Cls4 Nov Hdl gd-fm £4,165

5/03 Hrfd 2m3½f Cls4 Nov Hdl gd-sft £3,907
Total win prize-money £12,798
GF-HRD 1-2-8 GS-HVY 2-3-12 Course 0-0-0 Dist 1-0-10

22 Mar Ludlow 2m5f Cls4 91-114 Hdl Hcap £4,554
17 ran GOOD 11hdls Time 5m 9.10s (slw 14.10s)
1 Ordre de Bataille 5 11-6 ....Mark Bradburne.11/1
2 Blaeberry 6 11-12 ....Barry Fenton 11/2J
3 Musally 10 10-10 ....Warren Marston 33/1
11 CASHEL DANCER 8 10-1 Joffret Huet (3) 66/1
midfield, lost place 7th, no danger after
btn 66 lengths [RPR32 OR92]
Dist: 1¾-11-4-6-5 RACE RPR: 116+/116/92+
Racecheck: Wins - Pl 1 Unpl -

7 Dec 06 Ludlow 2m4f Cls4 Nov 74-100 Ch Hcap
£4,697
11 ran GD-SFT 17fncs Time 5m 24.00s (slw 32.00s)
1 Fight The Feeling 8 10-2 ....G Lee 13/2
2 Castle Frome 7 10-0 p ow1 Lee Stephens (5) 8/1
3 Lyon 6 10-13 ....Lee Edwards (10) 40/1
P CASHEL DANCER 7 11-1 ..Joffret Huet (3) 33/1
always behind, pulled up before 4 out [OR92]
Dist: 2-5-26-7-44 RACE RPR: 85+/85+/100+
Racecheck: Wins - Pl 1 Unpl 13

20 Nov 06 Ludlow 2m4f Cls4 Ch £5,010
11 ran GOOD 17fncs Time 5m 8.00s (slw 16.00s)

1 Fourty Acers 6 11-6 t..............A P McCoy 5/4J
2 Down's Folly 6 11-6 ....Mark Bradburne 5/4J
3 Secured 6 11-6 ....David Dennis 12/1
6 CASHEL DANCER 7 10-10 Joffret Huet (3) 50/1
held up, ridden after 7th, toiling final circuit
[RPR82 TS58]
Dist: 5-16-½-10-1 RACE RPR: 122+/118+/100
Racecheck: Wins - Pl 2 Unpl 11

Auditor   10-0

8-y-o b g Polish Precedent - Annaba (In The Wings)
S T Lewis Colin Bolger (3)
Placings: 4P98552-783PP825U666

OR60	H66	Starts	1st	2nd	3rd	Win & Pl
Chase		38	1	3	3	£13,219
All Jumps races		43	1	3	3	£13,219

89 11/04 Towc 2m½f Cls4 79-105 Ch Hcap good £4,648
GF-HRD 0-3-16 GS-HVY 0-1-12 Course 1-1-17 Dist 0-2-11

19 Nov 06 Towcester 2m1½f Cls5 62-88 Cond Ch Hcap
£3,253
10 ran SOFT 12fncs Time 4m 24.20s (slw 20.20s)
1 Billy Bray 6 11-9 ....Liam Treadwell (3) 33/1
2 Glen Thyne 6 11-9 b ....Nick Williams 6/4F
3 Taksina 7 10-13 t ....,..James White (3) 12/1

6 AUDITOR 7 9-9 b oh3 Ryan Cummings (5) 18/1
held up, ridden 6th, mistake 8th, weakened 3
out [RPR48 TS42 OR62] [op 20/1]
Dist: 11-2-¾-1½-16 RACE RPR: 107+/+93+/82
Racecheck: Wins 1 (1) Pl 1 Unpl 8

9 Nov 06 Taunton 2m7½f Cls4 78-111 Ch Hcap £4,554
6 ran GOOD 17fncs Time 6m 11.00s (slw 34.00s)
1 Kerstino Two 9 12-0 ex7 Mr J Snowden (5) 4/7F
2 Fluff 'N' Puff 12 10-11 ....A P McCoy 9/2
3 Sam Adamson 11 9-11 t oh5 ....
.....................................Richard Young (3) 10/1
6 AUDITOR 7 9-9 p oh18 Wayne Kavanagh (5) 50/1
hit 10th, always in rear [RPR49 OR78][op 40/1]
Dist: 10-5-20-7-4 RACE RPR: 128+/+97+/83+
Racecheck: Wins - Pl 3 Unpl 4

15 Oct 06 Hereford 2m3f Cls4 85-110 Ch Hcap £5,205
10 ran GD-FM 14fncs Time 4m 43.00s (slw 12.00s)
1 Butler's Cabin 6 11-7 ....Noel Fehily 3/1
2 Jarro 10 11-9 ....Sam Thomas 7/1
3 No Way Back 6 11-12 t ....Barry Fenton 7/1
6 AUDITOR 7 9-12 p ow1 oh24 ....
..................................Colin Bolger (3) 66/1
always behind [RPR57 TS22 OR85] [op 50/1]
Dist: 7-2½-hd-13-16 RACE RPR: 119+/111/112
Racecheck: Wins 4 (4) Pl 2 Unpl 8

Form Reading	**ROMNEY MARSH**
Spotlight	No closer than 8th on two occasions she has completed the course over hurdles.
Handicap Ratings	No handicap chase marks. Allocated a mark of 75 for today's contest, the value of which is hard to assess.
Significant Items of Form	Six year old with no wins and a best placing of 4th in only 9 runs to date. Current campaign started on 12.02.07 at Plumpton when pulled up before the 5th in a Class 5 Handicap Hurdle over 2 miles on Heavy. However next and last run also at Plumpton (Heavy) on 26.02.07, in a Class 4 Handicap Hurdle over 2m5f was a much better effort where led until 3 out at a decent pace before weakening and pulled up before last.
Verdict	Given the fact that current campaign followed a six week break, the indications are that the horse's fitness is improving and the switch to fences from hurdles should mean that it has shown promise to its trainer over fences at home. Last run was in a Class 4 Handicap Hurdle and, given the fact that this is a Class 5 Handicap Chase, it is not stretching the imagination too far to see a competitive performance on a track which is famous for suiting long priced outsiders.
Decision:	One look at the last six or seven placings of all the runners shows that it isn't going to be a huge surprise whichever of them make the top three placings.
Hence:	SELECT.

Form Reading	**CASHEL DANCER**
Spotlight	Failed to take advantage of slipping handicap mark over hurdles last season and no hint of a revival over fences/ hurdles this term.
Handicap Ratings	Ran off a mark of 92 two outings ago when pulled up, which was only Handicap Chase race in last six outings. Down to a mark of 85 today, which is probably insufficient reduction to spark a revival in form.
Significant Items of Form	Eight year old with three hurdle wins from 2 miles to 2m4½f on Good to Firm and Good to Soft in Class 4 Novice Hurdles (twice) and a Class 3 Handicap Hurdle (latest, February 2005), two of which were on right hand tracks. Only three runs

current season, first two of which were in Class 4 Chases in October/November 2006, both at Ludlow, and both over 2m4f on Good and Good to Soft resulting in 6th of 11 runners, beaten 32½ lengths and pulled up (always behind). Last run was on 22.03.07 again at Ludlow over 2m5f in a Class 4 Handicap Hurdle when 11th of 17 runners, beaten 66 lengths.

Verdict	Nothing in recent form to indicate this horse is becoming competitive.
Hence:	DISMISS.

Form Reading	**AUDITOR**
Spotlight	Gained only jumping wins here more than there years ago.
Handicap Ratings	Has run off marks of 86 (placed 5th) and 85 (placed 8th) in last six outings and down to a mark of 60 for today's race which looks generous as only 1lb out of the weights.
Significant Items of Form	Eight year old with one win at Towcester (November 2004) in a Class 4 Handicap Chase over 2m½f on Good. Towcester specialist having had 17 runs at today's course with one top three placing and one win. Last three runs in October and November 2006 were in Class 4 (twice) and Class 5 Handicap Chases, all on right hand courses where 6th of 10 runners, beaten 38½ lengths, 6th of 6 runners, beaten 46 lengths and 6th of 10 runners, beaten 31 lengths, over distances from 2m½ f to 2 m7½f.
Verdict	No evidence from *Racing Post* form information that horse goes well fresh but the plus points to its recent form is that it has been finishing its last three Chases and given its Towcester record, a top three placing in today's Class 5 Chase is a possiblity at least.
Decision:	Worth taking a chance that 130 day break will assist.
Hence:	SELECT.

Overall Comment

This was one of the races where, if you noted the fact that this was a Class 5 Chase and you then looked at the last six or seven placings alongside each of the listed runners, you would have seen that the form of the runners, with the exception of the paper favourite, Ballyaabutt, was nothing to write home about.

Although I strongly advise you not to chose races on the basis of whether or not you consider the favourite to be 'a good thing', if you had taken the trouble to glance at Ballyaabutt's form, you would have seen that it had never run at Towcester before.

Towcester, with its unique and thoroughly testing hill, is a graveyard for fancied horses so it would have been totally wrong to have passed the race over because the favourite was 5/4 when probably a price of 4/1 against would have been far more realistic.

The winner, Romney Marsh, was also a horse with no previous runs at Towcester but the big clue to this horse was the quality of its last run at Plumpton on Heavy in a Class 4 Handicap Hurdle over 2m5½f when it was still in front 3 out before being pulled up. This run showed that it was approaching peak fitness and this is the type of form profile you should be constantly on the lookout for.

For the record, the forecast of the winner with the favourite, Lusaka de Pembo, paid £199.20 for the Tote Exacta and £114.61 for the Computer Straight Forecast.

EXAMPLE 24

11.10.06 Wetherby – Good – Class 3 – Handicap Chase – 2m
Winner   ARCHIE BABE – 20/1

4.10 RACE 4
totesport.com Handicap Hurdle (Class 3) RUK
Winner £6,506   2m

£10000 guaranteed **For** 4yo+ Rated 0-135 **Minimum Weight** 10-0 **Penalties** after September 30th, a winner of a hurdle 7lb Aleron's Handicap Mark 134 **Entries** 14 pay £30 **Penalty value 1st** £6,506 **2nd** £1,910 **3rd** £955 **4th** £477

1 41F-021 **ALERON** (IRE) 18 CD p 8 11-12
b g Sadler's Wells-High Hawk Russ Garritty (136)
J J Quinn Grahame Liles

2 119F54- **TOWN CRIER** (IRE) 172 CD 11 11-6
br g Beau Sher-Ballymacarett David O'Meara (142)
Mrs S J Smith Trevor Hemmings

3 PF-P3P7 **PORTAVADIE** 18 D 7 11-6
b g Rakaposhi King-Woodland Flower Fergus King(3) (135)
J M Jefferson Ashleybank Investments Limited

4 26155-2 **CIRCASSIAN** (IRE) 154 D 5 11-5
b g Groom Dancer-Daraliya P J Brennan (135)
J Howard Johnson Andrea & Graham Wylie

5 B95-199 **CRATHORNE** (IRE) 52 (41F) CD 6 11-2
b g Alzao-Shirley Blue Dominic Elsworth (135)
M Todhunter The Centaur Group Partnership IX

6 -103515 **HILLTIME** (IRE) 8 D 6 10-10
b g Danetime-Ceannanas Phil Kinsella(5) (137)
J S Wainwright J S Wainwright

7 41/13- **INDUSTRIAL STAR** (IRE) 200 (74F) D 5 10-6
ch g Singspiel-Faribole G Lee (136)
M D Hammond Racing Management & Training Ltd

8 961/0-3 **ARCHIE BABE** (IRE) 144 (16F) CD 10 10-4
ch g Archway-Frensham Manor Dougie Costello(3) (131)
J J Quinn Bowett Lamb & Kelly

9 15846-0 **ICE AND SODA** (IRE) 143 D 6 10-2
b g Arctic Lord-Another Vodka Robert Thornton (131)
B G Powell Mrs A Ellis

10 /P668-6 **ALPINE HIDEAWAY** (IRE) 46 CD 13 10-0
b g Tirol-Arbour Patrick McDonald(5) (111)
J S Wainwright Peter Easterby

LONG HANDICAP: Alpine Hideaway 8-4

2005 (11 ran) Crathorne M Todhunter 5 10-2 11/2   Tony Dobbin OR108

BETTING FORECAST: 11-4 Circassian, 9-2 Industrial Star, Town Crier, 7 Aleron, 8 Hilltime, 9 Crathorne, 10 Portavadie, 14 Ice And Soda, 16 Archie Babe, 66 Alpine Hideaway.

SPOTLIGHT

Aleron In top form lately and followed a good second at Bangor with quite an emphatic success in a valuable race at Market Rasen last month; up 7lb for that but shorter trip no real problem and no ground worries either, so entitled to be in the shake-up.

Town Crier Versatile (though better as a chaser) and improved again last season, romping to a C&D success over hurdles in January; raised 12lb for that and worth remembering he was well beaten in this on his seasonal return a year ago off 114, so will need to be in peak order to defy this mark.

Portavadie Mixed fortunes over fences last season but returned to hurdling with an excellent effort at Market Rasen in July before running poorly next time; better display behind Aleron on latest start and as he is perhaps best on ground near to good, may well be able to build on that.

Circassian Found wanting in top novice company last season but performed creditably most starts and an easy winner when against modest rivals at Haydock last December; should be more to come and stable just hitting form but suspicion 2m on good ground may not be enough of a test; still an interesting contender.

Crathorne Has improved since winning this last year off 18lb lower and probably capable of a strong showing off this mark based on his win at Southwell in June; major worry is the ground - has done all his winning on good to firm so any rain would count against.

Hilltime Consistent and followed quite an impressive win on his chasing debut last month with a perfectly decent display back over hurdles eight days ago; would not want the ground any softer than good but no surprise to see him in the firing line if conditions remain in his favour.

Industrial Star Interesting profile, having had just ten career starts and only two over hurdles, which include a very solid effort under a penalty at Newbury in March; has his foibles (often hangs left) but successful on the Flat this summer so one for the short list off a reasonable mark for handicap debut; good ground ideal.

Archie Babe Has done connections proud over the years but did not look quite the same force in limited appearances on the Flat this summer; usually finds this grade beyond him over hurdles and as he is still 7lb higher than when last scoring 19 months ago, will do well to win.

Ice And Soda Ex-Irish; won a bumper (heavy) for Charlie Swan last December and a couple of his efforts in novice hurdles, when just out of the placings, look solid; probably weighted right up to his best for British/handicap debut.

Alpine Hideaway Last hurdling win was gained in a seller more than three years ago and will struggle from well out of the weights.

VERDICT **Circassian** mixed it with the best in novice events last season and makes plenty of appeal from this mark but another handicap debutant, **INDUSTRIAL STAR**, also looks on a handy rating and with Graham Lee booked, can make a successful return to hurdling.[JN]

OFFICIAL RATINGS							4.10	HANDICAP		RP RATING		
LAST SIX OUTINGS-LATEST ON RIGHT									TODAY FUTURE	LATEST	BEST	ADJUSTED
—	—	—	128⁹	125²	127¹	Aleron	...11-12	134		133	133	136
—	116¹	—	—	—	—	Town Crier	...11-6	128		—	147 ◄	142 ◄
—	—	—	126³	130ᴾ	130⁷	Portavadie	...11-6	128		128	135	135
—	—	—	—	—	—	Circassian	...11-5	127		114	135	135
118⁶	118⁹	116⁵	117¹	125⁹	125⁹	Crathorne	...11-2	124		118	135	135
117¹	121⁰	119³	118⁵	—	118⁶	Hilltime	...10-10	118		136 ◄	137	137
—	—	—	—	—	—	Industrial Star	...10-6	114		136 ◄	136	136
114⁰	110⁹	108⁶	105¹	115⁰	112³	Archie Babe	...10-4	112		127	127	131
—	—	—	—	—	—	Ice And Soda	...10-2	110		—	131	131
94²	95ᴾ	95⁵	94⁶	93⁸	87⁶	Alpine Hideaway	...8-4	108 -24		96	106	111

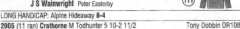

Alpine Hideaway   10-0

13-y-o *b g Tirol - Arbour (Graustark)*
J S Wainwright   Patrick McDonald (5)

Placings: 6/84214/23242/P668-6

OR**108**F45	Starts	1st	2nd	3rd	Win & Pl
Hurdles	41	4	4	5	£15,746
All Jumps races	43	4	4	5	£15,746
80 8/03 Sedg	2m1f Cls5 76-95 Sell Hdl Hcap gd-fm				
					£2,359
101 6/98 MRas	2m1½f Cls4 90-118 Hdl Hcap good				
					£2,903
5/98 Weth	2m Cls3 Nov Hdl gd-fm £2,698				
3/98 Newc	2m Cls4 Nov Claim Hdl gd-fm £1,896				
	Total win prize-money £10,056				

GF-HRD 3-4-15 GS-HVY 0-2-11 Course 1-0-6 Dist 2-2-18

26 Aug Market Rasen 2m3½f Cls5 85-91 Hdl Hcap
£3,083
9 ran GOOD   10hdls   Time 5m 9.80s (slw 36.80s)
1 Black Rainbow 8 11-2 ...Miss T Jackson (7) 11/2
2 Gondolin 6 11-6 ....S Durack 9/1
3 Erins Lass 9 10-13 v1 Joseph Stevenson 5/1
6 ALPINE HIDEAWAY 13 11-8 ....G Lee 22/1
in touch, effort 7th, lost place after next
[RPR68 OR87]   [op 14/1]
Dist: nk-11-¾-6-4   RACE RPR: 91/91+/81+
Racecheck: Wins - Pl - Unpl 4

17 Nov 05 Market Rasen 2m1½f Cls4 78-100 Hdl
Hcap £3,268
9 ran GD-SFT   8hdls   Time 4m 22.50s (slw 19.50s)
1 Parisienne Gale 6 10-9 ....
...............................Miss Caroline Hurley (7) 5/6F
2 Upswing 8 9-11 ow1 ...Miss C Metcalfe (7) 11/2
3 Nobel 4 11-5 ....Miss R Davidson (7) 11/2
8 ALPINE HIDEAWAY 12 10-12 p ....
....................................Miss S Brotherton (7) 25/1
*in rear, pushed along 3rd, behind from 5th
(jockey received caution: used whip when out
of contention)*

16 Oct 05 Market Rasen 2m1½f Cls5 68-94 Sell Hdl
Hcap £2,331
17 ran GOOD   8hdls   Time 4m 19.60s (slw 16.60s)
1 Sheer Guts 6 11-9 tv ......Andrew Thornton 8/1
2 Aleemdar 9 10-4 p ....Derek Laverty (5) 6/1F
3 Irish Blessing 8 11-3 tp ......Leighton Aspell 7/1
6 ALPINE HIDEAWAY 12 11-9 p ....
..................................Mr T Greenall (3) 12/1
in rear, headway 3 out, never near leaders
[RPR78 TS58 OR94]   [op 8/1]
Dist: ½-10-3-shd-7   RACE RPR: 96+/81/80+
Racecheck: Wins 3 (3) Pl 2 Unpl 17

Archie Babe   10-4

10-y-o *ch g Archway - Frensham Manor (Le Johnstan)*
J J Quinn   Dougie Costello (3)

Placings: F44/1423/50961/0-3

OR**112**F49	Starts	1st	2nd	3rd	Win & Pl
All Jumps races	14	2	1	2	£11,347
105 3/05 Towc	2m Cls4 84-110 Hdl Hcap soft £3,465				
11/03 Weth	2m Cls3 Nov Hdl gd-sft £4,069				
	Total win prize-money £7,534				

GF-HRD 0-0-0 GS-HVY 2-2-11 Course 1-1-5 Dist 2-2-10

20 May Bangor-On-Dee 2m1f Cls3 104-118 Hdl Hcap
£6,994
9 ran SOFT   8hdls   Time 4m 15.90s (slw 20.40s)
1 Red Moor 6 11-4 ....Benjamin Hitchcott 10/1
2 Cunning Pursuit 5 11-2 t ....P J Brennan 20/1
3 ARCHIE BABE 10 11-6 ....Russ Garritty 5/1
*prominent, ridden and outpaced after 6th,
weakened 2 out* [RPR103 TS93 OR112] [op 11/2]
Dist: 2½-10-17-8-3   RACE RPR: 113/109/103
Racecheck: Wins 1 Pl - Unpl 6

13 Mar Stratford 2m1½f Cls3 104-124 Hdl Hcap £10,021
13 ran GD-SFT   9hdls   Time 3m 58.50s (slw 10.50s)

1 Rojabaa 7 10-6 ....Richard Hobson 20/1
2 Caraman 8 10-9 ....Dougie Costello (5) 12/1
3 Lysander 7 10-2 ....Charlie Poste (5) 14/1
10 ARCHIE BABE 10 11-3 ......Russ Garritty 40/1
always behind
btn 28 lengths [RPR90 TS81 OR115] [op 33/1]
Dist: nk-2½-6-1¾-9   RACE RPR: 108/116/108+
Racecheck: Wins 3 (1) Pl 8 Unpl 5

10 Mar 05 Towcester 2m Cls4 84-110 Hdl Hcap £3,465
10 ran SOFT   8hdls   Time 4m 14.30s (slw 25.80s)
1 ARCHIE BABE 9 11-7 ....Russ Garritty 8/1
*chased leader, led 5th, ridden clear
approaching last, eased close home*
[RPR114 TS111 OR105]   [op 7/1]
2 Mr Bigglesworth 7 10-12 ....Henry Oliver 2/1F
3 Mnason 5 11-5 ....Mr P Cowley (7) 15/2
Dist: 13-2-9-5-13   RACE RPR: 114+/90+/102
Racecheck: Wins 2 (2) Pl 3 Unpl 14

Flat Form

25 Sep Hamilton 1m3f Cls6 49-63 App Hcap £3,239
14 ran GD-SFT   Time 2m 30.71s (slw 8.71s)
1 Cleaver 5 9-11 ....Andrew Elliott 5 6/1
2 Peas 'N Beans 3 8-1 ......Luke Morris (6) 12/1
3 Gigs Magic 3 8-3 ....William Carson (5) 7 14/1
8 ARCHIE BABE 10 9-0 Michael J Stainton 11 10/1
*tracked leaders, ridden along over 3f out, soon
weakened*
btn 12½ lengths [RPR42 TS38 OR51] [tchd 11/1]
Dist: 1½-2½-2½-½-1   RACE RPR: 73/60/57
Racecheck: Wins - Pl 1 Unpl 1

Form Reading	**ALPINE HIDEAWAY**
Spotlight	Last hurdle win was gained in a Seller more than three years ago.
Handicap Ratings	Has run off marks from 87 to 95 in last six outings, but allocated a mark of 108 for today's Class 3 contest, which puts the horse 24lbs out of the weights and seemingly in an impossible situation.
Significant Items of Form	Thirteen year old with four hurdle wins, the last being in August 2003 in a Class 5 Selling Handicap Hurdle over 2m1f on Good to Firm. All three other wins, which include a Class 3 Novice Hurdle at Wetherby over 2 miles, were in 1998. Two of last three runs were in October and November 2005 when 6th of 17 in a Class 5 Selling Hurdle and 8th of 9 in a Class 4 Handicap Hurdle, beaten 20 lengths and 31 lengths respectively. Last run on 26.08.06 was in a Class 5 Handicap Hurdle at Market Rasen (Good) over 2m3½f when 6th of 9 runners, beaten 22 lengths.
Verdict	Thirteen year olds and even older horses sometimes win races and so do horses that are many pounds out of the weights, but in the case of Alpine Hideaway a Class 3 contest must surely be out of reach for a horse that is currently finding it difficult to be competitive in Class 5 events.
Decision:	DISMISS.

Form Reading	**ARCHIE BABE**
Spotlight	7lbs higher than when last scoring nineteen months ago.
Handicap Ratings	Won off a mark of 105 three outings ago. Allocated a mark of 112 for today's outing, which is the same as its mark for its last outing, when placed 3rd.
Significant Items of Form	Ten year old with a Class 3 Novice Hurdle win over 2 miles at today's course

Wetherby (Good to Soft) November 2003. He had one other win in a Class 4 Handicap Hurdle at Towcester (Soft) over 2 miles in March 2005. Record at Wetherby is five runs, 1 place, 1 win. Last run in a National Hunt event was on 20.05.06 when 3rd of 9 runners in a Class 3 Handicap Hurdle at Bangor (Soft) over 2m1f, beaten 12 ½ lengths. Prior to its last run, horse had only run once in March 2006 since its win at Towcester 2005. Horse was given a fitness sharpener in a 1m3f Class 6 Apprentice Handicap flat race at Hamilton on 25.09.06 when 8th of 14 runners, beaten 12½ lengths.

Verdict   Course winner that has had only three runs in last nineteen months, but 3rd place at Bangor in a Class 3 Handicap Hurdle in May 2006 and flat run on 25.09.06 when only beaten 12½ lengths have demonstrated horse has a good chance of a top three placing in today's event when course, distance and going will all suit.

Hence: SELECT.

Overall Comment

This is an example of a Non-Preferred racecourse (Wetherby) but a Preferred Class and Type of race (Class 3 Handicap Chase).

The form of the winner, Archie Babe, is slightly unusual insofar as it had two easily identifiable positives rather than just one, which is normally the case, and this was sufficient reason to ignore the fact the race was at a Non-Preferred venue.

The two identifiable positives were, firstly, good course form, which is so frequently a significant feature in the form of winning 'outsiders'; the second was a recent flat run for form sharpening purposes where its finishing position was within 12 lengths of the winner.

In my experience a recent flat race run can be interpreted as a positive sign if the horse in question has finished within 10 to 12 lengths of the winner or, alternatively, it has either led or been very prominent until fairly close to the finish before weakening and losing ground, the amount of which is unimportant.

In the case of Alpine Hideaway, which was DISMISSED, I am always hesitant to leave out Course Winners because a return to a horse's favourite track can often bring about an improvement in form.

However, the form of Alpine Hideaway had been so far below the level required to feature in this particular race that a DISMISS decision was relatively easy.

For the record the Forecast Archie Babe with Aleron paid £56.10 for the Tote Exacta and £148.82 for the Computer Straight Forecast.

EXAMPLE 25

08.11.06   Lingfield – Good – Class 5 – Handicap Chase – 2m4½f
Winner   THE HARDY BOY – 66/1

2.30 RACE 4
Lingfield Park For Christmas Parties Handicap Chase (Class 5)
Winner £2,602.40   **ATR   2m4½f**

£4000 guaranteed For 4yo+ Rated 0-90 Minimum Weight 10-0 Penalties after October 28th, a winner of a chase 7lb Anshabil's Handicap Mark 90 Entries 34 pay £15 Penalty value 1st £2,602.40 2nd £764 3rd £382 4th £190.80

No	Form	Horse	Jockey	Wt	Rating
1	40P/FP-	**ANSHABIL** (IRE) 519 BF — br g Anshan-Billeragh Thyne — A King Jerry Wright	Wayne Hutchinson	7 11-11	105
2	647140-	**BACK IN BUSINESS** (IRE) 203 D — b/br g Bob Back-Rose Of Burnett — Evan Williams W Ralph Thomas	Paul Moloney	6 11-12	—
3	5P3037-	**THIEVES'GLEN** (IRE) 197 BF — b g Teenoso-Hollow Creek — H Morrison Mrs M D W Morrison	Andrew Tinkler	8 11-12	101
4	4UP25-7	**MYSON** (IRE) 180 D — ch g Accordion-Ah Suzie — G L Moore R Winchester & Son	Jamie Moore	7 11-10	106
5	1/P48-6	**GIMMEABREAK** (IRE) 186 — b g Beneficial-Gentle Eyre — Miss E C Lavelle Five Arrows Racing	Barry Fenton	6 11-9	—
6	0606P-U	**BELUGA** (IRE) 153 — gr g John French-Mesena — Carl Llewellyn Malcolm C Denmark	Robert Lucey-Butler(5)	7 11-9	83
7	32P5P-P	**LOST IN NORMANDY** (IRE) 18 D — b g Treasure Hunter-Auntie Honnie — Mrs L Williamson Please Hold UK	R J Greene	9 11-8	96
8	00F397-	**THE LAYING HEN** (IRE) 209 — ch m Anshan-Glacial Run — D P Keane Wincanton Race Club	Neil Mulholland	6 11-7	—
9	P/U3FP-	**LA SOURCE A GOLD** (IRE) 207 — br g Octagonal-Coral Sound — Nick Williams Mrs Alurie O'Sullivan	Willie McCarthy(7)	7 11-3	98
10	4211U5-	**MOSCOW GOLD** (IRE) 196 D — ch g Moscow Society-Vesper Time — A E Price Mrs Carol Davis	Owyn Nelmes(3)	9 11-1	100
11	38050-	**MISS CHIPPY** (IRE) 258 — ch m Mister Lord-My Alanna — T R Georgo Timothy N Chick	Noel Fehily	6 11-0	—
12	2737-P1	**OPPORTUNITY KNOCKS** 23 D — gr g Wace-Madame Ruby — N J Hawke Mrs D A Wetherall	Daryl Jacob(3) p6	10-13	95
13	505P3-P	**BALLY RAINEY** (IRE) 182 — b/br g Carroll House-Foxborough Lady — Mrs L C Jewell K Johnson, K Jessup	Leighton Aspell	7 10-13	94
14	FP1762-	**NEW LEADER** (IRE) 231 BF — b g Supreme Leader-Two Spots — Mrs L Richards E T Wright	Colin Bolger(3)	9 10-7	99
15	6764-5U	**THE HARDY BOY** 19 66/1 — br g Overbury-Miss Nero — Miss A M Newton-Smith Mrs John Grist	Henry Oliver	6 10-2	94

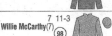

Lost In Normandy   11-8

9-y-o b g Treasure Hunter - Auntie Honnie (Radical)
Mrs L Williamson   R J Greene

Placings: 88P2/PP22374132P5P-P

OR86	H75	Starts	1st	2nd	3rd	Win & Pl
Chase		27	3	6	3	£20,374
All Jumps races		36	3	6	3	£20,374

79 12/05 Bang 2m4½f Cls4 79-105 Ch Hcap soft £4,167
75 10/03 Sthl 3m2f Cls4 67-83 Ch Hcap gd-fm £2,898
70 9/03 Bang 3m1½f Cls4 Nov 70-96 Ch Hcap good ....
....£4,134
Total win prize-money £11,199
GF-HRD 1-0-8   GS-HVY 1-1-10   Course 0-0-0   Dist 1-2-5

21 Oct Kelso 3m1f   Cls4 79-105 Ch Hcap £4,554
10 ran GD-SFT   15fncs Time 6m 33.60s (slw 31.60s)
1 Another Promise 7 11-12 ....G Lee 5/4F
2 Hugo de Grez 11 10-4 ....Dominic Elsworth 14/1
3 Another Taipan 6 10-0 oh10 Peter Buchanan 14/1
P LOST IN NORMANDY 9 10-8 T J Dreaper (3) 25/1
always behind, tailed off when pulled up 4 out

SPOTLIGHT

Anshabil Not quite so bad as grim recent form figures imply and had jumped well until departing two out when holding every chance in Stratford novice handicap chase in May last year; not seen since going wrong the following month but been given a chance by handicapper.

Back In Business Convincing winner over 2m4f on soft over hurdles in Ireland early this year and reported to have schooled well over fences for new trainer who has proved so consistently good with other stables' castoffs, so has to be considered.

Thieves'glen Disappointing favourite at Towcester in April when last seen and won only once in 24 starts in a varied career under Rules and between flags, but don't doubt he has it in him to land race like this if everything happened to fall just right.

Myson Held his form for a while after winning over this trip at Plumpton in March last year for David Feek but eventually lost his way over fences; potentially well treated if new trainer has rekindled his enthusiasm.

Gimmeabreak Jumped well when winning point in Ireland last year but didn't make massive impact over hurdles; has the build that suggests he's likely to be seen to much better effect now chasing and one to consider if there's any market confidence.

Beluga In contention but too early to say what would have happened had he not unseated seven out off this mark in novice handicap chase (16/1) at Uttoxeter in June; hard to assess.

Lost In Normandy In good form on soft ground in December/January last season, but well below par last four starts, including on reappearance, and has it to prove now even though back down to mark off which he was close second at Wetherby early in year.

The Laying Hen Limitations exposed in bumpers and over hurdles, with best effort a modest third in mares only novice at Wincanton in February; may well improve for fences but needs to.

La Source A Gold Difficult to pin down precise merit over fences and certainly nothing to admire in final outing when he was tailed off and pulled up before two out (tried tongue tied) in Newton Abbot handicap in April.

Moscow Gold Picked up two novice handicaps under this rider last December but way below par in April when last seen and still 8lb higher than for last success.

Miss Chippy Hasn't fulfilled promise of her bumper.debut third (well behind The Laying Hen in one hurdle race) and the hope must be that fences will be the making of her.

Opportunity Knocks Return of cheekpieces brought him fortunate success at Plumpton last month and the horse who ought to have won that contest flopped at Kempton yesterday; could easily be vulnerable off 8lb higher mark.

Bally Rainey Won maiden Irish point in mud but has looked limited over regulation fences in Britain, though had excuse of bleeding from nose when 40/1 for Fakenham handicap chase off this mark in May.

New Leader Got his jumping act together when winning off 7lb lower mark over 3m1f at Folkestone and rounded off last season with creditable Towcester second over much shorter trip; looks one of the likelier ones if stripping fit.

The Hardy Boy Useful front-running display to win maiden Irish point last year but only ordinary form over fences in Britain and closely weighted with Bally Rainey on Plumpton maiden chase running in April.

VERDICT **Anshabil** has much better prospects than his alphabet form figures imply but **MYSON** is handicapped to win races this season if Gary Moore has been able to relight his fire. Another must for the shortlist is **Back In Business**.[PJ]

BETTING FORECAST: 9-2 Myson, 5 Back In Business, 8 Anshabil, Gimmeabreak, 9 Opportunity Knocks, 10 Moscow Gold, New Leader, 12 Beluga, Miss Chippy, Thieves'glen, 14 The Laying Hen, 16 La Source A Gold, The Hardy Boy, 33 Bally Rainey, Lost In Normandy.

OFFICIAL RATINGS LAST SIX OUTINGS-LATEST ON RIGHT						2.30 HANDICAP		TODAY FUTURE	RP RATING LATEST / BEST / ADJUSTED		
				95	95P	Anshabil	11-12	90	—	—	105
						Back In Business	11-12	90	—	—	—
110F	104⁵			92⁷		Thieves'glen	11-12	90	85	85	101
101⁴	100U	99P		94⁵		Myson	11-10	88	—	111 ◀106◀
						Gimmeabreak	11-9	87	—	—	—
—	—	—	90⁶		87U	Beluga	11-9	87	—	83	83
74³	86²	92P	92⁵	90P		Lost In Normandy	11-8	86	—	96	96
						The Laying Hen	11-7	85	—	—	—
					86P	La Source A Gold	11-3	81	—	98	98
64⁴	63²	64¹	71¹	81U	81⁵	Moscow Gold	11-1	79	76	100	100
						Miss Chippy	11-0	78	—	—	—
73²	73⁷	73³	72⁷	70P	69¹	Opportunity Knocks	10-13	77	95 ◀	95	95
					77P	Bally Rainey	10-13	77	—	94	94
69F	65P	64¹	69⁷	69⁶	69²	New Leader	10-7	71	94	99	99
					69U	The Hardy Boy	10-2	66	—	94	94

[OR90]   [op 28/1 tchd 22/1]

Dist: 9-5-46   RACE RPR: 130+/83/75+
Racecheck: Wins - Pl - Unpl -

29 Apr Market Rasen 3m1f   Cls4 78-104 Ch Hcap
£4,111
13 ran GOOD   17fncs Time 6m 34.20s (slw 28.20s)
1 Over The Storm 9 10-13 b¹ ..David O'Meara 12/1
2 Runaway Bishop 11 10-9 ..Richard Hobson 10/1
3 Tee-Jay 10 11-1 ....Barry Keniry 8/1

P **LOST IN NORMANDY** 9 10-12 b Dave Crosse 16/1
*in touch, reminders and lost place 9th, soon
behind, pulled up before 12th (jockey said
gelding was never travelling) [or90]*
Dist: 1-8-5-9-hd   RACE RPR: 102+/97+/94
Racecheck: Wins - Pl 1 Unpl 14

18 Mar Uttoxeter 2m5f   Cls4 78-104 Ch Hcap £4,384
8 ran   HEAVY   16fncs Time 6m 0.70s (slw 1m 1.70s)
1 Young Lorcan 10 11-5 ......Richard Spate (7) 7/2
2 Major Belle 7 10-0 oh2 ....Henry Oliver 20/1
3 Pardini 7 10-1 v ....Charlie Poste (5) 10/1
5 LOST IN NORMANDY 9 11-0 b Dave Crosse 7/1
*chased leaders until weakened approaching 4
out [RPR85 TS22 OR92]*   [op 6/1]
Dist: hd-4-1¼-11-6   RACE RPR: 113/87/90+
Racecheck: Wins-1 Pl 1 Unpl 8

Bally Rainey   10-13

7-y-o bb g Carroll House - Foxborough Lady (Crash
Course)
Mrs L C Jewell   Leighton Aspell

Placings: U3F525/1505P3-P

OR77   Starts 1st 2nd 3rd   Win & Pl
Chase   4   –   –   1   £708
All Jumps races 6   –   –   1   £708
GF-HRD 0-0-1 GS-HVY 0-1-3 Course 0-0-0 Dist 0-1-3

10 May Fakenham 2m5½f Cls5 56-79 Ch Hcap £3,253
11 ran GD-FM   16fncs Time 5m 28.70s (slw 10.70s)
1 Galapiat Du Mesnil 12 11-10 .....Joe Tizzard 7/1
2 Tacita 11 9-11 ....Mr M Wall (7) 12/1
3 Chain 9 11-1 t ....Lee Vickers (3) 9/2J

P **BALLY RAINEY** 7 11-8 .....Leighton Aspell 12/1
*held up, blundered 9th, lost touch 11th, tailed
off and pulled up 13th, broke blood vessel
(jockey said gelding bled from the nose)
[OR77]*
Dist: 2½-3½-13-7-11   RACE RPR: 86/67+/75+
Racecheck: Wins - Pl 1 Unpl 5

17 Apr Plumpton 2m4f   Cls5 Mdn Ch £3,457
8 ran   GD-SFT   14fncs Time 5m 13.00s (slw 23.00s)
1 Saddlers Cloth 6 10-7 ....Marcus Foley 15/8F
2 Missyl 6 11-0 ....Andrew Thornton 100/30
3 BALLY RAINEY 7 11-0 ....James Davies 33/1
*chased leaders, outpaced after 10th, ridden to
chase winner 3 out, no impression, lost 2nd last
strides [RPR79 TS65 OR77]*   [op 25/1]
4 THE HARDY BOY 6 11-0 Matthew Batchelor 16/1
*led to 4th, led 8th to 10th, soon hard ridden,
weakened 3 out [RPR68 TS53 OR66]* [op 20/1]
Dist: 20-nk-11-16.   RACE RPR: 97+/79/79
Racecheck: Wins - Pl 2 Unpl 6

31 Jan Folkestone 2m5f   Cls4 Mdn Ch £3,904
7 ran   GD-SFT   15fncs Time 5m 33.60s (slw 27.60s)
1 The Outlier 8 11-2 ....Sam Thomas 8/13F
2 Sett Aside 8 11-2 p ....Benjamin Hitchcott 12/1
3 Twenty Degrees 8 11-2 b ....Jamie Moore 5/1
P BALLY RAINEY 7 11-2 .....Leighton Aspell 33/1
*not fluent, took keen hold, with leader 5th to
11th, with winner 3 out, weakened rapidly, poor
4th when mistake 2 out and pulled up [op 25/1]*
Dist: 6-3-dist   RACE RPR: 100+/82/81+
Racecheck: Wins 2 (2) Pl 3 Unpl 7

The Hardy Boy   10-2

6-y-o br g Overbury - Miss Nero (Crozier)
Miss A M Newton-Smith   Henry Oliver

Placings: P3555331/2P6764-5U

OR66   Starts 1st 2nd 3rd   Win & Pl
Chase   5   –   –   –   £558
All Jumps races 7   –   –   –   £558
GF-HRD 0-0-1 GS-HVY 0-0-2 Course 0-0-0 Dist 0-0-4

20 Oct Fakenham 2m5½f Cls4 69-95 Ch Hcap £6,506
9 ran   GOOD   15fncs Time 5m 40.00s (slw 22.00s)
1 Herecomestanley 7 11-5 h .....Dave Crosse 3/1F
2 Miss Wizadora 11 10-9 ......Richard Johnson 4/1
3 General Hopkins 11 10-1 ow8 oh28 ....
....Mr G Pewter (7) 100/1
U THE HARDY BOY 6 10-0 oh3 Henry Oliver 11/1
*chased leaders, 4th when mistake and unseated
rider 3rd [OR69]*
Dist: 45-33-34   RACE RPR: 114+/79+/25
Racecheck: Wins 2 (1) Pl - Unpl 4

14 May Plumpton 3m2f   Cls4 Ch £5,029
7 ran   GD-FM   18fncs Time 6m 28.30s (slw 6.30s)
1 Floreana 5 10-0 ....Dave Crosse EvensF
2 Redhouse Chevalier 7 10-7 b C M Studd (7) 33/1
3 Herecomestanley 7 10-9 h Charlie Poste (5) 13/2
5 THE HARDY BOY 6 11-0 Matthew Batchelor 33/1
*led to 12th, soon weakened, tailed off
[RPR29 TS29 OR66]*
Dist: 7-6-46-17   RACE RPR: 99+/98/94+
Racecheck: Wins 1 (1) Pl 1 Unpl 8

17 Apr Plumpton   4th, see BALLY RAINEY

Form Reading	**LOST IN NORMANDY**
Spotlight	In good form on Soft ground in December and January last season.
Handicap Ratings	Ran off a mark of 74 six outings ago (placed 3rd) which was raised to 86 for next outing (placed 2nd) and raised again to 92 for next outing (pulled up). Pulled up in last two outings, both on a mark of 90, and down to a mark of 86 today which indicates a degree of leniency if fit enough to take advantage.
Significant Items of Form	Nine year old with three Handicap Chase wins, all Class 4, over distances from 2m4½f to 3m2f on Good to Firm, Good, and Soft, last of which was in December 2005 at Bangor. Latest run on 21.10.06, which followed a six month break, resulted in pulling up 4 out in a Class 4 Handicap Chase at Kelso over 3m1f on Good to Soft.
Verdict	Since 2nd place, which Spotlight tells us was in early 2006, has been pulled up in three runs out of four. However these pulled ups appear to have occurred either at the end or start of a campaign and therefore appear understandable. Horse should strip fitter for latest run and reduction in distance to 2m4½f today should help on going that will suit, but on a course which is untried. Undoubtedly has the ability to finish in first three if it can recapture its form of twelve months ago, so worth taking a chance.
Hence:	SELECT.

Form Reading	**BILLY RAINEY**
Spotlight	Won Maiden Irish Point in mud.
Handicap Ratings	Only one Handicap Chase in last six outings and that was latest run when off a mark of 77 (pulled up). Same mark for today's event and no real way of knowing if this is favourable.

Significant Items of Form	Seven year old with one Irish Point win which, looking at placings record, was probably in early part of 2005/2006 season. Ran in a Class 4 Maiden Chase at Folkestone on 31.01.06 over 2m5f when although pulled up was with winner until 3 out. Had a 2½ month break before running in a Class 5 Maiden Chase at Plumpton over 2m4f on Good to Soft when lost second place in last stride, finishing 20 lengths down on the winner of 8 runner contest. Pulled up at Fakenham in last outing on 10.05.06, a Class 5 Handicap Chase over 2m5½f, after breaking blood vessel.
Verdict	The fact that horse's 3rd place at Plumpton was after a 2½ month break is probably sufficient evidence that it can go well in today's contest after a six month break and although no experience of Lingfield (left hand undulating track), Plumpton racetrack is not too dissimilar. Going and distance shouldn't be a problem and considering this is a Class 5 Chase, a place in the first three has to be a genuine possibility,
Hence:	SELECT.

Form Reading	**THE HARDY BOY**
Spotlight	Useful front running display to win Maiden Irish Point last year.
Handicap Ratings	Only one run in a Handicap Chase in its last six outings and that was its most recent when ran off a mark of 69. Down to a mark of 66 for today's contest which gives horse bottom weight at 10st 2lbs.
Significant Items of Form	Six year old with one Irish Point win towards the end of 2005/2006 season. Finished 4th, 11 lengths behind Bally Rainey (placed 3rd) on 17.04.06 in Class 5 Maiden Chase at Plumpton (Good to Soft) over 2m4f when both carried 11 stone. (NB The Hardy Boy is 11lbs better off today.) Finished 5th of 7 runners in a Class 4 Chase at Plumpton on 14.05.06 over 3m2f on Good to Firm, beaten 76 lengths after leading to the 12th. Given a five month break before running in a Class 4 Handicap Chase at Fakenham (Good) on 20.10.06 when unseated at the 3rd, when lying 4th of 7.
Verdict	Horse's two recent runs at Plumpton indicate that a top three placing in today's Class 5 contest is a reasonable possibility considering distance, going and left hand track.
Decision:	SELECT.

Overall Comment

Another contest were it was necessary to remind yourself of the fact that you are dealing with a Class 5 contest when you are reading the form.

Both the winner, The Hardy Boy, and Bally Rainey had Irish Point wins before moving to Britain and the fact that it was taking both of them time to adjust to the British scene is a familiar tale that should not put you off backing horses with a similar background.

The form of all three selections was nothing to write home about but was not far removed from the form of the other runners, a situation which could be gleaned by looking at the last six placings printed alongside the list of runners and riders.

Of considerable interest is the fact that the Forecast of the winner with the favourite paid £331.50 for the Tote Exacta and £288.25 for the Computer Straight Forecast.

EXAMPLE 26

19.11.06 Towcester – Soft – Class 5 – Conditional Jockey's Handicap Chase – 2m½f
Winner BILLY BRAY – 33/1

12.10 *gg.com Conditional Jockeys' Handicap Chase (Class 5)* ATR
RACE 1 *Winner £3,253* **2m½f**

£5000 guaranteed **For** 4yo+ Rated 0-90 **Weights raised** 1lb **Minimum Weight** 10 0 **Penalties** after November 11th, a winner of a chase 7lb **Billy Bray's Handicap Mark** 88 **Allowances** riders who, prior to November 16th, 2006, have not ridden more than 20 winners under any Rules of Racing 3lb; more than 10 such winners 5lb; any such winner 7lb; those riding for their own stable allowed an additional 3lb **Entries** 20 pay £15 **Penalty value 1st** £3,253 **2nd** £955 **3rd** £477.50 **4th** £238.50

PP/P0-8 **BILLY BRAY** 19 33/1 6 11-12
1 *b g Alflora-Chacewater* **Liam Treadwell**(3)
Miss Venetia Williams James Williams

0/006-3 **THATS MORE LIKE IT** (IRE) 23 7 11-11
2 *ch g Accordion-What It Takes* **J W Farrelly**(8) (86)
Jonjo O'Neill John P McManus

351-433 **GLEN THYNE** (IRE) 14 (CD)(BF) 2ND b6 11-9
3 *b g Good Thyne-Glen Laura* 6/4 **Nick Williams** (96)
Mrs Caroline Bailey Mrs Susan Carlsberg

P382312 **JUST REUBEN** (IRE) 16 11 11-2
4 *gr g Roselier-Sharp Mama VII* **John Kington**(3) (95)
R H Alner Alvin Trowbridge

454-616 **TAKSINA** 12 (D) 3RD t7 11-2
5 *b m Wace-Quago* 12/1 **James White**(3) (96)
R H Buckler Mrs Timothy Lewis

2-P6F63 **YAIYNA TANGO** (FR) 18 (D) 11 10-10
6 *br g Fijar Tango-Yaiyna* **Willie McCarthy**(3) (95)
Miss L Day Miss L Day

P0PU-74 **KIRBY'S VIC** (IRE) 14 b6 10-9
7 *b g Old Vic-Just Affable* **Bernie Wharfe**(6) (92)
N A Twiston-Davies Paul & Vivien Kirby

4P-6PU5 **HARRIHAWKAN** 12 (BF) 8 10-7
8 *b g Alflora-Beatle Song* **Gerard Tumelty**(3) (93)
A King McNeill Racing

4P8P/P- **CRUSOE** (IRE) 216 (5F) 9 10-3
9 *b g Turtle Island-Self Reliance* **Richard Collinson**(5)
A Sadik A Sadik

P825U66 **AUDITOR** 10 (CD) b7 10-0
10 *b g Polish Precedent-Annaba* **Ryan Cummings**(5) (95)
S T Lewis Simon T Lewis

LONG HANDICAP: Auditor **9-11**

BETTING FORECAST: 2 Glen Thyne, 4 Harrihawkan, 5 Thats More Like It, 13-2 Kirby's Vic, 8 Just Reuben, 10 Taksina, 14 Auditor, Yaiyna Tango, 20 Billy Bray, 33 Crusoe.

SPOTLIGHT

Billy Bray Modest in points and no better as yet under Rules, well beaten at huge prices in three hurdle events; fair chance he'll fare better as a chaser but hardly a rock-solid betting proposition as things stand.

Thats More Like It Only a glimmer of ability in a bumper and three novice hurdles in Ireland for Edward O'Grady; never really dangerous on chasing/handicap bow at Uttoxeter but did at least show more and shorter trip shouldn't bother too much around here.

Glen Thyne Both career wins achieved over C&D for Kim Bailey; has made a pleasing start for current handler and didn't do much wrong when failing to justify market support at Market Rasen last time; clear chance off the same mark returning to his favourite hunting ground.

Just Reuben Made all for a wide-margin win at Wincanton on penultimate start and claims on that form despite this 9lb higher mark, yet remainder of efforts during past year not as inspiring; this trip short of his best and essentially a fast-ground performer, so conditions a concern.

Taksina Exploited sliding mark over this trip on good/soft at Worcester and ground probably livelier than ideal when not so good next time; likes to boss it from the front though and easy lead highly unlikely on this occasion; now goes in a tongue tie.

Yaiyna Tango Quite lightly raced for an 11yo but nevertheless thoroughly exposed as modest and not so good over fences as hurdles; latest third came in a selling event and, though return to a right-handed track should help (jumped that way on latter occasion), he's not one to be getting stuck into.

Kirby's Vic Disappointing sort but blinkers brought about some improvement at Market Rasen, where he didn't quite last home having tried to make all over 2m4f (behind Glen Thyne); dropped in trip here but stiff finish could again see him vulnerable.

Harrihawkan 2m4f maiden point winner in May last year; jumping not always foot-perfect under Rules but has been backed on both his runs for this yard and this easier ground could be the key having not looked happy on good/firm at Exeter latest; respected under one of the better conditionals.

Crusoe Prolific winner on the AW but not even placed over hurdles in nine attempts and beaten in a selling event earlier this year; nowhere in a Flat seller the other day on first run since and no appeal here on chasing debut.

Auditor Capable of the odd decent display and now has the blinkers back on (regularly swaps various aids) but mighty hard to catch right and really needs better ground.

VERDICT **Harrihawkan** is one to consider off his light weight with today's easier ground possibly what he needs, but there are less doubts about **GLEN THYNE**, who returns to his favourite patch on the back of a solid performance at Market Rasen.[AWJ]

OFFICIAL RATINGS LAST SIX OUTINGS-LATEST ON RIGHT						12.10 HANDICAP		TODAY	FUTURE	RP RATING LATEST	BEST	ADJUSTED
—	—	—	—	—	—	Billy Bray	11-12	88		—	—	—
—	—	—	—	—	88³	Thats More Like It	11-11	87		86	86	86
75³	75⁵	76¹	85⁴	85³	85³	Glen Thyne	11-9	85		96◄	96	96◄
71³	73⁸	67²	73³	69¹	78²	Just Reuben	11-2	78		90	97	95
77⁴	84⁵	73⁴	73⁶	71¹	78⁶	Taksina	11-2	78		90	98	96◄
—	—	83⁶	78ᶠ	78⁶	75³	Yaiyna Tango	10-10	72		95	95	95
—	—	80ᴾ	84ᵁ	75⁷	72⁴	Kirby's Vic	10-9	71		92	92	92
—	—	76⁶	71ᴾ	69ᵁ	69⁵	Harrihawkan	10-7	69		93	93	93
—	—	—	—	—	—	Crusoe	10-3	65		—	—	—
68⁸	60²	86⁵	65ᵁ	85⁶	78⁶	Auditor	9-11	62	-3	77	107◄	95

Crusoe 10-3
9-y-o b g Turtle Island - Self Reliance (Never So Bold)
A Sadik Richard Collinson (5)

Placings: P0804P/8/P/P-

OR65 H65	Starts	1st	2nd	3rd	Win & Pl
All Jumps races	9	-	-	-	-

GF-HRD 0-0-1 GS-HVY 0-0-6 Course 0-0-0 Dist 0-0-9

17 Apr Huntingdon 2m½f Cls5 64-90 Sell Hdl Hcap £2,741
14 ran GD-FM 8hdls Time 3m 54.90s (slw 14.90s)
1 Quotable 5 11-2 ....Leighton Aspell 6/1
2 After Lent 5 11-2 .....Andrew Glassonbury (7) 9/2
3 Southern Bazaar 5 9-12 ..P J McDonald (7) 7/2F
P **CRUSOE** 9 10-1 ....Andrew Tinkler 12/1
behind from 5th, tailed off when pulled up before 2 out (jockey said gelding lost its action)
[OR65] [op 9/1]
Dist: 3-14-8-1¼-shd RACE RPR: 94+/98/66
Racecheck: Wins 3 (3) Pl 1 Unpl 10

20 Dec 03 Warwick 2m Cls4 72-98 Hdl Hcap £2,436
13 ran GD-SFT 8hdls Time 4m 8.10s (slw 31.10s)
1 Just Superb 4 9-7 oh8 Tom Greenway (7) 100/1
2 Knightsbridge King 7 11-2 R I Mackenzie (7) 20/1
3 Gingko 6 11-9 ....J A McCarthy 4/1
P **CRUSOE** 6 9-11 b oh7 .Miss E J Jones (3) 12/1
pulled hard and prominent, weakened 4th, tailed off when pulled up before 3 out
[OR72] [tchd 14/1 & 10/1]
Dist: 10-6-1¼-9-¾ RACE RPR: 92+/100/94
Racecheck: Wins 3 (2) Pl 4 Unpl 15

21 Nov 02 Hereford 2m1f Cls5 69-92 Sell Hdl Hcap £2,044
15 ran SOFT 8hdls Time 4m 11.30s (slw 21.30s)
1 Kaid 7 11-7 ....T J Phelan (5) 11/2
2 Indian Sun 5 10-3 t ....Warren Marston 12/1
3 Orange Tree Lad 4 9-12 ow5 oh12
....Mr J Barnes (7) 33/1
8 **CRUSOE** 5 10-3 ....Ollie McPhail 25/1
always behind
btn 28 lengths [RPR49 TS41 OR69] [tchd 33/1]
Dist: 5-¾-2½-2½-5 RACE RPR: 99+/71/73
Racecheck: Wins 1 (1) Pl 6 Unpl 18

Billy Bray 11-12
6-y-o b g Alflora - Chacewater (Electric)
Miss Venetia Williams Liam Treadwell (3)

Placings: PP/P0-8

OR88 H88	Starts	1st	2nd	3rd	Win & Pl
All Jumps races	3	-	-	-	-

GF-HRD 0-0-0 GS-HVY 0-0-1 Course 0-0-0 Dist 0-0-2

31 Oct Exeter 2m1f Cls3 Nov Hdl £5,205
16 ran GOOD 8hdls Time 4m 9.20s (slw 16.20s)
1 Beau Michel 4 10-12 ....R Walsh EvensF
2 Giveusaclue 5 10-12 ....A P McCoy 15/8
3 Annie Fleetwood 8 10-11 ..Andrew Thornton 9/1
8 **BILLY BRAY** 6 10-12 ....Sam Thomas 100/1
held up in mid-division, ridden after 5th, no headway btn 24 lengths [RPR78 TS33]
Dist: 6-2-¾-13-nk RACE RPR: 103+/96+/93
Racecheck: Wins - Pl - Unpl 1

18 Apr Chepstow 2m½f Cls4 Mdn Hdl £2,602
15 ran GOOD 8hdls Time 3m 57.00s (slw 9.00s)
1 Star Shot 5 11-3 ....Tom Doyle 4/1F
2 Turnberry Bay 5 11-3 ....Tom Scudamore 11/2

3 Golden Crew 6 10-12 ....Daryl Jacob (5) 9/2
10 **BILLY BRAY** 6 11-3 ....Sam Thomas 28/1
always towards rear
btn 54 lengths [ʀᴘʀ51]   [op 20/1]
Dist: 1-14-hd-4-8   RACE RPR: 107+/104/91+
Racecheck: Wins 1 (1) Pl 4 Unpl 13

30 Mar Wincanton 2m6f   Cls4 Nov Hdl £3,253
15 ran SOFT   11hdls Time 5m 31.00s (slw 22.00s)
1 The Luder 5 11-5 b¹ ....R Walsh EvensF
2 Surface To Air 5 10-5 ...Angharad Frieze (7) 14/1
3 Portland Bill 6 10-12 ....Robert Thornton 6/1
P **BILLY BRAY** 6 10-12 ....Sam Thomas 100/1

*with winner until 6th, gradually faded, tailed off
and pulled up before 2 out*   [op 66/1]
Dist: 8-7-hd-9-3½   RACE RPR: 127+/105+/98
Racecheck: Wins 4 (3) Pl 4 Unpl 9

Form Reading	**CRUSOE**
Spotlight	Prolific winner on the AW but unplaced over hurdles in 9 attempts, chasing debut.
Handicap Ratings	No previous Handicap Chase runs, allocated a mark of 63 for today's contest.
Significant Items of Form	Nine year old with no wins or top three placings. Placings record over nine starts shows four pulled ups, two 0's, two 8th places, and one 4th place. Last National Hunt run was on 17.04.06 when pulled up before 2 out in a Selling Handicap Hurdle (Class 5) over 2m½f at Huntingdon. Previous run was in a Class 4 Handicap Hurdle in December 2003 and run before that was in November 2002 in a Class 5 Hurdle at Hereford, when 8th of 15.
Verdict	Although given a satisfactory outing on the all weather five days ago, there is nothing in its hurdle form to indicate that this horse will change its spots on today's run over fences.
Hence:	DISMISS.

Form Reading	**BILLY BRAY**
Spotlight	Modest in Points, well beaten at huge prices in three hurdle events.
Handicap Ratings	No previous Handicap Chase ratings, mark of 88 for today's outing which puts it on top weight.
Significant Items of Form	Six year old who has had, according to the placings record, only five outings with a best of 8th place. Last three runs have all been over hurdles, first of which was on 30.03.06 over 2m6f at Wincanton in a Class 4 event (Soft) when with the winner until 6th before being pulled up before 2 out. Next run at Chepstow on 18.04.06 demonstrated nothing of importance but its following, and most recent run on 31.10.06 at Exeter over 2m1f on Good in a Class 3 hurdle resulted in an 8th of 16 runners, beaten 24 lengths.
Verdict	There are no obvious clues in the form published by the *Racing Post* to indicate why the horse has been allocated a mark of 88, making it top weight. However there must be a reason for this situation and you have to assume that it is connected to its unpublished form as well as its last run at Exeter (right hand track, tough course) where only beaten 24 lengths in a Class 3 contest, when returning from a six month break. Course (tough, right handed) should suit and although we know nothing about its Point form, we must assume that it is capable of tackling fences because it would be a folly to run an extremely inexperienced jumper over such a tough course early in its career. No direct evidence, but all the clues point to a top three placing.
Hence:	SELECT.

Overall Comment

This was one of those races where you needed to put your Sherlock Holmes hat on when reading the form.

Although it wasn't possible to solve the mystery with the limited information available, the lack of answers led you to ask the question as to why the top weighted horse with a very respectable midfield run last outing in a Class 3 event was available at a price of 33/1.

What made the situation even more surprising was the fact that the horse was trained by one of the country's most respected top trainers, who is certainly not the type of person to submit a young jumper to the type of test provided by the Towcester track without having considerable confidence in the horse's abilities.

Billy Bray's victory provided two important lessons. Firstly, always be prepared to have a bet when the price being offered appears high compared to what you have deduced about the horse. Secondly, and yet again, the midfield finishing position in its last outing, following a long break, proved to be extremely significant and a pointer to better to come.

It is also important to point out that the Forecast of Billy Bray with the favourite Glen Thyne paid out £101.60 on the Tote Exacta and £86.70 via the Computer Straight Forecast.

EXAMPLE 27

22.07.06   Market Rasen – Good – Class 2 – Handicap Hurdle – 2m1½f
Winner   TYCOON HALL – 33/1

SPOTLIGHT

Fair Along Very smart front-running juvenile last season, running best race when second in the Triumph at Cheltenham in March; recent run on the Flat should have teed him up nicely for this but weighted up to best on balance and vulnerable to something better handicapped picking him off late on.

Crossbow Creek May well be happier back over hurdles after last season's chase campaign went a bit amiss and recent Flat run should have put him right for this, but looks another weighted up to best; capable of running well but probably has bit too much weight to win.

Neveesou Never looked entirely happy over the brush hurdles at Southwell last time and better judged on previous second in well-contested handicap at Stratford in May, when he did particularly well considering he was lumping a big weight in very soft ground; this ground is an unknown but capable of bold show if handling it.

Paddy The Piper Decent strike-rate and has dropped to a more realistic mark; however, guesswork involved as to what form he'll be in after two down-the-field runs in top handicaps this spring and this trip could well be on the short side too.

O'Toole Career-best run when winning well in fair race at Worcester in May but has paid for it with 12lb higher mark, which is probably enough to stop him playing major role here, even though ground is ideal and return to hurdles (beaten favourite over fences last time) is a plus too.

Aleron Versatile sort who comes here fit from the Flat (winner at 1m3f at Hamilton in May); cheekpieces back on for this return to hurdling but weighted right up to best and no scope for improvement as a fully exposed 8yo.

Lord Baskerville Significant improvement of late, completing hat-trick in useful Stratford novice last month before running creditably when conceding lot of weight to the winner until departing at the last at Uttoxeter last time; wouldn't want to become embroiled in fight for the lead here and needs to show confidence is unimpaired but capable of bold show otherwise.

East Tycoon Always had a touch of class about him and having had a distinctly chequered time of it over fences, seemed happier back over hurdles when winning nicely in fair race at Stratford on Sunday; claims on that despite a 5lb penalty but suspicion that he is best on a left-handed track.

Portavadie Another failure to complete when pulled up in Stratford handicap chase last time and, weighted up to best for this return to hurdles, will do well to be involved in a very competitive race.

Crathorne Versatile sort who has been mixing hurdles and Flat runs, last hurdles start yielding a win in a well-contested Southwell handicap; drop in trip no problem and capable of running well but 8lb rise demands further progress if he is to take this.

Ela Re Settled better than has sometimes been the case en route to clearcut win back from eight months off at Hexham last month; still has possibilities on pick of his old form despite being 12lb higher here but strong suspicion that bit more dig in the ground suits ideally.

Hilltime Quietly progressive over hurdles, second in this last year and, having had just one Flat run in the interim, sticking on well to win reasonable contest over C&D last month; bit more needed off 4lb higher but going the right way and wouldn't rule out.

Wee Dinns One blip on soft ground apart, has really found her form over hurdles of late, four wins since April and looking on a nice mark on the form of her win in a Newton Abbot novice last month; trip/ground should suit and leading player for team Pipe, which has won this three times since 1999.

Double Vodka Creditable third off this mark in top Aintree handicap in April, not needing to run to that form when winning a novice there the following month; more needed even on that April form and didn't run very well on the Flat recently.

Dune Raider Fairly useful Flat handicapper who made it three from three over hurdles with workmanlike win at Uttoxeter last month; this is much tougher and, off high enough mark on the bare form, will need to find more to be leading player.

Albarino Back from two runs over fences with decent enough third to Hilltime off this mark over C&D last time; no certainty to reverse the form with that quietly progressive winner with 4lb pull and needs to pull out more if he is to win more competitive race here.

Tycoon Hall Two wins on decent ground over hurdles in Ireland last year but off for 11 months until this month's two down-the-field runs, one on the Flat and last time over hurdles; limited appeal in very competitive race here.

Sun King Running as well as he has ever done of late, last time staying on to snatch fair Perth handicap in last stride; shade more needed off 3lb higher in stronger race but decent-paced race at this trip on this ground will suit and very much one to consider.

VERDICT A strong field, featuring eight last-time-out winners plus a clutch of others of interest. The really interesting one is **WEE DINNS (nap)**, who has found her form with a vengeance and is on a nice mark judged on last month's win in a decent Newton Abbot novice. Team Pipe has won this three times since 1999 and she has good prospects of landing this again for them. There are numerous viable alternatives, with last year's second **Hilltime** the most interesting of them. [MCu]

OFFICIAL RATINGS LAST SIX OUTINGS-LATEST ON RIGHT						2.05 HANDICAP		TODAY	FUTURE	RP RATING LATEST	BEST	ADJUSTED
—	—	—	—	—	—	Fair Along	11-12	141	-6	122	146	146
135^{3}	—	—	—	—	—	Crossbow Creek	11-6	133	+2	—	—	143
—	—	128^{2}	128^{0}	126^{2}	—	Neveesou	11-5	132		124	142	142
—	138^{3}	138^{6}	135^{6}	135^{0}	133^{0}	Paddy The Piper	11-3	130		134	139	143
—	—	—	—	117^{1}	—	O'Toole	11-2	129		—	139	139
—	—	—	—	—	—	Aleron	11-1	128		—	—	141
88^{5}	—	90^{1}	—	—	—	Lord Baskerville	11-0	127		134	134	134
—	—	—	—	—	122^{1}	East Tycoon (5x)	11-0	127	-5	140	140	142
—	—	—	—	—	—	Portavadie	10-13	126		—	139	139
108^{1}	118^{4}	118^{B}	118^{9}	116^{5}	117^{1}	Crathorne	10-12	125		139	139	139
—	—	106^{P}	—	105^{F}	110^{1}	Ela Re	10-9	122		137	137	137
—	105^{0}	103^{1}	111^{3}	113^{2}	117^{1}	Hilltime	10-8	121		139	139	139
—	101^{1}	108^{1}	117^{6}	—	—	Wee Dinns	10-7	120		138	139	139
—	—	111^{5}	—	119^{3}	—	Double Vodka	10-6	119		128	142	142
—	—	—	—	—	—	Dune Raider	10-6	119		131	131	134
107^{1}	—	120^{0}	—	—	118^{3}	Albarino	10-5	118		141 ◀	148 ◀	148 ◀
—	—	—	—	—	115^{9}	Tycoon Hall	10-2	115		108	136	140
97^{4}	99^{1}	107^{7}	105^{2}	109^{3}	110^{1}	Sun King	10-0	113		141 ◀	141	141

Tycoon Hall 10-2

6-y-o ch h Halling - Tycooness (Last Tycoon)

P Bowen T J O'Brien (3)

Placings: 72632/0116-9

OR115 F70	Starts	1st	2nd	3rd	Win & Pl
All Jumps races	10	2	2	1	£13,865

6/05 Wxfd 2m Nov Hdl gd-fm £6,371
5/05 Wxfd 2m Mdn Hdl 5yo good £3,921
Total win prize-money £10,292

GF-HRD 1-0-3 GS-HVY 0-3-6 Course 0-0-0 Dist 0-0-2

17 Jul Newton Abbot 2m1f Cls4 89-115 Hdl Hcap £4,229
12 ran GD-FM 8hdls Time 3m 57.00s (slw 6.00s)
1 Space Cowboy 6 11-2 b ....Philip Hide 16/1
2 Cream Cracker 8 10-11 ....Daryl Jacob (5) 9/2
3 Iffy 5 11-0 ....Robert Thornton 11/2
9 **TYCOON HALL** 6 11-12 ..Richard Johnson 16/1
led until approaching 2 out, soon weakened and eased
btn 34 lengths [RPR82 TS61 OR115] [op 20/1]
Dist: 3/4-1/2-nk-3/4-7 RACE RPR: 108+/106/103
Racecheck: Wins - Pl - Unpl -

27 Aug 05 Wexford 2m Nov Hdl £6,371
11 ran GD-FM Time 3m 37.70s (fst 1.30s)
1 Articulation 4 11-1 b1 ....D N Russell 100/30
2 Emeranna 5 11-1 ....J M Allen (3) 8/1
3 Keelaghan 5 11-6 ....C O'Dwyer 4/1
6 **TYCOON HALL** 5 11-9 ....B J Geraghty 11/4F
close 2nd, challenged 3 out, 3rd under pressure next, soon no extra [RPR110] [op 3/1]
Dist: 2-3-1-1/2-4 RACE RPR: 112/113/112
Racecheck: Wins - Pl 4 Unpl 10

10 Jun 05 Wexford 2m Nov Hdl £6,371
16 ran GD-FM Time 3m 50.90s (slw 11.90s)
1 **TYCOON HALL** 5 11-4 ....T P Treacy 3/1
made all, slight mistake 5th, strongly pressed and briefly headed straight, on terms at last, stayed on best run-in to edge ahead close home [RPR111]
2 Pepperwood 5 11-1 ....D F O'Regan (3) 5/1
3 Articulation 4 10-11 ....D N Russell 6/4F
Dist: shd-4 1/2-nk-3 1/2-20 RACE RPR: 111/111/99
Racecheck: Wins 3 Pl 5 Unpl 15

13 May 05 Wexford 2m Mdn Hdl 5yo £3,921
15 ran GOOD Time 3m 46.40s (slw 7.40s)
1 **TYCOON HALL** 5 11-12 ....B J Geraghty 9/4J
close up in 2nd, led 3 out, ridden and strongly pressed after 2 out, kept on well from last (trainer's representative said, regarding the improved form shown, the better ground, sharper track and a change in tactics all helped) [RPR108] [op 3/1]
2 Feel Good Factor 5 11-4 ....D N Russell 9/4J
3 Faayej 5 11-7 ....Johnny Levins (5) 20/1
Dist: 1 1/2-2 1/2-6-1/2-shd RACE RPR: 108/99/104
Racecheck: Wins 4 Pl 5 Unpl 16

Portavadie 10-13

7-y-o b g Rakaposhi King - Woodland Flower (Furry Glen)

J M Jefferson Noel Fehily

Placings: 32411/124133PF-P

OR126	Starts	1st	2nd	3rd	Win & Pl
Hurdles	4	2	1	-	£10,060
All Jumps races	14	4	2	3	£23,150

12/05 Newc 2m1/2f Cls3 Nov Ch heavy £7,779
5/05 Hexm 2m1/2f Cls4 Nov Hdl good £3,052
4/05 Kels 2m1/2f Cls4 Nov Hdl good £3,731
2/05 Hayd 2m Cls6 NHF 4-6yo soft £1,904
Total win prize-money £16,466

GF-HRD 0-0-2 GS-HVY 2-0-5 Course 0-0-0 Dist 0-0-1

11 Jun Stratford 2m1 1/2f Cls3 104-130 Ch Hcap £7,829
10 ran GD-FM 13fncs Time 4m 2.90s (fst 0.10s)
1 Rookery Lad 8 11-0 ....T J O'Brien (3) 9/2F
2 Master Rex 11 11-5 ....Noel Fehily 11/2
3 Lindsay 7 10-12 ....Mark Bradburne 8/1
P **PORTAVADIE** 7 11-9 .....Andrew Thornton 13/2
held up, hit 1st, headway 5th, weakened 8th, behind when jumped right next, soon pulled up [OR127] [op 6/1 tchd 7/1]
Dist: 5-8-5-1 1/4-1/2 RACE RPR: 132/129/116+
Racecheck: Wins - Pl 1 Unpl 4

28 Apr Perth 2m Cls3 Nov Ch £6,506
9 ran GD-FM 12fncs Time 3m 57.30s (slw 3.30s)
1 Green Tango 7 11-8 ....Mark Bradburne 8/13F
2 Coat Of Honour 6 11-4 ..Peter Buchanan 100/30
3 The Biker 9 10-2 ....David Da Silva (10) 20/1
F **PORTAVADIE** 7 11-3 ....T J Dreaper (5) 6/1
led, headed and ridden when blundered 2 out, 2 lengths down and held when fell last [RPR129 OR127] [tchd 11/2 & 7/1]
Dist: 2-15-12-19-1 RACE RPR: 133+/123/102
Racecheck: Wins 2 (1) Pl 1 Unpl 5

17 Mar Cheltenham 2m1/2f Cls1 Gd3 126-147 Ch Hcap £42,765
23 ran GOOD 14fncs Time 3m 55.90s (fst 3.10s)
1 Greenhope 8 10-11 ....Andrew Tinkler 20/1
2 Tiger Cry 8 10-13 ....D J Casey 6/1
3 Madison Du Berlais 5 10-4 ex3 ....Tom Scudamore 11/1
P **PORTAVADIE** 7 10-7 ....Tony Dobbin 50/1
chased leaders, hit 7th and next, soon weakened, tailed off when pulled up before 3 out [RPR- OR128] [op 66/1]
Dist: 2-1-1 1/4-3/4-1/2 RACE RPR: 144+/143/138+
Racecheck: Wins 3 Pl 6 Unpl 19

14 Jan Carlisle 2m Cls3 Nov Ch £6,506
7 ran HEAVY 11fncs Time 4m 21.60s (slw 20.60s)
1 Iron Man 5 10-7 ....Tony Dobbin 4/7F
2 Great As Gold 7 11-2 b .....Wilson Renwick 20/1
3 **PORTAVADIE** 7 11-7 ....T J Dreaper (5) 5/2
chased leaders, went 2nd 6th, effort when hit 3 out and next, lost 2nd towards finish [RPR129 TS125] [op 2/1]
Dist: 6-1 3/4-23-12-7 RACE RPR: 123+/117/129+
Racecheck: Wins - Pl 4 Unpl 10

Sun King					10-0

9-y-o ch g Zilzal - Opus One (Slip Anchor)
K G Reveley   James Reveley (7)

Placings: 33476000/22/44172-31

OR113F51		Starts	1st	2nd	3rd	Win & Pl
Hurdles		30	5	6	5	£39,621
All Jumps races		33	6	7	5	£41,651
110	7/06	Prth	2m¹/₂f Cls3 101-127 Hdl Hcap gd-fm			
						£7,807
99	2/06	Muss	2m Cls3 99-125 Hdl Hcap good ..£7,807			
	5/02	Towc	2m Cls3 Nov Hdl good £3,150			
	5/02	Weth	2m Cls4 Nov Cond Hdl gd-fm £2,562			
	4/02	MRas	2m3¹/₂f Cls3 Nov Hdl gd-fm £3,780			
	6/01	Worc	2m Cls6 NHF 4-6yo gd-fm £1,537			
			Total win prize-money £26,643			

GF-HRD 4-5-14   GS-HVY 0-2-4   Course 1-2-5   Dist 0-2-4

6 Jul Perth 2m¹/₂f   Cls3 101-127 Hdl Hcap £7,807
8 ran   GD-FM   8hdls   Time 3m 44.10s (fst 2.90s)
1 **SUN KING** 9 10-2 t ....James Reveley (7) 3/1
held up in touch, headway after 3 out, effort and

every chance last, stayed on to lead post
[RPR113 TS114 OR110]   [op 9/2]
2 Gone Too Far 8 1·   5/2F
3 Critical Stage 7 10-··· ....---   ï) 8/1
Dist: shd-9-2¹/₂-1³/₄-10   RACE RPR: 113/121/103+
Racecheck: Wins - Pl - Unpl 2

11 Jun Perth 2m¹/₂f   Cls4 88-114 Hdl Hcap £5,205
13 ran   GD-FM   8hdls   Time 3m 50.70s (slw 3.70s)
1 Arresting 6 10-2 ....Richard Johnson 7/2F
2 Acceleration 6 10-0 t ....G Lee 7/1
3 **SUN KING** 9 11-0 t ....James Reveley (7) 11/2
chased leaders, kept on same pace from 2 out
[RPR11 1 TS85 OR109]   [op 6/1]
Dist: 8-1¹/₄-2¹/₂-5-hd   RACE RPR: 105+/91/111
Racecheck: Wins 3 (2) Pl 2 Unpl 5

26 Apr Perth 2m¹/₂f   Cls3 95-120 Hdl Hcap £7,807
15 ran   GOOD   8hdls   Time 3m 52.50s (slw 5.50s)
1 Lennon 6 11-2 ....Brian Hughes (5) 9/1
2 **SUN KING** 9 10-1 t ....James Reveley (10) 9/1
in touch, smooth headway before 2 out, led run-in, kept on, headed close home

[RPR109 TS109 OR105]   [op 10/1 tchd 8/1]
3 Billyandi 6 10-5 ....Marc Goldstein (7) 15/2
5 **CRATHORNE** 6 11-3 ....T J Dreaper (5) 12/1
behind, headway before 2 out, edged right, kep on from last [RPR118 TS119 OR116]   [op 8/1]
Dist: ¹/₂-¹/₂-1-hd-14   RACE RPR: 119/109/110+
Racecheck: Wins 4 (2) Pl 4 Unpl 7

24 Mar Newbury 2m¹/₂f Cls3 107-133 Hdl Hcap £6,500
11 ran   GOOD   8hdls   Time 3m 58.50s (slw 5.50s)
1 Motorway 5 10-12 ....Richard Johnson 4/6F
2 Bound 8 11-1 t ....Leighton Aspell 25/1
3 Pepe Galvez 9 11-0 ....A P McCoy 11/1
7 **SUN KING** 9 9-4 t oh2 James Reveley (10) 14/1
held up in mid-division, some headway approaching 3 out, never reached leaders, weakened 2 out
btn 18 lengths [RPR97 TS66 OR107] [op 12/1]
Dist: hd-8-2¹/₂-3¹/₂-1   RACE RPR: 127/130/121
Racecheck: Wins - Pl 3 Unpl 11

Form Reading	**TYCOON HALL**
Spotlight	Two wins on decent ground in Ireland last year but off for eleven months until this month's two down the field runs, one on the flat and the last time over hurdles.
Handicap Ratings	Only Handicap Hurdle rating in the last six outings was for its last outing, when allocated a mark of 115 (placed 9th). Running off same mark, 115 today, which puts it 2lbs above bottom weight. Very difficult to rate the value of 115 mark as previous runs were in Ireland.
Significant Items of Form	Six year old with two hurdle wins at Wexford (Ireland) in May and June 2005 on Good and Good to Firm. Last campaign in Ireland finished in August 2005 at Wexford (Good to Firm) in a Novice Hurdle over 2 miles when 6th of 11 runners, beaten 10½ lengths, after being a close 2nd until 3 out. Previous two runs were its 2 wins at Wexford, both over 2 miles in fields of 15 and 16 runners. Gap of nearly eleven months between last outing in latest Irish campaign and first National Hunt run in Britain on 17.07.06 Newton Abbot (Good to Firm) when 9th of 12, beaten 34 lengths after leading to 2 out in a Class 4 Handicap Hurdle over 2m1f.
Verdict	Although quality of Irish wins is hard to assess, 1st prize of £6,371 and a field of 16 for latest victory indicates it was a decent contest which should put it in with a shout for today's contest, assuming the bounce back factor does not affect its second National Hunt run in Britain. Coming after a near eleven month break its latest run at Newton Abbot was a good warm up for today's contest and the quality of that run points to further improvement today. Considering the fact that Tycoon Hall has carried 11st 12lb, 11st 4lb, 11st 9lb and 11st 12lb for last four outings, today's weight of 10st 2lb will appear to be of the feather variety and in this setting a top three placing must be a reasonable possibility.
Hence:	SELECT.

Form Reading	**PORTAVADIE**
Spotlight	Pulled up in Stratford Handicap Chase last time and weighed up to best for this return to hurdles.
Handicap Ratings	No Handicap Hurdle runs in last six outings and allocated mark of 126 for today's contest, the value of which is impossible to assess because even the trainer cannot be sure that a return to the small obstacles will bring about an immediate

improvement in performance, considering the lengthy time gap since its last run over hurdles. (NB Very difficult to determine the time gap from *Racing Post*'s published information but must be at least six months.)

Significant Items of Form	Seven year old with one Class 3 Novice Chase victory over 2m½f December 2005, two Class 4 Novice Hurdle wins over 2m½f April and May 2005 and one Bumper win February 2005. Has won on Good (twice), Soft and Heavy, all on left hand tracks and has run twice on Good to Firm and Hard going. Of the horse's last four runs between January and June 2006, three have been in Class 3 Chases and one in a Class 1 Chase at the Cheltenham Festival. Of interest is the fact that the best two runs of these last four have been on right hand courses. (NB Market Rasen is right handed.) On 14.01.06 finished 3rd of 7 runners in a Class 3 Novice Chase at Carlisle (2 miles) on Heavy, beaten 7¾ lengths and on 28.04.06 was lying second of 9 runners in a Class 3 Novice Chase at Perth (2 miles) on Good to Firm when fell at the last when 2 lengths down.
Verdict	As a seven year old with both Hurdle (Class 4) and Chase (Class 3) wins, the horse undoubtedly has ability and, though it is by no means certain that horse will respond to a return to hurdling in what is, after all, a Class 2 event, you have got to assume that his trainer knows what he is doing. The gap between its most recent races (approximately six to eight weeks) indicates horse is not over raced and as right hand course and Good to Firm going should suit, a top three placing is not an unreasonable possibility.
Hence:	SELECT.

Form Reading	**SUN KING**
Note	Having made two selections, option has been taken to read the form of the longest priced course winner.
Spotlight	Last time stayed on to snatch fair Perth Handicap in last stride.
Handicap Ratings	Has improved from a mark of 97 six outings ago, (placed 4th) to a mark of 110 for last outing when won. Raised to a mark of 113 for today's contest which is probably insufficient to seriously damage horse's chances.
Significant Items of Form	Nine year old with five Hurdle wins (four of them Class 3) and one Bumper win on Good and Good to Firm going over distances from 2 miles to 2m3½f, four of which have been at right hand tracks including Market Rasen (today's course). Recent form has been good with last outing on 06.07.06 resulting in a win at Perth (right hand track) in a Class 3 Handicap Hurdle over 2m½f on Good to Firm. Previous two runs, both at Perth, resulted in a 3rd of 13 runners in a Class 4 Handicap Hurdle over 2m½f (Good to Firm) on 11.06.06 and a 2nd of 15 runners in a Class 3 Handicap Hurdle over 2m½f (Good) on 26.04.06.
Verdict	Based on recent form a top three placing must be a good possibility.
Hence:	SELECT.

Overall Comment

As a Class 2 contest this was a Non-Preferred event as far as The Tail End System is concerned, but one look at the last half dozen placings of each of them, alongside the list of runners and riders, showed that between them they had amassed a total of 32 wins and therefore there was a good chance that the winner could come from virtually any position in the Betting Forecast. So it proved, with the first and the second coming from opposite ends of the Betting Forecast and the third placed horse occupying next to last position in the Betting Forecast.

The winner was yet another example of a horse with Irish form moving over to Britain and having the value of that form underestimated by the handicapper and the market makers.

As a result of this undervaluation, the forecast Tycoon Hall with the paper favourite Wee Dinns, paid £503.30 for the Tote Exacta and £250.27 for the Computer Straight Forecast.

Given the fact that Portavadie took 3rd place at 50/1, the Tricast was also achievable and that paid £11,180.75.

EXAMPLE 28

10.09.06   Stratford – Good to Firm – Class 4 – Handicap Hurdle – 2m½f
Winner   FLAMAND – 25/1

4.10 RACE 4

Join Liz Kershaw For Breakfast Handicap Hurdle (Class 4)   ATR
Winner £5,070.40   2m½f

£8000 guaranteed For 4yo+ Rated 0-110 Minimum Weight 10-0 Penalties after September 2nd, a winner of a hurdle 7lb Harry Potter's Handicap Mark 116 Entries 24 pay £20 Penalty value 1st £5,070.40 2nd £1,497.60 3rd £748.80 4th £374.40 5th £187.20

1 -UP1131 **HARRY POTTER** (GER) (7ex) [7] [c][d]
b g Platini-Heavenly Storm   Mr N Williams(5)   7 12-5 (113)
Evan Williams   Billy Evans And Gareth Morse

2 1-4124F **AVESOMEOFTHAT** (IRE) [17] [d][bf]
b g Lahib-Lacinia   Robert Thornton   5 11-11 (111)
J W Mullins   K J Pike

3 2361 **ROBINZAL** [19] [d]
b g Zilzal-Sulitelma   Noel Fehily   14 11-5 (104)
C J Mann   A F Merritt, D Burgess & P Cook

4 746-137 **CANADIAN STORM** [63] [d]
gr g With Approval-Sheer Gold   Liam Heard(5)   p 5 11-5 (104)
A G Juckes   A G Juckes

5 183-14U **MASTER NIMBUS** [17] [d]
b g Cloudings-Miss Charlie   Dougie Costello(3)   6 11-2 (109)
J J Quinn   J H Hewitt

6 01-483S **YOUNG TOT** (IRE) [13] [d]
b g Torus-Lady-K   David Dennis   8 11-1 (108)
M Sheppard   Out Of Bounds Racing Club

7 133-252 **NESNAAS** (USA) [7] [d]
ch g Gulch-Sedrah   Jamie Moore   5 10-12 (113)
M G Rimell   Mark Rimell

8 24-6063 **SECRET'S OUT** [13]
b g Polish Precedent-Secret Obsession   NON-RUNNER   10 10-11 (111)
F Lloyd   F Lloyd

9 RF65-4P **BRAVE DANE** (IRE) [17] [c][d]
b g Danehill-Nuriva   Antony Evans   8 10-9 (110)
A W Carroll   Exhall Dodgers

10 4078700 **FORZACURITY** [7] [d]
ch g Forzando-Nice Lady   Tom Messenger(5)   7 10-2 (111)
D Burchell   Don Gould, Mervyn Phillips

11 649-PP7 **FLAMAND** (FR) [67]
b g Double Bed-Rays Honor   Gerard Tumelty(5)   t5 10-1 (109)
C P Morlock   Simon Philip

12 27P-1PP **MUNADIL** [53] [d]
ch g Nashwan-Bintalshaati   William Kennedy(3)   t8 10-0 (103)
A M Hales   Mon Cheval Charmant

LONG HANDICAP: Munadil **9-9**

2005 (10 ran) **Mister Moussac** Miss Kariana Key 6 10-9 4/1   Robert Thornton OR91

BETTING FORECAST: 7-2 Master Nimbus, 9-2 Harry Potter, 5 Avesomeofthat, Nesnaas, 7 Robinzal, 10 Munadil, 12 Young Tot, 14 Canadian Storm, 20 Flamand, 33 Brave Dane, Forzacurity.

SPOTLIGHT

Harry Potter Winning chaser who looked on a nice mark for return to hurdles at Fontwell last weekend and duly exploited it, though didn't have masses in hand of the second whose previous victory had come in a seller; penalised and may find this a tad tougher.

Avesomeofthat Been maintaining his progressive profile and might have gone in again at Fontwell last time but for falling at the last when still marginally ahead; 2lb rise a bit annoying but this track should suit his front-running style and chance in confidence unaffected.

Robinzal Just about stays this trip over hurdles but everything fell into place when picking up a modest maiden event at Worcester (first-time tongue strap) and doesn't look that well treated now sent handicapping.

Canadian Storm Not really fulfilled initial promise over hurdles for Venetia Williams and contested a number of poor races before landing a claimer for this yard in April; comfortably held back in a handicap last time and this surely too competitive.

Master Nimbus Won three of his last six completed starts over hurdles and might have enhanced that strike-rate further here last time, when still bang in contention and travelling well at point of departure; previous defeat off this mark came in a better race so entitled to plenty of respect on ground he'll like.

Young Tot 9lb higher than when victorious on firm ground at Exeter in April but disappointing he hasn't been able to cash in on a much lower chase mark since then and looks to face stiff competition for the lead here, so passed over.

Nesnaas Needs conditions on top to get out over jumps, sole win coming on lightning quick ground around Wincanton; reasonable efforts of late over hurdles/fences and placed off similar marks, so enters the equation for sure.

Brave Dane Won a couple of Banded events during the spring but not the most reliable, as he's reminded us the last twice (didn't want to know here last time); much too risky.

Forzacurity Has come right down the weights since returning to action in March but no sign of light at the end of the tunnel just yet and readily passed over.

Flamand Possibilities on a fourth in a novice event at Taunton in December but has suffered some disappointments since, showing very little in handicaps; not easily fancied.

Munadil Likes coming off a strong pace on quick ground, as was the case when taking a classified chase at Worcester in May; not completed since but reverts to hurdling off a potentially lucrative mark even allowing for being a little out of the weights; not ruled out.

VERDICT This can go to **MASTER NIMBUS**, who has been in good form under both codes for a while now and still looks competitively handicapped in the right company. **Nesnaas** should also be thereabouts. [AWJ]

OFFICIAL RATINGS									RP RATING		
LAST SIX OUTINGS-LATEST ON RIGHT						4.10 HANDICAP		TODAY FUTURE	LATEST / BEST / ADJUSTED		
—	—	—	—	—	109¹	Harry Potter (7x)	12-5	116	-7	111 ◀ 111	113 ◀
93¹	93⁴	99¹	103²	105⁴	106²	Avesomeofthat	11-11	108		109	109	111
—	—	—	—	—	—	Robinzal	11-5	102		88	98	104
—	88⁴	94⁶	—	—	104⁷	Canadian Storm	11-5	102		98	104	104
86¹	93⁸	93³	95¹	99⁴	99ᵁ	Master Nimbus	11-2	99		—	109	109
—	89¹	—	—	—	—	Young Tot	11-1	98		—	108	108
85¹	93³	95³	96²	96⁵	—	Nesnaas	10-12	95		—	113	113 ◀
94²	94⁴	—	94⁰	—	90³	Secret's Out	10-11	94		111 ◀ 111	111
100⁶	100⁶	99⁶	97⁵	93⁴	92ᴾ	Brave Dane	10-9	92		—	106	110
95⁰	92⁷	100⁸	103⁷	89⁰	85⁰	Forzacurity	10-2	85		73	114 ◀ 111
—	—	—	88ᴾ	88ᴾ	85⁷	Flamand	10-1	84		91	109	109
—	—	—	—	—	—	Munadil	9-9	83	-5	—	103	103

Forzacurity   10-2

7-y-o ch g Forzando - Nice Lady (Connaught)
D Burchell   Tom Messenger (5)

Placings: 0005F489P00-44078700

OR85	F57	Starts	1st	2nd	3rd	Win & Pl
All Jumps races		35	3	2	2	£19,309
96	5/05	Bang	2m1f Cls3 95-113 Hdl Hcap good £6,479			
95	2/04	Hrfd	2m1f Cls4 92-110 Hdl Hcap gd-sft £4,596			
	11/03	NAbb	2m1f Cls5 Sell Hdl 4-7yo good ...£2,898			

Total win prize-money £13,973
GF-HRD 0-2-12 GS-HVY 1-2-12 Course 0-0-5 Dist 3-4-28

3 Sep Worcester 2m4f Cls4 84-110 Hdl Hcap £3,904
17 ran GOOD   10hdls   Time 4m 43.00s (slw 5.00s)
1 Rabbit 5 10-6 ....P J Brennan 15/2
2 Veverka 5 10-3 ....Sean Curran 20/1
3 Orion Express 5 10-7 ....Liam Heard (5) 7/2F
15 FORZACURITY 7 10-1 ......Antony Evans 28/1
  chased leaders until weakened approaching 6th
  btn 43 lengths [RPR47 TS12 OR85]   [op 25/1]
Dist: 5-1½-nk-3-1½   RACE RPR: 96+/88+/96+
Racecheck: Wins - Pl - Unpl -

                £4,229
12 ran GD-FM   8hdls   Time 3m 57.00s (slw 6.00s)
1 Space Cowboy 6 11-2 b ....Philip Hide 16/1
2 Cream Cracker 8 10-11 ....Daryl Jacob (5) 9/2
3 Iffy 5 11-0 ....Robert Thornton 11/2
4 AVESOMEOFTHAT 5 10-13 .T J O'Brien (3) 9/2
  always prominent, ridden to lead approaching 2
  out, soon headed, not quicken flat
  [RPR106 TS87 OR105]   [op 5/1]
12 FORZACURITY 7 9-9 .Tom Messenger (5) 33/1
  chased leaders until weakened approaching 5th
  btn 43 lengths [RPR48 TS25 OR89] [op 25/1]
Dist: ¾-½-nk-¾-7   RACE RPR: 109+/107/104
Racecheck: Wins 4 (3) Pl 3 Unpl 6

5 Jul Worcester 2m4f Cls3 103-129 Hdl Hcap £6,506
8 ran GD-FM   10hdls   Time 4m 43.10s (slw 5.10s)
1 The Names Bond 8 10-3 Miss R Davidson (7) 11/2
2 Marrel 8 10-12 v ....Antony Evans 12/1
3 Sky Warrior 8 10-6 ....S Durack 11/1
7 FORZACURITY 7 9-11 t oh14 ....
  ....Owyn Nelmes (3) 50/1
  chased leader, led 3rd until approaching 5th,
  soon weakened, tailed off
  btn 81 lengths [RPR27 OR103]   [tchd 66/1]
Dist: 1¾-4-21-nk-21   RACE RPR: 119+/118/108
Racecheck: Wins 2 Pl - Unpl 7

28 Jul 05 Stratford 2m½f Cls3 97-118 Hdl Hcap £6,131
9 ran GD-SFT   9hdls   Time 4m 2.70s (slw 14.70s)

---

1 Dominican Monk 6 11-11 ....Tom Doyle 8/1
2 Imperial Rocket 8 10-10 t ...Richard Johnson 6/1
3 Old Marsh 9 11-7 ....Mr C J Sweeney (5) 3/1F
4 FORZACURITY 6 10-7 ....Lee Stephens (5) 16/1
  chased leaders until ridden and weakened after
  3 out [RPR90 TS46 OR104]   [op 14/1]
5 BRAVE DANE 7 9-12 ......Charlie Studd (7) 33/1
  led into start, always behind
  [RPR54 OR97]   [op 28/1]
Dist: 3-15-1¼-29-8   RACE RPR: 122/104/105
Racecheck: Wins - Pl 1 Unpl 11

Brave Dane   10-9

8-y-o b g Danehill - Nuriva (Woodman)
A W Carroll   Antony Evans

Placings: 0PF05/U0/114/RF65-4P

OR92	F60	Starts	1st	2nd	3rd	Win & Pl
All Jumps races		16	2	–	–	£12,034
92	5/04	Strf	2m½f Cls4 Nov 88-98 Hdl Hcap gd-fm			
						...£4,290
84	5/04	Ludl	2m Cls3 Nov 84-105 Hdl Hcap good			
						...£6,825

Total win prize-money £11,115
GF-HRD 1-0-3 GS-HVY 0-0-7 Course 1-0-4 Dist 2-0-14

24 Aug Stratford 2m½f Cls4 91-104 Cond Hdl Hcap
                £3,904
9 ran GD-FM   9hdls   Time 3m 48.50s (slw 0.50s)
1 Jacaranda 6 11-6 ....T J O'Brien (3) 2/1F
2 Meltonian 9 10-3 ....Matt Crawley (10) 14/1
3 Golden Square 4 11-4 ....Owyn Nelmes 9/1
P BRAVE DANE 8 11-0 ....Tom Messenger 15/2
  reluctant to race, pulled up after 1st
  [OR92]   [op 13/2 tchd 6/1]
U MASTER NIMBUS 6 11-4 Dougie Costello (3) 7/2
  held up, in touch when blundered and unseated
  rider 5th [OR99]   [op 1/1]
Dist: 9-7-1½-5-2½   RACE RPR: 117+/91/89
Racecheck: Wins 1 (1) Pl - Unpl 1

14 Aug Southwell 2m Cls3 93-119 Hdl Hcap £5,205
8 ran   GOOD   9hdls   Time 3m 53.30s (slw 12.30s)
1 Cream Cracker 8 10-9 ....Daryl Jacob (5) 15/8F
2 Orpen Wide 4 10-13 ....Derek Laverty (5) 14/1
3 Hilltime 6 11-5 ....Mr R Tierney (7) 7/1
4 BRAVE DANE 8 10-0 oh1 ...Timmy Murphy 7/2
  reluctant early and tailed himself off, coaxed into
  touch by 4th, brief effort after 3 out but soon
  found nil, some renewed progress (jockey said
  gelding was reluctant to line up and start)
  [RPR87 TS17 OR93]   [op 100/30] .
5 NESNAAS 5 10-3 ....Jamie Moore 11/2
  close up, driven after 3 out, weakened next
  [RPR88 TS17 OR96]   [op 5/1]

Dist: 2½-6-1¾-2½-1¼ RACE RPR: 120+/114+/115
Racecheck: Wins 1 (1) Pl - Unpl 3

28 Jul 05 Stratford   5th, see FORZACURITY

Flamand   10-1

5-y-o b g Double Bed - Rays Honor (Ahonoora)
C P Morlock   Gerard Tumelty (5)

Placings: 00/649-PP7

OR84		Starts	1st	2nd	3rd	Win & Pl
Hurdles		6	–	–	–	£475
All Jumps races		6	–	–	–	£475

GF-HRD 0-0-1 GS-HVY 0-0-4 Course 0-0-1 Dist 0-0-7

5 Jul Stratford 2m1½f Cls4 Nov 81-94 Hdl Hcap £4,554
14 ran GOOD   9hdls   Time 3m 55.80s (slw 7.80s)
1 Monsieur 6 11-5 ....A P McCoy 7/2F
2 Smoothly Does It 5 11-12 .....Jason Maguire 12/1
3 Dubai Dreams 6 10-13 tp ....P J Brennan 10/1
7 FLAMAND 5 11-3 t ....Jimmy McCarthy 16/1
  held up, headway 6th, weakened after 3 out
  btn 27 lengths [RPR64.TS59 OR85] [op 25/1]
Dist: 2½-11-8-1½-3½   RACE RPR: 97+/98/74
Racecheck: Wins - Pl - Unpl 14

14 Jun Hereford 2m1f   Cls4 Nov 82-105 Hdl Hcap
                £3,578
10 ran GD-FM   8hdls   Time 3m 53.50s (slw 3.50s)
1 Megaton 5 11-8 ....A P McCoy 5/2J
2 Sun Hill 6 10-7 ....Ollie McPhail 12/1
3 La Dolfina 6 11-9 ....T J O'Brien (3) 5/2J
P FLAMAND 5 10-9 ....Jimmy McCarthy 50/1
  held up, headway 4th, soon ridden, weakened 3
  out, behind when pulled up before last
  [OR88]   [op 33/1]
Dist: 1-10-10-13-1¾   RACE RPR: 106+/90+/98
Racecheck: Wins 5 (5) Pl 3 Unpl 5

2 May Wincanton 2m Cls4 74-97 Hdl Hcap £3,426
17 ran GOOD   8hdls   Time 3m 48.90s (slw 11.90s)
1 Long Road 5 11-8 ....A P McCoy 11/4F
2 Brown Fox 5 10-1 t ....Owyn Nelmes (3) 16/1
3 Without Pretense 8 9-12 ow2 Mark Nicolls (5) 14/1
4 AVESOMEOFTHAT 5 11-1 ....
  ....Wayne Kavanagh (7) 4/1
  soon led, 7 lengths clear 3rd, headed and
  weakened approaching 2 out
  [RPR92 TS77 OR93]   [op 7/2 tchd 9/2]
P FLAMAND 5 11-3 ....Jimmy McCarthy 25/1
  always behind, tailed off when pulled up before
  2 out [OR88]   [op 20/1]
Dist: hd-8-3½-½-shd   RACE RPR: 103+/84/75
Racecheck: Wins 4 (2) Pl 5 Unpl 16

Form Reading	**FORZACURITY**
Spotlight	Has come right down the weights since returning to action in July 2006.
Handicap Ratings	On a mark of 95 (unplaced) six outings ago which then rose to a mark of 103 (placed 7th) three outings ago. Down to a mark of 85 for today's outing, which is a very significant drop if able to recapture lost form.
Significant Items of Form	Seven year old with three hurdle wins all at 2m1f on Good and Good to Soft in Class 5, Class 4 and Class 3 (latest) events, the last of which was in May 2005. Current campaign started on 05.07.06 after twelve months off and with 7th of 8 (beaten 81 lengths), last of 12 (beaten 43 lengths) and 15th of 17 (beaten 43 lengths) in a Class 3 and two Class 4 Handicap Hurdles, shows no sign of recapturing form.
Verdict	No glimmer of light at the end of the tunnel in form reading process.
Hence:	DISMISS

Form Reading	**BRAVE DANE**
Spotlight	Won a couple of banded events in the Spring.
Handicap Ratings	Ran off a mark of 100 six outings ago but marks of 93 (placed 4th) and 92 (pulled up) for last two outings. Mark of 92 for today's event.
Significant Items of Form	Eight year old with Class 3 and Class 4 Handicap Hurdle victories over 2 miles and 2m½f on Good and Good to Firm at Ludlow and Stratford (today's course), both in May 2004. Current campaign, after a twelve month break, started on 14.08.06 at Southwell in a Class 3 Handicap Hurdle over 2 miles (Good) when 4th of 8 runners, beaten 10 lengths after being reluctant to race but making late progress. Last run on 24.08.06 at Stratford in a Class 4 Handicap Hurdle, was again reluctant to race and pulled up after first.
Verdict	No point in risking money on horse that doesn't want to race at present.
Hence:	DISMISS.

Form Reading	**FLAMAND**
Spotlight	Possibilities on a 4th in a Novice event at Taunton in December 2005.
Handicap Ratings	Marks of 88, 88 and 85 (7th) for last three outings. Mark of 84 for today's event.
Significant Items of Form	Five year old with no wins and only eight outings which has produced one 4th place (see Spotlight). Although pulled up in first two Handicap Hurdle (Class 4) events of current campaign on 02.05.06 and 14.06.06 there were signs in latest race on 05.07.06 that it was getting the hang of things when 7th of 14 in a 2m½fClass 4 Handicap Hurdle at today's course (Stratford) after making headway at the 6th before weakening after 3 out.
Verdict	Midfield finishing position in last race, coupled with the fact that the race was at Stratford, are both good signs. Ran on Good to Firm at Hereford on next to last race on 14.06.06 when made headway at 4th before being pulled up before last, therefore today's going should not be a problem and suitability of today's course is proven by last run. Horse carried 11st 3lbs on last run at Stratford, and today with a 5lb claimer on board, means it will only be carrying 9st 10lbs so a top three placing has got to be a reasonable possibility.
Hence:	SELECT.

Overall Comment

Flamand won by 11 lengths going away at the finish and the *Racing Post* report on the race stated it had improved by one stone and it was the horse's first run following a wind operation. This last bit of information, which was not made available to the punters by the *Racing Post* on the day of the race, could mean that the signs of improvement spotted in the form reading were just a coincidence and not really relevant to the horse's winning run.

Whether they were or they weren't in my view is unimportant because you can only draw your conclusions from the factual form information printed in the *Racing Post*.

Furthermore, there are so many cases where winning form includes a midfield run in its last outing and/or previous run/s at the relevant course that you would be categorically wrong to exclude this information from the decision making process.

Returning to the subject of Flamand's Stratford race, it should be noted that the forecast of Flamand with Nesnaas the Favourite paid £159.20 for the Tote Exacta and £90.03 for the Computer Straight Forecast.

EXAMPLE 29

09.04.07   Fakenham – Good – Class 4 – Novice Handicap Hurdle – 2m4f

Winner   JENDALI LAD – 20/1

3.10
RACE 3

Betfair Novices' Handicap Hurdle ATR
(Class 4)
Winner £3,903.60   2m4f

£6000 guaranteed For 4yo+ Rated 0-105 Weights raised 3lb Minimum Weight 10-0 Penalties after March 1st, a winner of a hurdle 7lb **Patrixtoo's** Handicap Mark 102 Entries 35 Penalty value 1st £3,903.60 2nd £1,146 3rd £573 4th £286.20

F/80-04 **PATRIXTOO** (FR) [46]	6 11-12
gr g Linamix-Maradadi	Padge Whelan
T J FitzGerald P Stoner	(100)
0866 **LADY ROISIN** (IRE) [14]	5 11-5
b m Luso-Curracloe Rose	Matty Roe (10)
Mrs L Wadham The Not Over Big Partnership	(84)
-327PP **AKASH** (IRE) [59] (25F)	t7 11-5
b g Dr Devious-Akilara	Owyn Nelmes (3)
Miss J Feilden Oceans Eleven	(99)
4-P4P3 **THAT MAN FOX** [84]	b6 11-4
b g Sovereign Water-Oh No Rosie	Tom Messenger (5)
P S McEntee Roger Clarke	(100)
4097 **MAJOR FAUX PAS** (IRE) [12]	t5 11-5
b g Berathea-Edwina	Leighton Aspell
O Sherwood The St Joseph Partnership	(101)
4-35P **SIMPLY ST LUCIA** [25]	5 10-11
b m Charnwood Forest-Mubadara	Wilson Renwick
J R Weymes Mrs M Ashby	(97)
P-PP83 **VICKY BEE** [15]	t8 10-7
b m Alflora-Mighty Frolic	Sean Fox
K F Clutterbuck Fare Dealing Partnership	(100)
J6P9PP **WATER PISTOL** [41] (5F)	5 10-3
b g Double Trigger-Water Flower	David Cullinane (7)
M C Chapman David A Wilson	(102)
-F0048 **STOP THE PIGEON** [10]	p9 10-1
gr g Norton Challenger-New Dawning Miss S Phizacklea (7)	
N J Pomfret Mrs Nicolas Townsend	(93)
0009U9 **JENDALI LAD** [27]	6 10-0
b/br g Jendali-Magic Lake	Tjade Collier (7)
R C Guest White Horse Racing Club	(86)

LONG HANDICAP: Jendali Lad **9-11**

2006 (12 ran) Colophony K A Morgan 6 11-4 7/1   Johnny Levins (5) OR94

BETTING FORECAST: 100-30 Patrixtoo, 4 Major Faux Pas, Vicky Bee, 5 Lady Roisin, 7 Water Pistol, 10 Simply St Lucia, 12 That Man Fox, 16 Akash, 25 Stop The Pigeon, 33 Jendali Lad.

SPOTLIGHT

Patrixtoo Been rather luckless in his time under different codes and ground often slower than ideal over hurdles; however looks on fair mark and latest run at Huntingdon suggests he should have more to offer at this level; decent chance of staying longer trip on tight track like this and respected on ground that will suit.

Lady Roisin Very lightly raced but beginning to get the hang of things, shown some promise in novice/maiden hurdles at around 2m the last twice; could be interesting now handicapping as the longer trip will suit on pedigree and rider can claim the full allowance.

Akash Running better last April/May than he is now, pulled up in handicap hurdles the last twice and no better on sand last time; said to have had breathing problems once but tongue tie not helped the last twice and main hope is he'll be better for return to quicker ground.

That Man Fox Shown minor ability at up to about 2m2f, including on this ground, but connections still experimenting with trip and didn't seem to go that kindly in first-time headgear when last seen in January; possibilities now handicapping after a break but risky enough.

Major Faux Pas Dual winner at up to 1m on sand at two; back from long absence over hurdles this winter and not disgraced after a break in Kempton conditionals handicap latest; may be worth another chance upped in trip with stronger handling and tongue tie on for first time.

Simply St Lucia Has won on slow ground on the Flat (turf and sand) so disappointing she didn't do better on her handicap hurdle debut at Hexham last month; better than that but not convinced a longer trip is the answer.

Vicky Bee Not looked anything special in most of her handicap runs though appeared to appreciate the return to farther on quick ground in mares handicap at Southwell recently (33-1); at least on the right tracks but this is potentially stronger.

Water Pistol Could appreciate the return to this ground after struggling on soft surfaces over jumps but probably not in much form anyway judged on the way he ran back on the Flat at Catterick less than a week ago (that that was potentially tough).

Stop The Pigeon Failed to complete in four maiden points in 2005-06 and yet to show much in novice/maiden hurdles this winter, the last twice in cheekpieces; this is much more realistic but plenty to prove still.

Jendali Lad Minor form in a handful of runs, no better when handicapping for the first time at Sedgefield last month (out of the weights, as today); up against it again.

> **VERDICT**   Several of these are open to improvement but **PATRIXTOO** (nap) shaped quite nicely at Huntingdon in February and there's every chance he can build on that now he's back on more suitable ground. [EMW]

OFFICIAL RATINGS					3.10	HANDICAP		TODAY FUTURE	RP RATING		
LAST SIX OUTINGS-LATEST ON RIGHT									LATEST / BEST / ADJUSTED		
—	—	—	—	105[0]	102[4]	Patrixtoo	11-12	102	96	96	100
—	—	—	—	—	95	Lady Roisin	11-5	95	82	82	84
—	—	—	100[P]	100[P]		Akash	11-5	95	—	104	99
—	—	—	—	—	94	That Man Fox	11-4	94	86	100	100
—	—	—	—	—	93[7]	Major Faux Pas	11-5	90	92	101	101
—	—	—	—	—	90[P]	Simply St Lucia	10-11	87	97	97	97
84[2]	89[P]	85[P]	—	85[8]		Vicky Bee	10-7	83	100 ◄	100	100
—	—	112[P]	85[9]	—	82[P]	Water Pistol	10-3	79	—	106 ◄	102 ◄
—	—	—	—	—		Stop The Pigeon	10-1	77	85	93	93
—	—	—	—	—	80[9]	Jendali Lad	9-11	76 -3	41	86	86

Jendali Lad   10-0

6-y-o bb g Jendali - Magic Lake (Primo Dominie)
R C Guest   Tjade Collier (7)

Placings: 0-0009U9

OR76   Starts   1st   2nd   3rd   Win & Pl
Hurdles 4   –   –   –   –
All Jumps races 7   –   –   –   –
GF-HRD 0-0-1   GS-HVY 0-0-3   Course 0-0-0   Dist 0-0-1

3 Mar Sedgefield 2m1f   Cls4 Nov 79-105 Hdl Hcap £2,928
7 ran   GOOD   7hdls   Time 4m 9.50s (slw 18.00s)
Miss Pross 7 11-6 ....Robert Walford 2/1F
Square Dealer 6 10-0 b¹ oh3 Paddy Aspell 22/1
Pass The Class 7 10-10 Michael O'Connell (7) 6/1
JENDALI LAD 6 10-1 ow1 oh6 ....
....Larry McGrath 50/1
chased leader, weakened 3 out, soon behind, tailed off next
btn 74 lengths [RPR13 OR80]   [op 28/1]

Dist: ¾-nk-13-2½-2¾   RACE RPR: 106+/85/103+
Racecheck: Wins - Pl 1 Unpl 4

19 Jan Musselburgh 2m   Cls3 Nov Hdl £5,205
14 ran   GD-SFT   9hdls   Time 3m 52.10s (slw 10.10s)
1 Pevensey 5 11-10 ....G Lee 4/7F
2 Modicum 5 10-13 ....Miss R Davidson (5) 11/2
3 King Daniel 6 11-7 ....Michael McAlister (3) 11/2
U **JENDALI LAD** 6 11-4 ....Larry McGrath 150/1
in touch when hampered and unseated rider 3rd

Dist: ¾-15-nk-11-3½ RACE RPR: 122+/108/102+
Racecheck: Wins 1 Pl 3 Unpl 14

5 Jan Musselburgh 2m   Cls4 Nov Hdl £2,602
12 ran   GOOD   9hdls   Time 3m 52.60s (slw 10.60s)
1, Purple Moon 4 10-7 ....Tony Dobbin 4/6F
2 Make A Mark 7 11-5 ....G Lee 40/1
3 Scutch Mill 5 11-5 t ....Barry Keniry 20/1
9 **JENDALI LAD** 6 11-5 .....Warren Marston 150/1
prominent, ridden along and lost place halfway, behind from 4 out
btn 40 lengths [RPR58 TS41]   [op 100/1]

Dist: 3-6-shd-5-1¾   RACE RPR: 93+/95/89
Racecheck: Wins - Pl 1 Unpl 11

Stop The Pigeon   10-1

9-y-o gr g Norton Challenger - New Dawning (Deep Run)
N J Pomfret   Miss S Phizacklea (7)

Placings: B/PP-F0048

OR77   Starts   1st   2nd   3rd   Win & Pl
All Jumps races 4   –   –   –   £248
GF-HRD 0-0-0   GS-HVY 0-0-3   Course 0-0-1   Dist 0-0-0

30 Mar Ascot 2m   Cls3 Nov Hdl £6,263
9 ran   GOOD   9hdls   Time 3m 46.40s (slw 1.40s)
1 Mendo 7 11-0 ....Tom Doyle 8/13F
2 Modicum 5 11-1 ....Miss R Davidson (5) 5/1
3 Globel Trucker 5 11-0 ....R M Power 9/1
8 **STOP THE PIGEON** 9 10-9 p ....
....Tom Messenger (5) 100/1
hit 2nd, chased leader until after 5th, weakened quickly 4 out
btn 61 lengths [RPR58 TS44 OR77]   [op 66/1]

Dist: ½-8-2½-13-6   RACE RPR: 119/125/111
Racecheck: Wins - Pl - Unpl.-

28 Dec 06 Catterick 2m Cls4 Mdn Hdl £2,602
15 ran GD-SFT 8hdls Time 3m 53.90s (slw 9.90s)
1 Marine Life 4 10-12 v¹ ....James Davies 14/1
2 Primus Inter Pares 5 10-12 Wilson Renwick 12/1
3 Blue Buster 6 10-12 ....Mr T Greenall 5/2F
12 STOP THE PIGEON 8 10-9 ow4 ....
....................................Mr M Mackley (7) 150/1
behind, hit 2nd, no chance from halfway
btn 85 lengths [RPR29 TS5] [op 200/1]
Dist: 4-7-10-3½-3 RACE RPR: 111+/105/100+
Racecheck: Wins 1 (1) Pl - Unpl 13

15 Jan Fakenham 2m Cls4 Nov Hdl £3,383
10 ran GD-SFT 6hdls Time 4m 10.90s (slw 22.90s)
1 Ship's Hill 6 11-5 ....Mick FitzGerald 2/5F
2 Noble Ben 5 11-5 ....Timmy Murphy 7/2
3 THAT MAN FOX 6 11-5 b¹ ..Antony Procter 50/1
led until 2nd, driven and looked awkward after
omitted 5th, no chance with leading pair from 3
out [RPR76 TS47 OR102] [op 66/1]
4 STOP THE PIGEON 9 10-12 p ....
....................................Mr M Mackley (7) 100/1
chased leaders until 6th, struggled on in
hopeless pursuit from 3 out [RPR66 TS33]
Dist: 21-22-10-13-20 RACE RPR: 119+/99+/76
Racecheck: Wins - Pl - Unpl 7

Akash 11-5

7-y-o b g Dr Devious - Akilara (Kahyasi)
Miss J Feilden Owyn Nelmes (3)

Placings: 36-327PP

OR**95** F58 Starts 1st 2nd 3rd Win & Pl
All Jumps races .... 7 – 1 2 £1,804
GF-HRD 0-1-2 GS-HVY 0-1-4 Course 0-1-1 Dist 0-0-0

9 Feb Kempton 2m5f Cls4 Nov 93-105 Hdl Hcap £3,904
14 ran GD-SFT 10hdls Time 5m 40.10s (slw 30.10s)
1 Nudge And Nurdle 6 11-9 ....Tony Evans 9/1
2 Supreme Copper 7 11-11 ......Barry Fenton 6/1J
3 Flying Forme 7 10-7 .....Darren O'Dwyer (7) 20/1
P AKASH 7 11-4 t ....Owyn Nelmes (3) 33/1
held up, ridden after 5th and struggling, tailing
off when pulled up before 3 out [OR100]

Dist: 19-12-6-5-11 RACE RPR: 112+/98+/67
Racecheck: Wins - Pl 2 Unpl 5

2 Jan Folkestone 2m1½f Cls4 80-100 Hdl Hcap £4,229
9 ran SOFT 6hdls Time 4m 38.20s (slw 30.20s)
1 Mount Benger 7 10-13 p ex7 Richard Johnson 7/2
2 Corker 5 11-7 ....Tom Scudamore 9/1
3 Asaateel 5 10-3 b ....Jamie Moore 6/1
P AKASH 7 11-4 ....Owyn Nelmes (3) 9/1
close up until weakened rapidly after 2 out,
tailed off when pulled up before last (jockey
said gelding had breathing problems)
[OR100] [op 11/1 tchd 14/1]
Dist: 2-5-hd-16-3½ RACE RPR: 100+/105+/81
Racecheck: Wins 2 (1) Pl 4 Unpl 8

13 Dec 06 Newbury 2m1½f Cls4 Mdn Hdl £4,229
21 ran SOFT 8hdls Time 4m 13.20s (slw 20.20s)
1 Climate Change 4 11-0 ....Sam Thomas 8/1
2 Magical Quest 6 11-0 ....Richard Johnson 4/1
3 Oco 4 11-0 ....Robert Thornton 5/2F
7 AKASH 6 10-11 ....Owyn Nelmes (3) 50/1
chased leaders until outpaced 3 out, stayed on
again run-in
btn 23 lengths [RPR95 TS89 OR105] [op 40/1]
Dist: 4-4-8-2-5 RACE RPR: 121+/116+/111+
Racecheck: Wins - Pl 4 Unpl 23

Flat Form

15 Mar Southwell (AW) 1m3f Cls6 51-65 Hcap £2,267
12 ran STAND Time 2m 28.05s (slw 4.05s)
1 Shape Up 7 8-12 v ....Paul Fessey 2 16/1
2 Starcross Maid 5 8-3 ....Chris Catlin 4 15/2
3 Eforetta 5 8-13 ....Edward Creighton 3 10/1
9 AKASH 7 8-12 t ....James Doyle (3) 7 33/1
mid-division, ridden and weakened over 4f out
btn 33 lengths [RPR16 TS9 OR63] [tchd 40/1]
Dist: 1¼-1¼-2-15-9 RACE RPR: 69/58/66+
Racecheck: Wins 1 (1) Pl 3 Unpl 4

That Man Fox 11-4

6-y-o b g Sovereign Water - Oh No Rosie (Vital
Season)
P S McEntee Tom Messenger (5)

OR**94** Starts 1st 2nd 3rd Win & Pl
Hurdles .... 6 – – 1 £949
All Jumps races .... 7 – – 1 £949
GF-HRD 0-0-1 GS-HVY 0-1-4 Course 0-1-2 Dist 0-0-1

15 Jan Fakenham 2m Cls4 Nov Hdl £3,383
10 ran GD-SFT 6hdls Time 4m 10.90s (slw 22.90s)
1 Ship's Hill 6 11-5 ....Mick FitzGerald 2/5F
2 Noble Ben 5 11-5 ....Timmy Murphy 7/2
3 THAT MAN FOX 6 11-5 b¹ ..Antony Procter 50/1
led until 2nd, driven and looked awkward after
omitted 5th, no chance with leading pair from 3
out [RPR76 TS47 OR102] [op 66/1]
4 STOP THE PIGEON 9 10-12 p ....
....................................Mr M Mackley (7) 100/1
chased leaders until 6th, struggled on in
hopeless pursuit from 3 out [RPR66 TS33]
Dist: 21-22-10-13-20 RACE RPR: 119+/99+/76
Racecheck: Wins - Pl - Unpl 7

26 Dec 06 Huntingdon 3m2f Cls4 Nov Hdl £3,904
11 ran GOOD 12hdls Time 6m 29.00s (slw 31.00s)
1 Very Special One 6 10-5 v ....Alan O'Keeffe 11/2
2 Old Benny 5 10-12 ....J A McCarthy 7/2
3 Christdalo 6 10-11 ....Jamie Moore EvensF
P THAT MAN FOX 5 10-12 ..Antony Procter 50/1
jumped right 1st, mistakes, led until 8th, soon
weakened, tailed off and pulled up 2 out
[OR102]
Dist: 16-10-15-5 RACE RPR: 119+/108+/99+
Racecheck: Wins 3 (3) Pl 2 Unpl 9

9 Dec 06 Market Rasen 2m1½f Cls4 Nov Hdl £2,928
11 ran GD-SFT 8hdls Time 4m 13.70s (slw 10.70s)
1 Leslingtaylor 4 10-12 ....G Lee 5/4
2 Indian Pipe Dream 4 10-12 Dominic Elsworth 6/5F
3 Plenty Cried Wolf 4 10-12 ......Anthony Ross 8/1
4 THAT MAN FOX 5 10-12 ....Antony Procter 66/1
led, headed approaching 2 out, weakened last
[RPR90 TS85]
Dist: shd-10-hd-5-6 RACE RPR: 100+/100+/90
Racecheck: Wins 1 (1) Pl 4 Unpl 15

	JENDALI LAD
Form Reading	
Spotlight	Minor form in a handful of runs, no better when handicapping for first time at Sedgefield last month.
Handicap Ratings	Mark of 80 for first Handicap Hurdle race last outing (placed 9th). Down to a mark of 76 today which puts it 3lbs below the weights.
Significant Items of Form	Six year old with no wins and only seven outings, best of which were two 9th places, one of which was last outing on 13.03.07 at Sedgefield, a Class 4 Novice Handicap Hurdle over 2m1f on Good. The description of that last race 'chased leader, weakened 3 out, soon behind, tailed off next, beaten 74 lengths' was to be expected because on previous run on 19.01.07 in a Class 3 Novice Hurdle was hampered and unseated rider at 3rd when in touch. Run before that on 05.01.07 was in a Class 4 Novice Hurdle over 2m (Good) at Musselburgh when 9th of 12 after being prominent before losing place halfway and beaten 40 lengths.
Verdict	Considering the fact that this horse is six years old and inexperienced, and considering also that there was a two month one week gap between outings on 05.01.07 and 13.03.07, and with the 19.01.07 outing (unseated at 3rd) having contributed little if anything to level of fitness, it is safe to assume that the horse was not fit enough to show its true capabilities when it last ran. Run on 19.01.07 when unseated, was in a Class 3 contest which suggests its trainer believes it has potential above bottom two classes. Horse carried 11st 5lbs and 11st 4lbs in last two Non Handicap contests and with 7lbs claiming jockey ensuring a weight

of 9st 7lbs in today's contest, it has the conditions to take advantage of an improved level of fitness generated by last run twenty seven days ago. The weight advantage provided by the 7lb claimer could well be sufficient to obtain a top three placing in a race where, just looking at the last six placings of each of the runners, it appears to be wide open.

Hence: SELECT.

Form Reading	**STOP THE PIGEON**
Spotlight	Failed to complete in four maiden points in 2005/2006 and yet to show much in novice/maiden hurdles this winter.
Handicap Ratings	No previous handicap hurdle races in last six outings so whether today's mark of 77 is a fair assessment of current form is difficult to assess.
Significant Items of Form	Nine year old whose last run was a Class 3 Novice Hurdle at Ascot on 30.03.07 when 8th of 9, beaten 61 lengths, and two previous runs on 15.01.07 at Fakenham and on 26.12.06 at Catterick were in a Class 4 Novice Hurdle (4th of 10, beaten 53 lengths) and a Class 4 Maiden Hurdle (12th of 15, beaten 85 lengths).
Verdict	Although starting prices can be very misleading the fact that this horse has started at 100/1 in last three races demonstrates that neither the bookies nor the punters have spotted any form of significance in at least the last four outings of a racing career that has only involved eight races. Given the fact that this horse is now nine years old, you would expect the handicapper to have sufficient information on the horse's abilities to be able to make a fair assessment of its handicap mark. Nothing in the form to indicate improvement is likely.
Hence:	DISMISS.

Form Reading	**AKASH**
Spotlight	Running better last April/May than he is now, pulled up in Handicap Hurdles the last twice.
Handicap Ratings	Mark of 100 for the last two outings when pulled up on each occasion. Eased to a mark of 95 for today's race.
Significant Items of Form	Seven year old whose most recent campaign looked as if it started on 13.12.06 in a Class 4 Maiden Hurdle at Newbury when finished a respectable 7th of 21 on Soft in a 2m½f Class 4 Maiden Hurdle, beaten 23 lengths, after staying on again run in. However next two runs, on 02.01.07 at Folkestone in a Class 4 Handicap Hurdle on Soft over 2m1f and on 09.02.07 at Kempton in a Class 4 Novice Handicap Hurdle on Good to Soft over 2m5f, both resulted in it being pulled up. Horse's last outing was on the All Weather on 15.03.07 in a Class 6 1m3f Handicap when beaten 33 lengths after weakening 4 furlongs out.
Verdict	Although horse's first four career placings read 36-32, its subsequent three hurdle runs and one All Weather outing (latest) have not shown that its form is about to improve significantly at present, despite the fact it is only seven years old and has previously had a top three placing at today's course.
Hence:	DISMISS.

Form Reading	**THAT MAN FOX**
Spotlight	Shown minor ability at up to about 2m2f including on this ground.
Handicap Ratings	No handicap hurdle runs in last six months; allocated a mark of 94 for today's

	race which is below best previous rating of 100 but above latest rating of 86.
Significant Items of Form	Six year old whose last run of 15.01.07 was at today's course (Fakenham) when placed 3rd of 10 in a Class 4 Novice Hurdle on Good to Soft, beaten 43 lengths, after leading race in the early stages. Previous run on 26.12.06 was in a 3m2f Class 4 Novice Hurdle at Huntingdon (Good) when led until 8th before weakening and pulled up 2 out. Run before that at Market Rasen (Good to Soft) on 09.12.06 in a 2m1½f Class 4 Novice Hurdle resulted in a 4th place, beaten 10 lengths, after leading until 2 out.
Verdict	Form reads like a keen front runner that will be suited by today's course and going and should get today's distance of 2m4f. Top three placing a definite possibility even allowing for the fact that today's race is a Handicap and considering it has been given almost three months off the track to freshen up.
Decision:	SELECT.

Overall Comment

Yet another contest where the most recent placing of the winner, Jandali Lad, was 9th place, a placing which, like 6th, 7th and 8th, frequently appears in the form book as being the most recent placing of long priced outsiders that manage to get their heads in front at the right time.

The key to the selection of Jendali Lad was analysing from the form reading process that, although it had been beaten 74 lengths in its last race, it had chased the leader until 3 out and therefore you got the impression that its form could very well be improving. This impression contrasted with the form of Akash, where a return to form looked unlikely and a racing career in the case of Stop the Pigeon that showed no sign of going anywhere at present.

One other factor of significance in the case of Jendali Lad, which was not mentioned in the Verdict, was the fact that the horse's trainer, Richard Guest, had emerged from a long running quiet spell by landing two winners at Kelso only seven days previously. The knowledge that Guest's stable was starting to fire on all cylinders gave some kind of credence to the form based view that Jendali Lad could strip fitter than its last outing and so it proved.

I would make the point however, and this is very important, that you should never, ever dismiss a horse from the reckoning if its form is telling you it could obtain a top three placing when you know for a fact that its trainer's stable is doing badly.

Such a move could be a recipe for disaster because there are numerous examples of long priced winners occurring when a stable is in the doldrums. Conversely, if a trainer's stable is running well and you are looking at one of his/her horses whose form is difficult to make a positive decision about, then you can allow the extra bit of knowledge you possess to make the decision for you. I pass these observations on to you with reservations because you must not fall into the trap of thinking it is essential that you know the current form of all trainers in order to make your selection decisions.

The Tail End System is primarily about letting a horse's form speak for itself without unwarranted interference for reasons that are not necessarily directly related, and this is a principle you should be keen to uphold. However, by the process of following the Jump Racing results on a daily basis, you will pick up snippets of information about the form of trainers that you could use to your advantage when you are finding difficulty in making your mind up about the form of a horse.

Returning to the subject of this particular race, I have a comment to make about That Man Fox because, although this horse's forecast price was 12/1, when the actual betting started after a reformed betting market, it was backed down from a price of 9/1 to one of 11/2. Given this situation a decision had to be made as to whether to back the horse for a win at a price which was below the ideal minimum of 10/1.

For me personally I am quite happy in such circumstances to back a horse for a win at the best price I can obtain, providing it is at least 5/1 or more. If it fell below 5/1 I would restrict my interest in the horse to its inclusion in a reverse forecast with my other selections.

For the record, the forecast of Jendali Lad with That Man Fox paid £304.90 for the Tote Exacta and £132.19 for the Computer Straight Forecast.

EXAMPLE 30

23.04.07	Hexham – Good to Firm – Class 4 – Novice Handicap Chase – 3m1f
Winner	PANAMA AT ONCE – 25/1

2.30
RACE 1

Northern Media Novices' Handicap Chase (Class 4)
Winner £3,578.30

ATR
3m1f

£5500 guaranteed **For** 5yo+ Rated 0-100 **Minimum Weight** 10-0 **Penalties** after April 14th, a winner of a chase 7lb Star Fever's Handicap Mark 100 Entries 29 pay £15 Penalty value 1st £3,578.30 2nd £1,050.50 3rd £525.25 4th £262.35

1 0-36136 **STAR FEVER** (IRE) [16] [D][BF] 6 11-12
b g Saddlers' Hall-Phenico Allstar · Miss R Davidson(5) 7b (106)
N G Richards Mr & Mrs Duncan Davidson

2 3335U2F **HOLD THE BID** (IRE) [20] 7 11-9
b/br g Lusc-Killesk Castle David O'Meara (106)
Mrs S J Smith Formulated Polymer Products Ltd

3 F375P21 **MR TWINS** (ARG) (7ex) [7] t6 11-7
ch g Numerous-Twins Parade Michael McAlister(3) (97)
M A Barnes Alex Singar

4 -378653 **TOMILLIELOU** [55] 6 11-6
gr g I'm Supposin-Belle Rose Dougie Costello(3)
G A Swinbank Dom Flit One

5 3-P0424 **JERINGA** [27] 8 11-5
b g Karinga Bay-Jervandha Mr C Dawson(7) (104)
J Wade John Wade

6 334F352 **DUNGUAIRE LADY** (IRE) [16] [C] 8 11-2
ch m Toulon-Why Me Linda Barry Keniry (107)
P Needham P Needham

7 9/F1423 **COPPLESTONE** (IRF) [16] [C] p11 10-11
b g Second Set-Queen Of The Brush Ewan Whillans(7) (103)
A C Whillans J D Wright

8 2FP8PP9 **CORBIE LYNN** [16] 10 10-8
ch m Kinane-Kilkenny Gorge P J McDonald(5) (110)
W S Coltherd J R Cheyna

9 5664665 **PANAMA AT ONCE** [62] p7 10-8
ch g Commanche Run-Cherry Sip Tom Messenger(5)
J M Saville Ownaracehorse.Co.UK (Panama)

10 0384674 **CASH ON FRIDAY** [20] 6 10-4
b g Bishop Of Cashel-Till Friday Timmy Murphy
R C Guest The South And North Partnership

11 -214FP4 **CUL LA BALLA** [21] 7 10-4
b g Hubbly Bubbly-Belon Breeze Brian Harding
M Todhunter Mrs J Mandle

12 /P0P6F2 **MORANDI** (IRE) [27] 9 10-0
b g Insan-Eliza Everett Phil Kinsella(3) (105)
A Parker A Parker

13 -573P0P **SUPER REVO** [16] 6 10-0
b g Revoque-Kingdom Princess Larry McGrath
Mrs K Walton The White Liners

14 69/U06U **IMPACT CRUSHER** (IRE) [27] 7 10-0
b g Sri Pekan-Costume Drama Peter Buchanan
J Wade John Wade

LONG HANDICAP: Morandi 9-10 Super Revo 9-9 Impact Crusher 9-9
2006 (12 ran) **Bafana Boy** N G Richards 6 10-6 14/1 . Alan Dempsey OR82

BETTING FORECAST: 9-2 Star Fever, 5 Hold The Bid, Tomillielou, 15-2 Dunguaire Lady, Mr Twins, 8 Copplestone, Morandi, 10 Jeringa, 14 Cash On Friday, 33 bar.

SPOTLIGHT

Star Fever Won a 3m handicap hurdle in January; solid effort over inadequate 2m on first run over fences last month and surely failed to run his race when favourite here next time (2m4f), finishing behind some of these; unwise to rule out a revival on ground he shouldn't mind.

Hold The Bid Yet to win a race but his Catterick second on heavy was promising enough and seemed to be coping with the quicker ground next time at Wetherby until crashing out on the second circuit; handicap bow in this discipline and competitive off higher marks as a hurdler.

Mr Twins Apparent improvement against higher-rated opposition in beginners events the last twice, though last week's Wetherby affair probably ultimately took little winning; prefer to see progress confirmed in a handicap before giving him benefit of the doubt.

Tomillielou Maiden hurdler but a sound effort in fair company two runs back and then placed off a similar mark on his handicap debut (3m1f; heavy); considered more of a chasing type and every chance on breeding that he'll go on the ground.

Jeringa Bumper winner on heavy and a maiden over jumps; bumped into a progressive rival on chasing debut and a reasonable switch to handicaps at Sedgefield off what looked a high enough mark; 2lb lower here but work to do with runner-up Morandi.

Dunguaire Lady Won novice hurdle here, sole win to date; these conditions suit and didn't do a lot wrong when coming from off the pace at Carlisle last time, yet stamina needs to be taken on trust at this trip and the track might not help.

Copplestone Might have needed it on first run for six months when close up behind Dunguaire Lady at Carlisle, a commendable effort given he was never far away off a strong pace (second came from behind); never won beyond extended 2m1f, and that's the worry.

Corbie Lynn Dual hurdle winner in 2004 but not progressed since, failing to build on some initial promise over fences; no better back on quicker ground last time and lots to prove.

Panama At Once Struggled to make any impact in novice/maiden hurdles and not a lot better when sent handicapping last time off a light weight, though heavy ground might not have suited; cheekpieces applied for chasing debut and can only be watched.

Cash On Friday Yet to win a race of any type and found nothing for pressure having travelled best at Ayr two runs back; expected more of him on better ground at Wetherby last time (sported an eyeshield) and now looks risky kicking off over fences.

Cul La Balla Good-ground Irish maiden point winner last year but offered little encouragement so far under Rules for current yard and jumping has been an issue; no obvious appeal now handicapping.

Morandi Lightly raced since winning an Irish point in 2004 but went close on second chase start at Sedgefield last month off 1lb lower mark; that form pretty weak but today's extra yardage should benefit.

Super Revo Second in a fast-ground bumper on debut but failed to win over hurdles and always looked in trouble on chasing debut here earlier this month.

Impact Crusher Well beaten at big prices over hurdles and too early to tell what might have happened on chasing debut when a 50/1 chance; not really bred for today's longer trip.

VERDICT **STAR FEVER** deserves another chance to confirm the promise of his chasing debut at Ayr, as his flop here earlier this month was simply too bad to be true. **Tomillielou** is feared most.[AWJ]

OFFICIAL RATINGS LAST SIX OUTINGS-LATEST ON RIGHT						2.30	HANDICAP	TODAY FUTURE	RP RATING LATEST / BEST / ADJUSTED		
—	—	—	—	100³	100⁶	Star Fever	11-12	100	76	106	106
—	—	—	—	—	—	Hold The Bid	11-9	97	—	106	106
80³	—	76⁵	—	—	—	Mr Twins (7x)	11-7	95 -7	97	97	97
—	—	—	—	—	—	Tomillielou	11-6	94	—	—	—
—	—	—	—	—	95⁴	Jeringa	11-5	93	104	104	104
—	95⁴	—	—	—	90²	Dunguaire Lady	11-2	90	105◄107	107
—	73ᶠ	73¹	86⁴	83²	85³	Copplestone	10-11	85	103	103	103
—	—	105⁸	99ᴾ	99ᴾ	91⁹	Corbie Lynn	10-8	82	50	124◄	110◄
—	—	—	—	—	—	Panama At Once	10-8	82	—	—	—
—	—	—	—	—	—	Cash On Friday	10-4	78	—	—	—
—	—	—	—	—	—	Cul La Balla	10-4	78	—	49	—
—	—	—	—	69ᶠ	69²	Morandi	9-10	74 -4	105◄105	105
—	—	—	—	—	74ᴾ	Super Revo	9-9	74 -5	—	—	—
—	—	—	—	—	69ᵁ	Impact Crusher	9-9	74 -5	—	—	—

Impact Crusher   10-0

7-y-o b g Sri Pekan - Costume Drama (Alleged)
J Wade   Peter Buchanan

Placings: 669/U06U

OR74		Starts	1st	2nd	3rd	Win & Pl
Chase		1	–	–	–	–
All Jumps races		7	–	–	–	–
GF-HRD 0-0-2	GS-HVY 0-0-3	Course 0-0-2		Dist 0-0-0		

27 Mar Sedgefield 2m4f Cls5 69-95 Ch Hcap £2,602
14 ran GD-FM   14fncs Time 5m 13.30s (slw 27.30s)
1 Whatcanyasay 6 9-11 p oh3 ....
....Michael McAlister (3) 8/1
2 **MORANDI** 9 9-11 ....Phil Kinsella (3) 25/1
mid-division, headway 9th, went 2nd after 2 out,
kept on same pace [RPR95 TS18 OR95]
3 Reasonably Sure 7 11-6 b ..Mr T Greenall 5/2F
4 **JERINGA** 8 11-12 ....Paddy Aspell 7/1
chased leaders, one pace from 3 out
[RPR95 TS18 OR95]   [op 8/1]
U **IMPACT CRUSHER** 7 10-0 Wilson Renwick 50/1
in touch when stumbled landing and unseated
rider 5th [OR69]
Dist: 5-hd-8-9-2½   RACE RPR: 83+/77/98+
Racecheck: Wins 3 (3) Pl – Unpl 4

5 Feb Hexham 2m1½f   Cls5 Mdn Hdl £1,627
10 ran SOFT   6hdls   Time 4m 42.20s (slw 43.20s)
1 Bedlam Boy 6 11-3 ....Tony Dobbin 8/13F
2 Ocarina 5 11-0 ....Gary Berridge (3) 9/2
3 Dawn Ride 6 11-3 ....Wilson Renwick 40/1
6 **IMPACT CRUSHER** 7 11-3 ...Paddy Aspell 66/1
prominent to 3rd, weakened from next
[RPR29]   [op 50/1]
Dist: 18-7-12-14-23   RACE RPR: 115+/85/78
Racecheck: Wins 1 (1) Pl 1 Unpl 9 –

12 Jan Kelso 2m2f   Cls4 Nov Hdl 4-7yo £3,253
16 ran HEAVY   8hdls   Time 5m 2.30s (slw 49.30s)
1 Role On 5 11-5 ....Tony Dobbin 5/1
2 Cavers Glen 5 11-5 ....Barry Keniry 5/1
3 Nelson Du Ronceray 6 10-12 ....
....David Da Silva (7) 11/1
11 **IMPACT CRUSHER** 7 11-5 Paddy Aspell 100/1
chased leaders until weakened before 3 out
btn 72 lengths [RPR32]
Dist: 7-4-1½-19-1¾   RACE RPR: 109+/99/93
Racecheck: Wins – Pl 4 Unpl 16

Super Revo   10-0

6-y-o b g Revoque - Kingdom Princess (Forzando)
Mrs K Walton   Larry McGrath

Placings: 250679P-573P0P

OR74	H74	Starts	1st	2nd	3rd	Win & Pl
Chase		1	–	–	–	–
All Jumps races		13	–	1	1	£1,041
GF-HRD 0-1-1	GS-HVY 0-1-8	Course 0-0-0		Dist 0-0-2		

7 Apr Carlisle 2m4f Cls4 Nov 74-100 Ch Hcap £3,253
15 ran GOOD   16fncs Time 5m 13.30s (slw 16.30s)
1 Ballynure 9 10-4 v ....Peter Buchanan 11/1
2 **DUNGUAIRE LADY** 8 11-2 ....Fergus King 25/1
in midfield, headway to chase winner before 4
out, one pace from 2 out [RPR93 TS46 OR90]
3 **COPPLESTONE** 11 10-4 p Ewan Whillans (7) 10/1
led to 8th, soon ridden but stayed prominent,
kept on from 2 out, no impression (jockey
received one-day ban: careless riding (tbn))
[RPR86 TS39 OR85]   [op 11/1]
6 **STAR FEVER** 6 11-7 ...Miss R Davidson (5) 4/1 J
held up, ridden 10th, never on terms (trainer
had no explanation for the poor form shown
other than the gelding may be better suited by a
longer trip) (jockey received one-day ban:
careless riding (tbn)) [RPR74 TS25 OR100]
P **SUPER REVO** 6 10-0 p ......Larry McGrath 20/1
always behind; tailed off when pulled up 11th
[OR74]
Dist: 9-1¾-23-2½-1¾   RACE RPR: 90+/93/86
Racecheck: Wins – Pl – Unpl 1

17 Mar Newcastle 2m4f Cls5 Nov 79-101 Hdl Hcap
£1,952
16 ran GOOD   11hdls   Time 5m 2.50s (slw 19.50s)
1 Barracat 10 10-6 ....Tom Greenway (5) 17/2
2 Bright Sparky 4 11-10 ....Alan Dempsey 5/1 J
3 Stravaigin 7 10-13 ....David O'Meara 20/1
12 **SUPER REVO** 6 10-10 ....Keith Mercer 9/1
held up, struggling from 6th
btn 48 lengths [RPR38 OR79]   [op 11/1]
Dist: 1¼-1¾-nk-10-1¼ RACE RPR: 88+/100+/82+
Racecheck: Wins 1 (1) Pl 1 Unpl 5

2 Jan Ayr 3m1½f   Cls5 72-95 Hdl Hcap £2,056
20 ran HEAVY   10hdls Time 6m 47.50s (slw 1m 2.50s)
1 Em's Royalty 10 11-7 ....Phil Kinsella (5) 40/1
2 Sea Laughter 9 11-6 ....Anthony Ross 10/1
3 Tobesure 13 11-6 ....Jan Faltejsek (3) 16/1
P **SUPER REVO** 6 11-1 p ....Dominic Elsworth 7/1
in rear, reminders 2nd and 5th, behind when
pulled up before 3 out [OR84][op 8/1 tchd 9/1]
Dist: 13-½-shd-10-nk   RACE RPR: 101/83+/85
Racecheck: Wins 1 (1) Pl 5 Unpl 19

Cul La Balla   10-4

7-y-o b g Hubbly Bubbly - Belon Breeze (Strong
Gale)
M Todhunter   Brian Harding

Placings: 2-214FP4

OR78		Starts	1st	2nd	3rd	Win & Pl
All Jumps races		4	–	–	–	£860
GF-HRD 0-0-0	GS-HVY 0-0-3	Course 0-0-1		Dist 0-0-0		

2 Apr Kelso 3m1f   Cls4 Ch £4,554
10 ran GOOD   18fncs   Time 6m 28.00s (slw 26.00s)
1 Noir Et Vert 6 11-2 ....G Lee 10/11F

2 Bog Oak 7 11-2 ....D J Casey 8/1
3 Uncle Neil 10 11-2 ....Wilson Renwick 22/1
4 CUL LA BALLA 7 11-2 ....Brian Harding 33/1
in touch until outpaced from halfway [RPR25]
Dist: 5-5-69-10   RACE RPR: 111+/102+/94
Racecheck: Wins 1 (1) Pl – Unpl 2

12 Dec 06 Sedgefield 3m3f   Cls4 Ch £5,437
7 ran HEAVY   21fncs Time 7m 30.70s (slw 1m 8.70s)
1 Kilty Storm 7 11-6 t ....A P McCoy 4/7F
2 Noir Et Vert 5 11-6 ....G Lee 5/2
3 Iron Warrior 6 11-6 ....Barry Keniry 28/1
P **CUL LA BALLA** 6 11-6 ...Dominic Elsworth 12/1
not fluent, in touch, mistake 8th, jumped left and
weakened from 10th, tailed off when pulled up
before 14th   [op 14/1]
Dist: 4-14-66   RACE RPR: 115+/111/97
Racecheck: Wins 1 (1) Pl – Unpl 5

5 Dec 06 Sedgefield 3m3f   Cls4 Mdn Ch £4,478
12 ran SOFT   18fncs Time 7m 25.50s (slw 1m 3.50s)
1 Lucky Nellerie 7 10-9 ......P J McDonald (5) 13/2
2 The Poser 5 11-0 ....Paddy Aspell 28/1
3 Woodstock Lass 7 10-0 tp Mr N T Slevin (7) 25/1
F **CUL LA BALLA** 6 11-0 ...Dominic Elsworth 11/2
chased leaders, hit 10th, close third when fell
next   [op 6/1 tchd 5/1]
Dist: 30-15-64   RACE RPR: 98+/68/62
Racecheck: Wins 2 (1) Pl 3 Unpl 13

Panama At Once   10-8

7-y-o ch g Commanche Run - Cherry Sip (Nearly A
Hand)
J M Saville   Tom Messenger (5)

Placings: 9-5664665

OR82	H82	Starts	1st	2nd	3rd	Win & Pl
All Jumps races		8	–	–	–	–
GF-HRD 0-0-0	GS-HVY 0-0-7	Course 0-0-2		Dist 0-0-0		

20 Feb Sedgefield 3m3½f Cls4 84-110 Hdl Hcap
£2,928
15 ran HEAVY   13hdls Time 7m 32.70s (slw 1m 9.70s)
1 Top Cloud 6 11-7 ....G Lee 5/2F
2 Oscar The Boxer 8 10-8 ....Fergus King 6/1
3 Our Joycey 6 10-5 ....S J Craine (3) 14/1
5 **PANAMA AT ONCE** 7 9-12 Joffret Huet (3) 12/1
held up, went prominent 5th, weakened after 3
out [RPR30 TS4 OR85]   [tchd 14/1]
Dist: 6-28-18-13-1   RACE RPR: 117+/96/84
Racecheck: Wins – Pl 2 Unpl 8

17 Jan Newcastle 3m   Cls3 Nov Hdl £4,697
13 ran SOFT   13hdls Time 6m 19.10s (slw 45.10s)
1 Allegedly So 6 10-12 t .....Peter Buchanan 100/1
2 Fastaffaran 6 10-9 .....Michael McAlister (3) 10/1
3 The Whisperer 6 10-13 Miss R Davidson (5) 4/7F
6 **PANAMA AT ONCE** 7 10-12 ....
....Dominic Elsworth 66/1
towards rear, driven 8th, never dangerous
[RPR69 TS40 OR88]
Dist: ½-3-12-6-17   RACE RPR: 108/107/111+
Racecheck: Wins 2 Pl 3 Unpl 8

15 Dec 06 Uttoxeter 2m4½f   Cls4 Mdn Hdl £3,253
14 ran HEAVY   10hdls Time 5m 44.90s (slw 58.90s)
1 Aitch Doubleyou 6 10-12 ..Dominic Elsworth 7/2
2 Obaki de Grissay 4 10-12 ..Richard Johnson 4/1
3 Maktu 4 10-7 ....Gerard Tumelty (5) 80/1
6 **PANAMA AT ONCE** 6 10-9 Joffret Huet (3) 40/1
held up, ridden 4 out, never on terms
[RPR63 TS12 OR86]
Dist: 1¼-2½-10-13-15 RACE RPR: 107+/105+/101
Racecheck: Wins 2 (2) Pl 7 Unpl 10

Form Reading	**IMPACT CRUSHER**
Spotlight	Well beaten at big prices over hurdles and too early to tell what might have happened on chasing debut when a 50/1 chance.
Handicap Ratings	Mark of 69 for last outing, its handicap chase debut. Mark of 74 for today's race, which puts it 5lb out of the weights.
Significant Items of Form	Seven year old whose last run on 27.03.07 was its handicap chase debut at Sedgefield (Good to Firm) in a Class 5 contest over 2m4f when unseated at 5th. Previous run on 05.03.07 was in a Class 5 Maiden Hurdle at today's course (Hexam, Soft) where 6th of 10 runners, beaten 74 lengths. Run prior to that at Kelso (Heavy) in a Class 4 Novice Hurdle resulted in an 11th of 16 runners, beaten 72 lengths.
Verdict	No indication in last three outings that it has the ability to feature in a Class 4, 3m1f Chase.
Decision:	DISMISS.

Form Reading	**SUPER REVO**
Spotlight	Failed to win over hurdles and always looked in trouble on chasing debut here earlier this month.
Handicap Ratings	Mark of 74 for last outing (chasing debut) when pulled up. Same mark for today's race, which puts it 5lb out of the weights.
Significant Items of Form	Six year old whose chasing debut, last outing, on 07.04.07 at Carlisle (Good) in a 2m4f Novice Handicap Chase was unimpressive, 'always behind, pulled up 11th'. Previous two runs on 17.03.07 at Newcastle (Good) in a Class 4 Novice Handicap Hurdle over 2m4f when 12th of 16, beaten 48 lengths, and on 02.01.07 at Ayr (Heavy) in a Class 5 Handicap Hurdle over 3m½f when pulled up before 3 out, were both equally unimpressive.
Verdict	Nothing in form to give confidence for today's contest.
Hence:	DISMISS.

Form Reading	**CUL LA BALLA**
Spotlight	Good ground Irish Maiden Point winner last year but offered little encouragement so far under rules for current yard.
Handicap Ratings	No handicap chase runs in last six outings. Mark of 78 for today's outing, which gives it a weight of 10st 4lb.
Significant Items of Form	Seven year old whose placings record since Point to Point win (see Spotlight) read 4FP4. Last three runs, all at either Sedgefield or Kelso (latest), have been in Class 4 chases of 3m3f (Soft and Heavy) and 3m1f (Good) during the period from 15.12.06 to 02.04.07. Although the first of these runs resulted in a fall at the 11th and the next in being pulled up before the 14th, the horse's latest run after a 3½ month break when 4th of 10, beaten 79 lengths, was respectable.
Verdict	Given the fact the horse has moved to Britain from Ireland relatively recently, a period of adaptation is to be expected and therefore its results so far are certainly not disappointing and improvement can be expected. Whether a top three placing can be obtained in today's race is by no means certain but, given the fact that the horse's course records show it has already run at Hexham, and as

improvement on its last run at Kelso is also highly likely, a SELECT decision would appear to be the most sensible and safest option.

Decision: SELECT.

Form Reading	**PANAMA AT ONCE**
Spotlight	Struggled to make any impact on novice/maiden hurdles and not a lot better when sent handicapping last time. Cheek pieces applied for chasing debut.
Handicap Ratings	Mark of 82 and a weight of 10st 8lb for chase debut.
Significant Items of Form	Seven year old with what looks like a consistent if unspectacular placings record over hurdles, which reads 664665, for last six outings. Its last two runs are of interest particularly because it has been campaigned over 3m at Newcastle (Soft) in a Class 3 Novice Hurdle when 6th of 13, beaten 38½ lengths, and over 3m3½f at Sedgefield (Heavy) when 5th of 15, beaten 65 lengths, prominent from 5th, weakened 3 out.
Verdict	Trainer is unlikely to be giving his horse its chasing debut at such a tough track as Hexham if he didn't think it was likely to be suited to both challenges. This horse has already run at Hexham twice and judging by its last two runs, today's distance will not be problem. The fact that the horse has been finishing all its races is a good sign and as there are plenty of horses that become far better chasers than hurdlers and vice versa, the chase debut factor should not be regarded as a negative. The trainer has given his horse a two month break since its last outing, so with a bit of luck a top three placing could well be within its grasp.
Hence:	SELECT.

Overall Comment

Although I have never visited Hexham track, viewing the course on the TV leaves you with the impression that its ups and downs make it a severe test, probably not as hard as Towcester, but not far off. As a result, it throws up some good long priced winners on a regular basis and the racing from there for those not able to attend always makes for good viewing, courtesy of At the Races, in what is a fabulous setting high on the fells.

This particular race, a Class 4 Chase over 3m1f, had all the ingredients necessary to produce an upset, so the fact that the winner came from the BAR group of the Betting Forecast was no great surprise.

For the record, after selecting Cul La Balla and Panama at Once, I had the option of making a further selection/selections by considering in their correct sequence the two Course Winners in the field, namely Copplestone and Danguaire Lady, which although less than 10/1 in the Betting Forecast, were hovering close to 10/1 when actual betting opened up.

Alternatively I had the option of considering the one remaining horse in the BAR group (last in consideration because it was highest weighted), namely Corbie Lynn, before moving on to the last named horse in the Betting Forecast, Cash on Friday.

As things transpired, I decided to be satisfied with my first two selections, having looked at first Copplestone and then Danguaire Lady and deciding that, although previous Course Winners, they could both have a problem with the distance of 3m1f.

I also looked at the alternative option and decided that, as Corbie Lynn was distinctly out of form and Cash in Hand was struggling to make any sort of impression in Class 5 Hurdles, I was best off saving my money.

On this occasion I was proved correct but I should make it clear that if any one of these alternatives had given me the impression that it could do the business, I would have been more than happy to have backed it for insurance purposes, together with my first two selections.

For the record, Panama At Once won by 28 lengths; Corbie Lynn was 6th at 42¾ lengths, never on terms; Danguaire Lady, was 7th at 107¾ lengths, never on terms; Cash on Friday was pulled up after 4 out; and my first selection, Cul La Balla, was pulled up at the 14th.

The forecast Panama at Once, with Tomillielou, paid £438.50 for the Tote Exacta and £126.73 for the Computer Straight Forecast.

EXAMPLE 31

20.04.07　Hereford – Good to Firm – Class 5 – Handicap Chase – 2m
Winner　PAUNTLEY GOFA – 20/1

6.30 RACE 3 — *SIS Best For Data Handicap Chase (Class 5)* — Winner £3,578.30 — ATR — 2m

£5500 guaranteed For 5yo+ Rated 0-90 Minimum Weight 10-0 Penalties after April 7th, a winner of a chase 7lb Giust In Temp's Handicap Mark 89 Entries 23 pay £10 Penalty value 1st £3,578.30 2nd £1,050.50 3rd £525.25 4th £262.35

No	Form	Horse	Wt	Jockey
1	5446356	**GIUST IN TEMP** (IRE) ³ ⑱ — b g Polish Precedent-Blue Stricks — Mrs K M Sanderson　Mrs K M Sanderson	8 11-12	Mr I Chanin(7) 93
2	88P2101	**TRAVELLO** (GER) (7ex) ¹¹ ⑱ — b g Bakharoff-Trevista — M F Harris　Milton Harris Racing Club	t7 11-9	Dave Crosse 91
3	9-F5U01	**BOLLITREE BOB** (7ex) ¹¹ ⑱ — b g Bob's Return-Lady Prunella — M Scudamore　Mrs P de W Johnson	6 11-9	Tom Scudamore 95
4	-6F425U	**THIEVES'GLEN** ¹⁰ ⑱ — b g Teenoso-Hollow Creek — Mrs K Waldron　Nick Shutts	9 11-8	Andrew Tinkler 98
5	U-00P0P	**MARKANDA** (IRE) ²² — b h Marju-Shakanda — A L T Moore (IRE)　J D Moore	tp7 11-5	J W Farrelly(7)
6	48-PPP6	**PAUNTLEY GOFA** ⁹⁸ ⑱ — b g Afzal-Gotageton — S J Gilmore　Gofa Fun Partnership	11 11-2	Andrew Thornton 98
7	4473032	**JUST MUCKIN AROUND** (IRE) ³³ ⑱ — gr g Callo Rufo-Cousin Muck — R H Buckler　Pride Of The West Racing Club	t11 11-1	Daryl Jacob(3) 101
8	P-PF978	**IRISH TOTTY** ¹⁵ — b m Glacial Storm-Elver Season — C J Down　Mrs S Cork	t8 10-11	Chris Honour(3)
9	55PP/P-	**WOT NO CASH** ³⁶⁷ — gr g Ballecashtal-Madame Non — R C Harper　R C Harper	15 10-3	James White(5)
10	OF-PPU	**SCANIA CLASSIC** ⁵³ — gr g Thethingaboutitis-Gifted Gale — M Scudamore　Clive Price	t6 10-0	John Kington(7) 75
11	5P464F5	**STAR GALAXY** (IRE) ²² — b g Fourstars Allstar-Raven Night — M A Doyle　Donald Gould,David Prince,Mark Wadley	7 10-0	Jamie Moore 96

LONG HANDICAP: Scania Classic 9-5 Star Galaxy 9-1
2006 (12 ran) Twentytwosilver D B Feek 6 11-1 9/1　Robert Lucey-Butler (5) OR84

BETTING FORECAST: 9-4 Bollitree Bob, 4 Travello, 9-2 Just Muckin Around, 5 Thieves'glen, 8 Markanda, 16 Giust In Temp, Irish Totty, 25 Star Galaxy, 33 bar.

SPOTLIGHT

Giust In Temp Comfortably held in low-grade contests since taking a maiden hurdle at Worcester in August 2005 (2m, good to firm) and hard to fancy on just his third chase start after a lacklustre run in a handicap hurdle at Exeter on Tuesday.

Travello Burst a blood vessel at Newton Abbot two starts ago but back to form when equipped with a tongue-tie in a selling handicap chase at Plumpton last time; 7lb penalty makes this tougher and remains to be seen if his problems resurface when he comes under pressure.

Bollitree Bob Jumping had let him down in three previous attempts over fences but he put up an impressive display at Huntingdon last time (2m1f, good to firm); 3lb well in under a penalty and should make a bold bid to follow up.

Thieves'glen Unseated mid-race last time out but had previously been in fair form, with his best recent effort coming when just failing to make all over C&D in January; no problem with the ground but has always struggled to get his head in front; probably playing for minor honours.

Markanda Longstanding maiden who is hard to fancy on his Irish form, but gets a tongue tie and cheekpieces added for the first time and Irish trainer took a similarly weak contest at Chepstow last week with a well-backed raider, so one to note in the betting.

Pauntley Gofa Looked a fair prospect in his youth but has suffered an interrupted career; fourth in a better contest over C&D last March was a reasonable effort and now 18lb lower, but has shown nothing since and hard to fancy.

Just Muckin Around Down to a fair handicap mark and two latest efforts, including on unsuitable soft ground over C&D in February, have suggested his turn is not far away; one of the more likely contenders.

Irish Totty Fell at the first on chase debut in January (200/1) but not disgraced from out of the handicap over hurdles most recently, when encountering 2m on fast ground for the first time; conditions fine but more needed.

Wot No Cash Hasn't been seen since pulling up in a selling handicap chase at Chepstow a year ago when returning from another lengthy layoff; impossible to fancy.

Scania Classic Tongue tie fitted for the first time but only finished one of his five starts under Rules and impossible to fancy from out of the handicap.

Star Galaxy Poor maiden whose most recent run was over 3m2f; highly unlikely to make it 20th time lucky from well out of the handicap.

VERDICT — Plenty who like to force the pace and that should suit **JUST MUCKIN AROUND**, who had the misfortune to meet an in-form rival at Fontwell last time. **Bollitree Bob** will rightly be popular after an impressive win last week, but his jumping will be tested in this bigger field.[SR]

	OFFICIAL RATINGS LAST SIX OUTINGS-LATEST ON RIGHT					6.30 HANDICAP	TODAY FUTURE	RP RATING LATEST / BEST / ADJUSTED		
—	—	—	94³	—	—	Giust In Temp 11-12	89	—	93	93
86⁶	90ᵖ	—	—	—	79¹	Travello (7x) 11-9	86　-2	91	91	91
—	87ᶠ	82⁵	79ᵁ	—	79¹	Bollitree Bob (7x) 11-9	86　+3	95◄	95	95
90⁶	118²	84⁴	82²	85⁵	85ᵁ	Thieves'glen 11-8	85	—	98	98
—	—	—	—	—	87ᵖ	Markanda 11-5	82	—	21	—
97⁴	95⁸	91ᵖ	—	89ᵖ	84⁶	Pauntley Gofa 11-2	79	32	32	98
88⁴	86⁷	84³	84⁰	80³	78²	Just Muckin Around 11-1	78	95◄	113◄	101◄
—	—	—	—	—	—	Irish Totty 10-11	74	—	—	—
73⁷	—	83⁵	—	81ᵖ	72ᵖ	Wot No Cash 10-3	66	—	—	—
—	—	—	—	—	67ᵁ	Scania Classic 9-5	63　-9	75	75	75
—	66⁴	63⁶	64⁴	61ᶠ	61⁵	Star Galaxy 9-1	63　-13	65	98	98

Scania Classic 10-0

6-y-o *gr g Thethingaboutitis - Gifted Gale (Aird Point)*

M Scudamore John Kington (7)

Placings: 0F-PPU

OR63 H54	Starts	1st	2nd	3rd	Win & Pl
Chase	2	–	–	–	–
All Jumps races	5	–	–	–	–

GF-HRD 0-0-0 **GS-HVY** 0-0-5 **Course** 0-0-1 **Dist** 0-0-3

26 Feb Hereford 2m Cls5 67-93 Ch Hcap £2,602
10 ran SOFT 12fncs Time 4m 13.50s (slw 22.50s)
1 Femme d'Avril 5 10-12 ....A P McCoy 13/8F
2 Thievery 6 10-2 p ....Richard Johnson 16/1
3 **JUST MUCKIN AROUND** 11 10-10 t ....Daryl Jacob (3) 22/1
held up in touch, one pace from 3 out
[RPR86 TS73 OR80] [tchd 20/1 & 25/1]
5 **THIEVES'GLEN** 9 11-4 ....Andrew Tinkler 6/1
led, soon clear, headed 4 out, weakened 3 out, soon eased
[RPR75 TS51 OR85] [op 15/2 tchd 8/1]
U **SCANIA CLASSIC** 6 9-7 oh13 ....John Kington (7) 100/1
held up in touch, jumped right 8th, weakened after 4 out, behind when stumbled and unseated rider last [RPR47 OR67]
U **BOLLITREE BOB** 6 10-12 Tom Scudamore 11/1
held up and behind, headway approaching 3 out, soon ridden, 10 lengths 4th and weakening when blundered and unseated rider last
[RPR79 OR79] [op 14/1]
Dist: 2½-3½-7-13 RACE RPR: 95+/79/86
Racecheck: Wins 1 (1) Pl 1 Unpl 8

13 Jan Kempton 2m Cls2 Nov Ch £11,315
6 ran GD-SFT 12fncs Time 4m 5.85s (slw 14.85s)
1 Royal Shakespeare 8 11-2 Richard Johnson 6/4J
2 Trouble At Bay 7 11-7 ...Wayne Hutchinson 6/4J
3 Ofarel d'Airy 5 10-12 ....Sam Thomas 6/1
P **SCANIA CLASSIC** 6 11-2 ..John Kington 200/1
jumped poorly in rear, tailed off from 6th, pulled up before last [op 100/1]
Dist: 10-nk-24-84 RACE RPR: 149+/143+/135+
Racecheck: Wins - Pl 3 Unpl 5

16 Dec 06 Haydock 2m4f Cls4 Nov Hdl 4-7yo £4,554
16 ran HEAVY 10hdls Time 5m 16.20s (slw 38.20s)
1 Anglicisme 4 10-12 ......Wayne Hutchinson 33/1
2 Hills Of Aran 4 10-12 ....Sam Thomas 16/1
3 Mr Strachan 5 10-12 .Michael O'Connell (7) 5/2F
P **SCANIA CLASSIC** 5 10-5 John Kington (7) 100/1
always behind, tailed off when pulled up before 2 out
Dist: 1¼-8-10-7-4 RACE RPR: 115/114/115+
Racecheck: Wins 2 (2) Pl 4 Unpl 18

Wot No Cash 10-3

15-y-o *gr g Ballacashtal - Madame Non (My Swanee)*

R C Harper James White (5)

Placings: /44213FF63P/755PP/P-

OR66 H72	Starts	1st	2nd	3rd	Win & Pl
Chase	31	2	2	3	£7,716
All Jumps races	34	2	2	3	**£7,716**

72 10/03 Chep 2m3½f Cls5 62-88 Sell Ch Hcap gd-fm £2,002
64 5/01 Font 2m2f Cls5 60-78 Sell Ch Hcap gd-fm £2,384
Total win prize-money £4,386

GF-HRD 2-3-21 **GS-HVY** 0-2-6 **Course** 0-0-2 **Dist** 0-3-10

18 Apr 06 Chepstow 2m3½f Cls5 63-89 Sell Ch Hcap £2,277
16 ran GOOD 16fncs Time 4m 59.40s (slw 12.40s)
1 Collinstown 10 10-12 ....Noel Fehily 4/1F
2 Mill Bank 11 11-12 p ....Paul Moloney 13/2
3 Blazing Batman 13 9-10 ow1 ....Dr P Pritchard (5) 11/1
P **WOT NO CASH** 14 10-4 ...Mark Nicolls (5) 66/1
prominent, led 4th until after 5th, weakened 6th, tailed off when pulled up before 4 out
[OR72] [op 33/1]
Dist: 2-3-½-1¼-1 RACE RPR: 87+/100+/70
Racecheck: Wins 5 (4) Pl 1 Unpl 9

12 Sep 04 Hexham 2m4½f Cls4 65-91 Am Ch Hcap £3,486
13 ran GD-FM 15fncs Time 5m 11.40s (slw 11.40s)
1 Harem Scarem 13 9-9 ......Ewan Whillans (7) 8/1
2 York Rite 8 10-0 tp ....Robert Stephens (3) 4/1
3 Noble Colours 11 9-7 oh1 ....Miss Faye Bramley (7) 50/1
P **WOT NO CASH** 12 10-9 ow9 ....Mr J Newbold (7) 33/1
behind, weakened 9th, pulled up before 2 out
[OR81]
Dist: 2½-7-13-6-4 RACE RPR: 79/78/69+
Racecheck: Wins 2 (2) Pl 7 Unpl 11

16 Jun 04 Worcester 2m Cls5 64-85 Sell Hdl Hcap £2,660
17 ran GD-FM 8hdls Time 3m 45.60s (slw 2.60s)
1 Dance Of Life 5 10-5 b ....Leighton Aspell 14/1
2 Young Owen 6 11-1 ....Mark Bradburne 13/2
3 Ardwelshin 6 10-11 p ......James Davies (3) 33/1
P **WOT NO CASH** 12 10-11 Mr J Newbold (7) 33/1
held up in touch, weakened approaching 5th, behind when pulled up before 3 out [OR77]
Dist: 5-18-6-shd-1½ RACE RPR: 78+/83/64
Racecheck: Wins 1 (1) Pl - Unpl 25

Pauntley Gofa 11-2

11-y-o *b g Afzal - Gotageton (Oats)*

S J Gilmore Andrew Thornton

Placings: /4313/7/PPPPU48-PPP6

OR79 H109	Starts	1st	2nd	3rd	Win & Pl
Chase	12	1	–	2	£5,750
All Jumps races	23	3	2	3	**£14,012**

6/02 MRas 2m1½f Cls3 Nov Ch gd-fm £4,310
11/01 Ludl 2m Cls3 Nov Hdl 4-6yo gd-fm £3,559
5/01 MRas 2m1½f Cls4 Mdn Hdl good £2,914
Total win prize-money £10,783

GF-HRD 2-3-7 **GS-HVY** 0-0-5 **Course** 0-1-4 **Dist** 1-3-11

12 Jan Huntingdon 2m½f Cls4 84-105 Ch Hcap £3,904
7 ran SOFT 11fncs Time 4m 21.50s (slw 23.50s)
1 Elgar 10 11-12 t ....T J O'Brien 4/1
2 Dalriath 8 10-4 ....David Cullinane (7) 4/1
3 Salinas 8 11-12 ....Dave Crosse 9/1
6 **PAUNTLEY GOFA** 11 10-0 James White (5) 25/1
held up, behind from 6th
[RPR20 OR84] [tchd 22/1]
Dist: 1-3½-23-26-20 RACE RPR: 115+/102+/110
Racecheck: Wins 1 (1) Pl 3 Unpl 4

7 Dec 06 Huntingdon 2m½f Cls4 82-101 Cond Ch Hcap £4,554
7 ran GD-SFT 12fncs Time 4m 22.90s (slw 24.90s)
1 Elgar 9 11-6 t ....T J O'Brien 5/2F
2 In Extra Time 7 10-5 ....J W Farrelly (8) 13/2
3 Adecco 7 11-3 b ....Eamon Dehdashti (3) 4/1
P **PAUNTLEY GOFA** 10 11-0 ....S P Walsh 25/1
led until 6th, chased winner until 8th, ridden and mistake 10th, weakened next, tailed off and pulled up 2 out [OR89]
Dist: 9-¾-3-20 RACE RPR: 107+/90/98+
Racecheck: Wins 1 (1) Pl 3 Unpl 6

19 Nov 06 Towcester 2m3½f Cls5 Ch £3,253
10 ran SOFT 14fncs Time 5m 30.60s (slw 39.60s)
1 Carnt Spell 5 10-5 ....Adam Hawkins (7) 12/1
2 Ask The Umpire 11 10-12 b ....Henry Oliver 10/1
3 Clockers Corner 9 10-5 ....Mr A Merriam (7) 20/1
P **PAUNTLEY GOFA** 10 10-5 James White (7) 50/1
led to 8th, weakened after 3 out, pulled up before next [OR91]
Dist: 5-5-13 RACE RPR: 85+/77/74+
Racecheck: Wins 1 (1) Pl 1 Unpl 14

Star Galaxy 10-0

7-y-o *b g Fourstars Allstar - Raven Night (Mandalus)*

M A Doyle Jamie Moore

Placings: 9/0P07PU9P-025P464F5

OR63 H72	Starts	1st	2nd	3rd	Win & Pl
Chase	11	–	1	–	£1,407
All Jumps races	19	–	1	–	**£1,407**

GF-HRD 0-0-3 **GS-HVY** 0-1-13 **Course** 0-0-3 **Dist** 0-0-6

29 Mar Hereford 3m1½f Cls5 58-84 Ch Hcap £3,253
8 ran GD-FM 19fncs Time 6m 24.00s (slw 12.00s)
1 Back In Business 7 11-12 .....Paul Moloney 3/1F
2 Mountsorrel 8 10-0 oh6 ....Dave Crosse 7/1
3 Young Cuthbert 9 11-2 t ...Richard Hobson 14/1
5 **STAR GALAXY** 7 9-12 ow2 ...S P Walsh (5) 4/1
held up and behind, shortlived effort 12th
[RPR37 TS23 OR61] [op 11/2]
Dist: 24-6-1¼-6 RACE RPR: 100+/54+/70+
Racecheck: Wins - Pl 1 Unpl 2

27 Feb Leicester 2m4½f Cls5 Nov 61-87 Ch Hcap £2,928
10 ran SOFT 12fncs Time 5m 28.40s (slw 31.40s)
1 Surfboard 6 11-12 ....Mark Bradburne 9/1
2 Ballyaahbutt 8 10-1 b ....S P Jones (5) 7/4F
3 Mountsorrel 8 10-0 oh1 ....Dave Crosse 66/1
F **STAR GALAXY** 7 9-9 oh2 Tom Messenger (5) 9/1
prominent, chased leader 5th, close 2nd when fell 3 out. [OR61] [op 11/1]
Dist: 2-35-9-23 RACE RPR: 103+/81+/39
Racecheck: Wins 2 (2) Pl 3 Unpl 7

15 Feb Chepstow 2m½f Cls5 64-90 Ch Hcap £3,569
9 ran HEAVY 12fncs Time 4m 29.40s (slw 27.40s)
1 All Sonsilver 10 10-7 ....Derek Laverty (5) 16/1
2 Femme d'Avril 5 10-3 Andrew Glassonbury (5) 7/4F
3 Caislean Na Deirge 9 11-12 ....Paul Moloney 5/1
4 **STAR GALAXY** 7 9-9 oh5 ...S P Walsh (5) 14/1
behind, ridden and stayed on from 3 out but never going pace to reach leaders
[RPR66 TS58 OR64] [op 16/1 tchd 12/1]
Dist: ½-7-7-1-8 RACE RPR: 93/88+/100+
Racecheck: Wins 1 (1) Pl 2 Unpl 9

11 Jan Hereford 2m Cls5 66-88 Ch Hcap £2,602
9 ran HEAVY 12fncs Time 4m 23.70s (slw 32.70s)
1 Milton Des Bieffes 7 11-4 ..Tom Malone (3) 3/1F
2 **THIEVES'GLEN** 9 11-6 ....Andrew Tinkler 7/1
led to 6th, chased winner, kept on same pace flat [RPR92 TS89 OR82] [op 13/2 tchd 8/1]
3 Brigadier Du Bois 8 11-4 .....Leighton Aspell 4/1
4 **STAR GALAXY** 7 9-13 .Tom Messenger (5) 17/2
prominent until weakened after 4 out
[RPR56 TS46 OR66] [op 9/1 tchd 8/1]
Dist: 2½-11-9 RACE RPR: 97+/92/81+
Racecheck: Wins 1 (1) Pl 1 Unpl 7

Form Reading	**SCANIA CLASSIC**
Spotlight	Tongue tie fitted for the first time but only finished one of his five starts under rules.
Handicap Ratings	Mark of 67 for handicap chase debut (last outing) when unseated. Mark of 63 for today's outing, which puts it 9lbs out of the weights.
Significant Items of Form	Six year old whose placings record reads OF-PPU. Ran at today's course (Hereford) on 26.02.07 in a very similar contest to today's race, a Class 5 Handicap Chase over 2m on Soft, when weakened at the 4th and unseated at the last. Previous two contests on 13.01.07 at Kempton (Good to Soft) in a Class 2 Novice Chase over 2m 'tailed off from 6th, pulled up before last' and on 16.12.06 at Haydock (Heavy) in a Class 4 Novice Hurdle over 2m4f 'always behind, pulled up before 2 out' were both singularly unimpressive.
Verdict	Being out of the weights is not a problem, but poor form is.
Decision:	DISMISS.

Form Reading	**WOT NO CASH**
Spotlight	Hasn't been seen since pulling up in a Selling Handicap Chase at Chepstow a year ago when returning from another lengthy lay off.
Handicap Ratings	Allocated a mark of 83 four outings ago (placed 5th), down to a mark of 72 for last outing (pulled up) and reduced still further to a mark of 66 today, which gives it a weight of 10st 3lbs.
Significant Items of Form	Fifteen year old whose last run on 18.04.06 was in a Selling Handicap Chase (Class 5) at Chepstow over 2m3½f (Good) where 'weakened 6th and pulled up before 4 out'. Run prior to that was on 12.09.04 in a Class 4 Handicap Chase at Hexham (Good to Firm) over 2m4½f where 'weakened 9th, pulled up before 2 out'.
Verdict	Very unlikely to see a fifteen year old stage a remarkable comeback on first outing after twelve months lay off.
Hence:	DISMISS.

Form Reading	**PAUNTLEY GOFA**
Spotlight	Fourth in a better contest over course and distance last March was a reasonable effort, now 18lb lower.
Handicap Ratings	Mark of 97 six outings ago (placed 4th) which was down to a mark of 84 for last outing (placed 6th). Mark of 79 for today's race, which puts it 18lb lower than six outings ago.
Significant Items of Form	Eleven year old with one Class 3 Novice Chase victory over 2m1½f at Market Rasen (Good to Firm), June 2002 and two hurdle wins at Ludlow (2m, Class 3, Good to Firm) and Market Rasen (2m1½f, Class 4, Good), both in 2001. Last three runs, on 19.11.06, 07.12.06 and 12.01.07, have all been in Chases on right hand tracks, on either Soft or Good to Soft going, and over either 2m3½f (once) or 2m½f (twice). Although pulled up in the first two of those last three runs, it finished its last race on 12.01.07 6th of 7 runners, beaten 73½ lengths, 'held up, behind from 6th'.
Verdict	Having regard to Spotlight comment that horse was '4th in a better contest over

C&D last March, is now 18lb lower' and having regard also to the fact that horse finished its last race on Soft going, albeit a long way behind, there is a case for optimism. The horse's wins and form show it likes Good to Firm going, right hand tracks and a distance of 2m, all of which it will get today at Hereford, where it has previously run four times, with one top three placing. The trainer has given his charge a three month break and the handicapper has given it a real chance to perform in what is a very low grade contest. Top three placing must be a good possibility.

Hence: SELECT.

Form Reading	**STAR GALAXY**
Spotlight	Poor maiden whose most recent run was over 3m2f.
Handicap Ratings	On a mark of 66 five outings ago (placed 4th) which was down to 61 for last outing (placed 5th). Mark of 63 for today's race, which puts it 13lbs out of the weights.
Significant Items of Form	Seven year old with no wins but a record of some consistency in its most recent campaign from 11.01.07 to 29.03.07 that has consisted of four Class 5 Handicap Chases and placings of 4th of 9 (Hereford, Heavy, 2m); 4th of 9 (Chepstow, Heavy, 2m½f); Fell 3 out (Leicester, Soft 2m4½f); and 5th of 8 (Hereford, Good to Firm, 3m1½f) latest. In its last race at Hereford, 22 days ago, although 5th of 8, it was only beaten 37¼ lengths over a distance of 3m1½f and given race report stated 'held up and behind short lived effort 12th', there is a distinct possibility that it will provide a better account of itself over a shorter distance.
Verdict	The fact that horse is 13lbs out of the handicap is far less important than what its recent form has been like. Trainer has obviously decided the horse likes Hereford and the fact that he is dropping it back in distance to 2m could be significant. Its last run at Hereford on Good to Firm was the first time in four outings that it had handled anything better than Soft conditions, so assuming the ground suited its last run, improvement could be expected today. Top three placing is a reasonable possibility.
Hence:	SELECT.

Overall Comment

The key to cracking this contest was identifying the fact that Pauntley Gofa was thrown in at the weights if it could only reproduce its previous form.

Spotting the fact that it had been running on Soft ground in its last three runs when it really wanted Good or Good to Firm, meant you knew that it had been given its ideal conditions at last. The fact that it made all, rode away from the paper favourite approaching the last and won by 10 lengths says it all. Star Galaxy also performed well, finishing 4th at 18 lengths.

The forecast of Pauntley Gofa with Bullitree Bob paid £114.00 for the Tote Exacta and £78.53 for the Computer Straight Forecast.

EXAMPLE 32

23.04.07 Sedgefield – Good to Firm – Class 5 – Handicap Chase – 2m½f
Winner CHUKCHI COUNTRY – 40/1

7.40 RACE 5
Racecourse Video Services Handicap Chase (Class 5) **ATR**
Winner £3,485.90 **2m½f**

£5500 guaranteed For 5yo+ Rated 0-85 Minimum Weight 10-0 Penalties after April 14th, a winner of a chase 7lb Bolshoi Ballet's Handicap Mark 85 Entries 32 pay £10 Penalty value 1st £3,485.90 2nd £1,029.60 3rd £514.80 4th £257.40 5th £128.70

1 8560699 **BOLSHOI BALLET** 40 [D] p 9 11-12
b g Dancing Spree-Broom Isle Michael O'Connell(7)
Miss J E Foster The Golden Syndicate

2 5-P5375 **KNOCK DAVRON** (IRE) 14 p 8 11-8
ch g Beneficial-Chestnut Shoon Mr P Callaghan(7) 93
W Storey V Thompson

3 0498560 **LERIDA** 21 [D] 5 11-7
ch g Groom Dancer-Cataionia Peter Buchanan
Miss Lucinda V Russell D G Pryde

4 4-P3F32 **JIMMYS DUKY** (IRE) 82 [BF] 9 11-5
b g Duky-Harvey's Cream Dougie Costello(3) 94
D M Forster D M Forster

5 5-POP5P **CHUKCHI COUNTRY** (IRE) 104 b 9 11-1
b g Arctic Lord-Ann's Queen J L Cullen 87
J J Lambe (IRE) J P Kearney

6 00P/2P2 **SEA COVE** 8 [BF] 7 11-0
b m Tarimon-Regal Pursuit Tony Dobbin
G A Swinbank James Bousfield

7 P56P-P6 **PUCKS COURT** 116 10 10-11
b g Nomadic Way-Miss Puck P J McDonald(5)
I A Brown W Brown

8 PP4P9 **DOUBLE PAST** 21 5 10-11
b g Yaheeb-Gale Blazer Mr R Wakeham(7) 50
P Beaumont Percy's Punters

9 0P20754 **BARNEY** (IRE) 14 [BF] 6 10-11
b g Basanta-Double Or Nothing Michael McAlister(3)
Mrs E Slack A Slack

10 46P0876 **DELAWARE TRAIL** 37 t 8 10-11
b g Catrail-Dilwara Kenny Johnson 100
R Johnson Toon Racing

11 F80PPPP **SPORTULA** 14 b 6 10-10
b m Silver Patriarch-Portent Gary Berridge(3)
B Storey B Storey & T Hunter

12 U3FP-PP **LA SOURCE A GOLD** (IRE) 39 8 10-9
br g Octagonal-Coral Sound Andrew Tinkler
P C Haslam Mrs Alurie O'Sullivan

13 0-06836 **TUDOR OAK** (IRE) 60 5 10-7
b g Woods Of Windsor-Techeo David Cullinane(7) 91
Mark Campion Wolfracing UK

14 0-8703P **VILLA MARA** (IRE) 111 7 10-5
b g Alflora-Claudia Dilwara Miss L Horner(7)
G Brown Miss L Horner

15 P-87PPP **FLASHY FILLY** 199 p 7 10-2
b m Puissance-Tempted Ewan Whillans(7)
J C Haynes J C Haynes

16 P8735UU **THEONEBEHIND** (IRE) 247 (16P) v1 7 10-0
b g Wercraft-Kelly's Bridge Brian Hughes(5) 72
J W F Aynsley Heads Or Harps Syndicate

LONG HANDICAP: Theonebehind 9-13

2006 (11 ran) Drumossie R C Guest 6 10-6 15/2 Kenny Johnson OR79

BETTING FORECAST: 3 Barney, 100-30 Jimmys Duky, 4 Sea Cove, 10 Knock Davron, 12 Delaware Trail, 14 Lerida, Villa Mara, 16 Pucks Court, 25 Bolshoi Ballet, Tudor Oak, 33 Chukchi Country, Double Past, La Source A Gold, Theonebehind, 50 Flashy Filly, Sportula.

SPOTLIGHT

Bolshoi Ballet On a losing run Flat and jumps, unable to cash in on sliding handicap mark in either sphere; stiff task when last of seven only attempt over fences almost two years ago; effective on good to firm and usually wears headgear of some description (has won in cheekpieces).

Knock Davron Winning pointer in Ireland but no success in that sphere or, more recently, in novice chases in Britain; this will be less demanding, acts on good to firm and possible first-time cheekpieces will bring about some improvement.

Lerida Unplaced 10 attempts over hurdles, tried over further and dropped to selling company latterly, since gaining only success on good ground last season; no obvious reason for confidence on chasing debut.

Jimmys Duky Exposed maiden over fences, in good form but found wanting off lower marks at up to 2m4f in December/January; most form on soft surface but probably acts on good to firm, should run his race and be thereabouts.

Chukchi Country Irish challenger whose only win from 46 attempts was more than two years ago; offered no encouragement at 25-1 last two outings in Britain and has to show he handles firmer than good.

Sea Cove Poor maiden plater on the Flat and over hurdles; recent efforts reflect preference for good/good to firm, second off this mark at Market Rasen latest, and should be involved if proving equally effective over fences.

Pucks Court Ageing maiden plater over hurdles; bit below par in December after six months off; another absence since but will appreciate quicker ground here.

Double Past Lightly raced; no worthwhile form at big odds over hurdles/fences.

Barney Both hurdling wins on this course last May/June and creditable effort back here recently more than three months off; pulled up last season only try over fences but that was on unsuitably soft ground and handicapper taken a chance allotting him a mark 15lb lower than over hurdles.

Delaware Trail Tried on the Flat, in points, over hurdles and fences but remains a maiden after 33 starts; latest run (over hurdles) was respectable by his standards but not hard to look elsewhere; acts on good to firm.

Sportula Poor maiden; failed to complete eight of 13 attempts over hurdles/fences, pulled up in seven (reportedly bled from nose on chasing debut latest).

La Source A Gold Outclassed and tailed-off last of three only completed chases.

Tudor Oak Maiden; well held off 6lb higher in selling company last hurdles start; remote both outings over fences but out of depth and this at least is more realistic.

Villa Mara Poor in bumpers and over hurdles for Sylvester Kirk, coming up short off this mark in selling company over longer distances last twice.

Flashy Filly Unplaced in 16 outings in bumper and over hurdles.

Theonebehind Firm-ground maiden point winner a year ago but nothing to recommend him since; pulled up in maiden company only attempt over hurdles.

VERDICT Dire stuff and few that can be seriously considered. The handicapper has taken a chance with **BARNEY** who will find conditions more suitable than on his only previous start over fences.[FC]

LAST SIX OUTINGS-LATEST ON RIGHT						7.40 HANDICAP	TODAY	FUTURE	LATEST / BEST / ADJUSTED		
—	—	—	—	—	—	Bolshoi Ballet 11-12	85		—	—	—
—	—	—	—	—	—	Knock Davron 11-8	81		37	93	93
—	—	—	—	—	—	Lerida 11-7	83		—	—	—
—	67P	74³	73F	71³	73²	Jimmys Duky 11-5	78		91 ◄	91	94
81⁵	—	—	—	94⁵	79P	Chukchi Country 11-1	74		—	61	87
—	—	—	—	—	—	Sea Cove 11-0	73		—	—	—
—	—	—	—	—	—	Pucks Court 10-11	70		—	—	—
—	—	—	—	—	80⁹	Double Past 10-11	73		50	50	50
—	—	—	—	—	—	Barney 10-11	70		—	—	—
79⁶	76P	—	—	—	—	Delaware Trail 10-11	70		—	100 ◄	100 ◄
—	—	—	—	—	—	Sportula 10-10	69		—	—	—
—	—	86P	81P	73F	La Source A Gold 10-9		68		—	—	—
—	—	—	—	—	—	Tudor Oak 10-7	69		80	91	91
—	—	—	—	—	—	Villa Mara 10-5	64		—	—	—
—	—	—	—	—	—	Flashy Filly 10-2	61		—	—	—
—	—	—	—	—	66⁷	Theonebehind 9-13	59 -1		—	72	72

Sportula 10-10

6-y-o b m Silver Patriarch - Portent (Most Welcome)
B Storey — Gary Berridge (3)

Placings: 3/P52PP-F80PPPP

OR69 H69	Starts	1st	2nd	3rd	Win & Pl
Chase	1	-	-	-	-
All Jumps races	13	-	1	1	£1,750

GF-HRD 0-0-2 GS-HVY 0-2-10 Course 0-0-1 Dist 0-0-1

9 Apr Sedgefield 2m4f Cls4 Ch £3,803
9 ran GD-FM 14fncs Time 5m 1.90s (slw 15.90s)
1 Bestofthebrownies 6 11-2 ......P J Brennan 5/4F
2 Mr Twins 6 10-13 t ....Michael McAlister (3) 11/1
3 Imtihan 8 11-2 ....David O'Meara 2/1
5 KNOCK DAVRON 8 10-11 ....
.......................Mr M Thompson (5) 11/1
*prominent, challenged 5th to 7th, weakened
from 9th* [RPR31 TS11 OR81]
P SPORTULA 6 10-6 p .....Gary Berridge (3) 66/1
*chased leaders, lost place 6th, struggling when
pulled up before 9th (jockey said mare led
from the nose)* [OR69]   [op 50/1]
Dist: 7-5-nk-54-31   RACE RPR: 104+/90/85
Racecheck: Wins 1 (1) Pl - Unpl -

27 Feb Catterick 2m3f Cls5 63-82 Sell Hdl Hcap £2,056
13 ran HEAVY 10hdls Time 5m 6.00s (slw 38.00s)
1 Minster Abbi 7 10-7 p ......Miss J Riding (7) 5/1J
2 Frankincense 11 10-10 Miss Angela Barnes (7) 7/1
3 Square Dealer 6 10-12 v Miss S Sharratt (7) 28/1
P SPORTULA 6 10-8 p ......Miss J Foster (7) 33/1
*chased leaders, mistake 3rd, soon lost place
and behind, pulled up before 2 out*
[OR72]   [op 40/1]
P SEA COVE 7 10-11 ...Miss S Brotherton (5) 5/1J
*towards rear, hit 4th, soon ridden along and
behind from 7th, pulled up before 2 out (jockey
said gelding was unsuited by the heavy (soft in
places) ground)* [OR73]   [op 4/1]
Dist: 3½-13-16-12-17 RACE RPR: 82+/81/71+
Racecheck: Wins 2 (2) Pl 4 Unpl 6

17 Jan Newcastle 2m4f Cls5 69-95 Cond Sell Hdl Hcap
£1,757
10 ran SOFT 10hdls Time 5m 33.60s (slw 50.60s)
1 Over To Joe 7 10-0 b1 oh5 ....Phil Kinsella 14/1
2 College City 8 11-3 p ......David Cullinane (3) 5/1
3 Baligrundle 7 10-0 ....Brian Hughes 33/1
P SPORTULA 6 10-6 b1 .....Gary Berridge (3) 20/1
*led to 4 out, soon weakened, pulled up before
next* [OR78]   [op 16/1]
Dist: 1¼-7-27-2-11   RACE RPR: 73/92/67+
Racecheck: Wins Pl 3 Unpl 7

29 Sep 06 Hexham   Fell, see FLASHY FILLY

Flashy Filly 10-2

7-y-o b m Puissance - Tempted (Invited)
J C Haynes — Ewan Whillans (7)

Placings: PP0/P070477P-87PPP

OR61 H61	Starts	1st	2nd	3rd	Win & Pl
All Jumps races	16	-	-	-	£262

GF-HRD 0-0-6 GS-HVY 0-0-6 Course 0-0-3 Dist 0-0-9

6 Oct 06 Carlisle 2m4f Cls5 Nov 64-90 Hdl Hcap £2,741
13 ran GD-SFT 9hdls Time 5m 26.50s (slw 37.50s)
1 Nicozetto 6 10-5 ow1 ....Dale Jewett (5) 12/1
2 My Good Lord 7 11-12 p ....T J O'Brien 5/2F
3 Loscar 7 10-4 ....Brian Harding 11/2
P FLASHY FILLY 6 9-13 p ow2 oh3 ....
.....................Michael McAlister (3) 100/1
*always behind, tailed off when pulled up before
last* [OR64]   [op 66/1]
Dist: 7-5-3-5-5   RACE RPR: 85+/94+/68+
Racecheck: Wins 3 (3) Pl 4 Unpl 12

29 Sep 06 Hexham 2m4½f Cls4 Nov Hdl £3,220
8 ran GD-FM 10hdls Time 5m 1.20s (slw 8.20s)
1 Delray Beach 4 11-3 ....G Lee 17/2
2 Another Jameson 6 10-7 ...T J Dreaper (3) 10/1
3 Rising Tempest 5 10-7 ......Joffret Huet (3) 25/1

F SPORTULA 5 10-7 ....Gary Berridge (3) 33/1
close up, disputing 2nd when fell 3 out
[OR90]   [op 25/1]
P FLASHY FILLY 6 10-7 e/s1 ....
...................Michael McAlister (3) 100/1
*took keen hold, led to 5th, close up until
weakened 3 out, tailed off when pulled up
before last* [OR61]
Dist: 2½-3½-hd-1½-20 RACE RPR: 92+/83/81+
Racecheck: Wins - Pl 4 Unpl 9

28 Aug 06 Cartmel 2m6f Cls4 Nov Hdl £3,578
5 ran GD-SFT 11hdls Time 5m 42.90s (slw 28.90s)
1 Solway Sunset 7 10-7 ....Dale Jewett (5) 5/2
2 Paint The Lily 5 10-12 ....Paddy Aspell 8/1
3 Dunguaire Lady 7 11-5 t Richard McGrath EvensF
P FLASHY FILLY 6 10-9 Michael McAlister (3) 25/1
*led, blundered 7th, soon headed, weakened
quickly next, tailed off when pulled up before 3
out* [OR61]   [op 20/1]
Dist: 1-1½-48   RACE RPR: 91+/87/92
Racecheck: Wins - Pl 1 Unpl 7

Theonebehind 10-0

7-y-o b g Warcraft - Kelly's Bridge (Netherkelly)
J W F Aynsley — Brian Hughes (5)

Placings: PPP/721-90P8735UU

OR59	Starts	1st	2nd	3rd	Win & Pl
Chase	4	-	-	-	-
All Jumps races	5	-	-	-	-

GF-HRD 0-0-3 GS-HVY 0-0-1 Course 0-0-1 Dist 0-0-1

7 Apr Alnwick (PTP) 3m   Memb Hunt
7 ran FIRM   Time 6m 8.00s
1 Floritchel 10 12-4 ....C Gillon 4/6F
2 Know The Ropes 7 12-0 ....R Green 6/1
3 Jupiter Jo 11 12-0 ....T Oates 5/2
U THEONEBEHIND 7 12-0 ....A Nicol 7/1
trckd ldr; led 8 til ur 15
Dist: nk-15-8
Racecheck: Wins - Pl - Unpl -

31 Mar Friars Haugh (PTP) 3m   Rest
1 Battle Of Song 7 12-5 ....D Halley 5/2F
2 Nimbu 7 12-5 ....A Findlay 3/1
3 Half Of Nothing 11 12-5 ....A Richardson 4/1
U THEONEBEHIND 7 12-5 p ....A Nicol 6/1
bhnd til ur 7
Dist: 10-2½-8-3-20
Racecheck: Wins - Pl - Unpl -

17 Mar Friars Haugh (PTP) 3m   Mens Open
7 ran GOOD   Time 7m 5.00s
1 Natiain 8 12-5 ....M Ellwood 4/9F
2 Albatros 10 12-5 ....H Trotter 10/1
3 Garden Feature 9 11-12 ....T Oates 6/1
5 THEONEBEHIND 7 12-5 ....A Nicol 33/1
a bhnd
Dist: 5-20-6-3-10
Racecheck: Wins 2 Pl - Unpl 1

Rules Form

19 Aug 06 Market Rasen 3m1f Cls5 64-93 Ch Hcap
£3,578
9 ran GD-SFT 17fncs Time 6m 27.20s (slw 21.20s)
1 Mollycarrsbrekfast 11 10-3 ....P J Brennan 7/1
2 Luckycharm 7 9-4 oh7 J W Stevenson (10) 11/1
3 Fibre Optics 6 12-1 p ......Mick FitzGerald 5/1
7 THEONEBEHIND 6 10-2 b1 ..Paddy Aspell 33/1
behind when hit 8th, tailed off from 12th
btn 83 lengths [RPR- TS2 OR66]
Dist: 3½-2-6-nk-hd-49 RACE RPR: 84+/72/95
Racecheck: Wins - Pl 2 Unpl 7

La Source A Gold 10-9

8-y-o br g Octagonal - Coral Sound (Glow)
P C Haslam — Andrew Tinkler

Placings: B/4P/U3FP-PP

OR68	Starts	1st	2nd	3rd	Win & Pl
All Jumps races	6	-	-	1	£1,619

GF-HRD 0-0-1 GS-HVY 0-0-4 Course 0-0-0 Dist 0-0-2

15 Mar Hexham 2m4½f Cls5 68-94 Ch Hcap £3,083
12 ran SOFT 12fncs Time 5m 43.60s (slw 43.60s)
1 Loscar 8 10-0 ....Brian Harding 12/1
2 Mister Magnum 9 9-12 ...David Da Silva (7) 11/2
3 Seymar Lad 7 11-8 ....Russ Garritty 8/1
P LA SOURCE A GOLD 8 10-0 ....
......................Willie McCarthy (5) 16/1
*in touch, lost place 8th, tailed off when pulled
up before 2 out* [OR73]   [tchd 20/1]
Dist: 10-nk-1-4-12.   RACE RPR: 82+/75/94+
Racecheck: Wins - Pl 1 Unpl 7

8 Nov 06 Lingfield 2m4½f Cls5 66-90 Ch Hcap £2,602
15 ran GOOD 14fncs Time 5m 5.80s (slw 0.80s)
1 The Hardy Boy 6 10-2 ....Henry Oliver 66/1
2 Myson 7 11-10 ....Jamie Moore 100/30F
3 Beluga 7 11-4 ......Robert Lucey-Butler (5) 10/1
P LA SOURCE A GOLD 7 10-10 ....
......................Willie McCarthy (7) 25/1
*waited with in midfield, hampered 1st, ridden
and struggling 8th, tailed off and pulled up 3 out*
[OR81]   [op 33/1 tchd 50/1]
Dist: 9-1¼-21-1¾-5   RACE RPR: 83+/99+/94+
Racecheck: Wins 4 (4) Pl 3 Unpl 14

15 Apr 06 Newton Abbot 2m½f Cls4 86-109 Ch Hcap
£5,205
7 ran GD-FM 13fncs Time 3m 58.70s (slw 3.70s)
1 Wild Power 8 10-7 ....Owyn Nelmes (3) 9/2
2 Jupon Vert 9 10-10 ....Tom Scudamore 9/1
3 O'Toole 7 11-12 ....Richard Johnson 13/8F
P LA SOURCE A GOLD 9 10-10 ow3 ....
.....................Willie McCarthy (7) 8/1
*towards rear, lost touch 8th, tailed off and pulled
up before 2 out* [OR86]   [op 16/1]
Dist: ½-1¾-5-12   RACE RPR: 100/100/116+
Racecheck: Wins 2 (2) Pl 2 Unpl 7

Double Past 10-11

5-y-o b g Yaheeb - Gale Blazer (Strong Gale)
P Beaumont — Mr R Wakeham (7)

Placings: PP4P9

OR73	Starts	1st	2nd	3rd	Win & Pl
Chase	2	-	-	-	-
All Jumps races	5	-	-	-	£119

GF-HRD 0-0-0 GS-HVY 0-0-4 Course 0-0-0 Dist 0-0-0

2 Apr Kelso 2m1f Cls4 74-100 Ch Hcap £4,554
12 ran GOOD 12fncs Time 4m 16.40s (slw 8.40s)
1 Insurgent 5 10-7 p ....David Cullinane (7) 7/1
2 Yankee Holiday 7 10-9 ...Mark Bradburne 4/1F
3 Darnley 10 10-3 ow2 ....Gerry Supple 14/1
9 DOUBLE PAST 5 10-3 ....Anthony Ross 33/1
always behind, no chance from halfway
btn 48 lengths [RPR33 TS24 OR80]
Dist: 3-1-7-9-1   RACE RPR: 93+/88+/77
Racecheck: Wins - Pl 1 Unpl 2

15 Mar Hexham 2m½f   Cls3 Nov Ch £5,855
8 ran SOFT 11fncs Time 4m 28.20s (slw 28.20s)
1 Lankawi 5 11-3 ....T J O'Brien 11/8F
2 Torkinking 8 10-13 t ..Michael McAlister (3) 11/4
3 Andre Chenier 6 11-2 ....Wilson Renwick 10/1
P DOUBLE PAST 5 10-4 Mr R Wakeham (7) 100/1
in touch, mistake 4th, soon outpaced,

5 Feb Hexham 2m½f   Cls5 Mdn Hdl £1,627
10 ran SOFT 6hdls Time 4m 42.20s (slw 43.20s)
1 Bedlam Boy 6 11-3 ....Tony Dobbin 8/13F
2 Ocarina 5 11-0 ....Gary Berridge (3) 9/2
3 Dawn Ride 6 11-3 ....Wilson Renwick 40/1
4 DOUBLE PAST 5 10-10 Mr R Wakeham (7) 100/1
held up, outpaced before 2 out, never on terms
[RPR66]
Dist: 18-7-12-14-23   RACE RPR: 115+/85/78
Racecheck: Wins 1 (1) Pl 1 Unpl 9

Chukchi Country 11-1

9-y-o b g Arctic Lord - Ann's Queen (Rhoman Rule)
J J Lambe (IRE) — J L Cullen

Placings: 44FP0/06306005-P0P5P

OR74 H78		Starts	1st	2nd	3rd	Win & Pl
Chase		22	1	–	1	£9,161
All Jumps races		44	1	1	3	£12,731
88 11/04 Thur 2m2f 72-96 Ch Hcap yield						£7,299
GF-HRD 0-0-3 GS-HVY 1-4-37 Course 0-0-1 Dist 0-2-22

9 Jan Sedgefield 2m4f Cls5 71-95 Ch Hcap £2,602
10 ran HEAVY 16fncs Time 5m 28.40s (slw 42.40s)
1 Cloudmor 6 11-8 ....Keith Mercer 7/4F
2 Marshall Hall 6 11-2 ....G Lee 9/2
3 JIMMYS DUKY 9 10-2 ......Richard McGrath 2/1
chased leaders, challenged 2 out, upsides
when hit last, faded [RPR82 TS78 OR71] [op 5/2]
P CHUKCHI COUNTRY 9 10-7 b P C O'Neill (3) 25/1
chased leaders, lost place 12th, behind when
pulled up before 3 out [OR79] [op 16/1]

Dist: 1¼-2½-41-26-17 RACE RPR: 105+/97/82+
Racecheck: Wins 2 {2} Pl 4 Unpl 9

21 Sep 06 Perth 2m Cls3 94-120 Ch Hcap £6,506
6 ran SOFT. 12fncs Time 4m 11.60s (slw 17.60s)
1 Jaìlastep 9 10-2 ....Richard McGrath 3/1
2 South Bronx 7 11-12 t ....Mark Bradburne 9/2
3 Jefertiti 9 10-3 ....Peter Buchanan 2/1F
5 CHUKCHI COUNTRY 8 10-0 tb oh9 ....
....Tom Siddall 25/1
held up in touch, effort 8th, outpaced next, not
fluent 3 out, soon beaten
[RPR48 TS28 OR94] [op 16/1]
Dist: hd-1½-41-13 RACE RPR: 105/129/105
After a stewards' inquiry, the placings remained unaltered
Racecheck: Wins 2 Pl 2 Unpl 6

13 Sep 06 Sligo 2m2f 74-92 Hdl Hcap £3,812
16 ran SOFT Time 4m 43.60s (slw 19.60s)
1 Jigalo 5 11-7 p ....D N Russell 11/8F
2 Royal Mount Loftus 7 10-12 ....T G M Ryan 16/1
3 The Wrens Nest 7 10-11 ....A E Lynch (5) 12/1
P CHUKCHI COUNTRY 8 10-3 b ....
....Miss J A Kidd (7) 20/1
led, slight mistake 3rd and soon headed, slight
mistake next, remained prominent, lost place
after next, pulled up before 2 out [OR79]
Dist: 1½-hd-3-½-1¼ RACE RPR: 98/88/91
Racecheck: Wins 2 Pl 5 Unpl 12

Form Reading	**SPORTULA**
Spotlight	Poor maiden; failed to complete eight of thirteen attempts over hurdles/fences.
Handicap Ratings	No handicap chase ratings.
Significant Items of Form	Six year old whose last seven placings read F80PPPP. Of last four runs only most recent was in a Class 4 Chase at today's course (Sedgefield) where struggled from 6th before pulling up from before 9th (bled from the nose).
Verdict	No cause for optimism.
Hence:	DISMISS.

Form Reading	**FLASHY FILLY**
Spotlight	Unplaced in sixteen outings in bumper and over hurdles.
Handicap Ratings	No handicap chase ratings.
Significant Items of Form	Seven year old whose last five placings read 87PPP. Last three runs in August, September and October 2006 were in Class 4 Novice Hurdles and a Class 5 Novice Handicap Hurdle (latest) and all gave no indication of future improvement.
Verdict	Based on what it's shown so far, a run of promise in today's chase would be amazing.
Hence:	DISMISS.

Form Reading	**THE ONE BEHIND**
Spotlight	Firm ground maiden point winner a year ago but nothing to recommend him since.
Handicap Ratings	Mark of 66 for last National Hunt outing, a Class 5 Handicap Chase over 3m1f at Market Rasen (Good to Soft) on 19.08.06 when 7th of 9, beaten 83 lengths. Down to a mark of 59 for today's contest, which leaves it 1lb out of the weights.
Significant Items of Form	Seven year old whose last three outings at least have been in Point to Points, the best of which was its last run on 07.04.07 in a 3m contest at Alnwick where it led from the 8th to the 15th before unseating.
Verdict	It if cannot make at least some impression in Point to Points it should have very little chance in today's contest.
Hence:	DISMISS.

Form Reading	**LA SOURCE A GOLD**
Spotlight	Out classed and tailed off last of three only completed chases.
Handicap Ratings	Mark of 86 three outings ago (pulled up) down to 73 last outing (also pulled up). Mark of 68 for today's contest.
Significant Items of Form	Eight year old whose last six placings read U3FP-PP. Last two runs on 08.11.06 and 15.03.06 were in Class 5 Handicap Chases at Lingfield (2m4½f, Good, struggling 8th, pulled up 3 out) and Hexham, latest (2m4½f, Soft, tailed off 8th, pulled up before 2 out).
Verdict	Horse could benefit from reduced distance but difficult to see sufficient improvement to achieve top three placing.
Hence:	DISMISS.

Form Reading	**DOUBLE PAST**
Spotlight	Lightly raced; no worthwhile form at big odds over hurdles/ fences.
Handicap Ratings	Mark of 80 for last outing (placed 9th) which was only handicap chase outing in last six races.
Significant Items of Form	Five year old whose placings to date read PP4P9. Looking at last three races: On 05.02.07 was 4th of 10, beaten 37 lengths, in a Class 5 Maiden Hurdle at Hexham (Soft) over 2m½f 'held up, outpaced before 2 out, never on terms'. On 15.03.07 also at Hexham (Soft) was pulled up approaching last in a Class 3 Novice Chase over 2m½f when lying a distant 5th. On 02.04.07 at Kelso (Good) in a Class 4 Handicap Chase over 2m1f was 9th of 12, beaten 48 lengths, after being always behind.
Verdict	Form reads like a five year old learning the ropes and though finished last race, (a Handicap Chase), no positive indication that it is ready to compete for a top three place in a chase quite yet.
Hence:	DISMISS.

Form Reading	**CHUKCHI COUNTRY**
Spotlight	Irish challenger whose only win in 46 attempts was more than two years ago. Offered no encouragement at 25/1 last two outings in Britain, has to show he handles firmer than good.
Handicap Ratings	Mark of 81 six outings ago (placed 5th) which was raised to 94 for next handicap chase two outings ago (placed 5th). Down to a mark of 79 for next (most recent) race (pulled up). Down still further to a mark of 74 today, which seems to indicate a very lenient approach by the handicapper.
Significant Items of Form	Nine year old Irish trained horse with one win in a 72 to 96 rated Handicap Chase at Thurles in Ireland over 2m2f on yielding going in November 2004. Last run in Ireland was on 13.09.06 at Sligo (Soft) over 2m2f when pulled up in a 74 to 92 rated Handicap Hurdle. Next run on 21.09.06 was in Britain at Perth (Soft) in a Class 3 Handicap Chase over 2m where 5th of 6, beaten 55½ lengths, after being in touch and making an effort at the 8th. Next and most recent run on 09.01.07 was in a Class 5 Handicap Chase at today's course (Sedgefield) on Heavy over 2m4f when chased leaders before lost place 12th and pulled up before 3 out.

Verdict The form items of most significance are: the fact that it finished its Class 3 Handicap Chase at Perth after making an effort at the 8th; the fact that it was given a three month break before being given a serious try out at today's course when it was probably below full race fitness; the horse has now been given another break of fifteen weeks and, in consideration of the saying 'beware the Irish Raider', you've got to work on the basis than an improved performance should be expected. And finally, the horse has had three previous runs on Good to Firm – Hard and therefore you have to assume that such going will suit, otherwise why would its trainer have made today's decision to run? Assuming only half the above observations/assumptions are correct, a place in the first three has got to be a reasonable possibility.

Hence: SELECT.

Overall Comment

Chukchi Country's victory has been included in the race examples because, although Irish Raider wins are fairly common, it is quite surprising how often the form of the winner is disguised to an extent, where the vast majority of punters are wrong footed and a big priced winner results.

This particular race is a good example of such a situation occurring and I must make the point that I am no longer surprised when indifferent Irish form is found to be sufficient to capture British races even if they are in the lowest classes. One other point that is worth making is the fact that once again the winner is a horse which has been able to demonstrate the benefits of previous course experience.

For the record, the Forecast Chukchi Country with Barney the paper favourite paid £656.20 for the Tote Exacta and £153.20 for the Computer Straight Forecast.

EXAMPLE 33

14.04.07   Aintree – Good – Class 1 – Handicap Chase – The Grand National – 4m4f
Winner   SILVER BIRCH – 33/1

OFFICIAL RATINGS LAST SIX OUTINGS-LATEST ON RIGHT						4.15 HANDICAP	TODAY	FUTURE	RP RATING LATEST / BEST / ADJUSTED		
—	—	—	156²	—	—	Hedgehunter	11-12 158	+8	—	—	170
—	125⁴	122¹	135¹	148ᴾ	147¹	Eurotrek	11-8 154	+4	173◄	173◄	173◄
—	—	—	—	—	—	L'Ami	11-8 154		168	169	169
—	—	167³	—	—	—	Monkerhostin	11-6 152	+8	172	172	172
—	157ᶠ	—	157⁵	—	—	Thisthatandtother	11-5 151	+4	156	167	167
—	141⁹	140ᵁ	140⁵	139¹	—	Billyvoddan	11-4 150	+5	170	170	170
—	—	138¹	—	—	—	Numbersixvalverde	11-3 149	-2	150	150	165
—	144⁴	142²	144⁶	—	—	Idle Talk	11-2 148		—	167	167
159⁰	156⁶	—	150⁷	—	143⁶	Royal Auclair	11-1 147		135	170	170
—	—	—	—	—	—	Cloudy Bays	11-0 146	+1	—	160	163
138ᶠ	138²	142²	—	148⁸	—	Knowhere	10-13 145		144	168	168
130³	133¹	139³	144⁹	139²	139ᴾ	Kelami	10-12 144	-5	159	165	165
—	—	136ᴮ	136¹	—	—	Point Barrow	10-12 144	-2	—	165	165
—	—	—	144²	146⁰	143ᴾ	Celtic Son	10-11 143	-3	—	—	167
121¹	130⁵	127²	130⁶	132¹	143¹	Simon	10-11 143	+9	172	172	172
146²	146⁰	145ᴾ	144⁵	—	140⁰	Ballycassidy	10-9 141	-3	—	171	171
—	—	140³	—	143ᶠ	143ᴾ	Clan Royal	10-9 141	-1	—	—	170
120¹	—	132⁵	132¹	137³	141⁷	Gallant Approach	10-9 141	-2	154	163	163
—	—	—	133²	—	141⁰	Livingstonebramble	10-9 141	-2	144	165	165
137⁷	—	138ᶠ	—	—	—	Dun Doire	10-8 140	-3	164	164	164
149⁴	—	—	136⁷	132¹	140⁰	Kandjar d'Allier	10-8 140	-2	87	162	165
—	—	—	—	140ᶠ	140⁵	Slim Pickings	10-8 140	+2	167	167	167
—	—	141⁹	140²	—	140²	Zabenz	10-8 140		165	165	165
—	—	—	140⁴	138²	139⁹	Bewleys Berry	10-7 139	-1	131	167	167
126ᴾ	124¹	133⁴	137⁶	133⁷	130¹	Longshanks	10-7 139		161	161	161
120⁵	121¹	127¹	136⁵	—	140ᴾ	Bothar Na	10-6 138	-2	—	167	167
132¹	140⁶	140³	139⁵	139³	138ᵁ	Graphic Approach	10-6 138		—	167	167
—	—	127⁰	125ᶠ	125¹	—	Homer Wells	10-6 138	+4	166	166	166
132⁸	130¹	139⁴	141⁴	—	138⁹	Liberthine	10-6 138	-1	147	164	164
—	142ᶠ	142⁸	—	—	138²	Silver Birch	10-6 138	+4	170	170	170
133ᴾ	128²	131¹	138ᴾ	138⁶	137⁸	Philson Run	10-5 137	-1	148	148	166
142⁰	134⁵	—	131²	137⁷	135ᴾ	Puntal	10-5 137	-5	—	165	165
114¹	125ᴿ	125²	129¹	137ᴾ	137ᴾ	The Outlier	10-5 137		—	171	168
—	146⁸	150⁰	139⁴	138⁴	137⁰	Tikram	10-5 137	-1	153	166	166
131²	131⁴	130¹	138⁷	137⁶	—	McKelvey	10-4 136		—	167	170
119¹	126¹	131⁵	135³	136⁰	136ᴾ	Naunton Brook	10-4 136	-1	—	168	168
—	141⁰	137⁰	133⁴	135⁷	—	Jack High	10-3 135	+3	167	167	167
142ᴾ	140⁰	136⁵	—	—	—	Sonevafushi	10-3 135	-5	123	153	163
—	140⁷	137⁶	134⁷	131⁸	130¹	Joes Edge	10-2 134	+5	166	166	168
138ᵁ	140ᵁ	—	136⁷	134⁴	134³	Le Duc	10-2 134		157	162	170

SPOTLIGHT THE POST'S HORSE-BY-HORSE ASSESSMENT

1 Hedgehunter   11-1

Winner of this in 2005 and second to Numbersixvalverde last year, when overnight rain counted against him (handy 9lb pull now); weighted to be a major player if at his best after knee problem has restricted him to two runs over hurdles since; drying weather a help and, with his accurate jumping such a plus, high on the shortlist.
3m+ chase wins: 4;
Fell/unseated/refused (F/U/R): 1

2 Eurotrek   16-1

Has had leg, heart and blood vessel problems at one time or another, hence he has managed only 11 career starts; won five of them, including Becher Chase in clear-cut style here in November; 7lb rise makes things tougher and far from sure that the quicker ground will be in this fragile sort's favour.
3m+ chase wins: 4; F/U/R: 0

3 L'Ami   16-1

Ran Kauto Star close at Newbury two starts back and can be excused latest defeat in somewhat muddling race for the Cheltenham Gold Cup; old jumping frailties seem to have been eradicated with experience, and a staying-on effort over 3m4f at Auteuil in November 2005 suggests stamina ought not to be an issue and weighted to go very well for Tony McCoy if showing best in first-time cheekpieces.
3m+ chase wins: 2;
Fell/unseated/refused F/U/R: 3

4 Monkerhostin   25-1

Back to something close to his classy best on return from a break when staying-on fourth in the Gold Cup last time, again raising hopes that extreme trip will be within range; fairly weighted, too, and couldn't be ruled out, provided jumping, which is still prone to the odd blunder, holds up.
3m+ chase wins: 1;
Fell/unseated/refused F/U/R: 1

5 Thisthatandtother   66-1

Not quite the force of old this season on return from a year off and seemed a non-stayer at 3m1f once (longest trip he has tried), so stamina is a massive issue.
3m+ chase wins: 0;
Fell/unseated/refused F/U/R: 2

6 Billyvoddan   14-1

Improved for the recent fitting of blinkers, coming on again when close third in Ryanair Chase last time (5lb well-in here); has claims on that but stamina very much to prove on first try beyond 3m1f, while this will be only his tenth chase and, at age of eight, it's possible this may come too soon.
3m+ chase wins: 1;
Fell/unseated/refused F/U/R: 1

7 Numbersixvalverde   12-1

Proven marathon runner, winning 2005 Irish National and also taking this race last year; trained with this race in mind since, while proven stamina and jumping ability are notable pluses, but 11lb rise since last year makes for stiffer task and is well suited by plenty of give, so needs to show he is as effective on quicker surface.
3m+ chase wins: 4;
Fell/unseated/refused F/U/R: 0

8 Idle Talk   16-1

Thorough stayer who quickly made up into useful sort in first season over fences last term but strong suspicion things will happen too quickly for him on drying surface here, looks weighted up to the hilt and, having unseated in last two outings, confidence a concern.
3m+ chase wins: 2;
Fell/unseated/refused F/U/R: 2

9 Royal Auclair   33-1

Fine second to runaway winner Hedgehunter in this in 2005 but though drying ground is a plus for him, he doesn't seem as good as he was and it'll be a surprise if he can figure anything like as prominently this time.
3m+ chase wins: 2;
Fell/unseated/refused F/U/R: 4

10 Cloudy Bays   66-1

Not quite the horse he was and big doubts as to whether this race will suit, untried beyond 3m1f (though should stay further) and with these fences to negotiate (eight falls over jumps, including over hurdles last time).
3m+ chase wins: 3;
Fell/unseated/refused F/U/R: 5

11 Knowhere   80-1

Novice whose second, splitting top-class chasers, in big 2m5f Cheltenham handicap in December reads very well but form has tailed off since, jumping less than fluently, and lot to prove upped dramatically in trip over these fences.
3m+ chase wins: 0;
Fell/unseated/refused F/U/R: 1

12 Kelami   33-1

On a high enough mark but fair bit going for him otherwise, back to form at Auteuil last time, having shaped as if extreme trip can prove within range, ground fine and basically a sound jumper (one fall in 28 chases).
3m+ chase wins: 2;
Fell/unseated/refused F/U/R: 1

13 Point Barrow   9-1

Proved his effectiveness in big-field marathon when taking last season's Irish National (good) and every bit as good this time round, winning useful Leopardstown handicap in January and running highly promising prep for this over hurdles last time; sound jumper (yet to fall or unseat in 16 chases) and all set fair for very bold bid.
3m+ chase wins: 5;
Fell/unseated/refused F/U/R: 0

14 Celtic Son   100-1

Looked a potential star when easy winner of a Grade 2 on last season's chase debut but hasn't gone on from that in six starts since, pulled up on belated seasonal debut in February; 3m has seemed upper limit of stamina range.
3m+ chase wins: 0;
Fell/unseated/refused F/U/R: 0

15 Simon   14-1

Stepped up significantly in bagging big handicaps in two latest outings, last time off same mark as today when grinding his way to ultimately clear-cut success in the Racing Post Chase in February; officially 9lb well-in but tendency to make a serious mistake a definite concern here and suited by lot of give, so needs to prove he is as effective on much quicker surface.
3m+ chase wins: 4;
Fell/unseated/refused F/U/R: 0

16 Ballycassidy   50-1

Didn't show much spark back from a winter break on ground (as today) that ought to have suited last time; however, was still in front when falling six out on unsuitably soft ground in this last year (also unseated at the second in 2005), so not entirely without hope.

3m+ chase wins: 6;
Fell/unseated/refused F/U/R: 3

17 Clan Royal 22-1

Mostly fine record over these fences, two placed runs in this, including a third last year; however, clear signs that age has caught up with him and no surprise that Tony McCoy has jumped ship for L'Ami.

3m+ chase wins: 1;
Fell/unseated/refused F/U/R: 1

18 Gallant Approach 50-1

Quickly made up into decent handicapper over fences but stamina to prove beyond 3m and thrown in at the deep end after only six chase runs.

3m+ chase wins: 2;
Fell/unseated/refused F/U/R: 0

19 Livingstonebramble 66-1

Much better jumper nowadays but bit to prove overall, easier ground probably ideal, untried beyond 3m and good midwinter form tailing off of late.

3m+ chase wins: 0;
Fell/unseated/refused F/U/R: 3

20 Dun Doire 14-1

Interesting on his improved form in 2006, notably when staying on well for an unlikely win at the Cheltenham Festival; however, laboured effort when winning his prep race for this back over fences at Down Royal last month and definite concern he will lack the pace to hold a competitive position on drying surface here; fell in Becher Chase here in November.

3m+ chase wins: 4;
Fell/unseated/refused F/U/R: 1

21 Kandjar D'Allier 50-1

Useful handicapper but weighted up to best, bit more give suits, 3m has seemed limit of stamina range and though a better jumper of late, this will be a big test for him.

3m+ chase wins: 1;
Fell/unseated/refused F/U/R: 3

22 Slim Pickings 28-1

Useful novice last season who has run

two promising races for new stable of late and not a forlorn hope if stamina lasts on first try beyond 3m on ground he handles, provided jumping (two falls in 12 chase runs, including on penultimate start) holds up.

3m+ chase wins: 1;
Fell/unseated/refused F/U/R: 2

23 Zabenz 40-1

Sound enough jumper and goes on the ground but stamina very much to prove beyond 3m1f and also weighted up to best.

3m+ chase wins: 1;
Fell/unseated/refused F/U/R: 1

24 Bewleys Berry 22-1

Exuberant round of jumping from the front when eventually second in the Becher Chase here in November and can be excused latest defeat in a heavy-ground slog; could go well for a long way, though will be entering uncharted waters stamina-wise over the last mile.

3m+ chase wins: 2;
Fell/unseated/refused F/U/R: 0

25 Longshanks 22-1

Delicate sort who has made the track only twice in last two years and runs off career-high mark; far from fully exposed over fences, though, and showed an affinity for the track when making frame twice in the Topham; shaped as if an extreme trip may well be within range, so interesting for a trainer/jockey who have tasted success separately in this.

3m+ chase wins: 2;
Fell/unseated/refused F/U/R: 0

26 Bothar Na 18-1

Improved to pick up two useful handicaps in Ireland late last summer but lost his way afterwards, significant jumping errors creeping in; unproven beyond 3m1f and not easy to fancy.

3m+ chase wins: 4;
Fell/unseated/refused F/U/R: 2

27 Graphic Approach 50-1

Decent second-season handicapper at up to 3m but weighted up to best, far from sure he will last extreme trip and jumping was chancy before unseating when tried in blinkers (left off now) last time, so highly speculative.

3m+ chase wins: 2;
Fell/unseated/refused F/U/R: 2

28 Homer Wells 28-1

Fell three starts back but generally a sound jumper and in fine form when last seen out, taking Fairyhouse Grade 2 on heavy on disadvantageous terms (three of these behind); ground here will be vastly different and opposable.

3m+ chase wins: 3;
Fell/unseated/refused F/U/R: 1

29 Liberthine 25-1

Took last season's Topham over these fences under this young amateur rider but doubts about current form and stamina (3m5f seemed bit too far in last season's Betfred Gold Cup).

3m+ chase wins: 0;
Fell/unseated/refused F/U/R: 1

30 Silver Birch 25-1

Took 2004 Becher Chase here for Paul Nicholls and out of sorts last season (fell at the Chair in this) on return from a year off with leg injury; back to form in soft/heavy ground cross-country chases of late but this demands more, while quicker ground an issue.

3m+ chase wins: 4;
Fell/unseated/refused F/U/R: 1

31 Philson Run 50-1

Has two important marathons in his trophy cabinet but this fragile sort is suited by lots of give and fell at the first in one previous try over these fences, so doubts as to whether this will suit.

3m+ chase wins: 4;
Fell/unseated/refused F/U/R: 1

32 Puntal 80-1

Not easy to predict nowadays and quite possible his mood will take exception to all the hullabaloo but has shown up well in two previous tries in this, last year fading into distant sixth back from 16 months off the track; race-fit this time and not totally impossible he could take a hand.

3m+ chase wins: 1;
Fell/unseated/refused F/U/R: 2

33 The Outlier 100-1

Good run of form on favoured testing ground in midwinter and strong chance he will have the necessary stamina but seems to have gone off the boil and ground against him.

3m+ chase wins: 1;
Fell/unseated/refused F/U/R: 1

34 Tikram 66-1

Capable handicapper at up to around 3m but prone to the odd mistake and big doubt about his jumping around here over a trip likely to be beyond him; blinkers left off.

3m+ chase wins: 0;
Fell/unseated/refused F/U/R: 0

35 McKelvey 14-1

Jumping not always the best (has had back trouble) but jumped these fences well when sixth in the Becher Chase in November; stays extreme trips, goes on the ground and decent prep for this when winning over hurdles back from a break last time, so possibilities.

3m+ chase wins: 3;
Fell/unseated/refused F/U/R: 2

36 Naunton Brook 66-1

Thorough stayer looked to be feeling the effects of tough season with below-par efforts in last two runs and opposable in first-time blinkers off high enough mark on ground quicker than ideal.

3m+ chase wins: 4;
Fell/unseated/refused F/U/R: 0

37 Jack High 25-1

In-and-out of late and recent fitting of blinkers reinforces the suspicion that he has good days and bad days into veteran stage; sound jumper despite unseating in this last year and, with extreme trip/decent ground no problem, would have a chance on pick of this season's form.

3m+ chase wins: 3;
Fell/unseated/refused F/U/R: 4

38 Sonevafushi 150-1

Just a fairly useful hunter chaser nowadays; probably needs to dominate and this is likely to be altogether too competitive for him.

3m+ chase wins: 4;
Fell/unseated/refused F/U/R: 0

39 Joes Edge 7-1

Sounder jumper nowadays, two clear rounds over these fences to his name, including when seventh on unsuitably slow ground in this last year; 2005 Scottish National winner was back to form with a vengeance in top Cheltenham handicap last time and very much one to consider under National-winning rider.

3m+ chase wins: 2;
Fell/unseated/refused F/U/R: 1

40 Le Duc 50-1

Twice placed in competitive handicaps at shorter trips here but Canal Turn has caused him problems on latest two visits, recent form in cross-country chases leaves him vulnerable and stamina to prove.

3m+ chase wins: 0;
Fell/unseated/refused F/U/R: 5

Sonevafushi 10-3

9-y-o *b g Ganges - For Kicks (Top Ville)*
Miss Venetia Williams Mr T Greenall

Placings: 1213303/P311PP0-5129

OR135 H129	Starts	1st	2nd	3rd	Win & Pl
Chase	20	6	3	4	£55,614
All Jumps races	42	8	7	7	£92,490

	2/07	Winc	3m1½f Cls6 Am Hunt Ch gd-sft	£1,648
132	1/06	Tntn	3m3f Cls3 109-132 Ch Hcap gd-sft	£7,807
125	1/06	Newb	3m Cls3 99-125 Ch Hcap gd-sft	£6,506
	12/04	Wwck	3m½f Cls3 Nov Ch soft	£10,140
	11/04	Hayd	2m6f Cls3 Nov Ch soft	£10,917
	10/04	Font	2m6f Cls4 Ch gd-sft	£3,994
	5/02	Sthl	2m4½f Cls4 Hdl good	£2,667
	1/02	Newb	2m½f Cls3 Nov Hdl 4yo gd-sft	£4,180

Total win prize-money £47,859

GF-HRD 0-0-3 GS-HVY 7-6-26 Course 0-0-0 Dist 0-0-0

16 Mar Cheltenham 3m2½f Cls2 Hunt Ch £24,008
24 ran GD-SFT 22fncs Time 6m 46.60s (slw 7.60s)
1 Drombeag 9 12-0 p ....Mr J T McNamara 20/1
2 Whyso Mayo 10 12-0 ....Mr D Murphy 2/1F
3 Ned Kelly 11 12-0 ....Mr K E Power 20/1
9 **SONEVAFUSHI** 9 12-0 ....Mr T Greenall 16/1
prominent, led 5th, headed 12th, ridden after 15th, weakened after 3 out
btn 36 lengths [RPR98 TS98 OR132]
Dist: ½-15-1½-nk-5 RACE RPR: 134+/139+/120+
Racecheck: Wins - Pl - Unpl 8

13 Feb Folkestone 3m1f Cls6 Am Hunt Ch £1,648
4 ran HEAVY 18fncs Time 6m 56.50s (slw 49.50s)
1 Honourable Spider 8 12-4 ......Mr P Bull (3) 17/2
2 **SONEVAFUSHI** 9 12-7 ....Mr T Greenall 4/6F
reluctant to line up or race, rousted to lead 2nd, headed 13th, readily outbattled by winner from 3 out [RPR117 TS70 OR135] [op 8/13 tchd 8/11]
3 Knife Edge 12 12-7 p ....Mr A J Berry 15/8
Dist: 2-22 RACE RPR: 118+/117+/96+
Racecheck: Wins - Pl - Unpl 3

1 Feb Wincanton 3m1½f Cls6 Am Hunt Ch £1,648
8 ran GD-SFT 21fncs Time 6m 42.30s (slw 24.30s)
1 **SONEVAFUSHI** 9 12-7 ....Mr T Greenall 7/4F
prominent, led 4th until 10th, tracked leaders, ridden to lead 3 out, driven out
[RPR133 TS112 OR135][op 15/8 tchd 2/1 & 13/8]
2 Back Nine 10 12-0 ....Miss P Gundry 14/1
3 Risk Accessor 12 12-4 ......Mr A J Berry (3) 11/4
Dist: 1¼-3-7-19-4 RACE RPR: 133+/123/129+
Racecheck: Wins 2 (2) Pl 7 Unpl 3

6 May 06 Uttoxeter 3m Cls2 119-146 Ch Hcap £12,526
8 ran GD-FM 18fncs Time 6m 9.70s (slw 23.70s)
1 Sir Rembrandt 10 11-12 ....Andrew Thornton 9/2
2 See You Sometime 11 10-7 ....Wayne Kavanagh (7) 8/1
3 Gumley Gale 11 10-0 t oh1 .....R J Greene 28/1
4 **BALLYCASSIDY** 10 11-13 ......A P McCoy 2/1F
chased leaders, shaken up 6th, soon driven, hit 10th, lost place 12th, rallied 2 out, kept on
[RPR150 TS68 OR146] [op 7/4]
5 **SONEVAFUSHI** 8 11-3 b ......Sam Thomas 20/1
led, went clear after 14th, weakened 3 out, headed approaching next, stopped to nothing
[RPR128 TS47 OR136] [op 14/1]
Dist: hd-2-3-13-51 RACE RPR: 155+/142/127+
Racecheck: Wins 1 (1) Pl 4 Unpl 7

19 Apr 06 Cheltenham 3m1½f Cls2 114-140 Ch Hcap £12,526
17 ran GOOD 21fncs Time 6m 29.50s (slw 10.50s)
1 Sweet Diversion 7 11-2 t ....R Walsh 9/2F
2 Parsons Legacy 8 10-10 ....P J Brennan 16/1
3 Fork Lightning 10 11-7 .....Robert Thornton 15/2
14 **SONEVAFUSHI** 8 11-12 .....Sam Thomas 33/1
hit 7th and 11th, always in rear
btn 58 lengths [RPR92 TS80 OR140]
16 **NAUNTON BROOK** 7 10-11 t Tony Evans 11/1
always behind, tailed off from 15th
btn 69 lengths [RPR66 TS55 OR125][tchd 12/1]
Dist: 6-5-2½-4-shd RACE RPR: 144+/129+/136+
Racecheck: Wins 1 (1) Pl 6 Unpl 23

18 Feb 06 Wincanton 3m1½f Cls1 List 126-144 Ch Hcap £28,644
9 ran SOFT 21fncs Time 6m 45.50s (slw 27.50s)
1 All In The Stars 8 10-7 ....Daryl Jacob (5) 8/1
2 **CELTIC SON** 7 11-10 t ......Tom Scudamore 8/1
held up, hit 15th, headway next, led after 4 out, soon ridden, headed soon after 2 out, no extra
[RPR148 TS98 OR144]
3 Horus 11 10-12 v ....R J Greene 33/1
P **SONEVAFUSHI** 8 11-8 ....Sam Thomas 8/1
led until 3rd, chased leader until 14th, soon weakened, pulled up before 4 out
[OR142] [op 7/1]
P **SILVER BIRCH** 9 11-8 ....Joe Tizzard 2/1F
in touch, mistake 9th, dropped to rear 12th, soon lost touch, pulled up before 16th (trainer was unable to explain the poor run)
[OR142] [tchd 7/4]
Dist: 7-4-dist-dist RACE RPR: 141+/148+/130
Racecheck: Wins 1 (1) Pl 1 Unpl 16

The Outlier 10-5

9-y-o *gr g Roselier - Shuil A Cuig (Quayside)*
Miss Venetia Williams P C O'Neill

Placings: /4433/U21183-41O21PP

OR137 H107	Starts	1st	2nd	3rd	Win & Pl
Chase	13	4	2	1	£67,379
All Jumps races	19	4	3	3	£70,327

129	1/07	Hayd	3m Cls1 Gd2 127-147 Ch Hcap heavy	£42,765
114	11/06	Towc	2m6f Cls4 98-114 Ch Hcap heavy	£6,397
107	2/06	Towc	2m3½f Cls4 89-115 Ch Hcap soft	£6,338
	1/06	Folk	2m5f Cls4 Mdn Ch gd-sft	£3,904

Total win prize-money £59,404

GF-HRD 0-0-0 GS-HVY 4-4-13 Course 0-0-0 Dist 0-0-0

17 Mar Uttoxeter Pulled Up, see **PUNTAL**

17 Feb Haydock Pulled Up, see **PHILSON RUN**

20 Jan Haydock 3m Cls1 Gd2 127-147 Ch Hcap £42,765
9 ran   HEAVY   16fncs   Time 6m 44.80s (slw 44.80s)
1 **THE OUTLIER** 9 10-3 ....P C O'Neill (3) 8/1
always prominent, mistake 9th (water), led after 4 out, ridden approaching 2 out, stayed on well to draw clear run-in (jockey received three-day ban: used whip with excessive frequency (Jan 31, Feb 1-2)) [RPR148 TS148 OR129]
2 Turpin Green 8 11-10 ....Tony Dobbin 11/2
3 Truckers Tavern 12 10-4 t .....David O'Meara 14/1
Dist: 12-2-11-2½-6 RACE RPR: 148+/154+/132+
Racecheck: Wins 1 Pl 4 Unpl 6

30 Dec 06 Haydock 3m Cls3 99-125 Ch Hcap £16,265
8 ran   HEAVY   18fncs   Time 6m 54.40s (slw 54.40s)
1 Sharp Belline 9 10-10 ....David O'Meara 14/1
2 **THE OUTLIER** 8 11-12 ....Sam Thomas 15/2
held up, headway 8th, headway 12th, ridden to chase winner approaching 2 out, every chance last, kept on under pressure run-in
[RPR139 TS103 OR125] [op 8/1]
3 King Bee 9 11-2 ....Mark Bradburne 7/2
Dist: 2-37-37-10 RACE RPR: 126+/139/92
Racecheck: Wins 2 (2) Pl - Unpl 12

13 Dec 06 Newbury 3m2½f Cls3 117-129 Ch Hcap £9,759
7 ran   SOFT   21fncs   Time 7m 0.40s (slw 25.40s)
1 Latimer's Place 10 11-8 ....S E Durack 8/1
2 Kerstino Two 9 11-7 ....Mr J Snowden (5) 3/1F
3 Tanterari 8 11-7 t ....Timmy Murphy 9/2
O **THE OUTLIER** 8 11-8 ....Sam Thomas 7/2
in touch, hit 12th, chasing leaders when hit 16th, ridden to challenge from 4 out until ran out next [OR125] [op 100/30 tchd 3/1]
Dist: 16-29-shd RACE RPR: 140+/126+/91
Racecheck: Wins 2 (2) Pl 2 Unpl 6

25 Nov 06 Towcester 2m6f Cls4 98-114 Ch Hcap £6,397
5 ran   HEAVY   11fncs   Time 6m 4.40s (slw 37.40s)
1 **THE OUTLIER** 8 11-9 ....P C O'Neill (3) 5/1
made all, ridden clear approaching last, stayed on well [RPR143 TS112 OR109] [op 11/2]
2 What'sonyourmind 6 10-3 ....J W Farrelly 7/2
3 Fill The Bunker 6 10-13 .Wayne Hutchinson 9/4J
Dist: 30-¹⁄₂-nk RACE RPR: 143+/97/100
Racecheck: Wins - Pl 4 Unpl 5

Celtic Son   10-11

8-y-o b g Celtic Arms - For Kicks (Top Ville)
D E Pipe   Timmy Murphy
Placings: 5812111123P/124420-P

OR143	H138		Starts	1st	2nd	3rd	Win & Pl
Chase			7	1	2	-	£35,312
All Jumps races			23	7	4	1	£82,478
11/05	Winc	2m5f Cls1 Nov Gd2 Ch good ...£19,957
2/05	Kemp	3m1½f Cls3 Nov Hdl gd-sft £4,983
121 1/05	Wwck	3m1f Cls2 109-135 Hdl Hcap soft £14,019
105 1/05	Nowb	3m1½f Cls4 84-110 Cond Hdl Hcap gd-sft
							£3,780
105 1/05	Tntn	3m1½f Cls4 83-105 Hdl Hcap gd-sft £3,965
98 1/05	Extr	2m6½f Cls4 Nov 74-100 Hdl Hcap gd-sft
							£3,850
2/03	Thur	2m NHF 4yo sft-hvy £3,584
		Total win prize-money £54,138

3F-HRD 0-0-1   GS-HVY 6-3-12   Course 0-0-0   Dist 0-0-0

24 Feb Kempton 3m Cls1 Gd3 124-150 Ch Hcap £57,020
10 ran   SOFT   18fncs   Time 6m 42.34s (slw 42.34s)
1 **SIMON** 8 11-5 ....Andrew Thornton 11/2
in rear, headway 9th, went 2nd 11th, hit next, lost 2nd 4 out, headway and hampered approaching next, led approaching 2 out, hit rails run-in, driven out
[RPR155 TS122 OR143] [op 6/1]
2 Cornish Sett 8 11-7 b ....R Walsh 25/1
3 Lacdoudal 8 11-12 ....Richard Johnson 8/1
7 **PUNTAL** 11 10-13 tp ....A P McCoy 16/1
chased leader, challenged 7th to 9th, lost place under pressure 12th, never in contention after btn 32 lengths [RPR116 TS86 OR137]
P **CELTIC SON** 8 11-5 t ....Timmy Murphy 8/1
hit 10th, always towards rear, tailed off when pulled up before 15th
[OR143] [op 7/1 tchd 13/2]
Dist: 10-¹⁄₂-2-13-2¹⁄₂ RACE RPR: 155+/146/152+

---

16 Mar 06 Cheltenham 2m5f Cls1 Nov List 126-146 Ch Hcap £45,616
18 ran   GOOD   17fncs   Time 5m 5.00s (fst 3.00s)
1 Reveillez 7 10-11 ....A P McCoy 9/2F
2 Copsale Lad 9 11-0 ....Mick FitzGerald 8/1
3 Tumbling Dice 7 11-1 p ....B J Geraghty 14/1
14 **CELTIC SON** 7 11-10 tp ...Timmy Murphy 14/1
not fluent 7th, always behind
btn 90 lengths [RPR70 TS73 OR146] [tchd 16/1]
Dist: 1¹⁄₄-9-shd-7-1³⁄₄ RACE RPR: 150+/149/142+
Racecheck: Wins 5 Pl 9 Unpl 19

18 Feb 06 Wincanton 3m1¹⁄₂f Cls1 List 126-144 Ch Hcap £28,644
9 ran   SOFT   21fncs   Time 6m 45.50s (slw 27.50s)
1 All In The Stars 8 10-7 ....Daryl Jacob (5) 8/1
2 **CELTIC SON** 7 11-10 t ......Tom Scudamore 8/1
held up, hit 15th, headway next, led after 4 out, soon ridden, headed soon after 2 out, no extra
[RPR148 TS98 OR144]
3 Horus 11 10-12 v ....R J Greene 33/1
P **SONEVAFUSHI** 8 11-8 ....Sam Thomas 8/1
led until 3rd, chased leader until 14th, soon weakened, pulled up before 4 out
[OR142] [op 7/1]
P **SILVER BIRCH** 9 11-8 ....Joe Tizzard 2/1F
in touch, mistake 9th, dropped to rear 12th, soon lost touch, pulled up before 16th (trainer was unable to explain the poor run)
[OR142] [tchd 7/4]
Dist: 7-4-dist-dist RACE RPR: 141+/148+/130
Racecheck: Wins 1 (1) Pl 1 Unpl 16

11 Jan 06 Newbury 2m1f Cls3 Nov Ch £7,807
6 ran   GD-SFT   13fncs   Time 4m 14.80s (slw 10.80s)
1 Justified 7 11-12 ....A P McCoy 8/13F
2 Cornish Sett 7 11-8 b ....Christian Williams 9/2
3 Hors La Loi III 11 11-12 ....D Gallagher 11/1
4 **CELTIC SON** 7 11-12 t ....Timmy Murphy 5/1
chased leaders, soon niggled along to go pace, lost touch after 8th [op 9/2]
Dist: 2¹⁄₂-7-dist-dist RACE RPR: 151+/144+/142+
Racecheck: Wins 2 (1) Pl 3 Unpl 5

10 Dec 05 Cheltenham 2m5f Cls2 Nov Ch £9,864
4 ran   GD-SFT   17fncs   Time 5m 19.40s (slw 11.40s)
1 Exotic Dancer 5 11-0 ....A P McCoy 4/1
2 BEWLEYS BERRY 7 11-5 ....G Lee 5/2
led until headed after 2 out, rallied and kept on gamely run-in to re-take 2nd last strides, no impression on winner
[RPR146 TS133] [op 9/4 tchd 11/4]
3 Albuhera 7 11-8 t ....Joe Tizzard 3/1
4 **CELTIC SON** 6 11-8 t ....Timmy Murphy 2/1F
disputed lead, hit 4 out and next, challenged after 3 out, ridden and soon beaten next, tailed off (trainer was unable to explain the poor form shown) [RPR134] [tchd 9/4 & 13/5]
Dist: 1¹⁄₄-hd-dist RACE RPR: 144+/146+/149+
Racecheck: Wins - Pl 2 Unpl 8

11 Nov 05 Cheltenham 3m1¹⁄₂f Cls2 Nov Ch £10,522
7 ran   GD-SFT   19fncs   Time 6m 41.80s (slw 36.80s)
1 Church Island 6 11-8 ....D F O'Regan 12/1
2 **CELTIC SON** 6 11-8 t ......Timmy Murphy 8/13F
held up in touch, not fluent 7th, headway 12th, hit 3 out, staying on when left 2nd and slightly hampered 2 out, ridden and found no extra run-in [RPR140 TS45] [op 4/7 tchd 4/6 & 1/2]
3 Red Georgie 7 11-5 ....Carl Llewellyn 10/1
Dist: 8-dist-dist RACE RPR: 146+/140+/116
Racecheck: Wins 1 Pl 2 Unpl 10

Puntal   10-5

11-y-o b g Bering - Saveur (Ardross)
D E Pipe   Tom Scudamore
Placings: 11415UU1/68/60-5527P

OR137	H142		Starts	1st	2nd	3rd	Win & Pl
Chase			26	5	4	-	£193,762
All Jumps races			43	11	8	2	£278,875
142 4/04	Sand	3m5½f Cls1 Gd3 121-147 Ch gd-fm
							£87,000
1/04	Asct	2m Cls3 Nov Ch soft £8,093
11/03	Newb	2m4f Cls1 Nov List Ch gd-sft ...£16,286
11/03	Chel	2m4½f Cls2 Nov Ch good £16,614
10/03	Chel	2m Cls3 Nov Ch gd-fm £10,603
2/03	Kemp	2m Cls1 Nov Gd2 Hdl good £17,400

135	7/02	MRas	2m1½f Cls2 113-135 Hdl Hcap gd-sft ....
			£23,200
5/02	Strf	2m½f Cls3 Nov Hdl gd-fm £4,323
5/02	Worc	2m Cls4 Nov Hdl good £2,709
5/02	Hrfd	2m1f Cls4 Nov Hdl good £3,189
5/02	Sthl	2m Cls3 Nov Hdl good £3,469
		Total win prize-money £192,886

GF-HRD 3-0-5   GS-HVY 3-9-24   Course 0-0-2   Dist 0-0-2

17 Mar Uttoxeter 4m1¹⁄₂f Cls1 List 122-148 Ch Hcap £57,020
18 ran   SOFT   24fncs   Time 9m 1.50s (slw 31.50s)
1 Baron Windrush 9 10-9 ....Jason Maguire 12/1
2 d'Argent 10 11-5 ....Robert Thornton 40/1
3 Newbay Prop 8 9-11 oh1 .R C Colgan (3) 11/2J
P **PUNTAL** 11 10-13 tp ....Timmy Murphy 33/1
disputed lead to 9th, weakened after 12th, tailed off when pulled up before 18th [OR135]
P **THE OUTLIER** 9 11-1 ....Sam Thomas 20/1
chased leaders, mistake 14th, weakened 6 out, tailed off when pulled up before 4 out
[OR137] [op 25/1]
Dist: 12-nk-12-3¹⁄₂-4 RACE RPR: 148+/145/127+
Racecheck: Wins - Pl 1 Unpl 2

24 Feb Kempton 3m Cls1 Gd3 124-150 Ch Hcap £57,020
10 ran   SOFT   18fncs   Time 6m 42.34s (slw 42.34s)
1 **SIMON** 8 11-5 ....Andrew Thornton 11/2
in rear, headway 9th, went 2nd 11th, hit next, lost 2nd 4 out, headway and hampered approaching next, led approaching 2 out, hit rails run-in, driven out
[RPR155 TS122 OR143] [op 6/1]
2 Cornish Sett 8 11-7 b ....R Walsh 25/1
3 Lacdoudal 8 11-12 ....Richard Johnson 8/1
7 **PUNTAL** 11 10-13 tp ....A P McCoy 16/1
chased leader, challenged 7th to 9th, lost place under pressure 12th, never in contention after btn 32 lengths [RPR116 TS86 OR137]
P **CELTIC SON** 8 11-5 t ....Timmy Murphy 8/1
hit 10th, always towards rear, tailed off when pulled up before 15th
[OR143] [op 7/1 tchd 13/2]
Dist: 10-¹⁄₂-2-13-2¹⁄₂ RACE RPR: 155+/146/152+
Racecheck: Wins - Pl - Unpl 5

20 Jan Wincanton 3m1¹⁄₂f Cls3 115-135 Ch Hcap £22,002
11 ran   SOFT   21fncs   Time 6m 50.80s (slw 32.80s)
1 Maletton 7 11-3 ex7 ....Sam Thomas 5/2F
2 **PUNTAL** 11 11-8 tp ....Timmy Murphy 8/1
prominent, led 4th to 15th, hampered by loose horse bend approaching 3 out, slightly hampered by loose horse last, rallied flat
[RPR142 TS119 OR131] [op 10/1]
3 Le Jaguar 7 10-11 tb ....Liam Heard (3) 10/1
Dist: ³⁄₄-20-13-5 RACE RPR: 137+/142+/111
Racecheck: Wins - Pl 3 Unpl 11

26 Dec 06 Kempton 3m Cls1 Gd1 Ch £114,040
9 ran   GD-SFT   18fncs   Time 6m 5.70s (slw 5.70s)
1 Kauto Star 6 11-10 t ....R Walsh 8/13F
2 Exotic Dancer 6 11-10 p ....A P McCoy 9/1
3 Racing Demon 6 11-10. ....Timmy Murphy 7/1
4 **MONKERHOSTIN** 9 11-10 Richard Johnson 14/1
held up in rear, progress 12th, not fluent 14th, driven and not always fluent next, well beaten from 3 out [RPR152 TS143 OR163] [op 16/1]
5 **PUNTAL** 10 11-10 t ....N P Madden 100/1
chased leading pair to 7th, soon ridden, dropped to last of main group 11th, soon well beaten, kept on again from 3 out
[RPR140 TS86 OR134]
P **BALLYCASSIDY** 10 11-10 .Nick Williams 100/1
dropped to last pair and struggling 6th, tailed off when jumped badly left 11th, pulled up before next [OR144]
Dist: 8-1¹⁄₄-20-9-14 RACE RPR: 180+/171+/169
Racecheck: Wins 4 (4) Pl 2 Unpl 6

8 Dec 06 Cheltenham   5th, see LIBERTHINE
29 Apr 06 Sandown   10th, see LIBERTHINE

8 Apr 06 Aintree 4m4f Cls1 Gd3 134-156 Ch Hcap £399,140
40 ran GD-SFT 30fncs Time 9m 41.00s (slw 27.00s)
1 NUMBERSIXVALVERDE 10 10-8 ....
....N P Madden 11/1
*held up, smooth headway 17th, soon tracking
leaders going well, led last, shaken up and
stayed on strongly to forge clear*
[RPR154 TS151 OR138] [tchd 12/1]
2 HEDGEHUNTER 10 11-12 ....R Walsh 5/1J
*with leaders, left in lead 25th (2nd Valentines),
headed last, no extra*
[RPR166 TS165 OR156] [op 11/2 tchd 6/1]
3 CLAN ROYAL 11 10-10 ....A P McCoy 5/1J
*held up, headway to chase leaders 17th,
blundered 19th, challenged 3 out, rallied to take
3rd on line* [RPR151 TS149 OR140] [op 11/2]
6 PUNTAL 10 10-12 t ....B J Geraghty 66/1
*chased leaders, weakened 23rd (2nd
Foinavon), kept on from 2 out* [RPR97 OR142]
7 JOES EDGE 9 10-10 ....D N Russell 20/1
*mid-division, headway 17th, mistake 19th, lost
place approaching 2 out*
btn 56+ lengths [RPR95 OR140] [tchd 25/1]
F ROYAL AUCLAIR 9 11-12 t Christian Williams 33/1
fell 1st [OR156]
F SILVER BIRCH 9 10-12 t .....Sam Thomas 40/1
in touch until hampered and fell 15th (Chair)
[OR142] [op 33/1]
U JACK HIGH 11 10-7 ....D J Casey 9/1
*in rear until blundered and unseated rider 15th
(Chair)* [OR137] [op 12/1]
U LE DUC 7 10-10 ....Jamie Moore 33/1
*mid-division, blundered, rider lost iron and
unseated rider 8th (Canal Turn)* [OR140]
F BALLYCASSIDY 10 10-9 ...Leighton Aspell 80/1
*prominent, led 9th (1st Valentines), 6 lengths
clear when fell 25th (2nd Valentines)* [OR139]
Dist: 6-1¼-shd-dist-16 RACE RPR:
154+/166+/151+
Racecheck: Wins 2 Pl 5 Unpl 53

Knowhere   10-13

9-y-o *b g Lord Americo - Andarta (Ballymore)*
N A Twiston-Davies Tom Doyle

Placings: 1/11/P-11F22380

OR**145**	Starts	1st	2nd	3rd	Win & Pl
Chase	9	2	2	1	£69,381
All Jumps races	11	4	2	1	£90,460
10/06	Bang	2m4½f Cls3 Nov Ch gd-sft £8,133
9/06	Prth	2m4½f Cls3 Nov Ch soft £6,506
10/04	Chep	2m4f Cls1 Nov Gd2 Hdl soft £17,400
10/04	Hexm	2m4½f Cls4 Nov Hdl good £3,679
		Total win prize-money £35,718
GF-HRD 0-0-0 GS-HVY 3-2-10 Course 0-0-0 Dist 0-0-0

14 Mar Cheltenham 3m1½f Cls1 Gd1 Ch £96,934
17 ran GD-SFT 19fncs Time 6m 6.80s (slw 14.40s)
1 Denman 7 11-4 ....R Walsh 6/5F
2 Snowy Morning 7 11-4 ......Mick FitzGerald 10/1
3 According To John 9 11-4 ....Tony Dobbin 66/1
12 KNOWHERE 9 11-4 ....Tony Evans 28/1
*chased leaders but blundered his way around,
weakened from 16th (jockey received two-day
ban: used whip when out of contention (Mar
25-26))*
btn 37 lengths [RPR129 TS127 OR145] [tchd
25/1]
Dist: 10-3½-nk-1½-4 RACE RPR: 165+/154+/151+
Racecheck: Wins - Pl - Unpl 4

27 Jan Cheltenham 2m5f Cls1 Gd3 124-150 Ch Hcap
£31,361
10 ran HEAVY 11fncs Time 5m 37.13s (slw 29.13s)
1 Whispered Secret 8 10-3 ....R J Greene 8/1
2 New Alco 6 11-1 ....G Lee 4/1
3 Idole First 8 10-12 ....Alan O'Keeffe 6/1
7 ROYAL AUCLAIR 10 11-9 t Liam Heard (3) 33/1
hit 5th and 7th, behind most of way
btn 24 lengths [RPR137 TS123 OR150][op 40/1]

8 KNOWHERE 9 11-10 ....Tony Evans 8/1
*blundered and in rear 1st, hit 4th, headway 7th,
weakened well before bypassed 2nd last*
btn 49 lengths [RPR107 TS94 OR148][tchd 17/2]

Dist: ½-3-1¾-3-3½ RACE RPR: 135+/147+/141+
Racecheck: Wins 1 (1) Pl 1 Unpl 10

26 Dec 06 Kempton 3m Cls1 Nov Gd1 Ch £40,102
6 ran GD-SFT 18fncs Time 6m 10.50s (slw 10.50s)
1 Ungaro 7 11-7 ....Mick FitzGerald 14/1
2 Boychuk 5 11-7 ....Richard Johnson 5/1
3 KNOWHERE 8 11-7 ....Tony Evans 5/1
*sometimes jumped left, tracked leader, led 9th,
driven and headed 3 out, beaten next, mistake
last* [RPR142 TS133 OR148] [op 4/1]
Dist: 10-5-13-35 RACE RPR: 155+/144+/142+
Racecheck: Wins - Pl 1 Unpl 9

9 Dec 06 Cheltenham 2m5f Cls1 Gd3 131-157 Ch
Hcap £85,530
12 ran SOFT 17fncs Time 5m 34.00s (slw 26.00s)
1 Exotic Dancer 6 11-4 p ....Tony Dobbin 8/1
2 KNOWHERE 8 10-11 ....Tony Evans 10/1
*chased leader, hit 6th, led 12th, hit next, mistake
4 out, ridden and hit 2 out, headed and not
fluent last, kept on gamely but always held by
winner*
[RPR153 TS148 OR142] [op 11/1 tchd 12/1]
3 Taranis 5 11-4 t ....R Walsh 3/1F
4 TIKRAM 9 10-8 ....Robert Thornton 14/1
*chased leaders, ridden from 3 out and stayed
on same pace*
[RPR139 TS136 OR139] [tchd 16/1]
5 THISTHATANDTOTHER 10 11-9 ....
....Liam Heard (3) 12/1
*chased leaders, ridden to dispute 2nd after 3
out, weakened from next*
[RPR157 TS154 OR157] [tchd 11/1]
Dist: 1½-3½-2-5-1-2-7 RACE RPR: 160+/153+/155+
Racecheck: Wins 5 (2) Pl 3 Unpl 8

18 Nov 06 Ascot 2m3f Cls1 Gd2 128-146 Ch Hcap
£39,914
9 ran SOFT 16fncs Time 4m 47.60s (slw 13.60s)
1 Cerium 5 11-8 ....Sam Thomas 12/1
2 KNOWHERE 8 10-11 .....Mr D England (5) 4/1J
*jumped left early, led until mistake and rider lost
iron 4th, led 8th until 11th, blundered 3 out, one
pace, left 2nd and beaten last*
[RPR147 TS132 OR138] [op 5/1]
3 Hoo La Baloo 5 11-5 ....Liam Heard (5) 20/1
5 BILLYVODDAN 7 11-4 .....Mark Bradburne 14/1
*towards rear, mistake 8th, ridden 9th, never
reached leaders*
[RPR127 TS113 OR140][op 11/1 tchd 12/1 & 9/1]
Dist: 3½-8-11-shd-4 RACE RPR: 154+/147+/144+
Racecheck: Wins 1 (1) Pl 4 Unpl 10

11 Nov 06 Cheltenham Fell, see GRAPHIC
APPROACH

Tikram   10-5

10-y-o *ch g Lycius - Black Fighter (Secretariat)*
A King Wayne Hutchinson

Placings: 12/7552461/2008-0440

OR**137**H135	Starts	1st	2nd	3rd	Win & Pl
Chase	22	4	5	–	£132,807
All Jumps races	42	6	9	4	£207,230
139	4/05	Sand	2m4½f Cls2 120-145 Ch Hcap good .....
			£15,614
133	3/04	Chel	2m4½f Cls1 Gd3 133-159 Ch Hcap good .....
			£43,500
	2/04	Font	2m4f Cls3 Nov Ch good £9,937
	1/04	Font	2m6f Cls4 Ch good £4,381
120	12/02	Font	2m2½f Cls3 100-121 Hdl Hcap good .....
			£12,087
	1/01	Donc	2m1½f Cls3 Nov Hdl 4yo good £6,305
			Total win prize-money £91,824
GF-HRD 0-2-3 GS-HVY 0-7-16 Course 0-0-0 Dist 0-0-0

15 Mar Cheltenham 2m5f Cls1 Gd3 129-155 Ch Hcap
£57,020
23 ran GD-SFT 17fncs Time 5m 11.40s (slw 3.40s)
1 Idole First 8 10-7 ....Alan O'Keeffe 12/1
2 Palarshan 9 10-5 p ....Richard Johnson 28/1
3 Mariah Rollins 9 10-7 ......Mick FitzGerald 20/1
5 SLIM PICKINGS 8 10-11 .....B J Geraghty 33/1
*midfield, hit 5th, headway 10th, going well
before 3 out, not fluent 2 out and soon
outpaced, stayed on again towards finish*
[RPR147 TS141 OR140]
12 TIKRAM 10 10-8 b ....Robert Thornton 9/1
*in rear division, no impression when blundered
2 out*
btn 18½ lengths [RPR130 TS127 OR137] [op
10/1 tchd 11/1]
16 LIVINGSTONEBRAMBLE 11 10-12 ....
....D J Condon 50/1
midfield, not fluent 10th, behind from 11th
btn 28 lengths [RPR125 TS122 OR141][op 40/1]
U GRAPHIC APPROACH 9 10-9 b1 ....
....P J Brennan 16/1
*midfield, hit 1st and 5th, mistake and unseated
rdier 11th* [OR138]
Dist: 4-1¼-hd-¾-½ RACE RPR: 149+/141+/142
Racecheck: Wins - Pl - Unpl 2

3 Feb Sandown 3m½f Cls2 122-145 Ch Hcap £25,052
18 ran GD-SFT 18fncs Time 6m 15.50s (slw 12.50s)
1 Rambling Minster 9 10-5 ...Richard McGrath 15/2
2 KELAMI 9 11-3 ....A Duchene (3) 25/1
*mistake 1st, held up well in rear, still plenty to
do after 17th (2 out), good progress from 3f out
to lead after last, headed and not quicken flat*
[RPR149 TS119 OR139]
3 Briery Fox 9 11-1 ....Mark Bradburne 40/1
4 TIKRAM 10 11-5 ....A P McCoy 11/2F
*held up just behind leaders, still well there when
blundered 16th (3 out), effort again by-passing 2
out, weakened last*
[RPR143 TS113 OR138] [op 7/1]
Dist: ¾-4-6-¾-5-3 RACE RPR: 137+/149/139+
Racecheck: Wins 1 Pl 4 Unpl 14

9 Dec 06 Cheltenham 4th, see KNOWHERE

22 Jul 06 Market Rasen 2m6½f Cls1 Cls1 120-146 Ch
Hcap £37,063
14 ran GOOD 14fncs Time 5m 33.00s (slw 3.00s)
1 Yes Sir 7 10-10 ....A P McCoy 3/1F
2 BALLYCASSIDY 10 10-12 ...Jason Maguire 20/1
*chased leaders, driven and outpaced 8th, only
10th 4 out, 6th last, stayed on strongly to take
2nd towards finish* [RPR152 TS152 OR146]
3 Mr Fluffy 9 10-0 ....Tom Messenger (5) 50/1
10 TIKRAM 9 11-11 eb ....Jamie Moore 20/1
in touch, blundered 3rd, lost place after 7th
btn 35 lengths [RPR125 TS125 OR145][op 25/1
tchd 28/1]
Dist: 6-1¼-nk-1-8 RACE RPR: 152+/152/130
Racecheck: Wins 5 Pl 4 Unpl 15

7 Apr 06 Aintree 3m1f Cls2 128-152 Ch Hcap £31,315
18 ran GOOD 19fncs Time 6m 29.20s (slw 20.20s)
1 State Of Play 6 10-2 ....Paul Moloney 22/1
2 Lacdoudal 7 11-12 ....Richard Johnson 13/2
3 Aristoxene 6 10-6 ....Marcus Foley 40/1
8 TIKRAM 9 11-6 b ....Jamie Moore 16/1
mid-division, ridden after 11th, headway 13th
btn 53 lengths [RPR115 TS82 OR146][op 18/1]
U MCKELVEY 7 10-5 ....Christian Williams 16/1
blundered and unseated rider 2nd [OR131]
U BILLYVODDAN 7 11-0 ....Robert Thornton 14/1
*led 2nd to next, chased leaders, ridden 12th,
weakened 15th, hampered and unseated rider 2
out* [OR140]
Dist: 16-7-nk-hd-15 RACE RPR: 160+/164+/133+
Racecheck: Wins 6 (5) Pl 3 Unpl 19

17 Mar 06 Cheltenham 3m2½f Cls1 Gd1 Ch £228,080
22 ran GOOD 21fncs Time 6m 31.70s (fst 7.30s)
1 War Of Attrition 7 11-10 ....C O'Dwyer 15/2
2 **HEDGEHUNTER** 10 11-10 ....R Walsh 16/1
held up in rear, headway 16th, chased leaders and bypassed 3rd last, chased winner 2 out, kept on run-in but no impression near finish
[RPR170 TS151] [op 14/1 tchd 20/1]
3 Forget The Past 8 11-10 ....B J Geraghty 9/1
4 **L'AMI** 7 11-10 ....Mick FitzGerald 10/1
tracked leaders, ridden 4 out, outpaced at bypassed 3rd last, kept on again run-in but not a danger [RPR163 TS146] [op 9/1]
6 **MONKERHOSTIN** 9 11-10 Richard Johnson 13/2
in rear when blundered badly 5th, hit next, ridden and headway 16th, hard driven and kept on from bypassed 3rd last, ran on run-in, not reach leaders
[RPR164 TS145 OR166] [tchd 7/1 & 15/2]
9 **ROYAL AUCLAIR** 9 11-10 t Christian Williams 20/1
chased leaders until lost place 14th, kept on again from bypassed 3rd last, kept on run-in but never a danger
btn 16 lengths [RPR157 TS141 OR160]
12 **TIKRAM** 9 11-10 b ....Jamie Moore 100/1
hit 1st, mid-division, headway and in touch 13th, ridden after 18th, soon weakened
btn 36 lengths [RPR137 TS127 OR146]
13 **JOES EDGE** 9 11-10 ....Keith Mercer 100/1
behind from 7th
btn 37 lengths [RPR135 TS125 OR140]
14 **BALLYCASSIDY** 10 11-10 ....G Lee 100/1
in rear and hit 13th, ridden next, never in contention
btn 44 lengths [RPR128 TS120 OR139]
Dist: 2½-7-¾-½-½ RACE RPR: 173+/170+/165+
Racecheck: Wins 7 (1) Pl 6 Unpl 29

Naunton Brook 10-4

8-y-o *b g Alderbrook - Give Me An Answer (True Song)*
N A Twiston-Davies Noel Fehily

Placings: 1P/1P7P6130-8411530P

OR136H110	Starts	1st	2nd	3rd	Win & Pl
Chase	18	5	–	2	£56,552
All Jumps races	24	6	1	3	£62,420

126	12/06	Extr	3m1½f Cls3 107-133 Ch Hcap soft	£7,807
119	11/06	Hexm	4m Cls3 109-135 Ch Hcap soft	£18,789
118	2/06	MRas	3m1f Cls3 92-118 Ch Hcap soft	£6,506
116	10/05	Towc	2m6f Cls3 96-120 Ch Hcap good	£5,512
	10/04	Worc	2m7½f Cls3 Nov Ch good	£5,434
	3/04	Wwck	3m1f Cls4 Nov Hdl good	£3,794

Total win prize-money £47,842
GF-HRD 0-0-0 GS-HVY 3-3-13 Course 0-0-0 Dist 0-0-0

14 Mar Cheltenham Pulled Up, see **LIBERTHINE**

17 Feb Haydock 12th, see **PHILSON RUN**

13 Jan Warwick 3m5f Cls1 Gd3 125-151 Ch Hcap £39,914
13 ran HEAVY 22fncs Time 7m 41.60s (slw 26.60s)
1 Ladalko 8 11-1 ....R Walsh 9/2F
2 Mon Mome 7 11-1 ....Sam Thomas 5/1
3 **NAUNTON BROOK** 8 10-5 t Mr D England (5) 14/1
led 2nd, ridden and headed last, no extra
[RPR144 TS133 OR135] [op 11/1]
Dist: 4-1-9-17-hd RACE RPR: 152+/149+/144+
Racecheck: Wins 3 (2) Pl 5 Unpl 11

27 Dec 06 Chepstow 3m5½f Cls1 Gd3 130-151 Ch Hcap £57,020
18 ran SOFT 22fncs Time 7m 40.90s (slw 10.90s)
1 Halcon Genelardais 6 11-3 Wayne Hutchinson 7/1
2 Mon Mome 6 10-3 ....Liam Treadwell (3) 14/1
3 Juveigneur 9 11-3 ....Mick FitzGerald 11/1
5 **NAUNTON BROOK** 7 9-10 t ex5 ....Mr D England (5) 12/1
chased leader, led after 6th, hit 5 out, ridden and headed approaching 3 out, weakened approaching last
[RPR136 TS134 OR131] [op 16/1]

6 **SIMON** 7 10-2 ow2 oh3 Andrew Thornton 11/2F
prominent, hit 5th, weakened 17th
[RPR132 TS132 OR130] [op 7/1]
Dist: 4-6-4-2-3 RACE RPR: 165+/150/155
Racecheck: Wins 2 (2) Pl 6 Unpl 18

14 Dec 06 Exeter 3m1½f Cls3 107-133 Ch Hcap £7,807
8 ran SOFT 19fncs Time 6m 36.30s (slw 26.30s)
1 **NAUNTON BROOK** 7 11-0 t ....Mr D England (5) 11/4F
led to 10th, led approaching 12th, clear 2 out, stayed on well
[RPR142 TS120 OR126] [op 3/1 tchd 100/30]
2 Kock De La Vesvre 8 11-4 ......Sam Thomas 4/1
3 Keepatem 10 11-2 ....A P McCoy 12/1
Dist: 9-5-2½-4-15 RACE RPR: 142+/131/125+
Racecheck: Wins - Pl 4 Unpl 8

15 Nov 06 Hexham 4m Cls3 109-135 Ch Hcap £18,789
12 ran SOFT 25fncs Time 8m 55.40s (slw 43.40s)
1 **NAUNTON BROOK** 7 10-5 t Mr D England (5) 10/1
led 4th, made rest, hung right run-in, stayed on strongly [RPR134 TS102 OR119] [op 12/1]
2 Kinburn 7 11-12 ....P J Brennan 3/1F
3 High Cotton 11 9-9 ....James Reveley (7) 8/1
Dist: 1½-1-23-8-9 RACE RPR: 134+/149+/120
Racecheck: Wins 1 (1) Pl 2 Unpl 16

19 Apr 06 Cheltenham 16th, see **SONEVAFUSHI**

Cloudy Bays 11-0

10-y-o *ch g Hubbly Bubbly - Bellteen (Beau Charmeur)*
C Byrnes (IRE) Andrew J McNamara

Placings: 0241432541143/8FP18F

OR146H129	Starts	1st	2nd	3rd	Win & Pl
Chase	30	6	3	5	£187,912
All Jumps races	46	9	4	6	£226,771

	1/07	Tram	2m6f List Ch heavy	£17,594
117	1/05	Leop	3m 98-124 Hdl Hcap sft-hvy	£15,698
	1/05	Tram	2m6f List Ch heavy	£19,603
110	9/04	List	2m4f 106-136 Hdl Hcap heavy	£16,046
135	1/04	Leop	3m 131-159 Ch Hcap soft	£45,775
119	11/03	Navn	3m 114-142 Ch Hcap gd-yld	£33,768
105	7/03	Tipp	2m4f 103-138 Ch Hcap heavy	£13,506
	9/02	List	2m6f Ch firm	£6,561
	6/02	Wxfd	2m Mdn Hdl 5yo soft	£3,810

Total win prize-money £172,359
GF-HRD 1-2-11 GS-HVY 8-5-30 Course 0-0-0 Dist 0-0-0

15 Mar Cheltenham 3m Cls1 List 131-157 Hdl Hcap £39,914
24 ran GD-SFT 11hdls Time 5m 46.20s (slw 8.20s)
1 Oscar Park 8 10-9 t ....Tom Doyle 14/1
2 Material World 9 10-9 e .....Colin Bolger (3) 14/1
3 Adamant Approach 13 10-13 ....Mr P W Mullins (7) 16/1
F **CLOUDY BAYS** 10 10-4 p ow2 D N Russell 14/1
led until fell 5th [OR135] [op 16/1 tchd 18/1]
Dist: ½-3½-½-3½-3½ RACE RPR: 147+/149/153
Racecheck: Wins 1 Pl - Unpl 2

14 Jan Leopardstown 3m 114-144 Hdl Hcap £14,955
27 ran SFT-HVY 12hdls Time 6m 11.80s (slw 24.80s)
1 Adamant Approach 13 11-1 Mr P W Mullins (7) 16/1
2 Artiste Bay 5 9-6 ow1 ....E M Butterly (5) 10/1
3 Amalfitano 7 10-3 ow1 ....D F O'Regan 20/1
8 **CLOUDY BAYS** 10 10-12 p .....D N Russell 12/1
soon led, headed 7th, remained close up, 3rd approaching 2 out, weakened straight
btn 11½ lengths [RPR126 TS74 OR130] [op 8/1]
Dist: hd-1½-2-1¾-1¾ RACE RPR: 147/122/127
Racecheck: Wins 3 Pl 4 Unpl 25

1 Jan Tramore 2m6f List Ch £17,594
7 ran HEAVY Time 5m 34.10s (slw 22.10s)
1 **CLOUDY BAYS** 10 11-9 p ....D N Russell 5/1
tracked leaders, disputed lead briefly 6th, ridden in 3rd 3 out, moderate 3rd before last, stayed on strongly to lead close home
[RPR146 TS142 OR149] [op 100/30]
2 Mossy Green 13 11-9 ....D J Condon 11/8F
3 Public Reaction 9 11-5 ....Mr J J King (7) 7/2
Dist: 1-1-17-3½-14 RACE RPR: 146+/145/147
Racecheck: Wins 1 Pl 1 Unpl 7

10 Dec 06 Cork 2m Gd2 Ch £26,938
11 ran HEAVY 11fncs Time 4m 15.40s (slw 22.40s)
1 Tumbling Dice 7 11-4 p ......S M McGovern 10/1
2 Jim 9 11-4 ....A E Lynch 7/2
3 Steel Band 8 11-4 ....D N Russell 12/1
P **CLOUDY BAYS** 9 11-4 b ....B M Cash 14/1
prominent, mistake 4th, lost place quickly, tailed off when pulled up before 4 out [OR150]
Dist: 10-11-1¾-15-6 RACE RPR: 153/143/132
Racecheck: Wins 1 Pl 1 Unpl 12

4 Nov 06 Down Royal 3m Gd1 Ch £60,345
7 ran YLD-SFT Time 6m 35.20s (slw 36.20s)
1 Beef Or Salmon 10 11-10 p ....Andrew J McNamara 11/4
2 War Of Attrition 7 11-10 ....C O'Dwyer 4/7F
3 Justified 7 11-10 ....P Carberry 5/1
F **CLOUDY BAYS** 9 11-10 p ......D N Russell 33/1
led, headed 4 out, ridden and weakened before 3 out, moderate 4th when fell 2 out
U **BOTHAR NA** 7 11-10 ....D J Condon 33/1
raced mainly in 4th, 5th from 9th, ridden and no extra before 3 out, moderate 5th when unseated rider 2 out [OR136]
Dist: nk-13-24-5 RACE RPR: 162+/162+/157+
Racecheck: Wins 1 Pl 3 Unpl 7

7 Oct 06 Gowran Park 3m 103-131 Hdl Hcap £17,959
13 ran GOOD Time 5m 43.90s (slw 3.90s)
1 Sonne Cinq 7 9-10 ....D J Condon 6/1
2 Yarra Maguire 7 10-13 ....P Carberry 7/2F
3 Emotional Article 6 10-11 ....N P Madden 4/1
8 **CLOUDY BAYS** 9 11-10 Andrew J McNamara 14/1
soon led, headed before 7th, 4th and ridden 5 out, soon weakened
btn 25 lengths [RPR116 TS77 OR131] [op 12/1]
Dist: 1½-4-4-shd-4 RACE RPR: 115+/128+/122+
Racecheck: Wins - Pl 2 Unpl 14

Thisthatandtother 11-5

11-y-o *b g Bob Back - Baden (Furry Glen)*
P F Nicholls Sam Thomas

Placings: 121F22/22214/3F-2527

OR151H146	Starts	1st	2nd	3rd	Win & Pl
Chase	19	5	8	1	£314,028
All Jumps races	30	9	12	1	£381,029

3/05	Chel	2m5f Cls1 Gd2 Ch good	£87,000
2/04	Winc	2m Cls3 Nov Ch good	£10,847
12/03	Sand	2m Cls1 Nov Gd2 Ch good	£17,400
11/03	Chel	2m Cls1 Nov Gd2 Ch good	£20,825
10/03	Bang	2m1½f Cls3 Ch good	£4,225
1/03	Winc	2m Cls1 Gd1 Hdl gd-sft	£23,800
11/02	Winc	2m Cls3 Nov Hdl 4-6yo good	£4,891
10/02	Winc	2m Cls3 Nov Hdl good	£3,916
2/02	Winc	2m Cls6 NHF 4-6yo soft	£1,736

Total win prize-money £174,640
GF-HRD 0-0-0 GS-HVY 2-5-12 Course 0-0-0 Dist 0-0-0

15 Mar Cheltenham 2m5f Cls1 Gd2 Ch £99,785
9 ran GD-SFT 17fncs Time 5m 10.60s (slw 2.60s)
1 Taranis 6 11-0 t ....R Walsh 9/2
2 Our Vic 9 11-5 ....Timmy Murphy 7/2
3 **BILLYVODDAN** 8 11-0 b .Richard Johnson 20/1
soon chased leader, mistake 12th, over 1 length up when hampered and lost place 4 out, rallied to chase winner 2 out, stayed on, lost 2nd close home [RPR160 TS153 OR150]
7 **THISTHATANDTOTHER** 11 11-0 ....Sam Thomas 16/1
in touch, hit 1st, headway 4 out, ridden approaching 3 out, weakened before last
btn 12½ lengths [RPR147 TS142 OR155]
Dist: nk-½-3½-¾-7 RACE RPR: 160+/165+/160+
Racecheck: Wins - Pl - Unpl 1

17 Feb Ascot 2m3f Cls1 Gd1 Ch £84,675
7 ran GD-SFT 16fncs Time 4m 50.40s (slw 16.40s)
1 Monet's Garden 9 11-7 .....Tony Dobbin 11/10F
2 **THISTHATANDTOTHER** 11 11-7 ...R Walsh 4/1
chased leading pair, lost place 10th, ridden 12th, stayed on to chase winner between last 2, no impression
[RPR158 TS130 OR155] [op 7/2 tchd 9/2]
3 River City 10 11-7 ....Tom Doyle 20/1
Dist: 8-3-3-1½-24 RACE RPR: 165+/158+/153

9 Dec 06 Cheltenham 5th, see KNOWHERE

18 Nov 06 Huntingdon 2m4½f Cls1 Gd2 Ch £43,268
5 ran GOOD 16fncs Time 5m 1.10s (slw 10.10s)
1 Racing Demon 6 11-5 ....G Lee 13/8J
2 **THISTHATANDTOTHER** 10 11-0 ....Wayne Hutchinson 4/1
led, headed approaching last, no extra
[RPR158 TS139] [op 11/4]
3 **MONKERHOSTIN** 9 11-6 ......T J O'Brien 13/8J
chased leaders, 3rd and held when hit last
[RPR162 TS140 OR163] [op 15/8 tchd 2/1]
Dist: 4-5-40 RACE RPR: 168+/158/162+
Racecheck: Wins 1 Pl 2 Unpl 5

10 Dec 05 Cheltenham 2m5f Cls1 Gd3 132-158 Ch Hcap £62,722
16 ran GD-SFT 17fncs Time 5m 15.00s (slw 7.00s)
1 Sir Oj 8 10-0 b oh2 ....P Carberry 16/1
2 Le Passing 6 10-9 b ....Joe Tizzard 20/1
3 Lacdoudal 6 11-3 ex6 ......Richard Johnson 8/1
F **THISTHATANDTOTHER** 9 11-11 ....Christian Williams 15/2
chased leaders, 1 length 2nd and staying on well when fell 3 out [OR157] [op 7/1]
Dist: 1-5-shd-5-5 RACE RPR: 142+/150+/152
Racecheck: Wins 4 (3) Pl 3 Unpl 23

19 Nov 05 Huntingdon 2m4½f Cls1 Gd2 Ch £42,195
11 ran GOOD 16fncs Time 5m 0.60s (slw 9.60s)
1 Impek 9 11-6 ....A P McCoy 5/1
2 **MONKERHOSTIN** 8 11-6 Richard Johnson 5/2F
held up and behind, headway on inside 12th, ridden approaching 2 out, one pace
[RPR160 TS110 OR154] [op 2/1]
3 **THISTHATANDTOTHER** 9 11-10 ...R Walsh 3/1
held up, ridden and headway after 3 out, kept on flat [RPR158 TS111 OR159] [op 11/4]
Dist: 5-3½-3½-¾-24 RACE RPR: 166+/160+/158
Racecheck: Wins 1 (1) Pl 4 Unpl 15

Livingstonebramble 10-9

11-y-o *b g Supreme Leader - Killiney Side (General Ironside)*
W P Mullins (IRE) D N Russell
Placings: 45F2/12014-359442250

OR141 H118	Starts	1st	2nd	3rd	Win & Pl
Chase	20	3	4	2	£76,314
All Jumps races	29	4	6	2	£91,548

128 4/06 Fair 2m1f 125-141 Ch Hcap gd-yld ...£31,428
4/05 Punc 2m2f Nov Ch yld-sft ...£12,697
11/04 Wxfd 2m4f Ch soft ...£5,839
4/02 Fair 2m4f Mdn Hdl 6yo yield ...£7,196
Total win prize-money £57,160
GF-HRD 0-0-0 GS-HVY 4-8-27 Course 0-0-0 Dist 0-0-0

15 Mar Cheltenham 2m5f Cls1 Gd3 129-155 Ch Hcap £57,020
23 ran GD-SFT 17fncs Time 5m 11.40s (slw 3.40s)
1 Idole First 8 10-7 ....Alan O'Keeffe 12/1
2 Palarshan 9 10-5 p ....Richard Johnson 28/1
3 Mariah Rollins 9 10-7 ....Mick FitzGerald 20/1
5 **SLIM PICKINGS** 8 10-11 ......B J Geraghty 33/1
midfield, hit 5th, headway 10th, going well before 3 out, not fluent 2 out and soon outpaced, stayed on again towards finish
[RPR147 TS141 OR140]
12 **TIKRAM** 10 10-8 b ....Robert Thornton 9/1
in rear division, no impression when blundered 2 out
btn 18½ lengths [RPR130 TS127 OR137] [op 10/1 tchd 11/1]
16 **LIVINGSTONEBRAMBLE** 11 10-12 ....D J Condon 50/1
midfield, not fluent 10th, behind from 11th
btn 28 lengths [RPR125 TS122 OR141] [op 40/1]
U **GRAPHIC APPROACH** 9 10-9 b1 ....P J Brennan 16/1
midfield, hit 1st and 5th, mistake and unseated rdier 11th [OR138]
Dist: 4-1¼-hd-¾-½ RACE RPR: 149+/141+/142
Racecheck: Wins - Pl - Unpl 2

21 Feb Punchestown 5th, see SILVER BIRCH

25 Jan Gowran Park 3m 119-147 Ch Hcap £43,919
16 ran HEAVY Time 6m 35.20s (slw 45.20s)
1 **HOMER WELLS** 9 10-2 ....D J Condon 16/1
tracked leaders, 7th before halfway, 5th 5 out, close up after 4 out, led after 3 out, ridden and strongly pressed after next, edged slightly left after last, stayed on well (trainer said, regarding the improved form shown, gelding was in the process of running a good race last time out at Leopardstown until falling, while its previous run at Navan was its first of the year)
[RPR143 TS124 OR125]
2 **LIVINGSTONEBRAMBLE** 11 10-10 ....D N Russell 14/1
mid-division, 7th and progress after 4 out, 3rd 2 out, soon challenged, 2nd before last, slightly hampered and checked run-in, kept on
[RPR146 TS129 OR133]
3 Well Tutored 8 10-1 ....P A Carberry 15/2
F **SLIM PICKINGS** 8 11-3 ....B J Geraghty 16/1
held up towards rear, progress on outer 5 out, 5th approaching 3 out, soon ridden and no impression, staying on when fell last [OR140]
Dist: 3½-4-3-1½-6 RACE RPR: 143+/146/133
After a steward's inquiry, the placings remained unaltered.
Racecheck: Wins 1 Pl 2 Unpl 11

27 Dec 06 Leopardstown 3m 103-131 Hdl Hcap £13,918
21 ran HEAVY 12hdls Time 6m 31.40s (slw 44.40s)
1 Dosco 7 9-3 ex17 ....C D Maxwell (7) 9/4F
2 **LIVINGSTONEBRAMBLE** 10 10-8 ....D J Condon 12/1
held up, 11th 4 out, headway 2 out, 3rd straight, stayed on from last, no chance with winner
[RPR123 TS120 OR115]
3 Kylegarra Lady 7 9-7 ....A E Lynch (3) 33/1
4 **NUMBERSIXVALVERDE** 10 10-12 ....N P Madden 14/1
held up towards rear, 12th approaching 4 out, progress 2 out, moderate 5th before last, kept on [RPR117 TS115 OR119]
Dist: 4-1¼-9-nk-18 RACE RPR: 115+/123/110
Racecheck: Wins - Pl 4 Unpl 17

16 Dec 06 Fairyhouse 2m2f Hdl £8,578
11 ran HEAVY 10hdls Time 4m 41.50s (slw 30.50s)
1 Beef Or Salmon 10 11-2 Andrew J McNamara 7/4F
2 You Sir 6 11-6 ....B J Geraghty 4/1
3 Cadogan 6 11-6 ....P W Flood 7/1
4 **LIVINGSTONEBRAMBLE** 10 10-11 ....R J Kiely (5) 10/1
held up, 8th 3 out, 6th next, kept on
[RPR118 TS120 OR115] [op 8/1]
Dist: 1½-3½-2½-5-3 RACE RPR: 132+/128+/125+
Racecheck: Wins 1 Pl 5 Unpl 8

10 Dec 06 Punchestown 2m4f 91-114 Hdl Hcap £9,054
18 ran HEAVY Time 5m 41.10s (slw 1m 0.10s)
1 View Mount Prince 5 10-3 P A Carberry 100/30F
2 Spring The Que 7 10-10 ......P T Enright (7) 25/1
3 Patsy Bee 5 11-0 ....P W Flood 14/1
4 **LIVINGSTONEBRAMBLE** 10 11-5 R Walsh 12/1
mid-division, 5th and progress 3 out, 4th after 2 out, kept on from last
[RPR111 TS20 OR114] [op 8/1]
Dist: 2½-1¼-1¾-3½-nk RACE RPR: 107+/112/108
Racecheck: Wins 6 Pl 4 Unpl 15

Graphic Approach 10-6

9-y-o *b g King's Ride - Sharp Approach (Crash Course)*
C R Egerton Paul Moloney
Placings: 3/11F3/113U/2163-53U

OR138 H123	Starts	1st	2nd	3rd	Win & Pl
Chase	11	3	1	3	£63,861
All Jumps races	17	5	1	5	£71,378

132 1/06 Sand 3m½f Cls2 113-138 Ch Hcap gd-sft ...£25,052
1/05 Sthl 3m½f Cls3 Nov Ch good ...£9,184
1/05 Hrfd 2m3f Cls4 Ch soft ...£4,882
1/04 Weth 2m4½f Cls4 Nov Hdl gd-sft ...£4,446
12/03 Hrfd 2m1f Cls6 NHF 4-6yo gd-sft ...£1,694
Total win prize-money £45,258
GF-HRD 0-0-0 GS-HVY 4-3-13 Course 0-0-0 Dist 0-0-0

15 Mar Cheltenham 2m5f Cls1 Gd3 129-155 Ch Hcap £57,020
23 ran GD-SFT 17fncs Time 5m 11.40s (slw 3.40s)
1 Idole First 8 10-7 ....Alan O'Keeffe 12/1
2 Palarshan 9 10-5 p ....Richard Johnson 28/1
3 Mariah Rollins 9 10-7 ....Mick FitzGerald 20/1
5 **SLIM PICKINGS** 8 10-11 ......B J Geraghty 33/1
midfield, hit 5th, headway 10th, going well before 3 out, not fluent 2 out and soon outpaced, stayed on again towards finish
[RPR147 TS141 OR140]
12 **TIKRAM** 10 10-8 b ....Robert Thornton 9/1
in rear division, no impression when blundered 2 out
btn 18½ lengths [RPR130 TS127 OR137] [op 10/1 tchd 11/1]
16 **LIVINGSTONEBRAMBLE** 11 10-12 ....D J Condon 50/1
midfield, not fluent 10th, behind from 11th
btn 28 lengths [RPR125 TS122 OR141] [op 40/1]
U **GRAPHIC APPROACH** 9 10-9 b1 ....P J Brennan 16/1
midfield, hit 1st and 5th, mistake and unseated rdier 11th [OR138]
Dist: 4-1¼-hd-¾-½ RACE RPR: 149+/141+/142
Racecheck: Wins - Pl - Unpl 2

16 Dec 06 Ascot 3m Cls1 List 130-153 Ch Hcap £39,438
18 ran GD-SFT 20fncs Time 6m 8.60s (slw 22.60s)
1 **BILLYVODDAN** 7 10-12 b1 Leighton Aspell 25/1
badly hampered 3rd and settled towards rear after, headway 13th, led 4 out, drew clear after next, comfortably [RPR157 TS95 OR139]
2 **ZABENZ** 9 10-13 b ....Barry Fenton 16/1
prominent, led 15th, hit next, headed 4 out, soon outpaced by winner [RPR145 TS85 OR140]
3 **GRAPHIC APPROACH** 8 10-12 Paul Moloney 15/2
held up and behind, headway 15th, kept on from 4 out, no impression
[RPR141 TS83 OR139] [op 13/2]
9 **KELAMI** 8 10-12 ....A Duchene (5) 18/1
towards rear most of way, ridden and no danger from 16th
btn 28 lengths [RPR132 TS76 OR144] [op 16/1]
P **CLAN ROYAL** 11 11-2 ....A P McCoy 25/1
always well behind, pulled up before 11th [OR143]
Dist: 12-2-2-6-½ RACE RPR: 157+/145+/141
Racecheck: Wins - Pl 7 Unpl 9

11 Nov 06 Cheltenham 2m4½f Cls1 Gd3 123-149 Ch Hcap £62,722
16 ran GD-SFT 15fncs Time 5m 20.30s (slw 20.30s)
1 Exotic Dancer 6 11-2 p ....A P McCoy 16/1
2 Vodka Bleu 7 10-11 ....Timmy Murphy 4/1F
3 New Alco 5 10-7 ....G Lee 16/1
5 **GRAPHIC APPROACH** 8 11-2 Noel Fehily 14/1
always close up, ridden and outpaced 2 out, kept on same pace after [RPR145 TS102 OR139]
7 **KANDJAR D'ALLIER** 8 10-13 Robert Thornton 9/1
held up in rear on inner, progress 11th, ridden before 3 out and not quicken, one pace after
btn 14½ lengths [RPR138 TS95 OR136] [op 8/1]
F **KNOWHERE** 8 11-1 ....Tony Evans 17/2
made most at steady pace until fell 8th
[OR138] [op 10/1 tchd 11/1 & 8/1]
Dist: 3-½-3½-2½-¾ RACE RPR: 155+/146/142
Racecheck: Wins 7 (3) Pl 7 Unpl 16

16 Mar 06 Cheltenham 2m5f Cls1 Gd3 127-146 Ch Hcap £42,765
24 ran GOOD 17fncs Time 5m 5.20s (fst 2.80s)
1 Non So 8 11-3 ....Mick FitzGerald 14/1
2 Kelrev 8 11-1 ....Sam Thomas 50/1
3 **GRAPHIC APPROACH** 8 11-6 A P McCoy 11/1
prominent, chased leader and mistake 12th, driven and lost 2nd 3 out, soon outpaced
[RPR140 TS140 OR140] [op 10/1 tchd 12/1]
9 **BILLYVODDAN** 7 11-7 ....Richard Johnson 13/2
chased leader to 4th, with leading group until weakened from 13th
btn 26 lengths [RPR130 TS132 OR141] [tchd 7/1]
Dist: 9-7-hd-½-1¼ RACE RPR: 155+/141/140+
Racecheck: Wins 6 (1) Pl 6 Unpl 25

25 Feb 06 Sandown 3m¹⁄₂f Cls1 Gd3 129-155 Ch Hcap
£57,020
15 ran SOFT 22fncs Time 6m 19.80s (slw 16.80s)
1 Innox 10 11-0 b ....A P McCoy 8/1
2 **L'AMI** 7 11-7 ....A Duchene (5) 8/1
*held up towards rear, steady headway from
16th, chased leaders approaching 3 out, soon
ridden, stayed on to go 2nd run-in*
[RPR163 TS165 OR155]
3 My Will 6 11-4 ....Joe Tizzard 8/1
5 **BALLYCASSIDY** 10 10-10 Jason Maguire 100/1
*led 3rd until after 13th, led 4 out, ridden and
headed next, kept on no extra run-in (jockey
received one-day ban: disobeyed starter's
orders (Mar 8))* [RPR146 TS148 OR139]
6 **GRAPHIC APPROACH** 8 10-11 P J Brennan 8/1
*mid-division, smooth headway to track leaders
16th, ridden after 3 out, weakened last*
[RPR126 TS124 OR140] [op 7/1]
Dist: 2¹⁄₂-¹⁄₂-³⁄₄-³⁄₄-29 RACE RPR: 154+/163/156+
Racecheck: Wins - Pl 10 Unpl 18

7 Jan 06 Sandown 3m¹⁄₂f Cls2 113-138 Ch Hcap
£25,052
14 ran GD-SFT 22fncs Time 6m 24.90s (slw 21.90s)
1 **GRAPHIC APPROACH** 8 11-6 ..A P McCoy 7/1
*held up in mid-division, headway 12th, driven to
chase leader and 3 lengths down but staying on
when left in lead 2-out, ridden and ran on well
run-in* [RPR145 TS113 OR132] [tchd 13/2]
2 Shalako 8 10-4 ....P J Brennan 10/1
3 Jakari 9 11-4 ....Mark Bradbume 22/1
5 **LIBERTHINE** 7 11-1 ..Mr S Waley-Cohen (7) 9/2
*in touch, headway 12th, chased leaders next,
weakened 3 out*
[RPR129 TS101 OR134] [op 4/1 tchd 5/1]
Dist: 3¹⁄₂-1¹⁄₂-8-4-2¹⁄₂ RACE RPR: 145+/123/137+
Racecheck: Wins 2 (1) Pl 7 Unpl 18

Gallant Approach 10-9

8-y-o ch g Roselier - *Nicks Approach (Dry Dock)*
C R Egerton J A McCarthy

Placings: 21/5/1125-137

OR141   Starts 1st 2nd 3rd Win & Pl
Chase 6 2 1 1 £49,970
All Jumps races 8 3 1 1 £53,485
132 11/06 Newb 2m4f Cls2 125-143 Ch Hcap soft £31,315
120 12/05 Newb 3m Cls3 Nov 107-123 Ch Hcap gd-sft ...
£7,352
11/05 Hntg 2m¹⁄₂f Cls4 Nov Hdl gd-sft £3,515
Total win prize-money £42,182
GF-HRD 0-0-0 GS-HVY 3-2-7 Course 0-0-0

13 Mar 06 Cheltenham 3m¹⁄₂f Cls1 Gd3 130-150 Ch Hcap
£48,467
23 ran GD-SFT 19fncs Time 6m 15.94s (slw 10.94s)
1 **JOES EDGE** 10 10-6 ....D N Russell 50/1
*towards rear until headway 4 out, stayed on
under pressure from 3 out but still plenty to do
approaching last, stayed on under pressure to
lead last stride* [RPR140 TS106 OR130] [op 40/1]
2 Juveigneur 10 11-9 ....Mick FitzGerald 7/1C
3 Distant Thunder 9 10-11 Andrew J McNamara 7/1C
4 **GALLANT APPROACH** 8 11-3 P J Brennan 20/1
*chased leaders, ridden 3 out, hampered next
and soon beaten*
btn 17¹⁄₂ lengths [RPR135 TS103 OR141] [op
16/1]
17 **BALLYCASSIDY** 11 11-2 p ....T J O'Brien 50/1
*in touch until ridden and weakened 11th, tailed
off* btn 76 lengths [TS51 OR140] [op 66/1]
Dist: shd-shd-8-2-shd RACE RPR: 140+/156/144
Racecheck: Wins - Pl 1 Unpl 6

16 Dec 06 Haydock 3m Cls2 121-140 Ch Hcap £19,518
14 ran HEAVY 18fncs Time 6m 41.00s (slw 41.00s)
1 **KANDJAR D'ALLIER** 8 11-4 ....
.......................Wayne Hutchinson 10/1
*midfield, headway 14th, led approaching 2 out,
edged left towards finish, all out*
[RPR142 TS72 OR132] [op 8/1]
2 Wild Cane Ridge 7 11-12 ....Keith Mercer 10/1

3 GALLANT APPROACH 7 11-9 J A McCarthy 7/2F
*midfield, headway 8th, outpaced after 4 out,
rallied 2 out, went 2nd last, stayed
on run-in, lost 2nd and no extra towards finish*
[RPR144 TS76 OR137] [op 4/1]
Dist: ¹⁄₂-nk-11-6-2 RACE RPR: 142+/148+/144
Racecheck: Wins 1 Pl 2 Unpl 19

25 Nov 06 Newbury 2m4f Cls2 125-143 Ch Hcap
£31,315
10 ran SOFT 16fncs Time 5m 17.10s (slw 26.10s)
1 **GALLANT APPROACH** 7 11-1 J A McCarthy 7/2J
*led 4th, ridden 4 out, not fluent next, narrowly
headed after last, not much room on rail and
rallied gamely to lead again near finish*
[RPR143 TS90 OR132] [tchd 4/1]
2 No Full 5 10-11 ....Mick FitzGerald 8/1
3 Patman Du Charmil 4 9-9 oh2 ....
.......................Mr D England (5) 7/1
Dist: ¹⁄₂-3¹⁄₂-3¹⁄₂-14-11 RACE RPR: 143+/138+/123+
Racecheck: Wins 1 (1) Pl 1 Unpl 14

28 Apr 06 Punchestown 3m1f Nov 123-144 Ch Hcap
£42,759
9 ran GOOD Time 6m 15.20s (fst 4.80s)
1 Olney Lad 7 10-11 b ....J A McCarthy 25/1
2 Wolf Creek 6 10-3 ....P W Flood 7/1
3 Oulart 7 10-0 ....R Loughran (3) 100/30F
5 **GALLANT APPROACH** 7 10-12 .A P McCoy 5/1
*towards rear, slight mistake 3rd, 6th and some
progress 4 out, 5th and ridden 3 out, kept on
same pace* [RPR130 TS114 OR132]
Dist: 1¹⁄₂-5¹⁄₂-4-3-7 RACE RPR: 143+/134+/128+
Racecheck: Wins - Pl 1 Unpl 6

25 Feb 06 Sandown 2m4¹⁄₂f Cls1 Nov Gd2 Ch £18,461
5 ran SOFT 17fncs Time 5m 22.30s (slw 20.30s)
1 Napolitain 5 11-3 ....Christian Williams 2/1
2 **GALLANT APPROACH** 7 11-7 A P McCoy 4/5F
*tracked winner, disputing lead when blundered
11th, every chance 2 out, soon ridden, no extra
and soon held* [RPR139 TS128 OR132] [op 8/11]
3 Lago d'Oro 6 10-10 ....James Davies 66/1
Dist: 5-30-6 RACE RPR: 137/139+/95
Racecheck: Wins 1 Pl 1 Unpl 6

14 Dec 05 Newbury 3m Cls3 Nov 107-123 Ch Hcap
£7,352
9 ran GD-SFT 18fncs Time 6m 3.10s (slw 13.10s)
1 **GALLANT APPROACH** 6 11-7 Andrew Tinkler 7/2
*held up in touch, headway to track leader 8th,
led after 14th, shaken up run-in, stayed on well*
[RPR143 TS115 OR120] [op 3/1 tchd 11/4]
2 He's The Guv'nor 6 10-11 Benjamin Hitchcott 12/1
3 Bob The Builder 6 10-8 ....Tony Evans 7/2
Dist: 1¹⁄₂-15-5-4 RACE RPR: 143+/128+/113+
Racecheck: Wins 5 (2) Pl 2 Unpl 6

Philson Run 10-5

11-y-o b g Un Desperado - *Isis (Deep Run)*
Nick Williams Daryl Jacob

Placings: 1/P117/8FP21P6-8

OR137   Starts 1st 2nd 3rd Win & Pl
All Jumps races ...... 13 4 1 - £116,955
131 2/06 Newc 4m1f Cls2 111-137 Ch Hcap heavy .....
£46,479
123 3/05 Uttx 4m1¹⁄₂f Cls1 List 121-147 Ch Hcap gd-sft
£58,000
112 2/05 Chep 3m2¹⁄₂f Cls3 104-118 Ch Hcap soft £5,908
2/04 Winc 3m1¹⁄₂f Cls6 Am Hunt Ch good ...£1,561
Total win prize-money £111,947
GF-HRD 0-0-0 GS-HVY 3-1-9 Course 0-0-1 Dist 0-0-0

17 Feb 06 Haydock 3m4¹⁄₂f Cls1 Gd3 121-150 Ch Hcap
£71,275
16 ran HEAVY 20fncs Time 7m 32.20s (slw 17.20s)
1 Heltornic 7 10-0 ex5 ....Tom Scudamore 12/1
2 L'Aventure 8 10-1 t ....Paddy Merrigan 33/1
3 Mon Mome 7 10-11 ....Mr W Biddick (7) 12/1
8 **PHILSON RUN** 10 10-13 ....P A Carberry 33/1
*behind, headway 16th, closing and 5 lengths off
pace when blundered 2 out, weakened last*
btn 34 lengths [RPR125 TS84 OR137]
9 **BEWLEYS BERRY** 9 11-1 ......P J Brennan 11/1
*midfield, headway 9th, hit 10th, led after 14th,
headed approaching 16th, ridden 3 out, hit 2
out, soon weakened*
btn 48 lengths [RPR110 TS115 OR139] [op 12/1]

11 KANDJAR D'ALLIER 9 11-2 ....
.......................Robert Thornton 16/1
*held up, headway 4 out, ridden 3 out, weakened
approaching 2 out, tailed off*
btn 90 lengths [RPR67 TS84 OR140][tchd 14/1]
12 **NAUNTON BROOK** 8 10-12 t Tony Evans 14/1
*prominent, reminders after 13th (water),
weakened 14th, tailed off (jockey received
caution: used whip when out of contention)*
btn 91 lengths [RPR63 TS79 OR136]
P **KELAMI** 9 11-1 ....Jacques Ricou 8/1
*held up, headway approaching 14th, mistake
16th, weakened after 13th (water),
pulled up before 2 out* [OR139] [op 9/1]
P **THE OUTLIER** 9 10-10 .....P C O'Neill (3) 11/2J
*in touch, pecked 9th, ridden after 13th (water),
mistake 14th, weakened 16th, tailed off when
pulled up before 3 out (trainer's rep had no
explanation for the poor form shown)*
[OR137] [op 13/2 tchd 7/1]
Dist: 1¹⁄₄-15-2¹⁄₂-7-2¹⁄₂ RACE RPR: 143+/144/143
Racecheck: Wins 2 (1) Pl 11 Unpl 34

22 Apr 06 Ayr 4m1f Cls1 Gd3 133-159 Ch Hcap £91,232
30 ran GOOD 27fncs Time 8m 35.10s (slw 28.10s)
1 Run For Paddy 10 10-2 ....Carl Llewellyn 33/1
2 Ladalko 7 10-4 ....R Walsh 7/1J
3 Royal Emperor 10 11-4 ...Dominic Elsworth 50/1
4 **IDLE TALK** 7 10-11 ....Jason Maguire 8/1
*in touch, mistake 15th, led 21st to 23rd, stayed
upsides, weakened after 2 out*
[RPR146 TS84 OR144] [tchd 10/1]
6 **PHILSON RUN** 10 10-5 ....Keith Mercer 33/1
held up, ridden 22nd, never reached leaders
[RPR118 TS66 OR138] [tchd 40/1]
9 **ZABENZ** 9 10-8 b ....Richard Johnson 66/1
*towards rear, headway after 18th, weakened
from 21st*
btn 32 lengths [RPR118 TS67 OR141][op 50/1]
13 **ROYAL AUCLAIR** 9 11-7 t Liam Heard (5) 20/1
*held up in midfield, ridden and weakened after
22nd*
btn 50 lengths [RPR118 TS73 OR159] [op 25/1
tchd 28/1]
Dist: shd-¹⁄₂-10-18-1 RACE RPR: 147+/148+/161+
Racecheck: Wins 2 (1) Pl 11 Unpl 34

18 Mar 06 Uttoxeter 4m1¹⁄₂f Cls1 List 120-145 Ch Hcap
£62,027
18 ran HEAVY 24fncs Time 9m 30.60s (slw 1m 0.60s)
3 G V A Ireland 8 10-3 ....R Walsh 5/1F
2 Ossmoses 9 11-5 ....Richard McGrath 9/1
3 L'Aventure 7 11-2 tb ....Liam Heard 5) 16/1
P **PHILSON RUN** 10 11-5 ....P Carberry 7/1
*held up, hit 18th, always in rear, behind when
pulled up before 4 out*
[OR138] [op 9/1 tchd 10/1]
Dist: 4-14-6-17-2¹⁄₂ RACE RPR: 140+/153+/140
Racecheck: Wins - Pl 1 Unpl 26

25 Feb 06 Newcastle 4m1f Cls2 111-137 Ch Hcap
£46,478
17 ran HEAVY 22fncs Time 9m 3.80s (slw 40.80s)
1 **PHILSON RUN** 10 11-6 ....G Lee 10/1
*held up, headway halfway, led 3 out, soon hard
pressed, driven out run-in*
[RPR143 TS128 OR131] [tchd 11/1]
2 High Cotton 11 9-4 oh9 James Reveley (10) 12/1
3 Korelo 8 11-4 ....Timmy Murphy 7/2F
Dist: 1¹⁄₄-¹⁄₂-1¹⁄₄-dist-13 RACE RPR: 143+/120/140+
Racecheck: Wins 2 Pl 5 Unpl 21

12 Feb 06 Exeter 3m1¹⁄₄f Cls3 112-128 Ch Hcap £9,759
12 ran GD-SFT 19fncs Time 6m 44.80s (slw 34.80s)
1 Gunther McBride 11 11-8 ..Richard Johnson 5/1
2 **PHILSON RUN** 10 11-3 ....Liam Heard (5) 16/1
*held up towards rear, steady headway from
11th, chased winner after 15th, soon ridden,
kept on, held when not fluent last*
[RPR136 TS110 OR128] [tchd 20/1]
3 World Wide Web 10 11-3 b Mick FitzGerald 14/1
Dist: 2-25-3-2-dist RACE RPR: 140+/136+/105
Racecheck: Wins 2 (2) Pl 6 Unpl 11

27 Dec 05 Chepstow 3m5½f Cls1 Gd3 127-153 Ch Hcap £57,020
18 ran GD-SFT 22fncs Time 7m 38.90s (slw 8.90s)
1 L'Aventure 6 10-4 tb ....Leighton Aspell 14/1
2 Heros Collonges 10 10-11 Christian Williams 25/1
3 Cornish Rebel 8 11-12 ....R Walsh 9/2J
P **PHILSON RUN** 9 10-6 ow5 ....Tom Doyle 25/1
always behind, mistake 15th, tailed off when pulled up before 17th [RPR- OR133] [op 20/1]
P **MCKELVEY** 6 10-8 ....Tony Dobbin 8/1
mid-division, mistake 16th, soon behind, tailed off when pulled up before 5 out [RPR- OR135]
Dist: dist-nk-1¾-3-1½ RACE RPR: 151+/124/138
Racecheck: Wins 2 Pl 6 Unpl 23

16 Apr 05 Ayr 4m1f Cls1 Gd3 132-163 Ch Hcap £70,000
20 ran GOOD 27fncs Time 8m 23.80s (slw 16.80s)
1 **JOES EDGE** 8 9-11 ex5 oh5 Keith Mercer (3) 20/1
held up and behind, headway 19th, led 2 out to after last, rallied gamely to lead close home
[RPR145 TS76 OR132]
2 Cornish Rebel 8 10-7 ....R Walsh 9/2
3 Another Rum 7 10-0 oh17 ..Anthony Ross 10/1
6 **LONGSHANKS** 8 10-0 oh4 ...Carl Llewellyn 9/1
took keen hold, mistakes, held up, effort 22nd, never reached leaders
[RPR111 TS55 OR137] [op 10/1]
7 **PHILSON RUN** 9 10-0 oh5 .....S E Durack 12/1
held up in midfield, ridden 19th, soon outpaced
btn 34 lengths [RPR111 TS55 OR137]
Dist: shd-10-3½-3-17 RACE RPR: 145+/153+/136+
Racecheck: Wins 2 (1) Pl 11 Unpl 22

Silver Birch 10-6

10-y-o *b g Clearly Bust - All Gone (Giolla Mear)*
Gordon Elliott (IRE) R M Power

Placings: 3124P/111/4PPF-38242

OR138H111	Starts	1st	2nd	3rd	Win & Pl
Chase	13	4	3	1	£127,130
All Jumps races	20	6	3	2	**£138,364**

132	12/04	Chep	3m5½f Cls1 Gd3 126-153 Ch Hcap heavy £58,000
123	11/04	Aint	3m3f Cls2 122-146 Ch Hcap soft £43,500
119	11/04	NAbb	3m2½f Cls3 93-119 Ch Hcap soft £6,895
	1/04	Chep	3m2½f Cls4 Ch soft £3,907
	1/03	Plum	3m1½f Cls3 Nov Hdl heavy £5,473
	11/02	Chep	2m4f Cls3 Nov Hdl soft £4,232

Total win prize-money £122,007

GF-HRD 0-0-0 **GS-HVY** 6-4-18 **Course** 1-0-2 **Dist** 0-0-1

13 Mar Cheltenham X-Cntry 3m7f Cls2 124-150 Ch Hcap £28,184
16 ran SOFT 32fncs Time 8m 43.80s (slw 33.80s)
1 Heads Onthe Ground 10 10-2 Miss N Carberry 5/2F
2 **SILVER BIRCH** 10 11-0 t ....Jason Maguire 14/1
prominent, chased leader 6 out, ridden and lost 2nd 2 out, rallied to chase winner last, kept on but no real impression [RPR148 TS50 OR138]
3 **LE DUC** 8 10-10 ....Sam Thomas 8/1
prominent, tracked leader 24th, led 6 out, driven 2 out, headed and weakened well before last (jockey received two-day ban: careless riding (Mar 24-25))
[RPR131 TS37 OR134] [tchd 9/1 & 10/1]
6 **ROYAL AUCLAIR** 10 11-5 t .....Joe Tizzard 10/1
tracked leader, led 22nd until headed and blundered 24th, lost place rapidly, blundered 6 out, no chance after, ran on near finish
[RPR122 TS31 OR143]
Dist: 3½-12-5-5-11 RACE RPR: 143+/148+/131
Racecheck: Wins - Pl 1 Unpl 6

21 Feb Punchestown 2m4f Hdl £8,171
12 ran HEAVY Time 5m 33.20s (slw 52.20s)
1 Wheresben 8 10-13 ....Mr J A Fahey (7) 9/2
2 Baron de Feypo 9 11-2 ....J L Cullen 11/1
3 Pearly Jack 9 10-11 Mr M J O'Connor (5) 100/30
4 **SILVER BIRCH** 10 10-9 t ....D P Fahy (7) 14/1
in rear of mid-division, progress from before 3 out, moderate 5th approaching straight, kept on without threatening under pressure
[RPR120 TS83]

5 **LIVINGSTONEBRAMBLE** 11 10-11 ....R J Kiely (5) 5/2F
mid-division, 7th approaching 2 out, soon no impression under pressure, kept on without threatening
[RPR118 TS81 OR119] [op 3/1 tchd 100/30]
Dist: ½-5-2-2-5½ RACE RPR: 132/127/122
Racecheck: Wins 2 Pl 2 Unpl 4

4 Feb Punchestown 3m Ch £7,003
23 ran SOFT Time 6m 42.70s (slw 32.70s)
1 Heads Onthe Ground 10 11-4 ....Mr J T McNamara 3/1F
2 **SILVER BIRCH** 10 11-4 t ....R M Power 8/1
always prominent, 4th 6 out, improved into 2nd 2 out, soon ridden and outpaced, kept on from last [RPR117 TS117] [op 9/1]
3 Never Compromise 12 11-6 ..Ms K Walsh (3) 5/1
Dist: 10-15-5-2-4 RACE RPR: 127+/117/107
Racecheck: Wins 1 Pl 2 Unpl 7

8 Dec 06 Cheltenham X-Cntry 3m7f Cls2 118-144 Ch Hcap £14,405
12 ran SOFT 32fncs Time 9m 15.20s (slw 1m 5.20s)
1 Spot Thedifference 13 11-12 p ....Mr J T McNamara 6/1
2 Plum'tee 11 10-4 ....Jacques Ricou 9/2
3 Heads Onthe Ground 9 10-3 p P Carberry 100/30F
4 **LE DUC** 7 11-2 ....Sam Thomas 8/1
held up towards rear, not fluent 18th, mistake 21st, headway 25th, hard ridden approaching last, one pace flat [RPR136 TS63 OR134]
8 **SILVER BIRCH** 9 11-10 t ....Jason Maguire 33/1
held up in touch, every chance 2 out, weakened approaching last
btn 8 lengths [RPR137 TS67 OR142] [op 25/1]
Dist: 1-1¼-½-4-½ RACE RPR: 147+/125+/122
Racecheck: Wins 1 Pl 8 Unpl 7

19 Nov 06 Castletown-Geoghegan (PTP) 3m
7 ran SOFT Time 6m 58.00s
1 Captain Moonlight 10 12-0 ....G Mangan 4/1
2 Native Leisure 11 12-0 ....J T Carroll 5/1
3 **SILVER BIRCH** 9 12-0 ....J T McNamara 5/4F
sn 2nd, flatfooted 3out, eff to be 2nd at last, onepcd on flat [RPR93]
Dist: 7-¾ RACE RPR: 110/94/93
Racecheck: Wins 1 Pl 2 Unpl 4

8 Apr 06 Aintree 4m4f Cls1 Gd3 134-156 Ch Hcap £399,140
40 ran GD-SFT 30fncs Time 9m 41.00s (slw 27.00s)
1 **NUMBERSIXVALVERDE** 10 10-8 ....N P Madden 11/1
held up, smooth headway 17th, soon tracking leaders going well, led last, shaken up and stayed on strongly to forge clear
[RPR154 TS151 OR138] [tchd 12/1]
2 **HEDGEHUNTER** 10 11-12 ....R Walsh 5/1J
with leaders, left in lead 25th (2nd Valentines), headed last, no extra
[RPR166 TS165 OR156] [op 11/2 tchd 6/1]
3 **CLAN ROYAL** 11 10-10 ....A P McCoy 5/1J
held up, headway to chase leaders 17th, blundered 19th, challenged 3 out, rallied to take 3rd on line [RPR151 TS149 OR140] [op 11/2]
6 **PUNTAL** 10 10-12 t ....B J Geraghty 66/1
chased leaders, weakened 23rd (2nd Foinavon), kept on from 2 out [RPR97 OR142]
7 **JOES EDGE** 9 10-10 ....D N Russell 20/1
mid-division, headway 17th, mistake 19th, lost place approaching 2 out
btn 56+ lengths [RPR95 OR140] [tchd 25/1]
F **ROYAL AUCLAIR** 9 11-12 t Christian Williams 33/1
fell 1st [OR156]
F **SILVER BIRCH** 9 10-12 t .....Sam Thomas 40/1
in touch until hampered and fell 15th (Chair)
[OR142] [op 33/1]

U **JACK HIGH** 11 10-7 ....D J Casey 9/
in rear until blundered and unseated rider 15t (Chair) [OR137] [op 12/1
U **LE DUC** 7 10-10 ....Jamie Moore 33/
mid-division, blundered, rider lost iron and unseated rider 8th (Canal Turn) [OR140] [50
F **BALLYCASSIDY** 10 10-9 ...Leighton Aspell 80/
prominent, led 9th (1st Valentines), 6 lengths clear when fell 25th (2nd Valentines) [OR139
Dist: 6-1¼-shd-dist-16 RACE RPF
154+/166+/151+
Racecheck: Wins 2 Pl 5 Unpl 53

18 Feb 06 Wincanton Pulled Up, see **CELTIC SON**

26 Jan 06 Warwick 3m1f Cls3 95-120 Hdl Hcap £5,20
16 ran SOFT 12hdls Time 6m 22.00s (slw 34.00s
1 Passenger Omar 8 10-4 t .W T Kennedy (3) 4/1
2 Jiver 7 11-2 v1 ....Tom Scudamore 25/
3 **CLAN ROYAL** 11 11-1 ....A P McCoy 13/
held up and behind, headway approaching 8th ridden after 3 out, weakened approaching las
[RPR105 TS77 OR109] [op 6/1]
4 **SILVER BIRCH** 9 11-5 ...Christian Williams 4/1
led approaching 2nd to 3 out, soon ridden, weakened approaching last
[RPR108 TS81 OR113] [op 7/2 tchd 9/2]
Dist: ½-12-hd-3½-hd RACE RPR: 111+/117/105+
Racecheck: Wins 1 Pl 6 Unpl 17

Liberthine 10-6

8-y-o *b m Chamberlin - Libertina (Balsamo)*
N J Henderson Mr S Waley-Coher

Placings: 14/238410/7U5814-489

OR138H130	Starts	1st	2nd	3rd	Win & P
Chase	16	3	1	1	£137,155
All Jumps races	24	6	2	1	**£183,360**

130	4/06	Aint	2m5½f Cls2 119-145 Ch Hcap good £62,63
128	3/05	Chel	2m5f Cls1 Gd3 120-146 Ch Hcap good £43,50
	3/04	Strf	2m4f Cls3 Ch good £5,56
	9/02	Autl	2m2f Hdl 3yo v soft £19,14
	7/02	Autl	2m1½f Hdl 3yo v soft £11,779
	6/02	Diep	1m7f Hdl 3yo good £4,12

Total win prize-money £146,73

GF-HRD 0-1-1 **GS-HVY** 2-2-16 **Course** 1-0-2 **Dist** 0-0-

14 Mar Cheltenham 3m½f Cls2 123-139 Am Ch Hcap £33,01
24 ran GD-SFT 19fncs Time 6m 16.51s (slw 11.51s
1 Cloudy Lane 7 10-11 ....Mr R Burton 15/2F
2 Parsons Legacy 9 11-3 Mr Derek O'Connor 12/1
3 Cheeky Lady 10 10-7 ....Mr R O'Sullivan (3) 20/1
9 **LIBERTHINE** 8 11-8 ..Mr S Waley-Cohen (3) 9/1
always towards rear and never in contention
btn 22 lengths [RPR125 TS107 OR138] [op 8/1 tchd 10/1 & 11/1]
P **NAUNTON BROOK** 8 11-6 t Mr R Morgan (3) 33/1
always towards rear, tailed off when pulled up before 3 out [OR136]
Dist: ¾-2-½-1½-1¾ RACE RPR: 135+/139+/130+
Racecheck: Wins - Pl 1 Unpl 6

10 Feb Newbury 3m½f Cls3 108-130 Hdl Hcap £6,263
16 ran SOFT 12hdls Time 5m 57.30s (slw 7.80s)
1 Copsale Lad 10 11-7 ....Andrew Tinkler 14/1
2 Minella Tipperary 6 10-10 Richard Johnson 9/2F
3 Isle de Maurice 5 10-4 b ....Jamie Moore 15/2
8 **LIBERTHINE** 8 11-5 ..Mr S Waley-Cohen (7) 8/1
in touch, headway 6th, ridden approaching 3 out and soon weakened
btn 47 lengths [RPR100 TS107 OR130]
Dist: 5-15-¾-5-3 RACE RPR: 145+/126/108+
Racecheck: Wins 3 (3) Pl 4 Unpl 6

8 Dec 06 Cheltenham 3m1½f Cls1 List 131-156 Ch Hcap £57,020
15 ran SOFT 21fncs Time 6m 59.90s (slw 40.90s)
1 d'Argent 9 10-5 ....Robert Thornton 10/1
2 New Alco 5 10-5 ....G Lee 6/1J
3 My Will 6 11-12 ....R Walsh 6/1J
4 **LIBERTHINE** 7 10-4 ow3 ....Mr S Waley-Cohen (7) 10/1
chased leaders, ridden and hit 3 out, outpaced from next [RPR142 TS101 OR141] [tchd 12/1]

12 **JACK HIGH** 11 10-11 ....D N Russell 40/1
*in rear when hit 12th and 14th, some headway 4
out, never in contention, no chance when badly
hampered 2 out*
    btn 45 lengths [RPR108 TS69 OR141][op 50/1]
Dist: shd-shd-8-3-4   RACE RPR: 145+/144+/164
After a stewards' inquiry, the placings remained unaltered
Racecheck: Wins 2 Pl 6 Unpl 20

29 Apr 06 Sandown 3m5½f   Cls1 Gd3 133-159 Ch
                                          Hcap £91,232
18 ran GD-FM   24fncs   Time 7m 18.80s (slw 1.80s)
1 Lacdoudal 7 11-5 ....Richard Johnson 10/1
2 Eric's Charm 8 10-7 ....Leighton Aspell 8/1
3 My Will 6 11-2 ....R Walsh 8/1
4 **LIBERTHINE** 7 9-13 ow6 oh3 ....
...............................Mr S Waley-Cohen (7) 10/1
*not always fluent, well in touch, effort to chase
leading pair 19th, no impression and lost 3rd 3
out, faded*
    [RPR139 TS100 OR139]   [op 8/1 tchd 11/1]
9 **JACK HIGH** 11 10-7 ....G Cotter 10/1
*always well in rear, lost touch with leading
group from 17th, under pressure and tail
swishing furiously before 2 out*
    btn 39 lengths [RPR110 TS82 OR140][tchd 9/1]

10 **PUNTAL** 10 10-9 t ....Tom Scudamore 12/1
*tracked leading pair to 11th, soon ridden, losing
place when mistake 14th, toiling in rear from
17th*
    btn 45 lengths [RPR106 TS79 OR142][op 10/1]
12 **ROYAL AUCLAIR** 9 11-7 t Liam Heard (5) 25/1
*always well in rear, struggling and jumped
slowly 14th, well behind after*
    btn 54 lengths [RPR115 TS91 OR159]
Dist: 1¼-hd-10-2-1½   RACE RPR: 164+/149+/158+
Racecheck: Wins 2 (1) Pl 3 Unpl 20

7 Apr 06 Aintree 2m5½f   Cls2 119-145 Ch Hcap
                                          £62,630
29 ran GOOD   18fncs   Time 5m 36.00s (slw 11.00s)
1 **LIBERTHINE** 7 10-4 .Mr S Waley-Cohen (7) 16/1
*chased leaders, challenged 2 out, jumped right
and led last, stayed on gamely*
    [RPR147 TS146 OR130]
2 Hakim 12 10-6 ....P J Brennan 13/2F
3 Pak Jack 6 10-0 oh1 ....Timmy Murphy 25/1
Dist: 1½-5-2½-1½-5   RACE RPR: 147+/138/127
Racecheck: Wins 7 Pl 7 Unpl 30

15 Mar 06 Cheltenham 3m1½f Cls2 118-139 Am Ch
                                          Hcap £30,010
21 ran GOOD   19fncs   Time 6m 10.30s (slw 5.30s)
1 You're Special 9 10-12 t ....Mr R O Harding 33/1

2 Mon Mome 6 10-5 ....Mr W Biddick (7) 11/1
3 Undeniable 8 10-9 ....Miss N Carberry 16/1
8 **LIBERTHINE** 7 11-0 .Mr S Waley-Cohen (5) 7/1J
*behind, ridden 4 out, moderate progress 3 out
but never in contention*
    btn 18½ lengths [RPR132 TS119 OR132]   [op
11/2 tchd 15/2]
Dist: 3½-8-1½-shd-1¼ RACE RPR: 146+/143+/130
Racecheck: Wins 6 (3) Pl 8 Unpl 22

7 Jan 06 Sandown 5th, see GRAPHIC APPROACH

8 Apr 05 Aintree 2m5½f   Cls2 119-145 Ch Hcap
                                          £46,400
30 ran GD-GD   18fncs   Time 5m 31.80s (slw 6.80s)
1 Cregg House 10 10-5 ow1 .....D N Russell 50/1
2 Haut de Gamme 10 10-10 .Keith Mercer (3) 25/1
3 **LE DUC** 6 11-3 ....R Walsh 20/1
*held up, headway 14th, stayed on same pace
between last 2* [RPR141 TS136 OR136][op 16/1]
4 **LONGSHANKS** 8 11-0 ....John McNamara 9/2F
chased leaders, led 2 out to last, one pace
    [RPR136 TS133 OR133]   [op 11/2 tchd 6/1]
14 **LIBERTHINE** 6 10-12 Mr S Waley-Cohen (7) 10/1
*in rear when hampered 9th and 10th (Bechers),
kept on from 3 out, never on terms*
    btn 44 lengths [RPR109 TS101 OR138][op 12/1]
Dist: 1-5-nk-2-2½   RACE RPR: 134+/140/141+
Racecheck: Wins 2 (1) Pl 8 Unpl 38

Form Reading	**SONEVAFUSHI**
Spotlight	Fairly useful hunter chaser nowadays.
Handicap Ratings	Mark of 136 four outings ago, 135 today.
Significant Items of Form	Nine year old with six chase wins, last of which in February 2007 was in an Amateur Riders Hunter Chase.
Verdict	Most unlikely that a horse being campaigned in low grade hunter chases is going to have the ability to be in the places in this contest.
Decision:	DISMISS

Form Reading	**THE OUTLIER**
Spotlight	Good run of form on favoured testing ground in mid winter.
Handicap Ratings	Highest mark in last six outings of 137, which was mark for last two outings (pulled up both races). Same mark for today's race.
Significant Items of Form	Nine year old with four chase wins, the first three of which were Class 4 contests. Last win in Janary 2007 however was a Class 1 Handicap Chase over 3m at Haydock (Heavy) with 9 runners. All form on Good to Soft – Heavy. Last two runs on 17.03.07 and 17.02.07 on favoured ground were both poor (pulled up both times).
Verdict	Out of form, ground not ideal, distance unproven.
Hence:	DISMISS.

Form Reading	**CELTIC SON**
Spotlight	Easy winner of a Grade 2 on last season's chase debut, but hasn't gone on from that in six starts.
Handicap Ratings	Mark of 144 three outings ago (placed 2nd) and mark of 143 for last outing (pulled up); same mark today.
Significant Items of Form	Eight year old with five hurdle wins and one Class 1 chase win, Wincanton (Good), November 2005. Only one run since March 2006 and that was on

	14.02.07 in a Class 1 Handicap Chase at Kempton (Soft) when pulled up, 'always towards rear',
Verdict	Insufficient experience to figure in this contest.
Hence:	DISMISS.

Form Reading	**PUNTAL**
Spotlight	Has shown up well in two previous tries in this, last year fading into distant 6th back from sixteen months off the track.
Handicap Ratings	Allocated a mark of 142 for run which followed its 6th place in last year's Grand National. Mark of 137 for today's contest.
Significant Items of Form	Eleven year old with five chase wins, the best of which was in the Whitbread Gold Cup in April 2004. Last two runs were on 24.02.07 when 7th of 10 in a Class 1 Handicap Chase at Kempton (Soft) over 3m, beaten 32 lengths and on 17.03.07 when pulled up before 18th in the Midlands National at Uttoxeter.
Verdict	Although last year's 6th in the Grand National was impressive, horse's current form is not. Difficult to see sufficient form improvement to figure in this year's running.
Hence:	DISMISS.

Form Reading	**KNOWHERE**
Spotlight	Novice whose second, splitting top class chasers, in big 2m5f Cheltenham Handicap in December reads very well but form has tailed off since.
Handicap Ratings	Mark of 148 two outings ago (placed 8th). Mark of 145 for today's race.
Significant Items of Form	Nine year old with two chase wins, the last of which was in a Class 3 Novice Chase at Bangor over 2m4½f in October 2006. Good run at Cheltenham when 2nd to Exotic Dancer over 2m5f in December 2006, but three runs since then at Cheltenham and Kempton, albeit in Class 1 contents, have all been unconvincing.
Verdict	Everything says experience is insufficient for today's contest and recent form endorses that viewpoint.
Hence:	DISMISS.

Form Reading	**TIKRAM**
Spotlight	Capable handicapper at up to around 3m.
Handicap Ratings	Mark of 146 five outings ago (placed 8th). Mark of 137 for today's race.
Significant Items of Form	Ten year old with four chase wins including a win over 2m4½f in a Class 1 event at Cheltenham Festival in March 2004 over 2m4½f and a Class 2 win at Sandown in April 2005 over the same distance. Placings since that last win read 2008-0440. Two runs in 2007 at Sandown (Good to Soft) on 03.02.07 in a Class 2 Handicap over 3m½f when 4th of 18, beaten 7½ lengths, and Cheltenham (Good to Soft) on 15.03.07 in a Class 1 Handicap Chase over 2m5f when 12th of 23, beaten 18½ lengths.
Verdict	Difficult to envisage horse in its current form raising its game sufficiently, over a much longer distance than it is normally used to, to trouble principals.
Decision:	DISMISS.

Form Reading	**NAUNTON BROOK**
Spotlight	Thorough stayer, looked to be feeling the effects of a long season, with below par efforts in last two runs.
Handicap Ratings	Has improved from a mark of 119 when winning six outings ago to a mark of 136 today.
Significant Items of Form	Eight year old with five chase wins, all of them in Class 3 events, the last three of which were secured in 2006 and included a 4m win at Hexham. Since last win at Exeter on 14.12.06, form has tailed off and last two runs at Haydock on 17.02.07 in a Class 1 Handicap Chase over 3m4½f on Heavy (12th of 16, beaten 91 lengths) and at Cheltenham on 14.03.07 in a Class 2 Handicap Chase over 3m½f on Good to Soft (pulled up before 3 out) have been unimpressive.
Verdict	Has not had a decent break since Winning Spree in November/December 2006 so sensible to assume will not be returning to form today.
Hence:	DISMISS.

Form Reading	**CLOUDY BAYS**
Spotlight	Not quite the horse he was, untried over 3m1f.
Handicap Ratings	No handicap chases in last six outings. Mark of 146 for today's race.
Significant Items of Form	Ten year old with six chase victories all in Ireland, most recent of which was in a £17,000 Listed Chase at Tranmore in January 2007 over 2m6f. Two runs since that win, at Leopardstown on 14.01.07 and Cheltenham 15.03.07 have both been in hurdle events and unimpressive (8th of 27 and fell 5th respectively).
Verdict	Though hurdle races can be the correct preparation for today's race, overall form record would surely have to be a lot better than that possessed by Cloudy Bays to figure in today's race.
Hence:	DISMISS decision is the only logical one to make.

Form Reading	**THISTHATANDTOTHER**
Spotlight	Not quite the force of old this season on return from a year off.
Handicap Ratings	Mark of 157 three outings ago (placed 5th). Down to a mark of 151 today.
Significant Items of Form	Eleven year old with five chase and three hurdle wins, six of which have been at 2m and longest 2m5f. Second in a Class 1 Chase at Ascot (Good to Soft) over 2m3f in February 2007 and 7th of 9 runners in a Class 1 Chase at Cheltenham Festival over 2m5f on 15.03.07 (latest).
Verdict	I know 2½ milers can make the transition to the 4½m distance of the National in some instances but this is an eleven year old 2 miler and the chances of it being competitive are zilch!
Decision:	DISMISS.

Form Reading	**LIVINGSTONEBRAMBLE**
Spotlight	Much better jumper nowadays; untried beyond 3m and good mid winter form tailing off of late.
Handicap Ratings	Mark of 133 three outings ago (placed 2nd), which was raised to 141 for last outing (placed 16th); same mark for today's race.
Significant Items of Form	Eleven year old with three chase victories in Ireland, longest distance 2m4f, last of which was in April 2006. Last two runs on 21.02.07 at Punchestown (Heavy)

when 5th of 12 runners in a 2m4f hurdle and on 15.03.07 at Cheltenham (Good to Soft) when 16th of 23 runners in a Class 1 2m5f Handicap Chase have provided no evidence that this horse is any different than its form figures indicate.

Verdict	Out of its depth in this race.
Hence:	DISMISS.

Form Reading	**GRAPHIC APPROACH**
Spotlight	Decent second season handicapper at up to 3m but weighted up to best.
Handicap Ratings	Mark of 132 six outings ago (placed first); now on a mark of 138.
Significant Items of Form	Nine year old with three chase wins between January 2005 and January 2006, the best of which was a Class 2 Handicap Chase at Sandown (Good to Soft) over 3m½f. Most recent campaign started on 11.11.06 at Cheltenham in a Class 1 Chase when 5th to Exotic Dancer and that was followed by a Class 1 Handicap Chase at Ascot on 16.12.06 when 3rd of 18, beaten 14 lengths. Last run was at Cheltenham Festival on 15.03.06, again a Class 1 Handicap Chase, was a poor performance culminating in unseating at the 11th in what was a 2m5f contest.
Verdict	Recent form does nothing to indicate that horse has any sort of chance in today's contest.
Hence:	DISMISS.

Form Reading	**GALLANT APPROACH**
Spotlight	Decent handicapper over fences; stamina to prove over 3m; only six chase runs.
Handicap Ratings	On a mark of 120 six outings ago (placed 1st) and ran off a mark of 141 last outing (placed 7th) which is also today's mark.
Significant Items of Form	Eight year old with two chase victories (Class 3 and Class 2) in December 2005 and November 2006, both at Newbury over 2m4f and 3m, as well as one Class 4 Novice Hurdle win in November 2005 at Huntingdon. Current campaign started on 25.11.06 after a seven month break with a win at Newbury in a Class 2 Handicap Chase over 2m4f on Soft. Ran next at Haydock 0n 16.12.06 when 3rd in a Class 2 Handicap Chase on Heavy over 3m when only beaten half a length plus a neck. Rested until the Cheltenham Festival on 13.03.07 when finished 7th of 23 in a Class 1 Handicap Chase over 3m½f, beaten 17½ lengths, after being hampered 2 out when being ridden.
Verdict	All the form indicators, including rocketing handicap ratings, describe a rapidly improving chaser that likes flat courses. How the horse will cope with the unique National fences at Aintree is anybody's guess and although the horse is very short on experience, it definitely looks like it is one for the future and who is to say that it won't run on for a place in today's contest. If it likes Newbury, left handed, flat and stiff fences, and if it takes to the National fences it could well excel at Aintree.
Hence:	SELECT.

Form Reading	**PHILSON RUN**
Spotlight	Has two important marathons in his trophy cabinet. Fell at the first in one previous try over these fences.
Handicap Ratings	Ran off a mark of 131 four outings ago (placed 1st) which was raised to 138 for next outing. Mark of 137 for today's race.
Significant Items of Form	Eleven year old with four Chase wins, the last two of which have been in major long distance contests, the Midlands National over 4m1½f at Uttoxeter (good to soft) in March 2005, a £58,000 Class 1 contest and a 4m1f race at Newcastle (Heavy) in February 2006, a £46,000 Class 2 contest. Following its Newcastle win it had only two more runs in 2006, the Midlands National at Uttoxeter (heavy) on 18.03.06 when pulled up before 4 out and the Scottish National over 4m1f at Ayr (good) on 22.04.06 when 6th of 30, beaten 29½ lengths. Ten month break followed until 17.02.07 when 8th of 16 in a Class 1 £71,000 Handicap Chase at Haydock (heavy) over 3m4½f, beaten 34 lengths after 'headway 16th closing and 5 lengths off pace when blundered 2 out'.
Verdict	Although this horse's only visits to today's course and fences resulted in a fall at the first, its form at extended distances and at Newcastle, Haydock and Ayr (all left hand flat courses) indicates that Aintree should suit, as should today's going (Good) based on its Ayr April 2006 run. Looking at its most recent form, its latest run on 17.02.07 after a 10 month break was full of promise until blunder 2 out, and with a further 2 month break to prepare for today's toughest of challenges its form should be spot on. Top 3 placing a definite possibility.
Fence:	SELECT.

Form Reading	**SILVER BIRCH**
	(Courtesy Of Course Winner Option)
Spotlight	Took 2004 Becher Chase here for Paul Nicholls. Out of sorts last season on return from a year off with a leg injury, back to form in soft/heavy ground cross country chases of late.
Handicap Ratings	On a mark of 142 five outings ago and a mark of 138 for last outing (placed 2nd), same mark today.
Significant Items of Form	Ten year old with 4 chase wins including the Welsh National at Chepstow (Heavy) in December 2004 and the Becher Chase at Aintree (Soft) in November 2004. Most recent campaign started on 04.02.07 when 2nd of 23 in a 3m chase at Punchestown (Soft) and that was followed on 21.02.07 by a 4th of 12 in a 2m4f hurdle also at Punchestown (heavy), beaten 30 lengths. Next and most recent race was the 3m7f Cross Country Chase at the Cheltenham Festival (Soft) on 13.03.07 when 2nd of 16 runners, beaten 3½ lengths.
Verdict	Just over two years ago this horse had all the credentials necessary to be a strongly fancied runner in the Grand National, before a leg injury intervened. All the signs are this horse is returning to its former form at just the right time for a course and fences over which it has race winning form and over a distance and on going which should not be a problem. Top three placing a definite possibility.
Fence:	SELECT.

Form Reading	**LIBERTHINE**
	(Courtesy of Course Winner Option)
Spotlight	Took last season's Topham over these fences under this young amateur rider.
Handicap Ratings	Mark of 130 five outings ago (placed 1st) which had been raised to 141 three outings ago (placed 4th). Mark of 138 for last outing (placed 9th) and same mark today.
Significant Items of Form	Eight year old with three chase wins, the most important of which were a Class 1 Handicap Chase over 2m5f at the Cheltenham Festival (Good) in March 2005 and a Class 2 Handicap Chase (The Topham Chase) of 2m5½f over the National fences at Aintree (Good) in April 2006. Most recent campaign started on 08.12.06 at Cheltenham (Soft) when 4th of 15, beaten 8 lengths in a Class 1 Chase over 3m1½f. Ran next on 10.02.07 at Newbury (Soft) when 8th of 16 in a Class 3 Handicap Hurdle and that was followed on 14.03.07 by a Class 2 Handicap Chase of 3m½f at Cheltenham Festival (Good to Soft) when 9th of 24 runners, beaten 22 lengths.
Verdict	Although recent form has not been as good as when winning at Aintree in April 2006 it would be a hard call to pass by a young up and coming chaser who has already demonstrated that the National fences are not a problem and good going will suit. Horse was close enough, 11½ lengths, when finishing 4th in a Class 1 Handicap Chase over 3m5½f at Sandown (Good to Firm) in April 2006 to indicate that today's distance of 4½ miles will not necessarily be a problem. Having had a month's break since its last run at Cheltenham, a top 3 placing has got to be a reasonable possibility.
Hence:	SELECT.

Overall Comment

I was obviously delighted that The Tail End System came up trumps and produced not only the winner, Silver Birch at 33/1, but also the fourth, Philson Run at 100/1 and the fifth Libertine at 40/1.

What I was most chuffed about was dismissing eleven horses in the form reading process before selecting Gallant Approach (finished 12th) and Philson Run, though, having said that, I found that the dismissal decisions made themselves quite easily.

After making my first two selections, choosing the Course Winner option for my next two selections was a very easy one to make for two reasons.

Firstly, when I need to make more than two selections I always opt to pursue the Course Winner Option route first of all (assuming it is available) because my experience has taught me that course form of any description is extremely important and frequently gives horses the edge over the remainder of the field.

Secondly, because the fences at Aintree on the National course are unique and quite unlike fences anywhere else in Britain, the value of course form is probably worth double its normal value.

However, before I wax too lyrical about the result on this occasion, I must point out that, in my view, the chance of similar success using The Tail End System in the Grand National in the foreseeable future is quite remote. The Grand National over the last few years has, with the exception of Red Marauder, not been won by what you would genuinely term an 'outsider' and therefore a good few years could well pass before The Tail End System provides the winner again.

What is far more likely, however, is that The Tail End System could repeat the feat of throwing up at least one over long priced 'outsider' in the placings, particularly as some of the bookies are now offering each way odds on the first five finishers.

Nevertheless, despite this story of success in 2007 it hasn't altered my view that the Grand National, given its 40 runners, is a bookie's benefit and the majority of starting prices on offer represent very poor value. In this setting you should always approach the race with a good degree of realism and appreciate the fact that you could have selected ten horses and still not found the winner.

It is for all these reasons that Aintree does not appear on the Preferred List of Racecourses and another reason why Class 1 and Class 2 races are not Preferred contests as far as The Tail End System is concerned.

For the record, the Forecast of Silver Birch with McKelvey (8th horse in the Betting Forecast and 5th in the actual betting on the day) paid £667.60 for the Tote Exacta and £369.65 for the Computer Straight Forecast.

Chapter 24
THE HIGH PROFILE TRACKS AND MEETINGS

As a follower of sport I class myself as a grateful traditionalist because all three sports which receive the majority of my attention, namely jump racing, professional cycling and golf, all offer history, tradition, legendary names and sporting occasions of the type which produce golden moments by the cartload and tears of emotion by the bucketful.

However, over the years I have learned to recognise that in jump racing, for all the reasons I have just mentioned, it is all too easy to get over excited about the big meetings and the big races to an extent where you lose touch with reality, throw caution to the winds and end up losing a pile of money on sporting contests which quite frankly are almost a bridge too far for whatever type of betting system you employ.

The type of betting challenges which are presented by the Class 1 and Class 2 events (regardless of whether they are level weight or handicap contests) at the big meetings are, in the main, extremely difficult to solve because the prize money and kudos of winning ensures that practically every runner has been laid out for the race concerned.

The degree of difficulty in picking horses at a decent enough price to make any financial involvement worthwhile is highlighted by the following chart, giving a summary of events at the 2007 Cheltenham Festival and the Aintree Grand National 3-Day meeting, excluding any Hunter Chases (there were only a total of two such events at both festivals) and National Hunt flat/bumper races.

CHELTENHAM FESTIVAL AND AINTREE GRAND NATIONAL THREE DAY MEETING 2007

	Handicap Races			Non Handicap Races		
Cheltenham Festival	No of Races	Average No of Runners	Average Starting Price of Winn.ers	No of Races	Average No of Runners	Average Starting Price of Winners
Day 1	3	21	19/1	3	15	19/1
Day 2	2	26	8/1	3	14	8/1
Day 3	4	21	20/1	2	11	5/1
Day 4	2	25	12/1	3	20	5/2
Aintree Grand National Three Day Meeting	No of Races	Average No of Runners	Average Starting Price of Winners	No of Races	Average No of Runners	Average Starting Price of Winners
Day 1	2	18	16/1	4	8	7/4
Day 2	2	23	15/1	4	8	10/1
Day 3	4	23	16/1	2	8	7/1

Special Note: All of the above races were either Class 1 or Class 2 races.

Looking at the above chart from a pure betting point of view, and disregarding completely any particular system of selection, I think you have to conclude that the vast majority of the races this year did not offer a particularly brilliant betting opportunity if you were attempting to come away from any one day at either of those Festivals with a reasonable level of profit.

The Handicap Races, which in theory should be easier to sort out than the Non Handicap

Races, had an average field of twenty-two runners and with those types of numbers you could make half a dozen selections per race and still miss the winners.

The other problem that was present was a range of starting prices, which were skinny to say the least, and did not reflect in any way, shape or form the degree of difficulty involved in these contests. The problem which exists is one where our two main festivals of racing are getting more and more popular with the betting public and with the bookies knowing that the vast majority of punters will get caught up with the excitement and carry on punting regardless, they are shortening their prices.

Looking to the future, I cannot, unfortunately, see any significant alteration to this disturbing trend of reducing value and although the Tote and the Exchanges can frequently provide a better alternative than the bookies, they are not always a feasible alternative for many.

Concentrating for a moment on The Tail End System and how it fares in sorting out the big races, the biggest problem it has is in being effective in a situation where there are twenty plus fields of runners, because even if you are making up to four selections in the form reading/selection process, you could still not move far enough down the list of longest priced runners in the betting forecast to unearth a 33/1 shot which goes on to win. It is for this reason, coupled with the intense competition aspect of Class 1 and Class 2 races that these contests have been excluded from the Preferred Class and Preferred Type of races.

Cheltenham, Aintree, Haydock, Sandown, Kempton and Ascot all appear on the Non-Preferred List of Racecourses because, as high profile tracks primarily concerned with the provision of high class racing, they are providing the type of contests which generally make it far more difficult for long priced 'outsiders' to succeed.

It is in recognition of the situation that I have described that, as the creator of a betting system designed to win money, I am duty bound to steer system followers away from the toughest betting challenges because these events could very well affect your ability to achieve an overall profit situation over the period of the racing year.

Having said what I find necessary to say I should add that as a traditionalist with a twenty year spell of attending the Cheltenham Festival, it doesn't stop me being a huge supporter of what both Cheltenham and Aintree have to offer because they are providing, together with the Punchestown Festival, what is undoubtedly the most competitive and most excellent jump racing on offer in any part of the world.

Given this situation, the best advice I can give is to recognise the additional difficulties of winning at the Festivals and on the big races, recognise the fact that The Tail End System is more likely to be unsuccessful than successful in such circumstances and adjust your betting strategy accordingly. If you decide, that despite the difficulties, you want to bet, try to be very selective with the races you choose, give first consideration to the handicap events and keep your stakes on the low side.

Chapter 25
MAKING THE BEST USE OF THE TAIL END SYSTEM

In using The Tail End System to its best advantage you always have to be aware of both its strengths and its weaknesses.

The System's principal strength is that it enables the punter, by the process of diligent form reading, to identify long priced horses that have a reasonable chance of finishing in the first three places. Assuming that you have selected a race which produces a long priced winner, there are normally only three factors which can result in a failure to make a correct selection. These are:

a) The horse's form gives no indication that a top three placing is a reasonable possibility and is dismissed in the form reading process for that reason.

b) Insufficient selections are made to enable the winning horse to be considered in the selection process.

c) The winner's starting price was significantly longer than its Betting Forecast price.

In the case of a) above, you have to accept sometimes that a horse with totally diabolical form, which you have dismissed in the form reading process, will win a race. It is probably best that you do accept this situation as to take any different action will probably mean drastically reducing your selection standards and this could cost you far too much money in the long run. It could be more costly because by selecting horses with sub-standard form, you will inevitably be denying yourself the opportunity of selecting other horses whose form is reasonable enough to achieve a top three placing.

Fortunately, there are not that many long priced winners in the Class 3, 4 and 5 handicap races where their form does not give at least one clue to their top three place potential. In those cases where there are no clues in the form it sometimes pays to deviate from the strict written words of the System by taking into account the horse's trainer, particularly if you are aware that he or she has a tendency to spring long priced surprises every so often. If you do deviate from the System in such a manner it is probably best to treat your selection as an additional bet and move on to consider the next horse in the Betting Forecast as if you had dismissed the previous horse.

In the case of b) (see above) 'insufficient selections' there will always be cases occurring where if you made four, five, six or even seven or eight selections you still would not have moved far enough down the Betting Forecast to have considered the form of the winner. These sort of situations, which are most likely to occur in the big field handicaps when there are 16 or more runners, are best accepted rather than try to drastically alter your preferred number of selections and find that you have exceeded your betting budget.

Personally, for the vast majority of races which I select for betting purposes, I try to keep my selections to either one, two or three horses per race with the determining factor on number of bets being solely related to how happy I feel about the form of my selected horses as I work my way through the form reading process. There are occasions when I will select four or even five horses in a race but this happens very infrequently and is usually related to an exceptionally large field at one of the smaller tracks or one of the large handicaps at either Cheltenham or Aintree.

As far as c) above is concerned, where a horse's starting price is significantly higher than its Betting Forecast price, this is not a usual occurrence but where it does occur it can make the operation of The Tail End System a non event. In the majority of cases where I have seen it happen the situation is due to the horse's price drifting in the betting in the ten minutes before the race commences. If you are a punter that follows the price movements on either Teletext on the television or on the Tote screens or Bookmakers' price boards at the track itself, you will normally be alerted by the fact that there is a horse in the race, whose form you have not read, which is showing a price as long as the horses you have considered. Given such a situation you do not deviate from the strict written word of the System, but you study the form of the price drifting horse and if it impresses, place an additional bet as an 'insurance measure'.

The Tail End System's principal weakness is the fact that it is unable to provide a better idea as to which races to bet on other than to guide you to the Class 3, 4 and 5 handicap races at the preferred tracks. Having said that, the principal problem facing all punters is choosing which races to bet on, and, as I have stated earlier in the book, the form reading process will help you recognise strong reasons for selecting a race, particularly after a few months of following the System.

The very fact that you know that only one race in six produces an 'outsider' victory, that the Class 3, 4 and 5 handicaps at the preferred tracks are the best betting races, that the form reading process can guide you in selecting and dismissing races as well as horses, means that you will, in a relatively short period of time, become very selective about your choice of races as your experience increases.

Before launching into actual betting using The Tail End System, I would advise all readers of this book, regardless of the extent of their jump racing experience, to purchase the *Racing Post* on a daily basis and, for two to three months at least, study the position in the Betting Forecast and the form of all the outsiders which finish in the first three in all jump races.

By studying the results in this fashion, you will see for yourself how the system works and why the Class 3, 4 and 5 handicap races at the preferred tracks are the recommended contests for betting purposes. Most importantly you will start to consider the whole question of which races to select for betting purposes, as well as determining your betting strategy for when you start to work to the System.

As far as betting with The Tail End System is concerned, the following options are available to you:

1) Win Betting

When placing bets on long priced horses there can be big differences in the prices which are on offer so ideally you need to be in a position where you can place a bet with either a Bookmaker, the Tote or a Betting Exchange and take the best price available.

There is no way of knowing which of the three alternatives will offer the best price but as I have, on a number of occasions, seen prices which are more than twice and three times greater than the alternatives on offer, this is a critical issue which you will need to address.

In operating The Tail End System, I automatically place a win bet on all my selections simply because I have found it the most profitable course of action in a situation where you can never be entirely sure that a horse which you believe has a reasonable chance of achieving a top three placing will not win the contest as well.

It is my experience that where I have made more than one selection in a race it is a very difficult call to say that one will win, and the other selections will only be placed. For this reason therefore, I always back all selections to win, though where I am particularly keen on the chances of one particular horse I will increase the size of my win stake on that selection.

2) Place Betting

I must confess that I am primarily a 'bet on the nose' punter but because many of my selections achieve top three/four placings at very long odds, I am duty bound to point out that The Tail End System offers a lot of potential for place only backers.

Place only betting is available both on and off course with the Tote (Tote Sport as it is called now) and on the internet with certain betting exchanges.

For my own part I have no fixed rules about when I will or won't back each way as opposed to win only on any of my selections, but I usually start to consider the possibility of betting for a place when the win odds are 50/1 or greater. One of my selections, Leap Year Lass, a few seasons back finished third in a hurdle race at Tote place odds of £70 to a £1 unit so you can see that the system does offer the potential of a place betting coup on certain occasions.

3) Forecast Betting

In the same way as I have confessed to being a 'bet on the nose' punter I have to admit that I am an eternal optimist when it comes to forecast betting where you have the task of predicting the first two horses across the line in the correct order.

The Tote forecast is called an exacta if you nominate the first and second, or a reverse exacta if you want all of your selections to be covered to finish either first or second. The bookmakers' forecast is called a computer straight forecast or a reverse computer straight forecast.

Unless you are pretty damned sure which horse is going to win, either a reverse exacta or a reverse computer straight forecast is going to be your bet with:

two selections involving 2 bets
three selections involving 6 bets
four selections involving 12 bets
five selections involving 20 bets

Although forecast betting is extremely difficult to get right, the rewards can, on occasions, be incredibly high, particularly when long priced 'outsiders' fill the first two places, and still extremely attractive when a long priced outsider and one of the fancied runners are the two horses involved.

When you give consideration to the fact that a very rough guide to forecast payouts is a multiplication of the starting price of the two horses involved (eg 25/1 and 5/1 equals 125/1) it becomes clear that when operating to The Tail End System, forecast betting can be worth serious consideration.

I must, however, add some words of caution because all forecasts are extremely difficult to get right and the type of odds on offer frequently reflect the degree of difficulty involved.

In my experience, there are not many occasions when two of my system selections fill the first two places but there are numerous occasions where one of my selections finishes in the first two alongside one of the more fancied runners. Obviously, the task of picking one of the more fancied runners is in itself a difficult one, but the form reading skills which you will have acquired by following The Tail End System will undoubtedly be of assistance to you. The problem is, of course, that when you are considering the first four or five horses in the betting you can't apply The Tail End System selection criteria (ie 'a reasonable chance of achieving a top three placing') because practically all the fancied horses would fit that criteria and you would find yourself always picking the first horse in the Betting Forecast.

The situation is therefore a difficult one to solve, primarily because the majority of forecasts require total flexibility of thinking and flashes of genius type inspiration to achieve a result. The good news is the fact that The Tail End System is as good as any at picking 'outsiders' to put in the forecast, which leaves you, the punter, with the necessary freedom to select a horse or horses to go with one or more of your Tail End System selections.

In a situation where sometimes the most bizarre type of reasoning will provide the result you are looking for, I am genuinely loathe to make suggestions on how to pick horses to be paired with 'outsider' selections, particularly because any type of selection system you use is liable to fall foul of 'Sod's law'. However, given the fact that this book is aimed at experienced and inexperienced punters alike, some of whom will be keen to get involved with forecast betting for the first time, I feel duty bound to provide some practical advice on the subject, and it is as follows:

Selecting Shorter Priced Horses for Forecast Betting Purposes

a) Before getting involved in forecast betting it is well worth studying the results, particularly in Class 3, 4 and 5 handicap races at the preferred tracks so that you get an idea of the positions in the Betting Forecast which were occupied by the first two finishers in each race, and also the Tote Exacta and Computer Straight Forecasts which were payable. By studying the statistics in this way you can work out how you can achieve success while at the same time picking up dividends, which will make the exercise a profitable one within a reasonable number of bets.

The important point to remember is that you have to be very careful with forecast betting because it is all too easy to find you are including too many horses in the forecast to give yourself a reasonable chance of making a profit on a long term basis.

To give yourself an idea of what you are up against I will quote you the results of the last three handicap races at Plumpton on 27 March 2006 (which is the day I wrote this Chapter) because it gives you an idea of the challenge involved when The Tail End System is working well.

Selling Handicap Hurdle. 2m. Class 5. 11 runners. Frogmore Flyer (second in Betting Forecast) won at 7/1 beating Dirty Sanchez (next to last in Betting Forecast) 16/1. Tote Exacta of £77.60 Computer Straight Forecast £101.53.

Handicap Hurdle. 2m5f. Class 4. 11 runners. Brendar (last in Betting Forecast) won at 14/1 beating Myson (fourth in Betting Forecast) 7/1. Tote Exacta £220.90 Computer Straight Forecast £106.22.

Novices Handicap Chase. 2m4f. Class 4. 11 runners. Kirov King (last in Betting Forecast) won at 33/1 beating Denarius Secundus (8th in the Betting Forecast) 6/1. Tote Exacta of £291.20. Computer Straight Forecast £210.89. As you can see, in all three races either the last or the next to last in the Betting Forecast made the top two finishing positions, which meant that The Tail End System gave you every chance of selecting the outsider in the forecast in all three races.

As far as the shortest price horse in the forecast was concerned, getting the selection right was far more difficult because it meant picking the 2nd, the 4th and the 8th in the Betting Forecast.

Let us assume that you were prepared to invest in a reverse forecast covering three horses in each race, which would involve six bets at a cost of £6 if you were betting to a £1 unit.

Logic would suggest that, on the basis that it is always the 'outsiders' which make a forecast worth winning, at least two of your selections would be provided by The Tail End System which leaves you with just the one selection to either make a third Tail End System selection or make a selection not connected with The Tail End System.

There was a very good chance that if you had used The Tail End System to provide all three selections you would have been successful in the third race shown because by reading the form of the last four horses in the Betting Forecast you had every chance of selecting both Denarius Secundus and Kirov King.

b) If you have your own successful method or methods for selecting horses which finish in the first two places on a regular basis you should use it, because, combined with The Tail End System, you could have an extremely potent weapon at your disposal.

c) With forecast bets it can sometimes pay to pick a horse or horses by their position in the Betting Forecast without reading the form. It's a system which definitely works on occasions but you need to study the results over a reasonable period of time to ascertain the frequency with which you are likely to win and whether you could make a profit.

Certainly pairing say, the first two Tail End System selections with any one of the first half dozen horses in the Betting Forecast is a system which will throw up winners but you need to do your research to ascertain what is likely to be the most profitable route to follow.

d) If you consider yourself a reasonably lucky person you can pair your Tail End System selections with a random selection on your part which is based either on the form or alternatively on some kind of inspiration, knowledge or hunch which takes your fancy at the time.

e) You could select any one or more of the remaining horses in the field (remaining, that is, to The Tail End System horses already considered) by studying their form. You have to appreciate, however, that you are undertaking a big task and the time element involved will be considerable. You would also be risking the perils of Sod's law by making a selection of one horse by comparing its form with that of the other remaining horses.

In order to avoid the problems posed by Sod's law you could study the form by starting with the first horse in the Betting Forecast and asking the question 'Has this horse got the necessary form to win this race?'. If you answer is yes, you would select the horse, if your answer is no, you would dismiss the horse and move on to the next horse in the Betting Forecast in exactly the same way as you operate The Tail End System.

In conclusion, I would say that there is definitely money to be made by forecast betting which includes long priced horses but you need to study the results to determine the exact nature of the task which confronts you. Once you understand the task, you will find it far easier to work out a system which pairs Tail End System selections with a horse or horses from the remaining runners.

4) Tri-Casts

If you think forecast bets are difficult then tri-cast bets, where you are trying to pick the first three home in the correct order, have a degree of difficulty which can be roughly calculated by multiplying the starting prices of the three horses involved, eg 20/1 x 10/1 x 5/1 should yield a tri-cast dividend of approximately 1000/1.

I have got to be brutally honest and say that tri-cast bets are an excellent way of losing money, so you should only get involved if you fully appreciate the difficulties you face in achieving success.

Obviously there are occasions where the first three finishers are all 'outsiders' and there are numerous occasions where two 'outsiders' finish in the frame alongside a horse which was one of the first four listed in the Betting Forecast. Given the situation I have described there is obviously some merit in considering the inclusion of Tail End System selections in tri-cast bets on certain special occasions but you have got to be extremely lucky to make your involvement in such betting activities a profitable one.

5) Betting in Running

I must hold my hand up and say that I have never made use of the betting in running facility which is offered by some of the betting exchanges, but I can understand its popularity.

Whenever I think about Betting in Running I think about a couple of races, both involving lady jockeys, both 25/1 shots and both Tail End System selections which I happened to be on, which caused a bit of a stir amongst the betting in running fraternity.

In the one race at Exeter, the horse involved was lying third coming into the finishing straight for the final time but was so far behind the front two runners that it wasn't even in camera shot when the At The Races commentator suddenly said: 'Mr Woodland is starting to run on, in fact I think he could be involved in the finish.' By the time Mr Woodland did appear on screen he only had one horse to catch, which he duly did 50 yards from the line and his speed was such that he won the race by some five lengths easing down.

In the other race, at Bangor on Dee, the horse concerned, Two Timing Gent, was ten lengths down coming into the finishing straight and seemingly out of contention when it suddenly sprouted wings and overtook the two front runners in the last 100 yards.

I have mentioned these races because in both instances the *Racing Post* reported that the betting in running prices on Betfair which were available coming into the finishing straight were in excess of 300/1.

I can also think of numerous other Tail End System winners where it was very apparent a long way out from the finish that they had an extraordinarily good chance of winning the race.

I therefore feel certain that Tail End System followers have the potential to make serious amounts of money for a relatively small outlay by betting in running, particularly as the chances of rank outsiders are seriously underestimated by the majority of punters who will help to bolster the betting exchange payouts.

Although I know nothing about the difficulties involved in catching the maximum prices at the right time, I feel sure that betting in running is an area of betting for Tail End System followers which merits serious consideration.

However, Paul Haigh, in an article in the *Racing Post* recently, highlighted an area of concern with betting in running. He said that there was a very big potential problem for At The Races viewers who experience a three to four second real time delay in receiving their pictures and could therefore they could be making betting decisions not knowing that the horse had already fallen or shown signs of distress. I am sure many more words will be printed on this subject and I can only suggest that you appraise yourself fully of the situation before you participate.

Chapter 26

GETTING STARTED

Once you feel confident you have a reasonable understanding of how The Tail End System works, it is time to start your 'dry run' which will give you every opportunity to develop your race selection skills and form reading skills as well as your betting strategy before you actually start placing bets. Your 'dry run' will be a very important part of your development as a Tail End System follower and therefore the following points should be carefully noted:

a) You need to organise yourself so that on every day of the week you can study the *Racing Post*, sort out the races which you think have a reasonable chance of producing an outsider victory and then carry out the form reading procedure with a view to: 1) selecting horses for imaginary betting purposes and 2) making a final decision on whether or not you would be betting on the race if you were not on a dry run.

You will also need to study the results of all the races which, on the day, produced an 'outsider' result (win or place) and if it was not one of the races you had chosen for imaginary betting purposes, you need to consider the reasons why. Also, for all the races which produced an outsider result (win or place) you need to study whether and how The Tail End System could have picked up the 'outsider/s' in the field.

b) The duration of your Dry Run should be at least two months, simply because you need this type of period to cover a sufficient number of races to give you the kind of experience you will need to enter the betting arena.

c) You must have regard to when your Dry Run starts because if it happens to commence in the summer months, June to September, when there are far fewer races, you will need a longer period for the exercise.

d) An obvious problem you can encounter is if you are at work during the day and therefore unable to select races, study the form and make your selections and imaginary betting arrangements before the races actually take place. If you do have this difficulty, and to ensure that your Dry Run is a true test, you should make sure that you do not look at the results before you are able to find the time after the races have been run to carry out the complete procedure of selection and betting (imaginary).

e) Although you may not have the opportunity to view a race either at the course or on the television, it will make no difference to your ability to operate the system correctly, both in terms of making selections and reviewing the results. You should also note the fact that video data banks are now available which give you, the punter, the opportunity to view form races before an event and the race itself afterwards. Whilst this facility is to be welcomed from an enjoyment point of view, it is unlikely to improve the effectiveness of a system that has been designed to operate by reading the form, as opposed to viewing past races. The other problem with using videos of past races for form assessment purposes is the length of time the whole process takes and it is certainly a much longer method than the straightforward one of reading the form in the *Racing Post*.

f) Try and ensure during your dry run that you place the most emphasis on the Class 3, 4 and 5 Handicap Races at the Preferred Courses because these are the easiest route to a profitable system.

g) Take a good look at the results of the races that you had decided you were having an imaginary bet on. If an 'outsider' was successful but was not one of your selections, you need to determine the reason why, eg you didn't go far enough with the number of your selections to pick the winner up; you turned down the horse because you didn't think its form was good enough; the price of the horse was a lot longer than the *Racing Post*'s betting forecast had predicted.

Obviously there will be examples where you made the wrong decision, and this is all part and parcel of the learning process. There will be other examples, however, where you were quite correct in restricting the number of your selections to a figure that was more likely to keep you in profit on a long term basis and others where, if you dropped your form reading standards for selection purposes for no good reason, you would automatically create a position where you would be picking far too many 'no hopers' in the future.

h) Never spend a great deal of time worrying about selections that failed to win or be placed because such failure is only of importance if you misread the form and picked a horse which denied you the chance to make another selection which was successful.

Every race is a one off event, never to be repeated, and in this setting post race inquests should only be concerned with whether you operated The Tail End System in a manner which you feel was correct. Mistakes can and will be made and the lessons they teach you must be stored in the memory bank to help you in the future.

i) Particularly if you are already an experienced horse race punter you must discipline yourself to follow The Tail End System as it is written, rather than allow yourself to alter the System to accommodate your normal methods of selecting races and picking horses. It is, of course, very important that you do not select races for further consideration by trying to determine the chances of the shorter priced horses. Neither should you allow yourself to depart from the form reading procedure as it is written in order to consider horses which you feel could possibly be a better bet.

j) Because this is a dry run you should devote a considerable amount of time to working out whether win betting, place betting, forecast betting or betting in running is going to be your best route to financial success or, alternatively, a combination of the alternatives mentioned.

There is a lot to be said for adopting a very flexible approach to your betting arrangements by ensuring they are appropriate to the race in question and your selections.

k) Selectivity is very much the key to success with The Tail End System, so right from the start you should discipline yourself to keep the number of races you bet on as low as seems prudent and also to restrict the number of your bets in a race to a figure which feels appropriate to what your form reading is telling you about the chances of your selections.

l) Always pay a lot of attention to what is happening across the whole spectrum of jump racing on both a day by day and week by week basis, and be prepared to adopt a flexible approach by raising your activity level when the number of winning/placed 'outsiders' is high and reducing your activity level when the numbers are low.

m) Continuing the point about the need for flexibility in relation to the number of winning/placed 'outsiders' which are occurring, you must have regard to:

1) The lower level of activity in the summer months, June to September;

2) The blank spots which occur from time to time, not only at certain racetracks, but sometimes at all racetracks when the number of 'outsider' winners is down to a trickle;

3) The fact that, although Saturday racing normally has the most race meetings, it frequently does not produce the number of 'outsider' victories which occur during Monday to Friday racing. (Note: there are many reasons for this, some of which are connected to the fact that there are more high profile meetings, higher prize money and more higher class racing on a Saturday compared with the remainder of the week.)

4) The fact that Bank Holiday racing frequently produces very few 'outsider' victories.

In short, even in your dry run period, if you can start thinking like a professional gambler and plan to bet only when the time appears to be right and the right opportunities present themselves, you will be moving in the right direction.

n) Only move forward from the dry run into the Actual Betting Stage when you are confident about your understanding of The Tail End System and when you have proved to yourself that you can make it work.

The Actual Betting Stage

The Actual Betting Stage should not be remarkably different from the Dry Run, but the fact that you are placing bets will add importance to the task of ensuring that all of The Tail End System's decision making procedures are followed correctly.

When you are engaged in betting activities always have careful regard to the following points:

a) Always ensure that you give yourself ample time to select your races, study the form, select your horses and make your final decision as to whether to bet or not.

There is no worse a position than not having sufficient time because inevitably both situations will lead to mistakes which could prove very costly.

b) Always give yourself sufficient time to find out where the best prices are available, ie Bookmakers, Tote or Betting Exchanges, because again wrong decisions can prove costly.

Chapter 27

NORTON'S COIN

On the 15th March 1990 Norton's Coin climbed to the pinnacle of British National Hunt Racing by winning the Cheltenham Gold Cup, a Class 1 Chase and level weights contest staged over 3m2½f of the Prestbury Park Racecourse.

What was remarkable about the victory, which involved beating a total of eleven other horses including the legendary Desert Orchid, was the fact that Norton's Coin's trainer, a Welsh farmer by the name of Sirrell Griffiths, only had the one horse under training at the time.

Norton's Coin was a relatively lightly raced nine year old with only four victories to his name and although one of these was at Cheltenham, it was not expected by either the bookies or the public that he would be involved in the business end of proceedings. As a result he started the race at record odds of 100/1 after being freely available in places on the course at odds of 200/1. The result, which left many of the viewing public in total shock, was not a fluke created by some kind of mishap but a genuine hard fought victory orchestrated with aplomb by the horse's talented jockey, Graham McCourt.

I have always regretted the fact that I did not see this race live as I was at Cheltenham only the day before to see New Halen win the Mildmay of Flete at odds of 66/1. I did, however, see the race on television at the Coral betting shop in Cannon Street, Birmingham and not having had a bet on the race myself, my abiding memory is that of a tall West Indian gentleman entertaining everybody with a samba round the shop as he waved his £5 betting slip around for everybody to see whilst repeatedly saying: 'I never really thought it would win'.

Lest anybody thinks that the quality of Norton Coin's victory that day was in any way questionable, shown immediately below is the list of runners and riders for that race, together with Spotlight, Ratings and Form of the first three finishers.

3.30 13 DECLARED	Tote Cheltenham Gold Cup Chase (Championship Race)				3m2f New	TV BBC1

£100,000 added **For** five yrs old and upwards **Weights** 5-y-o. 11st 4lb; 6-y-o and up 12st **Allowances** mares allowed 5lb **Entries** 32 pay £245 **Forfeit** 23 pay £280 **Confirmed** 14 pay £175
Penalty Value 1st £67,003 **2nd** £24,98J **3rd** £12,140 **4th** £5,137 **5th** £2,218 **6th** £1,051

						POSTMARK
1	F13211 †**BARNBROOK AGAIN**[1] C Mel Davies —black, yellow cross belts and armlets.	D R C Elsworth	9 12-00		DOUBTFUL	166
2	148P-11 **BONANZA BOY**[82] CD S Dunster —pink, white stars, pink sleeves, purple armlets, pink cap, white star.	M C Pipe	9 12-00		P Scudamore	171
3	4121R-1 **CAVVIES CLOWN**[21] Mrs J Ollivant —green, pink cross-belts.	D R C Elsworth	10 12-00		G Bradley	163
4	F-12111 **DESERT ORCHID**[19] CD ⋅R Burridge —dark blue, grey sleeves and cap.	D R C Elsworth	11 12-00		R Dunwoody	183◀
5	42F3-F4 **KILDIMO**[12] CD Lady Harris —mauve and yellow check, yellow sleeves.	G B Balding	10 12-00		J Frost	164
6	2-32211 **NICK THE BRIEF**[26] CD John R Upson —white,dark green epaulets and star on cap.	John R Upson	8 12-00		M M Lynch	156
7	11-6923 **NORTON'S COIN**[33] C BF S G Griffiths —black, white hoops, black sleeves, emerald green and white quartered cap.	S G Griffiths	9 12-00		G McCourt	146
8	12P-152 **PEGWELL BAY**[63] C BF A K Barlow —yellow, black spots and sleeves, white cap.	T A Forster	9 12-00		B Powell	161

9	4321/11	**TEN OF SPADES**[36] CD	F Walwyn **10 12-00**	**K Mooney**	149
		W H Whitbread —*chocolate, yellow collar, cuffs and cap.*			
10	6111-67	**THE BAKEWELL BOY**[34] D	R G Frost **8 12-00**	**S Smith Eccles**	125
		N W Lake —*red, white sash, emerald green sleeves, emerald green and red check cap.*			
11	U1111U	**TOBY TOBIAS**[33] CD BF	Mrs J Pitman **8 12-00**	**M Pitman**	164
		Mrs Elizabeth Hitchins —*royal blue and red diamonds, royal blue sleeves, red cap, royal blue star.*			
12	P-3P332	**YAHOO**[33]	J A C Edwards **9 12-00 b[1]**	**T Morgan**	S-158
		Alan Parker —*yellow, white epaulets, yellow sleeves, black armlets, white cap.*			
13	111123	**MAID OF MONEY**[26]	J R H Fowler (IRE) **8 11-09**	**A Powell**	S-157
		Mrs H A McCormick —*yellow, black hooped sleeves & sash, black cap.*			

† Won 2.50 Cheltenham yesterday

LAST YEAR: **DESERT ORCHID**   D R C Elsworth 10 12 00   S Sherwood

BETTING FORECAST: 4-6 Desert Orchid, 7 Bonanza Boy, Toby Tobias, 8 Cavvies Clown, 12 Nick the Brief, 14 Pegwell Bay, 25 Ten Of Spades, Maid Of Money, 40 Yahoo, 66 Kildimo, 100 Norton's Coin, 200 The Bakewell Boy

TOPSPEED   Desert Orchid 181   Bonanza Boy 171   Nick The Brief 159

═══ 3.30 ═══

PEGWELL BAY, from an each-way betting point of view, looks an attractive proposition at this stage. While **Desert Orchid** towers over his rivals on all known form, only the grey's most ardent supporters will be interested in taking the odds. Pegwell Bay started second favourite behind jump racing's superstar in this season's King George, and he certainly looks over-priced by comparison with some others here.

The big factor in Pegwell Bay's favour is the fast ground, which he relishes. He was all at sea in the heavy here last year (pulled up before the last), but had earlier won the Mackeson and Budge Gold Cups in great style over the course and run Desert Orchid to ¾l at Sandown (3m 118yds).

Receiving 18lb, Pegwell Bay looked the winner half way up the run-in until Desert Orchid's famous battling qualities prevailed close home. But that showed Pegwell Bay did not lack stamina and, in the prevailing ground, he should see out the Gold Cup trip.

Tim Forster's bold jumper began this season with a good win at Kempton, but coughed after the King George, in which he could only finish fifth, and again lacked his usual bounce when beaten 8l by **Toby Tobias** (received 8lb) at Wincanton. Reported in top form again, Pegwell Bay can leave those efforts well behind.

Everything looks right for a repeat win for Desert Orchid, who overcame atrocious conditions to beat **Yahoo** 1½l last year. His 8l victory over Delius (received 2st) at Kempton last time was a superb display—and it also served to show how much better Desert Orchid is away from Cheltenham, given that Delius was beaten 10l by Yahoo (levels) at Liverpool.

Bonanza Boy, distant fourth here last year, would be fancied to finish much closer were it not for the fast ground. Much improved, Bonanza Boy could still go close but he is much better with give.

The same applies to **Nick The Brief**, who had **Maid of Money** 7½l away third when beating Carvill's Hill at Leopardstown. However, he has form on fast ground and may be a safer bet for the frame than Toby Tobias, whom he holds through Maid of Money. Yahoo has a 19lb pull for 8½l with Nick The Brief on Haydock running, but his form has been patchy this term and the ground is not in his favour. The blinkers may just sharpen him up.

Cavvies Clown, unlucky second in 1988, should be a bigger factor—provided he is on his best behaviour. He took little interest last year (tailed off when refusing at the last) and was reluctant to line up before going on to register an impressive win at Wincanton.

Jockey Club Adjusted Rating	3.30	POSTMARK
167 Barnbrook Again	12-00	166
166 Bonanza Boy	12-00	171
158 Cavvies Clown	12-00	163
182 Desert Orchid	12-00	183◀
158 Kildimo	12-00	164
164 Nick The Brief	12-00	156
145 Norton's Coin	12-00	146
163 Pegwell Bay	12-00	161
151 Ten of Spades	12-00	149
128 The Bakewell Boy	12-00	125
161 Toby Tobias	12-00	164
160 Yahoo	12-00	S158
Maid Of Money	11-09	S157

Norton's Coin

ch g Mount Cassino – Grove Chance
(St Columbus)
Placings: 51/32241211-6923

S G Griffiths   **9 12-0**

	Starts	1st	2nd	3rd	Win & Pl
	14	4	4	2	£33,454

	4/89 Chel	2m4f Featr Ch gd-sft £15,920
(R) 119	4/89 Newb	3m (0–70) Hcp Ch good...... £4,958
(R) 106	3/89 Bang	2m4f (0–45) Hcp Ch soft...... £2,023
	4/88 Chep	3m Hunt Ch gd-sft £882
		Total win prizemoney £23,783

10 Feb Newbury 2m4f   Hcp Ch £4,793
11 ran   HEAVY   16 fncs   Time 5m17.5s (slw20.3s)

1 Fu's Lady 8 10-6................ P Scudamore 4/1
2 One More Knight 7 10-4 .... L Harvey 9/2
3 **NORTON'S COIN** 9 11-8 ..... G McCourt 9/4F
steady headway approaching 11th, every
chance 3 out, ridden and weakened 2 out
[op 7/4 tchd 5/2]
Dist: ½-15-12-20-12   Postmark: 133/130/133

27 Jan Cheltenham 2m4f   Hcp Ch £5,640
9 ran   GOOD   17 fncs   Time 5m30.8s (slw24.9s)

1 Willsford 7 10-7 b .... D Gallagher EvensF
2 **NORTON'S COIN** 9 11-3 ..... G McCourt 13/2
held up, headway 12th, led and bumped 2
out, hard ridden and headed flat, ran on
[op 7/1 tchd 8/1 & 11/2]
3 Aughavogue 8 11-0 .... D Tegg 10/1
Dist: 1-12-6-5-2   Postmark: 137/146/131

13 Jan Ascot 2m   Hcp Ch £30,378
10 ran   GD-SFT   12 fncs   Time 3m55.6s (slw1.8s)

1 Meikleour 11 10-0 .... D Byrne 10/1
2 Feroda 9 10-0 .... J Osborne 11/2
3 Panto Prince 9 10-11 .... B Powell 4/1
9 **NORTON'S COIN** 9 10-0 ...... M Perrett 20/1
always behind, btn 18 lengths
[op 16/1 tchd 25/1]
Dist: 1½-7-½-5-1   Postmark: 153/151/155

26 Dec89 Kempton 3m   Champ Ch £40,986
sixth, see **DESERT ORCHID**

Toby Tobias

b g Furry Glen – Aurora Lady
(Beau Chapeau)
Placings: 1122115/1138F-U1111U

Mrs J Pitman   **8 12-0**

	Starts	1st	2nd	3rd	Win & Pl
	18	10	2	1	£34,976

	1/90 Chel	2m4f List Ch good.............. £10,016
	1/90 Winc	2m5f Ch good.................... £3,655
	12/89 Winc	2m5f Ch good.................... £5,754
(R) 124	12/89 Worc	2m4f (0–125) Hcp Ch gd-fm.. £3,392
	1/89 Leic	3m Nov Ch gd-sft £1,462
	1/89 Leic	2m4f Nov Ch gd-sft £2,525
	3/88 Leop	2m2f Hdl yield.................. £1,380
	2/88 Navn	2m2f Hdl soft................... £1,380
	3/87 Limk	2m NHF soft £966
	1/87 Punc	2m NHF gd-yld £966

10 Feb Newbury 3m   List Ch £11,030
4 ran   HEAVY   18 fncs   Time 6m20.6s (slw24.0s)

1 **BARNBROOK AGAIN** 9 11-12 H Davies 11/4
made all, left well clear 10th [op 7/4]
2 **YAHOO** 9 11-12 .... T Morgan 10/3
left poor second 10th
[op 7/2 tchd 4/1 & 3/1 plcs]
3 Golden Friend 12 11-4 .... G McCourt 25/1
U **TOBY TOBIAS** 8 11-6 ....° M Pitman 8/11F
went second 4th, with winner when
blundered and unseated rider 10th
[op 4/5 tchd 11/10 in a place]
Dist: dist-20   Postmark: 162/-/-/-

---

27 Jan Cheltenham 3m1f   List Ch £10,016
4 ran   GOOD   21 fncs   Time 6m49.8s (slw28.9s)

1 **TOBY TOBIAS** 8 11-6 .... M Pitman 5/4
always going well, led 17th, hit 2 out, ran on
well [op 5/4 tchd 11/10 & 11/8]
2 **MAID OF MONEY** 8 11-7 ... A Powell EvensF
joined leader 4th, mistake 9th, led 14th to
17th, mistake 18th, ridden approaching 2
out, one pace [op 10/11 tchd 6/5 in plcs]
3 Bigsun 9 11-8 .... R Dunwoody 9/1
Dist: 10-15-10   Postmark: 152/143/129

11 Jan Wincanton 2m5f   Ch £3,655
4 ran   GOOD   17 fncs   Time 5m16.3s (slw7.0s)

1 **TOBY TOBIAS** 8 11-6 .... M Pitman 6/5
held up, led 3 out, easily
[op 5/4 tchd 11/8 in plcs & Evens]
2 **PEGWELL BAY** 9 12-0 ...... C Llewellyn 8/11F
led to 3 out, beaten 2 out, mistake last
[op 4/6 tchd 5/6]
3 The Fruit 11 11-2 .... Mrs N Ledger 200/1
Dist: 8-dist-30   Postmark: 150/150/-

Desert Orchid

gr g Grey Mirage – Flower Child (Brother)
Placings: 1223221/111111F-12111

D R C Elsworth   **11 12-0**

	Starts	1st	2nd	3rd	Win & Pl
	60	31	10	5	£485,143

(R) 182	2/90 Kemp	3m List Hcp Ch good........ £24,100
	2/90 Winc	2m5f Ch gd-sft................. £3,850
	12/89 Kemp	3m Champ Ch good.......... £40,986
(R) 181	11/89 Winc	3m1f Lim Hcp Ch good....... £5,076
	3/89 Chel	3m2f Champ Ch heavy....... £68,371
(R) 180	2/89 Sand	3m118y Featr Lim Hcp Ch good
		£19,340
(R) 180	1/89 Asct	2m Hcp Ch good £21,950
	12/88 Kemp	3m Champ Ch gd-fm.......... £37,280
(R) 176	12/88 Sand	2m 18y List Lim Hcp Ch good £8,813
	10/88 Winc	2m5f Ch good.................... £3,694
(R) 170	4/88 Sand	3m5l18y List Hcp Ch gd-fm £45,000
	4/88 Lvpl	3m1f Featr Ch good.......... £16,040
	11/87 Kemp	2m4f Ch gd-sft £7,503
	10/87 Winc	2m5f Ch good £3,842
(R) 176	4/87 Asct	2m4f Hcp Ch gd-sft £7,142
	2/87 Winc	3m1f List Ch soft............... £6,323
(R) 171	2/87 Sand	3m118y Hcp Ch good......... £15,666
	12/86 Kemp	3m Ch soft...................... £13,696
(R) 144	12/86 Asct	2m Hcp Ch good................ £6,801
(R) 137	11/86 Sand	2m4f68y List Hcp Ch good... £4,950
	11/85 Asct	2m4f Nov Ch good £5,639
	11/85 Sand	2m18y Nov Ch good........... £3,759
	11/85 Asct	2m Nov Ch firm................. £7,987
	11/85 Devn	2m1f Nov Ch gd-fm........... £1,608
	2/85 Sand	2m Hdl gd-sft................... £4,417
	2/84 Winc	2m Hdl gd-sft £6,059
	2/84 Asct	2m Nov Hdl good £2,977
	1/84 Sand	2m Hdl good.................... £4,482
	12/83 Kemp	2m Nov Hdl good £3,548
	11/83 Asct	2m 4yo Hdl firm................ £2,317
	10/83 Asct	2m Nov Hdl firm................ £1,932
		Total win prizemoney £423,148

24 Feb Kempton 3m   List Hcp Ch £24,100
8 ran   GOOD   19 fncs   Time 6m00.10s (slw2.2s)

1 **DESERT ORCHID** 11 12-3⅔3
         R Dunwoody 8/11F
jumped well, led to 11th, led 3 out, soon
clear [op 4/6 tchd 4/5]
2 Delius 12 10-3 .... Peter Hobbs 6/1
3 Seagram 10 9-11 .... N Hawke(3) 33/1
Dist: 8-8-15-4-1   Postmark: 183/147/136

8 Feb Wincanton 2m5f   Ch £3,850
7 ran   GD-SFT   17 fncs   Time 5m25.2s (slw15.9s)

1 **DESERT ORCHID** 11 12-0
         R Dunwoody 3/10F
led to 5th, led 7th to 9th, led approaching 3
out, easily [op 1/4 tchd 1/3]
2 Bartres 11 12-0 .... M Bowlby 33/1
3 Mzima Spring 11 11-1 .... B Powell 16/1
Dist: 20-1½-5-1-25   Postmark: 145/125/110

---

26 Dec89 Kempton 3m   Champ Ch £40,986
6 ran   GOOD   19 fncs   Time 6m04.30s (slw6.4s)

1 **DESERT ORCHID** 10 11-10
         R Dunwoody 4/6F
made all, mistakes 12th and 13th, quickened
2 out, comfortably [op 4/6 tchd 8/11]
2 **BARNBROOK AGAIN** 8 11-10 B Powell 13/2
chased winner from 2 out, no impression
[op 7/2 tchd 7/1]
3 **YAHOO** 8 11-10 .... T Morgan 11/2
headway approaching 3 out, hard ridden
approaching 2 out, one pace
[op 6/1 tchd 7/1]
5 **PEGWELL BAY** 8 11-10 .... C Llewellyn 9/2
4th when mistake 15th, not recover
[op 5/1 tchd 6/1]
6 **NORTON'S COIN** 8 11-10 ... G McCourt 33/1
mistakes 4th, 6th and 8th, behind from 2 out
[op 66/1 tchd 150/1 in a place]
Dist: 8-7-3-6-15
Postmark: 168/160/153/150/144/129

2 Dec89 Sandown 2m18y
         List Lim Hcp Ch £10,040
4 ran   GD-FM   13 fncs   Time 3m57.1s (slw1.0s)

1 Long Engagement 8 10-0 .... B Powell 9/2
2 **DESERT ORCHID** 10 12-0 R Dunwoody 1/2F
led to last, unable to quicken
[op 1/3 tchd 4/7 in a place]
3 Prideaux Boy 11 10-0 .... J Short 4/1
Dist: 2½-2-8   Postmark: 151/176/146

16 Mar89 Cheltenham 3m2f
         Champ Ch £68,371
13 ran   HEAVY   22 fncs   Time 7m17.60s (slw40.4s)

1 **DESERT ORCHID** 10 12-0 . S Sherwood 5/2F
jumped well, led to 14th, left in lead 3 out,
soon headed, quickened and led flat
[op 11/4 tchd 7/2 in a place]
2 **YAHOO** 8 12-0 .... T Morgan 25/1
held up, chased leaders, led approaching 2
out until caught flat, ran on
[op 20/1 tchd 33/1]
3 Charter Party 11 12-0 .... R Dunwoody 14/1
4 **BONANZA BOY** 8 12-0 ... P Scudamore 15/2
mistake 9th, soon lost place, headway 14th,
weakened 16th, tailed off [op 7/1 tchd 10/1]
P **PEGWELL BAY** 8 12-0 ...... C Llewellyn 25/1
chased leaders to 14th, mistake 17th, soon
tailed off, pulled up before last
[op 20/1 tchd 33/1]
R **CAVVIES CLOWN** 9 12-0 .... R Arnott 8/1
headway 11th, joined leader 13th, soon lost
place, tailed off when refused¹ last
[op 6/1 tchd 10/1]
Dist: 1½-8-dist-dist   Postmark: 169/167/159

4 Feb89 Sandown 3m118y
         Featr Lim Hcp Ch £19,340
4 ran   GOOD   22 fncs   Time 6m18.8s (slw13.6s)

1 **DESERT ORCHID** 10 12-0 . S Sherwood 6/5F
led until 11th, led 2 out and last, quickened
and led near finish [op 1/1 tchd 5/4]
2 **PEGWELL BAY** 8 10-10 .... C Llewellyn 4/1
chased leaders, led 12th until 20th, ridden
approaching last, led flat, ran on well
[op 9/2 tchd 5/1 in plcs & 7/2]
3 **KILDIMO** 9 10-13 .... J Frost 2/1
mistakes 7th and 13th, headway 17th, ridden
20th, unable to quicken
[op 7/4 tchd 9/4 in a place]
Dist: ¾-2½-25   Postmark: 180/161/161

For the record, the result was first Norton's Coin 100/1, second Toby Tobias 8/1 at ¾ length, third Desert Orchard 10/11 at 4 lengths.

The wining time, which was on Good going, was 6 minutes 30.9 seconds, which compares very favourably with Kauto Star's Gold Cup wining time in 2007 on Good to Soft (Good in places) of 6 minutes 40.46 seconds.

Looking at the form of Norton's Coin, what stands out is not only its Cheltenham win in April 1989 in a £15,920 contest, but its close second to Willsford at Cheltenham on 27th January when giving away 10lbs. Its last run on 10th February at Newbury in a 2m4f Handicap Chase was on Heavy going, which he had not won on previously, so his 3rd place (beaten 15 lengths) behind horses receiving 1st 2lbs and 1st 4lbs should not necessarily have been interpreted as a cause for concern.

It is interesting that Spotlight made no mention of Norton's Coin, because in those days it did not automatically cover all of the horses in a race as it does now.

The fact that, as well as its very relevant Cheltenham form, Norton's Coin had also secured two Chase victories at 3m, meant that from a Tail End System form reading point of view you would have had ample reason to have concluded that a place in the first three was a reasonable possibility.

The quality of Norton's Coin's victory as a rank outsider that day can never be over estimated because it immediately posted a number of extremely important lessens to the racing public:

1) It demonstrated in the clearest fashion that 'outsiders' can achieve the unlikeliest victories at the highest level of our sport.

2) It was the best example I have witnessed for proving the point that, in non handicap races, you should never be using the ratings chart to assist your decisions when considering 'outsiders'. The adjusted Jockey Club ratings of 182 for Desert Orchard and 145 for Norton's Coin tell their own story.

3) Never be put off a horse by the fact that the horse's trainer has a small string or is virtually unknown.

4) Previous course form can be a highly significant factor in the form reading exercise.

5) Never be put off by a horse's starting price.

6) Never be put off a horse because the media has expressed negative opinions or alternatively decided to ignore the existence of the horse altogether.

7) It demonstrated in the clearest possible fashion that 'outsider' victories of the type where a horse produces a one off, career best, out of its skin type of performance, never to be repeated afterwards, is a feature of our sport which punters ignore at their peril.

All of the above lessons have already been highlighted at some stage in previous pages and I feel sure that you can appreciate how they have influenced the construction of The Tail End System. As a Tail End System follower, Norton's Coin's victory in the Gold Cup can undoubtedly help you in the future because it can give you all the confidence you need to suppress any feelings you may have that 'surely an upset can't happen?'

As you would have expected, on the day of Norton Coin's Gold Cup the *Racing Post*'s front page headline read: 'Desert Orchid to take the Gold Cup by storm.' This was followed by a number of articles supporting the legendary grey, none of which made mention of Norton's Coin. It is in situations such as these that you have to discipline yourself to ignore completely what the press has to say and let your form reading alone make the decisions for you.

Another and more recent classic example of the racing press/pundits/presenters/ experts wrong footing the racing public was the 2007 edition of the Cheltenham Champion Hurdle. With months to go before this race took place the media were already talking about it being the Champion Hurdle of the Century.

With a couple of weeks to go the Media had wound up the pre-race atmosphere to fever pitch proportions, to an extent where plane loads of pundits and jockeys were being flown over to Ireland for a series of Cheltenham previews aimed at uncovering the likely winner. Unfortunately, these previews, together with the English versions that were taking place around the same time, concluded in an extremely authoritative and professional manner that this race of the century concerned six horses only, namely Brave Inca (SP 11/2), Hardy Eustace (SP 3/1), Detroit City (SP 6/4), Straw Bear (SP 7/1) and finally Macs Joy and Harchibald (both eventual non runners).

Not having attended any of the said previews I cannot say for sure that there was no brave soul present to make a case for Sublimity, fourth in last season's Supreme Novices Hurdle. However, I cannot recall any of the *Racing Post* reports on these events making any mention of his name. With Sublimity (16/1) taking the race in grand style by three lengths from Brave Inca and Alfsoun (28/1) the lesson he provided is crystal clear, but please do not place any bets on similar upsets not happening again, and again, and again in the future.

Returning to the subject of Norton's Coin's Gold Cup, as time marches on the enormity of the achievement and the importance of its place in the illustrious history of British Jump Racing can only grow. I earnestly hope and pray that the Cheltenham Racecourse authorities will eventually commission a long overdue statue of Norton's Coin to be placed in a prominent place on the course it took by storm with the help of an epic riding performance by Graham McCourt and a legendary feat of training by Sirrell Griffiths.

Chapter 28
AN ENTIRELY DIFFERENT SET OF RULES

After Robert Cooper of At the Races gave me the idea to write this book, on the 19th April 2005, I set sail on a voyage to an unknown destination.

Over two years have elapsed since then, which has meant another two complete Jump Racing seasons, which provided me with another 6,000 plus races and more than 1,000 'outsider' victories to check and double check, whether the System I had put together in the early part of 2001 was still fit for purpose.

The voyage I refer to has been one of confirmation rather than discovery because the 'outsider' victories have continued to flow at the same annual rate, the average starting prices of those 'outsiders' are more or less unchanged and, most importantly, I have been unable to find any sound reasons to change any of the rules and guidelines which are an integral part of the System as it was first written.

When you think about the task of selecting a horse for betting purposes the only elements which can be of relevance are all aspects of the form of the horse, its breeding, its jockey, its trainer and other people's opinion on how the horse is likely to perform. If you want to consider all or any of the 'outsiders' in a particular race you have no alternative but to ignore its breeding, its jockey, its trainer and other people's opinion, because to do anything different will automatically eliminate from the reckoning a number of those 'outsiders' who could, however unlikely, go on to win the race or be placed.

Having eliminated those elements, all you are left with is all aspects of a horse's form and sheer common sense tells you that you cannot consider an 'outsider's' form against the form of more fancied horses in a race without immediately eliminating the 'outsider' from the reckoning.

Any successful system for selecting 'outsiders' must therefore be based on an entirely different set of rules than the type of rules that are likely to be attached to systems designed to select 'the most likely winner of the race'. If you accept this last statement as a fact then you should feel able to adopt The Tail End System with the type of confidence necessary to operate it as it is written, starting with a dry run.

Jump Racing for me has always been a fascinating and wonderful sport and one I have always felt immensely proud to be associated with. If this book provides you with many long priced winners and much enjoyment I will have achieved my objective.

Appendix
2006-2007 RACECOURSE 'OUTSIDER' STATISTICS

AINTREE

Date	Going	Class	Race Type	Distance	Winner	SP	Tote	2nd SP	3rd SP	Runners	No of Jump Races
19/05/06	Good	4	Handicap Hurdle	2m4f	Moon Catcher	11/1	12.70	7/2	16/1	11	6
19/05/06	Good	5	Novice Hunter Chase	2m4f	Kiora Bay	11/1	14.10	5/2	11/1	6	
21/10/06	Good		No Outsiders								6
22/10/06	Good to Soft		No Outsiders								5
19/11/06	Good	3	Handicap Chase	2m5f	I Hear Thunder	12/1	14.20	7/1	10/1	20	6
19/11/06	Good	1	Handicap Chase	3m2f	Eurotrek	25/1	38.90	14/1	14/1	21	
19/11/06	Good	3	Novices Handicap Hurdle	2m4f	Rothbury	20/1	32.40	22/1	6/1	20	
12/04/07	Good	1	Handicap Hurdle	2m4f	Two Miles West	25/1	48.60	33/1	10/1	22	7
13/04/07	Good	1	Novices Hurdle	3m	Chief Dan George	20/1	16.90	4/6	25/1	10	6
13/04/07	Good	2	Handicap Chase	2m5f	Dunbrody Millar	25/1	43.70	66/1	25/1	29	
13/04/07	Good	1	Novices Hurdle	2m	Blythe Knight	14/1	14.90	3/1	2/1	8	
14/04/07	Good	1	Handicap Hurdle	2m	Kings Quay	16/1	23.60	25/1	50/1	22	6
14/04/07	Good	1	Hurdle	2m4f	Al Eile	12/1	15.60	11/1	13/2	11	
14/04/07	Good	1	Grand National Handicap Chase	4m4f	Silver Birch	33/1	41.90	12/1	33/1	40	
14/04/07	Good	2	Con/Amateur Jockey Novice Handicap Chase	2m4f	Private Be	12/1	17.70	9/4	20/1	10	

2006/2007 STATISTICS

No of Races	'Outsider' Wins	SP Total	Average SP	'Outsider' Wins as a Percentage of Races	No of Blank Meetings
42	13	236	18/1	30.95%	2

'Outsider' Wins in Class of Race

Class 1	Class 2	Class 3	Class 4	Class 5	Class 6	Total
7	2	2	1	0	1	13

'Outsider' Wins – Type of Race

Handicap Chase	Handicap Hurdle	Non Handicap Chase	Non Handicap Hurdle
5	4	1	3

Calendar of 'Outsider' Wins

Apr	May	Jun	Jul	Aug	Sep	Oct	Nov	Dec	Jan	Feb	Mar	Apr
0	2	0	0	0	0	0	3	0	0	0	0	8

ASCOT

Date	Going	Class	Race Type	Distance	Winner	SP	Tote	2nd SP	3rd SP	Runners	No of Jump Races
28/10/06	Good to Firm	2	Handicap Chase	3m	See You Sometime	14/1	12.70	8/1	8/1	11	6
28/10/06	Good to Firm	3	Beginners Chase	2m3f	Time to Shine	12/1	11.10	7/2	6/4	4	
17/11/06	Good to Soft	2	Novices Hurdle	2m	Court Ruler	50/1	72.90	11/8	4/1	8	6

Date	Going	Race Type	Class	Winner	SP	Tote	2nd SP	3rd SP	Runners	No of Jump Races
18/11/06	Soft	Handicap Chase	1	Cerium	12/1	14.60	4/1	20/1	9	6
15/12/06	Good	Handicap Chase	2	Jericho III	16/1	9.30	12/1	40/1	12	6
16/12/06	Good to Soft	Handicap Chase	1	Billy Voddan	25/1	39.40	16/1	15/2	18	5
30/12/06	Good to Soft	No Outsiders								6
17/02/07	Good to Soft	No Outsiders								6
30/03/07	Good	No Outsiders								6
31/03/07	Good	Novices Chase	2	Bally Foy	33/1	16.70	8/15	5/1	3	6
31/03/07	Good	Handicap Chase	2	Misty Dancer	10/1	15.00	9/2	14/1	12	

2006/2007 STATISTICS

No of Races	'Outsider' Wins	Average SP	SP Total	'Outsider' Wins as a Percentage of Races	No of Blank Meetings
53	8	21/1	172	15.09%	3

'Outsider' Wins in Class of Race

Class 1	Class 2	Class 3	Class 4	Class 5	Class 6	Total
2	4	2	0	0	0	8

'Outsider' Wins – Type of Race

Handicap Chase	Non Handicap Chase	Handicap Hurdle	Non Handicap Hurdle
5	2	0	1

Calendar of 'Outsider' Wins

Apr	May	Jun	Jul	Aug	Sep	Oct	Nov	Dec	Jan	Feb	Mar	Apr
0	0	0	0	0	0	2	2	2	0	0	2	0

AYR

Date	Going	Class	Race Type	Distance	Winner	SP	Tote	2nd SP	3rd SP	Runners	No of Jump Races
29/11/06	Soft		No Outsiders								6
11/12/06	Heavy	4	Beginners Chase	2m	Mitey Perk	33/1	17.50	10/1	8/15	4	6
11/12/06	Heavy	4	Handicap Hurdle	2m4f	Kempski	12/1	14.70	50/1	16/1	11	
11/12/06	Heavy	3	Handicap Chase	3m1f	Devil's Run	18/1	11.90	3/1	15/8	6	
19/12/6	Heavy	5	Con Jockeys Handicap Hurdle	2m	Roadworthy	12/1	14.60	20/1	5/2	15	7
02/01/07	Heavy	4	Juvenile Novices Hurdle	2m	Storm Prospect	14/1	14.60	7/2	33/1	9	7
02/01/07	Heavy	5	Handicap Hurdle	3m	EMS Royalty	40/1	47.70	10/1	16/1	20	
02/03/07	Soft	5	Con/Amateur Jockeys Handicap Hurdle	2m4f	Something Silver	14/1	13.60	7/1	28/1	18	6
09/03/07	Heavy	5	Con Jockeys Handicap Hurdle	3m	Dalawan	20/1	22.90	9/2	33/1	11	7
10/03/07	Heavy		No Outsiders								6
22/03/07	Soft		No Outsiders								6

Date	Going	Class	Race Type	Distance	Winner	SP	Tote	2nd SP	3rd SP	Runners	No of Jump Races
20/04/07	Good to Firm	2	Mares Only Handicap Hurdle	2m	River Alder	16/1	22.90	12/1	7/4	7	7
21/04/07	Good to Firm	1	National Handicap Chase	4m	Hot Weld	14/1	16.50	5/1	8/1	23	7

2006/2007 STATISTICS

No of Races	'Outsider' Wins	SPTotal	Average SP	'Outsider' Wins as a Percentage of Races	No of Blank Meetings
65	10	193	19/1	15.38%	3

'Outsider' Wins in Class of Race

Class 1	Class 2	Class 3	Class 4	Class 5	Class 6	Total
1	1	1	3	4	0	10

'Outsider' Wins – Type of Race

Handicap Chase	Handicap Hurdle	Non Handicap Chase	Non Handicap Hurdle
2	6	1	1

Calendar of 'Outsider' Wins

Apr	May	Jun	Jul	Aug	Sep	Oct	Nov	Dec	Jan	Feb	Mar	Apr
0	0	0	0	0	0	0	0	4	2	0	2	2

BANGOR

Date	Going	Class	Race Type	Distance	Winner	SP	Tote	2nd SP	3rd SP	Runners	No of Jump Races
05/05/06	Good	5	Handicap Hurdle	2m4f	Tunes of Glory	16/1	25.50	22/1	14/1	15	6
05/05/06	Good	6	Novices Hunter Chase	3m	Abbey Days	20/1	23.30	10/11	13/2	13	
20/05/06	Soft	3	Handicap Hurdle	2m	Red Moor	10/1	13.10	20/1	5/1	9	6
25/07/06	Good to Firm		No Outsiders								6
04/08/06	Good to Firm		No Outsiders								6
19/08/06	Good to Soft	4	Novices Handicap Hurdle	2m1f	Troodos Jet	20/1	34.80	3/1	7/1	9	6
08/09/06	Good to Firm	4	Handicap Chase	3m	Hehasalife	16/1	20.80	13/2	6/1	12	7
08/09/06	Good to Firm	4	Novices Hurdle	2m1f	Red Scally	10/1	12.10	33/1	6/1	10	
08/09/06	Good to Firm	4	Handicap Hurdle	2m4f	Huckster	10/1	14.20	9/1	100/30	8	
07/10/06	Good to Soft	4	Novices Hurdle	2m1f	Royal Attraction	10/1	13.90	25/1	5/1	7	6
08/11/06	Good to Soft		No Outsiders								7
23/12/06	Soft	5	Handicap Hurdle	2m1f	Eastern Dagger	11/1	10.90	5/4	33/1	9	6
04/03/07	Heavy	4	Juvenile Maiden Hurdle	2m1f	Midnight Diamond	22/1	16.30	8/11	9/2	6	7
24/03/07	Good	4	Handicap Chase	2m1f	Brown Teddy	12/1	10.60	11/8	14/1	12	6
21/04/07	Good		No Outsiders								6

2006/2007 STATISTICS

No of Races	'Outsider' Wins	SP Total	Average SP	'Outsider' Wins as a Percentage of Races	No of Blank Meetings
75	11	157	14/1	14.66%	4

'Outsider' Wins in Class of Race

Class 1	Class 2	Class 3	Class 4	Class 5	Class 6
0	0	1	7	2	1

'Outsider' Wins – Type of Race

Handicap Chase	Handicap Hurdle	Non Handicap Chase	Non Handicap Hurdle
2	5	1	3

Calendar of 'Outsider' Wins

Apr	May	Jun	Jul	Aug	Sep	Oct	Nov	Dec	Jan	Feb	Mar	Apr	Total
0	3	0	0	1	3	1	0	1	0	0	2	0	11

CARLISLE

Date	Going	Class	Race Type	Distance	Winner	SP	Tote	2nd SP	3rd SP	Runners	No of Jump Races
06/10/06	Good to Soft	5	Novices Handicap Hurdle	2m4f	Nicozetto	12/1	14.70	5/2	11/2	13	6
15/10/06	Soft	4	Novices Handicap Hurdle	2m4f	Red Scally	16/1	13.00	50/1	9/2	18	6
29/10/06	Heavy		No Outsiders								6
06/11/06	Soft	4	Beginners Chase	2m	Tidal Fury	10/1	9.90	9/2	9/2	10	7
12/11/06	Heavy	3	Handicap Chase	3m2f	Datito	16/1	29.20	14/1	11/4	15	6
12/11/06	Heavy	4	Novice Hurdle	2m1f	Open de L'Isle	33/1	95.70	5/1	10/1	13	
19/02/07	Soft	4	Novice Hurdle	2m4f	Double Eagle	16/1	21.00	11/2	9/1	17	6
19/02/07	Soft	3	Handicap Chase	3m4f	See You There	10/1	11.20	7/4	9/1	7	
19/02/07	Soft	4	Handicap Chase	2m4f	Sands Rising	12/1	11.60	11/8	3/1	7	
18/03/07	Heavy	4	Novices Handicap Hurdle	2m4f	Minster Aboi	11/1	14.40	25/1	6/1	13	5
18/03/07	Heavy	4	Handicap Hurdle	3m1f	Carapuce	16/1	19.00	3/1	9/1	12	
07/04/07	Good	5	Handicap Chase	3m2f	Old Noddy	16/1	31.00	20/1	50/1	17	7
07/04/07	Good	4	Novices Handicap Chase	2m4f	Ballynure	11/1	17.30	25/1	10/1	15	

2006/2007 STATISTICS

No of Races	'Outsider' Wins	SP Total	Average SP	'Outsider' Wins as a Percentage of Races	No of Blank Meetings
49	12	179	14/1	24.48%	1

'Outsider' Wins in Class of Race

Class 1	Class 2	Class 3	Class 4	Class 5	Class 6	Total
0	0	2	8	2	0	12

'Outsider' Wins – Type of Race

Handicap Chase	Handicap Hurdle	Non Handicap Chase	Non Handicap Hurdle
5	4	1	2

Calendar of 'Outsider' Wins

Apr	May	Jun	Jul	Aug	Sep	Oct	Nov	Dec	Jan	Feb	Mar	Apr	Total
0	0	0	0	0	0	2	3	0	0	3	2	2	12

CARTMEL

Date	Going	Class	Race Type	Distance	Winner	SP	Tote	2nd SP	3rd SP	Runners	No of Jump Races
27/05/06	Soft	5	Handicap Chase	3m2f	Trovalo	10/1	12.80	9/2	11/2	12	6
29/05/06	Good to Soft		No Outsiders								6
31/05/06	Good		No Outsiders								7
20/07/06	Good to Firm	4	Beginners Chase	2m1f	Lutea	14/1	17.90	100/30	13/2	8	6
26/08/06	Good to Firm	4	Novices Handicap Hurdle	2m1f	Oniz Tiptoes	33/1	53.50	12/1	11/2	14	6
28/08/06	Good to Soft	4	Handicap Chase	2m5f	Incas	10/1	10.20	100/30	9/4	6	6

2006/2007 STATISTICS

No of Races	'Outsider' Wins	SP Total	Average SP	'Outsider' Wins as a Percentage of Races	No of Blank Meetings
37	4	67	16/1	10.81%	2

'Outsider' Wins in Class of Race

Class 1	Class 2	Class 3	Class 4	Class 5	Class 6	Total
0	0	0	3	1	0	4

'Outsider' Wins – Type of Race

Handicap Chase	Handicap Hurdle	Non Handicap Chase	Non Handicap Hurdle
2	1	1	0

Calendar of 'Outsider' Wins

Apr	May	Jun	Jul	Aug	Sep	Oct	Nov	Dec	Jan	Feb	Mar	Apr
0	1	0	1	2	0	0	0	0	0	0	0	0

CATTERICK

Date	Going	Race Type	Class	Distance	Winner	SP	Tote	2nd SP	3rd SP	Runners	No of Jump Races
29/11/06	Good to Soft	Handicap Chase	4	3m1f	Rival Bidder	14/1	17.10	14/1	7/1	10	6
29/11/06	Good to Soft	Juvenile Novices Hurdle	3	2m	Impeccable Guest	14/1	12.50	7/2	3/1	16	
14/12/06	Soft	No Outsiders									6
28/12/06	Good to Soft	Maiden Hurdle	4	2m	Marine Life	14/1	11.80	12/1	5/2	15	6
28/12/06	Good to Soft	Handicap Chase	4	3m1f	Bang and Blame	10/1	12.40	7/2	14/1	9	7
28/12/06	Good to Soft	Handicap Chase	4	2m3f	Emerald Destiny	25/1	29.80	8/1	14/1	13	
01/01/07	Soft	Handicap Hurdle	5	2m3f	Needwood Spirit	18/1	19.90	8/1	12/1	9	6
01/01/07	Soft	Handicap Chase	3	2m3f	Welcome to Unos	11/1	12.30	8/1	5/2	7	
24/01/07	Soft	(S) Handicap Hurdle	5	2m	Karyon	10/1	10.00	14/1	20/1	12	6
24/01/07	Soft	Handicap Chase	3	3m6f	Bang and Blame	10/1	12.50	14/1	7/1	14	
02/02/07	Good	(S) Con Jockeys Handicap Hurdle	5	2m3f	Southern Bazaar	10/1	15.20	8/1	13/2	12	6
07/03/07	Soft	No Outsiders									6

2006/2007 STATISTICS

No of Races	'Outsider' Wins	SP Total	Average SP	'Outsicer' Wins as a Percentage of Races	No of Blank Meetings
43	10	136	13/1	23.25%	2

'Outsider' Wins in Class of Race

Class 1	Class 2	Class 3	Class 4	Class 5	Class 6	Total
0	0	3	4	3	0	10

'Outsider' Wins – Type of Race

Handicap Chase	Handicap Hurdle	Non Handicap Chase	Non Handicap Hurdle
5	3	0	2

Calendar of 'Outsider' Wins

Apr	May	Jun	Jul	Aug	Sep	Oct	Nov	Dec	Jan	Feb	Mar	Apr
0	0	0	0	0	0	0	2	3	4	1	0	0

CHELTENHAM

Date	Going	Race Type	Class	Distance	Winner	SP	Tote	2nd SP	3rd SP	Runners	No of Jump Races
03/05/06	Good	Hunter Chase	5	2m5f	Derrintogher Yank	12/1	16.60	11/1	11/4	17	6
24/10/06	Good	Handicap Hurdle	2	2m5f	Monolith	20/1	26.30	5/1	7/1	19	6
24/10/06	Good	Con Jockey Handicap Hurdle	3	2m	O'Toole	25/1	33.30	9/2	10/2	12	
25/10/06	Good to Soft	Handicap Hurdle	2	2m	Dhehdaah	16/1	20.80	4/1	2/1	15	6
10/11/06	Good	Novices Hurdle	1	2m	Moon over Miami	16/1	18.80	16/1	20/1	9	6

Date	Going		Race Type	Horse	Dist		SP				
11/11/06	Good to Soft	1	Handicap Chase	Exotic Dancer	2m4f	14.80	16/1	4/1	16/1	16	6
12/11/06	Good to Soft	3	Handicap Hurdle	Mth Hill	2m5f	74.20	40/1	6/1	33/1	16	5
08/12/06	Soft	1	Handicap Chase	D'Argent	3m1f	13.60	10/1	6/1	6/1	15	7
08/12/06	Soft	3	Handicap Hurdle	Border Castle	2m1f	15.80	12/1	33/1	5/1	16	
09/12/06	Soft	1	Novices Hurdle	Flight Leader	3m	18.80	16/1	13/8	13/2	8	7
01/01/07	Heavy	2	Handicap Hurdle	Just Beth	3m	11.00	10/1	100/30	11/4	10	6
27/01/07	Heavy	1	Hurdle	Blazing Bailey	3m	19.30	14/1	9/2	7/1	9	7
13/03/07	Soft	1	Novices Hurdle	Ebaziyan	2m	78.80	40/1	15/2	2/1	22	6
13/03/07	Soft	1	Champion Hurdle	Sublimity	2m	16.20	16/1	11/2	28/1	10	
13/03/07	Soft	1	Handicap Chase	Joes Edge	3m	61.00	50/1	7/1	7/1	23	
14/03/07	Good to Soft	1	Novices Hurdle	Massinis Maguire	2m5f	26.70	20/1	10/1	7/1	15	5
14/03/07	Good to Soft	1	Handicap Hurdle	Burnt Oak Boy	2m5f	14.20	10/1	12/1	20/1	28	
15/03/07	Good to Soft	1	Novices Handicap Chase	L'Antartique	2m5f	26.20	20/1	10/1	20/1	19	6
15/03/07	Good to Soft	1	Handicap Chase	Idole First	2m5f	16.50	12/1	28/1	20/1	23	
15/03/07	Good to Soft	2	Amateur Riders Novice Chase	Butler's Cabin	4m1f	45.10	33/1	7/1	100/1	19	
15/03/07	Good to Soft	1	Handicap Hurdle	Oscar Park	3m	19.90	14/1	14/1	16/1	24	
16/03/07	Good to Soft	2	Hunter Chase	Drombeag	3m2f	35.60	20/1	2/1	20/1	24	
15/03/07	Good to Soft	1	Handicap Chase	Andreas	2m	18.60	12/1	8/1	33/1	23	6
15/03/07	Good to Soft	2	Handicap Hurdle	Pedrobob	2m1f	16.10	12/1	11/2	100/1	28	
18/04/07	Good		No Outsiders								7
19/04/07	Good	3	Handicap Chase	Glengarra	2m	16.50	12/1	16/1	11/1	12	6

2006/2007 STATISTICS

No of Races	'Outsider' Wins	Average SP	SP Total	'Outsider' Wins as a Percentage of Races	No of Blank Meetings
98	25	19/1	478	25.51%	1

'Outsider' Wins in Class of Race

Class 1	Class 2	Class 3	Class 4	Class 5	Class 6	Total
15	4	4	0	0	2	25

'Outsider' Wins – Type of Race

Handicap Chase	Handicap Hurdle	Non Handicap Chase	Non Handicap Hurdle
7	9	3	6

Calendar of 'Outsider' Wins

Apr	May	Jun	Jul	Aug	Sep	Oct	Nov	Dec	Jan	Feb	Mar	Apr
0	1	0	0	0	0	3	3	3	2	0	12	1

CHEPSTOW

Date	Going	Class	Race Type	Winner	Distance	SP	Tote	2nd SP	3rd SP	Runners	No of Jump Races
07/10/06	Good	2	Handicap Chase	Tribal Venture	3m	11/1	11.70	5/1	10/1	14	6
21/10/06	Good to Soft	1	Novices Hurdle	Kanpai	2m4f	12/1	10.70	100/30	4/7	7	7
21/10/06	Good to Soft	2	Handicap Hurdle	Desert Tommy	3m	12/1	16.00	8/1	14/1	16	
21/10/06	Good to Soft	3	Handicap Chase	Mr Dow Jones	3m	33/1	32.40	9/2	7/2	11	
21/10/06	Good to Soft	5	Maiden Hurdle	Flight Leader	3m	18/1	17.30	13/8	13/2	13	
01/11/06	Good to Soft	5	Maiden Hurdle	Carnival Town	2m4f	14/1	12.00	4/9	33/1	16	6
01/11/06	Good to Soft	5	Maiden Hurdle	Hawridge Star	2m	10/1	10.30	18/1	14/1	10	
22/11/06	Soft		No Outsiders								6
02/12/06	Soft		No Outsiders								7
27/12/06	Soft	3	Handicap Chase	Nadover	2m3f	16/1	20.60	11/4	4/1	14	6
27/12/06	Soft	3	Handicap Hurdle	The Real Deal	3m	18/1	23.90	15/2	10/1	17	
27/12/06	Soft	4	Novices Hurdle	Nictos de Bersey	2m4f	14/1	23.00	2/1	4/1	16	
02/02/07	Soft		No Outsiders								6
15/02/07	Heavy	5	Maiden Hurdle	Back Among Friends	2m	11/1	11.90	8/13	20/1	12	7
15/02/07	Heavy	5	Handicap Chase	All Sonsilver	2m	16/1	23.60	7/4	5/1	9	
10/03/07	Heavy	5	(S) Handicap Hurdle	Pop Gun	2m4f	12/1	14.30	9/2	40/1	12	6
21/03/07	Good		No Outsiders								6
10/04/07	Good	4	Handicap Chase	Hillcrest	3m	20/1	22.90	16/1	5/1	13	5
14/04/07	Good	3	Handicap Hurdle	Monticelli	2m4f	16/1	14.00	7/2	8/1	8	6
27/4/07	Good	4	Novices Hurdle	Ballamusic	2m4f	10/1	5.60	1/2	20/1	15	6

2006/2007 STATISTICS

No of Races	'Outsider' Wins	SP Total	Average SP	No of Blank Meetings	'Outsider' Wins as a Percentage of Races
80	16	243	15/1	4	20.00%

'Outsider' Wins in Class of Race

Class 1	Class 2	Class 3	Class 4	Class 5	Class 6	Total
1	2	4	3	6	0	16

'Outsider' Wins – Type of Race

Handicap Chase	Handicap Hurdle	Non Handicap Chase	Non Handicap Hurdle
5	4	0	7

Calendar of 'Outsider' Wins

Apr	May	Jun	Jul	Aug	Sep	Oct	Nov	Dec	Jan	Feb	Mar	Apr
0	0	0	0	0	0	5	2	3	0	2	1	3

EXETER

Date	Going	Class	Race Type	Distance	Winner	SP	Tote	2nd SP	3rd SP	Runners	No of Jump Races
09/05/06	Good to Firm	5	Handicap Chase	2m7f	Eveon	16/1	20.20	11/2	33/1	15	6
09/05/06	Good to Firm	5	Con Jockey Novice Handicap Hurdle	2m3f	Sultan Fontenaille	20/1	21.90	4/1	12/1	11	
17/05/06	Good to Firm		No Outsiders								6
04/10/06	Good to Firm		No Outsiders								6
17/10/06	Good	4	Novices Hurdle	2m1f	Wotchalike	10/1	10.90	9/4	33/1	12	6
17/10/06	Good	4	Handicap Hurdle	2m3f	Bishops Bridge	10/1	12.70	100/30	8/1	15	
31/10/06	Good	4	Handicap Hurdle	3m	Blaeberry	14/1	15.50	5/4	10/1	14	6
07/11/07	Good to Firm	5	Handicap Chase	2m3f	Joe Deane	10/1	10.70	6/1	7/1	11	6
17/11/06	Good to Soft	4	Novices Hurdle	2m1f	Only for Sue	25/1	23.10	9/2	11/2	17	6
01/12/06	Soft	4	Novices Handicap Chase	2m7f	Zimbabwe	10/1	16.40	12/1	16/1	13	6
14/12/06	Soft	4	Novices Hurdle	2m3f	Saratogane	14/1	22.20	20/1	8/1	15	7
21/12/06	Good to Soft	3	Handicap Hurdle	2m1f	Master Mahogany	14/1	12.90	5/6	14/1	11	6
21/12/06	Good to Soft	3	Handicap Chase	2m3f	Avitta	14/1	14.10	7/2	5/2	8	
01/01/07	Heavy		No Outsiders								6
25/02/07	Heavy		No Outsiders								5
20/03/07	Good to Soft	4	Handicap Hurdle	2m1f	Flaming Weapon	16/1	17.80	11/4	8/1	13	6
11/04/07	Firm		No Outsiders								6
17/04/07	Good to Firm	4	Novices Hurdle	2m6f	Bubbs	33/1	11.20	1/1	100/30	5	6
17/04/07	Good to Firm	5	Con Jockeys Handicap Hurdle	3m	Bite Un Fight	16/1	12.70	11/1	16/1	8	

2006/2007 STATISTICS

No of Races	'Outsider' Wins	SP Total	Average SP	'Outsider' Wins as a Percentage of Races	No of Blank Meetings
90	14	222	15/1	15.55%	4

'Outsider' Wins in Class of Race

Class 1	Class 2	Class 3	Class 4	Class 5	Class 6	Total
0	0	2	8	4	0	14

'Outsider' Wins – Type of Race

Handicap Chase	Handicap Hurdle	Non Handicap Chase	Non Handicap Hurdle
4	6	0	4

Calendar of 'Outsider' Wins

Apr	May	Jun	Jul	Aug	Sep	Oct	Nov	Dec	Jan	Feb	Mar	Apr
0	2	0	0	0	0	3	2	4	0	0	1	2

FAKENHAM

Date	Going	Class	Race Type	Distance	Winner	SP	Tote	2nd SP	3rd SP	Runners	No of Jump Races
10/05/06	Good to Firm	5	Hurdle	2m	Silvo	14/1	17.00	5/6	40/1	13	6
10/05/06	Good to Firm	5	Mares Only Handicap Hurdle	2m4f	Dalriath	14/1	13.80	10/1	5/1	8	
21/05/06	Good		No Outsiders								7
20/10/06	Good	5	(S) Con Jockeys Handicap Hurdle	2m	Escobar	11/1	11.90	4/1	7/2	12	6
20/10/06	Good	4	Handicap Hurdle	2m	Blushing Prince	25/1	25.50	9/1	5/1	11	
14/11/06	Good		No Outsiders								6
04/12/06	Good to Soft	4	Handicap Hurdle	2m7f	Letitia's Loss	20/1	23.90	11/2	13/2	8	6
15/01/07	Good to Soft		No Outsiders								6
16/02/07	Good to Soft	5	(S) Handicap Hurdle	2m	Queen Tara	66/1	53.90	20/1	16/1	14	6
16/03/07	Good	5	(S) Handicap Hurdle	2m	Princess Stephanie	20/1	27.90	33/1	5/1	11	7
16/03/07	Good	3	Handicap Hurdle	2m	Festive Chimes	16/1	30.30	25/1	7/1	12	
09/04/07	Good	4	Novices Handicap Hurdle	2m4f	Jendali Lad	20/1	42.60	11/2	5/1	9	6

2006/2007 STATISTICS

No of Races	'Outsider' Wins	SPTotal	Average SP	'Outsider' Wins as a Percentage of Races	No of Blank Meetings
56	9	206	22/1	16.07%	3

'Outsider' Wins in Class of Race

Class 1	Class 2	Class 3	Class 4	Class 5	Class 6	Total
0	0	1	3	5	0	9

'Outsider' Wins – Type of Race

Handicap Chase	Handicap Hurdle	Non Handicap Chase	Non Handicap Hurdle
0	8	0	1

Calendar of 'Outsider' Wins

Apr	May	Jun	Jul	Aug	Sep	Oct	Nov	Dec	Jan	Feb	Mar	Apr
0	2	0	0	0	0	2	0	1	0	1	2	1

FOLKESTONE

Date	Going	Class	Race Type	Distance	Winner	SP	Tote	2nd SP	3rd SP	Runners	No of Jump Races
24/05/06	Good		No Outsiders								6
14/11/06	Good	3	Handicap Chase	2m	Jericho III	10/1	10.80	9/4	15/8	5	6
27/11/06	Good to Soft	5	Novices Handicap Chase	2m5f	Gerrard	16/1	18.60	12/1	5/2	12	6
12/12/06	Heavy	5	Novices Handicap Hurdle	2m6f	Eastern Point	20/1	18.70	11/10	7/1	9	7
12/12/06	Heavy	5	Novices Handicap Chase	2m	Bally Rainey	10/1	15.90	11/1	3/1	6	

Date	Going	Class	Race Type	Winner	Distance	SP	Tote	2nd SP	3rd SP	Runners	No of Jump Races
02/01/07	Soft	4	Novices Hurdle	Shardakhan	2m6f	14/1	27.80	8/11	5/2	8	7
16/01/07	Soft		No Outsiders								5
30/01/07	Good to Soft		No Outsiders								6
13/02/07	Heavy	4	Maiden Hurdle	Sydney	2m4f	20/1	19.00	5/1	6/1	12	6
13/02/07	Heavy	4	Novices Hurdle	Safari Adventures	2m1f	25/1	33.10	7/2	6/1	10	6

2006/2007 STATISTICS

No of Races	'Outsider' Wins	SPTotal	Average SP	No of Blank Meetings	'Outsider' Wins as a Percentage of Races
49	7	115	16/1	3	14.28%

'Outsider' Wins in Class of Race

Class 1	Class 2	Class 3	Class 4	Class 5	Class 6	Total
0	0	1	3	3	0	7

'Outsider' Wins – Type of Race

Handicap Chase	Handicap Hurdle	Non Handicap Chase	Non Handicap Hurdle
3	1	0	3

Calendar of 'Outsider' Wins

Apr	May	Jun	Jul	Aug	Sep	Oct	Nov	Dec	Jan	Feb	Mar	Apr
0	0	0	0	0	0	0	2	2	1	2	0	0

FONTWELL

Date	Going	Class	Race Type	Winner	Distance	SP	Tote	2nd SP	3rd SP	Runners	No of Jump Races
05/05/06	Good to Firm	4	Handicap Chase	Primrose Park	3m2f	33/1	62.30	20/1	5/1	10	6
28/05/06	Good		No Outsiders								6
06/06/06	Good to Firm	5	Con Jockeys Handicap Hurdle	Zeloso	2m6f	16/1	26.90	17/2	9/4	14	6
24/08/06	Good to Firm		No Outsiders								6
03/09/06	Good to Firm		No Outsiders								7
21/09/06	Good to Firm	4	Novices Hurdle	Irish Whispers	2m2f	12/1	10.80	2/7	6/1	7	7
21/09/06	Good to Firm	4	Novices Hurdle	Sonoma	2m6f	10/1	13.00	13/8	9/2	5	
30/09/06	Good to Firm	4	Handicap Hurdle	Madiba	2m2f	10/1	13.50	8/1	40/1	11	6
03/11/06	Good		No Outsiders								6
12/11/06	Good		No Outsiders								7
26/11/06	Good to Soft	4	Mares Only Maiden Hurdle	Joli Classical	2m2f	20/1	38.10	2/1	7/1	11	6
05/12/06	Soft	4	Con Jockeys Handicap Hurdle	Pearly Star	2m6f	16/1	14.30	9/4	3/1	9	7
23/12/06	Good to Soft	2	Handicap Hurdle	Take a Mile	2m4f	14/1	12.80	5/1	8/1	8	6
04/01/07	Soft		No Outsiders								6
25/01/07	Soft		No Outsiders								6
04/02/07	Good to Soft		No Outsiders								6

Date	Going	Class	Race Type	Winner	Distance	SP	Tote	2nd SP	3rd SP	Runners	No of Jump Races
18/02/07	Soft	4	Hunter Chase	Deckie	3m2f	16/1	18.40	8/1	8/1	6	6
07/03/07	Heavy		No Outsiders								5
18/03/07	Good	5	(S) Hurdle	Atlantic Rhapsody	2m2f	11/1	12.40	7/2	11/4	9	7
10/04/07	Good to Firm		No Outsiders								5
26/04/07	Good to Firm	4	Handicap Hurdle	Callman	3m3f	12/1	16.40	5/1	9/1	12	6

2006/2007 STATISTICS

No of Races: 123

'Outsider' Wins in Class of Race

Class 1	Class 2	Class 3	Class 4	Class 5	Class 6	Total
0	1	0	7	2	1	11

'Outsider' Wins – Type of Race

Handicap Chase	Non Handicap Chase	Handicap Hurdle	Non Handicap Hurdle	Total
1	1	5	4	11

Calendar of 'Outsider' Wins

Apr	May	Jun	Jul	Aug	Sep	Oct	Nov	Dec	Jan	Feb	Mar
0	1	1	0	1	2	1	1	1	1	1	

'Outsider' Wins: 11
SP Total: 170
Average SP: 15/1
'Outsider' Wins as a Percentage of Races: 8.94%
No of Blank Meetings: 7

HAYDOCK

Date	Going	Class	Race Type	Winner	Distance	SP	Tote	2nd SP	3rd SP	Runners	No of Jump Races
06/05/06	Good	2	Handicap Hurdle	Westender	2m7f	20/1	24.40	13/2	9/2	12	2
06/05/06	Good	1	Handicap Hurdle	Acambo	2m	16/1	19.20	15/2	8/1	21	
19/10/06	Good	4	Handicap Chase	Arumun	2m4f	14/1	16.00	12/1	1/1	7	6
02/11/06	Good	4	Novices Hurdle	Nevertika	2m4f	50/1	69.10	7/2	16/1	15	6
18/11/06	Good to Soft		No Outsiders								6
16/12/06	Heavy	2	Handicap Chase	Kandar D'Allier	3m	10/1	10.70	10/1	7/2	14	6
16/12/06	Heavy	4	Novices Hurdle	Anglicisme	2m2f	33/1	51.40	16/1	5/2	16	
30/12/06	Heavy	3	Handicap Chase	Sharp Belline	3m	11/1	14.20	15/2	7/2	8	7
30/12/06	Heavy	2	Chase	Limerick Boy	2m6f	10/1	7.80	7/2	11/8	5	
06/01/07	Heavy	4	Novices Hurdle	Mister Potter	2m4f	16/1	11.90	7/2	100/1	10	6
20/01/07	Heavy	3	Handicap Chase	Ichi Beau	2m	16/1	16.70	7/2	8/1	5	6
17/02/07	Heavy	1	Handicap Chase	Heltornic	3m4f	12/1	15.00	14/1	12/1	16	7
17/02/07	Heavy	2	Handicap Hurdle	Millenium Royal	2m7f	33/1	38.20	25/1	13/2	20	
22/02/07	Heavy	4	Novices Handicap Chase	Auntie Kathleen	2m6f	20/1	20.80	8/1	15/2	12	6

Date	Going	Class	Race Type	Distance	Winner	SP	Tote	2nd SP	3rd SP	Runners	No of Jump Races
22/02/07	Heavy	3	Hunters Chase	2m6f	Cobreces	16/1	16.10	11/1	66/1	11	6
07/04/07	Good	4	Handicap Chase	3m4f	I Love Turtle	12/1	16.00	4/1	6/1	15	
07/04/07	Good	2	Handicap Novices Hurdle	2m4f	Or Jaune	11/1	14.80	14/1	12/1	16	
07/04/07	Good	4	Handicap Hurdle	2m4f	Eleazar	18/1	25.70	9/4	20/1	17	

2006/2007 STATISTICS

No of Races	'Outsider' Wins	SP Total	Average SP	'Outsider' Wins as a Percentage of Races	No of Blank Meetings
64	17	318	18/1	26.56%	0

'Outsider' Wins in Class of Race

Class 1	Class 2	Class 3	Class 4	Class 5	Class 6	Total
2	5	2	7	0	1	17

'Outsider' Wins – Type of Race

Handicap Chase	Non Handicap Chase	Handicap Hurdle	Non Handicap Hurdle
7	2	5	3

Calendar of 'Outsider' Wins

Apr	May	Jun	Jul	Aug	Sep	Oct	Nov	Dec	Jan	Feb	Mar	Apr
0	2	0	0	0	0	1	1	4	2	4	0	3

HEREFORD

Date	Going	Class	Race Type	Distance	Winner	SP	Tote	2nd SP	3rd SP	Runners	No of Jump Races
04/05/06	Good to Firm		No Outsiders								7
17/05/06	Good	5	Hurdle	3m2f	The Wife's Sister	11/1	5.40	40/1	3/1	11	5
17/05/06	Good	5	Handicap Chase	3m1f	Test of Friendship	16/1	17.20	9/2	8/1	17	
04/06/06	Good to Firm	3	Handicap Hurdle	2m1f	Mac Federal	25/1	35.90	9/4	14/1	15	6
04/06/06	Good to Firm	4	Handicap Chase	3m1f	Sungates	10/1	11.60	7/1	4/1	15	
14/06/06	Good to Firm	5	(S) Handicap Hurdle	2m1f	Dream On Maggie	16/1	10.50	33/1	8/1	14	6
19/06/06	Good to Firm	5	(S) Hurdle	2m1f	Airgusta	12/1	15.30	11/4	100/30	15	6
28/09/06	Good to Firm		No outsiders								6
15/10/06	Good to Firm	4	Handicap Hurdle	3m2f	Jug of Punch	50/1	53.70	22/1	5/4	16	6
05/11/06	Good to Firm	4	Juvenile Novices Hurdle	2m1f	Pukka Tique	12/1	12.20	9/2	18/1	11	6
05/11/06	Good to Firm	4	Maiden Hurdle	2m1f	Fantastic Arts	12/1	12.20	4/1	7/4	15	
16/11/06	Good to Soft		No Outsiders								6
28/11/06	Heavy		No Outsiders								6
22/12/06	Soft	4	Novices Chase	2m3f	Ice Bucket	12/1	19.80	11/2	4/1	10	7

Date	Going	Class	Race Type	Distance	Winner	SP	Tote	2nd SP	3rd SP	Runners	No of Jump Races
23/12/06	Good to Soft	5	Handicap Hurdle	3m2f	Radnor Lad	33/1	39.40	10/11	8/1	16	6
11/01/07	Heavy	3	No Outsiders								6
26/01/07	Soft	5	Handicap Chase	2m3f	Lucifer Bleu	28/1	28.10	1/1	7/2	8	6
29/03/07	Good to Firm	4	(S) Novices Hurdle	2m4f	Ricardo's Chance	14/1	18.00	8/1	10/11	13	6
11/04/07	Good to Firm		Maiden Hurdle	2m4f	Valuta	25/1	36.10	9/2	50/1	16	7
11/04/07	Good to Firm	4	Handicap Hurdle	2m4f	Kelv	10/1	9.30	16/1	14/1	18	
11/04/07	Good to Firm	5	Novices Handicap Chase	2m3f	Lyon	12/1	12.10	11/2	4/1	10	
20/04/07	Good to Firm	5	Handicap Chase	2m	Pauntley Gofa	20/1	17.60	3/1	11/4	10	
20/04/07	Good to Firm		Handicap Hurdle	3m2f	Dizzy Future	22/1	27.90	20/1	10/1	17	6

2006/2007 STATISTICS

No of Races	'Outsider' Wins	SP Total	Average SP	'Outsider' Wins as a Percentage of Races	No of Blank Meetings
104	18	340	18/1	17.30%	5

'Outsider' Wins in Class of Race

Class 1	Class 2	Class 3	Class 4	Class 5	Class 6	Total
0	0	2	8	8	0	18

'Outsider' Wins – Type of Race

Handicap Chase	Handicap Hurdle	Non Handicap Chase	Non Handicap Hurdle	Total
5	6	1	6	18

Calendar of 'Outsider' Wins

Apr	May	Jun	Jul	Aug	Sep	Oct	Nov	Dec	Jan	Feb	Mar	Apr
0	2	4	0	0	0	1	2	2	1	0	1	5

HEXHAM

Date	Going	Class	Race Type	Distance	Winner	SP	Tote	2nd SP	3rd SP	Runners	No of Jump Races
06/05/06	Good to Firm		No Outsiders								7
13/05/06	Good to Firm		No Outsiders								7
30/05/06	Good	4	Handicap Hurdle	3m	Eriskay	33/1	41.90	25/1	20/1	13	6
03/06/06	Good to Firm	4	Novices Chase	2m4f	Field Roller	20/1	30.40	3/1	25/1	11	6
03/06/06	Good to Firm	6	Hunter Chase	2m4f	Sajomi Rona	16/1	15.50	14/1	3/1	12	
17/06/06	Good to Firm		No Outsiders								6
25/06/06	Good to Soft	3	Novices Hurdle	2m	Lowsha Green	18/1	19.30	11/8	1/1	8	6
25/06/06	Good to Soft	5	(S) Handicap Hurdle	2m4f	Mags Two	14/1	12.80	10/1	5/1	12	
25/06/06	Good to Soft	4	Handicap Chase	3m1f	Fleetwood Mac	14/1	16.20	7/1	9/2	11	
29/09/06	Good to Firm	4	Novices Hurdle	3m	City Music	22/1	22.60	1/3	4/1	5	6

Date	Going	Class	Race Type	Distance	Winner	SP	Tote	2nd SP	3rd SP	Runners	No of Jump Races
07/10/06	Good	4	Novices Hurdle	2m	Alina Rheinberg	14/1	13.60	4/5	5/1	12	6
07/10/06	Good	4	Handicap Hurdle	3m	Top the Bill	12/1	19.00	7/2	16/1	12	6
03/11/06	Good to Soft		No Outsiders								6
15/11/06	Soft	4	Novices Hurdle	2m	Cedrus Libani	14/1	19.00	2/7	80/1	14	6
15/11/06	Soft	3	Handicap Chase	4m	Naunton Brook	10/1	14.10	3/1	8/1	12	
06/12/06	Heavy		No Outsiders								7
05/02/07	Soft	5	Maiden Hurdle	2m	Sowtary Palm	28/1	85.40	13/8	5/1	7	6
15/03/07	Soft	4	Handicap Chase	4m	Fleetwood Mac	10/1	12.20	15/2	3/1	10	6
15/03/07	Soft	5	Handicap Chase	2m4f	Loscar	12/1	20.40	11/2	8/1	12	
01/04/07	Soft		No Outsiders								6
23/04/07	Good to Firm	4	Novices Handicap Chase	3m1f	Panama At Once	25/1	41.90	4/1	7/1	13	5

2006/2007 STATISTICS

No of Races	'Outsider' Wins	SPTotal	Average SP	'Outsider' Wins as a Percentage of Races	No of Blank Meetings
98	15	262	17/1	15.30%	6

'Outsider' Wins in Class of Race

Class 1	Class 2	Class 3	Class 4	Class 5	Class 6	Total
0	0	2	9	3	1	15

'Outsider' Wins – Type of Race

Handicap Chase	Handicap Hurdle	Non Handicap Chase	Non Handicap Hurdle
5	3	2	5

Calendar of 'Outsider' Wins

Apr	May	Jun	Jul	Aug	Sep	Oct	Nov	Dec	Jan	Feb	Mar	Apr
0	1	5	0	0	1	2	2	0	0	1	2	1

HUNTINGDON

Date	Going	Class	Race Type	Distance	Winner	SP	Tote	2nd SP	3rd SP	Runners	No of Jump Races
04/05/06	Good to Firm		No Outsiders								6
16/05/06	Good to Firm	6	Hunter Chase	3m6f	April Spirit	12/1	13.00	15/2	7/2	8	6
08/06/06	Good to Firm	4	Handicap Chase	3m	Carricklee Boy	50/1	64.30	11/1	6/1	11	6
08/06/06	Good to Firm	4	Handicap Hurdle	2m4f	Gaelic Roulette	25/1	20.60	13/2	50/1	13	
28/08/06	Good to Firm	4	Handicap Chase	2m	Call Me Edward	20/1	15.20	18/1	13/2	8	6
24/09/06	Good to Firm		No Outsiders								6
03/10/06	Good to Firm	3	Handicap Hurdle	2m	Festive Chimes	28/1	23.80	4/1	18/1	11	5
01/11/06	Good to Firm		No Outsiders								6

Date	Going	Class	Race Type	Winner	Distance	SP	Tote	2nd SP	3rd SP	Runners	No of Jump Races
18/11/06	Good to Firm			No Outsiders							7
07/12/06	Good to Soft	4	Handicap Hurdle	Fleetwood Forest	2m5f	25/1	43.80	8/1	16/1	18	6
07/12/06	Good to Soft	3	Handicap Hurdle	Sunisa	2m	11/1	15.00	5/2	8/1	13	
07/12/06	Good to Soft	3	Mares Only Novices Hurdle	Le Dame Brune	2m4f	16/1	15.90	5/1	12/1	16	6
26/12/06	Good	4	Handicap Chase	Ground Breaker	2m	14/1	13.70	6/1	7/2	10	6
12/01/07	Soft	4	Novices Handicap Hurdle	Rebel Raider	2m	12/1	17.00	25/1	9/1	18	8
24/01/07	Soft			No Outsiders							7
22/02/07	Soft	4	Handicap Chase	It's Crucial	3m	14/1	19.00	5/1	31/2	9	
22/02/07	Soft	5	Novices Hunter Chase	Thompsons Wood	3m	10/1	19.90	4/1	25/1	8	
14/03/07	Good	4	Handicap Chase	Bronson F'Sure	3m	10/1	18.00	7/1	9/1	12	6
14/03/07	Good	4	Handicap Hurdle	Beauchamp Star	2m	11/1	15.30	10/1	100/30	12	
14/03/07	Good	4	Handicap Hurdle	Stars Delight	3m2f	16/1	23.10	14/1	11/1	17	
09/04/07	Good to Firm			No Outsiders							6

2006/2007 STATISTICS

No of Races	'Outsider' Wins	Average SP	'Outsider' Wins as a Percentage of Races	No of Blank Meetings
93	15	18/1	16.12%	6

SPTotal	Total
274	15

'Outsider' Wins in Class of Race

Class 1	Class 2	Class 3	Class 4	Class 5	Class 6
0	0	3	10	0	2

'Outsider' Wins – Type of Race

Handicap Chase	Handicap Hurdle	Non Handicap Chase	Non Handicap Hurdle
5	7	2	1

Calendar of 'Outsider' Wins

Apr	May	Jun	Jul	Aug	Sep	Oct	Nov	Dec	Jan	Feb	Mar	Apr
0	1	2	0	1	0	1	0	5	0	2	3	0

KELSO

Date	Going	Class	Race Type	Winner	Distance	SP	Tote	2nd SP	3rd SP	Runners	No of Jump Races
09/05/06	Good to Firm	4	Novices Handicap Hurdle	Heversham	2m6f	50/1	72.40	6/4	100/30	12	6
09/05/06	Good to Firm	3	Handicap Chase	Harlov	3m1f	16/1	26.10	8/1	11/2	8	
10/05/06	Good to Firm	4	Maiden Hurdle	Only Millie	2m	100/1	70.20	25/1	33/1	9	6
24/05/06	Good	4	Novices Handicap Hurdle	Fiddlers Creek	2m	14/1	13.40	3/1	16/1	16	6
01/10/06	Good	5	Novices Handicap Chase	Lambrini Mist	2m6f	14/1	13.30	12/1	5/1	12	7
01/10/06	Good	4	Novices Hurdle	Benny the Plier	2m6f	10/1	16.30	4/7	50/1	10	
01/10/06	Good	3	Handicap Hurdle	Front Rank	2m	16/1	20.10	7/1	12/1	15	
01/10/06	Good	4	Handicap Chase	Kids Inheritance	2m6f	16/1	26.10	7/2	9/2	7	

Date	Going	Class	Race Type	Winner	Distance	SP	Tote	2nd SP	3rd SP	Runners	No of Jump Races
21/10/06	Good to Soft	5	Maiden Hurdle	Smart Street	2m	16/1	21.70	5/6	14/1	15	6
21/10/06	Good to Soft	4	Handicap Hurdle	Classic Event	2m	12/1	23.40	13/2	20/1	12	
21/10/06	Good to Soft	4	Handicap Hurdle	College City	2m6f	10/1	12.40	12/1	25/1	13	
04/11/06	Good	3	Handicap Hurdle	Billy Bush	2m6f	40/1	40.30	7/2	6/1	10	7
04/11/06	Good	4	Con Jockeys Handicap Hurdle	Singhalongtasveer	2m2f	12/1	16.10	8/1	25/1	11	
17/11/06	Good to Soft	3	Handicap Hurdle	Hush Tiger	2m2f	12/1	16.60	12/1	7/1	10	7
03/12/06	Heavy	5	Amateur Riders Handicap Hurdle	Windygate	2m2f	12/1	11.00	100/1	8/1	17	7
12/01/07	Heavy	4	Mares Only Novices Chase	More Likely	2m6f	11/1	12.40	15/8	4/6	4	6
12/01/07	Heavy	3	Handicap Hurdle	Brave Vision	2m	12/1	12.60	11/4	6/1	11	
28/01/07	Soft		No outsiders								6
15/02/07	Soft	4	Juvenile Novices Hurdle	English City	2m2f	33/1	27.40	50/1	33/1	11	7
03/03/07	Heavy	4	Juvenile Novices Hurdle	Sobriquet	2m	16/1	16.80	4/1	10/11	9	7
02/04/07	Good	4	Handicap Hurdle	Kidithou	2m6f	20/1	26.20	5/1	20/1	17	7
15/04/07	Good		No Outsiders								7

2006/2007 STATISTICS

No of Races	'Outsider' Wins	Average SP	SP Total	No of Blank Meetings	'Outsider' Wins as a Percentage of Races
92	20	21/1	442	2	21.73%

'Outsider' Wins in Class of Race

Class 1	Class 2	Class 3	Class 4	Class 5	Class 6	Total
0	0	5	12	3	0	20

'Outsider' Wins – Type of Race

Handicap Chase	Handicap Hurdle	Non Handicap Chase	Non Handicap Hurdle
3	11	1	5

Calendar of 'Outsider' Wins

Apr	May	Jun	Jul	Aug	Sep	Oct	Nov	Dec	Jan	Feb	Mar	Apr
0	4	0	0	0	0	7	3	1	2	1	1	1

KEMPTON

Date	Going	Class	Race Type	Winner	Distance	SP	Tote	2nd SP	3rd SP	Runners	No of Jump Races
14/10/06	Good		No Outsiders								6
07/11/06	Good		No Outsiders								7
21/11/06	Good		No Outsiders								6
26/12/06	Good to Soft	1	Novices Chase	Ungaro	3m	14/1	17.50	5/1	5/1	6	6
26/12/06	Good to Soft	1	Hurdle	Jazz Messenger	2m	10/1	10.40	7/1	8/1	7	

Date	Going	Class	Race Type	Distance	Winner	SP	Tote	2nd SP	3rd SP	Runners	No of Jump Races
27/12/06	Good to Soft	3	Juvenile Novices Hurdle	2m	Poquelin	10/1	12.10	6/4	5/1	13	6
13/01/07	Good to Soft	3	Handicap Hurdle	2m	Romany Prince	40/1	45.60	8/13	25/1	7	7
13/01/07	Good to Soft	3	Novices Handicap Chase	3m	Lady of Scarvagh	50/1	62.80	11/2	100/1	11	
13/01/07	Good to Soft	2	Handicap Hurdle	2m5f	Verasi	20/1	27.60	25/1	9/1	17	
13/01/07	Good to Soft	3	Handicap Chase	2m4f	Idole First	12/1	12.70	15/2	4/1	12	
09/02/07	Good to Soft		No Outsiders								6
24/02/07	Soft	3	Handicap Hurdle	2m5f	Mac Federal	20/1	25.00	5/1	7/2	9	6
03/03/07	Heavy	3	Novices Chase	2m4f	Bible Lord	12/1	9.20	100/30	100/1	5	6
28/03/07	Good		No Outsiders								6

2006/2007 STATISTICS

No of Races	'Outsider' Wins	SP Total	Average SP	'Outsider' Wins as a Percentage of Races	No of Blank Meetings
62	9	188	20/1	14.50%	5

'Outsider' Wins in Class of Race

Class 1	Class 2	Class 3	Class 4	Class 5	Class 6	Total
2	1	6	0	0	0	9

'Outsider' Wins – Type of Race

Handicap Chase	Handicap Hurdle	Non Handicap Chase	Non Handicap Hurdle
2	3	2	2

Calendar of 'Outsider' Wins

Apr	May	Jun	Jul	Aug	Sep	Oct	Nov	Dec	Jan	Feb	Mar	Apr
0	0	0	0	0	0	0	0	3	4	1	1	0

LEICESTER

Date	Going	Class	Race Type	Distance	Winner	SP	Tote	2nd SP	3rd SP	Runners	No of Jump Races
3/11/06	Good to Soft	4	Mares Only Novices Handicap Hurdle	2m4f	Our Joycey	11/1	15.80	4/1	16/1	13	7
26/11/06	Good	4	Handicap Chase	2m7f	Curly Spencer	12/1	15.20	6/5	9/2	8	6
30/11/06	Soft	5	(S) Handicap Hurdle	2m4f	Paynestown Lad	25/1	26.70	8/1	10/1	14	6
06/12/06	Soft		No Outsiders								6
28/12/06	Soft	3	Handicap Chase	2m4f	Mokum	12/1	9.40	9/2	14/1	13	6
28/12/06	Soft	3	Handicap Hurdle	2m	Nikola	10/1	14.20	5/2	28/1	11	
31/01/07	Soft	4	Novices Claiming Hurdle	2m	Viscount Rossini	25/1	22.30	80/1	33/1	15	
14/02/07	Soft		No Outsiders								6
09/03/07	Heavy		No Outsiders								6

2006/2007 STATISTICS

No of Races	'Outsider' Wins	SP Total	Average SP	No of Blank Meetings	'Outsider' Wins as a Percentage of Races
49	6	95	15/1	3	12.24%

'Outsider' Wins in Class of Race

Class 1	Class 2	Class 3	Class 4	Class 5	Class 6
0	0	2	3	1	0

'Outsider' Wins – Type of Race

Handicap Chase	Handicap Hurdle	Non Handicap Chase	Non Handicap Hurdle	Total
2	3	1	0	6

Calendar of 'Outsider' Wins

Apr	May	Jun	Jul	Aug	Sep	Oct	Nov	Dec	Jan	Feb	Mar	Apr
0	0	0	0	0	0	0	3	2	1	0	0	0

LINGFIELD

Date	Going	Class	Race Type	Distance	Winner	SP	Tote	2nd SP	3rd SP	Runners	No of Jump Races
08/11/06	Good	5	Novices Handicap Chase	3m	Honor and Glory	10/1	10.20	9/1	6/1	16	6
08/11/06	Good	5	Handicap Chase	2m4f	The Hardy Boy	66/1	64.50	100/30	10/1	15	6
22/11/06	Soft		No Outsiders								6
04/01/07	Heavy	4	Novices Hurdle	2m	Grecian Groom	33/1	50.40	33/1	10/11	11	6
04/01/07	Heavy	5	Handicap Chase	3m	Star Glow	100/1	99.90	9/2	7/1	14	6
21/03/07	Soft	5	Handicap Hurdle	2m3f	Cleopatra's Therapy	16/1	20.50	9/4	9/2	15	5

2006/2007 STATISTICS

No of Races	'Outsider' Wins	SP Total	Average SP	No of Blank Meetings	'Outsider' Wins as a Percentage of Races
23	5	225	45/1	1	21.73%

'Outsider' Wins in Class of Race

Class 1	Class 2	Class 3	Class 4	Class 5	Class 6
0	0	0	1	4	0

'Outsider' Wins – Type of Race

Handicap Chase	Handicap Hurdle	Non Handicap Chase	Non Handicap Hurdle	Total
0	3	0	1	5

Calendar of 'Outsider' Wins

Apr	May	Jun	Jul	Aug	Sep	Oct	Nov	Dec	Jan	Feb	Mar	Apr
0												0

LUDLOW

Date	Going	Class	Race Type	Distance	Winner	SP	Tote	2nd SP	3rd SP	Runners	No of Jump Races
30/04/06	Good to Firm	3	Handicap Hurdle	2m5f	Kristoffersen	12/1	10.60	3/1	8/1	14	6
30/04/06	Good to Firm	5	Hunter Chase	3m1f	Tsar's Twist	12/1	7.10	4/1	15/8	8	
18/05/06	Good	4	Novices Handicap Hurdle	2m	La Dolfina	14/1	129.10	11/2	100/30	15	6
18/05/06	Good	3	Handicap Hurdle	3m	Business Traveller	10/1	13.60	9/1	7/2	5	
12/10/06	Good to Firm	4	Handicap Chase	3m	Meehan	10/1	12.70	6/1	15/2	10	6
12/10/06	Good to Firm	4	Beginners Chase	2m4f	Royal Katidoki	33/1	24.60	2/1	7/4	7	
19/10/06	Good to Firm	5	(S) Hurdle	2m5f	Ballito	14/1	11.30	9/2	100/30	10	7
09/11/06	Good to Firm		No Outsiders								6
20/11/06	Good		No Outsiders								6
07/12/06	Soft	4	Amateur Riders Handicap Hurdle	2m5f	Hello It's Me	12/1	17.20	2/1	9/2	16	6
21/12/06	Good to Soft	3	Novices Handicap Chase	2m4f	Art Virginia	14/1	23.90	10/1	13/8	13	6
21/12/06	Good to Soft	4	Handicap Hurdle	2m	Tora Petcha	10/1	11.40	25/1	9/4	16	
21/12/06	Good to Soft	3	Handicap Chase	3m	Touch Closer	22/1	20.60	3/1	4/1	9	
08/01/07	Good to Soft	4	Juvenile Novices Hurdle	2m	Altilhar	12/1	15.90	33/1	7/1	14	7
08/01/07	Good to Soft	5	Handicap Chase	3m	Tank Buster	16/1	16.50	15/2	25/1	17	
29/01/07	Good	4	Juvenile Novices Hurdle	2m	Punjabi	10/1	8.20	8/11	22/1	15	6
21/02/07	Good	4	Handicap Chase	2m	Glimmer of Light	40/1	31.60	12/1	7/1	11	7
21/02/07	Good	5	(S) Novices Hurdle	2m5f	Walton Way	18/1	23.70	18/1	4/1	14	
21/02/07	Good	4	Con Jockeys Handicap Chase	3m	Ca Na Trona	14/1	16.60	7/1	50/1	16	
21/02/07	Good	3	Handicap Hurdle	2m	Kickahead	11/1	12.30	5/6	7/2	8	
21/02/07	Good	5	Hunters Chase	2m4f	Viscount Bankes	33/1	51.30	7/2	9/2	15	
22/03/07	Good	4	Mares Only Novices Hurdle	3m	Ouh Jay	66/1	88.00	16/1	100/30	11	6
22/03/07	Good	4	Handicap Hurdle	2m5f	Ordre de Bataille	11/1	16.50	11/2	33/1	17	
05/04/07	Good to Firm	3	Handicap Chase	2m4f	Handy Money	12/1	14.30	3/1	11/4	6	7

2006/2007 STATISTICS

No of Races	'Outsider' Wins	SPTotal	Average SP	'Outsider' Wins as a Percentage of Races	No of Blank Meetings
82	22	406	18/1	26.82%	2

'Outsider' Wins in Class of Race

Class 1	Class 2	Class 3	Class 4	Class 5	Class 6	Total
0	0	6	11	3	2	22

'Outsider' Wins – Type of Race

Handicap Chase	Handicap Hurdle	Non Handicap Chase	Non Handicap Hurdle
7	7	3	5

Calendar of 'Outsider' Wins

Apr	May	Jun	Jul	Aug	Sep	Oct	Nov	Dec	Jan	Feb	Mar	Apr
2	0	0	0	0	0	3	0	4	3	5	2	1

MARKET RASEN

Date	Going	Class	Race Type	Distance	Winner	SP	Tote	2nd SP	3rd SP	Runners	No of Jump Races
21/05/06	Soft	4	Handicap Hurdle	2m1f	Toulouse Express	16/1	15.10	11/1	12/1	10	6
21/05/06	Soft	4	Handicap Hurdle	2m6f	Michael's Dream	11/1	10.20	6/1	18/1	9	
21/05/06	Soft	5	Handicap Chase	2m4f	Silver Dagger	50/1	51.30	2/1	20/1	12	
14/06/06	Good	5	(S) Handicap Hurdle	2m3f	Rushney River	10/1	15.60	13/2	50/1	17	6
30/06/06	Good to Firm	4	Novices Handicap Chase	2m6f	Rich Song	14/1	12.30	12/1	9/4	10	7
09/07/06	Good to Firm	4	Novices Hurdle	2m3f	Present Oriented	12/1	12.20	5/2	9/1	14	6
09/07/06	Good to Firm	4	Con Jockeys Handicap Hurdle	2m6f	Erins Lass	14/1	12.00	5/1	20/1	12	
22/07/06	Good	2	Handicap Hurdle	2m1f	Toycoon Hall	33/1	42.30	7/1	50/1	17	7
06/08/06	Good to Firm		No Outsiders								6
19/08/06	Good to Soft		No Outsiders								6
26/08/06	Good		No Outsiders								6
23/09/06	Good	2	Handicap Hurdle	2m3f	Aleron	14/1	15.20	12/1	9/4	12	6
01/10/06	Heavy		No Outsiders								6
05/11/06	Good		No Outsiders								7
16/11/06	Soft	3	Handicap Chase	2m6f	Iron Man	10/1	14.00	12/1	100/30	8	7
30/11/06	Soft	4	Juvenile Maiden Hurdle	2m1f	Olivair	100/1	80.40	11/8	10/11	10	6
09/12/06	Good to Soft		No Outsiders								7
26/12/06	Soft	4	Novices Handicap Chase	3m1f	I Love Turtle	12/1	18.20	100/30	7/2	7	7
19/02/07	Soft		No Outsiders								6
11/03/07	Soft		No Outsiders								7
19/03/07	Good to Soft	4	Juvenile Novices Hurdle	2m1f	River Logic	16/1	19.20	16/1	2/1	16	5
19/03/07	Good to Soft	5	Handicap Hurdle	2m1f	Shamrock Boy	12/1	19.00	6/1	28/1	19	
15/04/07	Good to Firm	4	Handicap Hurdle	2m6f	Fisby	14/1	13.70	4/1	5/1	8	6
28/04/07	Good	4	Con Jockeys Handicap Hurdle	2m6f	Fortunate Dave	25/1	26.40	16/1	8/1	17	6

2006/2007 STATISTICS

No of Races	'Outsider' Wins	SP Total	Average SP	'Outsider' Wins as a Percentage of Races	No of Blank Meetings
126	16	363	22/1	12.69%	8

'Outsider' Wins in Class of Race

Class 1	Class 2	Class 3	Class 4	Class 5	Class 6	Total
0	2	1	10	3	0	16

'Outsider' Wins – Type of Race

Handicap Chase	Handicap Hurdle	Non Handicap Chase	Non Handicap Hurdle
4	9	0	3

Calendar of 'Outsider' Wins

Apr	May	Jun	Jul	Aug	Sep	Oct	Nov	Dec	Jan	Feb	Mar	Apr
0	3	2	3	0	1	0	2	1	0	2	0	2

MUSSELBURGH

Date	Going	Class	Race Type	Distance	Winner	SP	Tote	2nd SP	3rd SP	Runners	No of Jump Races
24/11/06	Good	4	Novices Handicap Chase	2m4f	Barracat	40/1	55.00	11/10	20/1	12	6
24/11/06	Good	3	Handicap Hurdle	2m	Plica	12/1	12.20	14/1	6/5	11	
10/12/06	Good	5	Amateur Riders Handicap Chase	2m4f	Black Chalk	11/1	11.40	33/1	7/2	14	6
20/12/06	Good	5	Novices Handicap Chase	3m	Quibble	14/1	7.70	13/2	8/1	13	7
20/12/06	Good	3	Handicap Hurdle	2m	Majorca	12/1	15.80	10/1	11/4	13	
30/12/06	Good	5	Amateur Riders Handicap Chase	3m	Lethem Present	10/1	18.50	13/2	14/1	9	7
30/12/06	Good	3	Handicap Hurdle	2m	Double Vodka	14/1	14.50	10/1	4/1	10	
05/01/07	Good	4	Novices Handicap Hurdle	2m4f	Sybarite Chief	11/1	13.90	12/1	33/1	15	6
19/01/07	Good to Soft	4	Mares Only Novice Hurdle	2m4f	So Cloudy	12/1	11.20	2/1	50/1	13	6
19/01/07	Good to Soft	5	Con Jockeys Handicap Chase	3m	Woodstock Lass	20/1	22.10	17/2	8/1	12	
19/01/07	Good to Soft	4	Novices Handicap Chase	2m4f	Gastornis	33/1	36.00	7/1	14/1	8	
04/02/07	Good	4	Handicap Hurdle	2m4f	Kyber	10/1	10.80	11/4	50/1	16	6
14/02/07	Good to Soft	3	Novices Hurdle	2m	Sharp Reply	12/1	14.80	5/2	1/1	11	5
14/02/07	Good to Soft	3	Juvenile Novices Handicap Hurdle	2m	Patavium	10/1	16.40	8/1	15/2	7	

2006/2007 STATISTICS

No of Races	'Outsider' Wins	SP Total	Average SP	'Outsider' Wins as a Percentage of Races	No of Blank Meetings
49	14	221	15/1	28.57%	0

'Outsider' Wins in Class of Race

Class 1	Class 2	Class 3	Class 4	Class 5	Class 6
0	0	5	5	4	0

'Outsider' Wins – Type of Race

Handicap Chase	Handicap Hurdle	Non Handicap Chase	Non Handicap Hurdle
6	6	0	2

Calendar of 'Outsider' Wins

Apr	May	Jun	Jul	Aug	Sep	Oct	Nov	Dec	Jan	Feb	Mar	Apr	Total
0	0	0	0	0	0	0	2	5	4	3	0	0	14

NEWBURY

Date	Going	Class	Race Type	Winner	Distance	SP	Tote	2nd SP	3rd SP	Runners	No of Jump Races
24/11/06	Good to Soft		No Outsiders								6
25/11/06	Soft	1	Handicap Chase	State of Play	3m2f	10/1	11.60	12/1	12/1	16	6
26/11/06	Heavy		No Outsiders								7
13/12/06	Soft	4	Handicap Chase	Obelix de Longechaux	2m2f	16/1	22.50	16/1	14/1	12	6
22/12/06	Good to Soft		No Outsiders								6
17/01/07	Heavy	4	Con Jockeys Handicap Hurdle	Knighton Lad	3m	14/1	17.30	12/1	5/2	15	6
10/02/07	Soft	3	Handicap Hurdle	Copsale Lad	3m	14/1	18.00	9/2	15/2	16	6
10/02/07	Soft	1	Handicap Hurdle	Heathcote	2m	50/1	69.80	16/1	11/1	20	7
02/03/07	Soft	3	Handicap Chase	Magic Sky	2m1f	12/1	17.60	3/1	13/2	7	6
03/03/07	Soft	3	Novices Hurdle	Master Eddy	3m	10/1	6.40	1/1	25/1	6	
03/03/07	Soft	3	Handicap Chase	Green Belt Flyer	3m	20/1	23.00	7/1	7/2	7	
03/03/07	Soft	1	Handicap Chase	Madison du Berlais	2m4f	12/1	14.00	7/2	7/1	11	
23/03/07	Good		No Outsiders								6
24/03/07	Good	3	Novices Handicap Hurdle	Strawberry	2m	20/1	15.80	4/1	11/2	15	6

2006/2007 STATISTICS

No of Races	'Outsider' Wins	SP Total	Average SP	'Outsider' Wins as a Percentage of Races	No of Blank Meetings
68	10	178	17/1	14.7%	5

'Outsider' Wins in Class of Race

Class 1	Class 2	Class 3	Class 4	Class 5	Class 6	Total
3	0	5	2	0	0	10

'Outsider' Wins – Type of Race

Handicap Chase	Handicap Hurdle	Non Handicap Chase	Non Handicap Hurdle
5	4	0	1

Calendar of 'Outsider' Wins

Apr	May	Jun	Jul	Aug	Sep	Oct	Nov	Dec	Jan	Feb	Mar	Apr
0	0	0	0	0	0	0	1	1	1	2	5	0

NEWCASTLE

Date	Going	Class	Race Type	Distance	Winner	SP	Tote	2nd SP	3rd SP	Runners	No of Jump Races
10/11/06	Good		No Outsiders								6
25/11/06	Good to Soft		No Outsiders								7
16/12/06	Soft		No Outsiders								6
05/01/07	Soft		No Outsiders								6
17/01/07	Soft	3	Novices Hurdle	3m	Allegedly So	100/1	173.40	10/1	4/7	13	6
17/01/07	Soft	4	Handicap Hurdle	2m	Storymaker	10/1	14.20	16/1	9/1	14	
17/01/07	Soft	5	(S) Con Jockeys Handicap Hurdle	2m4f	Over to Joe	14/1	15.80	5/1	33/1	10	
31/01/07	Soft		No Outsiders								6
24/02/07	Heavy	3	Handicap Hurdle	2m	Through the Rye	12/1	12.80	15/8	3/1	7	6
06/03/07	Heavy	4	Novices Hurdle	2m	King Mak	100/1	126.10	6/4	5/2	14	6
17/03/07	Good	4	Handicap Chase	2m	Ton Chee	14/1	12.40	13/2	11/1	10	7

2006/2007 STATISTICS

No of Races	'Outsider' Wins	SP Total	Average SP	'Outsider' Wins as a Percentage of Races	No of Blank Meetings
56	6	250	41/1	10.71%	5

'Outsider' Wins in Class of Race

Class 1	Class 2	Class 3	Class 4	Class 5	Class 6	Total
0	0	2	3	1	0	6

'Outsider' Wins – Type of Race

Handicap Chase	Handicap Hurdle	Non Handicap Chase	Non Handicap Hurdle
1	3	0	2

Calendar of 'Outsider' Wins

Apr	May	Jun	Jul	Aug	Sep	Oct	Nov	Dec	Jan	Feb	Mar	Apr
0	0	0	0	0	0	0	0	0	3	1	2	0

NEWTON ABBOT

date	Going	Class	Race Type	Distance	Winner	SP	Tote	2nd SP	3rd SP	Runners	No of Jump Races
11/05/06	Good to Firm		No Outsiders								6
16/05/06	Good	4	Novices Handicap Hurdle		Fountain Crumble	11/1	9.20	1/1	12/1	6	6
08/0606	Good to Firm		No Outsiders								6
12/06/06	Good	4	Handicap Hurdle	2m6f	Zuletta	100/1	40.80	3/1	12/1	10	6
20/06/06	Good to Firm		No Outsiders								6
27/06/06	Soft	5	(S) Hurdle	2m3f	Galant Eye	16/1	11.50	2/1	10/1	13	5
17/07/07	Good to Firm	4	Handicap Hurdle	2m1f	Space Cowboy	16/1	19.90	9/2	11/2	12	6
23/07/07	Good to Firm		No Outsiders								5
02/08/06	Good	4	Con Jockeys Handicap Hurdle	2m3f	Dukes View	50/1	61.40	15/2	9/4	6	6
02/08/06	Good	4	Novices Hurdle	2m1f	Psycho Cat	20/1	21.40	4/1	7/1	10	
02/08/06	Good	3	Handicap Chase	2m	Scalloway	12/1	16.10	3/1	6/1	8	
02/08/06	Good	4	Maiden Hurdle	2m1f	Majestic Vision	20/1	37.00	6/1	5/1	11	
07/08/06	Good to Firm		No Outsiders								6
15/08/06	Good to Firm	3	Handicap Chase	2m5f	Sento	12/1	13.30	5/2	5/2	7	6
20/08/06	Good to Soft	2	Handicap Chase	2m5f	Kings Brook	11/1	14.30	6/1	25/1	14	6
21/08/06	Good to Soft		No Outsiders								6
26/08/06	Good to Firm	4	Novices Hurdle	2m1f	Left Hand Drive	16/1	25.50	15/2	20/1	11	6
01/04/07	Good to Firm	6	Novices Hunter Chase	2m5f	Alambique	10/1	8.70	11/10	9/1	8	7
07/04/07	Good	5	Novices Handicap Hurdle	2m6f	Alderman Rose	16/1	17.10	5/1	12/1	14	6
27/04/07	Good to Firm	4	Novices Handicap Hurdle	2m1f	Pocket Too	20/1	26.50	17/2	7/1	15	5

2006/2007 STATISTICS

No of Races	'Outsider' Wins	SPTotal	Average SP	'Outsider' Wins as a Percentage of Races	No of Blank Meetings
100	14	330	23/1	13.20%	6

'Outsider' Wins in Class of Race

Class 1	Class 2	Class 3	Class 4	Class 5	Class 6	Total
0	1	2	8	2	1	14

'Outsider' Wins – Type of Race

Handicap Chase	Handicap Hurdle	Non Handicap Chase	Non Handicap Hurdle
3	6	3	2

Calendar of 'Outsider' Wins

Apr	May	Jun	Jul	Aug	Sep	Oct	Nov	Dec	Jan	Feb	Mar	Apr
0	1	2	1	7	0	0	0	0	0	0	0	3

PERTH

Date	Going	Class	Race Type	Distance	Winner	SP	Tote	2nd SP	3rd SP	Runners	No of Jump Races
17/05/06	Soft	4	Handicap Hurdle	3m	Political Sox	12/1	14.80	10/1	5/1	13	6
17/05/06	Soft	5	Handicap Hurdle	2m	Arresting	20/1	27.40	11/1	11/4	18	
18/05/06	Soft	4	Handicap Hurdle	2m	Kiwijimbo	16/1	20.80	9/2	7/1	10	6
11/06/06	Good to Firm	4	Novices Hurdle	2m4f	Countrywide Sun	25/1	47.00	5/2	66/1	14	6
11/06/06	Good to Firm	2	Handicap Chase	3m	King Barry	14/1	16.70	6/1	7/2	15	
11/06/06	Good to Firm	3	Novices Handicap Chase	2m4f	Red Man	10/1	10.60	6/1	7/4	9	
06/07/06	Good to Firm		No Outsiders								6
16/07/06	Good to Firm	4	Handicap Hurdle	3m	Poor Tactics	12/1	19.80	8/1	14/1	14	6
01/08/06	Good to Firm	4	Handicap Hurdle	3m	Greenfort Brave	11/1	16.00	16/1	15/2	11	6
01/08/06	Good to Firm	4	Handicap Hurdle	2m	Supply and Fix	16/1	19.70	6/1	14/1	11	
22/08/06	Good		No Outsiders								6
20/09/06	Good		No Outsiders								6
21/09/06	Soft		No Outsiders								6
25/04/07	Soft	2	Novices Chase	3m	Caribou	11/1	16.20	1/1	8/1	7	7
25/04/07	Soft	4	Maiden Hurdle	2m4f	Brickies Mate	33/1	34.10	6/1	50/1	12	
26/04/07	Soft	3	Handicap Chase	2m	Terian	16/1	16.40	25/1	5/1	13	6
26/04/07	Soft	2	Handicap Chase	3m	Dream Alliance	12/1	19.80	9/2	8/1	15	
27/04/07	Good to Soft	4	Maiden Hurdle	2m	Midnight Chase	16/1	17.90	100/30	11/2	12	6

2006/2007 STATISTICS

No of Races	'Outsider' Wins	SPTotal	Average SP	'Outsider' Wins as a Percentage of Races	No of Blank Meetings
73	14	224	16/1	19.17%	4

'Outsider' Wins in Class of Race

Class 1	Class 2	Class 3	Class 4	Class 5	Class 6	Total
0	3	2	8	1	0	14

'Outsider' Wins – Type of Race

Handicap Chase	Handicap Hurdle	Non Handicap Chase	Non Handicap Hurdle
4	6	1	3

Calendar of 'Outsider' Wins

Apr	May	Jun	Jul	Aug	Sep	Oct	Nov	Dec	Jan	Feb	Mar	Apr
0	3	3	1	2	0	0	0	0	0	0	0	5

PLUMPTON

Date	Going	Class	Race Type	Distance	Winner	SP	Tote	2nd SP	3rd SP	Runners	No of Jump Races
14/05/06	Good to Firm	4	Amateur Riders Handicap Hurdle	2m5f	Canni Thinkaar	16/1	15.30	8/1	8/1	11	6
17/09/06	Good to Firm	3	Handicap Hurdle	2m	Creinch	12/1	12.40	9/2	13/2	7	7
16/10/06	Good	5	Maiden Hurdle	2m	Almanshood	18/1	20.50	5/1	5/1	14	6
16/10/06	Good	5	Handicap Chase	2m4f	Opportunity Knocks	14/1	15.80	17/2	9/1	12	
30/10/06	Good	4	Handicap Chase	2m4f	Master T	16/1	10.50	15/8	7/2	6	6
19/11/06	Good	3	Novices Hurdle	2m	Harcourt	20/1	21.90	66/1	25/1	10	7
29/11/06	Soft		No Outsiders								6
11/12/06	Heavy	3	Novices Chase	2m1f	Siberion	16/1	9.90	9/4	13/8	8	6
07/01/07	Soft		No Outsiders								6
15/01/07	Soft		No Outsiders								6
12/02/07	Heavy	4	Con/Amateur Jockeys Handicap Hurdle	2m	It's Rumoured	20/1	36.60	16/1	16/1	14	5
12/03/07	Soft		No Outsiders								7
26/03/07	Good		No Outsiders								6
08/04/07	Good to Firm	5	Classified Hurdle	2m	Zizou	25/1	24.70	9/4	11/4	8	7
09/04/07	Good to Firm		No Outsiders								6
23/04/07	Good to Firm	4	Handicap Chase	3m2f	Lets Go Dutch	12/1	12.20	7/4	16/1	6	7

2006/2007 STATISTICS

No of Races	'Outsider' Wins	SPTotal	Average SP	No of Blank Meetings	'Outsider' Wins as a Percentage of Races
94	10	169	16/1	6	10.63%

'Outsider' Wins in Class of Race

Class 1	Class 2	Class 3	Class 4	Class 5	Class 6	Total
0	0	3	3	4	0	10

'Outsider' Wins – Type of Race

Handicap Chase	Handicap Hurdle	Non Handicap Chase	Non Handicap Hurdle
3	3	1	3

Calendar of 'Outsider' Wins

Apr	May	Jun	Jul	Aug	Sep	Oct	Nov	Dec	Jan	Feb	Mar	Apr
0	1	0	0	0	1	3	1	1	0	1	0	2

SANDOWN

Date	Going	Class	Race Type	Distance	Winner	SP	Tote	2nd SP	3rd SP	Runners	No of Jump Races
04/11/06	Good		No Outsiders								6
01/12/06	Good to Soft		No Outsiders								6
06/01/07	Heavy	2	Handicap Chase	3m	Kerstino Two	16/1	24.30	9/4	9/2	12	6
03/02/07	Good to Soft		No Outsiders								7
16/02/07	Heavy	4	Novices Handicap Hurdle	2m4f	Scaramouche	25/1	28.80	16/1	9/1	13	6
10/03/07	Soft		No Outsiders								6
27/04/07	Good to Firm		No outsiders								3
28/04/07	Good to Firm		No outsiders								3

2006/2007 STATISTICS

No of Races	'Outsider' Wins	SPTotal	Average SP	'Outsider' Wins as a Percentage of Races	No of Blank Meetings
43	2	41	20.50	4.65%	6

'Outsider' Wins in Class of Race

Class 1	Class 2	Class 3	Class 4	Class 5	Class 6	Total
0	1	0	1	0	0	2

'Outsider' Wins – Type of Race

Handicap Chase	Handicap Hurdle	Non Handicap Chase	Non Handicap Hurdle
1	1	0	0

Calendar of 'Outsider' Wins

Apr	May	Jun	Jul	Aug	Sep	Oct	Nov	Dec	Jan	Feb	Mar	Apr
0	0	0	0	0	0	0	0	0	1	1	0	0

SEDGEFIELD

Date	Going	Class	Race Type	Distance	Winner	SP	Tote	2nd SP	3rd SP	Runners	No of Jump Races
01/05/06	Good to Firm		No Outsiders								5
24/05/06	Good	5	(S) Con Jockeys Handicap Hurdle	2m1f	Crosby Dancer	14/1	17.70	33/1	10/1	15	6
24/05/06	Good	4	Novices Handicap Hurdle	2m5f	Barney	18/1	19.00	6/1	28/1	8	
07/06/06	Good to Firm		No Outsiders								6
11/08/06	Good to Firm	4	Handicap Hurdle	2m4f	Ad Murum	20/1	21.30	2/1	7/2	14	6
29/08/06	Good to Firm	5	(S) Handicap Hurdle	2m1f	Tirailleur	10/1	13.10	5/1	8/1	14	6

Date	Going		Race	Dist	Horse						
26/09/06	Good to Firm	4	Handicap Hurdle	2m5f	Welsh Dream	12/1	12.80	8/1	16/1	14	7
26/09/06	Good to Firm	4	Handicap Chase	2m5f	Kerry's Blade	16/1	20.00	3/1	20/1	9	6
25/10/06	Soft	4	Novices Hurdle	2m1f	Le Rouge Fatal	16/1	19.60	8/11	10/1	10	5
07/11/06	Good		No Outsiders								
21/11/06	Good to Soft	4	Beginners Chase	2m4f	Day of Claies	16/1	21.30	2/5	14/1	10	7
05/12/06	Soft		No Outsiders								7
12/12/06	Heavy	3	Handicap Hurdle	2m4f	Tomenso	14/1	14.10	100/30	13/2	9	6
12/12/06	Heavy	3	Handicap Chase	2m	Transit	16/1	21.70	5/4	11/1	8	
26/12/06	Soft		No Outsiders								6
09/01/07	Heavy		No Outsiders								6
20/02/07	Heavy		No Outsiders								7
13/03/07	Good	4	Handicap Hurdle	2m5f	Political Pendant	10/1	15.10	100/30	5/6	7	6
13/03/07	Good	4	Handicap Chase	2m4f	Dumadic	12/1	18.10	11/4	9/2	6	
27/03/07	Good to Firm	5	(S) Handicap Hurdle	2m4f	Francincense	12/1	16.90	14/1	7/1	15	7
27/03/07	Good to Firm	4	Handicap Hurdle	3m3f	Ice Crystal	16/1	15.30	5/1	6/1	8	
27/03/07	Good to Firm	6	Hunter Chase	2m4f	Gangster's R Us	12/1	13.40	15/8	6/1	15	
09/04/07	Good to Firm	5	Novices Handicap Hurdle	2m1f	Blasting the Past	14/1	13.00	28/1	6/4	14	7
23/04/07	Good to Firm	5	Novices Handicap Chase	3m3f	Rainbow Tree	14/1	18.90	14/1	6/1	10	5
23/04/07	Good to Firm	5	Handicap Chase	2m	Chuckhi County	40/1	62.90	11/4	4/1	16	

2006/2007 STATISTICS

No of Races	'Outsider' Wins	SPTotal	Average SP	'Outsider' Wins as a Percentage of Races	No of Blank Meetings
111	18	282	15/1	16.21%	7

'Outsider' Wins in Class of Race

Class 1	Class 2	Class 3	Class 4	Class 5	Class 6	Total
0	0	2	9	6	1	18

'Outsider' Wins – Type of Race

Handicap Chase	Handicap Hurdle	Non Handicap Chase	Non Handicap Hurdle	Total
5	10	2	1	18

Calendar of 'Outsider' Wins

Apr	May	Jun	Jul	Aug	Sep	Oct	Nov	Dec	Jan	Feb	Mar	Apr
0	2	0	0	2	2	1	1	2	0	0	5	3

SOUTHWELL

Date	Going	Class	Race Type	Distance	Winner	SP	Tote	2nd SP	3rd SP	Runners	No of Jump Races
05/05/06	Good to Firm	3	Handicap Hurdle	3m2f	Enhancer	10/1	11.70	7/2	4/1	12	6
04/06/06	Good	4	Intermediate Hurdle	2m1f	Cherished Number	12/1	12.80	8/13	15/2	15	6
04/06/06	Good	4	Con Jockeys Handicap Hurdle	2m5f	Darab	12/1	12.00	5/1	13/2	14	
22/06/06	Good to Firm	3	Handicap Chase	2m4f	Tevere	10/1	10.30	16/1	11/2	13	6
22/06/06	Good to Firm	3	Handicap Hurdle	3m	Siegfried's Night	25/1	31.70	2/1	11/1	12	6
04/07/06	Good to Firm		No Outsiders								6
21/07/06	Good to Firm		No Outsiders								6
14/08/06	Good	5	Handicap Chase	2m4f	Magic Route	12/1	9.10	14/1	100/1	14	7
08/12/06	Good to Soft		No Outsiders								7
27/01/07	Soft		No Outsiders								6
25/03/07	Good to Firm		No Outsiders								6

2006/2007 STATISTICS

No of Races	'Outsider' Wins	SP Total	Average SP	No of Blank Meetings	'Outsider' Wins as a Percentage of Races
56	6	81	13/1	5	10.71%

'Outsider' Wins in Class of Race

Class 1	Class 2	Class 3	Class 4	Class 5	Class 6	Total
0	0	3	2	1	0	6

'Outsider' Wins – Type of Race

Handicap Chase	Handicap Hurdle	Non Handicap Chase	Non Handicap Hurdle
2	3	0	1

Calendar of 'Outsider' Wins

Apr	May	Jun	Jul	Aug	Sep	Oct	Nov	Dec	Jan	Feb	Mar	Apr
0	1	4	0	1	0	0	0	0	0	0	0	0

STRATFORD

Date	Going	Class	Race Type	Distance	Winner	SP	Tote	2nd SP	3rd SP	Runners	No of Jump Races
26/05/06	Soft	3	Novices Handicap Chase	2m5f	Isotop	14/1	12.40	7/2	11/2	8	6
26/05/06	Soft	2	Novices Hunter Chase	3m4f	Coomakista	14/1	16.10	14/1	7/2	10	

Date	Going	'Outsider' Wins	Race Type	Distance	Horse	SP	SP Value	Odds	Odds	Runners	Meeting Races
27/05/06	Soft		No Outsiders								7
11/06/06	Good to Firm		No Outsiders								5
18/06/06	Good to Firm	3	Novices Hurdle	2m	Lord Baskerville	16/1	22.90	8/11	7/2	12	6
05/07/06	Good	3	Handicap Chase	2m7f	On the Outside	12/1	13.30	4/1	7/2	11	6
05/07/06	Good	3	Handicap Hurdle	2m6f	Harrycat	20/1	18.70	33/1	10/1	15	
05/07/06	Good	4	Novices Handicap Chase	2m5f	Monty's Tan	16/1	19.50	14/1	5/1	9	
16/07/06	Good to Firm		No Outsiders								7
23/07/06	Good	4	Novices Handicap Hurdle	2m3f	M'Lord	18/1	29.50	13/2	66/1	12	6
03/08/06	Good to Firm		No Outsiders								6
24/08/06	Good to Firm	4	Handicap Chase	2m7f	Rash Moment	10/1	17.90	5/2	4/1	7	6
02/09/06	Good to Firm	5	(S) Con Jockeys Handicap Hurdle	2m6f	Dizzy Future	11/1	11/60	7/2	6/1	16	6
02/09/06	Good to Firm	3	Beginners Chase	2m5f	Reflex Blue	25/1	24.70	4/1	50/1	10	
02/09/06	Good to Firm	3	Handicap Chase	2m7f	Another Joker	16/1	18.70	4/1	12/1	9	
10/09/06	Good to Firm	4	Handicap Hurdle	2m	Flamand	25/1	23.80	11/4	10/1	9	5
14/10/06	Good	4	Maiden Hurdle	2m	Kontinent	16/1	13.20	10/1	16/1	15	7
14/10/06	Good	4	Lady Riders Handicap Hurdle	2m	Dishdash	12/1	16.90	3/1	9/1	15	
26/10/06	Soft	3	Novices Hurdle	2m	Thenford Flyer	14/1	14/70	16/1	16/1	12	7
03/02/07	Good to Soft		No Outsiders								6
26/03/07	Good to Soft	4	Beginners Chase	2m5f	Maldoun	40/1	59.20	33/1	5/2	7	7
26/03/07	Good to Soft	4	Maiden Hurdle	2m3f	Jump Jet	16/1	19.70	8/1	50/1	15	
26/03/07	Good to Soft	4	Handicap Hurdle	2m6f	Herne Bay	14/1	14.60	6/1	15/2	15	
22/04/07	Good		No Outsiders								6

2006/2007 STATISTICS

No of Races	'Outsider' Wins	SPTotal	Average SP	'Outsider' Wins as a Percentage of Races	No of Blank Meetings
99	18	309	17/1	18.18%	6

'Outsider' Wins in Class of Race

Class 1	Class 2	Class 3	Class 4	Class 5	Class 6	Total
0	7	7	9	1	1	18

'Outsider' Wins – Type of Race

Handicap Chase	Handicap Hurdle	Non Handicap Chase	Non Handicap Hurdle
5	6	3	4

Calendar of 'Outsider' Wins

Apr	May	Jun	Jul	Aug	Sep	Oct	Nov	Dec	Jan	Feb	Mar	Apr
0	2	1	4	1	4	3	0	0	0	0	3	0

TAUNTON

Date	Going	Class	Race Type	Distance	Winner	SP	Tote	2nd SP	3rd SP	Runners	No of Jump Races
26/10/06	Good	4	Beginners Chase	2m7f	Matt theThrasher	16/1	19.70	20/1	11/10	9	7
09/11/06	Good		No Outsiders								6
23/11/06	Good	3	Handicap Hurdle	2m3f	Ellway Prospect	16/1	12.50	9/1	25/1	16	6
07/12/06	Soft	3	Novices Hurdle	2m1f	De Soto	11/1	9.30	12/1	2/7	14	7
18/12/06	Good to Soft	4	Con Jockeys Handicap Chase	2m3f	Better Moment	25/1	19.50	100/1	16/1	14	7
29/12/06	Soft	4	Novices Hurdle	2m3f	City Streets	10/1	12.50	13/2	66/1	13	7
08/01/07	Soft	4	Handicap Hurdle	3m	Star's Delight	10/1	12.50	11/1	25/1	11	6
30/01/07	Soft	4	Beginners Chase	2m3f	Always Waining	28/1	32.10	1/2	5/2	8	6
30/01/07	Soft	4	Amateur Riders Handicap Hurdle	3m	Rocky's Girl	11/1	15.00	3/1	7/4	12	
30/01/07	Soft	3	Handicap Chase	2m3f	Malaga Boy	10/1	11.70	25/1	3/1	9	
08/02/07	Good to Soft	5	Mares Only Handicap Hurdle	3m	Topless	20/1	34.90	11/1	6/4	9	7
20/02/07	Soft	4	Maiden Hurdle	2m1f	Silver Sister	11/1	12.00	11/8	2/1	14	7
20/02/07	Soft	4	Handicap Chase	2m7f	Trading Up	16/1	14.40	10/1	33/1	12	
12/03/07	Soft		No Outsiders								7
25/03/07	Good	3	Novices Handicap Hurdle	3m	Fine By Me	11/1	10.70	6/1	9/1	12	
25/03/07	Good	5	Handicap Hurdle	2m3f	Native Commander	10/1	11.30	33/1	9/2	16	6

2006/2007 STATISTICS

No of Races	'Outsider' Wins	SP Total	Average SP	'Outsider' Wins as a Percentage of Races	No of Blank Meetings
79	14	205	14/1	17.72%	2

'Outsider' Wins in Class of Race

Class 1	Class 2	Class 3	Class 4	Class 5	Class 6	Total
0	0	4	8	2	0	14

'Outsider' Wins – Type of Race

Handicap Chase	Handicap Hurdle	Non Handicap Chase	Non Handicap Hurdle
3	6	2	3

Calendar of 'Outsider' Wins

Apr	May	Jun	Jul	Aug	Sep	Oct	Nov	Dec	Jan	Feb	Mar	Apr
0	0	0	0	0	0	1	1	3	4	3	2	0

TOWCESTER

Date	Going	Class	Race Type	Distance	Winner	SP	Tote	2nd SP	3rd SP	Runners	No of Jump Races
08/05/06	Soft		No Outsiders								6
15/05/06	Good to Soft	3	Hunter Chase	3m	Vinnie Boy	12/1	12.20	6/1	16/1	16	5
15/05/06	Good to Soft	4	Handicap Hurdle	2m	Merryvale Man	16/1	19.00	28/1	6/4	14	
23/05/06	Heavy	5	(S) Novice Hurdle	2m	Island of Memories	11/1	11.60	11/8	13/2	9	6
02/06/06	Good	5	Maiden Chase	2m3f	Caveman	12/1	14.50	3/1	11/4	12	6
02/06/06	Good	4	Handicap Chase	2m	Neltina	12/1	12.00	6/5	6/1	7	
02/06/06	Good	5	(S) Hurdle	2m3f	Tanning	18/1	20.90	4/1	12/1	12	
04/10/06	Good	4	Handicap Hurdle	2m	Optimum	14/1	19.50	3/1	7/1	15	6
04/10/06	Good	4	Handicap Chase	2m3f	Ice Melted	14/1	19.40	8/1	11/4	10	
22/10/06	Good to Soft	5	(S) Hurdle	2m	Aberdeen Park	16/1	24.40	20/1	5/1	11	7
02/11/06	Good to Soft	4	Mares Only Novices Hurdle	2m	Blackberry Thyne	16/1	22.60	7/2	16/1	14	5
02/11/06	Good to Soft	3	Handicap Hurdle	2m5f	Bring Me Sunshine	10/1	10.70	15/8	8/1	8	
02/11/06	Good to Soft	5	Con Jockeys Handicap Chase	2m	Billy Bray	33/1	20.60	6/4	12/1	10	
19/11/06	Soft	4	Handicap Chase	3m	Apple Joe	12/1	17.20	33/1	33/1	13	6
19/11/06	Soft	5	Classified Chase	2m3f	Carnt Spell	12/1	14.00	10/1	20/1	10	
25/11/06	Heavy	4	Handicap Hurdle	3m	Dinnie Flanagan	10/1	10.60	100/30	9/2	7	6
26/12/06	Soft		No Outsiders								5
21/01/07	Heavy		No Outsiders								6
01/02/07	Soft	4	Novices Hurdle	2m3f	Carrick Oscar	12/1	14.70	7/2	4/1	11	6
01/02/07	Soft	4	Beginners Chase	2m6f	Nonantais	12/1	15.40	8/1	16/1	8	
18/02/07	Heavy	5	(S) Handicap Hurdle	2m	Temper Lad	22/1	25.30	5/1	17/2	17	5
18/02/07	Heavy	4	Handicap Hurdle	3m	Whittford Don	33/1	46.40	33/1	9/2	16	
28/03/07	Good	4	Handicap Hurdle	2m	Another Burden	20/1	23.40	15/8	16/1	18	6
28/03/07	Good	4	Mares Only Novices Hurdle	2m5f	Heavenly Pleasure	33/1	40.50	11/1	8/11	8	
29/03/07	Good	5	Handicap Chase	2m3f	Romney Marsh	33/1	61.80	5/2	16/1	11	6

08/04/07	Good to Firm	4	Maiden Hurdle	2m3f	Give Me a Dime	12/1	10.40	11/4	4/1	16	6
24/04/07	Good to Firm	4	Handicap Chase	2m	Arctic Spirit	11/1	11.30	8/1	20/1	17	6
24/04/07	Good to Firm	6	Maiden Hunter Chase	2m3f	Howard Howard	10/1	12.70	7/1	20/1	12	

2006/2007 STATISTICS

No of Races	'Outsider' Wins	SPTotal	Average SP	'Outsider' Wins as a Percentage of Races
98	25	416	16/1	25.51%

'Outsider' Wins in Class of Race

Class 1	Class 2	Class 3	Class 4	Class 5	Class 6	Total
0	0	1	14	8	2	25

'Outsider' Wins – Type of Race

Handicap Chase	Handicap Hurdle	Non Handicap Chase	Non Handicap Hurdle
6	7	5	7

Calendar of 'Outsider' Wins

Apr	May	Jun	Jul	Aug	Sep	Oct	Nov	Dec	Jan	Feb	Mar	Apr
0	3	2	0	0	0	3	7	0	0	4	3	3

No of Blank Meetings: 3

UTTOXETER

Date	Going	Class	Race Type	Distance	Winner	SP	Tote	2nd SP	3rd SP	Runners	No of Jump Races
06/05/06	Good to Firm	4	Novices Hurdle	2m6f	Barfleur	33/1	66.00	9/2	11/8	12	6
14/05/06	Good	4	Novices Hurdle	3m	Mister Sher	25/1	30.50	11/4	11/4	9	6
14/05/06	Good	5	Handicap Hurdle	2m	Donie Dooley	33/1	38.80	25/1	20/1	15	
20/05/06	Heavy	4	Novices Hurdle	2m4f	Allistathebarrista	20/1	21.60	4/1	2/1	8	5
28/05/06	Soft		No Outsiders								6
08/06/06	Good	4	Novices Handicap Hurdle	2m4f	Sultan Fontenaille	12/1	15.60	7/1	28/1	16	6
15/06/06	Good	5	Handicap Hurdle	3m	Hylia	20/1	22.00	40/1	4/1	17	5
02/07/06	Good to Firm		No Outsiders								6
11/07/06	Good to Firm	4	Handicap Chase	2m	Barton Park	10/1	13.30	9/2	6/1	10	6
19/07/06	Good to Firm		No Outsiders								6
27/07/06	Good	5	Novices Handicap Hurdle	2m	Stokesies Boy	50/1	32.00	7/2	2/1	15	5
31/07/06	Good to Firm	5	Con Jockeys Novice Handicap Hurdle	2m4f	McQueen	10/1	7.40	7/2	25/1	9	6
06/09/06	Good	3	Handicap Hurdle	2m4f	Ragdale Hall	33/1	41.00	4/1	3/1	11	6
17/09/06	Good	5	(S) Handicap Hurdle	2m6f	Almabrook	14/1	22.00	22/1	7/1	16	7

Date	Going	Class	Race Type	Distance	Winner	SP	Tote	2nd SP	3rd SP	Runners	No of Jump Races
01/10/06	Good to Soft		No Outsiders								7
11/10/06	Soft		No Outsiders								6
27/10/06	Heavy	4	Handicap Chase	2m5f	Supreme Tadgh	22/1	28.30	9/1	10/11	10	6
11/11/06	Good to Soft		No Outsiders								6
23/11/06	Heavy	4	Novices Hurdle	2m	Little Rocker	20/1	25.20	5/2	4/7	12	7
23/11/06	Heavy	4	Novices Hurdle	3m	Desperate Dex	50/1	77.50	4.6	11/2	8	
15/12/06	Heavy	5	Maiden Hurdle	2m	Wizard of Us	40/1	75.60	4/1	100/1	17	6
15/12/06	Heavy	4	Handicap Chase	3m	Cinnamon Line	20/1	25.20	15/2	14/1	14	
27/01/07	Heavy		No Outsiders								5
17/02/07	Heavy	2	Handicap Hurdle	2m	Wizard of Us	12/1	14.20	11/4	9/2	8	6
17/03/07	Soft	1	Handicap Chase	4m1f	Baron Windrush	12/1	14.90	40/1	11/2	18	6
17/03/07	Soft	3	Novices Hurdle	2m4f	Jungleland	14/1	17.30	20/1	16/1	18	
31/03/07	Good	4	Maiden Hurdle	3m	Golden Parachute	11/1	14.40	2/1	5/2	13	6

2006/2007 STATISTICS

No of Races	'Outsider' Wins	SP Total	Average SP	'Outsider' Wins as a Percentage of Races	No of Blank Meetings
137	20	461	23/1	14.59%	7

'Outsider' Wins in Class of Race

Class 1	Class 2	Class 3	Class 4	Class 5	Class 6	Total
1	2	2	10	6	0	20

'Outsider' Wins – Type of Race

Handicap Chase	Handicap Hurdle	Non Handicap Chase	Non Handicap Hurdle	Total
4	8	0	8	20

Calendar of 'Outsider' Wins

Apr	May	Jun	Jul	Aug	Sep	Oct	Nov	Dec	Jan	Feb	Mar	Apr
0	4	2	3	0	2	1	2	2	0	1	3	0

WARWICK

Date	Going	Class	Race Type	Distance	Winner	SP	Tote	2nd SP	3rd SP	Runners	No of Jump Races
30/10/06	Good	4	Juvenile Novices Hurdle	2m	Cheveley Flyer	10/1	7.10	100/1	4/11	9	9
15/11/06	Good	4	Novices Hurdle	2m	Noble Raider	16/1	28.10	5/4	50/1	17	6
03/12/06	Soft	4	Handicap Hurdle	2m	Kickahead	12/1	20.80	100/1	12/1	20	6

Date	Going	Class	Race Type	Distance	Winner	SP	Tote	2nd SP	3rd SP	Runners	No of Jump Races
31/12/06	Heavy	5	Novices Handicap Hurdle	2m3f	Milton des Bieffes	10/1	13.00	9/1	9/2	13	6
13/01/07	Heavy		No Outsiders								6
25/01/07	Heavy	4	Handicap Chase	3m2f	Cinnamon Line	20/1	20.20	14/1	8/1	12	6
23/02/07	Hevy		No Outsiders								7
11/03/07	Soft	4	Con Jockeys Handicap Hurdle	2m	Ceoperk	12/1	10.80	16/1	2/1	14	6
20/03/07	Good		No Outsiders								7

2006/2007 STATISTICS

No of Races	'Outsider' Wins	'Outsider' Wins as a Percentage of Races
56	6	10.70%

Average SP	SPTotal	No of Blank Meetings
13/1	80	3

'Outsider' Wins in Class of Race

Class 1	Class 2	Class 3	Class 4	Class 5	Class 6	Total
0	0	0	5	1	0	6

'Outsider' Wins – Type of Race

Handicap Hurdle	Handicap Chase	Non Handicap Hurdle	Non Handicap Chase
3	1	2	0

Calendar of 'Outsider' Wins

Apr	May	Jun	Jul	Aug	Sep	Oct	Nov	Dec	Jan	Feb	Mar	Apr
0	0	0	0	0	0	1	1	2	1	0	1	0

WETHERBY

Date	Going	Class	Race Type	Distance	Winner	SP	Tote	2nd SP	3rd SP	Runners	No of Jump Races
30/04/06	Good to Firm	5	Handicap Hurdle	2m4f	Twist N Turn	12/1	14.50	8/1	6/1	12	7
30/04/06	Good to Firm	5	Amateur Riders Handicap Hurdle	2m	Only Words	14/1	20.70	15/2	13/2	21	
11/05/06	Good to Firm	4	Handicap Hurdle	2m	Etoile Russe	16/1	20.20	66/1	11/1	11	6
25/05/06	Heavy	4	Novice Hurdle	2m7f	Himalayan Trail	10/1	11.50	14/1	10/1	8	6
01/06/06	Good to Firm		No Outsiders								6
11/10/06	Good	3	Handicap Hurdle	2m	Archie Babe	20/1	17.00	15/2	3/1	9	7
27/10/06	Soft	4	Handicap Chase	3m1f	Bob's Buster	40/1	20.50	12/1	4/1	6	7
28/10/06	Soft	1	Hurdle	3m1f	Redemption	12/1	10.40	4/9	17/2	7	7
11/11/06	Good to Soft	4	Handicap Chase	3m5f	Celtic Flow	11/1	16.80	9/2	8/1	8	6
22/11/06	Soft	4	Novices Hurdle	2m	Springvic	18/1	25.50	2/1	11/1	20	6
02/12/06	Soft		No Outsiders								6

Date	Going	Class	Race Type	Winner	Distance	SP	Tote	2nd SP	3rd SP	Runners	No of Jump Races
26/12/06	Soft		No Outsiders								6
27/12/06	Soft	2	Handicap Chase	Catalagan	2m	14/1	22.80	7/2	8/1	7	6
03/01/07	Heavy		No Outsiders								6
13/01/07	Heavy	4	Con/Amateur Jockeys Handicap Hurdle	Clock House	2m	12/1	10.20	5/1	10/1	14	6
03/02/07	Good to Soft	3	Handicap Hurdle	Laertes	2m7f	14/1	15.20	5/1	16/1	8	6
03/02/07	Good to Soft	1	Novices Chase	Heltornic	3m1f	14/1	19.10	10/1	11/2	7	6
17/03/07	Good		No Outsiders								6
03/04/07	Good to Firm	4	Handicap Chase	Profowens	3m1f	12/1	17.30	7/2	13/2	9	6
16/04/07	Good	4	Handicap Hurdle	Dream Castle	2m	33/1	42.50	25/1	18/1	14	7

2006/2007 STATISTICS

No of Races	'Outsider' Wins	SP Total	Average SP	'Outsider' Wins as a Percentage of Races	No of Blank Meetings
113	15	252	16/1	13.27%	5

'Outsider' Wins in Class of Race

Class 1	Class 2	Class 3	Class 4	Class 5	Class 6	Total
2	1	2	8	2	0	15

'Outsider' Wins – Type of Race

Handicap Chase	Handicap Hurdle	Non Handicap Chase	Non Handicap Hurdle
4	7	1	3

Calendar of 'Outsider' Wins

Apr	May	Jun	Jul	Aug	Sep	Oct	Nov	Dec	Jan	Feb	Mar	Apr
2	2	0	0	0	0	3	2	1	1	2	0	2

WINCANTON

Date	Going	Class	Race Type	Winner	Distance	SP	Tote	2nd SP	3rd SP	Runners	No of Jump Races
02/05/06	Good		No Outsiders								6
12/05/06	Good to Firm	4	Novices Handicap Chase	John Foley	2m5f	22/1	34.60	8/1	5/2	9	6
05/10/06	Firm	4	Novices Handicap Hurdle	She's Our Daisy	2m	14/1	18.50	11/10	10/1	9	6
22/10/06	Good to Soft		No Outsiders								7
04/11/06	Good	1	Handicap Chase	Parson's Legacy	3m1f	16/1	20.10	14/1	16/1	12	6
16/11/06	Good		No Outsiders								6

Date	Going	No.	Race Type	Dist	Horse	SP	Avg			Runners	
30/11/06	Good to Soft		No Outsiders								6
26/12/06	Good	5	Novices Handicap Hurdle	2m	Femme D'Avril	11/1	11.00	8/1	13/2	16	6
26/12/06	Good	2	Handicap Hurdle	2m6f	Lord Sam	10/1	16.70	7/1	5/2	9	
26/12/06	Good	4	Handicap Chase	2m5f	Alphabetical	14/1	16.90	9/2	6/1	11	
10/01/07	Soft	5	Handicap Hurdle	2m6f	Celtic Major	50/1	93.40	7/2	3/1	16	7
10/01/07	Soft	4	Maiden Hurdle	2m	Le Burf	20/1	29.70	6/1	17/2	17	
20/01/07	Soft	4	Novices Hurdle	2m	Cherry D'Or	33/1	40.00	10/1	4/5	14	7
20/01/07	Soft	3	Handicap Hurdle	2m6f	Celtic Manor	12/1	15.80	13/8	7/2	15	
01/02/07	Good to Soft	4	Handicap Chase	3m1f	Wizard of Edge	25/1	26.30	12/1	11/2	12	6
01/02/07	Good to Soft	2	Novices Hurdle	2m6f	Marcus	50/1	47.90	3/1	4/1	16	
17/02/07	Soft		No Outsiders								7
08/03/07	Soft		No Outsiders								5
19/03/07	Good	5	Handicap Hurdle	2m	Tytheknot	20/1	27.90	8/1	3/1	16	6
19/03/07	Good	3	Handicap Hurdle	2m6f	Royal Katidoki	18/1	23.60	9/2	4/1	16	
05/04/07	Good to Firm	4	Handicap Hurdle	2m	John Charles	16/1	17.70	16/1	9/4	9	6
05/04/07	Good to Firm	4	Novices Handicap Hurdle	2m	Moon Star	10/1	9.80	33/1	7/1	16	
22/04/07	Firm		No Outsiders								

2006/2007 STATISTICS

No of Races	'Outsider' Wins	Average SP	SP Total	'Outsider' Wins as a Percentage of Races	No of Blank Meetings
99	16	21/1	341	16.16%	6

'Outsider' Wins in Class of Race

Class 1	Class 2	Class 3	Class 4	Class 5	Class 6	Total
1	2	2	8	3	0	16

'Outsider' Wins – Type of Race

Handicap Chase	Handicap Hurdle	Non Handicap Chase	Non Handicap Hurdle	Total
4	5	0	7	16

Calendar of 'Outsider' Wins

Apr	May	Jun	Jul	Aug	Sep	Oct	Nov	Dec	Jan	Feb	Mar	Apr
0	1	0	0	0	0	1	1	3	4	2	2	2

WORCESTER

Date	Going	Class	Race Type	Distance	Winner	SP	Tote	2nd SP	3rd SP	Runners	No of Jump Races
06/05/06	Good to Firm	5	Classified Chase	2m	Munadil	16/1	13.00	4/1	7/2	9	5
14/05/06	Good	4	Beginners Chase	2m7f	Oakfield Legend	33/1	43.10	11/4	14/1	12	5
14/05/06	Good	4	Mares Only Handicap Hurdle	3m	Lady of Scarvagh	20/1	20.80	11/2	17/2	15	
14/05/06	Good	4	Handicap Chase	2m	Sir Brastias	11/1	12.30	3/1	14/1	10	
20/05/06	Soft		No outsiders								5
03/06/06	Good to Firm	3	Handicap Chase	2m4f	Cameron Bridge	14/1	17.40	9/1	20/1	11	7
13/06/06	Good to Firm		No Outsiders								5
21/06/06	Good to Firm	4	Handicap Hurdle	2m4f	Harrycat	20/1	18.90	66/1	9/4	12	7
28/06/06	Good		No Outsiders								6
05/07/06	Good to Firm	4	Con Jockeys Novice Handicap Hurdle	2m4f	Joey	20/1	24.20	100/30	5/2	11	6
05/07/06	Good to Firm	4	Novices Hurdle	3m	Possextown	12/1	11.20	33/1	100/1	13	
12/07/06	Good	4	Novices Hurdle	2m4f	So Brash	11/1	10.80	11/8	14/1	11	6
12/07/06	Good	5	Novices Handicap Hurdle	3m	Idbury	22/1	52.30	9/2	5/2	14	
19/07/06	Good	5	Novices Handicap Chase	2m	Welsh Dane	12/1	19.80	18/1	9/4	8	6
26/07/06	Good to Firm		No Outsiders								6
01/08/06	Good	5	(S) Hurdle	2m4f	Seymour Weld	10/1	11.20	14/1	9/1	11	6
11/08/06	Good		No Outsiders								7
22/08/06	Good to Firm		No Outsiders								6
03/09/06	Good	4	Beginners Chase	2m	Fortune Point	28/1	22.50	6/1	10/11	8	7
03/09/06	Good	5	Handicap Chase	2m7	Sam Adamson	33/1	75.80	9/2	10/1	17	
22/09/06	Good to Soft	4	Novices Handicap Hurdle	2m	Walton Way	40/1	65.00	33/1	8/1	12	5
05/10/06	Good to Soft	4	Con Jockeys Handicap Chase	2m	Lascar de Ferbet	12/1	19.10	6/4	9/4	5	6
05/10/06	Good to Soft	4	Novices Handicap Chase	2m7f	Over the Blues	12/1	11.10	16/1	11/2	10	
18/10/06	Good to Soft	3	Handicap Chase	2m4f	Briery Fox	12/1	12.60	16/1	5/2	11	6
15/04/07	Good to Firm	4	Handicap Hurdle	3m	Natoumba	16/1	19.00	15/2	9/2	15	5
25/04/07	Good to Firm	4	Novices Handicap Chase	2m7f	Snipe	16/1	23.70	7/2	12/1	13	6
25/04/07	Good to Firm	5	Maiden Hurdle	2m4f	Ready Response	10/1	8.10	4/1	6/1	12	
25/04/07	Good to Firm	4	Handicap Chase	2m4f	Fieldsofclover	10/1	7.30	15/8	5/1	13	

2006/2007 STATISTICS

No of Races	'Outsider' Wins	SP Total	Average SP	'Outsider' Wins as a Percentage of Races	No of Blank Meetings
118	22	390	17/1	18.64%	6

'Outsider' Wins in Class of Race

Class 1	Class 2	Class 3	Class 4	Class 5	Class 6	Total
0	0	2	14	6	0	22

'Outsider' Wins – Type of Race

Handicap Chase	Handicap Hurdle	Non Handicap Chase	Non Handicap Hurdle
9	6	3	4

Calendar of 'Outsider' Wins

Apr	May	Jun	Jul	Aug	Sep	Oct	Nov	Dec	Jan	Feb	Mar	Apr
0	4	2	5	1	3	3	0	0	0	0	0	14

Notes

Notes

Notes